CW01395463

The World and Us

The World and Us

Roberto Mangabeira Unger

V
VERSO
London • New York

First published by Verso 2024
© Roberto Mangabeira Unger 2024

1 3 5 7 9 10 8 6 4 2

Verso
UK: 6 Meard Street, London W1F 0EG
US: 388 Atlantic Avenue, Brooklyn, NY 11217
versobooks.com

Verso is the imprint of New Left Books

ISBN-13: 978-1-80429-265-5
ISBN-13: 978-1-80429-266-2 (UK EBK)
ISBN-13: 978-1-80429-267-9 (US EBK)

British Library Cataloguing in Publication Data
A catalogue record for this book is available from the British Library

Library of Congress Cataloging-in-Publication Data

Names: Unger, Roberto Mangabeira, author.
Title: The world and us / Roberto Mangabeira Unger.
Description: London ; New York : Verso, 2024. | Includes index.
Identifiers: LCCN 2023034974 (print) | LCCN 2023034975 (ebook) | ISBN
    9781804292655 (hardback) | ISBN 9781804292679 (ebk)
Subjects: LCSH: Transcendence (Philosophy)
Classification: LCC BD362 .U54 2024 (print) | LCC BD362 (ebook) | DDC
    199/.81—dc23/eng/20231128
LC record available at https://lccn.loc.gov/2023034974
LC ebook record available at https://lccn.loc.gov/2023034975

Typeset in Minion Pro by MJ&N Gavan, Truro, Cornwall
Printed in the UK by CPI Group (UK) Ltd, Croydon CR0 4YY

FSC
www.fsc.org
MIX
Paper | Supporting
responsible forestry
FSC® C171272

Contents

3. The Human Condition: Becoming More Human by Becoming More Godlike

4. Ethics (as Clarity about the Conduct of Life)

Prologue: Finitude and Transcendence in Human Experience

Our Dreamlike and Vertiginous Existence

Suddenly, amid the tasks and distractions of another day, in the vanishing series of my days, I stop to think about the situation in which each of us finds himself. We are embodied, mortal organisms in a world the existence, beginning, and end of which remain—and may always remain for our species—an enigma that we cannot decipher.

Many great thinkers have claimed to show that the world must exist and even that it must be the way it is. Their arguments should strike us as childish: so strikingly fallacious as to betray a horror of our real circumstance. There is no reason why there should be something rather than nothing or why this something should not be radically different from what it is. The most important fact about the world is that it is what it is rather than something else. Given how things are, and have been, many possible ways in which they might now be otherwise may be excluded. But no reason that we can discern in all our discoveries and reasoning explains why the world might not have started out differently or even why, having started out the way it did, it may not have taken another turn.

The world is the way it is because it was the way it was. Everything changes sooner or later, including change itself: the kinds of things that there are, how they differ, and how they turn into one another or into new things—things that never existed before. Much of the natural science that we regard as fundamental, and of the philosophical speculation that it has inspired or from which it has drawn inspiration, holds that nature works with a stock of immutable elementary constituents, subject to regularities that are themselves changeless.

Although this view has almost always appealed, and continues to appeal, to many of the greatest scientists and philosophers, we have already discovered enough about nature and its history to doubt that it is true. The universe has a history and so does everything inside it. We human beings and our societies are no exception. If part of what we mean by the reality of time is the susceptibility of everything, including change itself, to change, then the world has no permanent structure.

We find ourselves trapped in our bodies and their limited perceptual apparatus. In our scientific practices we have learned to supplement that natural apparatus with observational, experimental, and computational equipment as well as with a dialectic between empirical investigation and theoretical speculation. In art we have opened another road into reality. But neither within natural science nor outside it does the growth of knowledge give us hope of coming closer to understanding the basis of reality or the beginning and end of time.

We are, in this sense, groundless. The framework of reality and therefore of our existence eludes us. We, and likely those who come after us, will never know it, and our discoveries seem to bring us no closer to grasping it.

Our groundlessness might seem to many of us only an idle curiosity if we were not mortal. One experience would come after another, with an open horizon to a future without end. The dramatic concentration of human life would no longer result in our inability to do it all over again, so long as the organization of society and of culture allowed us to reinvent ourselves. The questions—What does it all mean? Where does it all come from?—might lose their urgency. We might more readily reconcile ourselves to the just-so-ness of the world: its just happening to be what it is.

But we are not immortal: each of us is on the way to death. Our species may itself be ephemeral, even if it can survive, through our relocation to other parts of the universe, the eventual destruction of our planet and of the star that illuminates and heats it. But so long as our setting in the universe remains compatible with human life, the death of the individual organism remains—according to the rule that we observe all around us—a condition for the endurance of the species.

We have been able to extend the life span of a human being. Some even imagine that at some future time humanity will find ways to avoid or reverse aging, and to defeat death altogether. If that were ever to happen our lives and societies would change radically, in ways that might be full of evil as well as of good.

In the meantime, we remain death-bound. Death is for each of us an unimaginable event. If we are lucky, and not crushed, as much of humanity has been, under the weight of societies and cultures that leave us hapless placeholders in an order of social division and hierarchy, each of us embodies and encounters a trace of transcendence: the power to experience or foreshadow more than the established order of society or culture will countenance; the power to transgress, overcome, and surprise that we associate with life itself.

Death is the annihilation of all possible experience, an annihilation from which there is no appeal. It represents the definitive destruction not simply of an individual but also of the whole world represented in his consciousness, a world that will never come back to life. We are told that it is not so: that this world evoked in the mind of the individual will live on in other people or will be preserved in the creations and deeds of the dead. One must wonder whether anyone has ever believed in this meager and fanciful consolation, so blind as it is to the disproportion between life and its remnants.

Death is indescribably awful because it denies us a future, the continuance of experience, and because it denies us, one after another, those whom we love most. That it does so in the context of groundlessness, of the mysterious character of existence, only increases its terrors. We have priceless life, only to have it taken away from us, from ourselves and from our beloved. Although we can account for our mortality in natural-evolutionary terms, we cannot easily resign ourselves to it. If we can transcend, we may be, and have been, tempted to ask: Why can we not outlive?

The history of religion and philosophy, in the West and throughout the world, is filled with narratives that attempt to explain away the combination of groundlessness and mortality that casts so dark a shadow on our experience. These narratives profess to show us the basis of reality and existence and to offer us a route to eternal life: if not life as we know it, in our bodies and our temporal setting, among those whom we care about most, then life in some more shadowy form—better than nothing, but, even the believer may fear, a sorry substitute for the real thing.

However, the better the news delivered by these explanations, the greater the reason to suspect that what they deliver is too good to be true. The news becomes more credible as it becomes less encouraging.

Other sages, reluctant to be cast in the role of providing feel-good stories, have advised us to turn away from the confrontation with mortality. Spinoza, for example, wrote that a wise man thinks of life, not of death. But even the austere Spinoza combined his turning away from death with a denial of groundlessness: he explained to us the ultimate nature of reality and did so in a fashion that makes the cessation of life seem less complete, momentous, and unrequited.

For the most part, those who see no such answer to death and groundlessness have simply kept their silence and busied themselves with matters that lie more securely within our grasp. Yet a few have thought, with reason, that we need to reckon with groundlessness and mortality the better to resist the routines and the idols that deny us the more complete possession of life.

The recurrent character of our experience: finitude and transcendence. In the shadow of mortality and groundlessness, we live our lives. The elucidation of our experience and of our powers is the chief concern of philosophy.

In every department of existence, we encounter a reality—the reality of our experience and of its possible development—with the same perplexing features. I offer a preliminary account of this reality here and develop the account in the remainder of this book.

Incarnate in dying organisms (while conscious of being temporarily alive), and powerless to penetrate the riddle of the world and of our place in it (although we may flatter ourselves that this enigma has been deciphered), our most fundamental experience is finitude. Mortality and groundlessness are its most telling expressions. But they are only the beginning of our troubles and limitations.

Each of us has both a genetic and a social fate. Each is born into a particular historical and social situation, of parents we did not choose. None of us can leave his body and see the world as the God who many of us have imagined might see it. All of us are adrift, like the world itself, on a current of time that we are powerless to stop and that we foresee will eventually engulf us, all that is dear to us, and ultimately —long after we have ceased to exist and after all memory and trace of our existence have been erased—our planet, our universe, and even the world itself. The nailing of the self and its aspirations to a decaying body, to a social circumstance, to a time in human and natural history, to a series of particulars that are themselves limited and that impose limits on us—this is our finitude. Such limits are moveable—by how much we do not know—but we do not abolish them by moving them.

Our finitude has no constant measure. Unable to overcome it, we can nevertheless loosen its bonds. We can increase our powers of insight beyond what our frail capacities of perception allow, although the basis of being and existence continues to escape us. We can enlist natural forces to our benefit and intervene in the workings of nature. We can establish societies and cultures that express our humanity in different ways and develop them in divergent directions. And through these societies and cultures, as well as in our struggles against their arrangements and assumptions, we can create things, ideas, experiences, and arrangements that never existed before.

Alongside embodiment, there is empowerment; alongside confinement, correction; alongside finitude, transcendence—if by transcendence we mean overcoming what had seemed to be the inalterable limits of our powers and experience. Our ability to transcend is not unlimited but its limits are indefinite. Every attempt to define the outer reaches of those limits has, in time, been discredited.

The power of transcendence is vested in the individual human being as well as in the whole of humanity. Our institutions and dogmas have differed in the extent to which they recognize and nourish this power. But even when and where it has been least recognized and most suppressed, it has never been extinguished.

There is no universal and uncontestable form of social life or way of thinking. The social and conceptual worlds that we build and inhabit help make us who we are. But there is always more possibility of experience, feeling, connection, insight, and invention in each of us individually, as well as in all of us collectively, humanity, than there is, or ever can be, in those worlds. In the old vocabulary of Western philosophy and theology, these social and conceptual contexts of our experience are finite in relation to us, and we are infinite in relation to them.

We can, for example, make a discovery, or think a thought, that makes no sense according to our settled methods and established presuppositions, and then develop, retrospectively, the methods and presuppositions that allow us to make sense of it. We can experiment with a way of organizing our social life that has no prior institutional expression and then, after the fact, work out rules, institutions, and ideas that make our experiment regular, recurrent, legitimate, and intelligible. This power to exceed all the finite determinations of our existence, vested in us both as individual human beings and as humanity, is our transcendence.

The promise made by the unqualified use of this vocabulary cannot be kept. Our power to transcend the bounds of finitude in each area of our experience has no definite limits: no limits that we can specify from our vantage point in time. But to say that this power has no definite limits is not to imply that it is unlimited. Its exercise by the individual is hostage to all the frailties of mind and body and to the relentless oppression of society. Its exercise by the species is subject to the limits of our natural constitution and to the misadventures of our history.

Such limits are manifest in the immeasurable distance that always remains between our discoveries of the workings of nature outside and within us and our ignorance of the ground of being, of the framework of reality, of the beginning and end of time. The repeated exercise of our power to transcend the limits to insight never brings us any closer to what in the tradition of that same Western vocabulary was sometimes called absolute knowledge. It never frees us from our groundlessness. There may be thoughts that beings of our species can never have and discoveries that they can never make.

In this condition of ours, we remain perennially susceptible to two errors, common in the history of our attempts to make sense of our circumstances. On one side, we may mistake infirmities of perception, insight, and creation for inalterable constraints on our powers, failing to recognize the extent to which we can either overcome them or make up for them: for example, by way of the telescopes and microscopes, the computers and particle colliders, with which we have begun to go beyond the limits of our senses. On the other side, encouraged by our repeated acts of overcoming the limits to our understanding of reality, we may come to think of ourselves as sharers in the absolute knowledge possessed by the God of the believers. Such knowledge will be ours, we may flatter ourselves: not immediately, in the biographical time of the individual, but ultimately, in the historical time of the species.

The dialectic of embodiment and empowerment, confinement and correction, transcendence and finitude, which we undergo in the shadow of death and groundlessness, touches every aspect of existence and provides philosophy with a central part of its subject matter. But it is not the whole story, and it cannot all by itself provide a sufficient account of the concerns of philosophy.

We experience our finitude and go to our deaths as individuals. It is, however, through social practices, including the practices of natural science, that we push back the boundaries of finitude. The ability to push them back is granted to the individual as well as to the collectivities to which he belongs and to the entire human race. But it is only by acting through and against those practices—the methods of the different sciences and disciplines, the institutional arrangements of society, the roles and practices available to us, and the symbolic world in which all our activity is enveloped—that the individual can develop and exercise this power.

To the acknowledgment of our finitude, and of the loosening of the constraints that it imposes on us, we must add, to form a realistic view of ourselves, a recognition of our incompleteness as individuals and of our desperate longing to be completed by one another. We both need other people and we fear them. We are free only through our connection to others and engagement in a particular social world.

Every connection, however, seems to threaten us with subjugation and loss of distinction and freedom. And every engagement in a particular social world seems to require surrender to that world as the condition of engagement.

To be free, and to come more fully into the possession of life, we would need to connect without losing ourselves, and to engage in a social world without surrendering to it. We would need to find unconditional love and recognition in the embrace of another person, and to deny the last word to society and keep it for ourselves.

We complete ourselves only in others, but our connection to them is fraught at every turn with complication, misunderstanding, and disappointment. Faced with the prospect of death and the impenetrable enigma of existence, we look for assurance in one another's arms that there is, for each of us, an unconditional place in the world. But in those arms we find trouble as well as consolation. Our relations to one another, even at their deepest and most intimate, are tainted by an ambivalence from which we never gain unalloyed relief.

We live in societies and cultures that develop under the shield of belligerent states. Each of these experiments in humanity discourages, or forecloses, some forms of experience and existence that we may have reason to value, even as it makes others feasible. Within these warlike states, each individual is born with a social as well as a genetic fate, in class societies that shape the life chances of individuals and demand extraordinary trials of ingenuity and ambition, combined with luck, to climb over their hierarchies and divisions.

Even where our transcendence should be least constrained by social fate—in science and speculation—we find vision fastened to the cross of fossilized method and convention, and dissent punished by marginality or outright persecution.

Nowhere are we able to find completion in one another without suffering and confusion. The loosening of the restraints of finitude in the shadow of mortality and groundlessness is not a triumphal march, despite the experiences of love, insight, and joy that life may afford us.

The circumstances whose elements I have just described—the dialectic of finitude and transcendence; the social character of our efforts to loosen the restraints of finitude; the conflicted nature of our relation to one another; and the invisible circle of longing and love that nevertheless binds us to one another—reappear in every area of our experience.

What sense are we to make of our situation in a world adrift in time? In this world of ours, nothing lasts forever, and each of us plays a small and ephemeral part before going to his death, ignorant, though he may think otherwise, of the framework of existence and of the ground of being. How are we to respond to this reality, as individuals, as societies, and as the whole human race?

Such is the subject matter of philosophy, which, once described in these terms, may seem to be both inescapable and inaccessible.

Philosophy

This is a work of philosophy. It takes as its major theme our response to the dreamlike and vertiginous character of our lives, which we live on the way to death, uninformed of the ground of being and reality. I cannot carry out the task that I have set for myself here by relying on any of the conceptions of what philosophy is, and of what it can or should do, that have been prominent in the history of thought. Nevertheless, the view of philosophy that I embrace here has roots in that history. The best way to define philosophy is to do so by contrast to what, in its most recognized and influential forms, philosophy has been.

In the central tradition of Western philosophy, philosophy was a super-science practiced in the service of self-help. This super-science provided an explanation of the world, or at least of what was most important about it for the conduct of life and the governance of society. The self-help it offered was to assist us in dealing with the irreparable flaws in the human condition, beginning with our mortality and groundlessness, when custom, religion, and art seemed to fail us.

At its most ambitious, philosophy, conceived in this manner, claimed to present a view of the world and of our place in it. In pursuit of this ambition, it professed to explain both how and why the world is the way it is. It dealt with the foundations of both reality and of our understanding of it. It was not—even in the hands of philosophers like Aristotle who were interested in specialized disciplines or sciences and in the methods suitable to their distinct subject matters—simply an encyclopedia of the established knowledge of the time. Its concern was to account for reality as a whole, or for what was most significant to humanity about it, and to do so by way of procedures having the most general and reliable application.

In the most intransigent versions of this philosophical practice, a philosopher such as Leibniz or Spinoza might begin a book by informing us of the basic constitution of the world and then, later on in the same work or in its sequels, explain the implications of that foundational view for us and our interests. The practitioners of this super-science seem not always to have wholly convinced themselves of its claims to tell it as it is, if by *it* we mean the world as it really is, viewed with regard to the features that are central to its workings and that have the greatest bearing on our affairs.

Schopenhauer wrote in the preface to *The World as Will and Representation* that his philosophy was the definitive solution to the enigma of existence. Elsewhere, however, he remarked that a man's philosophy is the expression of his temperament. These two propositions cannot both be true, unless we suppose that there is a particular temperament whose possession happens to give admission to the secrets of the super-science.

The philosophers who worked in this tradition differed widely in the extent to which they provided explicit answers to the question: How do you know that your account of the way things are is true? Sometimes they were explicit about their choice and justification of a method that would be proof against skeptical objection. At other times they simply chose the method that seemed to reconcile the greatest rigor and precision in their reasoning with what seemed most suitable to their subject matter and to the way in which they approached it.

The implicit standard of success in this enterprise was the power of their ideas, taken as a whole, rather than proposition by proposition, to elucidate experience. In this respect, they required to be judged by a standard no different from the one applied to the natural science of the last few centuries. The difference is that they took everything for their subject matter.

The would-be practitioners of super-science often sought immunity against doubt by appealing to a supposedly special category of insight, as Descartes did in taking the certainty of his own existence as his point of departure. When they proceeded in this way, however, they soon discovered that no pretense of indubitable knowledge could discredit a sufficiently radical skepticism. Even if it could, it would fail to provide an adequate bridge to what the program of a super-science requires: an inclusive understanding of the world in which we find ourselves. It would be as if the mind were admitted to a safe room from which it could go nowhere else.

Other philosophical super-scientists dispensed, as Aristotle did, with the appeal to a special category of privileged insight and stood by the power of their system, taken as a whole, to account for reality. But there were too many different ways to formulate such accounts and no obvious way in which to arbitrate their competing merits. The history of philosophy as super-science consequently came to consist in a succession of incompatible world views: each one of them the handiwork of a great original mind, at once inimitable and imitated.

The only way to judge these comprehensive views of the world and to make them more useful to our collective self-understanding would be to come down from the lonely peaks of system and genius. It would be to engage what we have collectively discovered about the world and recorded in the ideas of the specialized sciences and disciplines. It would be, in other words, to abandon the idea of a super-science.

There is no higher understanding of reality that we can place, as the queen of the sciences, above the specialized disciplines through which we engage with reality, piece by piece, and try to make sense of it. If a more comprehensive and fundamental understanding is to emerge from such efforts, it will not result from the claim to be standing on a higher level of insight. It will not justify the practice of handing down, from that exalted position, accounts of ultimate reality to everyone else.

There is a salvageable remnant in the otherwise illusory and dangerous project of a philosophical super-science. It is the idea that the established fields of inquiry, including the natural and social sciences, fail to exhaust our power to press our understanding of reality and of its transformative possibilities to its uncertain limits. The inadequacy of the specialized fields of inquiry becomes more salient when our aim is to form a view of our situation as a whole: a view compatible with recognition of our groundlessness.

As with everything else in our experience, each of the specialized disciplines is the product of a distinct history shaped by confrontation between rival views of its subject matter as well as by the influence of the societies and cultures in which it developed. The division of labor among fields is not to be confused with a permanent organon of the faculties of the mind: it forms part of a contested and accidental history. In each of the natural and social sciences, we find a forced marriage between a method and a subject matter, even though the same subject matter might be approached by an entirely different method.

Fundamental physics, for example, proceeds by an anti-historical method, and takes as its subject the permanent and regular workings of nature, affirming the priority of structure over change and history. But evolutionary biology, since Darwin, has proceeded by a historical method. After the discovery in the 1920s of the historical character of the universe, we might have reason to view cosmology as a historical science and as the most fundamental of the natural sciences: if the universe has a history, so must every part of it, and, in every part of nature, history must be prior to structure rather than the other way around.

To dissolve the marriage of method and subject matter in each discipline is no easy matter. It requires intellectual revolution, defies the arrangements as well as the orthodoxies of the research universities, and unsettles the basis on which academic specialists have staked their careers.

If the confusion of method and subject matter is one reason to refuse allowing the specialized disciplines the last word over what the world is like and how things and people can change, another reason is the irreducible gap between our empirical findings and our theoretical constructions. We can always interpret the same findings through alternative theories. We cannot establish the superiority of one theory to another by observation but only by seeing how rival theories—each of them a complex body of ideas—bear on a large range of phenomena and comparing their usefulness and fecundity in the pursuit of an agenda of research and thought over time.

A theory, a way of thinking, is in the first instance an account of how things change. To understand a phenomenon, to have insight into how it works, is just to grasp what it can become under certain conditions or interventions. Not to grasp its transformative variations in the realm of the adjacent possible is just to stare at it, mistaking description or retrospective rationalization for explanation.[1]

But the price of this power to subsume the actual under a range of accessible possibilities is the distance taken from the phenomenon: the ability and the necessity to see it under the lens of some view whose advantages will have to be demonstrated over a large range of events and over time—not the time of these events but the time of alternative research programs. In each theory there will be a conception of what part of the world is like and of how the phenomena it studies behave and change. And in each such conception there will be the fragment or the hint of an ontology: an account of the protagonists of that part of reality and of how they interact.

These inexplicit ontologies will be metaphysical in the literal sense that they cannot be immediately derived from any piece of the manifest world. Yet it is only by trafficking in them that we can make sense of what we have observed or discovered.

The fragmentary ontologies of the different disciplines do not line up. They do not form subheadings of the same encyclopedia. They are adventures in thought, usually disguised as something else, and adventures in different directions rather than orchestrated steps taken in the same direction. The idea of a hierarchy of the forms of knowledge, in which science takes precedence over non-science, and fundamental physics takes precedence over all other sciences, may seem to contain the resulting disorder and impart to it the semblance of a coherent vision. But it is a paltry order, relying on a methodological and metaphysical prejudice—a certain idea of rank among fields

---

1. In the life sciences the concept of the adjacent possible has been developed by Stuart Kauffman. See his *Investigations: The Nature of Autonomous Agents and the Worlds They Mutually Create*, Santa Fe Institute working paper #96-08-72, 1996.

of knowledge—that lacks even the remote and conjectural relation of theory to fact that we find in the fragmentary ontologies of the different disciplines.

The relatively accidental character of the distinctions among specialized fields, the forced marriage of method and subject in each of them, and the inescapable presence of metaphysics within physics and every other branch of study, within and outside natural science, has implications for what can and should succeed philosophy as super-science. There can be no such super-science, offering a direct route to the understanding of fundamental reality.

We nevertheless have reason to resist allowing the specialized fields of inquiry to usurp the prerogative of thought. The sum of these fields fails to exhaust our powers of inquiry. We cannot collect their teachings into an ordered view of the world. We cannot even trust them completely with the interpretation of their own areas of interest. And we cannot expect them to give us ideas about what is common and fundamental to all our experience: ideas that can inform our response to the condition of mortality and groundlessness.

How can we abandon the project of a philosophical super-science without resigning ourselves to the exclusive rule of the specialized disciplines? The solution to this apparent dilemma is to understand philosophy as a bearer of our residual powers of insight: those that the specialized sciences fail to exhaust and that we identify with the imagination.

Two moves define the aspect of our mental experience that we call the imagination. The first move—the one emphasized by Kant—is distancing from the phenomenon. The second move—which Kant neglected—is the subsumption of the actual under a range of variations in the realm of the adjacent possibilities: what the actual can become next.

The two moves of the imagination do not apply only to nature and society around us and within us. The apply as well as to the conventional forms that the work of the imagination takes in each of the specialized fields of inquiry. The keynote of our reckoning with the real is insight into transformation. We understand the nature and limits of the established procedures by which we reckon with the real only to the extent that we subject them to the same imaginative pressure that we apply in the study of nature and society.

The activity in which we reckon most relentlessly and unconditionally with the real in the most unlimited form as well as with our ways of reckoning with the real is philosophy. Philosophy, understood in this way, is the central, albeit far from exclusive, seat of the imagination in our reasoning about the world. Understood in this way, philosophy may seem to be necessary. But is it possible?

In the imaginative activity of the mind, we can form ideas about the world that our established methods and assumptions fail to validate. We can grasp reality under an aspect that those assumptions and methods do not allow us to make sense of fully. And then we can develop retrospectively the ways of thinking that make sense of them.

This transgressive and transcending power of the imagination is not the exclusive privilege of philosophy. It is spread through all intellectual experience and is present, as a potential of thought, in every field. However, in philosophy this power appears in its least compromised and most concentrated form.

For one thing, no attempt to turn philosophy into another specialized discipline like the others has succeeded. There have been many such attempts (later I will refer to the most recent) but none of them have survived for long or found acceptance beyond provincial academic cultures. The first reason for their failure is that they pay the price of specialized and organized inquiry in their confinement to a limited stock of methods and moves, without the corresponding advantage of being recognized as useful by anyone other than their own agents.

For another thing, the core subject matter of philosophy is finitude and transcendence—in every facet of our experience, including our understanding of the real. What philosophy sees in all our experience, it must see in itself. If it fails to exemplify its theme of finitude and transcendence in its own practice, it cannot hope to do this theme justice.

The alternative to the project of a philosophical super-science is the idea of philosophy as the mind at war, pushing our ambition to understand and explain, and to act in the light of such insight, beyond the boundaries of the specialized disciplines and their methods and beyond the established arrangements and assumptions of society. Viewed in this way, philosophy comes as close as it can to the limit of our groundlessness—our ignorance of the ground of existence and reality. It insists on our prerogative to address what matters most by advancing into the outer reaches of our powers of reasoning and discovery, into the almost unthinkable and unspeakable, where our light begins to fail us. Such work is no super-science. But neither is it the surrender of our powers of insight to the account of the real supplied by the organized and established disciplines.

Philosophy, viewed and practiced in this way, represents our last and best chance to advance to the limits of thought. It advances with the risk that it may cross those limits unawares. In making this attempt to serve as the most direct and uncompromising expression of the struggle of transcendence with finitude in the life of the mind, it pays a heavy price. As the rebellion that it is—a rebellion against our limitations of insight about matters of ultimate concern—it is far more likely to fail than to succeed.

The idea of the super-science is the theoretical element in the classical conception of philosophy—the one that in the West has been predominant from the pre-Socratic philosophers to our own time. The practical element in this dominant tradition is the enlistment of the super-science in the service of a particular form of self-help. Philosophical super-science offers self-help in the face of the inescapable defects in the human condition: our mortality and groundlessness as well as our insatiability. Not only must we die and die ignorant of the ground of being and existence; we must also undergo the ordeal of insatiable desire.

Surrounded only by limited, finite things and by people who are both resistant and obscure to us, we desire the infinite, the absolute, the unconditional. This longing for the infinite, in the midst of the finite, is no minor or accidental feature of our attitudes; it is a manifestation, in the experience of desire, of the central dialectic of finitude and transcendence that is inscribed in our being. And because there are no desires without thoughts, it penetrates our thinking as well as our desiring and helps place the view of philosophy as the reserve army of thought in the setting of our experience as a whole.

Our insatiability enters as well into our dealings with others. In connecting with them and seeking a form of connection that reassures us in the sentiment of being, rather than robbing us of freedom and distinction, we demand of every other person a sign that there is an unconditional place for each of us in the world. This transaction can never be completed: the sign, even when given, is never enough, if only because it remains subject to the erosion of time. And the impossibility of obtaining the assurance we seek helps inspire the ambivalence that shadows our relations to one another.

Unable to find the infinite, the absolute, and the unconditional in a world that contains only the finite, the relative, and the conditional, we are perennially tempted to seize on some piece of the surrounding finite reality as if it were a token of the missing infinite. The history of thought is replete with words that designate this endless metonymy: words such as displacement, fetishism, reification, and idolatry. The result of this temptation is to mislead us into consuming our lives—when they are not wholly bent under material needs and social oppression—in repeated acts of what we might describe as false transcendence. Thus, we lose our freedom to a spiritual perversion.

The super-science has not been simply an expression of overweening intellectual ambition. It has also served as an antidote to these irreparable flaws in the human condition. The Semitic monotheisms—Judaism, and especially its successors, Christianity and Islam—promised a decisive antidote: eternal life, the grounding of our existence in a narrative of dealings between a creative God and mankind, beginning in historical time and outlasting it. Christianity, especially, made love for and by God the model for our love of one another and for our emancipation from insatiability, idolatry, and false transcendence.

As believers in one of these religions, the philosophers (including Maimonides, Aquinas, Averroes, and Nicholas of Cusa) sometimes tried to elucidate and uphold this promise in the discourse of philosophy and struggled with the tension between a way of thinking organized around impersonal being and structure, at least partly exempt from change and time, and a story of salvation formulated in the language of personality—with a theomorphic view of man and an anthropomorphic view of God, man and God acting in the medium of time.

But even when they were believers, the philosophers have more often continued to do what they did before these religions arose. They have taught us how to compose ourselves in the face of death or to turn away from death to life. They have translated the promise of eternal life into something other than our perpetual embodied existence. They have presented a view of the real—or at least of what is most real in our experience—that equates what is most real with what is least time-bound. And they have wanted to free us from our insatiability by turning us toward those abiding realities.

In all these ways the philosophers have persevered in the effort to provide us with means by which to deal with the irreparable defects in our situation. When they have been unable to deny those defects, they have advised us how to manage them by reinterpreting them or simply forgetting them. This advice has been the practical point of the philosophical super-science.

Only a few have refused to offer such consolation as the reward of philosophical enlightenment. If they were believers (like Pascal and Kierkegaard), they qualified faith in eternal life with uncertainty about salvation. If they were unbelievers (like Nietzsche and Heidegger), their refusal to console was bound up with their apostasy from the idea of the super-science and consequently from its use as the source of consolation.

The first and fundamental objection to such self-help is that it threatens to turn philosophy into a feel-good story. By so doing, it risks robbing philosophy of its integrity and diminishing its power, which is to help us live in the light of the truth. We are entitled to hope. But we have no reason that is good enough to deny the facts of mortality and groundlessness and to dismiss our insatiability as a bad habit or an illusion rather than to recognize in it an expression of our innermost identity.

We dare not allow fear—of death and of moral anarchy—and wishful thinking to suppress recognition of the most perplexing and frightening aspects of our situation. It is one thing for philosophy to serve as an auxiliary to theology. The argument about what we can hope for then turns into a contest over religion and its promises. It is another thing for philosophy to claim the powers of a revealed faith without being able to count on any of the means by which such a faith tries to show that our situation is not what it seems to be: an experience of revelation that has compelling immediacy and authority results from a transformative encounter with a God who breaks into history.

Facing death, recognizing groundlessness, and undergoing insatiability may be the indispensable conditions for awakening from the roles and routines that prevent us from entering more fully into the possession of life. These routines and roles lull us into a passivity that cheats us of the characteristic attributes of life—the surfeit of experience over established structure, the spontaneity of life and its capacity to surprise—and suppresses the repeated acts of transcendence that make us more human by making us more godlike. The result is to coax us into dying many small deaths beforehand, and to prevent us from dying all at once.

To turn against these roles and routines and affirm the power to transcend—in experience, not simply in doctrine—we must confront our mortality, groundlessness, and insatiability and reconcile ourselves to living in a world where everything changes sooner or later, where nothing is outside of time. Facing these incurable wounds in the human condition may be the first and indispensable step to our liberation—not from death but from the renunciation of life.

The classical conception of philosophy as a super-science in the service of self-help is far from exhausting what philosophy has been in the course of its history. Among alternative views, there is one that deserves special attention both because of its contemporary influence and because it highlights by its defects another way in which philosophy can go wrong by assuming a mistaken view of the relation between finitude and transcendence.

This view has often been labeled Analytical Philosophy and contrasted, given its ascendancy in the universities of English-speaking countries, to the afterlife enjoyed by the classical conception in continental Europe. Its central conceit, through the successive stages of its evolution, has been that once philosophy abandons the illusory pretensions of super-science, and the hope of passing judgment on what the specialized fields of inquiry can teach us about reality, it can justify its survival only by going in search of both a well-defined subject matter and a distinctive method.

The main candidate for the role of the subject matter is the nature of argument, justification, and the conveyance of meaning in all the specialized disciplines. When Analytical Philosophy has not been content to remain passive and descriptive, it has assumed the role of a thought police, proposing to expose the fallacies, chasten the unjustified knowledge, and dispel the confusions it has seen all around it in the established fields of inquiry. In this activist and admonitory role, it has provided a service with few takers. Its agents have been punished by being left to speak mainly with one another rather than with the intended clients of their police work.

Analytical Philosophy has gone through two stages: one empiricist, the other linguistic. In its empiricist phase, its temper was reductionist: to deflate knowledge claims that failed to enjoy an adequate and direct basis in our phenomenal experience. In its linguistic phase, it hoped to trace the mistakes of metaphysical super-science, and of its lesser forms in the established disciples and in everyday discourse, to confusions in the use of language.

It then entered a third stage (though the previous two live on), in which it abandoned the activist and revisionist task—the thought-police operation—and resigned itself to a passive role. Discounting transcendent claims to knowledge by even the hard sciences and mathematics, it presented those claims as gaining sense only in the context of certain social practices. It rejected the search, characteristic of the earlier forms of Analytical Philosophy as well as of philosophical super-science, for higher-order criteria by which to judge these practices—a meta-discourse.

The late philosophy of Wittgenstein was the most influential source of this third moment of Analytical Philosophy. The work of philosophers like Willard Quine in challenging the distinction between analytical and synthetic judgments—those that are true by definition and those whose truth depend on the facts of the matter—formed part of its background. This work denied Analytical Philosophy a domain that it might claim exclusively for itself. The teachings of other philosophers like Wilfrid Sellars—who attacked the idea that the mind can ever work with "givens" innocent of theoretical conceptions—supplied another part of the background. These teachings undermined confidence in our ability to settle intellectual disputes by recourse to a tribunal of the facts without prior commitments to clashing theories.

Against this background, philosophers like Richard Rorty argued that all we have to work with are different conversations, shaped by collective practices, and susceptible to challenge and change only from within. The attempt to judge these practices by higher-order criteria, imported from outside them, is simply a proposal to change a practice, disguised as a knowledge claim. The only legitimate meta-discourse is a meta-discourse useful in exhibiting other meta-discourses as such disguises.

This view, from late Wittgenstein to Rorty, fails to do justice to the relation between the human agent and the social practices and arrangements through which he must act in the world. When he engages such a regime of social practice—whether it is a stylized discourse or an organization of our life together, will he surrender to it? Or will he deny it the last word and keep that word to himself? Will the practice be arranged to facilitate its own revision, or will it be organized to entrench itself against challenge and change? Will the difference between our regime-preserving and our regime-changing moves be great, as when change requires revolution, open struggle, and genius in politics or in science? Or will that distance be narrowed so that our regime-changing moves arise more naturally and continuously from our regime-preserving ones, without requiring crisis as the condition of change, or conflict as its instrument? And if this distance fails to be narrowed, can the individual agent nevertheless seek to act as an insider who is also an outsider, and as the prophet of alternatives, informed by the memory or the intimation of other ways of doing things?

The standards to which the rebel or the prophet appeals, in thought as in politics, are not confined to those of the established practice or regime. But neither are they drawn from a higher realm of concepts and criteria that a philosophical super-science would be able to codify. They are informed by all our experience—the countercurrents, deviations, and anomalies within the established forms, and the knowledge, however remote and fragmentary, of other regimes and practices. They amount to an intimation of some form of practical or cognitive power that the present order suppresses.

The third stage of Analytical Philosophy commits a mistake that is the inverse of the mistake committed by the philosophical super-science. In its conception of the relation of our powers to our practices and regimes—what Wittgenstein called our forms of life—the super-science failed to recognize the true character of our transcendence. It mistook our ability to do more than the established regime of thought or of social life makes possible for an escape from our finitude and an approach to the ideal of absolute knowledge. Analytical Philosophy in this last variation taught that nothing lies beyond the horizon of our shared institutions, practices, or conversations. We may or may not be able to change them. But we cannot hope to base any effort to change them on claims to see beyond them, or to envision a different collective future and a different relation between us and them—one that recognizes and develops our structure-defying freedom. We would be misguided to see in our reconstruction of them any practical expression of our transcendence.

Philosophy finds its way by resisting all such mis-directions.

This Book: Its Scope, Plan, and Character

This is a general work of philosophy. It addresses each of the principal philosophical disciplines recognized in the tradition of Western philosophy: ontology, epistemology, ethics, politics, and what for want of a better term has sometimes been called philosophical anthropology—reflection on the human condition and human nature. But although it uses these labels, it gives each of them a meaning different from the one it has had in that tradition.

It enacts the conception of philosophy that I have just explained: philosophy as the expression of our residual power to advance beyond the specialized fields of discourse and their established methods and to address what should most concern us—our plight as mortal, groundless, and insatiable beings—and test the limits of what we can think and say. The way of thinking that informs this book lays claim to no source of insight different from the sources readily available to us in the specialized disciplines, in the history of society and of thought, and in our everyday experience. It proposes no system of ideas that would ground the groundless beings who we are. And it does not dictate from a plane of supposedly higher insight—the plane on which the super-science claimed to stand.

But neither does the argument of this book, or the idea of philosophy that it exemplifies, cower before our practices and specialties, as if each of them were a law unto itself. At each step, it claims for philosophy—which is to say for thought outside as well as within the disciplines—a power of revision. The mistake is to suppose that philosophy must either wear the crown of super-science or abdicate, together with this crown, that revisionist power.

A paradox of the tradition of philosophical super-science is that despite its claim to higher insight it was careful not to disagree with the prevailing interpretation of the most ambitious and influential natural science of its time: for example, the physics of Galileo or of Newton. It took that interpretation as a given, and then, through a process of metaphysical reverse engineering, tried to show how it could be inferred from a grander and more inclusive system of ideas.

The philosophical practice for which I speak strengthens, rather than weakens, its revisionist reach by abandoning the pretenses of philosophical super-science. It excludes nothing—not even mathematics and fundamental physics—from the scope of its revisionism. We do not need to make claims to foundational knowledge to question dominant ideas about either nature or humanity and to argue in favor of alternative ideas. All we need is a hard-won freedom from superstition and idolatry and an ability to discern the disputable metaphysical element in what are misrepresented as straightforward empirical discoveries in the sciences.

This book has a central subject, which it pursues—relentlessly—in each step of its argument. The subject is the one evoked at the beginning of this prologue: the coexistence of finitude and transcendence in every part of our experience, under the shadow of death, enigma, and insatiable desire; the social character of our efforts to loosen the bonds of finitude; and the direction that these efforts can and should take given the contradictory and ambivalent character of our relations to one another.

The view of what the world is like for which I argue might be described, in its account of reality, as a temporal naturalism, if this label, like every label, were not more dangerous than useful. It is a naturalism because it takes the most important feature of the world, and of humanity within it, to be that they are what they are rather than something else. It repudiates every trace of the attempt, characteristic of rationalist metaphysics, to show why the world must be what it is. It is also a naturalism in the sense that, in its conception of our natures and our place in the world, it rejects the dualisms that, in successive waves, have dominated Western philosophy: the attempt to find for us what Spinoza called a kingdom within a kingdom, exempt from the general regime of nature.

It is temporal because it argues—against what I will describe as the two dominant traditions in the world history of philosophy, as well as against the leading contemporary accounts of what science has discovered about the workings of nature—that nothing in the world is forever, not even its most elementary constituents and its most stable regularities: laws, symmetries, and constants. Everything changes sooner or later, including change itself.

The reality of time defines our experience. In biographical time, we as individuals die, and either live or fail to live in such a way as to die only once. In historical time, we struggle against our finitude and with one another. For each of us, time is our chief and, in a sense, our only resource, and the medium in which our lives acquire their fateful and concentrated form. Every conception of natural or human reality that undermines or qualifies recognition of the reality of time subtracts from our self-understanding and misleads us in the conduct of life.

Four themes run through the argument of this book, animating and unifying its many strands. They reappear, in one form or another, in every chapter.

The first is the theme that has figured prominently in this prologue: the vocation and future of philosophy. How can philosophy escape the illusions of philosophical super-science without abdicating its power to question the orthodoxies of the established disciplines? There is no intellectual space reserved for a supposed master discipline entitled to deal with the foundations of all the specialized areas of inquiry. But the absence of that space does not mean that there is nothing left to philosophy but to accept what the specialized fields of inquiry say. The issue is not the prerogative of a form of thought labeled philosophy; it is the use of the saving remnant of the mind, in its most ambitious and comprehensive endeavors, to examine and challenge the reigning ideas and methods in the specialties, including the natural and social sciences, and to open up questions that they have closed.

The second theme is that of the development and defense of a temporal naturalism as an alternative to two dominant traditions of thinking in the global history of philosophy: the philosophy of deep structure, which has been predominant in the West, from Aristotle to twentieth-century physics; and the philosophy of the timeless one, which has been a minor strand in Western philosophy but a major strand in other parts of the world. Both these dominant traditions deny or diminish the reality of time and associate what is most real with what is timeless. They provide an inadequate basis on which to understand a world in which everything changes sooner or later, and beings like ourselves for whom change, time, and causation are central to every part of their experience.

A consequence of the permanent campaign against time has been the diversion of much of modern Western philosophy into a series of dualisms that have served the purpose of carving out for ourselves a miraculous exception to the general regime of nature. Another consequence has been to associate explanatory ambition, in social thought as well as in natural science, with the search for regularities and structures that we mistakenly treat as immutable. On such a basis we cannot hope to make sense of our experience or to make the most of our moral and political prospects.

A third theme is that of the human being as what we might call—in the potent but also dangerous and misleading vocabulary of Christian theology and Christianized metaphysics—embodied spirit. He is embodied and therefore dying—the starkest expression of his finitude. And he is spirit in the sense of carrying the stigma of being unaccommodated and the power of transcending all the finite determinations of his existence. Spirit in this context is not an allusion to any dualism: a distinction between two kinds of reality—material and immaterial. It is the invocation of a power: the power to overcome, to transcend, to see, think, feel, connect, experience, innovate, and invent more than can be accepted and elucidated by the social and conceptual worlds in which the human agent moves. The individual human being does not exercise this power alone; he exercises it with others, as a social practice, in a social world, or not at all.

My aim is to give a naturalistic account of this idea of the human being—an account dispensing with miraculous dualisms but also forswearing any pretense of solving the riddles of the nature and origin of consciousness. This view of the person serves as the point of departure for thinking about the contradictory character of the conditions of selfhood (philosophical anthropology), the growth of our understanding of the world (epistemology), the conduct of life (ethics), and the organization of society (politics).

The conception of the human being as embodied spirit has been central to Western literature as well as to our moral and political ideas. Throughout this book I ask myself what we can and should make of it today, once we have restated and developed it in a form free of all theological presuppositions and resolved to recognize the complications of our relation to society and to nature.

It is a view of the human being that might be derided as provincial given its close association with religious and political ideas that have been predominant in the West. It has been disseminated throughout the world first by the Semitic monotheisms and later by the world revolution (the fourth theme of the book). But rather than seeing this view of the human being—creative, transformative, transcendent, and theomorphic—as a product of these influences, we have reason to see these influences as drawing much of their power from having given voice to an idea of our humanity that many have found irresistible— with good reason, I argue here. The idea resonates deeply with the experience of people all over the world.

The fourth theme, then, is the world revolution and its future. At least since the closing decades of the eighteenth century, the whole world has been set on a fire by a revolutionary movement. This movement has had two sides. Its political side, carried by democracy, liberalism, and socialism, has offered to lift the grid of entrenched social division and hierarchy weighing on humanity. Its personalist side, associated with romanticism, and especially with the worldwide popular romantic culture, has assured every man and woman that they have unlimited depth and can hope to come more fully into the possession of life.

This revolutionary movement continues to command the agenda of humanity: it has many enemies, but all of them respond to it. But if it continues to be strong, it is now also weak insofar as its adepts no longer know what its next steps might or should be on either its political or its personalist sides. It can live only if we reinvent it in both form and substance, practice and program. The world in which it has failed to be reinvented is now restless under the yoke of a dictatorship of no alternatives.

One way of understanding this book is to take it as an attempt to imagine the ideas that might help breathe new life and new meaning into the revolutionary project. These ideas concern the next steps of this movement on both its political and personalist sides—the subject matter of the later chapters. But they also include the account of the human condition at the center of my argument, the discussion of our powers of inquiry and discovery, and the view of what the world is like outlined in the early chapters. It matters whether we have, or can develop, the capabilities that the revolutionary program requires and whether we find ourselves in a world that has room for its novelties.

These four themes may seem to be only loosely associated. They are, however, closely connected in the arguments of this book. The reawakening and redefinition of the revolutionary movement gives moral and political consequence to an idea of ourselves as embodied spirit, struggling with the relation between our finitude and our transcendence. This idea, and the ways of thinking about how to live and organize society that it helps inspire, cannot easily be reconciled with either of the two dominant traditions in the world history of philosophy. Rejecting arbitrary exemptions from the general regime of nature, it requires, as its backdrop, another view of natural reality—the view that I label temporal naturalism.

Such a view, however, is not enough by itself to guide us in this endeavor. We also need a mode of thought that is free of any claim to be a science of the foundations of all the specialized fields of inquiry. This mode of thought must be unrestrained by any inhibition when it comes to criticizing the ideas of those disciplines and proposing alternative directions. In all its work, it must exemplify the central impulse of the imagination, which is to deepen our insight into the actual by developing our vision of what the actual can next become. It must put every orthodoxy through the skeptic's flame, risking nihilism for the sake of insight. I give the name philosophy to this mode of thought.

My argument develops in eight chapters.

Chapters 1 and 2 deal with the world and our knowledge of it, under the traditional headings of ontology and epistemology. These are the two parts of what, in the tradition of the super-science, we think of as theoretical philosophy. The chief aim of my argument in these chapters is nonetheless practical: to sweep away false obstacles to our engagement with the world as well as to our understanding of reality.

Chapter 1 reinterprets ontology as natural philosophy and social theory. Its aim is to propose an initial conception of the natural reality around and within us. We cannot make sense of our experience within the confines of the two major traditions in the world history of philosophy. Both these traditions deny, to a greater or lesser extent, the reality of time, and affirm, mistakenly, that what is most real is what changes least. Nor can we understand society if we continue to accept ideas that confer a halo of naturalness and necessity on the arrangements or structures of social life rather than recognizing them as the frozen fighting that they are: outcomes of the partial containment or temporary interruption of our struggles over the terms on which we enjoy access to one another.

The practical aim of ontology, reinterpreted in this way, is to free us from the illusions that keep us from understanding the real, in nature or society, by denying, understating, or misrepresenting its susceptibility to transformation. These illusions surround us with an army of phantasms and idols and cheat us of our freedom. Although they may claim to present us with a view of the world in the eyes of God—the absolute knowledge from which we seem to be, and are in fact, barred—their effect is the opposite: to prevent us, in one area of our experience after another, from exercising our power to loosen the constraints of our finitude.

Chapter 2 addresses, under the label epistemology, our understanding of the world. It redefines epistemology as inquiry about inquiry. The argument of this chapter has two aims.

Its first goal is to show how the growth of knowledge exemplifies the dialectic of finitude and transcendence. The stock controversies and options of epistemology, from radical skepticism to the claim to absolute knowledge, are one of the most sterile parts of the philosophical tradition. The misdirections and dead ends that make up most of the history of the philosophy of knowledge come down to two sets of mistakes. The first set of mistakes results from the adoption of a misguided standard of what knowledge would or should consist in, conceiving it as affording access to reality as it is, not simply from the perspective of the embodied organisms that we are—with the inevitable disappointment that follows at our inability to meet this standard. The second set of mistakes arises from underestimating our ability to push back our cognitive and even our perceptual limitations. One variant of this second family of mistakes is to identify the ways of thinking that come most naturally to us and suggest they constitute a world view so deeply implanted in our natural constitution that we are powerless to criticize, correct, and improve it.

An understanding of why these two sets of views are mistaken and of how we can avoid them requires us to achieve clarity about causation and about the relation of mathematics to science and to nature. Mathematics presents a simulacrum of the world, with time and phenomenal particularity sucked out of it. Consequently, mathematics holds the greatest interest for an approach to inquiry that places change and time as the most basic and enduring feature of reality.

The second goal of this chapter is the conversion of epistemology, once liberated from these opposing mistakes, into a practical theory of the growth of our insight into reality: transcendence in the realm of inquiry. Here the revisionist impulse of philosophy comes to the fore. Each of the natural and social sciences misrepresents in its own way the vital link between insight into the actual and imagination of what the actual can next become. The prevailing forms of education deny us the equipment that we need to correct these misrepresentations, both within and outside natural science.

Epistemology becomes, in this view, a program of cognitive empowerment. A working assumption of this program is that we can never know beforehand how far our theories and our observational, computational, and experimental equipment will allow us to move beyond the forms of perception and the ways of thinking that nature and history have together instilled in us.

Chapter 3, on the human condition, deals with what has sometimes been labeled philosophical anthropology or the doctrine of human nature. Although this label is the least familiar, in the philosophical canon, of my titles, the topic itself is the hinge on which philosophy turns: on one side of this hinge lies theoretical philosophy—ontology and epistemology; on the other side, practical philosophy—ethics and politics. The theoretical philosophy explored in the first two chapters has as one of its goals to remove obstacles to an understanding of who we are and can become. The practical philosophy explored in last five chapters, focusing on ethics and politics, is animated by that understanding. The argument of Chapter 3, on philosophical anthropology, advances in three steps.

In the first step, I return to the subject broached at the beginning of this prologue: the irreparable flaws in the human condition. Here I view these flaws in another light—as pointing to a world awash in time in which everything changes sooner or later. I relate them to the struggle of our transcendence with our finitude, in our constitution and in our efforts to make sense of the real. And I discuss the cost of not facing these flaws openly.

In the second step of the argument, I address the main ways in which philosophy and religion have sought to console us by either explaining these flaws away or supplying an antidote to their terrors. However, the better the news that these efforts at consolation bring, the less reason there is to believe them. Even a view recognizing that there is no one here but us, in a universe and an existence whose ground we cannot grasp, may divert us from the truth about our situation by teaching us always to look the other way, to our connections and engagements. We follow this advice, however, only at a terrible cost to our ascent to a higher form of life.

In the third step of the argument, having argued against all such solace, whether theological, metaphysical, or psychological, I turn to what stands here in place of a traditional doctrine of human nature: an account of the contradictory conditions of selfhood in the present moment—life right now, which is all we ever have. To be free, we must connect with others. But every such connection threatens us with loss of freedom and distinction. We must engage in a particular social and cultural world. But every such world seems to require, as the price of engagement, that we surrender to it, and take our cue from the script that it hands us. We must form a coherent way of being in the world. But every such way of being threatens to become a mummy, within which the context-transcending spirit begins to die many small deaths, rather than dying, as we should desire, only once.

To attenuate these contradictions—given that we cannot overcome them—in the historical time of political struggle as well as in the biographical time of our moral striving, is the path of our rise to a higher form of life.

Chapters 4, 5, and 6 deal with ethics. Chapter 4 develops a conception of ethics as clarity about the conduct of life. It is foolish to suppose that philosophy can legislate what each of us is to do with his own and only life and how he is to live. But it is equally wrong to accept the direction that moral philosophy has recently taken in the Anglo-American academy: the confinement of ethics to the deployment of methods that are supposed to specify our obligations to one another but that are silent about the conduct of life. The different schools of this meta-ethics (invoking Kant's categorical imperative, Bentham's felicific calculus, or Rousseau's social contract) express, through their focus on obligation-specifying devices, a legalistic moralism unsuited to the thing itself—the living, suffering, and aspiring human being, who is the protagonist of this book and ought to be the protagonist of ethics.

Philosophy cannot prescribe, from first principles, how we should live. Nor are we justified in reducing ethics to a book of accounts and to the supposedly impartial procedures that would apportion our moral liabilities and assets. We must find another basis on which to develop our ideas about the conduct of life.

In the spirit of the conception of philosophy defended here, we must engage the powerful moral visions in our historical moment and take their criticism and reconstruction as starting points. Such visions are not merely abstractions favored by isolated thinkers. To exert influence, they must be enacted in practices that reveal much of their meaning. They must draw much of their force from the needs of the societies in which they emerge, not simply from someone's ideas about how to settle guilt and innocence.

In this spirit, Chapter 5 addresses the two most important approaches to the conduct of life in the world today: an ethic of self-fashioning and non-conformity and an ethic of connection and responsibility. In their familiar forms, associated with particular modern or ancient thinkers, they are so obviously defective and incomplete as orientations to existence that to take them at the word of their famous ideologists would be to rehearse a battle of strawmen. They represent, amid the tribulations of real people in real societies, two ways of dealing with the contradictions of our need for other people, of our engagement in a social world, and of our relation to ourselves.

Chapter 6 completes the discussion of ethics by exploring the future of the contest between the ethics of self-fashioning and the ethics of connection. It shows how each of them has been shaped, or misshaped, by its relation to one of the two great powers of today: the United States and China. The privileged association of each of these moral visions with one of those powers is contingent and even subject to radical reversal and transvaluation. Moreover, it helps account for the most salient defects of these orientations to existence in the conventional form in which they have come to us. To strengthen each of these visions, we must revise them, and to revise them we must shake off this dust of history.

These two moral views would not command the influence they do if they were merely the outcome of powerful intellectual traditions, contingently associated with certain countries and their cultures. They derive their power from their relation to two major functional imperatives of contemporary societies: the enhancement of agency and the development of higher forms of cooperation. These two imperatives both sustain and contradict each other. The ways in which they combine or clash help set the course of our lives.

It is natural to think that we should be able to bring these ethics into a higher-order synthesis. But we cannot do this in any more than a superficial rhetorical sense. Behind the contest between these approaches to the conduct of life stands a deep and lasting duality in our moral consciousness. This duality allows us to see in a new light the relation between our finitude and our transcendence and the social character of our impulse to transcend.

Chapters 7 and 8 deal with politics, which, alongside ontology, epistemology, and ethics, completes the core of the classic philosophical encyclopedia. Thus, from theoretical philosophy—ontology and epistemology—we turn to practical philosophy—ethics and politics. The study of politics completes the program of practical philosophy in its ambition to mark the form of transcendence that is open to us in this one real world of ours. Our watchword, if we are to do justice to the dialectic of finitude and transcendence in political experience, should be the combination of uncompromising realism with transformative ambition.

Chapter 7 develops the idea of politics as a struggle over the future of society. It begins with the description of the two nightmares that beset our life in societies that are organized under the shield of states. In the history of civilization, all societies have been class societies: everyone in them is born into a place in a system that shapes his life chances, to a greater or lesser extent. As a result, our efforts at transcendence take place under the constraint of a force that most of us, for most of the time, in most societies, may be unable to overcome. Our one and only life may be extinguished before we have enjoyed any freedom comparable to the freedom that I exercise in writing this book.

To this first nightmare, the political life of humanity adds a second. Where there are civilized societies, there are also states. These states provide the protection that allows different parts of humanity to take different directions. And it is only by organizing social life in different ways, under different arrangements and assumptions, that we can develop the powers and potential of humanity.

There is no natural form of social life, and no regime that is neutral among conflicting forms of experience and visions of the good. The pretense of neutrality—of an impersonal right, contrasted with sectarian moral and material interests—serves its opposite. It entrenches a sectarian vision of our highest moral and material interests, and of the best way to satisfy them, against attack and revision.

Those who come to power in the armed and belligerent states in which humanity carries out its experiments in ways of being human regularly use this power to turn temporary advantage into lasting right. The result is to combine the two nightmares haunting our political life into one. It is in this harsh and unforgiving context that we pursue our political hopes.

To do so, however, it is not enough to infer an ideal from a conception of our humanity, such as the view developed in Chapter 3, on the human condition. We also need to have a way of thinking about structure in social life—the institutional and ideological regime of a society—that does not mislead us. The theory of regimes is the chief object of explanatory ambition in social theory just as the preservation or reconstruction of regimes is the overriding concern of practical ambition in politics.

To establish the basis of a program for the transformation of social life, we must combine a view of the making and reconstruction of regimes with the idea of a direction. Such an idea must be rooted in our understanding of ourselves and of our higher natures: it must be able to draw on insight into the contradictory conditions of our self-possession in the relation of the self to others, to society and culture, and to itself.

The argument of Chapter 7 develops the idea of a direction in successive steps: by drawing out the implications of the contradictory requirements of self-construction for politics; by proposing a way to understand the difference between conservatives and progressives, the Right and the Left, that makes explicit the political consequences of the ideas argued for in this book and focuses on the most fateful political choices before us; by relating the progressive cause to the past and future of the revolutionary project that has set the world on fire over the last two or three hundred years; and by identifying a conception that can serve as a bridge between these ways of thinking and a proposal to reshape both institutions and culture. These ideas lay a foundation for a way of opposing and surpassing the last great moment of institutional and ideological settlement in the history of the advanced societies: the institutionally conservative social democracy or social liberalism of the mid-twentieth century.

We need a bridge between these ideas about a direction and an institutional program that would implement these ideas in the circumstances of contemporary societies. That bridge between philosophy and program is the conception of the haven and the storm. The individual should be rendered capable and secure in a haven of safeguards against governmental and private oppression and of capability-ensuring endowments, so that he can move and thrive in the midst of a storm of perpetual experiment and innovation. The storm does not arise spontaneously in the absence of crisis, especially in the form of war or ruin. It needs to be arranged. Its arousal is the chief object of a politics of deep freedom.

Chapter 8 outlines the institutional program of such a politics. The program proposes a way to breathe new life and new meaning into the revolution that has agitated humanity over the last few centuries. And it responds to the three major forms of belittlement and estrangement in the societies of today and of the recent past: subjugation in class society; social disunion under the division of labor; and coldness, the denial of affect to our relations outside the sphere of intimacy—in these societies, we can become free only by becoming cold.

The argument of Chapter 8 explores change in four domains: the market economy, democratic politics, civil society outside the market and the state, and education. In all of them, it gives substance to the effort to arouse and arrange the storm, which, if it consists in the perpetual creation of the new—innovation and experimentalism— also, more deeply, expresses the transcendence of which we, without denying our finitude, are capable.

In the economy, this program looks to the democratization of the market order and the arrangements by which we can develop a knowledge economy for the many. Instead of freedom from the economy through the overcoming of scarcity, it promises freedom in the economy, despite the constraints of scarcity.

In politics (narrowly understood), it points to the development of a strong, high-energy democracy. Such a democracy, acting through a renewed conception of law, subjects the structure of society to challenge without requiring crisis as the condition of change. And it overthrows the rule of the living by the dead.

In civil society, it seeks to create social cohesion through the multi-plication of forms of collective action: the ways by which people do things together. It wants to build cohesion out of difference rather than out of sameness.

In education, and more generally in culture, it wants to generalize and radicalize the experimentalist impulse. It proposes a school that serves, under democracy, as the voice of the future rather than as the instrument of the state or the family, and that recognizes in every young person a tongue-tied prophet. To this end, it teaches every subject from contrasting points of view. By preparing ourselves to be unsettled makers of the new, through our institutions and our education, we come more fully into the possession of life and affirm our powers of transcendence.

Such is the plan of this book, which may seem unreasonable even to those who sympathize with the aspirations motivating it. The plan nevertheless follows from the view of the human condition and the conception of philosophy for which I have argued in this prologue.

1

Ontology (as Natural Philosophy and Social Theory)

The Study of What the World Is Like

The subject of this chapter is what the world is like: the nature of the reality that surrounds us and of which we are a very small part. Our understanding of ourselves and of the projects that we can pursue effectively must rely on such a view of what the world is like. But it can only be a view such as beings like us can hope to hold: susceptible to subversion and correction in light of new discoveries and ultimately limited by the ideas and experiences accessible to beings with our natural constitution. To recognize that these limits are indefinite—if we could define them, we would be seeing beyond them—is not to suggest that they are non-existent.

We may insist that human beings differ from everything else in the world, as the dualisms prominent in the history of Western philosophy assert. To support such claims, we must develop and defend a view of what distinguishes us from the rest of reality. Similarly, when we formulate and advance moral and political programs—approaches to the conduct of life and to the organization of society—we must have reason to believe that nothing in the nature of reality makes those programs unreasonable or futile.

In the tradition of philosophical super-science, the philosopher informs us about the basic constitution of the world: the kinds of beings that there are, what makes them more or less real, what governs their transformation or assures their immutability, and how they relate to the manifest phenomena that we can perceive or discover.

How does he know these things? If he infers his knowledge claims from the specialized fields of inquiry, they are no more than superficial summaries, interpretations, or extrapolations of what the underlying disciplines—the established fields of knowledge—have to tell us about reality. In the age of specialized science and research, such entries into an encyclopedia of universal knowledge amount to an idle pastime.

If, on the other hand, he claims for his insights a basis distinct from any that the sciences have to offer, we need to know the sources and procedures by which he arrived at his account of the world. We need to understand how his account relates to what the established disciplines of thought teach us about reality. By the time Kant formulated his attack on metaphysical dogmatism two-and-a-half centuries ago, it had already become clear that this was a hopeless task. The growth of scientific knowledge since then has made the attempt seem even more fanciful.

It does not follow, however, that in our efforts to form a view of what the world is like, all we can do is to study what the specialized disciplines teach and paste together their teachings in the spirit of the encyclopedia. We can reinterpret ontology as natural philosophy and social theory. We can conceive natural philosophy as the criticism of the contemporary natural sciences—or of the prevailing interpretation of the theories to which they are now committed—and social theory as the criticism of the social and behavioral sciences of today, of the ways in which they represent our social and historical experience. We can find a basis for the criticism and revision of the most influential pictures of the world without standing on the false authority of philosophical super-science.

There is space for movement, revision, and deepening in thought without laying claim to such higher insight. We know that there is such room for maneuver in thought thanks to two striking features of what the specialized disciplines tell us about the world.

For one thing, the images of reality that they present contradict one another, although the contradictions may be obscured by both differences of subject matter and distinctions of method. For another thing, each of these disciplines, shaped by the influences of its own history, presents material that enables us to question the way in which it approaches its problems. At the center of such questioning is the issue that is always most important in every branch of knowledge: the relation between what things are and what, under certain conditions, they might next become.

When this questioning deals with nature and natural science, it is natural philosophy. When it engages society and social science, it is social theory. Natural philosophy and social theory, viewed in the way that I have begun to describe, are not philosophical super-science: they do not pretend to stand above the organized fields of inquiry and to reveal the ultimate framework of natural and social reality. But neither are they limited to interpreting the current orthodoxy of each discipline. They can and should express the revisionist impulse of philosophy: the power of thought to transcend its established and specialized expressions.

Natural philosophy stands in contrast to the philosophy of science. The proximate subject matter of the philosophy of science is science. The proximate subject matter of the philosophy of nature is nature. The philosophy of nature, unlike the philosophy of science, shares its subject matter with science. Yet it cannot rely on either the observational, experimental, and computational equipment of natural science or its conceptual instruments, including mathematics. It argues about what science has actually discovered, sometimes in opposition to what scientists claim to have discovered.

Natural philosophy remained a recognized genre up to the middle of the nineteenth century: until then, the boundary between natural philosophy and natural science continued to be fluid. In physics, natural philosophy had a brief resurgence in the early twentieth century, with Ernst Mach and Henri Poincaré. In the life sciences, it was never interrupted.

In every scientific theory there is an implicit ontology: a conception of the kinds of things that there are and of how they interact. Quantum mechanics, for example, portrayed a world different from the world evoked by Newtonian mechanics. This implicit ontology is not a self-evident inference from empirical and experimental findings. It wins its authority, competing with rival conceptions, by its power to account, as a whole, for a wide range of phenomena, not proposition by proposition but in inclusive accounts of its subject matter. Once associated with a method that allows for their continued deployment and development by specialists, such ontological assumptions begin to be mistaken for the empirical discoveries that they help frame, and even for an understanding of reality with which nature has endowed us.

The work of natural philosophy is to deny this specious authority to such implicit ontologies and to the ways of thinking with which they are associated. It is to ask whether other ways of interpreting what a particular natural science has discovered about the world—as opposed to what it says it has discovered—may not fit better with what we have found out about the world in other areas of knowledge, as well as in the area that the science takes as its own. Moreover, it is to suggest, from such controversial beginnings, alternative research agendas. The more we come to understand that the implicit ontologies and the explicit methods of the sciences have been shaped by larger philosophical assumptions—about change, time, and reality—that matter to our understanding of ourselves as well as of the world, the stronger the reason to distinguish what science has found out about the world from what, with the help of such ontological framing, scientists say that it has found out.

Natural philosophy can degenerate into metaphysical dogmatism and undisciplined speculation. Without practicing it, however, under whatever name we do so, we are left defenseless against the impulse of each science to equate philosophical preconception and method- ological routine with truth about nature and its workings.

What natural philosophy can do for the natural sciences, social theory must do for the social sciences. To form a view of ourselves, of the direction of our empowerment, and of the terrain on which we reckon with one another, we must grasp the nature of the institutional and ideological regimes that represent the chief target of explanatory ambition in social thought and of transformative ambition in politics. Such an understanding must account for the distinctive features of our situation and our powers without alleging, on our behalf, a miraculous exemption from the general regime of nature.

Neither the social sciences of today nor classical European social theory, which found its consummate expression in Marx's work, accomplish this goal. Each of the social sciences severs in its own way the vital link between insight into the actual and imagination of the proximate and accessible possible. Each casts a retrospective halo of naturalness and necessity on the arrangements of contemporary societies. Each suppresses the imperative of structural imagination. Marx's theory of society and history, and much of classical European social theory along with it, dealt with structure, structural discontinuity, and structural change only by compromising the central insight of this social-theoretical tradition into the made and imagined character of the institutional and ideological regimes that shape each form of social life.

These theories did so by embracing a series of necessitarian illusions: that there is a closed list of regimes in history; that each of them forms an indivisible system; and that irresistible laws govern the foreordained succession of such regimes in history. Such laws put the script that history has in store for us in place of any program for our collective future that we might form ourselves.

Viewed in this way, natural philosophy and social theory become successors to what ontology was in the tradition of philosophical super-science. We must practice them as part of our struggle for reality. We need them to enlighten us and to free us from superstition disguised as orthodoxy. We also depend on them to throw light on our path, as we attempt to loosen the constraints of finitude and to address the contradictory conditions of our self-construction.

The Rejection of Metaphysical Rationalism

In 1697 Leibniz published his brief essay *On the Ultimate Origin of Things*.[1] It offers a clear and radical account of the nature of reality: the view that the world must exist and must be what it is. It is common to

---

1. Gottfried Wilhelm Leibniz, *De Rerum Originatione Radicali*, 1697, in *Opera Philosophica*, 1840, pp. 147–50.

emphasize, in the interpretation of Leibniz's doctrines, the idea that this is the best of all possible worlds. But what is most striking and important about his metaphysical rationalism is the idea that nothing in this world of ours just happens to be the way it is. Nothing could be different from how it is. Rejection of this view is the first step in facing reality as it is.

Imagine, wrote Leibniz, a book presenting the elements of geometry. Each copy is made from an earlier one, with no first copy. We can ask why there have always been such books, why they were written, and why they have the content that they do. Such, wrote Leibniz, is the relation between different states of the universe, each state copied from the one before.

Why is there any world at all? Why is it the way it is? These questions remain unanswered even if we assume that the world is eternal. The answer cannot lie within the world. Yet there must be an answer if we accept what Leibniz called the principle of sufficient reason: that there must always be a reason sufficient to explain why anything, including the world itself, exists and is what it is. Causes active within the world are a kind of reason but not the only kind.

Leibniz's answer is the core of his metaphysical rationalism. Everything that is possible strives to exist; Leibniz uses the term *conatus*, which also played a star role in Spinoza's version of metaphysical rationalism. We know the conatus as the striving or inclination toward the maintenance of existence that all living beings have, what in the vocabulary of today's life sciences we would call *homeostasis*. But Leibniz attributes such a striving—to maintain existence in fullest form but to also to achieve everything that is possible—not just to living beings. The world that exists is the *plenum*, the only world that reconciles the most varieties of being and thereby achieves the greatest measure of being.

An additional but distinct doctrine of Leibniz's is that these possible states of affairs and varieties of existence are ideas in the mind of God and that the perfection of the plenum is a maximization of good or salvation as well as of being. That is where the metaphysical rationalism turns into theodicy and only then provokes derision. For the concerns of this chapter, however, the earlier step is the decisive one.

Leibniz was right that the pursuit of causal inquiry about states of the world always remains unfinished and our explanation of the world incomplete. We can push back the frontiers of causal inquiry but we cannot reach the end point. That fact is one of the conditions for our incorrigible groundlessness. He was also right that to complete our explanation we cannot simply offer more causal inquiry; we must introduce a different mode of explanation and argument. If it is successful, it will allow us to elucidate the framework of existence and of being: the highest ambition of philosophical science, of which such metaphysical rationalism is the limiting case. If we succeed in this effort, we may remain mortal and even insatiable, but we will no longer be groundless. If we are lucky, we may also conclude, as Leibniz did, that we have reason to believe in eternal life as well as the means with which to free ourselves from insatiable desire.

To accomplish his purpose, Leibniz relies on two ideas. The first is the notion of a vast but fixed stock of possible things, beings, or states of affairs. The second is the attribution to such possible beings or states of affairs of a thrust toward actuality. Both these ideas are arbitrary fabrications. They gain whatever semblance of plausibility they may enjoy from a series of remote analogies (such as the analogy to the homeostasis characteristic of living beings) as well as from their combination with other ideas, equally factitious, in Leibniz's metaphysics. The threshold objection to them is that with a little bit of philosophical ingenuity, and freed from any constraint other than the consistency of our fabrications with one another, any of us could devise many other routes to the same outcome.

Leibniz pursues his metaphysical rationalism at the expense of two truths that we must recognize if we are to take the world for what it is. The first truth is the truth of groundlessness. We do not know the ground of existence and being, nor can we look into the beginning and end of time, although we can hope to discover more and more about the history of this universe of ours, and even about what may have preceded the present universe. The second truth is the truth of the just-so-ness of the world, of its brute givenness. The world is what it is rather than something else. The universe, we learned a hundred years ago, has a history.

And so—we have no good reason to deny—does everything in it and everything about it. We cannot, by successive extensions of our ability to explain the history of the universe and the ways in which nature works, reason away its just-so-ness. Nature and the universe are what they are because they were what they were. From the succession of Leibniz's copies of the book of geometry, there is no point at which we jump off into the explanation of everything.

We must therefore abandon the attempt to complete what is unavoidably incomplete and to pass from causal explanation, even at the scale of the whole universe and its history, to an account of why there is something rather than nothing and why the world can be only what it is. Such an attempt is not simply an exaggeration of our explanatory powers as if we had merely taken one step too many in accounting for reality. It is a basic misrepresentation of both the world and us. Ontology as natural philosophy must begin by rejecting it.

The spirit of metaphysical rationalism continues to live on, in a more qualified and less transparent form, in what have been the two major traditions in the world history of philosophy. After describing and criticizing the central idea of each of these two traditions and what, despite their differences, unites them, I go on to suggest the germ of an alternative.

The Philosophy of Deep Structure and Its Afterlife in Natural Science

There have been two major traditions in the world history of philosophy: major by their influence within and especially outside philosophical thought. Despite diverging radically, they share major tenets, which I argue to be false. To develop an adequate understanding of the world, as a terrain on which to enact the dialectic of finitude and transcendence and to come to terms with one another, it is not enough to cast aside metaphysical rationalism. We also need to reject both these approaches to reality and to put another one in their place. I will call one of these traditions the philosophy of deep structure and the other the philosophy of the timeless one.

The philosophy of deep structure might also be labeled the Greek philosophy of being, because Aristotle's metaphysics was not only its earliest systematic statement but also—until the last few centuries—its most influential expression. But with even greater accuracy it might be called the philosophy of fundamental physics: we can find its most complete development in physics from Newtonian mechanics to the physics of the twentieth century and of today: quantum mechanics, the particle physics to which it gives rise, and general relativity.

Its central idea is that, viewed at its deepest level, nature has an abiding structure. All explanations of how nature works that base their explanatory accounts on something other than this structure are less general and less fundamental than structure-based explanations. On this conception, history is derivative from structure and historical explanation from structural analysis.

This deep and abiding structure, which gives natural science its central subject matter, consists in two corresponding sets of realities. They are so intimately related that we may regard them as a single system. The first set consists in the ultimate constituents of nature. The second set consists in the regularities either governing the movements and interactions of these basic elements of nature or exhibited by them. In the science of the last few hundred years, such regularities are the laws, symmetries, and constants of nature.

In the tradition of the philosophy of deep structure, the picture of what these basic elements are has changed from Aristotle to today. It has varied, as well, from one moment in the history of fundamental physics to another: from Galileo to Newton, from Newton to statistical mechanics and thermodynamics, and from thermodynamics to quantum mechanics. In each of these moments, physics has worked with a different ontology: a distinctive picture of the kinds of things that there are and of how they interact. Each of these ontologies, however, has amounted to a variation on the idea of deep structure.

The physics of the last hundred years has seen increasingly less reason to distinguish between the two parts of the basic structure: the description of the kinds of things that there are and the account of their interactions. Entities and events have come to be seen as the same.

But throughout the evolution of the philosophy of deep structure, from Aristotle to quantum mechanics, something remains. The deep structure explains change. It does not itself change. The fundamental constituents of nature (as described today by the standard model of particle physics), and the regularities that govern these elements of nature (represented in modern science by the laws, symmetries, and constants of nature), are permanent features of the world. Time leaves them untouched.

By time I mean that feature of reality by virtue of which it is susceptible to change. I also mean that change is uneven and occurs in different forms and at different rates, so that we can clock the change of some things by the fixity, or different rate of change, of others. For the philosophy of deep structure, time is real but not completely real. It is not completely real because it is not inclusive. Something remains outside it: the basic structure of nature. Because this basic structure is the part of the world that does not change, it is also the most real part. It provides a basis on which we can explain change in the rest of reality.

At the core of the philosophy of deep structure is an association between reality and timelessness. The most real, with the greatest explanatory potency, is the least time-bound.

We already have reason to believe that, despite its central place in physics from Galileo and Newton to today, the ontology of deep structure fails to describe the world. Its chief mistake lies in its way of dealing with time and transformation.

In the 1920s, Lemaître and his contemporaries discovered that the universe has a history. At that time, Einstein and his peers had already proposed, on a non-historical basis, what have since then been the most successful theories in physics—quantum mechanics and relativity. The discovery of the historical character of the universe has implications for every part of nature and of science. If the universe has a history, so must everything in it.

We already know enough about that history to infer that neither part of the deep structure presented in the ontology of today's fundamental physics could have existed in the early moments of the present universe: neither the elementary constituents of nature, now described by the standard model of particle physics, nor the laws, constants, and symmetries of nature.

In the mature, cooled-down universe in which we find ourselves, nature is divided into discontinuous components—the particles and fields studied by particle physicists. More generally, it is populated by kinds of things and natural kinds, as Aristotle also thought it was. In this observed state, natural phenomena occur within a limited range of parameters of energy and temperature, displaying a potential for only a very limited range of transformations: the penumbra of the accessible alternatives around each phenomenon or state of affairs—what it can become, given its present state—remains thin and restricted. The laws of nature—both the effective laws operating in defined domains and the fundamental laws or principles (such as the principle of least action) cutting across domains—are clearly distinct from the phenomena that they govern or help explain. It is only a short step from these conceptions to the idea that changing states of affairs conform to unchanging laws.

For the philosophy of deep structure to provide an adequate template for the investigation and explanation of nature, this state of nature would need to be its only state, not just its most common state or the one that we most readily observe now. If it is not nature's only state, reliance on the ontology of deep structure as the keynote for our understanding of nature must be mistaken. We could not dismiss this mistake as a failure to make a minor, peripheral proviso—it would go to the essentials of our explanatory practice. It would be as if, in a narrow part of physics, we had a physics of liquids but no physics of phase transitions: the implications of this mistake taint our understanding of the whole world and everything in it.

Consider a modest and trivial example. We know that the chemical elements identified in the periodic table did not exist early in the history of the present universe. We even know something about their emergence. The discovery of the historical character of the universe suggests that the same may also be true of both the elementary constituents and the lawlike regularities of the cooled-down universe.

The universe seems to have had, according to now standard cosmological ideas, an early moment in which the structural distinctions among the elementary constituents of nature had broken down or not yet taken shape. In this other state of nature, the parameters of temperature and energy were extreme but not infinite (as they would be under the conception of a cosmological singularity), with the result that they are in principle open to causal and empirical investigation, whatever the obstacles to exploring them. There may have been a much wider range of accessible transformations than we currently observe in the cooled-down universe: the penumbra of the adjacent possible around each phenomenon would then have been thick and rich. The effective laws applicable to particular domains, if not the fundamental laws or principles cutting across domains, may have been barely distinguishable from the states of affairs that they governed. This other state of nature—presented schematically in this heuristic conception—may recur later in the course of the history of the present universe, in phenomena exhibiting extreme conditions (such as black holes) or in the universe as a whole late in its history.

It trivializes Lemaître's discovery to reduce it to the conjecture that the universe had, and may have again, a different structure. Rather, it had no structure at all if by structure we mean nature as represented by the regime of elementary constituents of nature, conforming to immutable regularities, that science in this tradition took to be the universal and eternal form of the natural world.

I have stated this idea of a different state of nature in a form that dispenses with the notion of an infinite singularity. The appeal to such a notion hides the early or alternative state of nature behind a screen that closes it to causal inquiry. It also contradicts what we may have better reason to believe: that there is no infinite in nature. But even if we were to accept the notion of the infinite singularity, we would still have to admit that in that moment the distinctions and interactions of our cooled-down universe could not have existed. Moreover, we would still need to understand how nature passed from its state behind the screen of the infinite to the finite realities in which we observe it.

A misrepresentation of the place of cosmology in science, together with two cosmological fallacies, help explain how the philosophy of deep structure has continued to coexist with the discovery of the historical character of the universe.

The misrepresentation is to view cosmology as large-scale astronomy rather than to understand it first as a historical science and second as a master science. It is a historical science in the sense that, properly considered, it affirms that history is prior to structure rather than—as a natural science based on the philosophy of deep structure claims—the other way around. It is also a master science: if the universe has a history that exempts nothing from change, every part or feature of nature must share the same character.

The marginalization of cosmology as a historical science helps make possible the perpetuation of deep-structure ontology in basic science. But what renews the force of deep-structure ontology in ordinary scientific practice is the endlessly repeated and unquestioned reenactment of two cosmological fallacies.[2]

The first cosmological fallacy is a fallacy of false universality. It applies to the whole world a way of thinking that makes sense only when applied to a piece of nature. If we cannot apply it to all of nature, we must qualify even what it can teach us about a piece of nature. I have called it elsewhere the Newtonian paradigm: it is the method of explanation deployed by physics and cosmology since the time of Galileo and Newton.

Under this Newtonian paradigm, we define a configuration space within which unchanging laws can explain the changes and movements of a certain range of phenomena. To this end, we stipulate certain facts: the initial conditions of the configuration space. We do so the better to explain the change or movement within the configuration space.

What belongs to the unexplained initial conditions in one instance of the Newtonian paradigm can become the phenomena to be explained in another instance. Science advances as if it were a searchlight shifting its focus: one part of nature after another comes into the area of light—the light of explanation—while other parts, including the stipulated initial conditions, remain in the dark. Eventually we—the collective we of science—hope to explain everything, part by part.

---

2. For a more developed discussion of these two cosmological fallacies, see Roberto Mangabeira Unger and Lee Smolin, *The Singular Universe and the Reality of Time: A Proposal in Natural Philosophy*, 2015, pp. 18–32.

The observer or scientist stands outside the configuration space, relating to it as God may relate to the world. The instrument with which he explains the phenomena within the configuration space are timeless laws. The laws have no history. To ask why they are what they are is to pose a question to which there can be no answer, other than their consistency with other such laws, in a science conforming to the Newtonian paradigm.

We cannot generalize this procedure to the study of the whole universe. In that study, we have no way of distinguishing the configuration space from what lies outside it.

The second cosmological fallacy is a fallacy of universal anachronism. It supposes that the form that nature displays in our cooled-down universe is the only form that it can exhibit. Consequently, it embraces an ontology and an explanatory practice that take this presentation of nature for granted. The ontology is the philosophy of deep structure in the successive versions through which it has passed in the course of the history of modern fundamental physics. The explanatory practice relies on the idea of immutable laws, symmetries, and constants.

The second cosmological fallacy is a cosmological fallacy because it can arise only within cosmology and as a result of its most significant discovery: the discovery that the universe has a history. It exposes the temporal parochialism of our predominant understanding of nature, a parochialism that fundamental physics has been reluctant to give up.

The first cosmological fallacy has the practice of science as its proximate topic and the workings of nature as its ulterior subject matter. The second cosmological fallacy concerns the facts of the matter directly and scientific method by implication. If time is inclusively real, and if we are mistaken about the temporal universality of prevailing conceptions of nature, then we fail to understand nature at its deepest level.

The ontology of deep structure is, then, not what its proponents claim it to be; it is an account of a special case—albeit the most common one in the natural world that we observe. And the method on which we rely as the touchstone of science is only a locally convenient proxy—local in time more than in space—for another way of understanding nature.

To be sure, everything that we can infer about what the universe —or, if we admit a succession of universes, about the present universe—was like at its earliest moments continues, for now, to be speculative. The basis for a positive conception of the workings of nature in those moments, or in counterparts to them later in the history of the universe, remains fragmentary and fragile. By contrast, we have strong reason to embrace the negative thesis that nature then must have been very different, and worked very differently, from what it is and how it works in the cooled-down universe.

At least some of the elements that we now identify as the building blocks of nature, and that are described at the most fundamental level by the standard model of particle physics and at a more superficial level by the periodic table, could not have existed early in the history of the present universe; even chemistry must be a historical science. And neither could many, or any, of the laws, symmetries, and constants characterizing the cooled-down universe have applied. They would be excluded regardless of whether we represent those other times under the veil of an infinite singularity or according to the picture of extreme density and temperature.

It is the whole conception of a differentiated structure, kept in order by perpetual regularities or recurrent interactions, that would then be undermined: the very image that the philosophy of deep structure, carried into the central tradition of modern science, takes to be the universal and permanent character of nature.

The two cosmological fallacies reinforce each other. They make each other seem natural or even unavoidable, and indispensable to the practice of science, rather than the contestable options that they in fact are.

The first cosmological fallacy presupposes a view of the workings of nature that makes any other view seem to be incompatible with scientific practice. By treating the piecemeal investigation of nature, under the technique of a well-defined configuration space, stipulated initial conditions, and an external observer who invokes immutable regularities to explain what goes on in the space, as the only possible approach of natural science, it leaves no room for the study of the whole universe and its history. It implies that a more inclusive understanding results from adding one focused explanatory exercise to another, turning what is stipulated as initial conditions in one iteration of the practice of explanation into the phenomenon to be explained in another iteration of that practice.

The closer we come to the perspective of true cosmology (as distinguished from large-scale astronomy), the less are we able to fulfill the requirements for the application of the Newtonian paradigm. We cannot then uphold the distinction between initial conditions and a local configuration space of law-governed phenomena. We cannot represent ourselves as observers external to the configuration space. And we cannot dismiss cosmology and its discoveries as peripheral to the concerns of natural science.

The second cosmological fallacy assures us that we will always encounter nature in a form to which the Newtonian paradigm applies. The well-differentiated structure of the cooled-down universe will appear to us not as one of the variations or disguises of nature but as its universal and eternal character. If our discoveries force us to recognize that the universe could not always have taken the form of a differentiated structure governed by changeless laws, we can limit the resulting trouble by placing any alternative form of nature behind the screen of an infinite singularity. There it remains forever closed to observation, experiment, and analysis; it is simply an inference from the equations we use to describe the workings of the cooled-down universe—specifically, for the science of the recent historical period, the equations of general relativity.

The second cosmological fallacy is more fundamental than the first. The first commits a mistake of method, with empirical implications. The second amounts to a mistake about natural reality, with far-reaching consequences for the practice of science.

The central issue in the acceptance of the philosophy of deep structure is its incompatibility with a full recognition of the reality of time. Is the world so constituted that its basic constituents and regularities remain changeless? Everything with which we have direct acquaintance changes sooner or later. The more we discover about the world, the more we find that aspects of reality we regarded as fixed are in fact susceptible to change. Now we know that both life and the universe have a history.

Even the ways in which reality changes change. For example, the "laws" of Mendelian genetics could not have preceded the emergence of life, unless, by sheer metaphysical conceit, we imagine them to have existed in some state of unrealized possibility, waiting for the material to which they would apply, or unless we attempt to infer them from a more basic and general regularity, such as the principle of least action.

Yet we find ourselves inhibited, by both a general and a particular embarrassment, from taking the reality of time and change to its last consequences. The general embarrassment is the thesis, explicitly defended by Poincaré and others, that the idea of immutable laws is indispensable to natural science. If everything changes, we would be unable to explain anything: the unchanging structures and regularities supposedly provide a basis for explaining the changing phenomena. What is necessary for scientific explanation to be possible, however, is only that change not be uniform in place, mode, and rate, as indeed it is not in the world that we observe.

More serious is the particular embarrassment: the bar that the dominant interpretation of general relativity seems to impose on acceptance of the inclusive reality of time. In showing, in the next few paragraphs, how we may hope to deal with this embarrassment, I risk resorting to a discourse that is too technical to be useful to the general reader but not technical enough to satisfy the physicist. Here, as in some other moments in the argument of this book, I see no readily available solution to this problem. But it is not on that account that I will quit living up to my word about the revisionist responsibility of natural philosophy.

The prevailing interpretation of general relativity combines distinct elements. We must disentangle them to judge whether the impediment should be taken to vindicate the idea of deep structure and to diminish or deny the reality of time. This abbreviated exercise serves as well to exemplify the meaning of revisionism in the relation of natural philosophy to the reigning orthodoxy in a science.

A first element in this theory is recognition of the local relativity of simultaneity coming from special relativity. A second element is the inference from the field equations of general relativity to the notion of an infinite initial singularity. This inference does not allude to any empirical or experimental evidence, other than the evidence adduced in support of general relativity. We can best understand it as the statement of certain temporal limits to the domain of application of general relativity. The third element is the addition of the Riemannian spacetime conception, more generally of the attempt to spatialize time (which Einstein himself denounced as a misunderstanding of "vulgarizers"), and the block universe view (spacetime as single, pre-determined grid), which brought out the supposed spatialization of time.[3] This third element is a metaphysical gloss on the hard empirical kernel of general relativity.

None of the (post-classical) empirical tests adduced in favor of general relativity—the perihelion precession of Mercury, the deflection of light by the Sun, and the observation of binary pulsars, for example—has any close relation to the Riemannian spacetime conception or the block universe idea. Of such empirical tests, the only one that might be claimed to lend support to these notions is Shapiro's time delay test, confirmed by very long baseline interferometry. Even this test, however, with its prediction of so-called time dilation in the movement of photons close to the surface of the Sun, can be accommodated by the part of general relativity bearing on the interaction between the physical nature of light and the gravitational potential of our star. It requires no reliance on those ideas or on the impulse to render time spatial.[4]

This third and indispensable element resulting in the opposition of general relativity, under its predominant interpretation, to full recognition of the reality of time results from what can properly be described as the metaphysical element, or the ontological image, in that interpretation. To call it metaphysical or ontological is not to criticize it. Science cannot advance, or formulate its most revolutionary theories, without resorting to metaphysical presuppositions.

---

3. See Albert Einstein, "À propos de la Deduction Rélativiste de M. Émile Myerson," *Revue Philosophique de la France et de l'Étranger*, 105 (1928), pp. 161–6.

4. I take this paragraph from Unger and Smolin, *The Singular Universe and the Reality of Time*, p. 191.

In this instance, as always, the metaphysical gloss calls into being a way of thinking and a vocabulary in which to express it. The data are always too fragmentary, and too susceptible to multiple interpretations, to speak for themselves. A conception of how to think and speak about a part of nature must mediate between empirical findings and theoretical explanation.

A theory must indeed prove itself at the tribunal of the facts as being more powerful than its rivals, not proposition by proposition but overall and at its periphery of empirical implication, and not in one instant but over time—the historical time of the development of large theories and research agendas. But it cannot achieve the clarity of claims that the tribunal requires without taking on a metaphysical gloss or ontological presuppositions. This gloss, these presuppositions, will have consequences, and impose limitations, that are rarely obvious when they are first made explicit. Then at some time, having yielded their explanatory advantage, they may exact their explanatory price. What started out as accommodating metaphor may end up as misleading preconception.

One of the implications of the metaphysical gloss is to ensure the possibility of alternative vocabularies and accounts as ways to reformulate, rather than to replace, an ambitious theory. It may be possible to convert the propositions of general relativity, without compromising their empirical success, into this different language—a language whose speakers need not deny, or diminish, the reality of time.

The Philosophy of the Timeless One

The other major answer to the question—What is the world like?—in the history of philosophy, and the chief alternative to the philosophy of deep structure, has been speculative monism: the doctrine of one and timeless being. I will deal it with it much more briefly than I have dealt with the philosophy of deep structure because it has had much less relevance to natural science and natural philosophy.

Its central idea is that the distinctions among things, among beings, and among selves—so central to our experience—are illusory or, if not wholly illusory, shallow. Behind the discriminate structure that seems to surround us on every side, and the dramatic conflicts and transformations that this discriminate structure seems to undergo, lies the eternal one. Change and time are therefore also unreal, or less real than they seem to be.

The philosophy of the timeless one is, in some respects, the very opposite of the philosophy of deep structure: it affirms the unreality, or the diminished reality, of what the philosophy of deep structure takes to be most real—the abiding organization of reality. Nevertheless, the philosophy of one and timeless being shares with the philosophy of deep structure a premise of decisive importance: the association of the most real with the least time-bound. For this speculative monism, the most real is being concealed under the veil of change and distinction. For the philosophy of deep structure, the most real is the basic constitution of the world as well as the regularities governing it.

In the West, the philosophy of one and timeless being has been, by comparison to the philosophy of deep structure, a dissident strand. In the philosophy of ancient India, it was the dominant tradition. The Indic Vedanta, the Upanishads, early Buddhism, and, in China, early Daoism, all thought and taught in this direction. This view had many metaphysical expressions, such as Nagarjuna's doctrine of emptiness (*sunyata*) within the Madhyamaka school of Indian Buddhism. In ancient Greece its philosophers included Parmenides, Plato—especially the Plato of the dialogue that carries Parmenides' name —the Stoics, and the Neoplatonists, beginning with Plotinus. In recent centuries, its supreme expression in the West is the philosophy of Schopenhauer. But we can find it expressed, in alternatives forms, in the monism of Spinoza and the relationalism of Leibniz.

Moreover, it has been the implicit metaphysic, sometimes made explicit, in the mystical countercurrents within Judaism, Christianity, and Islam. These countercurrents have always verged on heresy within the religions of the Bible. Their theology of mystical union and their pursuit of the theological *via negativa*—the definition of the divine as the negation of all discriminate being, whether personal or impersonal—have proved hard or impossible to reconcile with the narrative of God's saving work in history.

The philosophy of the timeless one has spoken in both radical and qualified forms. In its radical form, it holds that distinction and time are illusory, and it teaches that our sufferings and perversions result from entanglement in this illusion. These misleading appearances arouse insatiable desire. To overcome the will, which keeps us fastened to the treadmill of insatiability, we must see the world as it is. Only a sustained focus, a detached approach to reality through art, and sacrificial action animated by a vision of our unity with all life and being, can deliver us from our ordeal.

The qualified version of the philosophy of the timeless one affirms that there is a hierarchy or a chain of degrees of reality. The manifest phenomena, sunk in distinction and time, are, according to this view, epiphenomenal rather than wholly illusory. They are the rough, outward expressions of the archetypes or founts of beings. We have one version of this view in the middle Plato's doctrine of Forms and another in Plotinus's philosophy of emanations: the manifest world is the last stage in a series of emanations of the one.

The qualified version of the philosophy of the timeless one has its deepest and oldest roots in a way of thinking that was widespread among the Indo-European peoples in the ancient civilizations of Eurasia. In Plato's doctrine, the philosophical and political core of this vision appears clearly. There is a hierarchy in the soul, as well as in society, of both reality and value. In the individual human being, the rational understanding must prevail over the action-oriented impulses and these in turn over the carnal appetites. To this hierarchy of our faculties, there corresponds a hierarchy of casts or ranks in society: thinkers and priests; rulers and fighters; workers and peasants. The right view of the world helps uphold the hierarchy in the soul, which in turn sustains the hierarchy in society. And the connection goes in the opposite direction as well: from social to moral order, and from moral order to openness to reality.

The proponents of the philosophy of the timeless one can find much in our experience of life to encourage them in their view. These signs are more fundamental than the case for the ancient Indo-European doctrine of a reciprocally supporting moral and social hierarchy to which the qualified version of this metaphysic gave refined and elaborate expression. One of these inspirations is our sense of the unity of consciousness. Our experience of insight into one another suggests that our mental experience is shared. The struggle of the uncompromising mind with the awkward and decaying body reinforces the conviction in the power and unity of mind.

Another inspiration is the spectacle of the impermanence of everything in the world, including the body, melting away under our terrified eyes. Yet another is the ordeal that takes us from insatiable longing to boredom and back again, with no prospect of release until we have suppressed or mastered both our cravings and our illusions.

Despite its tie to inspirations that run so deep in our experience, the philosophy of the timeless one suffers from fundamental defects as an account of reality. These defects help explain how little it has influenced the scientific investigation of nature. They account, as well, for our trouble in taking the idea of the timeless one as a point of departure for a natural philosophy that has abandoned the pretense to be part of a philosophical super-science.

A threshold objection to this metaphysic is its failure to explain why one and timeless being appears to us under a form—that of time and distinction—which conceals its true nature. We might attribute the false appearance of the world to our nature as dying organisms with limited perceptual and cognitive equipment, enslaved by both our physical constitution and our natural history to desires that we cannot wholly escape and can barely master. Such a response, however, takes the philosophy of the timeless one further away from metaphysical rationalism and closer to the view that the world just happens to be the way it is: that the world is, in this sense, factitious. If that view is true, the only source of instruction we have is the investigation of nature and its workings.

At that point, however, the defects of speculative monism, as a basis on which to discover what the world is like, become evident. If the world has no real structure, then reality and change come down to the perpetual dissolution of false distinction. And if there is no time, then there can be no causal interaction among parts of the world; causation presupposes time. There can be only a timeless grid. The attempt to understand how things work by finding out how they change cannot even begin.

A defense of this view of the world may then shift ground: from super-science to self-help. Its true aim, according to this defense, is to liberate us from the insatiable will that torments us. It is to provide an antidote to nihilism—the belief that our lives and the world itself are meaningless.

It accomplishes this goal by placing us in contact with what it claims to be the ultimate source of reality and value. As a rescue from the despair of groundlessness, it suffers, however, from a fatal defect: the theoretical antidote to groundlessness that it proposes conflicts with the practical antidote that we learn from experience.

We are rescued from despair by our engagements and connections, by work and love: by commerce not with a hidden timeless being but with a real society and its struggles; not impersonal benevolence, born out of a metaphysic that proclaims our affinity with all beings, but actual love for someone original and unique in the eyes of love. What rescues us from despair and nihilism in fact is what the philosophy of the timeless one takes to be part of the veil of illusion that we must tear away.

Temporal Naturalism

The weakest voice, the strongest message. A third view of reality is the one in closest accord with our experience of the manifest world. It is also the one that we can most easily reconcile with what we have discovered about the universe and its history, about life and its evolution, and about society and its transformation. It saves us, as I later argue, from the successive philosophical dualisms that have claimed for us an exemption from what they represent to be the general government of nature. Despite its proximity to our experience, this third approach to reality speaks with the weakest voice in the world history of philosophy. It is nevertheless the foundation on which we should rebuild our view of nature and its workings.

Its central thesis is that everything changes sooner or later and nothing last forever. Even change changes. The transformation of transformation is one way of defining what time is. But nothing becomes less real by virtue of being ephemeral or susceptible to transformation into something else. This third view has no agreed upon or obviously suitable name. I call it here temporal naturalism to draw attention to the central importance that it gives to the reality of time as well as to its refusal to compromise with metaphysical rationalism. The most important feature of the world, it holds, is that it is what it is rather than something else.

Against the philosophy of deep structure, temporal naturalism teaches that nothing is exempt from change and time: not a basic constitution of the world nor laws of nature. Against the philosophy of the timeless one, it insists that nothing becomes less real by virtue of being and then not being. Against both these leading positions in the world history of philosophy, it rejects the idea that unites them: the association of reality with timelessness, the idea that the most real is the least time-bound.[5]

To say that this view has spoken with the weakest voice in the history of philosophy is not to say that it lacks representatives. The names that most readily occur in the West are Heraclitus, Hegel, and, in the philosophy of the twentieth century, Bergson and Whitehead. But this rarefied list also illustrates the ways in which a philosophy that emphasizes becoming over being and process over structure may nevertheless fail to exemplify what I have just described as temporal naturalism.

Thought loosely associated with a philosophy of becoming contradicts the tenets of a temporal naturalism if, in its devotion to process (or dialectic, or any of the other names by which change goes), it discounts the reality and significance of structure. In both natural science and social theory, everything turns on the effects of structure and of its variations and transformation. Structure loses neither significance nor reality by virtue of losing its exemption from time and change.

5. For a systematic account of the cosmological implications of temporal naturalism in two divergent voices and versions, see Unger and Smolin, *The Singular Universe and the Reality of Time*.

Moreover, the philosophers of becoming have been perennially tempted to conjure up a protagonist—mind, spirit, élan, God in the making—whose disguises and vicissitudes they depict as forming the stuff of the universal history of society and of nature. There is no such plot, no such suffering hero of a *Bildungsroman* of the world, along a route taking us from the pre-human to the super-human. The recruitment of such a plot by the philosophers signals the regression of the philosophy of becoming to metaphysical rationalism. The real world is what it is. Its characteristics and events cannot be deduced from any conception. But at any moment it can turn, or be turned, into something else all along the periphery of the accessible possibilities in nature or society.

In this misdirected version of temporal naturalism, however, the world is embarked on a trajectory of ascent. The trajectory follows a script that is known to the philosopher and enacted by the central protagonist of his story. At that point, philosophy begins to trade temporal naturalism for metaphysical rationalism. Time starts to lose its luster and reality: the script of ascent stands over and beyond it.

Why has a view that seems on its face to accord most closely with our experience of the manifest world and with both natural history and the history of human society had so much smaller a presence in the world history of philosophy than its two great rivals? Many factors seem to have played a part in this miscasting. Understanding them helps us comprehend this many-sided contest among approaches to reality.

A first reason is that no view close to what I have labeled temporal naturalism has played a role in fundamental physics, the branch of modern science that has been regarded as the gold standard of scientific practice. A second reason is the influence of a conception of the hierarchy of forms of inquiry, within and outside natural science, which insists that the power of a style of explaining is inversely related to its reliance on historical explanation. According to this view, as the importance of history increases, the level of explanatory ambition diminishes. A third reason is the central role and immense prestige of mathematics in natural science, and especially in fundamental physics. And mathematics, I argue later in this chapter, presents us with a simulacrum of the world from which time and particularity have been banished. A fourth reason is the fear that abandoning the idea of exemption from time and change may deny us access to a part of reality—the most real part—that can relieve us from our groundlessness, or even our mortality, and throw light on the conduct of life. The combined effect of these reasons has been to weaken the voice of the philosophy that seems easiest to reconcile with reality.

To save the thesis of temporal naturalism from falling for the philosophy of becoming or succumbing to metaphysical rationalism and the pretenses of philosophical super-science, I consider it in each of the main contexts of its application: natural history, cosmology, and social theory. From its development in these contexts there emerge the elements of a view of what the world is like that can and should replace the philosophies of deep structure and of the timeless one.

Temporal naturalism, natural history, and natural science. The part of the scientific study of nature that bears the strongest and most direct affinity to temporal naturalism is natural history: the old-fashioned label for what today are often called the earth and life sciences. The scope of the label is important because it does not draw its boundary at the division between life and non-life: it extends backward and forward to include the history of lifeless nature in geological time, and its characteristics are as clearly manifest in geology as they are in evolutionary biology. Nothing in this argument tends toward vitalism—the view that life differs from everything else and must be studied by unique methods. Everything draws attention to what unites the life sciences with the science of nature before life.

We are used to thinking of the characteristics of this form of study as being unique to sciences with explanatory ambitions more limited than those of either fundamental physics or the study of human society and history. And, indeed, the task of understanding differs in each of these areas. But in every area, we face the task of engaging with the world as it is without denying the reality of either time or structure. The methods of natural history suggest what the execution of that task requires in each branch of inquiry, from cosmology to the social sciences. Viewed from this perspective, natural history is not weaker than fundamental physics or more simple-minded than social science. It provides a model for relating history to structure that transcends the differences of method and subject matter among the established disciplines.

Three features of natural history exemplify its distinct approach to nature and its workings. The first principle is the mutability of types. According to this principle, there is no permanent and closed stock of natural kinds—of types of things—such as species in evolutionary biology or types of rocks in geology. The list of natural kinds is open. Not only may there emerge types of beings that never existed before, but the ways in which types differ, come into existence, and distinguish themselves also vary and change. Such differences may include how, how much, and for what reasons individual instances of the type differ from one another.

Once generalized, the principle of the mutability of types contradicts one of the main assumptions of the philosophy of deep structure: the idea that there is a timeless repertoire of the basic constituents of nature and of the regularities that they exhibit.

Consider, as an example, different kinds of rocks. Igneous rocks, crystallizing from a molten liquid, can be explained directly by reference to the composition, temperature, and cooling rate of the parent magma. There is a clear contrast—in terms of origins and of properties—between the phaneritic and aphanitic varieties.

For metamorphic rocks, resulting from the effects of temperature and cooling on preexisting rocks, the general forces shaping igneous rocks operate with much less determinant consequence. Other forces and circumstances may produce an effect, arranged in different sequences. The classification of metamorphic rocks into foliated and non-foliated is correspondingly less sharply drawn than is the distinction between the two main types of igneous rocks. Each individual metamorphic rock exhibits historical particularity to a greater extent than does each igneous rock. There are multiple pathways to the same individual piece of gneiss. Each specimen shows its history.

For sedimentary rocks, produced by the settling of particles through aqueous media, the influence of historical particularity is even stronger. The classifications developed by stratigraphy—the scientific study of such rocks—are rough and tentative. The characteristics of the kind pale in comparison to the distinctions of the specimen: each individual piece is more individual than is each specimen of an igneous or metamorphic rock.

The mutability of types, striking in the world of macroscopic objects, applies as well to the microscopic world, albeit on a very different time scale. The chemical elements described in the periodic table, and, at more fundamental level, the elementary particles described in today's science by the standard model of particle physics, could not have existed—as I have already remarked—in the earliest moments of the history of the present universe. We are not yet able fully to describe their genealogy.

The only reasonable conjecture, on the basis of our present knowledge, is that they too are susceptible to change, on a much larger time scale, as well as on a very short one through our forceful intervention. To think otherwise is to suppose that a natural kind with definite historical origins (although not ones that we are yet able fully to identify) has no future history and must remain forever stable and identical to itself.

All this changing variation in nature is adrift on a sea of time in the particular corner of the universe where the world is most directly present to us: our planet. In that world, viewed up close and macroscopically, there is no eternal, cast of characters. The argument of the second cosmological fallacy implies the same for the whole universe and its history: we too easily mistake relative stability in the cooled-down universe for eternity and immutable law. The mutability of types, most palpable in the readily visible objects of our planetary environment, extends outward, in both directions, the subatomic and the cosmological, to the Planck scale and the scale of universal history.

The second principle of natural history is path dependence. We might also call it hysteresis were it not for the special and distinct meanings that this word has acquired in cosmology and economics. Everything in the world and the world itself are what they are because they were what they were.

The question that immediately arises, in every branch of our account of reality, is how we are to understand the relation between structure and history. According to a presumption decisive in the fundamental physics of today, and characteristic of the philosophy of deep structure, structure precedes and commands history. Only if it does govern history can we, according to this presumption, hope to explain the workings of nature in ways that are comprehensive and fundamental.

This presumption conflicts with a pattern that recurs in every aspect of reality. We cannot infer the necessity of this pattern from any general conception, in the spirit of metaphysical rationalism; indeed, this pattern gives us more reason to believe that no account of the world designed in the spirit of metaphysical rationalism can be true.

There is a moment of fire or conflict in which every stable structure, if it existed before, melts down. In that moment, the range of the proximate possible—of what can happen next—expands, which is another way of saying that the power of the past to determine the future diminishes. Then the moment of incandescence—of the dissolution of structure—is partly contained, or temporarily interrupted. To that extent, structure emerges. Once it takes hold, through such containment or interruption, the phenomena exhibit regularities, which can in turn become the basis for causal explanations that invoke these regularities. The degree to which the long periods of relative stability contrast with the moments of breakdown and reshaping may vary in different parts of reality or in different periods of universal history. Such variations imply, as well, differences in the openness of states of affairs to subsequent change.

One of the main subjects on which this alternation between stability and reconstruction operates is the range of the kinds of things that there are. In the social and historical study of humanity, they are institutional and ideological regimes. In cosmology and fundamental physics, they are the elementary constituents of nature. In natural history, they are the types of things that exist in our planetary environment. Among such things are species. The prodigious history of speciation alternates—as the theory of punctuated equilibrium has shown—between long periods of stability, reinforced by the constancy of DNA, and moments rich in the destruction and creation of species.

The causal sequences through which the present emerges from the past may be more tightly or loosely tied together. Part of what is implied by the priority of history over structure is that transformation may result from distinct sequences of events that we cannot persuasively understand as steps in the enactment of a preset master plan.

Consider a stylized episode in mammalian evolution. The example trades on the loose relation between competitive selection in determining the characteristics of the higher mammals and the movement of the land masses on the surface of the planet as described by plate tectonics. Suppose that mammals in one isolated continent were subject to noncompetitive extinctions resulting from severe climatic conditions. As a result, they benefited from the development of cranial capacity and other advantages. And suppose further that these advantaged mammals happened to have been placentals. And suppose further that a marsupial mammal population had long since arrived in another continent, which, as a result of the movement of the continents, had afterward become completely isolated. Later the two continents joined. The more capable and versatile placentals liquidated their marsupial rivals, who survived only in other isolated parts of the world, where they were subject to no such challenge. The placentals then remained the main line of mammalian evolution. The influences of the floating of the continents had nothing do with the comparative potential of different types of mammals. They nevertheless exercised a major effect on the evolutionary outcome.

The significance of path dependence is also enhanced by the importance of the order in which events happen. For example, it is a commonplace of contemporary evolutionary biology that the average genetic structure of any biological population depends on the historical sequence of environments, not just on their static probability distribution. Gene frequency may respond more readily to recent environments. It will always be hard for the naturalist to tell which features of the natural world depend on such specific circumstances and which hold regardless of the order of such causal influences.

The principle of path dependence holds in spades for the historical experience of humanity and the alternatives with which it has experimented, or might next. But does it hold as well at the cosmological scale and on the cosmological time horizon? We cannot know for sure on the basis of our present knowledge of the history of the universe. But if that history sees swings between structure and its disruption, we have reason to suppose that the times and places where structure breaks down are also the ones in which the range of the adjacent possible expands and the importance of path dependence, irreducible to preexisting structure, increases.

The third principle of natural history is the coevolution of the laws and the phenomena of nature. I use laws here in a broad sense to include all the regularities—the recurrent forms of causal connection—exhibited by natural phenomena. The idea underlying this principle is the change of change: the phenomena change and so, together with them, does the way in which they change, which is another way of stating what I mean by the laws of nature. In natural history, change changes discontinuously and repeatedly.

The methods of change, which we may express as explanatory laws, change with the appearance of life. They change again with the emergence of multicellular organisms. And, again, with sexual reproduction and the Mendelian mechanisms. And then, once again, with the advent of consciousness and of language. In natural history, the change of the mechanisms of change is not limited to the history of life; it extends backward to the history of lifeless nature, in geology and earth science. In these contexts, it is closely associated with the principles of the mutability of types and of path dependence. For example, the formation of crystals represents a mechanism for the reproduction of invariance that displays regularities different from those found in the biosphere.

To affirm that these regularities in the workings and continuous transformation of nature preexist the appearance of the phenomena that exhibit them is not a conclusion supported by any empirical observation. It is a metaphysical postulate inspired by the philosophy of deep structure and its persistent interest in exempting the ultimate structure of nature and its regular workings from time and change.

The implication of this postulate is that the regularities were there waiting to exert their influence, even before the material to which that influence could be applied existed. Or, even more strongly, it is that everything was determined from the outset, in the spirit of Laplacian determinism or of what today is known as the block universe view: time can then be real only in a diminished sense, if at all. The universe cannot have a history in any developed sense of the term history. And the observations of the naturalist, informed by the three principles I have stated, must be dismissed as misrepresenting the deeper character and workings of nature.

How can we think historically and affirm the primacy of history over structure without abandoning our most ambitious explanatory projects in science? If change changes, how are we to approach the question of why change changes in the way it does rather than in some other way? If the laws coevolve together with the regularities, are there higher-order laws governing this coevolution? If there are, we have done nothing to escape the presumptions of the philosophy of deep structure and of the scientific practice that embodies it. If there are not, we seem to have abdicated the effort to explain natural phenomena in favor of radical chance in universal history.

Temporal naturalism and social theory. The relation between structure and history in our human experience suggests by analogy ways of thinking about these problems. The most important features of every society are its institutional arrangements and the ideological assumptions on which their representation and operation depend—its regime. A regime shapes the surface conflicts and exchanges of social life, especially those over the resources of power, capital, and cultural authority by which we make the social future within the social present. (The theme of the nature and transformation of regimes of thought and of social life will come up again briefly in Chapter 2, on epistemology, and at greater length in Chapter 7, on politics.)

Human history is a record of struggle over such regimes and their reconstruction. The long periods in which they are left in place alternate with more concentrated times of disruption. And, in those moments of disruption, it is not just the institutional and ideological order that is shaken; so too are the beliefs that each class or community has about its interests and its identity. They all lose some of their appearance of naturalness and necessity together. Our confidence in our ability to mark the boundaries of the accessible possibilities—the *theres* to which we can get from *here*—is shaken.

The true nature of institutional and ideological regimes is revealed in their hour of breakdown. It is then that we see clearly what we may forget, or find hidden from us, in the long times of misleading quiet. Regimes are not things. They are us. They mark the places at which our contests over the terms of our access to one another let up: temporarily interrupted and relatively contained. We can know them from within because they are our creations, to which we have lent a false semblance of naturalness and necessity. The advancement of our most basic material and moral interests depends not only our mastering these regimes but also on so designing them that they cease to imprison us. So that they do not imprison us, we must redesign them to facilitate their own revision in the light of experience.

In the history of the universe and of nature, we witness a similar oscillation between disruption and relative stability. In the most extreme forms of disruption, new phenomena are generated and, with them, in time, even new regularities. The penumbra of the accessible variations widens.

Even the distinction between the regularities and the phenomena may break down. In these states of highest temperature and energy, the two central protagonists of the philosophy of deep structure and of the scientific practice it informs—the elementary structure of nature and the laws, symmetries, and constants of nature—may fail.

The character of natural structures, and the methods by which we can hope to discover how they work and change, are different from the character of social structures and the methods by which we can grasp their workings and transformation. A chain of analogies nevertheless connects them. A striking feature of that chain is the mutability and relativity of what the philosophy of deep structure, in the conduct of its war against the reality of time, takes to be the most important part of the real: the part that does not change.

In nature, as in society, everything—including structures and regularities and even the forms of change themselves—changes sooner or later. The scope of mutability is unlimited. In nature, as in society, the extent to which reality presents itself in recurrent form, as a defined regime, with stable constituents and regularities, is variable. In society we can hope to achieve what nature gives no example of: to split the difference between regime and disruption, establishing a regime that facilitates its own reconstruction and invites the perpetual creation of the new.

And yet, despite their mutability and variability, the structures and the regularities of the natural world and of social life are not, as the philosophy of the timeless one supposes, the epiphenomenal or illusory manifestation of a reality beyond time and variation. They are as real as anything is, for as long as they last. It is only by studying their history and transformation and by extending our insight into the causal influences on their changes that we can develop our insight into what the world is like.

Mathematics: The World Emptied Out of Time and Phenomenal Particularity

Mathematics. The mistake that the philosophy of deep structure makes about the world is both expressed and instigated by ideas about mathematics and about the relation of mathematics to nature and science. Mathematics has been the most powerful instrument of natural science, the torch illuminating what otherwise seems impossible to retrieve from the shadows of the perceived world. But it offers natural science a poisoned gift: the idea of timeless laws of nature.

To understand why the gift is poisoned and how it may be washed clean of the poison, consider the attributes of mathematical reasoning. To do so, we must leave aside traditional disputes about whether mathematics is invention or discovery. These disputes about false alternatives have obscured what most needs to be understood about the relation of mathematics to the world in which we find ourselves.

The familiar attributes of mathematical reasoning are explication, recursive reasoning, and fertility in the making of equivalent propositions. Mathematics explicates by bringing out what is implicit in the conception of a structured whole or bundle of relations, stated in numerical or geometrical language. The world presents itself to us in spatial extension as a differentiated structure. As soon as there are space and complexity, there is also reason to count or to quantify. Numerical relations and spatial disposition are two sides of the same thing. Mathematics presents us with a growing stock of ideas about a reality from which everything except number and space has been removed. It then develops ways of reasoning about what is implicit in each of these ideas.

Mathematics relies on recursive reasoning; reasoning that takes itself for its subject and that applies to its own procedures. Through recursive reasoning we pass from enumerations to generalizations; we suggest the general rule implicit in what had been, up till then, an enumeration of particulars. We hope by such means to reach strong and rich conclusions supported by weak and parsimonious assumptions.

Fecundity in the statement of equivalent propositions also characterizes mathematics. A major part of mathematical reasoning consists in showing how one line of analysis can be restated in terms of another. Just as explication can be mistaken for deduction and recursive reasoning for induction, the multiplication of equivalent propositions can be mistaken for the marking of synonymy. The significance of this third characteristic of mathematics lies in the peril to which mathematics, more than any other branch of knowledge, is exposed by virtue of its abstraction: the danger of failing to distinguish between its conceptions and their conventional expression. Mathematics guards against this danger by restating its ideas in alternative and equivalent forms the better to see beyond form to substance.

These three characteristics begin to distinguish mathematics as a unique form of inquiry. They fail, however, to reach the feature of mathematics that accounts for both its power and its limitations. This additional attribute explains the role that mathematics has been made to serve in a natural science guided by the philosophy of deep structure.

Mathematics presents us with a simulacrum of the world from which time and phenomenal distinction have been removed. It does not offer us a vision of an ethereal world of mathematical objects, as the mathematical Platonist may be inclined to believe. Nor are we justified in treating it as an arbitrary set of conventions by which to develop and deploy deductive reasoning, or as a game whose rules we are free to reinvent so long as we agree on the changes of the rules. Neither of these two approaches to mathematics can account for its "unreasonable effectiveness": the mystery of its preternatural power not only to equip our physical theories but even to run ahead of them as scouts.

The subject matter of mathematics is the one real world—not another world or no world. But it is an imagined world that has been reduced to shadows by the expulsion from it of what fills the actual world: particulars moving in time. Phenomenal particularity and time are bound together. All phenomena have a history and an end; that is why the philosophies of deep structure and of the timeless one view them as less than something else—the structure and laws of nature or the undivided reality—that they mistakenly see as lying beyond the reach of time. The reality of time is inseparable from differential change among particulars. Phenomena change at different rates and in different ways: rates and ways that are themselves susceptible to change.

The abstraction of mathematics from time and particularity allows it to develop a stock of modes of thinking about whatever can be counted or projected in space. These modes of thinking are not tied to particular beings or situations. They nevertheless have for their subject matter the one real world at a second remove, cleansed of temporality and particularity.

This combination of attributes helps account for the prodigious usefulness of mathematics in natural science as a source of ways of representing and connecting parts of reality. By the same token, however, it also explains why there is no automatic correspondence between mathematical ideas or methods and the world restored to the flesh of time and particulars. There may or may not be such a corre-spondence in any given instance: the effectiveness of mathematics in natural science is reasonable because it is variable. It succeeds or fails.

We can also see why a capacity for logical or mathematical reason-ing confers on the being who possesses it a formidable evolutionary advantage: an ability to reason about the relations among things apart from any narrowly defined use or circumstances. This capacity is all the more useful for appearing to be useless: for not being bound to any context or limited set of contexts. It represents yet another example of our transcendence.

The reliance of natural science on mathematics, however, has implications that are not at first apparent. The relation among moves in mathematical reasoning (as in logic) is outside time. The conclusion of a syllogism, or a mathematical demonstration, is simultaneous with its premises even though its working out in the minds of human beings takes time. Causation, on the contrary, implies time: the effect must follow the cause.

Newton and Leibniz conceived the calculus—the most famous invention in the history of mathematics over the last several centuries—to describe movement and change in time. How can a form of reasoning that banishes time, and, alongside time, phenomenal particularity, play a central role in the scientific investigation of nature? This is the enigma that remains after we have cut the "unreasonable effectiveness of mathematics" down to size by affirming that it is reasonable only because it is relative. A mathematical connection may or may not serve to represent a connection in nature. And a connection in nature may or may not be susceptible to mathematical representation.

A gap opens between what the world is like and how it can be represented in mathematics. The source of the gap is the same as the basis for the irreplaceable service that mathematics renders to natural science: the making of a proxy for the world that is expunged of time and phenomenal distinction.

There are ultimately two ways to deal with the consequences of this gap. One way is to extract causality—and any view of laws of nature that relates to causal succession—from the explanatory practice of science. This is what the physics of the twentieth century largely accomplished. The result is to resolve a contradiction only at the cost of mistaking the simulacrum built by mathematics for the world.

The ideas and attitudes underlying this way of dealing with the gap in turn help account for the seductive force of two illusions. One illusion is to mistake the mathematical representation of reality for privileged insight into a separate, nature-transcending realm of mathematical truths and objects. The other illusion is to allow ourselves to be lulled into the belief that, at its most fundamental level—the level of basic constituents and regularities—nature shares the timelessness of mathematics.

The second response is to use what mathematics has to offer without converting into an ontology the limitations that explain its power. In this spirit, we would always insist on looking for the physical reasons that explain the conformity of a physical phenomenon to a mathematical expression. We will be quick to identify the metaphysical conception—such as the idea of spacetime as a four-dimensional pseudo-Riemannian manifold in general relativity—that superimposes on an empirical discovery an interpretation taking time out of a slice of nature. We will not allow ourselves to be dissuaded by the trouble that mathematics has with history from viewing nature and its transformations historically.

Logic. In its historical forms, logic has the same character as mathematics: the same abstraction from phenomenal particularity and time. The subject matter of logic, albeit just as abstract as that of mathematics, is even more general. It goes beyond number and space, beyond structured wholes and bundles of relations, to present a way of thinking about connection. If its proximate subject matter is connection in thought, its ultimate subject matter is connection in the world, viewed without regard to anything particular or to the changes to which all particulars are subject.

The premise of logic is a proto-ontology, reduced to three postulates. By the postulate of reality, there is something rather than nothing. By the postulate of plurality, there is more than one thing. By the postulate of connection, the plural things are connected. Logic is about their connection, both in thought and in the world.

Its greatest practical use in the discipline of thought about connection is to save us from contradiction. But its ability to illuminate the bearing of contradiction on change is limited by its inability to deal with time. Consider the violation of one of the cardinal principles of classical logic: the principle of non-contradiction, according to which two contradictory propositions cannot both be true.

Once we apply this principle and its violation to the temporal world, the world in which particulars undergo upheaval and transformation, it loses the rigorous meaning that it had when confined to a world without time or phenomenal distinction. In the course of the history of philosophy, many philosophers have employed ways of thinking that defy the principle of non-contradiction. But what does the violation of the principle imply for how we represent and understand change?

On one view—which we find, for example, in Meillassoux's defense (in *Après la Finitude*) of the fundamental importance of the principle of non-contradiction—the denial of this principle (for example in the philosophers of Jewish, Christian, and Muslim mysticism) makes change impossible to understand. If contradictions can coexist, change will never happen; it is because contradictions cannot coexist that change can happen. Change resolves untenable contradiction.[6]

Yet in Hegel's philosophy the violation of the principle of non-contradiction is the condition of change. Every form of life and consciousness—the forms of life and consciousness whose history Hegel explores in *The Phenomenology of Spirit*—consists in a set of contradictions between and within thought and experience. What logic will not allow is, on this view, a pervasive feature of reality. If Hegel later rejects the principle of non-contradiction at the beginning of his logic, it is because he understands logic to be simultaneously about the world and thought.

Meillassoux's and Hegel's theses are both true—a contradiction in the deployment of the principle of contradiction—because they do not define contradiction in the same way. The root of the confusion is that the principle of non-contradiction loses its clear meaning, and degenerates into metaphor, once we apply it to the world. It loses clear meaning because logic, like mathematics, has no grip on a time-drenched world in which everything real changes and nothing lasts forever.

---

6. Quentin Meillassoux, *Après la finitude: Essai sur la nécessité de la contingence*, 2006, pp. 103–9.

Causality and Time

If time is central to what the world is like, so is causality. The program of temporal naturalism cannot dispense with the idea of causality. And the denial of the reality of time invariably results in an attack on causality.

Time and causality are implicated in each other. Begin with a loose and approximate conception of causality as the influence that an event or state of affairs has on a later event or state of affairs. This initial definition is undeniably vague; it is meant to capture types of connection and of change that are significantly related to one another. Temporal succession is in every instance the requirement for their relation. But the vagueness imposed by this looseness is not the result of an irremediable defect in the concept of causation; it is a consequence of the mutability of causal change over time—of the change of change.

Causation presupposes time. A cause must precede an effect. The conclusion of a course of mathematical or logical reasoning is simultaneous with its premises. That difference is the basis for what is most puzzling about the use of mathematics in natural science: the application of an idea of timeless connections, in the language of mathematical functions, to the time-drenched processes of nature. And it explains the power of the tendency, in the leading tradition of fundamental science, to attribute to nature the attributes of its timeless mathematical proxy.

As causality presupposes time, time presupposes causality. Causality is connection in time. It unites distinct things or events in the world temporally. Without causation, under whatever name, nothing would unite moments in time. We could solve the resulting problem only by denying the reality of time, or—what is effectively the same thing—by embracing a view (such as the block universe view of the world, the contemporary counterpart to Laplacian determinism) that sees the universe at all moments of time as a single, predetermined entity.

In the philosophy of the West over the last few centuries, especially since Kant and Hume, two ideas about causality have been predominant. The development of a better view of causation requires us to reject both.

The first idea is that causation is a projection of the human mind. It is a way of understanding the world that is instilled in us, and for which we can have no substitute. How it relates to what the world is really like we cannot know because we do not, and never will, have access to things in themselves. It was Hume who opened the space for the development of this idea by doubting that we are entitled to infer causal connection inductively from the regular successions that we observe.

It is true that a sufficiently radical skepticism is unanswerable to the extent that it draws out the implications of our embodiment and of finitude. We cannot in fact jump out of ourselves and view the world with the eyes of God. But—and this is the initial objection to this first element in the predominant approach to causality in modern Western philosophy—there is no good reason to single out for privileged status skepticism about causality from skepticism about all the other discoveries that we make within and outside natural science.

Moreover, the claim that causality is a projection of the human understanding rather than a feature of reality itself contradicts two facts. One of them is incontestable. The other is a controversial tenet of the temporal naturalism defended in this chapter.

The incontestable fact is that our ideas about causation have a history: they have changed and continue to change. The way in which we develop, from childhood on, our understanding of the world around us—a topic investigated by developmental and cognitive psychology—may have inclined us to take as the model for all causal connections the relation between our intentional actions and their effects. Nevertheless, we can, and frequently do, revise our ideas about causality, as the history of natural philosophy, social theory, and natural science shows.

The controversial fact is that the forms of causal connection in nature—not just in our thinking about reality—have a history and are susceptible to transformation. This is the thesis that change varies among domains and changes over time. Kant developed his argument about causation as part of a response to empiricist skepticism, on one side, and rationalist dogmatism, on the other. But it is itself an instance of metaphysical dogmatism because it closes the intellectual space in which we might hope to study the diversity and transformability of causal connections.

The second idea that has shaped the predominant approach to causality in the history of modern philosophy is a view of the relation between causal explanations and laws of nature. According to this view, the laws of nature serve as warrants underlying causal connections. Every causal connection enacts a law of nature: a rule-like and recurrent relation between two kinds of events, involving a more or less broadly defined set of phenomena or beings, in nature. We can expand the concept of laws of nature to include constants and symmetries and refer to all three as regularities or simply as laws in an expanded sense. (A symmetry is a transformation that leaves all relevant structure intact. The concept of symmetry is intimately related to the idea of invariance.)

In this prevailing view, we take the laws of nature to be immutable as well as recurrent. Thus, together with the constituents of nature, they represent, according to the philosophy of deep structure, with which this view of causality is closely associated, the most real part of natural reality and the one with the greatest explanatory significance. Their special status is inseparable from their timelessness.

Although we often regard this way of relating causality to laws of nature as characteristic of thinking in natural science, as well as of philosophy over the last few centuries, it has in fact a particular and misunderstood history. And this history has philosophical significance. It was Collingwood who most forcefully pointed out that what we take to be the universal view of causality is in fact an episode in the history of natural philosophy and natural science.[7]

The idea that all causal connections are underwritten by laws of nature was Kant's view. It gained wide currency in nineteenth-century physics, despite the enigma presented by the seeming contradiction between the timeless character of mathematics and the time-bound nature of causal connections. That we need not adopt this view of the

---

7. R. G. Collingwood, *An Essay on Metaphysics*, 1940, chapter VI, pp. 49–57.

relation between causality and laws of nature is shown by its having been preceded and followed in the history of physics—widely seen as the most fundamental branch of natural science—by two different ways of thinking about connection in nature.

In Newtonian mechanics, causality and law are not related as correlates: the latter supplying a basis for the former. Instead, each applies to a different domain of phenomena and presents a distinct explanatory task to science. The laws apply to the clocklike workings of nature, without interruption or intervention: the world of constant motion. Causality comes into play when an event occurs that interrupts constant motion, as when an object strikes and deflects another. Where there is law, there is, on this way of thinking and talking, no cause, and where there is cause, there is no law.

In the physics of the twentieth century, the appeal to causality and to laws of nature, which Kant and the nineteenth century took to be the hallmark of natural science and an indispensable presupposition of our understanding, has waned or even entirely disappeared. It has been displaced by a way of thinking that is structural rather than historical and functional (in the mathematical sense) rather than causal. If the idea of laws of nature survives in this physics, it survives as a vestige to describe the formative and ultimate structure of nature. Time survives at best as an aspect of this essentially timeless structure. And causality vanishes, together with time, in the mathematical representation of reality.

Thus, we go from a way of thinking in which causality and law apply to different domains, to one in which they play distinct and complementary roles in all domains (laws of nature underwrite causal explanations), to one in which the laws of nature (reinterpreted) are everything, and causality (in its traditional sense) is nothing.

I have already anticipated one of the implications of this history: that it undermines the thesis that causality is an indispensable presupposition of the understanding. How can it serve as such a presupposition if its meaning has been radically contested and altered during the history of our inquiries into nature and if the science widely regarded as the most fundamental has now all but rejected it? As with everything else in this temporal world, our ideas about causality have a history. Whatever the approach to causality that is instilled in us as we pass through infancy and childhood, we can rise above it, and have risen above it, through the work of science.

The same history of ideas has an even more direct philosophical implication for the other major tenet of the modern approach to causality: the thesis that causal explanations depend on laws of nature; that the former enact the latter. What according to that tenet was the natural and necessary connection between causation and laws of nature turns out to be only a moment in the history of natural science and natural philosophy. That history of thought in turn leaves us free to reconsider causation in the light of the history of nature itself. If causation is a primitive feature of reality rather than an inbuilt assumption of the mind, and if our ideas about it have changed and will continue to change, then we need to ask which conception of causal connection comes closest to the facts of the matter—facts not about the mind but about nature.

Let us begin by considering, in this spirit, each of the three views of causality and law—let me call them for short the Newtonian, the Kantian, and the Einsteinian—that I have just recalled.

The explanatory practice of the Newtonian view depends on what I earlier called the Newtonian paradigm: the application of timeless laws to a configuration space describing a fragment of nature and bounded by stipulated factual conditions. Within that configuration space events can occur that modify the operation of the laws. Only then do we speak of causes and effects. The observer stands outside the configuration space, in the position of God with respect to those events and the laws to which they conform.

But this way of thinking cannot be extended to the whole universe; it applies only to pieces of nature, viewed successively. The stipulated, unexplained initial conditions in one iteration of this Newtonian paradigm become the explained subject matter in another. By this procedure, our understanding of nature becomes more comprehensive only by the accumulation of such piecemeal incursions.

If we want to account for the whole universe (the subject matter of cosmology), we cannot use this method. There is no place outside the configuration space in which the observer can stand in his godlike position, or from which he could prepare copies, or look for other instances, of the subject matter to be explained. When we turn to the entire universe, with the knowledge we already possess, we find that it has a history. What the Newtonian paradigm assumes to be the exclusive and permanent way in which nature works—through immutable laws whose application may be interrupted or deflected but never permanently suspended by events—turns out to be at best the way in which it works in the long, cooled-down, relatively stable stretches of its history. Whereas we cannot legitimately go from the piecemeal deployment of the Newtonian paradigm to the whole universe, we can and must go in the opposite direction from the universe to its parts and its movements. If the universe has a history, so must each of its parts and moments.

The Kantian view leaves no room for such transformation in the workings of nature. It assumes causality will always be recurrent and that its recurrence will be explicable only by the power of unchanging laws (and today we would add: by symmetries and constants). Either this unbreakable complementarity between causal connection and underlying laws is a necessary presupposition of the human understanding or it is a feature of the real. It cannot be the former, because our views of causal connection in nature continue to change, through our discoveries about the real, whatever the initial conception of causality that our development in the early stages of life instills in us.

Suppose we say that causal connections, based on immutable laws, are a feature of nature. Then, we have to reckon with change in the nature of those connections and in the content of those regularities. Such change may occur in the earliest moments of the present universe or in extreme circumstances that arise in the course of its history. Or it may result from the incessant emergence of new kinds of phenomena and beings, and new types of regularities—the traditional subject matter of natural history.

In the physics of the twentieth century, we witness the development of an approach to nature that dispenses with causality and laws altogether. The predominant interpretations of general relativity and the actual practice of particle physics dismiss causal thinking as an anthropomorphic perversion that science outgrows.

The understanding of nature takes on the features of the mathematical reasoning in which it is expressed. It views cosmology as large-scale astronomy and treats its incipient exploration of the history of the universe as a speculative sideshow to the work of fundamental physics. Causality as traditionally understood all but disappears. The laws of nature survive only in the sense of a basic structure, such as a pseudo-Riemannian four-dimensional manifold. Such a structure has no place for non-emergent, global, continuous, and irreversible time, or for the idea that nature—and everything in it—has a history. Both our discovery of the history of the universe and ordinary experience, however, suggest that everything changes sooner or later. Faced with this conflict of views, we must consider whether the denial of time is justified by our empirical findings or merely motivated by the marriage of mathematics and metaphysics in natural science.

The preceding argument about causation has been historical in a twofold sense. It has sought to make explicit the philosophical significance of the history of our ideas about causality and the laws of nature in natural science and natural philosophy. Moreover, it has looked to natural history, including cosmology, understood as a historical science, for what it may teach us about time and change.

The historical argument culminates in a series of stark choices. The first such choice has to do with the relation of causality to our understanding, on one side, and to nature, on the other. Either causality is a feature of nature, or it does not exist. We cannot save it by claiming, as Kant did, that it is an assumption without which we would be unable to form a coherent account of our experience.

Our ideas about causality, within and outside natural science, have been too diverse and contradictory to support the claim of unavoidable reliance on this assumption: the reference of the assumption remains unclear. And no matter how we choose to define the supposedly unavoidable presupposition, we will find in the history of science and philosophy examples of how people have learned to dispense with it and to think in another way. Thus, the first part of the approach to causality that has been dominant in natural science and natural philosophy—that causality is about how we think rather than about how nature works—fails.

But although the thesis that causality represents an indispensable requirement for making sense of experience is untenable, it contains an element of truth. We all learn as children to manipulate the word as well as to deal with the human agents around us, collaborating with them or resisting them. Piaget, Vygotsky, and other cognitive or evolutionary psychologists demonstrated that across a wide range of societies these capabilities pass through the same developmental stages. We can admit that a loose causal understanding of reality informs our experience of intentional action. However, this understanding, suggested by the pragmatic circumstances of human agency, enacts no particular idea of causality.

As soon as we begin to be exposed to the influences of the folk and scientific cultures in which we find ourselves, our ideas about how events connect in nature and society begins to shift. The pragmatics of agency is wedded to a folk science, influenced in turn by real science. From then on, the conversation between our pre-scientific and our scientific views of causality never stops. It may even result in the denial of causality, sometimes under the disguise of its radical reinterpretation. The proximate target of that denial is causation. The ulterior target is time.

This argument brings us to the threshold of what I shall call the false antinomy of causality. There is an apparent antinomy about causal connection. Once examined, however, it dissolves: the solution to it lies in one of its two sides.

The idea of causation stands accused of being irreparably vague and both anthropocentric and anthropomorphic. Its roots are said to lie in our experience of intervention in the workings of nature—in our reckoning with the resistance that the world and other people impose on our actions. As soon as we try to cleanse our idea of causality of its anthropomorphic and anthropocentric taints and make its meaning precise, it seems to dissolve into ambiguity and contradiction.

What exactly does it mean to say that an earlier event produces a later one? Must we presuppose a particular conception of necessity or probability? Must both the cause and the effect be recurrent events of some type? Is there a lapse of time between the cause and the effect? By what alchemy, in that lapse of time, does the cause become the effect? If there is no such lapse, how can the effect be distinguished from the cause? These questions may appear to have no acceptable answers: the conundrums that they imply result, according to the first leg of the antinomy, from the crude anthropomorphic and anthropocentric origins of causal thinking.

We then find ourselves led to the second leg of the antinomy. If the hopelessly vague and ambiguous idea of causality cannot be extricated from its anthropomorphic and anthropocentric roots, the solution may seem to be to abandon it and replace it by the mathematical idea of function and more generally by a mathematical and logical representation of connections in nature that makes no reference to causality. This solution is not simply a proposal made by the critics of causal thinking. It is the practice that has to a large extent been adapted by the fundamental physics of the last 100 years. Such an alternative presents no problem for those who are willing to give up the reality of time or to redefine that reality so radically that it breaks its connection with the temporal assumptions of causal thinking.

This antinomy—the choice between a view of causality that can never extricate itself from the situation of human agency and an escape from causality that is necessarily also a denial of the reality of time—is a false antinomy. It has two solutions: one for the disbeliever in the reality of time; the other, for the proponent of the reality of time.

The disbeliever must accept that the alternative to causality is also an alternative to time and to history—the history of nature and of the universe. If cosmology finds the universe to be historical, the disbeliever in the reality of time must treat the claim of universal history as a speculative afterthought to the main work of science and detach the micro view—the account of the elementary constituents of nature in particle physics at one level and chemistry at another—from the macro view or the narrative of the evolution of the whole universe. He must therefore also reckon with the widening of the gap between nature as science represents it beyond time and nature as we experience it in time. He dissolves the antinomy, but at a price.

The antinomy also has another solution, which presupposes, and helps develop, the temporal naturalism for which I argue. On this second solution, the rejection of causality on account of its contamination by our action-centered and self-referential perspective is twice wrong. It is wrong, first, because it amounts to a rejection of our finitude and, second, because it understates our powers of transcendence. Thus, the argument of the antinomy about causality and causal explanation makes the two main mistakes that we can make when representing our situation in the world.

It rejects our finitude by treating the rootedness of our causal ideas in the circumstance of agency as a defect. It denies our transcendence by failing to recognize that the point of departure need not be the point of arrival: as the history of our ideas about causality shows, we can change the ideas, or revise the assumptions, suggested to us by the circumstance of agency. We do not know, we never know beforehand, how far we can go in the exercise of this power of revision, which is, in this context, another name for transcendence. We know where it starts but not where it ends.

It is not just our causal thinking that remains entangled in the human perspective: in the situation of the embodied organism whose cognitive interests are joined to its practical ones and coeval with them. To associate this perspective with illusion is to uphold an idea of objectivity from an imaginary standpoint—the standpoint of God, the absolute, inhuman perspective. We then find ourselves deficient, by that criterion, in every facet of our engagement with reality.

But finitude can be the opposite of objectivity, rather than the beginning of the road to greater objectivity, only by a criterion suited to another being. It cannot be the opposite of objectivity for us. Nor can it be the opposite of objectivity for any being that we have ever encountered or that, on the analogy of such encounters, we can imagine as existing within the world and time rather than beyond them.

Thus, we gradually give the idea of causation a definite content in the specific contexts of our scientific and artistic attempts to engage the world. As even the simplified history of ideas about causes and laws of nature that I have outlined earlier shows, it is impossible, despite the efforts of Kant and others to the contrary, to separate approaches to causality and to the laws of nature from the substance of scientific theories and the ways in which they represent, or deny, causal connection.

The common element in ideas about causation is the recognition of time and of connection in time between a before and an after. In Newton's physics the reality of time is both recognized and circumscribed: the laws of nature are outside time but determine what happens within it, and the scientist views temporal reality from this atemporal standpoint. In Einstein's physics, causation gives way to mathematical function, and history to structure, because time ceases to have independent reality.

Kant had prepared the way by attributing causal connection to the unavoidable requirements of the human understanding rather than to the workings of nature. He had presented time, in the same spirit, as the medium of conscious experience rather than as the most fundamental aspect of reality: that everything changes sooner or later. And yet the historical consciousness, which Nietzsche called our third eye, flourished as never before in the nineteenth century in both natural history and social thought.

At every moment of this evolution, humanity demonstrated that it could either transform its understanding of causation or reject causation altogether. Our insight into how phenomena are connected, within or outside time, was not restricted to the incipient science of the earliest civilizations or to the natural philosophy of the child. Never did science demonstrate more conclusively our power to revise our spontaneous and unrefined causal thinking than when it rejected causation and even time altogether. It rejected them in the face of a stark contradiction between its resulting account of nature and the way in which we continue to experience the world.

The antinomy of causality is false. If time is unreal, or has only diminished reality, we can treat mathematical reasoning, with its timeless connections, as a foreshadowing of reality rather than as a simulacrum of the world from which time and phenomenal particularity have been sucked out. If time is real, we can go on to develop our ideas about causal connections in time-bound nature, limited only by our ignorance and infirmity, not by the causal preconceptions we had as children or that our ancestors entertained earlier during the rise of mankind.

There is no antinomy about causation. There is a dispute about the facts of the matter. The crux of the dispute is the reality of time and the meaning, scope, and consequences of its reality. That disagreement achieves its most general form in the contest between the philosophies of deep structure and temporal naturalism.

No Kingdom within a Kingdom: Deep Structure, Dualism, and Temporal Naturalism

The remainder of this chapter completes the ontological view set out in the preceding sections. It does so by exploring the place of humanity within this conception of what the world is like. The central question raised in this and in the next section is whether we form an exception to the basic regime of nature. The gist of the answer is that we do not. We are not, however, simply a continuation of what came before us; we bring novelties. And our greatest power consists in our ability to accelerate the making of the new.

But the world has been the scene of novelty all along, before us and beside us, only in other ways and by different measures. All along, in the kinds of beings that there are, there is a chain of analogies, of similarity and difference, not a wall between the human and the rest of reality.

The philosophy of deep structure, and the practice of natural science that it informs, are in manifest conflict with our lived experience. The issue on which the conflict comes to a head is time and the implications of denying its reality and of finding the most real in the least time-bound. And the conflict has been not simply with our subjective experience; it has been with the teachings of Christianity, of romanticism, of modernism—of all the movements of thought and sensibility that have had the greatest influence on our self-understanding as well as on their counterparts in other civilizations.

The result of this conflict has been the presence in the history of Western philosophy of a series of dualisms. The message of these dualisms is to distinguish in the world what Spinoza described as a kingdom within a kingdom.[8] These dualisms have come in four waves.

Each of these dualisms has its own assumptions, intentions, and claims. What they all share is the exemption that they accord to humanity—or to the part of human experience they regard as most significant and distinctive—from the general order of nature. The rules of the inner kingdom differ from the rules of the outer kingdom. And it is only by this coexistence of the general regime with the exceptional regime that it has been possible—at a cost we ought to judge unacceptable—to square the philosophy of deep structure with reality as we encounter it.

The view of what the world is like that I defend here has no need of the exceptional regime: it describes the general regime in a way that makes place for us, human beings, and for our powers of transformation and transcendence, without doing violence to existence as we live it. Consequently, it dispenses with the special pleading—the fallacies, evasions, and wishful thinking—on which each of the dualisms so prominent in the history of Western philosophy has depended.

The study of dualisms has philosophical interest. Each of them offers a view of what makes us more human and of why and how our humanity rebels against the general regime of nature. Each poses questions to which ontology as natural philosophy and social theory must give an answer. What would the world have to be like for us to make room for our humanity without having to allege in our favor a miraculous exception to the general regime? And is the world in fact like that, or can we make sense of ourselves only through a view that supplies such a carve out? The overcoming of dualism and the rejection of the philosophy of deep structure are two sides of the same endeavor. The reward of that endeavor is to free our self-understanding from what each of the dualisms has done in its own way: the conversion of a view of our distinctive powers into a rift within reality.[9]

8. Baruch Spinoza, *Ethics*, Part III, preface and subsequent argument against the "imperium in imperio," first published posthumously in 1677.

9. For a more developed discussion of the nature and consequences of these

The first wave of dualism in the history of Western philosophy from the fourth century to the twenty-first was the division, in late medieval scholasticism, between the realms of nature and of grace. It is traditionally described as nominalist but it might also be labeled simply dualist if that word did not carry such heavy baggage in the history of Christian orthodoxy and heresy. In the domain of grace, God's perfect freedom communicated with the flawed freedom of his human creatures, allowing them to increase their share in his life and in the experience of love and transcendence. Spiritless nature, in the contrasting domain, could become an object of scientific study and practical manipulation because it did not participate in that ascent.

The contrast between the orders of nature and grace verged on heresy. It continued the spirit of the Nestorian heresy, with its conception of an insuperable chasm between the human and divine natures of Christ. And it threatened Christians with God's breaking of his promise, in the Hebrew Bible, to pour out his spirit unto all flesh: the human being as embodied spirit could tolerate within himself no such cleavage between the spiritless body and the disembodied spirit. However, it created a conceptual space within which a view of the general advance of science acceptable to the philosophy of deep structure could advance.

The second wave of dualism came with Descartes' distinction between the mental and the physical: *res cogitans* and *res extensa*. It is only mental experience, when it has itself as its object, that we know free from radical doubt and from within. Physical stuff, even as the human body, we encounter as something alien to which we have no reliable access, except insofar as we can trust in a God who would not subject us to systematic delusion. Thus, the division between two orders of reality, which the nominalist dualism had placed at the boundary between God and humanity, is relocated within the embodied self.

The third wave of dualism appeared with Kant's distinction between the indispensable presuppositions of experience and things

successive dualisms, see Roberto Mangabeira Unger, *The Religion of the Future*, 2014, pp. 143–62.

in themselves, which remain forever unknowable to us. The second regime—the regime of our experience and of its self-grounding—is defined by the requirements of our ability to make sense of the world, regardless of what the world is actually like. Thus, Descartes' division between mind without extension and extension without mind gave way, with Kant, to a contrast between our experience, with its indispensable presuppositions, and the impenetrable non-human reality beyond our grasp. The procedure for defining the structure of the exceptional, human regime went backward from our experience to its universal enabling conditions—the transcendental method. And it viewed the experience whose enabling conditions it explored in the dimension of the individual self, taken as a prototype for all humanity, rather than in the shared life of a culture and a society.

It is precisely on this last point that the fourth wave of dualism—the historicist—moved in a different direction during the nineteenth and twentieth centuries. Historicist dualism locates the frontier between the two kingdoms in the division between our collective forms of life and consciousness and nature beyond society and culture. The distinction is both hermeneutic or epistemological and objective or ontological. Under our social arrangements and cultural assumptions, we acquire a second nature. Those arrangements and assumptions define the context within which we can assign meaning and value and make claims on one another. Without this second nature, we would be lost, and cease to be human. And we can know these social and cultural facts in a way in which we cannot hope to know natural phenomena: from within, as their creators. They are our collective constructions in historical time: the products of our ceaseless struggle with one another, as well as of its temporary interruption or relative containment.

The proponents of the historicist dualism teach us that the power that the dead exercise over the living, through the medium of these forms of collective life, is not to be confused with the constraints that non-human nature imposes on human experience. To mistake the former for the latter—treating the institutional arrangements and ideological assumptions of the established social order as part of the furniture of the universe, and allowing them to wear the false semblance of naturalness and necessity—is to bow down before an idol of our own making and to forfeit our freedom to that idol.

These four varieties of dualism have much in common, besides the fundamental polarity between a natural and a human world. They all make our individual and collective self-understanding depend on a miracle: the singular emergence within nature, and in a tiny corner of the evolving universe, of a reality operating under terms that diverge from those under which the rest of reality subsists and works. And they all produce this miracle by a variant of the same method.

The method is to convert anthropology and epistemology into ontology, inferring the frontiers and the structure of the kingdom within a kingdom from our powers and from the limits of the domains in which we exercise in them. In the nominalist dualism, they are the powers that we exercise jointly with God, or rather the powers of our conversation with him, and of his creative and redemptive action among us, in history. In the Cartesian dualism, they are the self-referential powers of consciousness. In the Kantian dualism, they are the powers by which we ground ourselves in a world to whose nature, apart from us, we can never hope to have access. In the historicist dualism, they are the powers by which we establish social and cultural regimes that give us a second nature—a nature beyond nature—and rescue us from the alienness and indifference of the non-human world and its inability to support the making of meaning and of value.

In each instance, we read a division of reality off from the exercise and the limitation of our powers. We proceed in the manner of a man who, finding that he can see up to a hundred meters ahead of him, imagines the world to be divided into two parts—the part that he can see and the part that he cannot—and supposes that they must be completely different. Then he picks up binoculars and sees further and announces that the division between the two parts of reality passes through a different place.

Our powers are limited. Their limitation is an expression of our finitude. But their limits are not fixed; they are movable, as the history of both science and art demonstrates. We cannot determine once and for all how far we will be able to move them. Our ability to enhance our powers, without overcoming our finitude, is a testament to our transcendence. We all know the truth of Pliny the Elder's remark: "Many things are considered impossible until they are done."

The consequence of the philosophy that represents the limit of our powers as a division within reality, converting anthropology and epistemology into ontology, is to contaminate our understanding of what the world is like with an element of arbitrariness. The range of our powers, and our views of what they are and of what they can become, are always changing. The philosophical dualisms, however, project these views onto a conception of the world and of its division into two kingdoms.

The temporal naturalism defended here dispenses with this projection. But once we dispense with the transmutation of an account of our powers into a contrast between two orders of reality, how are we to understand our place in a world that has no room for a kingdom within the kingdom?

The Human Difference, without Dualism

Structure and change. We must reject the dualisms that are required by attempts to reconcile the philosophy of deep structure with our experience. This rejection poses the question of the human difference and of its place in the world. There is no kingdom within a kingdom. However, the world witnesses an endless albeit discontinuous production of difference and novelty. The human difference forms part of that production, developing in time. And so, in different ways, does everything in the world.

In Chapter 3, on the human condition, I approach the human difference from the perspective of the irreparable flaws in the human condition—our mortality, our groundlessness, and our insatiability —as well as from the vantage point of what enables us to deal with them: our excess over circumstance, our ability to turn the tables on our setting, our unlimited need to be held in the arms of someone who loves us and whom we love.

In Chapter 7, on politics, I deal with the human difference as it expresses itself in our relation to the chief object of explanatory ambition in social thought and of transformative ambition in political activity: the institutional and ideological regimes that shape the practical and discursive routines of a society and set limits to the outcomes that they allow. These regimes give us our second nature and lay the basis for the only life acceptable to us, a life in society. To the extent that they become insulated against challenge and change, by ideas as well as by arrangements, they begin to wear the false semblance of naturalness and necessity. They are, however, nothing but our constructions run away from us. They are frozen fighting: the marks and residues of our temporarily interrupted and relatively contained struggles over the terms of our dealings with one another.

The regimes of social life mediate the effect of the constraints of non-human nature and modify the way in which we experience and address the unfixable defects in the human condition. For the sake of our interests in the development of our productive powers and the enhancement of our freedom, we have a stake in designing these regimes so that they allow us to engage in them without surrendering to them. Our interest is to reimagine and remake them, by steps, even as we go about the ordinary business of life. Here is something that did not exist before us and cannot exist apart from us or from beings like us.

In Chapter 2, on epistemology, interpreted as the theory and program of inquiry, I address the human difference from the angle of a type of knowledge that we can have of the institutional and ideological regimes shaping our existence in society. Such knowledge is unlike any that we can hope to have of non-human nature. We can know such regimes from within, as their creators: just as God, for a believer in one of the Semitic monotheisms, knows his creation.

The key to progress in every field of inquiry is the relation that it establishes between insight into the actual and imagination of the accessible variations of the actual. To grasp how a part of nature works is to understand what it can become under different provocations. This fact has consequences for the relation between our insight into social life and our attempts to reshape society: the attempts can sustain the insight, not just the other way around.

All these aspects of the human difference, explored later in this book, bear on my theme here: the placement of humanity in a world in which difference and novelty abound on every side but no simple line separates human experience from the rest of the real. The history of nature, once we view nature historically, anticipates each of the elements that make up the human difference.

Everything, according to the natural philosophy for which I argue, changes sooner or later, including change itself, and nothing is less real by virtue of being temporary. But change is discontinuous in every aspect of reality and in every part of the history of nature. Cosmologically, we see this succession of disruption and relative stability in the passage from the fiery early moments of the present universe, with its extremes of density, energy, and temperature, to the relatively stable regularities and elementary structures of the cooled-down universe. And within this cooled-down universe, we find the vestiges of the early violence recorded in the cosmic microwave radiation background that we observe, as well as in extreme events and conditions, such as the occurrence of black holes, in a universe that is no longer and not yet in the throes of radical disruption.

We see the perennial emergence of the new, out of the swing between structure and its disruption, on the scale of natural history. The earth and life sciences find it in the passage, back and forth, from concentrated upheaval in geological time to change that is much slower and more subtle. We encounter it as well in the prodigious history of speciation—the punctuated equilibrium that evolutionary biology studies, giving way to long-lasting species, reliant on DNA that is remarkably constant and on a relatively restricted repertoire of ways in which biological function is expressed in physical structure.

An analogous sequence of concentrated innovation in institutional and ideological regimes, followed by an afterlife of normalization that may seem destined to exist forever, and be readily mistaken for naturalness and necessity, marks human history. That history is in large part the record of the formative arrangements and assumptions that give shape to the practical and discursive routines of each society.

Marx and other European social theorists of the nineteenth and twentieth centuries mispresented that history. They did so, for example, by claiming that each regime is an indivisible system, which must be either managed (reformism) or replaced (revolution.) They nevertheless understood that structure—regime making and regime change—is the central topic of both political practice and social theory. By contrast, each of the social sciences that arose in the aftermath of the tradition of classical social theory has descended into the retrospective rationalization of the real. Each has done so by severing the vital link between insight into the actual and imagination of accessible possibility.

In every part of the natural and social worlds, the past shapes the future in time: that is the substance of causality. But in every part of reality this power of path dependency is variable rather than constant. In the extreme forms of nature—early in the formation of the universe, as well as later, during the history of the cooled-down universe, in the local resurgence of such extreme conditions—the range of the accessible possible, of the next steps to which you can get from here, grows. Laplacian determinism and its twentieth- and twenty-first-century successor—the conception of the block universe—have no place for such variation in the influence of the past on the future.

In human history the variable force of path dependency takes on another character—as with all other aspects of the human difference—distinct from what happens in non-human nature, yet analogous to it. It is as if everything that happens in this world—which is what it is rather than something else—runs the changes on the same themes, thus confirming that there is no kingdom within the kingdom.

The institutional and ideological regimes that so decisively influence social life differ, among other ways, both in the extent to which they resist revision and in the degree to which they determine their own sequel. These two differences are two aspects of the same thing: it is by giving the dead the power to rule the living that such regimes shape their own succession. And it is by remaking the regimes so that the distance between our ordinary regime-preserving routines and our exceptional regime-changing activities narrows that we disrupt the power of these institutional and ideological orders to shape the future and substitute our agency for their influence.

In all features and moments of the history of the world, whether natural or social, the extended periods of relative quiescence that alternate with the more concentrated moments of disruption display a stability that we can easily mistake for lawfulness. This misunderstanding sustains the view that timeless regularities—the laws, symmetries, and constants of nature—underlie causal connections and give warrant to causal explanation, and that such connections are always recurrent relations among stable categories of events or of phenomena. But both natural and social history suggest that this is only one of the forms of causal connection in time. There are states of nature, or times in the history of nature, in which causal connection takes no such recurrent form and no differentiated manifold of stable elements of reality takes hold.

If, in such states or times, the causal connections are not recurrent and the parts of nature that they connect are not subdivisions of a changeless elementary structure, then we have reason to reinterpret the relative stability of the cooled-down universe in which we find ourselves. What we used to describe as laws of nature (before the advent of a style of physics that has gone far toward dispensing with both laws and causes) may be in fact the relatively stable temporal connections that we observe. On this alternative view, they are stable until they are not. They describe recurrent connections in time in certain pictures of the workings of nature, such as Newton's world of forces and bodies at rest and in motion.

When applied to nature at the atomic and subatomic levels, these ideas may seem paradoxical and enigmatic. They have a more familiar meaning when explored in the macroscopic phenomena studied by the earth and life sciences. The natural-historical principle of the coevolution of the phenomena and of the regularities that they exhibit—as with the relation between the "laws" of Mendelian genetics and the emergence of multicellular organisms capable of sexual reproduction—already brings closer the causal connections and the laws that supposedly explain them. It places both the former and the latter in the flow of history. It subjects both the former and the latter to the sequence of concentrated disruption and temporary stability, easily mistaken for timeless lawfulness.

In human society, the historical relativity of laws, already manifest in natural history, becomes all the more striking. Every institutional and ideological regime imparts a semblance of lawfulness to a form of social life. The laws promulgated and enforced by the state form only a part of this lawfulness.

In the most democratic and in the most despotic regimes, the state—whether a "dictatorship of the law" or a would-be radical democracy—may aspire to shape all social practice. In fact, in all the states that have existed up to now, state-made law is no more than a series of episodic interventions in a preexisting world of social practice. The formative institutional arrangements and ideological assumptions, only partly expressed in that state-made law, are the basic source of lawful regularity in social life.

Every such regime is a product of practical and visionary strife and of its temporary interruption or relative containment. It is neither universal nor eternal—this is the central thesis of the single greatest achievement of classical European social theory, Marx's critique of English political economy.

But Marx's account of the nature of such regimes is, in every other vital respect, mistaken. Regimes are not indivisible systems with a logic that can be reduced to a series of propositions like Newton's laws of motion. The extent to which they resist transformation and determine their own sequel is variable and an object of struggle in both thought and politics. And there are no higher-order laws governing the sequence of regimes, although there are constraints on their reconstruction, which may be looser or tighter.

Regimes that allow for the greater development of our practical powers and our moral interests are more likely to flourish and be imitated. However, they are not selected from a closed list of possible regimes; no such list exists. The same functional advantage—of ability to sustain a certain level of development of the "forces of production" —may have different regimes for a basis. Moreover, regimes compete against the manifest alternatives, not against possible orders that have never become real. The idea of the set of all possible institutional orders is an empty fiction.

The lawfulness of social life—the power of regimes to give us our second natures and to shape a collective destiny—is a measure of the degree to which we remain unfree. The regime most conducive to freedom would be the one that allows us to cooperate without imposing on our cooperation a script that we did not choose and barely understand and that induces—or forces—us to mistake it for the freedom that it denies us. Our encounter with lawful regularity in human history gives clarity and intensity to what we already find foreshadowed in natural history.

The making of the new and the spectral idea of the possible. In every aspect of reality, the new can emerge. The idea of the emergence of the new is incompatible with the view that an unchanging script governs the transformations of reality. It is therefore also incompatible with any approach to reality that denies the radical and inclusive reality of time by holding that something outside time governs what takes place within it.

But it is not just these ideas that undermine recognition of the emergence of the new. It is also our conventional notion of the possible as a ghost stalking the world and waiting to come onto the stage of the actual. For that notion, there is a horizon of possible states of affairs: not just a penumbra of the accessible possibilities—the *theres* to which we can get from *here*—but also a well-defined set of all the events and states of affairs that could ever happen. Our knowledge of this horizon is, according to this view, always imperfect and tentative; it develops with the progress of scientific insight.

The idea of a horizon of possible states of affairs follows from the philosophy of deep structure. For that philosophy, every event is the actualization of a possibility that existed beforehand. The ultimate set of possibilities is determined forever. At most, there may be a measure of diversity and path dependency in the actualization of one possibility rather than another.

The possible states of affairs are then ghosts—the ghosts that haunt present reality. They wait off stage for their cue to come on to the stage of actuality. They have every attribute of a being, except the one that matters: being in fact.

This spectral idea of possibility refers to nothing that natural or social science has discovered about the world. It is a metaphysical conception. It has no place in a temporal naturalism, which is one of the reasons to prefer temporal naturalism to the philosophies of deep structure and of the timeless one. Its effect is to eviscerate the recognition of the new.

What underlies this criticism of the spectral idea of possibility are the views of causation and time for which I earlier argued. Causation is a primitive feature of nature in a world in which everything changes sooner or later, including change itself, rather than merely an indispensable presupposition of our understanding. In the history of the universe, causation also changes: the recurrent, lawlike variant of causal connection is not the only variant of causality. Moreover, apart from the natural history of causation, there is also a human history of our thinking about causal connections: even in the brief period of the last few hundred years our thinking about causality, the laws of nature, and the structure of reality has undergone repeated upheaval. A central element in this history has been our approach to time, and our recognition or denial of its reality and its sway.

Our ideas about the possible bear the imprint of our limited, defective insight into nature and its transformations. The conception of an ultimate horizon of possible states of affairs, suggested by the philosophy of deep structure, is misleading and dangerous for two reasons: because it disregards or circumscribes the susceptibility of everything to change, which is the meaning of time, and because it detaches the conception of possibility from the only context that gives it meaning—the context of the accessible transformations of some part of reality into something else—and leaves the idea of the possible floating, as if it had a meaning outside such definite contexts.

These remarks suggest a note of caution in distinguishing these views from views with which they have more than superficial similarities, such as Henri Bergson's ideas about the real and the possible.[10] The universe is not our partner in our struggle to rise to a higher form of being. It is not a factory of creativity and joy. What it has in store for us is annihilation. But for the same reason that, as Whitehead

---

10. Henri Bergson, *Le possible et le réel*, originally published in Nordisk Tidskrift in 1930.

reminded us, the business of the future is to be dangerous, nature is prodigal in the production of novelty.

In the history of nature, the new emerges at every scale. With each episode in the making of the new, the range of accessible transformations, which is the clearest and most definite sense of possibility, changes. The point is not just that our idea of what is possible changes in the light of change in the real. Something happens that makes things possible that were not possible before. Each episode in the emergence of the new changes the workings of the world in some way. In the renewed world, things can work in ways in which they did not previously work. Changes can take place that could not have occurred before the renewal. There is no real renewal, and there is no change in change, if the succession was predetermined and the difference between the earlier and later workings of nature or society amounts to an illusion.

The idea of the emergence of the new, taken in a sense incompatible with the spectral idea of possibility, leads, however, to an apparent antinomy: a second antinomy of causality. This second antinomy is just as false as the first one. Disarming it results in a vital clarification.

Suppose we reject every part of what we often take to be the widely shared approach to causality and the laws of nature but is in fact—as I earlier argued—only a moment in the history of natural science and natural philosophy: the moment associated with the philosophy of Kant and of nineteenth-century physics. One part of that view was the idea that causality is a presupposition of the human understanding rather than a feature of reality. Another part was the idea that laws of nature underwrite causal explanations. Every causal connection represents an instance of a law of nature at work.

The opposing view is that causal connections are primitive features of nature: they are the connections among events or states of affairs in time, in a world in which nothing is more real than time because everything, including the ways in which things change, changes sooner or later. Moreover, what we take to be the regularities of nature—its laws, symmetries, and constants—are descriptions of the recurrent form of causality among types of phenomena in the relatively stable, cooled-down universe that we observe.

Nature also has states in which causal connection lacks this recurrent and stereotypical form. Among those other states of nature are the ones that the present universe seems to have exhibited at its fiery beginning. Other such states reappear later in extreme natural phenomena in the course of cosmological history. No unchanging laws control these vicissitudes of causal connection in the history of nature and the universe. The new changes what is possible, which is tantamount to saying that it changes the laws.

This view may seem to fall victim to an antinomy, which is, however, as false as the antinomy of causation discussed earlier. Is the change of the laws itself governed by higher-order, unchanging laws? If so, we have not defeated the philosophy of deep structure and the spectral idea of possibility. Or is the change in the workings of nature undetermined—or at least underdetermined? If so, it seems that we have escaped from deep structure and spectral possibility only by an explanatory nihilism, placing inexplicable and therefore arbitrary change at the center of natural and cosmological history.

The first step to dismantling this apparent antinomy is to observe two different ways in which we find change changing, and creating the new, in nature. One way is when a state of affairs can have many different sequels and nothing determines that the result is one rather than another, except the particular sequence of interactions among the components of that state of affairs at a certain time. At the limit, we can describe such a circumstance as genuinely stochastic or random.

Such a circumstance may characterize nature in states or moments of extreme density and energy. It may occur as well in the cooled-down, well-differentiated universe at the subatomic level in the processes that are described by quantum mechanics—or at least by versions of quantum mechanics that do not appeal to "hidden variables" in an attempt to escape randomness. There is, then, indeed arbitrariness or indeterminacy. It is an arbitrariness that, in time, can result in new order and an indeterminacy that can end in a new form of determination.

The second way in which we can find change changing, and creating the new, is by the workings of the characteristic processes of natural history. Recall them in the inverse order in which I considered them earlier in this chapter: the coevolution of laws and of the phenomena that they govern; the crucial role of sequence or path dependency, magnified by the coexistence of causal sequences that may be relatively independent of one another rather than expressions of a unified system; and the mutability of types—implying the transience of natural kinds, even at the most basic levels of nature, as well as the occasional emergence of types of being that never existed before.

These processes are not random, but they can be fertile in the making of the new. By the operation of causal forces in natural-historical time, they can lead (through path dependency and the loose relation of causal sequences) to new phenomena (the mutability of types) and new regularities (the coevolution of the phenomena and of the laws, or regular causal connections, that they exhibit.) When the outcome is the creation of a type of being that embodies a new order, with the potential to endure and to recur, the spell of the preexisting order and its laws is broken: a different future becomes possible. Once again, the decisive condition for its occurrence is the passage of time. Without the passage of time, the creation of a new form of order, with staying power and the facility for recurrence, becomes incomprehensible.

Such an emergence of new causation and new order from preexisting order and causation is an event that has happened repeatedly in the history of nature. Each time it has been different, and it has resulted in new difference. It is not a break in causal connection. It represents an instance of causal connection, once we understand causality in its natural-historical expression rather than in the language of an explanatory practice that treats the idea of a historical science as an oxymoron.

It happened in the appearance of the subatomic order that particle physics treats as a permanent regime of nature; in the history of lifeless nature through the formation, for example, of crystals; in the arrival of life; in the emergence of mind and then of the human mind with the attribute of imagination—the ability to transgress its own settled methods and presuppositions; and in the development of human societies and cultures that make more or less room for the perpetual creation of the new. Thus, we might say that emergent order in nature has been a prophecy of life, life has been a prophecy of mind, and mind has been a prophecy of the imagination, which has the new for its subject, as a form of social life.

This way of talking about the turning points in natural history risks trouble: it can degenerate into an anthropomorphic mythology of hope, projecting onto nature what we have reason to want for ourselves. Nothing in the workings of nature guarantees an ascent if the measure of ascent is the power to innovate. Such a guarantee would amount to yet another version of the idea of a timeless script, expressed as a historical narrative—a narrative that in this form can have only one direction and one outcome.

The emergence of the new in nature includes the emergence of life on our planet—and thus creates the basis for our existence. Apart from that event, however, the transformations of nature are indifferent to our concerns, and not arranged to suit our (contradictory) conceptions of progress. For all we know, at any time the evolution of our universe could end badly for us (if we continue to exist) and take bad turns all along the way.

A temporal naturalism must guard vigilantly against the association of change in nature with our plans and preferences. Such an association results in the corruption of natural philosophy by wishful thinking and power worship. Under the disguise of piety, this corruption taints the pantheistic and panentheistic ideas that have attracted so many great philosophers.

The making of the new and the imagination. Nevertheless, with the development of the human mind and of our societies and cultures, the making of the new acquires distinct and powerful instruments. These instruments lack any close counterpart in nature before humanity. On one side, the mind resembles a machine. It is modular and formulaic, with parts that perform dedicated functions. The connection between mental function and brain structure is subject to modification by the remarkable plasticity of the brain. In this respect, however, the mind works by rule even when its rule-based working includes the power of recursive infinity: the ability to come up with something new through an endless recombination of familiar elements that may end up suggesting ideas and procedures that are both new and useful. Up to this point, everything in our mental experience conforms to a model common in the prior history of nature.

In other respects, however, the mind is an anti-machine. It is not modular or formulaic. It can see something, or envisage a transformation of established reality, or of our established way of understanding the real, not countenanced by the assumptions and methods on which we have relied in our ongoing practices of inquiry. Its discoveries may be in that way senseless. And then it may retrospectively develop the methods and assumptions that make sense of such otherwise senseless discoveries.

This second side of the mind is what we call the imagination. Two moves define it. The first move is the one that Kant emphasized: distancing from the phenomenon—an image is the memory of a perception. Such distancing represents, in our mental experience, the simplest and most basic form of transcendence: our removal from the immediate scene of perception and action.

We can best understand such distancing as a preliminary to the second move of the imagination: subsuming part of the manifest world under a range of transformative variation in the space of the proximate possible. Insight into the actual deepens only as imagination of the adjacent possible expands. As the manifest world loosens what had been for us some of its brute rigidity—its just thereness—we become able to stare less and to grasp more.

Nothing in the physical structure of the brain predetermines the relative power of these two sides of the mind—the mind as machine and the mind as imagination, which is to say the mind as agent of the perpetual creation of the new. The relative prominence of these two sides of the mind depends on the arrangements of society and culture. The history of politics is internal to the history of the mind.

The extent to which a social and ideological regime serves the perpetual creation of the new and expands the space for the transformative work of the imagination has decisive consequences for our most important interests in empowerment and freedom. (I consider them again in Chapter 7, on politics.) The individual agent must be secure in a haven of vital safeguards against oppression and capability-assuring endowments while all around this haven there rages a storm of innovation. This storm does not arise spontaneously: it results from the character of the political and economic institutions as well as from the nature of education and culture. It must be aroused.

The arrangements under which individual and collective agents gain access to the resources of economic capital, political power, and cultural authority by which we create the future within the present must not remain fastened to a single plan. Different forms of decentralized access to such resources should coexist experimentally: for example, different regimes of private and social property, and the contractual practices adapted to them, within the same market order.

The whole regime, in each of its parts, must be so designed that instead of entrenching itself against challenge and change it lays itself open to revision in the normal course of everyday life, without the provocation of crisis. Thus, the distance between our ordinary context-preserving routines and our exceptional context-changing initiatives narrows. And the ordering of our relations to one another sheds all mendacious semblance of naturalness and necessity.

Such a regime moves in the direction of a transcendence that develops in our life in common rather than being relegated to the dreams and longings of intimate experience. Such transcendence will count for nothing unless it leaves its mark on our institutions and practices. In becoming real, it widens the space for the work of the imagination and for the ceaseless making of the new.

This account is not the description of an actual form of life. It is a regulative ideal, informed by a view of humanity emphasizing our excess over the contexts that shape us. Our ability to create the new is an aspect, or an expression, of this vocation of ours. This regulative ideal would represent only an inconsequential utopia if the power to create the new were not so intimately related to the practical success of any society and to the development of our collective capacities to produce, invent, and destroy.

The Message of This Ontology

Six theses have been central to the argument of this chapter—an ontological argument recasting ontology as natural philosophy and social theory.

The first thesis is that of the facticity—the just-so-ness—of the world. The most important feature of the world is that it is what it is rather than something else. It is not arranged to suit our concerns: our practical interests, our spiritual longings, or our desire for pleasing intellectual symmetry. Above all else, the real is alien to us. The desire to represent it as arranged for our advantage is the beginning of all illusion. This theme stands in opposition to metaphysical rationalism, which wants to show, by philosophical speculation, why the world must be as it is. But the world is surprising: it conforms to no model that we can infer from reasoning about the real, with our eyes closed.

The second thesis is that of the inclusive reality of time. Everything changes sooner or later including change itself. The attempt to explain the world through immutable laws and constituents of nature—therefore through something outside time that holds the key to understanding what happens within time—disregards the reality of time, which is to say, the susceptibility of everything that exists to change. The timeless cannot explain the temporal because there is nothing timeless.

We are equipped with a way of thinking, in mathematics and logic, that presents us with a proxy for the world, from which time and phenomenal distinction have been taken out. This capacity for abstraction confers on us an enormous evolutionary advantage. It has endless uses in science, by suggesting to us new ways to represent connections in nature and by revealing the implications of our ideas and arguments. But we take a step in the wrong direction when we treat mathematics as the oracle of science and ascribe its distinctive and unnatural characteristics to nature.

The thesis of the inclusive reality of time challenges the philosophy of deep structure, which has been dominant, though never without opposition, in the Western philosophical tradition from the pre-Socratics to today. It takes causal connection in time to be a primitive feature of nature rather than just a presupposition of the human understanding. Causal connection changes, as does everything else. It varies in different states of nature and in different moments of natural history.

The third thesis is that of the repeated emergence of the new in the history of the universe, of nature, and of humanity. This thesis is an extension of the thesis of the inclusive reality of time and of the idea of the transformation of transformation. It contradicts Laplacian determinism and its successor, the block universe, and gives uncompromising expression to the view of cosmology as a historical science. However, it implies no break in causal connection over time. What it does require is the making of one form of order out of the accidents, anomalies, and involuntary experiments of another, through a combination of stochastic and non-stochastic causation. The emergent order results in connections and powers that the earlier one lacked, including the power to recur or reproduce itself in ways that never existed before.

The emergence of the new in nature through disruptive evolution began long before the emergence of life on our planet. It extends beyond the evolution of life forms into the history of humanity. In this history, the perpetual creation of the new is the measure of our empowerment and of our freedom. It is anchored in the mind as imagination and the remaking of the social order as a structure that invites its own revision in the light of experience and allows us to engage without surrendering.

The fourth thesis is that there is no kingdom within a kingdom: no human reality exempt from the general regime of nature. There is a human difference, which it is the task of ontology as social theory to explore. No bright line, however, separates the human from the non-human. There is only one regime in the world, not two.

Every aspect of the human difference is prefigured by events in the history of nature and of the universe that long preceded the emergence of the first human beings. The transmutation of a view of our powers into a categorical division within reality—turning anthropology into ontology—makes our self-understanding depend on our claim to embody, in part if not in all our experience, a miraculous exception to the workings of nature.

Yet it is hard to avoid making this claim if we understand reality through the lens of the philosophy of deep structure and of its expression in natural philosophy and natural science. Such an understanding is in such stark contradiction to our conscious experience of existence that it forces us either to reject our experience as illusory or to claim to be a mysterious exception to what the world is like. The sharp edge of this contradiction has been the issue of the reality of time. The dualisms that have shaped much of the history of Western philosophy over the last six centuries have been the major conceptual devices by which the philosophers have sought to exempt us from the general regime of nature.

There is only one regime in the world. But it is not the one that Spinoza—who tried to reconcile the philosophy of deep structure with the philosophy of the timeless one—described. And it exists in countless different forms, in a chain of analogies within which we form an extreme link. Everything that is real arises and changes or disappears in time. What came before shapes what came later, but not constantly, in the same way or to the same extent.

The fifth thesis is the incompatibility of such a temporal naturalism with the impulse to deify and to revere the world—just because it is bigger than we are and is the largest entity that we can conceive. This blasphemous impulse takes two main forms. One form is static; the other dynamic.

The static form treats the deep structure or the timeless one as the source of all value as well as the expression of what is most real. When a twentieth-century philosopher who always places time at the center of his thinking, such as the later Heidegger, reorganizes his ideas around the radiance of being, he is, through this neo-paganism, giving new expression to that ancient idea. And when another twentieth-century philosopher who has come to understand ideas as practices grounded in temporal reality, such as the later Wittgenstein, associates the mystical with a reality that is beyond thought and words because it encompasses everything, he is making a similar move in a different vocabulary.

The dynamic form of the impulse allows for time and history, but with a qualification that drastically reduces the significance of the concession: the ultimately real and valuable is the final state of the world, the end to which it is tending—creative nature become nature perfected, or man become God. It is reality plus—known in the history of philosophy as panentheism—in a pseudo-temporal or pseudo-historical form. It is pseudo because the narrative of inevitable ascent to a predetermined goal takes back with one hand what it gives with another: it gives us time but then takes it back by subjecting change to a script that is itself outside time. One by one the thinkers who have come closest to accepting temporal naturalism—Bergson, Whitehead, Teilhard de Chardin, for example—have succumbed to this equivocation.

The world is what it is rather than something else. It is productive of endless surprise, but it does not hand out its surprises according to rules outside time. It is full of wonderful things as well as of terrible ones. And the history of life, which has developed in our corner of the universe, displays the combination of the seductive and the repulsive, the creative and the destructive, that we see in the world before life.

Reverence for being, or for reality taken as a whole, or for the promised outcome of its universal history, is predicated on self-deception and wishful thinking. It is power worship under the disguise of piety. Each of us will be crushed and annihilated by this reality that we are expected to revere. Our brief, disoriented, marvelous, tormented experience of existence, the ground and framework of which lie forever beyond our comprehension, gives us no reason to abase ourselves worshipfully at the altar of the force that will also destroy us—first one by one, and later, in all probability, as a species. Such a bending of the neck under the yoke of the universal master—nature that makes and undoes—is inimical to the ideas, attitudes, and arrangements that can strengthen, in each domain of our existence, our ability to loosen, although we can never overcome, the restraints of finitude.

The sixth thesis is that of the need for a way of understanding and practicing philosophy that is as necessary as it may seem to be impossible. There is no philosophical super-science, no set of methods by which, apart from the practices and discoveries of the established fields of inquiry and of transformative engagement with reality, we can develop a reliable view of what the world is like. Yet it is also true that we must not allow the methods and conceptions of the existing disciplines to define the limits of accessible insight—not just in some future moment of the advance of science but also now.

In each natural science, the contingent marriage of method to subject matter is commonly treated as indissoluble. And the meaning of empirical discoveries depends on theoretical practices and traditions that are in turn informed by metaphysical preconceptions. In the social sciences and humanities, we can make no progress unless we resist the temptation to treat the institutional and ideological regimes that shape our lives as if they were natural phenomena rather than our own creations. To understand ourselves and develop our powers, we must tear from such regimes the mask of naturalness.

The struggle against such superstitions helps define the task of philosophy in making sense of what the world is like: to renounce the idea of a philosophical super-science without allowing the established forms of inquiry and discourse to circumscribe our understanding. Ontology, understood as natural philosophy and social theory, reckons with the unacceptable choice between these two errors and attempts to overcome it. In this perilous attempt, philosophy exemplifies both our finitude and our transcendence, the defining attributes of our humanity.

2

Epistemology (as Inquiry into Inquiry)

Epistemology and Its Discontents

Epistemology is traditionally defined as the philosophical study of knowledge. For centuries, and even in the hands of some of the greatest philosophers, it has consisted in the analysis of a small number of stock positions about the nature and limitations of our understanding of reality. Its ancient puzzles form the staple of schoolbook philosophy. What is knowledge and how do we know we have it? (We need the discrete sciences and other specialized forms of inquiry to make any progress in answering those questions.) Can we resist relentless skepticism and, if so, how? (We cannot.) How do we know that we are not being systematically fooled by some malevolent or benign power? (We do not, but it may not matter.) What should we do about our inability to escape the perceptual and cognitive limitations of our embodied state? (We go on living and try to loosen the restraints that they impose on us.)

Both the questions and the answers, or evasions of answers, have, with good reason, helped give philosophy in general, and epistemology specifically, a bad name. To those engaged in trying to make sense of some part of the world, or to change it, these fabricated conundrums, devoid of context and consequence, have seemed to lack even the seriousness, and the potential to surprise, instruct, and inspire, of child play.

Epistemology has acquired interest, and deserves attention, only when it has assumed at least one of two characters, and especially when it has assumed both. The first character is metaphysical rather than technical: taking our cognitive potential and limitations as revelatory of who we are and can become. Philosophers as different as Plato, Kant, and Schopenhauer have addressed epistemology in this metaphysical sense. The second character is programmatic rather than descriptive: exploring the steps by which, in many disciplines and across disciplines, we can expand our power to grasp more of reality and of how the world changes. We encounter epistemology in this programmatic version in, for example, Francis Bacon and Charles Sanders Peirce, and more generally in the reflections of many of the most ambitious scientists and humanists.

This remark about what has redeemed epistemology from the desiccation and triviality to which it has often abandoned itself helps explain the direction that I take here. This chapter has two themes: one metaphysical, the other programmatic. The metaphysical theme is the expression, in our attempts to make sense of the world, of the relation between finitude and transcendence that, together with our troubled relations to one another, shapes every part of our experience. The programmatic theme is the nature of the practices and ideas that might allow us to push back, in one form of engagement with reality after another, the limits to our understanding of the real.

Each of the two steps in the argument of this chapter—the theory of inquiry and the program of inquiry—addresses one of these themes. In developing the theory of inquiry, I begin by discussing the basic ways in which we can mischaracterize our epistemic situation. The rejection of those misdirections excludes much; a better direction emerges by contrast to them. I go on to describe our epistemic situation free from the influence of those detours and seen in relation to the temporal and embodied beings that we are. I continue to develop this view by contrasting it to errors that have been prominent in the history of epistemology for over 2000 years. They are, simultaneously, mistakes about the relation between finitude and transcendence in our experience, about our relation to one another and to our shared practices of inquiry and discourse, and about what the world is like.

In the second step of my argument—addressing the program of inquiry—I explore the implications of this view for our power to investigate nature and society and to intervene in them. Transformation is the key. It is by resisting or producing change that each of us first discovers, as a child, causal connection and tries to use it or to defend against it. We go on to form and test ideas about how transformation happens—about what can change into what, under what conditions. In this way, we increase our insight into change, and turn it, when we can, to our advantage.

The unavoidable dependence of our most ambitious explanatory projects on what are ultimately metaphysical conceptions, mediated through scientific theories and research programs, exposes every science to illusions dressed up as empirical discoveries. It can recognize these illusions only with difficulty thanks to the work of revolutionary genius. Such risks are aggravated by the equally inevitable specialization of inquiry, and the narrow association of the subject matter of each field with procedures that narrow its vision and inhibit it from changing itself.

We should ask what practice of inquiry and of education stands the best chance of diminishing our need to be rescued by genius. We ought to ask as well how, without retreating to the self-deception of philosophical super-science or denying the imperative of specialized knowledge, we can save our powers of discovery from becoming or remaining hostage to the marriage of method and subject matter in each discipline.

The study of nature and of society in the specialized fields of inquiry is not our only way of exploring the real. We also have art. This chapter ends with a coda: a reflection on art as it bears on our cognitive situation and on the pull within it between our finitude and our transcendence. Art is a promise of happiness, as well as a promise of insight. To evoke it at the end of this chapter is to ask questions that cannot be confined to epistemology, even when reinterpreted as the theory and program of inquiry. These questions carry us forward to thinking about the human condition, the topic of Chapter 3.

The Denial of Finitude and Transcendence in Epistemology

Epistemology has either denied our finitude or denied our transcendence. The characteristic way in which it has denied our finitude is by attributing to the human being a privileged experience of the world. Insofar as he has this privileged experience, he sees the world with the eyes of God: of an omniscient spirit who is able to look into the reality of things. He does not view the world with the flawed and fallible vision of the embodied creatures that we are.

This is an ideal of absolute knowledge, unthreatened by any of the weaknesses that result from our mortal state—as beings who are endowed with a limited perceptual and cognitive apparatus, apprehending the world through a veil and thinking certain thoughts but not others. According to the ideal of absolute knowledge, our privileged experience provides a gateway to a higher knowledge, as if it allowed us to escape the limitations of the body.

The two most famous examples in the history of Western philosophy are Plato's doctrine of the Forms and Descartes's idea of self-knowledge. To these, we might add another: Hegel's conception of a form of knowledge that becomes absolute at the end of the history of thought by resolving all the contradictions in our imperfect insight and subsuming our incomplete knowledge within a more inclusive understanding of reality. This is a different way of escaping finitude: not by a special gateway to privileged insight but by a jump at the end of the history of thinking from incomplete and imperfect knowledge to knowledge that is all inclusive.

The reverse side of the absolutist illusion is skepticism or reductionism. The disappointed absolutist about knowledge infers one of two conclusions from the failure of our explanatory projects to satisfy his absolute standard of knowledge. If he believes that nothing that fails to satisfy his standard of privileged experience deserves to count as reliable knowledge, he becomes a skeptic. If he thinks that something can be saved from the wreck of an absolutist epistemology, if only we bring our explanatory ambitions down to the level of what makes sense on the basis our observations and experiments, he becomes a reductionist. What these experiments and observations validate is, for him, the only reliable basis of knowledge.

Skepticism, we shall see, is irrefutable if it is comprehensive and thoroughgoing enough. But for the same reasons for which it is irrefutable, it also irrelevant. It sets a standard that we must disregard to continue making sense of the world and developing the fallible body of our scientific ideas.

Reductionism, on the other hand, contradicts the way knowledge grows in the very area in which reductionists put their faith: natural science. For in natural science all empirical observations and experiments rely on ontological pictures that we cannot infer from the empirical findings that they make sense of. Skepticism and reductionism are twin versions of the bad conscience of an absolutist epistemology.

In the history of modern epistemology, the denial of transcendence has taken two main forms: the transcendental and the social or perspectival.

The transcendental variant of the denial of transcendence is most famously represented by the argument of Kant's *Critique of Pure Reason*. Its most general and basic claim is the dependence of human knowledge on presuppositions that are immutable and without which we cannot make sense of the world or of our experience of it. These presuppositions relate (in Kant's Transcendental Aesthetic) to space and especially time—the principle of connection in consciousness— and (in his Transcendental Logic) to categories or ideas that allow us to build coherent images of the world or of parts of it. One of these categories is causality, and Kant's discussion of the complications of our causal understanding is the single most striking and influential part of the *Critique of Pure Reason*.[1]

We have, on this view, no access to what things are in themselves, but only to our experience of them. In this experience we remain forever hostage to the constitution of the human mind. But the

---

1. See the discussion of the second analogy of experience in the Transcendental Analytic, Immanuel Kant, *Kritik der Reinen Vernunft*, as revised for the 1787 edition.

transcendental thesis drastically underestimates our ability to revise or even to cast aside, in our attempts to explain how nature works, the ways of understanding the world that come naturally to us. The history of our thinking about causality—discussed in Chapter 1—is a preeminent example.

The way of understanding causal connection and its relation to laws of nature in nineteenth-century physics was different from what it had been in Newton's system. And even though Kant took Newton as his chief scientific reference, his way of understanding causality and its relation to laws of nature looks forward to nineteenth-century physics more than it looks back to Newtonian mechanics. Then physics in the twentieth century went one step further: it affirmed structure over history and placed its faith in the marriage of natural science to mathematics to such an extent that it came close to dispensing with causal explanation altogether.

In the predominant interpretations of general relativity, it radically reshaped what Kant had viewed as the most deep-seated and pervasive of our supposedly indispensable presuppositions: unified, continuous, and irreversible time. It is another matter to decide whether physics was justified, by the empirical discoveries that its proponents invoked, in this assault on our pre-theoretical experience of the world. What matters, for the issue at hand, is that it did so and in so doing defined the direction in which the natural science commonly regarded as the most fundamental evolved.

We are clearly not limited, in our explanatory endeavors in science—or, for that matter in art—by the ways of understanding the world that nature implants in the mind during our ontogenetic development. We can assess, on the basis of evidence, standards, and ideas that are always contestable and sooner or later contested, the distance between our explanatory conjectures and the way of understanding that comes naturally to us. We cannot resolve such contests by feigning imprisonment in inescapable presuppositions: the premise of the contest is that we have escaped them. (How far we can go in escaping them without increasing the risk of a drastically wrong turn in our ideas about reality is a question that I take up later in this chapter.) And the resolution of the contest turns on what we think the world is like, regardless of our untutored assumptions about nature and reality.

The root of the mistake made by the transcendental approach to our epistemic situation is the denial or understatement of our cognitive transcendence. Ultimately at stake is our self-transcendence: our power to venture beyond the view of the world that our embodied perceptual and cognitive apparatus suggests to us.

If the transcendental approach is one way to deny our transcendence over our practices of inquiry, another is the perspectival idea. Whereas the former emphasizes the relation between our cognitive engagement with the world and its universal enabling conditions, the latter focuses on our specific practices of inquiry—on the social character of our ways of investigating nature. These practices are inevitably collective: they involve discourse within a community.

The essence of the perspectival challenge to our cognitive transcendence is that there is nothing to counter or overrule a particular discourse except another discourse: the answer to one conversation is another conversation.

To challenge such a discourse from a place outside it must, according to this view, entail one of two things: either viewing it from a place above particular discourses by appealing to a level of reality and value that only a philosophical super-science could access, or challenging one discourse from the vantage point of another. But the first appeal is unavailable, and the second is ineffective. This view misrepresents the nature of our discursive practices, our relation to them, and the extent to which both the former and the latter can change.

Our discursive practices, including the methods of the specialized sciences, have no permanent structure or essence. We cannot legitimately, ask, for example, what legal reasoning is or requires. It exists only in the form of historically located and specific ways of making sense of the law and of applying law in specific settings. The question—What is it, in its inner nature?—mistakes its character. Instead of asking what its essence is, we can ask in what form we have received it and what we can and should turn it into. Our answer to this question is not arbitrary: it depends on what we think the law is for, as well as on what we believe can be accomplished by its transformation and the remaking of the practice by which we apply and elaborate it. In historical reality, the contest among these views takes a certain shape: clashing assumptions and visions, associated with different ideas about the past, present, and future of society.

In the natural sciences, the practice of inquiry and the standards of success are relatively more stable. Yet there is no more a scientific method than there is a practice of legal reasoning. Every major change in the leading theories of a science appears as a revision of its procedures. A historical natural science does not make the same assumptions about scientific method that a structural one does.

The contest of such conceptions is ultimately a dispute about what the world is like as well as the placement of bets on what is the most promising research agenda. Nothing in the practice of a science remains untouched by such disagreements: every part of the science, from its explanatory theories and their metaphysical assumptions to its criteria of empirical validation, remains always on the line and open to challenge.

The consequence of these facts is that our practices of inquiry, and the forms of life in which they are embedded, lack the integrity and constancy that would allow us to take any version of one of them as a tribunal of last resort. We might want to surrender our freedom to them but we cannot. Their nature does not allow them to take us prisoner, even though we may want them to do so and prefer to disguise our self-imprisonment as willing abandonment to them.

The Mistakes of Epistemology Further Examined

Every view of inquiry that denies, in our cognitive engagement with the world, either our finitude or our transcendence is false to the reality of our circumstances. The argument of this chapter began by defining the space for an understanding of our cognitive situation that acknowledges both our finitude and our transcendence and that recognizes the social character of our practices of inquiry without denying our ability to resist or revise them. Having approached epistemology as the theory and program of inquiry, I went on to offer a view of the resources and the perspective with which inquiry into reality begins, given our natural constitution.

In that view, we go beyond the cognitive bounds imposed on us by that constitution. In doing so, however, we never come any closer to absolute knowledge: insight from no specific perspective, unrestrained by the limitations of the embodied beings that we are. Here as elsewhere in our existence, we cannot overcome our finitude. But no specific limitations of insight and discovery mark its definitive and unsurpassable boundary.

Consider the many ways in which epistemology has misrepresented our condition and our prospects as knowers of the world. Taken together, these mistakes define what most of epistemology has been; their history is its history. To appreciate why we should reject them is to see the need for another direction, defined by their exclusion. Understanding the direction is more important than accepting any single way of taking it, including the way for which I have argued in the previous section.

Of the seven mistakes that I briefly address in the following pages, the first five mispresent the dialectic between finitude and transcendence in our cognitive situation. They also implicitly mischaracterize our relation to the social practices of inquiry. The last two mistakes misrepresent the relation of inquiry to these social practices. They also implicitly mischaracterize the dialectic between transcendence and finitude in our attempts to make sense of reality. All seven of them exemplify ways of thinking that prevent us from addressing and overcoming the two crises that have emerged in our contemporary view of reality: one in natural science, the other in social theory. They divert us from what we need to do to develop our understanding of the world and of ourselves.

A better theory of inquiry emerges by contrast to these seven mistakes. That view is made tangible in the subsequent discussion of the program of inquiry and of its implications for how we should deal with the two contemporary crises in the development of our understanding of the world.

⁂

Radical skepticism. A radical skepticism denies that we have any grounds on which to claim knowledge of reality. We can report on our experience, but what we are not entitled to do, according to the radical skeptic, is to trust in a link between reality and our experience. The tests by which we measure our tracking of reality are all unreliable. They point back to our experience; they do nothing to show that our experience reveals what the world is really like apart from that experience.

Not only may the deliverances of experience be detached from reality, they may also be systematically detached. They may line up with one another so neatly that they seem to support a view of the world, as if the fragments of our experience voted unanimously. All to no avail, according to radical skepticism. Their coherence with one another brings us no closer to reality. Out of misplaced confidence in our powers or in the benignity of nature or providence, we mistake this unanimous vote about the real for the opening of the curtain that conceals reality.

Nevertheless, in our impatience and our desire to misinterpret even our ignorance as a subject matter of intellectual ambition, we may look for reasons to explain how such a total divergence between how we experience the world and what it is really like could come about. In the long history of philosophy, a recurrent idea has been the conjecture that we may be victims of a demon with higher powers. For reasons beyond our understanding, he has chosen to toy with us by making us experience the world in a fashion that bears no relation to its reality.

I have included radical skepticism in this list of exemplary mistakes in epistemology. But such skepticism is not a mistake. In fact, it is irrefutable so long as it is relentless and comprehensive. It becomes susceptible to refutation only when it vacillates and blinks. If we are not just misguided by our experience but systematically and comprehensively misguided, and if nothing in that experience, not even the failure to use nature to our advantage, denounces our misconception, we are left defenseless against the skeptical challenge. But does it matter?

Skepticism is unanswerable if it is all inclusive. The mistake lies in the impression that such a radical skepticism changes anything in a naturalistic understanding of our epistemic situation. It is at most a reminder of our finitude, embodiment, and groundlessness.

If, to take one variant of radical skepticism, we are the victims of a demon who has lined up different parts of our experience only to delude us, then it should matter to us only if the demon were inconsistent and out of a surfeit of malevolence chose to vary the distance between experience and reality. But then, with our resources of ingenuity, we might end up finding him out. If he is consistent, everything goes on for us as if he did not exist, and we are back where we thought we were before arousing the specter of his meddling in our affairs.

Radical skepticism is the bad conscience of the ideal of absolute knowledge—the knowledge that an omniscient God might have of his creation, the knowledge possessed by those who need not rely on the resources (however augmented by theory and technology) of their limited, fragile, and dying bodies. Radical skepticism is irrefutable for the same reasons that absolute knowledge is inaccessible to us. For those same reasons, it is also irrelevant, except as a reminder of our groundlessness.

Reductionism. Reductionism, as I use the term in this context, is the limitation of our knowledge claims to propositions that can be supported by a strictly defined class of empirical evidence for those claims. Like radical skepticism, reductionism expresses a disappointment with our inability to fulfill the requirements of absolute knowledge. The radical skeptic responds by disputing the possibility of any reliable knowledge, given our failure to satisfy those conditions. The reductionist responds by deflating our pretenses to know and bringing them down to the level of what he regards as a robust basis for our knowledge claims. Whatever claims exceed his threshold, he can dismiss as baseless or even as nonsense. Reductionism had a heyday in the early twentieth century in logical positivism.

The first objection to reductionism is that we cannot reconcile it with the way in which knowledge, including natural science, has grown. In moving beyond our immediate acquaintance with reality, science relies on theory. Theory in turn relies on ontological models—conceptions of the kinds of things that there are and of the ways in which they interact. Such theories are vulnerable to challenge only at their periphery of empirical implication. And although their defenders habitually understate the extent to which the same observational and experimental findings to which they appeal might bear alternative theoretical interpretations, the truth is that every powerful explanatory agenda is a bet on the fecundity of a research program. If science, or knowledge more generally, were restrained by the shackles that the reductionist wants to impose on it (while pretending only to make explicit best scientific practice), we would never have had the theoretical systems of Newton, Darwin, or Einstein.

A second objection to reductionism is that its attempt to canonize a certain class of factual reports as a necessary and sufficient basis for our explanatory efforts is doomed to fail. It fails because of the nature of such reports as well as the way in which science and knowledge do and must develop. Even pre-scientific perception is already penetrated by ideas and influenced by conceptual assumptions. The reports produced in any real and rich setting of scientific work must be much more so. And outside the frontiers of natural science, the impossibility of marking any clear distinction between how we think and what we find is all the more obvious.

It is only in the context of a theoretical tradition and its idea-laden practices that any class of factual reports achieves special status. The attempt to hold constant the definition of that class is futile because it requires not just a pre-theoretical but a pre-conceptual engagement with events and phenomena.

These two objections to reductionism complement each other: if we hobble theory in the hope of providing knowledge with grounds more robust than those on which it would rest if unhobbled, we do so in vain. We inhibit or paralyze the theoretical imagination without reaping the benefit of the robust grounds.

Reductionism is a form of dogmatism. It is dogmatism about the limits to our insight into reality as well as about the means by which we extend those limits. It fails to give our cognitive transcendence its due. As a result, it also misrepresents the nature and consequences of our cognitive finitude.

❧

Indubitable knowledge, achieved through privileged experience. We do not give up the absolute standard of knowledge and reconcile ourselves to the cognitive consequences of our finitude lightly. One of the most persistent attempts in the history of philosophy to rescue that standard has been an appeal to privileged experience as a gateway to indubitable knowledge. It is in a sense the inverse of reductionism, with which, however, it shares a defining move. Like reductionism, it wants to canonize an element of experience. But whereas reductionism is deflationary and seeks to establish knowledge on a robust basis at the cost of severely limiting what we can hope to know and what we are entitled to say, this quest to canonize part of our experience has high cognitive hopes. By relying on a part of our experience that it assures us we have no reason to doubt, it wants to bring back what we may have given up: the search for an absolute frame of reference. As reductionism denies our transcendence, while implicitly misrepresenting our finitude, this search for the absolute framework of reference denies our finitude, while implicitly mischaracterizing our transcendence.

Earlier in this chapter, when I was marking out the intellectual space in which we need to look for an understanding of our epistemic situation, I mentioned Plato and Descartes as two widely different examples of this approach, having chosen them because in all other respects their philosophies are as far apart as one might imagine. I return to these examples now to illustrate the chief flaw in this plan to rescue us from our cognitive finitude.

For Plato—at least the Plato of the middle dialogues—the canonical experience was recognition of the Forms or Ideas as the formative and most real part of reality, behind the shadows of our phenomenal experience. For Descartes the canonical experience was our consciousness, and in particular our self-consciousness as thinking beings. And in both Plato and Descartes, identification of the most real part of reality—the Forms or my existence grasped through self-consciousness—was only the first step. Having found something indubitable, we could then begin to build an understanding of reality and shine a light on our experience that would remove the shadow of skepticism.

But we could not take this first step, nor the steps following, without the support of an ontology, a view of the world. For Plato the axis of this ontology was the relation of the Forms to everything else in our phenomenal experience. And the backdrop to this ontology was no mere philosophical conceit. It was a vision deeply rooted in the ancient civilizations of the Indo-European peoples. There was a hierarchy of classes or castes in society (priests, rulers and fighters, and workers) and of faculties in the human soul (reason, the action-impulses, and the sensual appetites). The moral and political hierarchies were intimately related. Discernment of the prototypes of reality and the sources of value by the priests and rulers would inform and support both these hierarchies and bring the world to order and to light.

For Descartes it was clear (as the argument of the *Meditations on First Philosophy* shows) that not even the first step of confidence in self-consciousness sufficed to save us from radical doubt without an ontological, indeed a theological, backdrop. We might be deluded even by self-consciousness. Only the existence of a benevolent providence could assure us that we would not be. It was the Christian view of the world that made this idea live with all but irresistible immediacy and authority.

The experience that served as the gateway to reality in both these— and in all other—instances of the search for an absolute frame of reference was trustworthy only against the background of the ontology or theology, and indeed of the larger vision of reality, into which it opened up. But how could we reach this vision in the first place (by secular reason rather than inspiration or revelation) unless we had identified and opened the path of reliable insight?

This is the ontological-epistemological circle that the quest for the absolute frame of reference is unable to break. It cannot break out of it unless it is already outside it. But whether we ever can be outside it is the issue in contention.

Better to acknowledge our cognitive fragility and work to lighten the burden of our ignorance than to pretend that we have a shortcut, especially if the pursuit of that shortcut depends on ideas about both knowledge and the world that devalue the means by which we can hope to advance our cognitive empowerment.

❧

Inescapable presuppositions of experience: the transcendental method.
Our experience of the world rests on certain presuppositions of perception and of thought with which we are endowed by nature. They
allow us to have a coherent view of our experience. We cannot escape
them. The world that we know or can ever come to know is the world
that they give us. What things are "in themselves," apart from these
presuppositions, we can never grasp. As they enable our experience,
they also set impassable bounds to it.

This is the transcendental epistemology associated with Kant, who
described in his Transcendental Aesthetic the role of space and above
all of time in the shaping of our basic perceptual experience, and in
his Transcendental Logic the role of categories such as substance,
causation, and reciprocal interdependence in forming our cognitive
experience. Kant's doctrine contains a powerful element of truth. In
his two-front war against metaphysical dogmatism and skepticism, he
rejects philosophical super-science. He faces the finite human being,
endowed with limited perceptual and cognitive equipment and forever
unable to view the world through the eyes of God.

This transcendental metaphysic—for it is a metaphysic, not just
a method—makes two connected mistakes. The first is to suppose
that our perceptual and cognitive presuppositions—those that come
to us from phylogeny and ontogeny—can never change, or that we
can never go beyond them, and correct the view of reality with which
they endow us. The history of knowledge in general, and of natural
science in particular, shows the opposite.

Science, we have seen, advances by correcting our natural experience and even by contradicting it. Its most ambitious explanatory
projects, informed by ontological models, take the place of our natural
experience. I have argued that, in the course of this advance, it has
come to a momentous choice of direction.

In one direction—which much of basic physics has in fact taken—it
even severs the link of its explanatory practice with the nexus of causation, time, and change, which Kant viewed as the inner sanctum of
our natural experience. As a result, it begins to offer accounts that we
may be unable even to translate from their mathematical expressions
into the language of experience. Their message is locked up in their

mathematical formulation, and any attempt to extract it from there amounts to crude metaphors and allegories.

Whether science is justified in severing this link to causation, change, and time, or has misjudged the costs of the severance for the future of inquiry, is another matter. That it can do so, and that in its most admired and influential field it has, demonstrates unequivocally the falsehood of the idea that our natural perceptual and cognitive presuppositions are incorrigible.

Moreover, these presuppositions—the perceptual as well as the cognitive ones—in addition to being corrigible are always penetrated by ideas. And ideas have a history that never stops. No insurmountable wall separates our ordinary experience from our adventures in thought. The latter remake the former, at first marginally but then ever more deeply.

In the light of these considerations, we can see that Kant did not in fact renounce completely the attempt to identify an absolute frame of reference; he naturalized it, cutting it down to the dimensions of our natural constitution. But in so doing, he greatly understated our powers of self-transcendence, in inquiry as in everything else.

The second mistake—a corollary to the first—in Kant's transcendental approach to knowledge is its assignment to the supposedly incorrigible conditions of experience what in fact belongs to nature itself, including causality (in his Transcendental Logic) and time (in his Transcendental Aesthetic). The metaphysical distinction between phenomenal experience and things in themselves led Kant to shrink from making claims about the workings of nature (a retreat that he partly undid in his very late work in natural philosophy). But how events or phenomena connect, whether causally in time or non-causally outside time, must be, and has been, one of the principal subjects that natural science investigates.

If there is a diversity of views of these matters, as the history of natural philosophy and natural science shows that there is, the relative merits of such views must be determined by their uses in the explanation of nature and the mobilization of natural forces to our benefit. If temporal naturalism draws us closer to the real than its rivals in the history of philosophy, then even change, and thus causal connection in time, changes. We can study this change in the history of nature and society. Setting a metaphysical bar to such an investigation, based on our imprisonment in supposedly inescapable conditions of experience, amounts to another form of dogmatism.

The mistake of the transcendental approach is its denial of our cognitive transcendence, motivated by an interest in recognizing our cognitive finitude. But like other such denials it misrepresents what that finitude is.

No object without a subject: idealism as correlationism. The mistake that I now describe goes under different labels, such as idealism or correlationism. Rather than being associated with a particular philosopher, it is a tendency widespread in the thinking of the last hundred years. It has a pre-history in the discussion, in early-modern European philosophy, of the distinction between primary and secondary qualities: those that belong to natural objects themselves and that may be described by mathematics and physics, and those that, although they may "correspond" to something in the natural world to which we attend, come from us. Kant foreshadowed it in his transcendental epistemology, but it has developed a message that is alien to his philosophy and is often associated with the mistake about the relation of knowledge to social practices that I take up next.

The central thesis of this position is that there is no subject without an object and no object without a subject. The subject is the human agent who forms himself in confronting other human agents and the world. And the object exists only as the object of a subject. All the concepts and categories by which we describe the world, including the idea of being, are our categories and concepts and have no meaning apart from language and practices. In every report about the world there is a double reference: to object and subject. The subject is collective—the community of a society and a culture or of a form of life. And the object is everything for which any report about the world accounts.

When we talk about objects as if they existed separately from subjects, we project the human subject on to an imaginary being and imagine ourselves grasping the world through his eyes. Is it like what happens when someone supposes himself dead and goes on in spectatorial-voyeuristic fashion to imagine himself looking on from non-being? No, it is not quite like that, because, in such a situation, there will continue to be other agents around confronting one another and the world. To imagine a world without subjects is to imagine a world in which our human discourse about reality—thoroughly motivated by our practical interests, formed during our evolution as natural beings—has ceased to have a place.

Although this thesis may seem at first to be only an idle speculation, it has implications that help account for its diffusion. It carries forward the renunciation of any attempt to establish an absolute frame of reference. It infers from that renunciation the need to carry an anthropocentric view of reality and inquiry to its ultimate consequences. And it supplies a basis for replacing, as a standard of the adequacy of ideas, "correspondence" to reality by diffusion within the community of life and discourse, and objectivity by intersubjectivity, joint intentionality, and shared practice.

Such correlationism does not then imply a metaphysical or objective idealism that disputes the reality of material things and affirms the supremacy of consciousness even in the constitution of the non-human world. Rather, it is what we might label a correlationist idealism, placing the correlation between subject and object at the center of its philosophical program. If we were to translate it into the old language or primary and secondary qualities, it evokes a world in which there are only secondary qualities. The principle of this world is, according to this view: no mind, no nature.

In this list of the mistakes of epistemology, it represents a bridge between the mistakes that are primarily about cognitive transcendence and finitude and the mistakes that are chiefly about the dependence of knowledge on shared practice or its independence from such practice.

Consider the reasons to reject correlationist idealism. We have overwhelming reason to believe that the universe and our planet existed long before the first human beings appeared: we have only to look at the geological record. What we know about the history and likely future of our solar system suggests that mankind will not survive the destruction of our star, if we have not disappeared, most likely by our own hand, long before then, and if we have not found a way to escape to another part of the universe before the self-destruction of the sun. There is no mechanism by which the universe could cease to exist just because we perished. From everything that we have discovered so far about nature, our existence as a species is—at least so far—an inconspicuous and inconsequential event in cosmological history.

The world is not what it seems; the history of inquiry has been a history of increasing divergence from our natural experience. A dangerous and perplexing moment in that divergence occurs when science threatens to take us in a direction that denies features lying at the center of how we experience reality. But any divergence is enough to show that an epistemology that denies the independence of nature from our consciousness and understanding, or that wants to set prior limits to how far the disconnection between subject and object may extend, must be false.

(The doctrine that all matter is mind—objective idealism or panpsychism—would require a different discussion. That discussion shares with this one, however, a major theme. By taking mind as pervasive in reality, and our mental experience as no more than a variant of this universal mental substance, we refuse to acknowledge the utter strangeness of the world, its indifference to our concerns, and its resistance to our understanding. Only philosophical super-science, with its groundless claims to higher insight, could teach such a doctrine.)

Correlationist idealism evades our finitude under the disguise of honoring our transcendence, which, however, it misrepresents. The world does not need us to exist, nor are we united to all that is reality by an experience of mind of which we are the supreme (albeit not the exclusive) embodiment. The moral color of our transcendence does not result from our power to confer, through our mental experience, or our share in universal mind, reality on what would otherwise remain in the limbo of non-being. It lies, instead, in our ability to live for the future and for one another as beings who are more than they seem to be and can never be exhausted by the present determinations of their existence.

∽

*Social practice and the conditions of insight: pragmatism and histor-
icism in epistemology.* The remaining two epistemological mistakes
that I address have as their immediate subject the relation of inquiry
to social practice. But just as the mistakes about cognitive transcendence and finitude imply mistakes about inquiry and practice, so the
mistakes about inquiry and practice imply mistakes about cognitive
transcendence and finitude.

For the view that I now consider, knowledge claims depend upon
the ability to generate and convey sense, and sense exists only in
communities of discourse and practice. A real society and a real
culture stand behind such communities. The theory of inquiry must
therefore be chiefly a theory of the shared practices by which inquiry
is conducted.

The first premise of this conception is the idea that inquiry, like
society, has no single natural form. There is no reason to expect convergence on a single idea of what society is and requires, or on a single
set of practices. The diversity of the communities of discourse and
practice in which people flourish is not a transitory characteristic of
our exploration of reality, destined to be superseded by convergence
on a single authoritative practice; it is a constitutive feature of our
cognitive approach to reality.

Within such communities we make claims to knowledge. But these
claims risk ceasing to make sense if they are transported from one
community to another. They acquire their sense from the practices
and the discourse of one such world. If they continue to make some
sense beyond the frontiers of that world, it cannot be as isolated
propositions. It can be only as the result of a new conversation—a
conversation between communities. Such a conversation is a proposal
to begin a new community.

A second premise concerns the test of cognitive success, given
that in this view it cannot be a simple correspondence of knowledge
claims to the facts of the matter. In between the inquiring mind and
the world stand the others: the community of discourse and its practices. The proximate test of cognitive success is not correspondence;
it is intersubjective agreement, acceptance within the community of
discourse and practice.

The ultimate test is practical success in achieving or developing some power that we did not possess before. In natural science, it is the power to intervene in the processes of nature in a way that mobilizes those forces to our benefit.

Those who want to save something from the wreck of metaphysical rationalism will insist that there must be something between the proximate test of agreement and the ultimate test of practical success, otherwise the agreement would be arbitrary and the practical success mysterious. And, indeed there is, but it is not any idea of correspondence. It is, according to this view, the exercise of a power. To understand a piece of reality—in nature or in society—is to understand how it changes, what can change it, and what it can next become given certain events in the world or interventions of our own. We jump onto this moving train and try to change its direction. We do not, on this view, need any idea of correspondence. The idea of correspondence dispels one mystery only by creating another.

Nothing prevents the members of such a community from changing their shared practices and discourse. But once again there will be no simple test of correspondence to the facts of the matter by which to validate or oppose such changes.

This activity of gaining power, which is not so much the result as it is the method of inquiry, exists only as a collective activity in the diverse communities of discourse and practice. We can admit the idea of knowledge claims, in this epistemological doctrine, only if we purge it of the reference to correspondence, wipe it clean of metaphysical rationalism, recognize that cognitive and practical empowerment are two sides of the same thing, and understand that we achieve it only in such communities and on the ground of their practices.

To this doctrine I give two labels—historicism and pragmatism. Neither of these labels is entirely adequate. But the otherwise unlabeled positions to which they refer have become a powerful element in thought worldwide at the time of the writing of this book. Historicism connotes the decisive role and the ineradicable diversity of the specific communities in which our exploration of reality advances, and the replacement of correspondence by convergence or agreement within such communities. Pragmatism evokes the intimate relation between our cognitive stake in understanding transformation—whether in nature or society—and our practical stake in directing it and in replacing correspondence by empowerment.

Those who have contributed to one or another version of this view include the later American pragmatists (Dewey, Mead, and Rorty), Wittgenstein in his late philosophy, and the contemporary sociologists of knowledge and historians and philosophers of science. It is a doctrine often dismissed as relativism or skepticism. Its whole point, however, is that we need not choose between skepticism and metaphysical rationalism so long as we grasp the implications of inquiry being a social practice, not an investigation of the world by individual minds that would be reduced to silence if they were not joined together.

Having stated the gist of this position in what I take to be its strongest form, I now say why I believe that we must nevertheless reject it. The objection relates to the nature of cognitive practices and of the thought regimes to which they belong. It also has to do with the nature and the implications of our relation to such regimes. (The ideas on which this argument against the adequacy of the historicist or pragmatist approaches to epistemology depend will have another use in a later section of this chapter, about the program of inquiry.)

For the historicist-pragmatist approach to work, each community of discourse and practice (or forms of life in Wittgenstein's phrase) must have a distinct personality, order, and logic. It must in effect be a little world of language and thought. We confront reality, according to this view, as members of such worlds. But for the little world to replace the big one as the principal setting of inquiry, it must have a certain coherence, even a logic of its own and implicit rules: its parts must be strongly connected, and its practices informed by unifying conceptions. It must be possible for the participants in the little world to appeal to these conceptions in their arguments with one another and to invoke their citizenship in it as sufficient justification for their actions and omissions. But is that what the communities of discourse and practice are like, even in the hardest of the hard sciences?

Our practices of inquiry are organized in thought regimes. These regimes are not theories, although developing and replacing theories may be one of their chief activities. To understand what they are like, begin by considering the nature of their counterparts in the organization of society rather than of inquiry: the institutional and ideological regimes that are the main target of transformative ambition in political practice and of explanatory ambition in social theory.

Such regimes exist, and have the significance that they do, because society has no single natural form. Each of them gives life to a particular version of the otherwise empty idea of society, a way of being human. Each weds institutional arrangements to ideological assumptions. The assumptions lend sense and authority to the arrangements.

The regimes form the routines of social life, including the procedures and conflicts by which we shape the future. They resist change, though the extent to which they do so is one of the most important ways in which they differ. But they are not systems, as if conceived by a single mind and will. Structural change, change in the regime, is almost always fragmentary. Regimes differ in the material and moral advantages that they confer. This difference helps explain why some develop, persist, and are imitated.

Similarly, thought regimes exist because inquiry and discourse have no natural form. They too shape practice and resist challenge and change, establishing a contrast between moves within the framework that they establish and moves intended to revise the framework. But the degree to which they increase or diminish the distance between the framework-conforming and the framework-revising moves is one of the most consequential ways in which thought regimes vary in the history of thought.

The historicist and pragmatist epistemology that I have described supposes that we can press knowledge claims and make sense only within one of these communities of discourse and practice. But in treating them in this manner we mistake their nature. Like social regimes, they are ramshackle collective artifacts, combining practices that have no essences. The difference between being inside one of these communities and being outside it, between conforming to its rules and routines and defying them, is never more than relative. They cannot perform the role that the historicist and the pragmatist want to assign to them: providing a ground on which to stand that dispenses with metaphysical rationalism without abandoning us to skepticism.

No institutional and ideological regime—however much it may wear the false semblance of naturalness and necessity and entrench itself by tangible and intangible means against challenge—exhausts our powers to imagine and arrange in another way our relations to one another. Similarly, no thought regime, regardless of the claim made on its behalf to represent one of the permanent modalities of human understanding, in some larger organon of knowledge, is more than a temporary resting place in our struggle to reckon with reality by gaining insight into transformation, and to use this insight to increase our practical powers.

It is in our interest to design our social regimes in such a way that they facilitate their own revision, diminishing the distance between the ordinary moves that we make within a framework of arrangements and assumptions that we take for granted and the extraordinary moves by which, from time to time, typically at the provocation of crisis, we challenge and changes pieces of the framework. Then we cease to be hostage to our institutional and ideological creations and can be insiders and outsiders at the same time. We can participate without surrendering.

The same goes for our relation to thought regimes. The less they oppose routine to revolution in thought and allow our normal practices of inquiry to acquire some of the traits of intellectual revolution, the less we, as sharers in their work, will allow a thought regime to be anything more than a provisional stand-in for the imagination. Every thought regime represents a particular way of representing the relation between a piece of reality and its transformative variations in the realm of the accessible possible. That is the central work of the imagination, undertaken to achieve more insight and power, and incapable of being fixed in a single and definitive form. Neither the character of nature nor the nature of mind will allow it.

The epistemology of historicism and pragmatism contributes to an understanding of our cognitive situation by highlighting the dependence of inquiry on social practice. The mistake made by its conventional formulations is to misrepresent our relation to these practices and to the thought regimes that organize this relation. A radicalized historicism and pragmatism would correct this mistake. It would describe the relation of inquiry to practice in such a way as to give our transcendence over practices and regimes its due. The program of inquiry outlined later in this chapter will show more clearly than the theory of inquiry can what such a turn implies and requires.

Escape from cognitive finitude in the future: absolute historicism. Thought is led by its contradictions and their resolution to a form of absolute knowledge—a frame of reference that we no longer have reason to dispute. Its progression to this final stage takes place in historical time—the history of our forms of life as well as of our ideas. The absolute standard of knowledge, which we had prematurely applied to our flawed ways of thinking along the path of this ascent, returns at the end: in a future that we can envision and that may already be upon us.

The setting of the ascent is history—not of a particular thought regime, science, culture, or society but of all mankind and of philosophy as the movement of thought through and beyond all its particular instances. The fuel of this movement of ascent is contradiction in our ideas as well as in their relation to our experience. The consequence of the central role played by contradiction and its resolution is that the path of our rise will be interrupted by successive disruptions. The consummation is the achievement of a form of thought that no longer needs to be disrupted because it has overcome all contradiction.

The chief exponent of this view in the history of philosophy was Hegel. For the early Hegel, of *The Phenomenology of Spirit*, the chief object of the dramatic ascent was the development of a form of life in which subjectivity—and our awareness of the infinite within the self—no longer needed to be at war with the institutions and practices of society. We would at last be at home in the world: at home without surrendering what in this book I call our impulse to transcendence.

For the late Hegel, of the *Logic* and the *Encyclopedia*, the object was our understanding of the world, including our scientific understanding and its power to account for the whole of reality in the discourse of reason, without relying on the metaphors of revealed religion or the magic of art. The practices and methods of thought, in each of the specialized areas in which it works, would then be wholly suited to its objects. Philosophical super-science would be reborn—not as a claim of instant access to higher insight but as the hard-won gift of a long and troubled advance in historical time. For both the early and the late Hegel, the consummation was not in some distant future; it was within reach, and he had at least begun to reach it.

Not one living person would be likely to accept absolute historicism in the dramatic and intransigent version in which I have described it. But it is worth considering because it lives on in many other more equivocating and veiled forms: for example, in Peirce's concept of truth as the ideal limit to which our practices of inquiry converge; or in the view that science has already (and even definitively) described the basic laws of nature or the ultimate constituents of the universe; or in the willingness to take the present practices of the specialized fields of thought, within and outside natural science, as reliable proxies for our powers of inquiry. The extremism of Hegel's project helps show what is at stake and what is wrong even in the much less ambitious versions of this doctrine.

Absolute historicism makes two connected mistakes. The first and most fundamental is to suppose, even as a regulative ideal or limit, that we can ever have a regime—of society or of thought—against which we have no reason to rebel. Such a regime would be an absolute frame of reference: a way of thinking, or a practice of inquiry, open to every discovery about the world; or an institutional and ideological ordering of social life that could accommodate and support every form of self-affirmation and connection with other people that we have reason to value and seek.

There is no such frame of reference in the past or future of society or of thought. There is none because there is always more in us—in each of us individually and in all of us collectively, humanity—than there is or ever can be in the social and conceptual worlds that we build and inhabit. That is the meaning of transcendence. Regimes of society and of thought—and the practices, methods, assumptions, and institutions that define them—are the temporary outcomes of a past history of conflict and exploration, truce lines in conflicts that can be temporarily interrupted or partly contained but never permanently suppressed. To mistake them for our definitive home would be a species of idolatry or false transcendence.

But to say that no such regime deserves to be taken as our definitive home is not the same thing as denying that some regimes are better than others in advancing our most important material, moral, and cognitive interests. One of the ways in which some may be better than others is by allowing us to participate in them without ceasing to resist and revise them. The next best thing to having a regime, of society or thought, that needs no correction is to have one that is corrigible.

The second mistake of absolute historicism is to rationalize the trajectory that brought us to the absolute framework, the real history of politics or of ideas. If prospectively each step was beset by conflict, confusion, and doubt, retrospectively the path may be represented as the enactment of a logic of development. Only at the end—when the "owl of Minerva" takes flight—does the meaning of the whole historical movement become clear. In this way, absolute historicism misdescribes what the history of regime change in society or in thought is really like: dominated at each turn by a contest among a small number of accessible options, in the organization of society or of inquiry, and marked at each turn by roads that were closed but may be reopened later on.

The first mistake of absolute historicism is to sin against the imperative of transcendence by projecting an order that we no longer need to transcend. The second mistake is to sin against the recognition of finitude by conferring on the path that brought us to the final outcome—a home in the world—a necessity or an authority that it does not deserve. That path does not represent the hand of God or of reason in history. It is simply the record of our attempts to push back the limits of finitude as we reckon with one another. There is no incontestable set of practices of inquiry or of arrangements for society. And neither is there a sacred history of steps in that direction.

An absolute historicism sins against both the imperative of transcendence and the recognition of finitude by envisaging a regime of thought that no longer requires disruption. It imagines mistakenly that there is, at the end of a long and troubled history of contradiction and struggle, a final and all-inclusive understanding that realizes the ideal of an absolute frame of reference. By the light of that understanding and with the help of the practices of inquiry that develop and sustain it, the mind at last sees reality for what it is and brings the project of philosophical super-science back to life. Absolute historicism also supposes that there is a path—unique and irreplaceable, unimaginable prospectively and necessary in retrospect—that carries us toward this end. And all the half-true ideas and flawed practices that we deploy along the way are steps along this path at the end of which we see the world with the eyes of God.

All seven misdirections of epistemology discussed in this section have a threefold nature. All misrepresent our transcendence or our finitude or the relation between them. All misdescribe the relation of inquiry to the social practices by which we conduct it. And all suffer the influence of mistakes about what the world, and our position within it, are like. If we did not misunderstand the world and the human condition so grievously, we would not have lost our way in epistemology.

The Agent of Inquiry and His Capabilities

The denial of finitude and of transcendence in the history of episte-mology points back to an agent: the man who searches. He is the one whose finitude and transcendence we must not deny. But who is he, and what are his abilities?

If he had never existed, the world would be much like what it is like now. And once he disappears, if he does, it will continue to be like what it was before he emerged in our corner of the universe. The hope that our evolution will one day intersect with the evolution of the universe and that our experience of consciousness will be found to have counterparts in many aspects of nature has no basis other than our sense of our own importance and our puzzlement over the mysteries of consciousness.

What we recognize as knowledge is knowledge such as an embod-ied and finite being like us, with limited perceptual and cognitive equipment, may achieve. It is as embodied and finite beings that we engage the world. Both the denial of our finitude and the denial of our transcendence are rooted in features of this cognitive situation of ours: the denial of our finitude in the tendency to extrapolate from our ability to subsume more limited views within more inclusive ones, and the denial of our transcendence in the social character of our sense-making practices.

Our cognitive engagement in the world is founded in a natural constitution in whose rudimentary forms we can distinguish three elements: our perpetual apparatus, our powers of reasoning, and what I shall describe as our higher-order cognitive capabilities.

Our perceptual apparatus already shows perception and mind working together. Our senses give us a schematic view of the world, probably very different from the sense that other animals have and heavily colored by the influence of the mind in the synthesis and interpretation of perceived experience. Our observational and experimental equipment allows us to reinforce our perceptual abilities just as our computational equipment helps us reinforce our cognitive powers.

The second element in the natural constitution of inquiry is our reasoning: the cognitive procedures by which we connect our ideas with one another and with our perceptions and draw inferences from them. Two forces distinct from each other, yet overlapping in ontogeny as well as in phylogeny, play a central role in the development of our powers of reasoning. One force is the attempt to intervene in the natural and social worlds around us to produce or to avoid certain effects. The other force is our participation in forms of social life that require not only cooperation but also what some students of the development of thinking have called joint intentionality: projects conceived and pursued in common, through forms of expression and communication—symbolic forms—that are external to the individual and incapable of being developed in a private language.

Action in the world to produce or resist an effect is the starting point of causal thinking. In its beginnings, in the experience of the individual mind or the history of human understanding, such thinking is both anthropomorphic and anthropocentric. But in both our individual and collective development it soon outreaches this origin and turns into a wider idea of causation and change.

We never succeed in completely expunging from the idea of causality its origins in our confrontation with a natural and a social world that resists and threatens us and from which we must obtain what we need. Nevertheless, we come, in historical time as collectivities and cultures, if not in biographical time as individuals, to take the idea of causation as the gateway to a more general way of understanding a world in which everything is susceptible to change. To understand something then becomes to understand what it takes to change it and what it can next turn into. This nexus among causation, transformation, and time lies at the center of the development of our thinking and of our powers of inference and connection.

But we could not grasp this force driving our cognitive development without considering the other force: the cognitive requirements and consequences of our engagement with one another. Everything in our practices of reasoning, from language to specialized method, serves our ability to cooperate.

What is obscure to the individual is then the brute residue of whatever in his consciousness—in his inner thoughts, longings, and anxieties—he cannot translate into the shared symbolic forms of a culture and interpret and deploy accordingly. What is clear and usable is whatever can be represented and explored in that common language and in those shared practices. When we read one another's minds, as we must in order to participate in this world of social practice and symbolic forms, we draw one another more closely to this shared light, and only intuit the unexpressed darkness that lies beyond it.

Our cooperative practices, including our discursive practices, require the refinement of our causal thinking. Such thinking in turn develops in a way that either equips us or leaves us unequipped to understand a social world by understanding how we change it and what we can change it into. These two forces—causality and cooperation—serve as bridges from the natural constitution of human knowledge to our higher-order cognitive capabilities.

If all we had were perception and reasoning, we could not grasp the nature of consciousness, the feeling of being alive. It would be as if we had two toolboxes—of perception and of reasoning—but missed what brings them to life and allows us to combine them, as conscious agents, in our encounter with the world. That third element, alongside reasoning and perception, is the synthetic construction of experience: the development of a coherent representation of the world—a world in which we are able to move and act.

The representation is synthetic because it combines our situation in space with our situation in time. It places our perceptions within a composite view of the manifest reality before us. The picture of that reality with which it presents us supplies the material on which the two forces that drive the development of our reasoning—the complex forms of sociability and cooperation and our causal intervention in reality—can go to work. Without this synthesis, which enters deeply and pervasively into the feeling of being alive, we could not act. The other elements of our epistemic situation would fall apart as if they were so many pieces of different puzzles, never meant to be put together.

Nothing in this description brings us any closer to having a well-founded response to the enigma of abiogenesis: of how consciousness could have arisen from matter in the first place. What it does do is to remind us of how much is implied in being conscious: much more than could ever be produced by simply adding up perception and reasoning.

The use of the term synthetic recalls Kant. It was Kant who, in his Transcendental Aesthetic, provided the most penetrating account in the history of philosophy of this foundational part of our cognitive experience. The work of this part of our cognitive encounter with the world is synthetic (rather than analytic) in the sense that it conjoins elements that cannot be inferred from one another. Kant's genius was to grasp the significance of such presuppositions of our experience. His mistake was to suppose that we are stuck with them—that we cannot criticize, revise, or go beyond them. He thought mistakenly that we cannot hope to set them aside, if not in our spontaneous consciousness then at least in our ideas about the world and our place in it. Having put them aside, we can consider how reality deviates from the picture that such in-built presuppositions present to us. To that extent, he underestimated our cognitive transcendence and mispresented the nature and limits of our cognitive finitude.

The non-Kantian view of our cognitive relation to the world that I have sketched, defined by the synthetic construction of experience as well as by our faculties of perception and reasoning, is still missing a crucial part: our higher-order cognitive capabilities. Until we include them, we cannot take the full measure of the dialectic of finitude and transcendence in our inquiries into the real.

Such cognitive capabilities are higher order in several related senses. They presuppose the basic natural constitution that I have just described and build on it. They express more directly and radically than anything else in our cognitive engagement with the world the impulse to transcendence, and they exemplify in that engagement a characteristic of all our existence: that everything in our experience points beyond itself. They are the seat of the human difference in our cognitive situation. The rest we share, to a greater or lesser extent, with other animals on our planet.

A first pair of high-order capabilities are discrete powers that nevertheless have very general implications for the nature and potential of human knowledge. One such capability is the recursive character of our reasoning. We can reason about our reasoning: we can formulate views, like the view I am presenting right now, that interpret the nature, potential, and limits of human understanding. These views can in turn inspire and inform programs for the development of inquiry. They can support our comparative assessment of the promise of such programs. They are thus direct manifestations of cognitive transcendence: their implication is that the way in which we think now is not the necessary one and need not be the eternal practice of human reason.

Another such discrete higher-order capability is mathematical reasoning. In Chapter 1, on ontology, I suggested a view of its central character: it is a way of thinking about the world wiped clean of phenomenal particularity and time. What remains of the world, once time and phenomenal particularity have been wiped away, is number and space, or structured wholes and bundles of relations. It turns out that a way of thinking about the real without time or phenomenal particularity is immensely useful to the exploration of a world with them.

We obtain this vast service, recorded in the history of the partnership between natural science (especially physics) and mathematics, at a price. The price is the risk of succumbing to one of the two illusions that have stalked that partnership from its beginning: the idea that mathematics is about a distinct realm of unchanging entities, and the idea that nature shares in the timeless character of mathematical and logical propositions. The latter illusion is the more consequential of the two because it strongly influences the direction of natural science. Its influence is manifest in the substitution, in much of basic physics, of thinking organized around causality and laws of nature by thinking organized around structure without causality. As a result of this substitution, mathematics ceases to be a mere instrument of science and becomes part of its substance: putting its stamp on nature by the hand of the most ambitious and encompassing physical theories.

Mathematics—contrary to the first illusion—is not about some other realm of being. It is about the only world that there is, the one in which we find ourselves. Our ability to build a proxy for the world from which time and phenomenal particularity have been erased is one of our higher-order cognitive powers. Its natural-evolutionary advantages are immense. By thinking about the connection among parts of reality in the context of this radically thinned-down simulacrum of nature, we have been able vastly to expand our ability to explore the actual and the possible transformative variations of nature, apart from the immediate scene of perception and action. But now we see that we have gained this advantage at the cost of risking seduction by those two ideas about mathematics and its relation to nature and science. I shall soon return to the implications of this fact for the theory and program of inquiry.

A second pair of higher-order cognitive capabilities, alongside recursive and mathematical reasoning, has even greater generality. These powers relate directly to the twin forces that drive the development of our reasoning and turn them into foundations of both inquiry and society. Together, they represent the most direct and radical expression of the impulse to transcendence in our cognitive situation.

One of these capabilities is the side of our mental experience that we know as the imagination. It deepens our early anthropomorphic and anthropocentric discovery of causality—of intervening in the natural and social world to get what we want. It carries the nexus of causation, change, and time far beyond any circumstance in which we have a direct interest and turns it into a basis of inquiry in art, science, natural philosophy, and social theory.

The imagination—I earlier remarked—works in two steps: by distancing from the phenomenon (the image as the memory of a perception), and by the subsumption of the distanced phenomenon under a range of transformative variation—what something can next turn into, given certain events or provocations. And it is only by insight into such accessible variations that we develop our understanding of the actual.

We do it differently in each domain. But this diversity in the way of connecting the actual to the possible is unavoidable. We could escape it only if a philosophical super-science were to usurp the place of the specialized sciences and forms of discourse, which it cannot legitimately do. Under cover of this diversity of approaches to the link between the actual and the possible, the link may be severed altogether. The result of severing it is the corruption of insight and its descent into a retrospective rationalization of the actual. By making the actual seem either necessary or random, and depriving it of any penumbra of transformative variation, we render it unimaginable. Our narratives risk becoming just-so stories. We see this perversion in much of the work of both the natural and the social sciences today, though always in forms so domain-specific that we fail to recognize what unites them.

Our other higher-order cognitive capability of general scope is the development of symbolic forms in language, law, religion, and art. These forms express both views of our relations to one another and assumptions about the human condition. They present us with images of what our dealings with one another can and should be like in different areas of social life. They may even invest us with divine powers. At the same time, they amount to reckonings with the dialectic of finitude and transcendence.

They are forms because they are enacted in speech, texts, rituals, practices, and institutions. They are symbolic because these artifacts and arrangements, and the discourse in which we represent, reproduce, and revise them, are more than practical solutions to the practical problems that the organization of social life presents to us. We understand and develop them as the outward expression of our ideas about what matters most: our expectations of one another and our assumptions about the human condition.

We have no social experience without them. And if we can have no social experience without them, we can have no first-person experience without them. Even in the most intimate recesses of self-consciousness and introspection, they provide the language and the terms on which we can begin to make sense of our experience. No one untouched by the symbolic forms can be human even if, biologically, he has the physical constitution and equipment of a human being. The second nature that they give us is, from the standpoint of our introduction to a world of human concern, our first nature.

Our ability to develop symbolic forms and our dependence on them are the foundation of our most far-reaching cognitive powers. They also provide the intangible basis for the cooperative practices on which we build civilization. However, they generate a problem that haunts our highest achievements.

Precisely because the symbolic forms are a collective construction, because they are external to any individual person, and because they are reproduced by discursive practices that are the common possession of a society and a culture, we may be tempted to mistake their nature. We may begin to treat them as if they were things, part of the furniture of the universe, rather than our own creation and expression. This reification—the transmutation of the symbolic forms into things driven by a logic of their own—is one of the great themes of politics and of social theory. I return to it in Chapter 7.

Our higher-order cognitive capabilities, and especially the pair last discussed—the work of the imagination linking the actual to the possible, and the development of the symbolic forms underlying human society—are the voice of the impulse to transcendence in our mental experience. It is time to look back and ask of them, as of every expression of transcendence considered in this book, to what kind of transcendence they give voice.

It is, first, a transcendence that reaffirms finitude rather than cancelling it out. With respect to its causal basis, our cognitive finitude lies in our natural condition of embodiment in a dying organism with limited perceptual and cognitive equipment, finding ourselves in a world in which everything changes sooner or later. With respect to its most unmistakable manifestation, such transcendence is confirmed by the unbridgeable gap between absolute knowledge—the knowledge possessed by an omniscient spirit—and the knowledge that finite beings can ever hope to acquire as we push back the bounds of our ignorance.

The transcendence to which our higher-order capabilities point is, moreover, a transcendence that consists in refusing to equate what we are and know now with what we can become and discover in the future. Transcendence means living for the future. Here, it is the future of inquiry as part of the future of human experience. But we do not live in the future. All any of us ever has is life right now. Living for the future must mean living in the present as a being not exhausted by the present circumstances of his existence.

The Idea of a Program of Inquiry

A view of inquiry lays a basis for a program of inquiry, which is a vision both of our future as knowers of the world and of a way to move toward this future. We should develop such a view in a form that is at once general and engaged with the established disciplines in the inquisitive and revisionist spirit that is suitable to philosophy. Such a program should seize the advantages of its disadvantages: what it lacks in contextual detail, related to the situation of each branch of inquiry, it can hope to regain in its conception of the movement of thought across disciplines.

The points of departure for this program lie in the understanding of what I described as the natural constitution of our cognitive circumstance. A first point of departure is our early experience, in the formation of every human being, of dealing with nature and with one another, and our encounter in this experience with causality, change, and time. We act to enlist nature or others, or to resist them, in the pursuit of our aims and desires. Our primitive assumptions about causation are anchored in this predicament.

The connection of causality with change and time reappears in even the most soaring endeavors of the imagination. Nothing so far in our empirical discoveries, by contrast to our interpretation of them through the lens of metaphysical presuppositions hostile to them, requires us to replace that foundation by ideas that deny the reality of time, causality, and change.

But physics, ordinarily regarded as the core of natural science, has embraced ideas that either deny the reality of time, causality, and change or radically reinterpret it in a way that jeopardizes the communion of natural science with our experience of the manifest world. The result is to produce the crisis in the development of our understanding that I next discuss.

A second point of departure for a program of inquiry is our ability to correct, on the basis of our theories and our observational, experimental, and computational equipment, the view of the world supported by the perceptual and cognitive resources with which we are naturally endowed. This ability is no less a part of our natural constitution than is our inability to view the world as the disembodied beings that we are not.

As embodied beings and figures in a world in which everything is transitory, we are finite. But the boundaries of our cognitive finitude, as of finitude in all other domains of life, are moveable. There are no foreordained limits to how far we can move them. A program of inquiry is a program for moving them. Nevertheless, no matter how far we move them, a distance that we cannot traverse always separates our empowered insight from absolute knowledge—the view of the world through the eyes of God or from the perspective of a being who, unlike us, knows the ground of being and the framework of its own existence.

A third point of departure, and the one from which we can begin to trace the elements of a program of inquiry, against the background of the other two, concerns the cognitive opportunities and dangers that arise along the way, as we go beyond our initial view of reality. These dangers and opportunities fall into two groups.

The first group has to do with the unavoidable dependence of ambitious insight, within and outside science, on metaphysical assumptions or ontological images. Such assumptions or images may prevent us from recognizing the extent to which we can explain the facts that established and influential theories claim to elucidate in other, very different ways.

This unavoidable reliance of our natural science on metaphysical presuppositions, and specifically on an ontological image of hidden nature, has implications for the choice of our practices, including our choice of practices of inquiry. One such practice is not as good as another. In the history of natural science, they succeed one another as one view subsumes a previous one of more limited scope: Aristotle's account of the workings of sublunary nature was subsumed within Newton's mechanics, and Newton's mechanics within both relativity and quantum mechanics.

We are not at the beck and call of these ontological images, informing our practices of inquiry. We can pass judgment on them. This power of judgment involves the use our higher-order conceptual capabilities, including recursive and mathematical reasoning. These higher-order capabilities help make possible our exploration of nature beyond the scale of perception and intervention that comes naturally to us.

The succession of explanatory research agendas, each one subsuming our earlier attempts at explanation under a more inclusive view of the workings of nature, demonstrates our powers of transcendence over any specific practice of inquiry. From the fact that we develop these ontological pictures, or metaphysical presuppositions, which have no necessary and intrinsic relation to the empirical findings that they marshal in support of their explanations, there results the possibility of error: instead of ascending to more inclusive accounts of natural reality, they may lead us further and further away from fertile engagement with nature.

In science we must rely on such presuppositions: images of what part of the world is like. Without such metaphysical presuppositions or ontological images, we would be unable to make theoretical sense of our empirical findings, or rather we would be able to make sense of them in too many different ways. For example, the ontological assumption that spacetime conforms to a four-dimensional pseudo-Riemannian manifold may allow us to narrow the conceptual space in which we connect the empirical findings invoked in support of general relativity to our accepted theories and exclude many ways of making explanatory sense of those findings that might be available to us on the basis of different ontological assumptions. The choice of ontological assumptions may in turn be retrospectively validated by the success of the theoretical view that it helps make possible: its explanatory and predictive success and its success as a fertile research agenda.

Alternative ontological assumptions may help make sense of the same empirical findings in a different way. Thus, to invoke an example to which I return in my discussion of the first crisis in the development of our understanding, shape dynamics is one of several rival ways of interpreting what general relativity discovered about what the world is like. It makes a different ontological assumption, neither more nor less factually validated than the ontological image that it would replace, but just as compatible with the hard empirical core of general relativity and of the empirical "proofs" invoked in its defense. In this sense, shape dynamics is equivalent to the most influential account of general relativity. In that account, size is universal and time is relative. In shape dynamics, time is universal and space is relative.

The second group of dangers relates to the consequences of the intellectual division of labor and the development of specialized sciences. Each science or branch of inquiry defines itself by the marriage of a method, or of a small set of methods, to a subject matter. The marriage of method to subject matter, as a principle of the design of the intellectual division of labor, may keep us from seeing how much more we might learn by dissolving this marriage and exploring a subject matter with the help of another method.

To push back the boundaries of our cognitive finitude we have a stake in developing practices of inquiry that loosen the restraints that these two dangers—the reliance of theory on ontology and the marriage of methods to subject matters—impose on the development of knowledge. We must try to loosen them without rejecting either the intellectual division of labor or the unavoidable reliance of theory on ontology.

The First Crisis: Fundamental Physics and Its Denial of Time, Change, and Causality

Natural science and natural experience. As theory in science moves further and further away from a pre-theoretical view of reality (a view already informed by the assumptions of a culture), its reliance on theory increases. And so will the reliance of theory on a view of the kinds of things that there are and of the ways in which in which they interact. Theory will need a language in which to express this conception. That conception, expressed in this language, is its ontology. Such an ontology stands in the place of a pre-theoretical view of reality.

If theory continues to acknowledge the reality of causation, change, and time, its dependence on an ontological conception will be clear for all to see. It may think of the world, for example, as Newton did, as a set of bodies and forces conforming to regular motions, like the parts and movements of a clock.

It may describe those regular motions mathematically. But there will always be something in the theory and its ontology that escapes its mathematical formulation, given that mathematics offers a simulacrum of the world from which time as well as phenomenal particularity have been banished. The physical image, and the physical intuition informing it, will be paramount. The mathematical formulation, however impressive and useful, will simply help bring it out.

But when science takes a further step away from our natural experience of the world, and severs the connection with change, time, and causality, the relation of mathematics to the physical picture is reversed. (Newtonian mechanics had begun this operation but not completed it.) Now the pure truth of the theory lies only in its mathematical expression, and all its non-mathematical versions are at best metaphorical approximations to that truth. Yet even then we can understand the application of the mathematics to physical reality only by forming a conception of the phenomena or events that compose that part of reality and of how they interact. That is the function of Riemannian spacetime (or more precisely a pseudo-Riemannian four-dimensional manifold) in the prevailing interpretations of general relativity. Such a conception—an unimaginable image of nature—will be more than mathematics. It will be an ontology performing the role I have described: that of replacing our pre-theoretical view of the world, the one that Kant said we could not escape but that science progresses by correcting.

Reliance on an ontology is not a problem to which a program of inquiry must provide a response. Such reliance is just the reverse side of the power of inquiry to overstep the boundaries of our natural experience. The problem lies in the relation between empirical discovery and ontological preconception. A characteristic tendency in the development of every science is to claim, or to imply, that the observational and experimental findings that its leading theories propose to elucidate justify its ontological assumptions and its choice of the language in which to state them.

In Chapter 1, on ontology, I offered an example in another context. None of the post-classical tests of general relativity (gravitational lensing, frame dragging, observation of binary pulsars, and even Shapiro's time delay test) has any close relation to the ontological conception of Riemannian spacetime. More generally, the facts that general relativity explains can be explained by alternative ontologies and languages. One such ontology is the one expressed in the language of shape dynamics. To recall a remark made in the previous section: whereas under the predominant interpretations of general relativity, which rely on the Riemannian spacetime conception, size is universal and time is relative, in space dynamics time is universal and space is relative. You can translate the propositions of general relativity, without loss of empirical success, into this different language and the view that it expresses.

It is true that the common description of the observational tests adduced in favor of general relativity is often couched in the language of geodesics of a spacetime continuum, connected with the ontological program of spatializing time. In every instance, however, what these tests show can be fully accounted for by aspects of the relativistic way of thinking that do not depend on Riemannian spacetime; they depend only on the equivalence of gravitational and inertial forces and their effects on the movement of everything, including clocks and human cells. There is nothing in these tests and in what they test that requires us to make the extra leap of regarding time as a merely local extension of space or as a fourth "dimension" of a spacetime continuum.

It is no more true to say that the successful application of general relativity to the phenomena that chiefly interest it supports the metaphysical conception of Riemannian spacetime than it would be to say that the similar explanatory success of classical mechanics in its core domain of application vindicated Newton's picture of a world of interacting forces and bodies against an independent background of space and time. In each instance we may have reason to ask when, and with what consequence, the marriage between the empirical substance or residue and the metaphysical vision in an ambitious scientific theory (like classical mechanics or general relativity) should end in divorce.

We must pay a price for our ability to push outward the frontiers of our cognitive finitude. The price is the unavoidable dependence of theory on metaphysical assumptions or ontological models. Such assumptions inform our interpretation of our empirical discoveries of nature and its workings and suppress alternative understandings of the significance of what we have discovered, as the interpretation of general relativity illustrates. We risk narrowing the range of ways in which to interpret what we have found out about a part of nature. As a result, we fail to formulate alternative theoretical explanations and to explore alternative research agendas. Our daring apostasy from our pre-theoretical view of reality may exact a high cost from us and weaken our campaign to loosen the restraints of our cognitive finitude.

Faced with this threat, the task of natural philosophy is not to legislate for the sciences in the bad old manner of philosophical super-science. It is to diminish the price that we must pay for our audacity and to strengthen the campaign to weaken the restraints of our cognitive finitude. It can do so in four related ways.

The first way is to provide the analytical instruments with which to distinguish in every theory what a science has actually discovered—the empirical-experimental residue or substance of its findings—from what its practitioners say they have discovered. Theory and ontology guide them in what they say they have discovered. The aim is to restore to the empirical findings something of their ambiguity and openness of theoretical significance. We never exercise an idea-free grip on what we suppose to be given. But we have reason to loosen the grip, the better to explore rival ways of understanding the significance of our empirical and experimental discoveries.

The second way is to probe the gap, or the loose links, between the empirical-experimental residue of a scientific theory and its explanatory claims, informed, inescapably, by metaphysical presuppositions that face only distant and oblique empirical challenge. Here natural philosophy considers how the factual findings to which a theory appeals—such as the "post-classical" tests invoked in favor of the dominant interpretations of general relativity—might give conflicting testimony.

The third way, which builds on the second as the second builds on the first, is to imagine alternative research agendas. Natural philosophy can do so motivated by the two forms of liberating skepticism that I discuss in this part of my argument: skepticism about the theoretical reading of what we have discovered about nature and skepticism about the marriage of method to subject matter in each science—the next topic addressed in this program of inquiry.

The fourth way—and the one that most concerns me given the scope of my argument—is to deal with the long-term direction of natural science and the most consequential turning points that it may face as it distances itself from our natural experience. One such inflection holds the greatest interest for the view of the world and of our place in it developed in this book: the choice between a direction that retains the connection of our explanatory projects to change, time, and causality—and consequently refuses to see the essence of our explanatory accounts as contained in their mathematical statement—and a view of the world that severs the connection of science with causality, change, and time, replaces causal explanation by functional analysis, subordinates history to structure, and treats the mathematical statement of theory as its only faithful rendition. Such a view takes every non-mathematical account of an explanatory theory in natural science as a metaphorical approximation to truths secluded in their mathematical statement. I will argue in the following pages that nothing in what we have found out so far about the world justifies, even in basic physics, choosing the second direction over the first.

In carrying out these four tasks natural philosophy fulfills the calling of philosophy in general, which is to represent in thought the impulse to transcendence without denying our finitude.

The thesis of the centrality of change, time, and causation in our experience. This first crisis in the growth of our understanding of the world does not occur in all the natural sciences. It happens in the part of natural science that is widely regarded as the most important: fundamental physics and its cosmological extension, when cosmology is not viewed and practiced, in the way it should be, as a historical science.

To explore the nature and consequences of this crisis, I now develop the discussion of the previous pages of this section into four theses. They are analytically distinct. Each of them has its separate justifications and implications. But it is only when we see them both separately and together that we can grasp the significance of this disturbance in the progress of inquiry.

The first thesis is the thesis of the centrality of the interrelated reality of change, time, and causation to our experience. They form the axis around which our experience is organized; we cannot pull this unifying thread out without undermining all our experience. They are rooted in our elementary enactment of agency and of resistance to agency, which runs through all our existence.

Change, or the susceptibility to change, is the most pervasive feature of the world that we encounter. The philosophy of the timeless one affirms that change is illusory or epiphenomenal. The philosophical tradition of deep structure, which set the philosophical horizon of the fundamental physics of the last few centuries, recognizes the reality of change but sees it as occurring within a changeless framework: the basic constituents and regularities of nature that it views as immutable.

Only a temporal naturalism recognizes the susceptibility to change of everything, including change itself, as a general feature of the real.

Regardless of whether we take this universal susceptibility to change as a feature of the world, what we cannot deny is that it is a central—indeed the central—feature of our experience and of consciousness, if consciousness is the awareness of being alive. Life is action, and we act to cause change or to avoid it. Action confirms us in the sentiment of being.

Time is the quality of reality by virtue of which everything real is susceptible to change. In another sense, it is the transformation of transformation. We can measure change because different parts of reality do not change at the same speed or in the same way: clocks are the expression of this differential or uneven character of change.

A view of nature that dismisses the reality of time, or even one that treats time as derivative or emergent from some more fundamental fact, or that in any other way undermines the continuity of temporal succession, contradicts a feature of our experience with which every other feature is directly or indirectly connected. In his Transcendental Aesthetic, Kant described time as the unifying element in our internal sense, faithful to the spirit of his transcendental method, which treated space, time, and causality as presuppositions of the way we understand and perceive the world. In this commitment, I argued previously, he committed a double error: attributing to consciousness what may be primitive features of nature and underestimating our power to develop ideas that revise, or even deny, some of these supposedly indispensable presuppositions.

Kant was not, however, mistaken in his claim that the unity of consciousness is essentially temporal. The truth of this claim leaves open the possibility that the world is not fundamentally temporal, or that time, as the prevailing interpretations of general relativity suggest, has a meaning that contradicts what we commonly suppose it to be.

Our sense of time is rooted in our encounter with the world as living and dying animals. Our lives have a characteristic arc, projected in time. All our efforts to achieve a goal or to protect what we have achieved or possess make sense to us only insofar as they are played out in time. Similarly, time is the medium of our collective efforts to build regimes and the forms of life that they shelter. And time is the ultimate enemy of all our collective constructions. But all these observations are about us: the question remains (and is addressed by thesis four as well as by the arguments of this chapter about the classic mistakes of epistemology): What is the relation between the structure of our experience and what the world is really like?

Causality is the third element in the triad that, together with change and time, makes up the axis organizing our experience. Causality presupposes time and is manifest as change. Every claim of causality assumes a before and after, temporal succession. For this reason, causal connection cannot be reduced to mathematical or logical implication, inference, or entailment. The latter, unlike the former, is atemporal. This difference gives rise to a riddle haunting physics at least from the seventeenth century to the beginning of the twentieth: How can mathematical reasoning, which is alien to time, represent change in time? The physics of the twentieth century came to suppress this enigma only to the extent that it dispenses with talk of causality altogether.

Our recognition of causality is anchored in the circumstances of agency. From early on, we act to produce or to avert effects and we analogize the workings of nature around us to our own experience of successful or frustrated agency. Cognitive psychologists have explored the steps by which the recognition of causal nexus and potency develops, always in close connection with our awareness of change and of time.

The natural history of this sense of causality arouses a familiar objection: that our attribution of causality to nature, inspired by experiences of successful and frustrated agency, is anthropomorphic as well as anthropocentric. But this objection begs the question of whether we have reason or not to work on the assumption of an affinity between our experience and the workings of nature. If we do, such an affinity is not the end of our struggles with the idea of causality; it is only the beginning. We do not, by virtue of asserting this affinity, abdicate our power to develop and complicate our views of causation in the light of our exploration of nature around us and within us.

᪅

The thesis of the significance of the contrast between affirming and denying, in natural science, the central element in our experience. The second thesis is that there is a consequential difference between a view, in natural science or natural philosophy, that accepts this axis of our experience—change, time, and causation—and one that rejects it. Here it is useful to distinguish two interpretations of what it would mean to reject it.

The minimalist interpretation is that rejecting that axis means denying the reality of the interrelated conceptions of change, time, and causation. It means, as well, denying that their centrality in our experience is a sign of their centrality to the workings of nature.

The maximalist interpretation is less precise but has decisive significance for an understanding of what I have described as the first crisis in epistemology. Whatever the message of a scientific theory that we entertain, it matters whether we can translate it, without loss of meaning, into terms that we can express in a language compatible with our grasp of the manifest world—a grasp in which the triad of change, time, and causality plays a decisive role.

For every account of part of reality in our theory that is formulated in mathematical language, there must be a corresponding account that can communicate with our physical perceptions and intuitions and, through them, connect with the experience-defining triad of change, time, and causation. Another way to make this point is to say that the message of a theory in natural science must not be locked up in the mathematical expression of that theory. The mathematical statement must have a parallel non-mathematical form: the only assurance that it can have a meaning within a discourse about our experience, forever organized around the axis of change, time, and causation. Rejecting the axis of time, change, and causality means, on this maximalist account, failing to live up to this standard.

Fundamental physics has now abandoned this ambition and accepted, as a consequence, that the truth of its central propositions is indeed arrested in their mathematical statement. On this view, any non-mathematical account of these propositions must resort to a series of metaphors that may seem, to the uninitiate in higher mathematics, to give the appearance of bridging a gap that is in fact unbridgeable. The result is to inaugurate a practice of natural science that no longer speaks the language of laws of nature underwriting causal explanations. Instead, this practice presents a structural, non-historical account of nature at both the sub-human and supra-human scales.

In such an account, time and history retain only a remote connection to what they mean to us. If time and history are represented at all, they are represented by mathematical expressions and metaphysical presuppositions that leave what we call time unrecognizable to a human being. In the world that such a view of nature describes, no role remains for physical intuition to perform.

In retrospect, this way of thinking may seem to be the foreseeable and even unavoidable outcome of the approach to science that Galileo helped begin in the late sixteenth and early seventeenth centuries, with its emphasis on quantities over qualities. It was not long ago, however, that Einstein, who stood at the origin of both signature endeavors of twentieth-century physics—relativity and quantum mechanics—insisted on the guiding role of physical intuition and the sovereignty of mysterious nature as the true subject matter of both physics and mathematics. He denounced the "spatialization of time" as an "extravagance" of vulgarizers, and in his unfinished and unpublished article for *Nature* of 1919/20 wrote that "in the end geometry is supposed to tell us about the behavior of the bodies of experience … This association makes geometry a science of experience in the truest sense, just like mechanics. The propositions of geometry can then be confirmed or falsified, just like the propositions of mechanics."

To apply to the forms and scales of reality with which Einstein dealt, the scientific imagination—supported by intuition, theoretical insight, and empirical investigations of the workings of nature—would have to extend outward a chain of analogies beginning in our experience of the manifest world. The link with that experience and that world would stretch but it would never—so Einstein hoped—break.

Now, however, it seems that it has broken. And the result is that in fundamental physics we have a science that has ceased to communicate using any language in which we can make sense of the world in terms that do not undermine how we make sense of our own action in the world. Nothing in this science allows us to remain in contact with the hallmarks of our experience—an experience afloat in time, in a universe in which everything changes sooner or later and in which what came before causes what comes after.

The thesis of the scientific and the existential cost of denying the central element in our experience. My third thesis about this first crisis in epistemology concerns the nature of the misfortune that we would face if fundamental physics turned out to be justified in its embrace of a view of the world that breaks with the axis—of change, time, and causation—around which we shape our experience.

If the facts of the matter supported such a view, we would face two misfortunes: one, narrower, regarding the practice of scientific inquiry; the other, wider, about our situation in the world.

The narrower misfortune is that science—or the part of it that embarked on such a program—would cease to have an anchor or a guide in physical intuition or in our experience of the manifest world informed by physical intuition. We know that our perceptual apparatus is limited and unreliable, and that it has emerged out of evolution to deal with the ordinary objects and states of affairs that we encounter at the habitual scale at which we act. There are colors that we cannot see and sounds that we cannot hear. As the example of the perceived flatness of our spherical planet shows, we use our observational and experimental equipment and our powers of inference from experience and experiment to correct the testimony of our eyes. But it is one thing to make such corrections, as we do constantly in the planetary and life sciences, and it is another thing to sever any link between our natural-scientific conceptions and our sense of the manifest world.

There will still be, you may say, the witness of experiments: showing whether, for example, we can or cannot detect at the Planck scale, through the use of a particle collider, a subatomic particle predicted to exist by the standard model of particle physics. But if the larger conception that this empirical discovery serves cuts its connection to an experience in which change, time, and causation play a central role, it will suggest that our whole sense of the manifest world is misleading. Nothing in our understanding of reality will be left undisturbed: the challenge will go to the basics of that understanding, not just to the reliability of our perceptions but to the basis on which we combine and interpret them.

The risk to which this situation exposes natural science is the danger of descending into directionless allegory. In literary allegory, our moral experience guides us in imagination and interpretation. But there is no counterpart to this guide in the allegorical turn of natural science.

We can distinguish three elements in the ideas and practice of any science: its interpreted empirical and experimental findings, its explanatory theory, and the ontological picture that connects this theory to those findings. In a science that has turned away from the recognition of time, change, and causality, our immediate apprehension of reality ceases to have any hold on this ontological picture. Its place is usurped by mathematical ideas to which we can give no verbal expression accounting for the reality that we observe and confront. The consequence is to open the door to fabrications and fantasies. Disguised as popularizations made necessary by the need to explain mathematics to the unmathematical, they are in fact free translations of views that have no meaning in our world into views that would have a meaning. They gain a meaning by appropriating some part of the discarded conceptions of change, time, and causation and using them in a narrative unsupported by the mathematical theories that they profess to popularize.

The greatest risk that befalls a science that has severed its link with our experience of the manifest word is not, however, the risk of meaninglessness or distorted meaning. It is the risk of sterility. Deprived of the incitements of physical intuition, grounded in our pre-theoretical sense of what the world is like, the scientific imagination loses its greatest inspiration.

It was a source to which physicists had constantly resorted before relativity—especially general relativity—and quantum mechanics. One of its characteristic expressions in the physics of earlier periods had been mechanical. Lord Kelvin reflected on the use of mechanics to ground theory in physical intuition when he said: "I am never content until I have constructed a mechanical model of the object that I am studying. If I succeed in making one, I understand; otherwise, I do not."[2] Indeed, the point of Newtonian mechanics had been to make such a model of the entire universe. A historian of physics and natural philosophy remarks: "The peculiar explanatory power of mechanics was held to reside in its *Anschaulichkeit*, its intuitive perceptibility. Mechanical models were palpable; they could be drawn, built, pictured in the mind."[3]

The larger misfortune that results from the denial of change, time, and causation has to do with the way we understand our situation in the world rather than with the practice and future of natural science. To appreciate what is at stake, consider the contrast between two views of this situation. They amount to two conceptions of our groundlessness.

On one image, we stand in a small clearing of uncertain light—our hard-won knowledge of the world, achieved by science, art, and all the forms of inquiry available to us. This clearing is surrounded on every side by measureless darkness. We are not even able to calculate the relation between the tiny zone of light and the vast darkness that surrounds it. But in the zone of light, we can elucidate part—if only a small part—of the world in which we find ourselves. We can make sense of it on terms that communicate with our experience.

On the other image—if science were our only resource of insight and within science only the fundamental physics of today counted—there is no such clearing of light. Our account of nature may allow us to make certain predictions that experiments confirm, and to harness some natural forces for our purposes. But it also suggests to us that, whatever the world is like, it is not arranged in a way that we can ever hope to understand on the terms that are central to our experience.

In such a universe, we must be exiles: exiles from a world in which what matters to us and what allows us to make sense of our relation to it and to one another is real. That world from which we are exiled would wear a human face. We would not need to pretend that it existed

2. William Thomson Kelvin, *Baltimore Lectures on Molecular Dynamics and the Wave Theory of Light*, 1904. And see Ludwig Boltzmann's entry "Model" in the 1902 edition of the *Encyclopedia Britannica*.

3. Edward Skidelsky, *Ernst Cassirer: The Last Philosopher of Culture*, 2008, p. 13.

for our benefit, curiosity, and pleasure. But whatever secrets it yielded would be ones that we could hope to make sense of on terms like the terms that we need and use to make sense of ourselves. In that other world, we could hope to establish and guard the clearing of light in the middle of the darkness that surrounds us.

The thesis that refusal to pay this cost cannot be justified by metaphysical rationalism but may be justified by the alliance of empirical discovery with philosophical criticism. The fourth thesis that helps explain the nature and significance of this first crisis in our present-day understanding of the world is that we have a stake in the truth of one of these two futures of inquiry. We have reason to prefer a practice of natural science that remains in communion with our central experiences of change, time, and causality to one that does not; reason to prefer a science that continues to be inspired by physical intuition nourished by engagement with the manifest world to one that leaves its message locked up in its mathematics; and reason to prefer the picture of a small clearing of light in the midst of boundless darkness to the image of banishment to a world in which our science fails to connect with our experience.

However, there is no reason why reality must vindicate us in these preferences. It all depends on what the world is really like. And the world does not need to be, and may not be, the way that these preferences require. The world just happens to be the way it is, and the most important fact about the world—the message the ontology of Chapter 1 proclaims—is that the world is what it is rather than something else.

To reason otherwise would be metaphysical rationalism—the attempt to infer the nature of the world from arguments of rational necessity prior to experience. Natural philosophy begins with the rejection of metaphysical rationalism, which pretends to offer us, in exchange for nothing but the bald assertion of this faculty, the power to discern what is and must be, the ground of being and the framework of reality.

In Chapter 1, on ontology, I have taken the position of temporal naturalism and argued that time is inclusively real, and that causality is a primitive feature of nature rather than just, as Kant and his successors held, a constant and indispensable presupposition of our understanding. If those claims are true, then our experience of the centrality of change, time, and causation accords with the way the world is. Views, including views in natural science, that deny it are, consequently, mistaken. But the thesis of temporal naturalism may turn out to be false. Even if it is true, it is not necessarily true and not a feature of a reality that could not be other than what it is.

Philosophy is powerless to abolish contingency—the brute given-ness of reality, its just happening to be one way rather than another. But it is not powerless to recognize the element of contingency in the development of natural science; to tally up the mounting costs of the direction that fundamental physics has taken; to arouse suspicion of the part that metaphysical and methodological prejudice, rather than empirical discoveries, has played in this choice of direction; and to suggest the initial steps of another path that would uphold the communion of natural science with our experience of the manifest world.

This is philosophy not as the old super-science in the service of self-help, nor as the self-appointed thought police always ready to root out fallacy and nonsense. This is philosophy engaged in the exercise of its revisionist mission. If it is not the instrument of metaphysical rationalism, neither is it required to identify our powers of reasoning and discoveries with the present orthodoxies of the specialized disciplines. It is especially attentive to the unavoidable but dangerous role of metaphysical and especially ontological assumptions in the evolution of the natural and social sciences. As natural philosophy in relation to the natural sciences and as social theory in relation to the social sciences, it expresses the aspiration to transcendence in the life of the mind. It is in this spirit that you should read this account of the first crisis in our understanding of reality today.

The Second Crisis: The Social Sciences and the Suppression of Structural Vision

The second crisis in our contemporary understanding of the world arises in the development of our ideas about society and ourselves. And like the first crisis, it concerns the future—now of our self-construction

as well as of our self-knowledge. It has to do not with the basic constituents of nature and how they work but with the institutional and
ideological framework of a particular society: the regime that shapes
its routines of exchange and conflict and the way in which it creates
its own future. This second crisis has direct consequences for the
future of our self-construction as well as of our self-understanding.

In fundamental physics, the sheer alienness of the subject matter
explains the need for a prop—the ontological image—on which we
can project our empirical findings about the workings of nature. When
addressing a regime of social life, the problem is reversed. It is not
alien; it is all too familiar. It surrounds us on every side: we know it as
the rules of the game, as the basic system of institutions and culture
that organizes our social experience. We speak its language as we
speak our mother tongue.

Yet everything in our experience conspires to disguise and misrepresent its true character. Instead of the ontological prop, standing
in for alien and unknowable nature and serving as a screen on which
to project our fragmentary and otherwise ambiguous empirical findings, we have a series of fabrications that present the regime of social
life as something other than what it is: the outcome of a temporary
interruption or partial containment of conflict over the terms of our
claims on one another.

Once again, we have the power to reject these fabrications, just
as we have the power to question, in natural science, the ontological
stand-in for the hidden constitution of nature. But now our rejection
is not simply a matter of measuring the consequences of taking one or
another direction in our investigation of nature. It is the condition of
our empowerment, the gateway to our liberation. The development
of a usable view of regimes—of their nature, their making, and their
reconstruction—is the indispensable instrument of a vision of the
remaking of society.

The second great crisis in our understanding of the world today lies
in our lacking a usable and credible view of regimes—of the formative
institutional and ideological contexts of a society—of how they get
made, of how they work, and of how they change. Without such a view,
we cannot make sense of our collective self-construction in history

or find ideas which, when married to a view of the direction and the ideal, can sustain a programmatic argument. We fall back on a fake criterion of political realism: proximity to the existent. We may treat a proposal as realistic (albeit trivial) if it comes close to what already exists. And we may dismiss it as utopian (albeit appealing) if it remains distant from what exists. We mistake programmatic arguments for blueprints rather than for successions, for architecture rather than music. Our error is aggravated by our failure to grasp the nature of regimes and of regime change. Today few believe in the heroic assumptions of Marx's theory of society and history. But the vocabulary of that theory survives without the theoretical conviction that gave those assumptions meaning. Deprived of a way of thinking about structural change and structural alternatives, we are left to mistake proximity to the existent for realism in our thinking about social alternatives.

In the study of society and history, the counterpart to the relation of natural philosophy to the natural sciences is the relation of social theory to the social sciences. And the counterpart to the role of an ontological model of part of nature in our most ambitious natural-scientific theories is the role of assumptions about institutional and ideological regimes in social and historical inquiry.

In the social sciences and the study of history, we do not move beyond our natural experience, for there our natural experience is our experience of life in society, which we cannot escape even if we wanted to. We have a kind of knowledge of this social experience that we cannot hope to have of natural phenomena—a knowledge from within. The most important part of social reality—the formative institutional and ideological framework of a society—is its deep structure. This structure shapes our practical and discursive routines including our contests over the resources of political power, economic capital, and cultural authority by which we make the social future within the social present. (This will form a major topic of Chapter 7, on politics.)

The institutional and ideological regime is the decisive element in social life. It is nothing but frozen politics: the outcome of the relative containment and temporary interruption of our ceaseless contest over the terms of our access to one another. We are collectively its creators.

But it is often what in society we least understand or even recognize. It is the central reality, at once hidden and powerful.

The assumptions that we make about these regimes—even by disregarding their existence or misrepresenting their nature—hold, in the social sciences, the place of ontological models in the natural sciences. For it is on the basis of such assumptions, mediated by the leading theories and explanatory practices of each branch of social and historical study, that the social sciences make sense of the facts that they claim to elucidate and take one or another direction.

Yet the history of thinking about the formative institutional arrangements and ideological assumptions of a society has always been and remains troubled. To this day, the social sciences and historiography continue to lack an adequate account of them, while, for the most part, not knowing that they lack it. Without such an account, however, they cannot grasp what is vital in all understanding of reality, whether natural or social: the relation between the actual and its accessible transformations.

Consider three moments in this troubled history of thinking about regimes: Montesquieu, Marx, and twenty-first-century social science. In Montesquieu the regimes are represented in the classical Aristotelian mode. They form part of a closed list, a small menu of historical options. Each is an indivisible system, with two aspects: an institutional order and a form of consciousness—a "spirit" or "principle" that it inspires and that helps maintain it.

In Marx, as in Montesquieu, the regimes, under the name of "modes of production," continue to be the most important element in social life, together with the varieties of class hierarchy and class conflict that they support. Again, they come from a closed menu of historical options. Again, they are indivisible systems. But now their foreordained succession in history is driven forward by laws: the fate of the "relations of production" that they organize depends on whatever is necessary, by way of social and economic organization, to make possible the maximal development of the "forces of production," always associated with the interests and the ascent of a class.

In this central tradition of Western social theory, from Montesquieu to Marx and beyond, the theory of structure or of regime is the chief site of explanatory ambition in social and historical thought. And with Marx, preceded by Hegel and Vico, comes the revolutionary insight that such regimes are just frozen politics, that they are our inventions, and that having made them, we can remake them, albeit under the unyielding constraints of social and historical reality. The theoretical and practical reach of this insight remains in thrall to necessitarian assumptions: the closed and short list of regimes, the indivisibility of each regime, and the laws of historical change that we can hope to ride but not to redirect. The link between insight into the actual and imagination of the proximate possible is at once affirmed and eviscerated by the necessitarian paraphernalia of this social-theoretical apparatus.

And what do we then find in the social sciences of the twenty-first century? Their predominant tendency is to suppress structural vision altogether rather than to radicalize the central insight of classical social theory into the made and imagined character of the structures of society, liberating that insight from the necessitarian illusions that corrupted it under the pretext of registering the constraints on the transformation of regimes and the construction of alternative ways to order social life. The result is to cut the connection between insight into the actual and imagination of the proximate alternative ways of shaping a society. Each social science cuts that connection in its own way. The effect is to lend to the present organization of social and economic life a false semblance of naturalness and necessity. It is right-wing Hegelianism—the principle that the real is rational, offered as social science.

In this circumstance, social theory must accomplish what social science has not. It must turn its attention to structural vision, structural discontinuity, and structural alternatives. There are two ways in which it can do so. One way is to appear as a theoretical endeavor distinct from the social sciences that carries on the project of classical European social theory—the project of which Marx's theory of society and history was the consummate but flawed expression. In Chapter 7 of this book, on politics, I offer the outline of such a view. The other way is to act not under the label of social theory at all but in the form of a contest within each discipline, including the two most important disciplines of power—law and economics. Philosophy as revisionist social theory must then meet each discipline on its own terms, rather than pretending to soar above it. And it must meet it on its own terms with the aim of recasting it in a form that allows it to serve the imagination of structure and of structural alternatives and to reestablish the severed link between insight into the actual and imagination of the accessible alternatives to the actual.

The intellectual practice that I am calling social theory hardly exists today. The label social theory is used to describe a canon of long dead great social thinkers, like Marx, Durkheim, and Weber, whose speculative work is thought to form part of the prehistory of the social sciences. But just as natural philosophy, another archaic label, must be reborn in another mode to challenge the natural sciences, from both outside them and within each of them, so social theory must be reborn in another mode to challenge the positive social sciences and the normative social disciplines (legal theory and political philosophy) from both outside and within each of them. Approached in this fashion, social theory is simply the name that philosophy assumes on one of the many fronts of its struggle to affirm transcendence in thought as well as in experience.

The Intellectual Division of Labor and the Marriage of Method to Subject Matter

The dangers and opportunities in the development of inquiry discussed in the immediately preceding pages all have to do with the consequences of the unavoidable reliance of thought on assumptions about the nature of the reality with which it deals. In the natural sciences, these assumptions are ontological, and the need to rely on them is triggered by the increasing distance of the most fundamental natural science from our immediate experience. In the social sciences, the assumptions are also ontological, and their subject is that which in society holds the place of the basic constitution of reality: the institutional and ideological regimes that give shape to a form of social life. In one case, we are offered an understanding of the subject matter that ceases to communicate with our experience of the manifest world. We cannot give the understanding a non-mathematical interpretation without loss of meaning. In the other case, the most salient aspect of the subject matter—regimes and their transformation—is all too obvious, but we now lack a credible way of thinking and talking about it. In both cases, philosophy, acting in one instance as natural philosophy and in the other as social theory, must come to the rescue.

I now turn to a second set of dangers and opportunities: those that result from the consequences of the intellectual division of labor and the existence of specialized branches of inquiry, including the natural and the social sciences. In each of those fields, method is wedded to subject matter: if not, as usually happens, one favored or exclusive method, then a small set of methods. The marriage of method to subject matter, often made to appear indissoluble, weakens the development of inquiry by denying us the insights that we may gain when we dissolve these forced marriages and approach each subject matter with the help of alternative methods.

Such recombinations of method and subject matter need not be idle exercises or mere gambles on an intellectual benefit that we are unable to define. They can, and often will, have a basis in the central problems of each of the specialized fields. Further consideration, from this perspective, of examples offered earlier in the argument will illustrate the point.

An example from the recent development of basic physics and cosmology goes straight to the heart of the most consequential issue in the contemporary development of natural science. Fundamental physics has opted for a method that is structural rather than historical, and functional (in the mathematical sense) rather than causal. Its message cannot be extricated from its mathematical formulation. Talk of laws of nature as well as of causation has either vanished or been radically reinterpreted. If the concept of laws of nature has any meaning in the science that has taken this fateful step, its meaning is the description of reciprocal connections in natural reality without any appeal to causal explanation, for such explanation presupposes the reality of time and for that very reason cannot be adequately described in mathematical terms.

Yet—as I remarked in Chapter 1, on ontology—cosmology has discovered that the universe has a history. On that basis, we have strong reason to believe that neither the basic constituents of nature, described by the standard model of particle physics, nor the regularities of nature (constants and symmetries as well as laws), could have been in the earliest moments of the present universe (or in later extreme variations of nature such as black holes) what they are in the more recent, cooled-down universe. To do justice to these discoveries, cosmology must be a historical science. It must exhibit, in a form suitable to its practices, the attributes of natural-historical study that I considered in Chapter 1. No historical science can tolerate the subordination of structure to history or the substitution of causal explanation by atemporal functional analysis. No historical science can abandon its central ideas to their mathematical formulation and treat mathematics as the oracle of nature rather than as a useful, even indispensable, but nevertheless limited instrument of its explanatory endeavors.

If the universe is historical, it must be historical in all its parts. And if cosmology is the historical science of the whole universe, it makes no sense to marginalize it as a speculative afterthought to physics or to demote it to the place of large-scale astronomy. The exclusive devotion of basic physics to structure over history, function over causality, and mathematical formalization over physical imagination must give way to a broader array of methods.

Evolutionary biology, on the other hand, has been a historical science since before Darwin. In the neo-Darwinian synthesis in the life sciences, however, ideas about structure, function, and the organization of complexity have come to play an increasing role in the evolutionary as well as in the genetic part of that synthesis. And with them has come the use of mathematics to represent and explore evolutionary dynamics.

Thus, the assignment of fundamental physics to structure and mathematical representation and of evolutionary biology to history and causation, studied by non-mathematical means, appears as an impediment to the advance of insight. Methods and subject matters must be recombined.

A similar situation takes place in the social sciences. For a long time, economics, to take the example of the most influential social science, has not been the study of the economy. It has been the study of a method pioneered by the marginalist theoreticians at the end of the nineteenth century. There is both plenty of formal analysis and empiricism in what contemporary economists have made of this method, but the empiricism and the deductive theorizing have little to do with each other. The resulting discipline is deficient in ideas that would contribute to what matters most: insight into the alternative institutional futures of the market order. In Chapter 7, on politics, in discussing the missing theory of regimes, I return to the reasons why economics is deficient in the imagination of institutional possibility and consequently deficient in insight into the world with which it deals.

Now let us step back and consider the relation of this part of the program of inquiry to the established division of intellectual labor in both the natural and social sciences and to the reproduction of the specialized disciplines that have come to form the backbone of academic culture. The point is not to abolish the specialized character of inquiry, organized as the different sciences, each defined by its ruling theories and methodological commitments. The dissolution of the specialized sciences into philosophical super-science, of the natural sciences into natural philosophy and of the social sciences into social theory, will never happen. It would represent a step back into obscurantism and deprive us of the knowledge that only long devotion to a well-defined set of problems can bring.

But with the dissolution of the marriage between method and subject that is the organizing principle of the present form of the intellectual division of labor, the boundaries that separate the disciplines from one another must lose some of their clarity. As they do so, the distinctions between the natural sciences and natural philosophy, on the one hand, and between the social sciences and social theory, on the other, will not vanish but will be relativized.

Such a change will be the equivalent, in the organization of knowledge, to what we observe in the contemporary reshaping of production. In what used to be the most advanced productive practice, industrial mass production, there was a stark contrast between the planning and the implementation of productive tasks. The reverse side of this contrast was the narrow specialization and repetitious character of the jobs of the workers charged with implementing the plan of production: each job being defined by its assigned place in the plan. Under this system the workers worked as if they were one of their machines: through formulaic movements mirroring the movements of the mechanical devices of industrial mass production.

Today, the most advanced productive practice, the knowledge economy, requires for its deepening and dissemination that production be marked by perpetual innovation and radical experimentalism. The contrast between planning and execution must be softened: each task contributes to the revision of the plan in the light of opportunities discovered in the process of implementing it.

In the inherited organization of knowledge, the plans are the leading theories and theoretical traditions, the planners are the rebels who become the authors of a new orthodoxy, the workers are everyone else, and the methods are the machines. Our intellectual life should resemble an inclusive, experimentalist knowledge economy, devoted to perpetual innovation in both its products and its practices, more than it resembles standardized mass production, with its stark specializations and hierarchies, and its routines broken only by occasional technological or economic revolution. The aim is not to destroy the principle of intellectual specialization. It is to render relative and open the boundaries separating the disciplines from one another and from philosophy: social theory for the social sciences and natural philosophy for the natural sciences.

Implications for Natural Science

The implications of this program for the practice of natural science can be summarized in a single conception, using and revising a contrast made famous by the historian of science, Thomas Kuhn: the contrast between normal science and scientific revolutions.[4] What he called

---

4. Thomas Kuhn, *The Structure of Scientific Revolutions*, 1962.

normal science I will call routine science. It is not, or should not be, normal for the practice of science to have only the characteristics that Kuhn described under that heading. And what he described as scientific revolutions, I will call transformative science. What it transforms in the first instance is not the world (though it ultimately helps do that) but itself. The practice of transformative science need not be the exclusive prerogative of a handful of scientific geniuses, such as Newton and Einstein, appearing as rare and isolated pinnacles in the history of their science.

The program of inquiry outlined in the previous pages implies that routine science can and should take on some of the features of transformative science. As a result, the distance between these two ways of doing science should narrow.

In his characterization of normal science, Kuhn emphasized the predominance of problem-solving under the aegis of an established theory, which he called a paradigm. Such problem-solving is a common but nevertheless relatively shallow trait of routine science. A deeper trait is its largely implicit reliance on an ontological picture of nature, or the part of it with which it deals. Against the background of such a picture it connects its explanatory theories with its empirical findings.

In routine scientific practice, the implicit ontology, the explicit theory, and the interpreted empirical and experimental findings appear to be seamlessly connected. Method remains married to subject matter: a single method or small set of methods prevails, as if it were the natural, exclusive, and indispensable road to insight in each science. Mastery of the method or methods serves as the essential condition for professional education and the main object of the training of the young scientist.

Reliance on the metaphysical or ontological assumptions—invisible and uncontested—allows the conversation between theory and empiricism to remain intimate and focused, discouraging any impulse to interpret in other ways the empirical and experimental observations at the top of the current research agenda or to see in those observations any reason to change the direction of theory. The marriage of method to subject matter removes what would be the most potent source of disturbance to this entente between theory and empiricism.

On each of these points, transformative science goes the other way. But it need not go the other way in long, revolutionary leaps. It may do so in small, cumulative steps and by a practice of fragmentary reconstruction of theory and empirical research in each science. The potential of such initiatives to result in far-reaching changes in our approach to inquiry may become clear only in retrospect. At each point along the way no one will be able to assess with confidence the transformative potential of such intellectual innovations. If we are to employ the political analogy built into the use of the word "revolution," we might call such a practice radical reform. When it persists, by fragmentary measures and piecemeal steps in a certain direction, it can produce an outcome that at the end we might describe as revolutionary.

Consider the example of the introduction into our thinking about natural evolution of ideas about the role of the limited palette of structures and of relations between structures and functions with which evolution works. Over the long term, these ideas point toward bodies of explanatory ideas and methods that have up to now played little role in the development of the half of the neo-Darwinian synthesis that deals with natural selection as opposed to the half that deals with genetic invariance, mutation, and recombination. The ideas may be those of theories of complexity and organization, imported from other disciplines. The recombination of methods and subject matters goes along with a revision of ontological assumptions: under the ideas about structural constraints in natural evolution, their functional consequences, and the management of complexity by emergent forms of life, our image of the pertinent part of nature and of how its pieces interact changes.

Early on in the application of these ideas and methods to the problems of evolution, it is impossible to say whether the outcome will be an enrichment of the neo-Darwinian synthesis, leaving most of its established explanations and methodological habits intact, or some more consequential change in the theory, methods, and empirical research agenda of the science. This outcome is neither what Kuhn described as normal science nor what he labeled a scientific revolution. We can more accurately describe it as a heightening of the powers of routine science as its ordinary practice takes on the transformative traits that I have just described.

Transformative science turns out not to be an opposite to routine science at all, as in the binary terminology of normal science and scientific revolutions. It is simply routine science taken to a higher level of ambition and capability, through practices that can be widely enacted within the community of a discipline rather than remaining the prerogative of individual genius.

Before being a proposal, this account of the modification of routine science is a description: the vast preponderance of scientific innovation overstepping the limits of the scientific practice that I have called routine takes this form rather than the form of what Kuhn named scientific revolutions and paradigm shifts. Such revolutions and shifts are simply a limiting case of such frequent and familiar innovations. The issue is not how to replace routine by revolution; it is how to elevate the nature of the normal in the practice of normal science.

Kuhn protested that such a cumulative modification of ordinary scientific practice contradicts what the history of science has shown to be a condition for the development of a robust and fertile science: rigorous training in a particular tradition within a science. Innovation in science, as in art, is more likely to flourish, according to this view, when enabled and chastened by mastery of an established canon of ideas and procedures.[5]

This objection contains an element of truth: if the mind travels amid a multitude of vaguely sketched theories and methods and fails clearly to grasp and understand any of them, its ability to innovate is likely to be weakened rather than strengthened. If, however, our aim is to raise the ordinary practice of inquiry to a higher level of awareness of assumptions and of openness to alternatives, there should be no such insuperable conflict.

Yes, the mind cannot resist or reinvent what it has failed fully to grasp. But, no, transformative practice is compatible with the pursuit

---

5. Thomas Kuhn, *The Essential Tension: Selected Studies in Scientific Tradition and Change*, 1977.

of such mastery. What such practice excludes is a species of mastery that equates command of a discipline with failure to recognize that both the ontological assumptions on which the established discipline relies and the methods to which is wedded are open to contest.

Moreover, the contrast between scientific revolutions and normal science, as Kuhn and others have developed it, suggests that the views of nature introduced by revolutionary "paradigm shifts" are incommensurable. The thesis of the incommensurability of paradigms is, however, false to the history of natural science. It also contradicts the grounds that we have for the hope of pushing back the boundaries of our cognitive finitude without ever abolishing them. If we cannot realize these hopes in the domain of natural science, how can we hope to realize them in any other part of our engagement with the world around and within us? Nothing in the picture of our cognitive situation set out earlier in this chapter justifies such a dismissal of the ideal of successive approaches, in natural science, to more inclusive truth about nature.

The history of the most ambitious explanatory projects is better described as a sequence of such successive approximations to more inclusive accounts of nature than as a series of substitutions of one incommensurable world view for another. Aristotle's physics offers an account of fundamental physical processes that holds good in the limited sublunary domain—of movement on earth within the medium of a fluid or gas—that they were formulated to explain. Newton's physics works over a wider expanse of natural phenomena, beyond our situation on earth, and preserves Aristotle's physics as an approximation valid for a more limited setting. Einstein's special and general relativity extends further the scope of the reality to which it applies and preserves Newtonian physics as an approximation valid within its domain, and in turn fails to apply beneath the Planck scale (though Einstein helped invent quantum mechanics as well as relativity). Each large advance has subsumed the earlier view as valid within its range of intended application. This is not a history of incommensurable paradigms; it is a history of repeated approaches to a more encompassing understanding.

Something is nevertheless missing from this interpretation of the history of natural science, as exemplified by the history of physics. What remains missing is recognition of the possibility that late in such a trajectory of successive advances toward a more complete approximation to the truth about nature and how it works, there may arise questions about the whole direction. In this sequence—from Aristotle to Newton and from Newton to Einstein—the question of greatest significance has two sides.

On one side is the reality of causality, change, and time. On the other side is the relation of mathematics to nature and natural science, and the view of mathematics as more than a useful or indispensable instrument of our explanatory projects: as the prophet of science and the oracle of nature. At each step in this trajectory, recognition of the inclusive reality of time has become more qualified and the willingness to take atemporal mathematical reasoning as a shortcut to an understanding of nature has become stronger.

But at what cost to our understanding of natural reality and its variations? The story is just beginning. The course of natural science remains subject to changes of direction. The views of the history of science as a succession of incommensurable paradigms and as an unbroken triumphal march, with no chance that the march might ever take a wrong turn, are both mistaken.

We can better understand the wider significance and motivations of the account of the advancement of science developed in the preceding pages by returning to the political analogy of established order, radical reform, and revolution. Ideas about society have often been modeled on ideas about nature, and social theory or social science on whatever conception of method in natural science happens to be most influential at a given time. But we have more reason to proceed in the opposite direction, from politics to science.

We can never depart from our experience of social life as much as natural science can carry us away from our pre-scientific view of natural reality. Contrary to common belief, we are less likely to be deluded in our assumptions about how we gain knowledge of society than in our assumptions about how we can acquire insight into nature. To understand the relation between routine and transformative science, we can look to politics and, more generally, to our relation to the conceptual and social worlds that we build and inhabit. Writing about another aspect of the empowerment of inquiry, Francis Bacon remarked: "What in some things is considered a secret has in others a manifest and well-known nature, which will never be recognized as long as the experiments and thoughts of men are engaged on the former only."[6]

In many respects, the conceptual worlds that we build and inhabit resemble the institutional and ideological ones—the regimes, which represent the fateful element in social life. One of the several ways in which classical European social theories, such as Marx's theory of society and history, misrepresented these regimes was to describe them as indivisible systems. From this thesis there resulted a binary view of politics: politics must consist in either the revolutionary substitution of one such regime (for Marx, the modes of production) by another or the reformist management of a regime. In fact, however, the formative institutional and ideological settings of social life are not such indivisible systems. Their parts often both reinforce and conflict with one another.

The way in which they change is almost always part by part. Thus, radical reform, a name for such structural but piecemeal remaking, is the main species of structural change. The total substitution of one system by another is only a limiting case. Today the chief rhetorical use of the idea of revolution has come to serve as an alibi for its opposite. As revolution is either inaccessible or too dangerous, what remains is to humanize the existing regime—typically through compensatory redistribution by progressive taxation and redistributive social spending. The result is to exclude from our practices, our ideas, and even our vocabulary, the chief instances of structural transformation.

And so it is with natural science. The binary classification of scientific practice into normal science and scientific revolutions becomes a pretext for its opposite. Scientific genius brings about revolution. Everyone else does normal science.

Our interest in society is to generate structural alternatives without succumbing to structural dogmatism, as the liberals and socialists

---

6. Francis Bacon, *Novum Organum*, section 58, originally published in 1620.

of the past often did. To this end, we should seek to design regimes that create ample opportunity for their own revision without requiring crisis, in the form of economic slumps and wars, to serve as the enabling condition of change. Thus, we may want high-energy democracies conducive to the repeated practice of radical reform, market orders that are no longer pinned to a single regime of property and contract, and cultures that radicalize experimentalism in every department of social life.

The larger idea, exemplified by these notions, is the narrowing of the distance between the ordinary moves in a context of arrangements and assumptions that we take for granted and the extraordinary moves by which we challenge and change pieces of this framework. The consequence is to bring our powers to a higher level of capability, to widen the scope of our concerns and ambitions, and to enhance the concentration and intensity of our experience. The acquisition by routine science of features of transformative science is the form that such an ascent can and should take in the advancement of scientific inquiry.

Implications for the Social Sciences, the Normative Public Disciplines, and the Humanities

The chief implication of this program of inquiry for the social sciences is the need to center their work on the development of ideas about structure (the institutional and ideological regimes with commanding influence on social life), structural discontinuity, and structural alternatives. We do so to reestablish the link, which the social sciences have broken, between insight into the actual form of society and imagination of its accessible alternative forms.

We now lack a usable view of structure and structural change. Classical European social theory, best represented by Marx's account of society and history, had such a view of the primacy of structure and structural change. However, it allowed the truth and force of this view to be compromised by its necessitarian assumptions. The social sciences that developed in the aftermath of this social-theoretical tradition freed themselves from these assumptions only by abandoning the structural focus. As a result, they descended, by many distinct paths, into the retrospective rationalization of social and historical experience and broke the link between established reality and its accessible transformations. I have already anticipated—and will explore further in Chapter 7, on politics—how we can hope to escape this detour in the development of our understanding of society and history.

This work cannot now be accomplished solely or chiefly in a detached intellectual space, floating over the separate social sciences, as if it were a philosophical afterthought. Its main form must be its intervention in the practice of each of these disciplines—now pseudo-sciences, given their deficit in this crucial area. Yet social theory can serve as the representative of philosophy and of its revisionist attitude to established arrangements and ideas. It will always remain the exceptional rather than the standard form of the intellectual practice to which this program of inquiry points across the whole range of social and historical studies. But it can nevertheless perform a unique role, which is to represent, in their most ambitious form, the two chief tasks of this program of inquiry for the social sciences.

The first task is to work toward a view of the formative institutional and ideological contexts of social life, the regimes, that does justice to their decisive importance without misrepresenting them as members of a short, closed list of alternative institutional and ideological orders, as indivisible systems, and as objects of imaginary laws of historical change. I take up this task in Chapter 7.

The second task is to dissolve, in each of the social sciences, the monogamous marriage of method to subject matter and to assert the primacy of the latter over the former. The agenda of inquiry is what matters. We must experiment with methods as often and as widely as suits the advancement of that agenda. The consequence over time is not the destruction of the boundaries among disciplines but their weakening. And, with that relativization of this division of intellectual labor, comes the attenuation of the frontier between the specialized social sciences and social theory, which speaks for philosophy and for the transformative imagination.

The implications of this program of inquiry reach beyond the positive social sciences to the normative disciplines of political philosophy and legal thought as well as to the humanities. Legal thought and normative political philosophy are shaped by assumptions about structure and structural alternatives. For example, the theories of distributive justice that exercised the greatest intellectual influence in the closing decades of the twentieth century—in the English-speaking countries and from that base throughout the world—offered a pseudo-philosophical gloss on compensatory redistribution, by tax-and-transfer, in the institutionally conservative social democracies or neoliberal economies of the late twentieth and early twenty-first centuries. Reliance on the established institutional arrangements of democracy and the market shaped their character and limited the potential of their recommendations.

Similarly, during this same historical period and in these same places, the most influential form of legal thought idealized the law as a flawed approximation to a system of impersonal principles and policies responsive to the collective interest and to conceptions of right neutral among sectarian visions of the good. The result was to present the rough-and-ready institutional and ideological settlement of the mid-twentieth century as if were a system with an ideal, albeit incompletely realized, moral and political logic. It was to mispresent the contradictory character of any body of law and empower a cadre of legal notables—judges and jurists—to make law on the pretext of putting the best face on the law. Above all, it was to squander the major comparative advantage of legal thought: its unfulfilled vocation as a practice of institutional imagination that projects alternative institutional possibilities and takes the variations and contradictions of established law as the point of departure for this transformative work.

The humanities share with the arts the effects of agnosticism or despair about the structure of society and its transformation. The parting of the ways between leftism and modernism at the beginning of the twentieth century created the setting for a circumstance that has ever since marked the high culture of the advanced societies. Leftism had a structural vision, albeit one flawed by the reliance of its most influential theoretical guide—Marx's social theory—on the idea that history has a preestablished script. But it continued to rely on a pre-modernist, primitive view of who we are. Modernism explored our ambivalences and inner conflicts but lacked any vision of society and its transformative possibilities.

Without insight into structure and structural alternatives, the humanities descend into a subjectivist adventurism lacking significance for the remaking of society. They teach us to sing in our chains—the chains of an order that we are powerless to reimagine and to remake. Everything that represents our highest hopes in art and religion is banished to private experience: the privatization of the sublime. They hand over public life and public discourse to the cold calculus of marginal gains in efficiency and equity when they do not surrender it to the harsh contest of organized interests.

The aspirations of humanity always remain nailed to the cross of the regimes that shape our life chances and define the terms of our claims on one another. Without a way of understanding them and imagining their transformation, our hopes will continue to be subject to the privatization of the sublime. And the romantic idea that we can be truly ourselves only in those brief interludes in which we shake the hold of established regimes and disrupt the established routines of social life—because spirit is irreconcilable with structure—will continue to misdescribe a political and spiritual failure as an inescapable fate.

Genius Reimagined

An objection to this program of inquiry is that it lacks realism because it supposes the collective pursuit of a task that only genius can carry out. Answering this objection provides an opportunity to place the program in the wider setting of an aspiration that should be shared by every aspect of the work of philosophy, a concern that philosophy in turn shares with democracy, as well as with religion and art: to raise human life up to a higher level of intensity, scope, reach, and power, and to do so in such a way that we rise together.

In the *World as Will and Representation*, Schopenhauer discussed the difference between talent and genius. The talented man, he wrote, is a marksman who hits a target that others cannot hit. The genius is a marksman who hits a target that others cannot see.[7] Genius, Schopenhauer understood, is not about intellectual facility; it is about vision. The program of inquiry that I have sketched in the preceding pages is an effort to deepen the visionary powers of humanity and to do so in a fashion that allows many to share in that deepening rather than leave it as the prerogative of a tiny band of geniuses.

For nineteenth-century romanticism, genius and vision stand in contrast to the tenor of our experience, characterized by the overwhelming predominance of routine and repetition, framed by structures of life and of thought that are left unchanged, unchallenged, and even unseen. Among such routines are the routine practices of the specialized branches of inquiry. The contrast between reform and revolution as the two forms of political activity gives expression to this idea in politics. The contrast between normal science and scientific revolutions gives expression to it in science.

In both instances, the contrast describes something real. There are revolutionary changes in politics and in thought. They are not, however, the primary form of change in either thought or politics. In both, the invocation of the idea of revolution—an anomalous, limiting case—supplies an excuse for all who fail to merit the label genius to resign themselves to a practice that is seen as lacking transformative potential. One way to describe the central aim of this program of inquiry is to say that it seeks to elevate the visionary aspect of our cognitive engagement with the world, and to do so in the interest of our rise to a higher form of life as well as in the interest of the development of our understanding of natural and social reality. Vision should penetrate the routines of inquiry and relativize the contrast between our ordinary moves within a regime of thought and our extraordinary regime-changing moves.

As the Protestant Reformation affirmed the priesthood of all believers, so our cognitive, moral, and political ascent now requires that prophetic powers be diffused within the whole of humanity. Genius,

---

7. Arthur Schopenhauer, *Die Welt as Wille und Vorstellung*, supplements to book 3, section XXXI, originally published in 1844.

vision, and prophecy are different names for the widening, in the domain of our cognitive relation to the world, of our share in the power of transcendence.

What is the subject to which such genius addresses itself? What is the object of the vision? What is the nature of the prophecy? What is the regulative ideal toward which this view of our cognitive empowerment tends? And how does this idea exemplify an experience of genius that can be shared? There are three seemingly distinct but in fact equivalent answers to these related questions. They suggest in what sense genius, vision, and prophetic power can penetrate our practices of inquiry and discourse and become a possession in which many can share.

The first answer has to do with the relation between the phenomena —natural and social—and their transformative variations. We must lift from the natural and social phenomena around us some of their brute facticity—their just-there-ness—and see them in the light of what they can become. Only in this light can we hope to deepen our insight into reality. An understanding that fails to intimate transformation is not an understanding. It is a redescription or a rationalization. But all insight into transformation—especially in the terrain of the accessible possibilities, where we seek to find out what can happen next—is insight into reality.

Thus, inquiry, when it is not a mode of mystification, must be prophetic. Prophecy is not prediction. It is the extension in thought of our primordial experience of discovering what the world is like by acting to mobilize or resist, in our favor, some piece of nature or society. When prophecy extends beyond the horizon of action, it imagines other events and forces that might take the place of the present human agent, provoking change in one or another direction. In action, we both discover and produce transformative possibility.

Prophecy and prediction would be the same thing if the new were impossible, if the set of adjacent possibilities were reduced to one, if the world had no room for the new, as supposed by Laplacian determinism in the past and by the block universe view of the world now. In such a world, there is space for oracles but not for prophecy.

A second answer builds on this thesis. The prophetic and visionary element in the development of our thinking has to do with our recognition of a feature of the world that we encounter: that it perpetually creates the new. It is because of this perpetual emergence of the new that we must reject the spectral idea of the possible. According to this spectral idea, the range of the possible has been forever set; possible states of affairs have every feature of being, except actual existence. They are ghosts waiting behind the curtain for cues to come onto the stage of actuality.

Our idea of the possible is an image of reality seen, as Bergson argued, in a rearview mirror: we continuously adjust it in the light of the new, unaccommodated by an established conception of possibility. And yet—Bergson should have gone on to concede—it is always also a prospective as well as a retrospective image if the new is embodied in a new ordering of natural phenomena. For so long as it lasts and for as far as it goes, such an order sets the limits of the accessible transformations of a part of nature: of what that part of nature can next become. If the image of the possible were not prospective as well as retrospective, the idea of the possible transformations of a phenomenon would be meaningless.[8]

How can it be that we must understand reality by exploring the accessible possible but that at the same time our ideas about the accessible possibilities are forever subject to revision in the light of the new—the new in the world, not simply the new in our ideas about the world? Both things must be true. That they must be true and that they can be true at the same time is something that we cannot avoid recognizing in our study of ourselves, of our societies, and of our history. This truth is manifest in natural history before life, and then even more in life, and then yet more again with the emergence of consciousness, and then with ever mounting force in our historical experience. At last, we conceive the aim of creating institutions and cultures that organize us without imprisoning us and that promise to deliver the perpetual creation of the new. Such institutions do more than bring us to order; they bring us more fully to life.

---

8. Bergson implied as much in his contrived distinction of the prospective virtual from the retrospective possible. See Gilles Deleuze, *Le Bergsonisme*, 1966, pp. 99–100.

We may be tempted to think that this feature of reality, and therefore of the ideas that we need to understand it, is a peculiarity of our human experience and of our place in the world. In the world before us or apart from us, it would have no place. Then we must either embrace the notion of a fundamental disconnection between human and non-human reality (the dualisms discussed and rejected in Chapter 1, on ontology, according to which ours is a kingdom within and kingdom—the outer one constituted on principles opposite to the inner one), or suppose, as Spinoza did and much of contemporary natural and behavioral science has, that the human world is just as alien to the creation of the new as the non-human one.

We have better reason to believe that the perpetual creation of the new, present in our experience, is already foreshadowed in nature before and beyond our human experience. We see it, and we come to want it, intensified. But it was always there in a universe that is indifferent to us but pregnant with possibility, fertile in novelty (although more in some of states and moments than in others), and for that very reason dangerous.

The openness to the new is just another name for what, in our experience, we recognize as transcendence. The prophetic and visionary element in the program of inquiry is, on this account, just this recognition that our transcendence is an accentuation of what happens in the one real world rather than a miraculous exception to the general regime of nature. In this sense, everything in our existence is both the consummation and the renewal of prophecy. Its watchword is: you haven't seen anything yet. Our thinking about the world is visionary and prophetic to the extent that it both elucidates and exemplifies the perpetual creation of the new.

A third answer to the question about the content of the vision and of the prophecy is that it concerns the promise of the ordinary: not as it is but as it might become, in our practices of inquiry as in every aspect of our existence. The ordinary has more promise than the noble: the transvaluation of values taught by Christianity against the established hierarchies of value. Visionary and prophetic power can be broadly spread in humanity, but only if it takes cooperative and collective form rather than appearing as the prerogative of a handful of inspired individuals. Orientation to the future can turn into a way of living in the present and coming more fully into the possession of life. Ordinary men and women will be found to be not so ordinary after all, and we shall find light in the shadowy world of the commonplace.

Our cognitive empowerment—purged of every Promethean delusion of future omniscience and omnipotence, of deathlessness and of clarity about the framework of existence, of final reconciliation with one another and with ourselves, forever denied us—rides on this wave.

A Coda to Epistemology: Art

In this book, art barely figures—not because it has little importance when dealing with the problems that philosophy addresses but because it has too much importance. It is a rival to philosophy: together with religion, the most powerful rival. In an age of half-belief, of the sentimental will to believe, philosophy, when it remains ambitious and claims to show us the way, becomes a successor (among several) rather than a rival to religion. But the ancient struggle of philosophy with art never ceases: art, like philosophy, deals with everything. Although it cannot become didactic without jeopardizing its power, it too has implications for the way we understand ourselves and live.

The contest between philosophy and art, however, has been lopsided. Art has usually disregarded philosophy, whatever the philosophical interests of individual artists. But philosophy has always been anxious about its relation to art. No wonder: if it retains anything of its old ambitions even after having abandoned the pretense to be a super-science, its claims outrun its seductions.

For philosophy to reduce art to the condition of one more subject of its work is for it to pretend to a power that its lacks. I nevertheless conclude this chapter on epistemology with some propositions about art because to omit them would be to be risk misinterpretation of my epistemological argument.

To restrict our cognitive engagement with the world to science, or even to our practices of reasoned argument, would be to form a false view of the resources available to us to investigate reality. Such a confinement of the road to insight would not be science; it would be scientism. And scientism stands to science as militarism stands to the army: as an overreach that threatens to pervert rather than to magnify what it does, by alleging a baseless prerogative.

Nothing in science justifies a bid for superiority over art in making sense of our experience and exploring its transformative possibilities. Such a bid must rest on a metaphysical claim. That claim has no place in an epistemology that is open, against the background of a temporal naturalism, to both the progression of our understanding and the diversity of its forms. Art serves in this coda as the most salient and significant example of such diversity—another road to reality, incommensurable with the roads that this chapter has considered.

Art has a dual nature. It is about the world—the only world that there is—in its present reality and accessible variations. Even music, an art beyond language, and therefore in some sense beyond ideas, is, I argue further ahead, about something fundamental in the world and in our experience of it.

But art is also the creation of another world—a world that we imagine and invent in the medium of each art. In this second life, art is the creation of artifacts that stand as proxies for the world or for something in the world. The proxy may be tangible and visual, or spoken or written, or heard, by outer or inner hearing, and with or without enactment or performance. The immediate object of art is then the tangible or intangible artifact itself. But the ulterior object remains the one reality that we face—in nature, in society, or within each of us—and our relation to it.

Mathematics offers a simulacrum of the world, wiped clean of time and phenomenal particularity. It can bring us deeper into the real, both despite and because of its departure from reality. So it is with the arts. Their tangible and intangible artifacts are invented worlds of their own. The work of art commands and seduces us to lose ourselves in these invented worlds as if they were the real thing, and in a sense they are. Yet what goes on in them and in our relation to them can change our understanding of the one real world and of our place in it.

This dual nature of art—the fact that, like mathematics, it is about both the world as well as about itself—supplies a basis on which to begin understanding the history of art. A principle of stylistic change in art is the history of world views—the general conception of reality that is predominant in the society and culture in which the art is practiced. These world views are organized around fundamental themes that are at once metaphysical and social. A feature of such world views is, for example, the degree to which they accept conflict and contradiction as features of reality and as conditions of our ascent.

The sequence of styles in each art has a second source: a succession of stylistic vocabularies. Each such vocabulary must be at home in the specific medium of the art. The transformative variations of the real world are achieved with difficulty. They draw blood by the resistance that established reality opposes to them. But the variations of a stylistic canon encounter no such resistance. The art object has no presence in the world. It is a fabrication, and it offers little resistance to meddling by the fabricator.

This simple fact explains the degradation of styles. A stylistic vocabulary is played out until it is exhausted. Nothing opposes this succession of possible expressions of the style. The absence of effective resistance is the death of the style.

From these facts there results the heterogeneity of each artistic style. On the one hand, it is the expression of a world view—focused even on very general and abstract themes such as the way in which a certain artistic vision manages conflict and contradiction—and its implications for the organization of space (in the visual arts), the manifestation of character and its struggle with fate (in literature), and the presentation of consonance and dissonance (in music). On the other hand, a style is also the expression of a vocabulary—of a set of artistic moves and tropes—that may quickly run their course. So whereas the first source of style has the power to endure, presenting challenges to vision and understanding that may continue to resonate long after the style to which it was married has fallen into disuse, the second source of style is, by its nature, ephemeral and self-destructive, and carries the world view down in the wake of its self-destruction.

It may even happen that a crisis of confidence in the power of art to organize itself as a style results in the creation of an anti-style:

of a vocabulary in the visual, literary, or musical art that renounces altogether the attempt to present a coherent message. Then the fabricated realities of the artist may turn against themselves and deny the principle of art, which is the creation of a surrogate world, making explicit the possibilities of experience that lurk, undefined, in the world of reality. This message of negation may be like a flight of hope from the world, a disbelief in the power of art to evoke and to transfigure.

From the duality of art—that it is about both the world, the only world there is, and itself—there follows a duality in each of the arts. Each of them is ultimately about an aspect of our existence in the one real world. But each of them reaches this aspect of our existence through the application of its unique resources and in the vocabulary of a style suited to its medium.

For each of the arts, when it is confident in its powers, the intended goal is a particular form of happiness. Thus, art has been justly described as a promise of happiness. And the promise is to be kept by marshalling the special power that each art possesses: the power distinguishing it from all our other activities.

The visual and plastic arts promise to give us back the world that we perceive, with the bodies with which we are born. The happiness that they promise us is the happiness of our embodiment in an organism with a certain apparatus for seeing.

Civilization is a long trip away from the visionary immediacy of such a happiness: the happiness of a being who delights in the revelations that his eyes bring him. The two dominant traditions in the world history of philosophy, the philosophy of the timeless one and the philosophy of deep structure, deny or demote the reality of what our eyes see—the one by affirming the illusory or epiphenomenal character of the distinctions and changes that we perceive; the other by identifying the touchstone of reality with invisible and atemporal constituents and regularities of nature.

Where is the world of the child who awoke to the radiance of a reality made entirely of particulars and of the impressions that they caused in him? To be happy would be to inhabit one's body and its visual equipment without suspicion and to delight in what the body shows us.

The means by which the visual arts aim for this condition of happiness in the world is something peculiar to this art and to its creation of special objects that embody its promise of happiness. The means is an art that finds depth in surface. The depth is not beyond the surface; it lies in the surface. How the surface of things is to be approached depends on the resources and potential of each style. But in every instance the surface will yield its secrets if it is approached inquisitively. Nothing will be hidden from the onlooker, except what he chooses to hide from himself.

The visual arts—painting, drawing, and sculpture—engage us with the splendors of the world: of its sensuous forms, shapes, and colors, in their temporal and phenomenal particularity. Their premise is the depth of the surface. In philosophy and science, we move away from the visible surface of reality in the hope of revelations that will allow us to make sense of the surface. Along the way, we risk losing the world of phenomenal particulars, the world that we see.

The visual arts promise to give us the manifest world back. They do so by never distancing themselves from it in the first place. In this sense, they are the inverse of mathematics, which gives us the world without particulars or time.

The individual, wrote Aristotle, is ineffable; the particular slips through the sieve of every categorical scheme. But in the visual arts, the particular is the alpha and the omega, and the question is how it relates to a larger truth.

The visual arts are comic or tragic according to whether they express or deny that what is most real, valuable, and seductive can be fully expressed without sacrifice of reality. If what is human can be fully expressed in the quivering body and the objects that surround it, we can call the work comic or romantic: there is no distance between the human reality and its incarnate expression. If, on the contrary, the human is stylized, or transfigured on the screen of the sublime, and the infinite is projected and remote to us, there is a distance between the infinite self and its finite longings in the world. Here comic equals romantic, and tragic equals classical, but not in the sense in which these epithets are commonly used in art history. Classical is here not simply the art of the Greeks and Romans; it is the art of the sublime at cross-purposes to our ordinary humanity: for example, in Tiepolo's ceiling frescoes in Wurzburg. And romantic is more the painting of Rembrandt and late Titian than the painting of Delacroix. Much of the romantic painting of the nineteenth century undermines the expression of the particular by its servitude to tropes and formulas, whereas the portraits and self-portraits of Rembrandt achieve the romantic hope: the portrayal of unique and individual spirit in the tremulous, imperfect flesh.

Classical art is always sad even when it beckons with the prospect of our ascent to the ideal. It gives us back a sensuous world but not the sensuous world that we in fact possess. Romantic art is always joyous even when it suggests the sorrows of the mortal creature, to whose spirit it gives luscious form. The human being is the ultimate subject of both classical and romantic art: the infinite that must be expressed in either actual sensual form in romantic art or in idealized and remote sensual form in classical art. Both find depth in surface. But for classical art the deep surface is removed from the habitual occasions of life; for romantic art, it lives amid our longings and sorrows.

If Schopenhauer were right about the will-lessness of art, art could never wave Prospero's wand; its representations would never hold transformative promise, other than to liberate us from insatiable desire and the will to power, restoring us to an experience undisturbed by the temptations and sufferings of agency. It would be otherwise impotent.

To enjoy transformative power, the visual arts must be confident in their own power: the power to give us back the world that we are always losing to the abstractions of science and politics. It is the power to restore to us the visionary immediacy of the child, in the higher form that the child never had, the form that gives us the prophetic in the sensual.

The higher-order comic element in the visual arts is their confidence in representing the phenomenal and temporal world with such force that the representation changes our experience and arouses in us the hope that we will not lose that world. It will not recede from us, and its recession will not foretell our annihilation.

☙

In literature, we have a completely different art form. The happiness that it promises us is not chiefly of the person isolated in his body: it is of the person living a life among individual selves and struggling with his fate: his fate as a person in society and his fate as a dying organism. Literature engages us in a conversation about the variations of personal and social experience, beginning from where we are: the self in a moment. Its effect is to rob the actual self that each of us is—fixed at a certain place in the social division of labor and a certain moment in our life trajectory—of its brute facticity, of its just-there-ness, and to surround that actual course of life with a series of variations, of possible lives and possible experience. Thus, an exchange takes place: the actual life begins to seem like a variation on these possible human experiences, and the possible lives, narrated in the literary work, borrow some of the weight of actuality.

To understand what makes us so happy in the possession of these narratives of possible experience, we must recognize the poisonous character of fate: the singular direction taken by our existence under the constraints of our social and genetic endowment and of the mixture of luck and misfortune in our lives. Literature relieves us of this sense of fatefulness by the hidden exchange that it promotes between the traits of actual and possible experience. Its narratives may come from a stock of epic or sacred plots that we—readers or listeners—could not easily imagine ourselves enacting. But the exchange between actual and possible experience nevertheless takes place in a nether world in which we shed our actual identities and assume the shapeless human identity that took one or another form in these narratives. For once, we are everyone. And our variations do not bear the resistance and sorrow that beset our attempts to resist fate in the actual world.

Literature gives us this happiness by engaging us in a conversation about our relation to other people, to society, and to ourselves. The conversation takes a comic or tragic turn according to whether it describes a series of transformations that reconcile the contradictory requirements of selfhood, or on the contrary exhibits these contradictions as inalterable features of our situation and shows how they can bring about our downfall.

In the tragic work of literature, we have both sides of a contradictory experience displayed. We can resist becoming half of a human being. Our ambivalence toward other people is portrayed remorselessly: each connection with another person brings a forestate of subjugation and loss of personal distinction. Our inability to be free in society is made manifest: we participate in the social order and pay, for our engagement, the terrible price of servitude, and we are never more servile than when we pretend to discharge a heroic office. Our incapacity to develop a coherent way of being in the world without surrendering to it—and having this rigidified version of the person turn into a surrogate for the living, spontaneous self, an idol of our own making—becomes plain for all to see.

In the tragic work, the author may depict a world in which we miss one another, and destruction results from our failures of recognition and of love. He may explore the expressions and consequences of our reciprocal ambivalence. He may show us seeking from one another what no one can give to another human being: an unconditional assurance of one's place in the world, acceptance untainted by failures of recognition.

Literature and drama show us dealing with these multiple rifts in our experience—in our relation to others, in our engagement in society and history, in our dealing with ourselves—in the setting of our enigmatic existence: on the way to death, unable to discern the ground of our existence and of reality (unless we accept some secular or sacred narrative of salvation), and bound to the wheel of insatiable desire, seeking (although we may not know it) the infinite in inadequate forms unless we can find it in another human or supra-human being. The literary work may show us as we really are: vacillating and confused, crushed by our social and historical fate, or the fate of the rigidified form of the self—the character consumed by acts of false transcendence and misplaced faith, or struggling to find a way to live through the medium of his attachments and engagements, while he plays a chosen or unchosen part in a larger historical narrative not of his own making.

When the work of literature is tragic it nevertheless gives us, in our daydreaming against fate, a picture of the whole of our experience.

And the comic resolution, missing in the experience of the protagonists, is nevertheless present in the relation of the author to his readers. In his work he affirms a belief in the possibility of a discourse that unites him with his invisible or even unborn readers and that promises the revelation of human truth, not just an exchange of self-projections and misunderstandings.

It is an untested communication because it is deficient in reciprocity. Even if the literary work is performed, as drama or epic narrative, before a live audience, they have only a derivative engagement. Neither they nor the author are in intimate jeopardy. The truth is proclaimed in a space far from danger, and filtered through the formal seductions of the literary work of art. The work allows us to relive, without actually reliving, a life in which we miss one another. By reliving it, we come closer to the truth about ourselves than we may be able to do in the middle of our suffering and struggles in society.

The literary work of art is comic insofar as it shows a possibility of resolution in these rifts of selfhood. The sign of resolution, in whatever domain of experience and to whatever degree, is another form of life and of consciousness. Such breakthroughs may be achieved through love and searching, or by the grace of forces, profane or sacred, that escape our control. And they may be represented either as a restoration (as in the ancient genre of the romance) or as the creation of something new, which allows those who experience it to come more fully into the possession of life.

The two questions decisive for the possibility of such a resolution are the same that were decisive for the romance: the possibility of love and the availability of an ennobling quest—of a work that justifies the expense of life.

The third art is music. It presents special problems, for it is at once the most physical and the most philosophical of the arts. It engages us in a conversation about whether we can feel and understand more than we can put into words. Can music outreach the boundaries of language and, to the extent that there is no thought without language, of thought itself?

This must be an art of peculiarly philosophical significance if our conception of philosophy is that it works at the boundary between the sayable and the unsayable, the thinkable and the unthinkable. For where philosophy cannot go—beyond that boundary—music may nevertheless be able to reach. Thus, music is the art that presents to us most directly the question of the relation of our transcendence to our finitude. In music, it seems, we outreach ourselves and apprehend more than we can express in words.

What is strange is that this ultra-philosophical art depends on a physical characteristic of our embodied self: the sense of hearing. There are sounds that we cannot hear, and of those that we can hear, some will be barely audible or may be heard only as the background humming of the universe in which we find ourselves.

The art of music promises a special form of happiness: that through this sense of sound and of hearing we will have an enlarged experience of life and be subjected to experiences of arousal and exultation that may defy all our powers of reasoning and interpretation. Nevertheless, we are happy: happy to enjoy this surfeit of susceptibility to arousal, happy to ride the wave of incantation, happy to be larger than our minds and our language.

The means by which music achieves this effect is the special province of its art: the interplay between consonance and dissonance. All other aspects of music—rhythm, melody, harmony, and counterpoint—are subsidiary to this master device.

Let us immediately face the problem with which the centrality of this interplay between consonance and dissonance presents us. There are no sounds—at least no sounds on the pentatonic scale—that are inherently dissonant. What is heard as dissonant in one period of music history may be heard in the next period as consonant: dissonance and consonance are always relative to each other and to an accepted canon of hearing.

If dissonance is heard as a disturbance of consonance, it makes consonant sound more interesting and seductive, without disturbing it to the point of destruction. We are entranced. Consonance without disturbance and variety would soon bore and repel us. But if we hear dissonance as a complication of consonance, and of melody and even rhythm, we are able to delight in the musical argument. We are saved from the sonic equivalent of staring.

What is it that we hear in this interplay between consonance and dissonance that casts further light on the special character of music's promise of happiness? We hear the promise of an association in experience between continuity and novelty, between repetition and transformation.

Repetition marks our experience in every domain of existence. Its chief expression is routine: the recurrent moves that we make within a framework of arrangements and assumptions that we take for granted. A defining conceit of romanticism (to the criticism of which I return at different moments in the argument of this book) is the contradiction between spirit and structure. According to this romantic conceit, we are fully human only in those interludes in which we temporarily shake the hold of routine on our experience.

Kierkegaard was right to remark that the war against repetition is a war against life. It is against the background of tradition, structure, and routine that innovation becomes possible. The mistake of the romantics was a mistake of despair. They despaired of changing the relation between structure and spirit. Structure is not only reimagined but also remade to become more hospitable to spirit: by allowing more space for variety and contradiction and by facilitating its own transformation. Spirit is pushed forward to the vanguard of experience. In the anti-romantic understanding of this romantic trope, spirit is another word for transcendence: for the failure of any structure definitively to accommodate us.

Music translates this struggle over repetition and disruption into an interplay between consonance and dissonance. The history of music is in large part the history of our expanding ability to hear dissonance as consonance and thereby to push out the frontier of the interplay between them. What some hear as dissonance, others hear as consonance. But no one can hear all sound as consonant or be indifferent to the distinction between consonance and dissonance, even though this distinction exists partly in the music and partly in the hearing of it.

In many conventional styles of music, including the so-called classical style that reached its apogee in Europe between 1770 and 1820, the difference between consonance and dissonance is both subtle and moveable. It is signaled by a sound difference that anyone unfamiliar with how this music sounds might miss: for example, the greater difference of pitch between notes in the minor keys. And this difference, already so limited, was covered over, in the immediately subsequent period, by the use that Wagner and others made of chromaticism.

The tragic element in the musical art work emerges when dissonance overwhelms consonance. Stylistic experimentation in music may always lead some to hear as dissonance what others hear—and the composer intended—as complementarity between consonance and dissonance. But at some point even the most practiced musical ear ceases to be able to translate unfamiliar sound into recognizable consonance. Dissonance takes over. The sound of disruption ceases to serve as a widening of the musical field on which we hear dissonance as an enrichment of consonance rather than as an attempt to undermine it.

This turn was prefigured by an ambiguity much earlier in the history of Western music. Even in the classical style of European music, music in the minor keys was heard, at the time of its composition, as an intimation of disaster. Its ambiguity helps account for the special quality of its fascination: the musical equivalent of living on a knife's edge between the improvement of consonance and its disruption.

When the pentatonic scale is left behind and music becomes atonal, the triumph of dissonance and of the tragic element in music becomes complete. Whatever the interest of the musical argument—and it may have many other claims to interest—we can no longer hear it as a promise of the reestablishment of consonance on a wider basis. And looking from music to existence, we can no longer take the music as a prophecy of the marriage of routine and novelty, structure and spirit.

Can we feel and even understand more than we can think and put into words? Can music outreach the boundaries of language and, to the extent that there is no thought without language, of thought itself? If we did not feel that it does, or that it might, if we did not respond to a sequence of sounds as if they admitted us to a celebration of powers and truths that none of us can adequately voice after the celebration ends, we would not return to it each time with Nietzsche's conviction that without music life would be a mistake.

The outcome is comic if we can, and tragic if we cannot, feel and know more through music than we can put in words. When we exhaust our ability to push outward the limits of our finitude, we find in music a second chance. Or do we?—protests the skeptic. Does such a hope mistake our susceptibility to be aroused through sound, as we are by each of our other senses, for the revelation that it cannot offer? What we cannot put adequately in words, the skeptic continues, we cannot truly think, and what we cannot think we should not mistake for discovery—other than the discovery of what moves us.

The proximity of music to philosophy, its rivalry with philosophy, arises from the facts that these enigmas address. Once philosophy abandons the pretense of being a super-science, but also rejects, as unworthy, service as an arsenal of argumentative and analytical skills, it becomes an attempt to continue thinking at the frontier of the almost unthinkable and unsayable. As it approaches this boundary, philosophy meets music.

3

The Human Condition: Becoming More Human by Becoming More Godlike

The Hinge of Philosophy

Thou art the thing itself. The central subject of philosophy and the chief concern of this work is the human condition: our situation in the world—and what we should make of it. What we should make of our situation means how we should understand it: the topic of theoretical philosophy—ontology (as natural philosophy and social theory) and epistemology (as the theory of inquiry). What we should make of it also means what we should do about it: the topic of practical philosophy—ethics (as an approach to the conduct of life) and politics (as a program for the organization of society).

Thus, a view of the human condition is the hinge of philosophy. Theoretical and practical philosophy lie on either side and relate to it in different ways.

In ontology we ask what the world is really like. If our view of our situation clashes with our understanding of what the world is really like, one of the two must be mistaken. The views of reality that have been dominant in the worldwide history of philosophy—the philosophy of deep structure and the philosophy of the timeless one—conflict with the understanding of our situation that I defend here. Indeed, they are irreconcilable with many elements of our ordinary experience and of our action-oriented discourse, with its characteristic focus on the human person as an agent. They clash with our experience by dismissing or discounting the reality of time and by undermining the reality, and consequently the value, of our engagements and connections. They depict a world in which true novelty is impossible (in the philosophy of deep structure) or insubstantial (in the philosophy of the timeless one).

The successive dualisms that have shaped modern Western philosophy—between nature and grace, between physical and mental stuff, between the phenomenal and the noumenal, and between natural and human history—have dealt with this contradiction by seeking to justify a human exception: Spinoza's kingdom within a kingdom. In so doing, however, they have multiplied baseless, mysterious exemptions from the general regime of nature.

In epistemology we ask how we can and do make sense of the world and of our situation within it. The significance of an epistemology shows up in the agenda of inquiry that it implies. If the history of epistemology is a history of mistakes, that is because the philosophies of knowledge that have commanded the greatest influence have misrepresented the human condition. They have misrepresented it by falsifying the relation between our finitude and our transcendence in our cognitive engagement with reality.

Practical philosophy—ethics and politics—has a more intimate relation to ideas about the human condition than does theoretical philosophy. Theoretical philosophy must lay a basis on which we can understand ourselves. Our understanding of ourselves and of our situation in the world must inform our approach to the conduct of life as well as our projects for the organization of society. Otherwise, that approach and these projects would suit a being other than us. But the relation is also reciprocal: when we choose a way of living or of ordering our relations to one another in society we also choose to develop our humanity in a particular direction.

Running through the ideas about the human condition presented in this chapter is the major theme of this book: the dialectic of finitude and transcendence. We are beings who are shaped by history and context but who contain more, by way of possible experience, than any history can explain or any context can accommodate. Everything in our experience points beyond itself.

The core subject of ontology is how the workings of nature can have a place for a being with such powers and limitations. The major theme of epistemology is how to grasp and develop the understanding that is available to such a being in such a world. The central topic of ethics is the choice of a way of living for the context-shaped and context-transcending being who we are in a world that is what it is rather than something else—a contingent world in which the new can happen. The fundamental concern of politics is to arrange social life in a way that develops our faculties of transcendence without denying the reality of our finitude.

One of the many expressions of our finitude is that although we may have grounds for preferring one approach to the conduct of life to another, such grounds are always inconclusive. The question of how to live is the only question that no one can leave unanswered; he will answer it by the way he lives. Yet although we have reasons as well as influences and constraints in choosing how to live, the reasons are always inadequate to the weight of the choice.

Another expression of our finitude is the absence of any natural way of organizing society: an ordering of social life that supports all the forms of experience that we have reason to value and all the ways of empowering ourselves that we have reason to seek. How should we organize society and shape the relations among societies organized under the shield of states given that no ordering of social life can be neutral among conceptions of the good or of the direction in which best to develop our humanity? And how can our answer to this question recognize our individual and collective power to envision, create, and value more than any one order can allow or support?

I consider the human condition from two distinct but complementary perspectives. One perspective is that of the irreparable flaws in our situation: our groundlessness and mortality—the chief expressions of our finitude—and the endless work of insatiable desire, of restless imagination and of rebellion against the belittlement to which, in society, we always remain subject in our never-ending attempt to loosen the constraints on the expression of our transcendence.

The other perspective from which I develop a view of the human condition is that of the requirements for our experience of personality or selfhood. These requirements—in the relation of the self to other people, to a particular society and culture, and to itself—are contradictory. To be free, to come more fully into the possession of life, as the finite but transcendent beings who we are, we must be able to connect with other people without paying for that connection the price of subjugation or of loss of personal distinction. We must be able to engage in a social and cultural world without surrendering to that world. And we must be able to develop a coherent way of being without allowing that way of being to harden into a mummy—a rigidified version of the self—within which each of us suffocates and dies many small deaths.

An ordering of life in society can attenuate these contradictions but it cannot overcome or suppress them. What politics fails to achieve in its long historical time each of us must somehow accomplish in his brief biographical time on pain of failing to die only once.[1]

The plan of this chapter is simple. I begin by discussing the incurable defects in the human condition and their significance for the way in which we understand the dialectic between finitude and transcendence in our experience and deal with it. Later in the chapter I explore the human condition from the other standpoint, that of the conflicting requirements of personality. This second look shows in what sense we may hope to change the relation of transcendence to finitude in our experience, not just to understand it.

Between these two steps of the argument, I discuss the two principal attempts in the history of belief to deny the reality of the incurable defects in the human condition: the narrative of creation and redemption in the Semitic monotheisms, especially as exemplified by Christianity; and the philosophy/theology of universal union and renunciation—the creed and program of the mystical countercurrents within those same religions—seen now less as a metaphysic (the philosophy of the timeless one) than as another road to salvation. This road is an alternative approach to the rescue also promised by Christianity and its sister religions: salvation from death and darkness.

---

1. For an account of the human being focusing neither on the irreparable flaws in the human condition nor on the contradictory requirements of selfhood but on our passions and their message, see my book *Passion: An Essay on Personality*, 1984. It is my "treatise on human nature."

What can we hope for if we conclude, as I argue we must, that despite their riches of insight and their immense influence on the spiritual history of mankind, neither of these traditions deserve now to guide us in dealing with the human condition? Our hope need not depend on illusion. To emerge chastened and strengthened, however, it must risk destruction.

A view of the human condition, represented from these two complementary perspectives, is not the same thing as an account of human nature. To present a view of our situation—of its irreparable flaws and insuperable contradictions—is not to offer an account of who we essentially are. There are fatal objections to any such view; nothing in my argument presupposes such an account.

We cannot divide the attributes of humanity into two classes: those that are universal and eternal and those that are variable and circumstantial. Any such division contradicts the workings of nature in a world in which everything changes sooner or later. It contradicts as well the social and historical character of all our experience. There is nothing in that experience that is not susceptible to modification by society and culture: everything—even our most intimate experiences, say of jealousy or despair—is on the line in history. For that reason, the idea, central to classical liberal political philosophy, that a free society can distinguish the sectarian good from the impersonal right and establish institutions that are neutral among visions of the direction for humanity is false; every institutional order tilts the scales, encouraging some varieties of experience and discouraging others. The claim of neutrality always serves the opposite of what its adherents profess to support; it entrenches a particular ordering of social life against criticism and revision.

Nevertheless, the false and dangerous idea of neutrality bears kinship to an idea that is justified and even indispensable: an ordering of society should be open to a wide range of contradictory life. Above all, it should be readily corrigible in the light of experience. Openness and corrigibility are the legitimate counterparts to the illegitimate idea of neutrality.

On the other hand, however, we are not a plastic clay to be reshaped readily and at will. We change only with difficulty and at the margin. It is harder to change an individual than to change a country. To change a country, it suffices to be a statesman, supported by a movement. To change a person, it is necessary to be a prophet and a savior.

The dialectic of transcendence and finitude, running as a central theme through all human existence, does not contradict this rejection of an essentialist conception of human nature. Our natural finitude is expressed in our resistance to transformation and in the influence of history and context; our transcendence is expressed in our ability to resist that influence and to create ways of organizing society and of living that limit the power of the past to shape the future and of the established order of society and culture to inhibit the further ascent of an individual agent or of a people.

Thinking about the human condition can best begin in the recognition of the unspeakable mystery that surrounds us on every side. To live in the light of the truth and to approach the sacred flame of life, we should acknowledge this mystery, and accept its terrors as well as its wonders, rather than try to explain it away.

Impenetrable Darkness: The Amazing Situation

Philosophy, Plato said, begins in wonder. What should most amaze us is not any single part of reality; it is our situation in the world and the world itself. Much of the history of philosophy and religion has passed in attempts to explain away what is inexplicable about our circumstance. This conversion of darkness into false clarity denies us the benefit of the amazement and lays a basis for our moral and political endeavors that is tainted by self-deception. Whatever consolation the false clarity may give us is poisonous.

What should amaze us, and what we are unable to make sense of, is the coexistence in our experience of two ways of encountering the world and of comprehending our condition. Call them the internal and the external views. They are not, however, just contrasting conceptions; they are two sides of our experience. The elusive and troubling character of the relation between them is rooted in our natural condition as the finite beings who we are, with the powers that we possess.

We are conscious: that is to say, we are aware of being alive. Our awareness of being alive includes the sense of being embodied. We cannot view the vicissitudes of the body as if they were alien to us; they penetrate every aspect of the experience of being alive and it is through them that we encounter the world.

All around us lies the world. Pieces of it strike us with their impressions whether or not we go in search of them; the manifest world makes itself present to us. Later we may acquire ideas—scientific or philosophical—that may lead us to doubt the testimony of the senses—even to doubt them radically. But even these ideas would make little sense to us if we did not have, as part of the awareness of being alive, the experience of the world making itself present to us in ways that we can learn to disregard or reinterpret only with difficulty.

The assurance of being alive and embodied in a world that makes itself present, as light does, is sustained and deepened by the engagement with the real that also forms part of the awareness of being alive. It is by acting in the world—by facing resistance and seeking to produce effects—that we confirm and strengthen both our awareness of being alive and our experience of the reality of the manifest world. The work of the imagination, anticipated in even the most rudimentary moves of perception, shadows our engagement.

The awareness of being alive in a world that makes itself selectively present to us and that we begin to understand by imagining it changed finds further reinforcement in our encounters with other people and with all sentient life. Both our need for others—of their help, recognition, and love—and our fear of them—of the countless tangible and intangible dangers that they create for us—inhabit our consciousness to such an extent that our recognition of this need and of these dangers becomes inseparable from the sense of being alive.

This consciousness of living incarnate in a particular body and at a particular time and place, and of being incomplete, in need of other people, is from early in life associated with a certainty that our discoveries and convictions may challenge or qualify but can never wholly suppress. There is a world that extends outward from each of us—the embodied person on the way to death.

Each of us learns early on that he is not the center of the world and that some form of annihilation awaits him, even if it is an exchange of one state of being for another. He is made to discover that he is in the hands of fate or of chance, that he is not indestructible or invulnerable but on the contrary subject at any moment to dissolution, and that, with this dissolution, it is not only his own existence that will disappear but the whole world that was represented in the theater of his mind and that will never exist again, just as it never existed before.

This consciousness of finitude forms part of the awareness of being alive and precedes any philosophical or religious teaching to which the human agent may be exposed. It requires no more than the observation of what happens to all of us. The evidence of our vulnerability and dissolution may be radically reinterpreted but it can never be successfully disguised. In every age and place, and notwithstanding what any savior or seer teaches, it is the open secret that leaves us hapless and abashed, shivering and astonished in the dark.

The revelation of finitude, which enters deeply, against all opposition by feel-good philosophy and religion, into our awareness of being alive, endures side by side with another part of our consciousness. Life surprises. Its power to surprise is no mere accidental feature of life. It is the tangible and immediate expression of our transcendence. One of its signs is its surfeit over structure: its power to outreach structure, the ordered regimes of society and culture, of thought and character, that shape our experience but can never shape it completely or definitively. Another sign is our power, as both collectivities and as individuals, to alter the force of path dependency—the influence of the past on the future—and to resist an apparent fate. Thus, transcendence appears in our experience in the charming disguise of spontaneity as well as in the menacing and hieratic costume of prophetic non-conformity.

The constraints of need, oppression, and dogma, which have narrowed throughout history the room for maneuver open to the ordinary man and woman, may seem to make of this power of transgression, recognized in only its showiest forms, the prerogative of an elite of privilege or of heroic defiance. Yet it is present in every corner of the common experience of everyone who has lived, even in chains, with a trace of agency: present in the experience of our cravings and perceptions and of our discoveries and disappointments in life among other people, as well as in the activity of thought or the contests of society and politics.

It is there with us wherever the awareness of being alive survives. Even when established belief in science or politics teaches the opposite, it makes it hard for us to see ourselves, from within our experience, as mere instances of a collective category or products of a set of historical forces. We may be weak, subject to fortune, and predestined to annihilation. But we also experience, as part of being alive, a fecundity that meets us in experience even when we determine to turn away from it in thought.

All this begins to compose the first, internal side of our situation in the world: the substance of our awareness of being alive. It coexists with a view from the outside. The subject matter of this external view is not what it feels like to be alive. It is what, regardless of this feeling, our situation in the world actually is. The coexistence of that situation, as we can best understand it, with what it is like to feel alive—the experience of consciousness—is what ought most to amaze us, and amaze us to a degree that goes beyond any specific fear or perplexity. It is too terrible to be compared to any common fear and too puzzling to be placed alongside our ordinary enigmas.

On this external view—the view of what the world is like that is suggested by common observation as well as by the best science available to us in our time—reality no longer appears as if organized around each of us. The awareness of being alive—consciousness—has already come with intimations of finitude, inseparable from our condition as natural beings subject to the vicissitudes of the body and their expression in the changes of our mental experience. Now, when we consider our situation as figures in a world in which each of us plays a brief, minute, and accidental part, a different picture emerges. The development and details of this picture will depend on the range of our experience and knowledge, as well as on the advance of science in our time, our mastery of that science, and our position in its internal debates. But something of this external view is open to anyone, anywhere, anytime, who has not allowed his experience of nature and of life to be replaced (rather than corrected and deepened) by a faith that promises us some form of liberation from the consequences of our finitude. (Later in this chapter I discuss the two most influential examples of such a faith.)

When we consider our situation in this way, we find that nature is indifferent to our concerns. It has given us life but only to decree our destruction—as individuals and probably as a species as well. Its workings take place on a scale vastly larger than that of our experience.

In this world so alien to us, everything changes sooner or later, including change itself, although the philosophy of deep structure and the traditions of the sciences that this philosophy informs deny it. Time, whose sway has been questioned by the philosophy of deep structure and by the tradition of fundamental physics, envelops everything that is real.

We occupy a little corner of the universe—a planet that orbits around our star—ignorant of whether other life forms may have arisen in other parts of our universe. The life sciences have taught us that every species, like our planet and the universe itself, has a history. The practice of the life forms is that the individual dies so that the species may live. At any given time on our planet, as Schopenhauer reminded us, countless animals are tearing each other apart in an effort to live a little longer. But we animals all die, after such struggles, anyway.

The appearance of life, and thus our own appearance on this earth of ours, may seem extraordinarily improbable. On the other hand, the eventual extinction of our species seems likely if only because our star and planet themselves, like everything else in the world, are destined for destruction. Our species might prolong its existence by escaping from our precarious and transient place in the universe, provided that our murderous conflicts do not put an end to humanity before then.

The extreme improbability of our existence has encouraged some to argue that we cannot be as accidental and inconsequential as we seem to be on the fragmentary evidence before us. The universe must have somehow been arranged, or have evolved, to produce beings who can understand it—although an embarrassment to this idea is that we have not understood it and, it seems, never will. In the meantime, despite our curiosity about the existence of sentient and thinking life in other parts of the universe, we are left, for the moment, with the sobering conclusion that there might be no one here but us.

Our insight into the workings of nature will doubtless continue to grow. Future generations may, if our species survives long enough, recall our own beliefs about those workings with bemusement. But to understand how something came out of nothing, or why the world exists at all, and to look into the beginning and the end of time, we would need an understanding radically different from the one with which our natural history has equipped us or that the machines we design can provide at our behest. We will not achieve such an understanding just because we want to. It is much more likely that, so long as our species survives, we will continue to go to our graves unenlightened about the foundation of reality or the ground of being and existence.

One of the effects of our natural history has been to equip us with minds capable of abstracting from the immediate context of action. The ability to develop ideas about structured wholes and bundles of relations is the faculty that underlies our logical and mathematical reasoning. Through such reasoning we make a simulacrum of the world from which time and phenomenal particularity, omnipresent in nature, have been removed. It is the very remoteness of these ideas from the temporal particulars of the natural world that makes them so powerful an instrument of inquiry into that same world. Thanks to its generality and versatility, we can think about relations among pieces of reality in many different ways.

This instrument is so powerful, and has so many uses, that its possession can induce us to embrace a twofold illusion: that mathematical and logical reasoning offers us a shortcut to the understanding of reality, and that its distinctive characteristics—its banishment of time and phenomenal particularity—are features of nature itself. The most important instance of the second illusion is the idea of timeless laws of nature, written in the atemporal language of mathematics.

Our ability to understand the actual by subsuming it under a range of accessible states of affairs represents a yet more basic and general example of our power to exceed the context—a natural expression of transcendence in our cognitive engagement with reality. Nothing, however, justifies us in seeing in this ability a promise that we will be able to unlock what Leibniz described as the ultimate origin of reality or to discern the ground of being and existence.

When we consider this aspect of our situation—the aspect that has to do with our cognitive engagement with the world—from the external point of view, as minute, marginal protagonists in natural history, we find ourselves forced to accept a causal picture of our perceptual experience. That experience, into which we must ultimately translate all our conjectures about the workings of nature, is the product of the ramshackle perceptual and cognitive equipment with which the natural evolution of our species has endowed us. We could not have survived if our perceptions bore no relation to what the world is really like—at least to the point of guiding action and averting danger. Our perceptions and ideas cannot give us the world as it really is, in each of its minute parts as well as in its most basic and inaccessible framework. Like a blind man feeling his way with a walking stick we can make inferences about what the world is really like and formulate them in a language useful to our movements. What we cannot do is to see and understand the world as it might appear to a being with better or even different perceptual and cognitive equipment: we cannot see it and understand it as if we were not the finite, embodied, and dying beings that we are.

As I argued in Chapter 2, on epistemology, it matters whether our ideas about the workings of nature continue to be organized around the overlapping themes of change, time, and causality. If they are, then we can translate them, by intermediate steps, into terms that we can make sense of in the language of our experience. Our scientific ideas will continue to be in dialogue with physical intuition, and the world as it looks from the internal point of view with the world as it is represented from the external one. But once the scientific study of nature severs its link with change, time, and causation, and the meaning of our scientific propositions remains locked up in their mathematical statement, natural science will no longer be able to drink at the well of physical intuition. The internal point of view will appear to be an illusion rather than a first step toward cumulative discovery and enlightenment. And we will have a motive to distrust the whole picture of the manifest world conjured up by our senses.

We have motives to hope that the former picture is correct rather than the latter, and some reason to think that its rejection by the fundamental physics of the twentieth century is the result of metaphysical prejudice rather than of empirical discovery apart from such prejudice. But our hope may nevertheless be disappointed. The features of reality that are central to our experience of agency—change, time, and causation—may not be reaffirmed, or be reaffirmed only in a way that radically alters their meaning, in the ways nature works. After all, the world does not exist for our benefit or for our explanations of it, and it just is what it is.

To define the amazing situation in which we find ourselves, all we need to do is to put together, as each of us does in his own way, the internal and external views that I have described, subject to the divergence about the reality and centrality of change, time, and causation I have just recalled. Aware of being alive, experiencing in life a force that seems always able to exceed any structure designed to contain it, and finding a piece of reality, our world, organized around each of us, how could we ever accept our undoing and the undoing of mankind? What is the point of all the striving and suffering, the revelations and the joy, which, in the course of an ordinary life, most of us will experience? And if it makes no sense to ask for its point, because it is what is it is, driven by causation rather than by purpose, how should we respond to its pointlessness?

If the most important characteristic of the universe is that it is what it is rather than something else, and if its evolution in time has no relation to our concerns, other than to impose stringent limits on our ability to achieve them, then the cradle must rock in a void of meaning. All our moral and political projects, and, most likely, our species itself, must come to nothing. Because these projects serve us, we may be able to sustain a sense of their value. But when they vanish together with us and our civilizations, no one will be there to remember and mourn them.

If metaphysical rationalism—the attempt to show, by the exercise of reasoning, that the world must exist and be what it is rather than something else—is bound to fail, the world might just as well never have existed or have existed in a different way, and with a different content, than the way in which it in fact exists, with the features that it in fact possesses. We have no good reason to expect that we will ever be able to find our way out of the amazing situation, despite the growth of our understanding, the lengthening of our lives, and the diversification of our experience.

Seen in these terms, without the benefit of any of the feel-good stories that occupy much of the history of philosophy and religion, our situation may seem frightening. It is, however, stranger and more puzzling than it is frightening. It may terrorize us because it threatens us with the extinction not only of our own existence, returned to the nothing from which it emerged, but also of everyone and everything that we love and cherish. But if we have either a speculative or a calculating turn of mind, we may conclude that it might have been worse: we might never have existed in the first place—neither each of us nor all those we value and love, nor our states and civilizations and the products of our genius. In fact, by the application of probability in cosmology, the appearance first of life and then of our species was preternaturally improbable. Moreover, each of us knows for a fact that his individual existence is the chance result of chance encounters between other men and women. Unless we regard life as suffering and a mistake, as many have, we may reckon that, by the simple fact of our existence, we have come out ahead in this cosmic distribution of lots of being and non-being.

Against the enigmatic character of our situation—its astonishing, dizzying, and dreamlike strangeness—we have no protection other than not to think about it or, in thinking about it, to accept one of the philosophical or theological systems that claim to elucidate it, replacing mystery with false clarity. The amazing situation is puzzling in a way that differs from all the riddles that we encounter in our experience: it is about the relation between the personal, agent-centered horizon of our experience, and what the world, apart from us and our interests and impressions, is really like. Because it has to do with the whole of our situation rather than with any aspect of it, it has implications for every aspect of it. What role can and should our confrontation with it play in our lives?

Many have advised us to disregard the amazing situation given that we cannot change it, and to turn away from it to the concerns of life—to the work at hand, the tasks we value, and the people we love. We should leave speculation about the amazing circumstance, they urge, to the idle curiosity of the philosophically minded.

It is true that, as Pascal reminded us, death is a sun at which we cannot look too directly and for too long. And what Pascal says about death might be applied as well to every feature of the circumstance in which we find ourselves: to life, and our passing encounter with it, as well as to the annihilation that awaits us, and to the relation between death and life against the background of the insuperable limits to our understanding. The awareness of having come from nothingness to life, if only we could hold it in our minds, might fill us with a joy no less intense and paralyzing than the anticipation of our coming death in a world that we can investigate but are unable ultimately to comprehend. To avert our gaze from the amazing situation would seem to be an indispensable protection with which our engagement in life equips us.

It is nevertheless a dangerous forgetfulness. It threatens to deny us a grasp of the relation between our finitude and our transcendence in the form that matters most: not as an empty abstraction but as truth manifest, in many different forms, in every aspect of our existence. It is a species of self-deception that may penetrate and pervert all our experience.

The first and most fundamental harm that it threatens to inflict is to weaken the incitement that recognition of the amazing situation provides to acknowledging both the dramatic concentration of existence and the inconclusive character of our grounds for seeking to live in one way rather than another. Life is now, and given to us, only once. We cannot live it twice or in reverse. And we shall never be able to lay our orientation to existence on an indubitable basis: the basis of an understanding of the ground of being and of our place in the history of the world.

We must accept the incompleteness and the inadequacy—the radical uncertainty, the residue of brute necessity or constraint, accidental history, and unjustifiable faith, in what we make of our time. Unadorned recognition of the amazing situation recalls us to the urgency of that time and the fateful consequences of our never adequately grounded decisions about how to use that time or how and how much to struggle with the constraints that society and our temperaments and bodies impose on its use. Two other harms deepen the significance of this injury. One of them has to do with our relation to society; the other, with our relation to other people.

Astonishment and anguish at our situation awaken us to our fleeting existence and to the concentrated and irreversible character of our share in it. As the proponents of one of the moral visions that I discuss in Chapter 5 always recognized, our reckoning with time, death, and groundlessness is our most powerful safeguard against surrender to the tropisms of society and culture that threaten to rob us of the experience of being alive. Awakened by terror and astonishment to the urgent press of our time of life, we cannot so easily surrender to the oblivion induced by the formulas of established society and culture. The end of all things and of our selves comes to the forefront of our attention and breaks the spell that the routines of society and the dogmas of culture cast on us.

The other injury done by failure to face the amazing situation is the threat that it poses to the quality of our relation to other people. Acknowledgment of the predicament that we share—the root expression of our finitude and transcendence—provides a basis for recognition and respect. The sharing is in a situation in the world, not in ideas about how to live and to organize society. It is compatible with the deepening of the differences of forms of life by which humanity develops its powers. And it ought to inspire an inclusive compassion founded on the acknowledgment of the one fate that we are powerless to overcome. Divided by the injustices of society and the caprice of fortune, the privileged and the oppressed, the lucky and the unfortunate alike, find themselves caught in the toils of that fate. They will all go to their deaths unenlightened about the nature of the world in which they have lived and died. They have a better chance of coming more fully into the possession of life and winning more freedom if they remember that fate than if they forget it.

Finitude: Groundlessness

Rejection of what have been the most influential ways to dispel the mysterious character of our place in the world leaves us in an uncertain place. Can we think our way out of the amazing situation? Are there principled and fundamental reasons to believe that we cannot? If, as I argue, there are such reasons, we must accept our groundlessness. We cannot understand the ultimate basis of being and the framework of existence: why the world is what it is and why it exists at all. We cannot discern within or beyond the world that lies open before us a force that creates the real out of nothing.

We are powerless to establish, on such an understanding, the basis for an orientation to the world and to life. We must continue to be astonished by our situation unless, immersed in our struggles, delights, and sufferings, we manage to forget about it. The conception of groundlessness thus includes both the character and the consequences of our inability to solve the riddle of the world, by looking behind the screen of reality as philosophical super-science and religious revelation have claimed to do.

Why is the world the way it is? There are two classes of answers. Each implies the other. Neither class of answers dispenses with the other. But each can be understood and combined with the other in different ways. These differences are decisive for our approach to the explanation of nature. No combination of these two kinds of answers holds the promise of explaining why the world is the way it is, much less why it exists at all, without eliciting further questions, which we are unable to answer.

One of these two approaches is historical: the world is the way it is because it was the way it was. The other approach is structural: the world is the way it is because it is made of a small number of elements, such as the subatomic particles, that combine and behave under the sway of regularities—the laws, symmetries, and constants of nature. The historical method invokes causation, and causation implies the regularities that underwrite causal connections unless these connections are a primitive feature of reality in a temporal world —a world in which everything may be emergent except time. At some point in our investigations of reality, the causal thread will run out; we will be unable to explain an after on the basis of a before. We will have to be content with saying there must have been a before that accounted for this after, but we will not know for sure what it was. We will not be able to say why the causal sequence in time began as it did rather than with some other content. We will have to say that it just was what it was.

The structural method may be used to explain how pieces of reality connect. If such connections are causal, they must work in time. And we will have reason to ask whether the enduring structure and regularities are immutable, as the philosophy and science of deep structure imply, or have a history. If they are unchanging, we will not be able to explain them except by reference to one another. If they have a history, we will either have to say that their history is governed by higher-order laws or that it is not. Either way, we will come to the end of road of understanding and explanation. We will just have to say: this is how things happen to be.

Some people may have a mystical vision of the world, expressed as art or as religion, into the unity and necessity of the real. They will think they see beyond the incomplete history or the timeless structure into the essence of reality. But if their vision is anything more than a variation on the idea of the timeless one, it will be incapable of translation into thoughts and words. The would-be seers will be deceiving themselves if they believe that they have seen into the ground of being. They will be locked into the amazing situation, just like the rest of us.

In the prologue to this book, I argued that the rejection of metaphysical rationalism is the beginning of an understanding of the world and of our place in it, and I cited Leibniz as having stated metaphysical rationalism in its most intransigent form. Metaphysical rationalism, as Leibniz understood and practiced it, is the belief that everything, including what the world is like, has a sufficient reason: a reason why it could not have been other than it is.

Take that conventional instance of transparency and necessity: geometry. Suppose that a book expounding the elements of geometry had always existed, in successive editions, with each edition a copy of earlier ones. Why does the book have the content that it has and why does it exist at all?

Leibniz found the answer to this question in a metaphysical doctrine of maximal actuality. The world is so arranged as to ensure a plenitude of being: the greatest expression of being that is most compatible with the expression and the coexistence of all the possible forms of being. But what determines the stock of possible beings? Where do the limits on how they can coexist, and by means of their coexistence, raise the level of plenitude, come from? And why should reality conform to this principle of plenitude rather than any number of other principles that one can imagine or that God at the creation might have chosen to exemplify and enact?

The spirit of metaphysical rationalism is to build an unbroken bridge from specific explanations to the explanation of reality as a whole, from particular reasons to all-inclusive sufficient reason. In the end, however, its arbitrariness stares us in the face. It cannot prevent us from reaching a point at which we must say: the world just is what it is.

To make his case, Leibniz needed to supplement his arguments with assumptions about God's motives and procedures in making the arrangements of reality. The idea of divine goodness that these theological assumptions embrace is no less arbitrary than the moves of the metaphysical rationalism.

This brute facticity of the world—the world's just being what it is rather than something else—is what metaphysical rationalism tries, and fails, to avoid. Even if metaphysical rationalism could succeed, we would not have freed ourselves from the puzzles of the amazing situation. We would have formed a view of all reality rather than merely of pieces of it, but our place in this reality, condemned to suffer, die, and misunderstand one another surrounded by the perfection and plenitude of being, would continue to baffle and disturb us. We might flatter ourselves that we had begun to think our way out of the darkness that surrounds us. But we cannot get to even this step in the elucidation of our circumstance without fooling ourselves.

From the strong form of metaphysical rationalism, we may retreat to weaker forms. They turn out to be no more than successful than the strong form. An example is anthropic reasoning, applied in any combination of the historical and structural methods. Observing the extreme improbability of our existence given the generally prevailing ideas of how nature works, and of how it has changed, we look back and ask how we would need to supplement these ideas to account for our existence. We turn a backward-looking teleology, an imaginary reverse engineering, into a principle of explanation. We hope to be able to tell a story that makes our existence seem to be something more than a wild fortuity. And we hope that the result will be to narrow the extent to which we must accept the brute facticity of the world: its just being the way it is.

This weakened form of metaphysical rationalism, however, can never be weak enough to survive scrutiny. The outcome—our existence—may have been the unlikely result of a cosmological and planetary history that might have taken many turns that would not have led to it. Or we may be only one of many forms of many conscious beings, stationed in different places in the universe, who are able to ask why they are who they are. And even if we accept the premise of the inverse teleology, an account of the workings and history of nature must explain how, against the apparently overwhelming odds, we came into existence. There may have been many combinations of events and of circumstances that would have produced us, or beings who share some of our characteristics.

In any of these ways, the weakened metaphysical rationalism fails to close the gap between causal explanations of discrete phenomena and events and a comprehensive account of either nature or of our place in it. Consequently, it fails to rob the world of its brute facticity: its just-so-happens-to-be-what-it-is character.

Temporal naturalism suggests an explanation, if an explanation is required, for the failure of metaphysical rationalism: the inability of science and philosophy to show (much less to prove) that the world is the way that it is for a reason. But temporal naturalism is natural philosophy, not natural science, although the frontier between natural science and natural philosophy is an open one and the difference in the nature and authority of their propositions is only relative. You can recognize the failure of metaphysical rationalism without accepting temporal naturalism. But temporal naturalism does provide an account of what metaphysical rationalism leaves unaccounted for. It does so without pretending that we can explain the ground of being.

Recall from the argument of Chapter 1, on ontology, the central tenets of temporal naturalism. Everything in the world changes sooner or later, including change itself. Contrary to the philosophy of deep structure—the predominant tradition by far in the history of Western philosophy and Western science—there is no rudimentary structure of reality, and there are no eternal laws of nature. Neither the types of things that exist nor the way in which they change are for keeps. But nothing is less real on account of being temporal, for time is inclusively real: nothing is outside it.

Mathematical reasoning, which allows us to think about structured wholes and bundles of relations abstracted from any context of action or observation, gives us a simulacrum of nature from which time and phenomenal particularity have been sucked out. Mathematics has proved so useful precisely because of its selectivity. But it is not the oracle of nature; it provides no shortcut to the understanding of nature. And it has given natural science, together with a powerful instrument, a poisoned chalice: the idea of timeless laws of nature, the conceit that natural reality participates in the atemporal character of mathematical and logical inferences.

A science bewitched by mathematics expresses causal connections in mathematical form. But causality presupposes the reality of time, to which mathematics is foreign even when it is used to explore change and movement. Rather than being underwritten by timeless laws of nature, causal connections are a primitive feature of a nature that is sometimes relatively stable and sometimes subject to relatively rapid and radical transformation.

In the world evoked by temporal naturalism the idea of historical science is not an oxymoron. Structure must be subordinate to history, not the other way around. The project of metaphysical rationalism can have no purchase on such a world: we must accept that causal inquiry will never be complete. It will never have for a subject matter or a result the permanent structure of nature. At some point we will always have to say: this is just what the world is like until it changes. And we will not be able to infer what the world is like from some supposed rational necessity that we find in mathematics or metaphysics. We will have to study the world, and each time we study it more we will be surprised and wonder some more about why it is the way it is rather than some other way.

Natural science and its extension in natural philosophy and social theory are not our only ways to study reality. We are also, for example, able to explore reality through art. But natural science and natural philosophy are the ways from which we may expect most help in postponing our confrontation with the brute facticity of the world. Though they postpone it, however, they do not avoid it. They cannot show why the world must exist and be the way it is. Temporal naturalism provides a way of thinking about this limitation that represents it as a consequence of how things are rather than simply as an infirmity of our cognitive powers.

We have no good reason to believe that the world will have evolved to produce beings equipped to elucidate its most important secrets and that we are those beings. Our cognitive equipment is the result of a series of evolutionary accidents and compromises. Even when extended by our observational, experimental, and computational devices, it bears the marks of its homely evolutionary origins. There may be many aspects of reality that, given the nature of that equipment and its great but not unlimited potential for development and correction, we will never be able to understand.

But if, given what we have discovered, temporal naturalism comes closer than its rivals to describing what the world is like, even beings with better cognitive equipment than ours would be unable achieve what metaphysical rationalism demands. Even they would have to acknowledge at some point: here we are in a world that just happens to be what it is. Like us, such creatures would be unable to base an orientation to their existence on a view of what reality must be. Like us, they would be groundless.

If nothing in the reality of an external world indifferent to our concerns can ground us, must we, and can we, ground ourselves? Can we, in this way, create meaning in an otherwise meaningless world and find direction in a world that offers us none?

Such a self-grounding will have a very different meaning from the meaning of the grounding that would come from outside us—from the ultimate nature of reality or from the transactions between God and humanity enveloping our secular experience. We will, in effect, be speaking to ourselves in a world that cannot speak to us. The practices by which we speak to ourselves, without any validation or echo coming from outside us, take the form of inconclusive arguments with ourselves.

In ethics (understood as thinking about the conduct of life) our ideas will be informed by assumptions about who we are and can and should become. They will offer us promises of happiness and serve as self-fulfilling prophecies. Act me out, each of them will say, and you make the world, or your situation in it, more like what I say it is. We have arguments about these promises of happiness. But although these arguments will have force, they will always be inconclusive. A gap will always remain between the significance of a decision to commit a human life in one direction or another and the adequacy of our justifications for what we decide to do. In that sense, we will remain groundless.

In politics, the premise of our argument must always be that there is no natural way of organizing society and that no way of organizing it—no institutional regime, no order of right—can be neutral among conflicting views of the good. People will struggle over both the moral and material interests that should be favored and the institutional arrangements that can favor them. The course of the struggle will be influenced by the ideas of human nature—of who we are and should become—that gain ascendancy. It will be shaped as well by the ability of different states and societies to deliver power and prosperity. This struggle will be interminable and, so long as the states that shelter these experiments in ways of being human and of organizing society remain armed, it will sometimes be violent.

If these claims about self-grounding in ethics and in politics are justified, self-grounding is not another form of grounding, and it fails to relieve us from our groundlessness or to deprive the human condition of its wonder and terror. It is what we do, what we can and must do given that we cannot find a basis for our orientation to existence outside us, in the nature of the world.

I will argue in the remaining chapters of this book, on ethics and politics, that we can hope for progress—for ascent to a higher form of life—in both the moral and the political domains. But this ascent is not assured, and it is forever susceptible to reversal. Because the diversity of its forms and directions forms part of the condition of its possibility, it is also always subject to contest: a contest that now and forever becomes an occasion for struggle within the mind of a single individual as well as within and among states and societies.

Thought and its vanguard, philosophy, speak in this contest, sometimes powerfully but always inconclusively, as their historical role in ethics and politics confirms. When it speaks, to such inconclusive and powerful effect, philosophy is faithful to its vocation as neither the servant of the established disciplines and their methods nor the master of a super-science. It pushes and tests the limits of what we can understand, think, and say. And it bears witness, in this paradoxical work, to both our finitude and our transcendence.

Finitude: Mortality

Awareness of being alive, which is the condition of all experience and the meaning of consciousness, may imply to the conscious agent that life is forever until he is forced to recognize that it is not. From the external point of view, which forms part of the amazing situation, we come to recognize the fact of death. But even when we embrace one of the visions that promise us eternal life, we may not be able to resign ourselves to death.

Who can blame us? Even if we can overcome the barriers to belief in one of the religious or philosophical faiths that offer us eternal life, we may be reluctant to exchange the mortal life evoked by consciousness for the promised deathless sequel.

An eternal beatitude, in the company of the God who made us, may seem a poor trade for an embodied life in the time of the historical world, surrounded by other people in a historical time that is irreversible and decisive. Literary representations of such a beatitude threaten us with the torture of an eternal boredom. Even when drawn by the hand of genius, they leave us cold when they are not repellent.

The equivalent promise made by the doctrine of the timeless one taxes our credulity less but offers us even less comfort. Describing our death as the inconsequential dissolution of epiphenomenal selfhood into the universal being that is the only ultimate reality, it adds insult to injury by informing us that we never had in the first place the independent existence whose destruction we fear.

When we are unable to trust these promises of an eternal life that awaits us, or that we already possess without recognizing it, we may be offered, instead, a secular consolation. The most common form of such a consolation is the idea that we will continue to live, albeit forgotten, in the collective endeavors to which we tried to contribute or, more broadly, in the life of a future humanity.

This consolation is so paltry, and reliant on assumptions so questionable, that the persistence with which it is adduced must be taken as a sign of our desperation in confronting death: the deaths of those we love and our own death. It extends to all humanity a pretense that up to now has been the prerogative of self-flattering elites: that they are setting their mark on the future. In fact, the greater our success in deepening political freedom, the less will the dead govern the living. And even the greatest influence is likely to be diluted, combined, and redirected in ways that we, the consoled, neither foresaw nor wanted. Moreover, we do not revoke the finality of death by awarding ourselves an afterlife in the lives of our descendants or of those whose lives ours may have touched. Our species, like our planet, is not eternal. The sacrificial impulse, which raises us up, should not need to be sustained by the idea of a legacy that survives us. Such a consolation is unresponsive to the horror that it would be used to assuage: the annihilation of the self, the extinction of consciousness embodied in an individual human organism, which wastes, dies, and is dissolved, never to live again.

Death is unimaginable. Its horror is the definitive manifestation of the finitude of a being that has the attribute of transcendence. There is always more in each of us than there is or ever can be in all the situations that formed us and that we inhabit: more possibility of experience and invention, of spontaneity and surprise. It is easy to mistake this surfeit of experience and possibility over structure and circumstance for a promise of unlimited life. Death, however, will put paid to this promise, and show that life was not, when it seemed to be endless, what we may have supposed it to be.

The bloating and rotting of the body that follows immediately on death, when the body is not incinerated or preserved in chemicals as the empty and ghastly shell of a vanished life, is the visible expression of this catastrophe. The decaying body, once revered, becomes a cause of revulsion.

And if we can somehow steel ourselves against our own dying, which when it comes may come as a relief from suffering, we will have no such recourse against the death of those whom we love. Our grief for the beloved will register the stark contradiction between the boundless life that she represented and brought to the lover and the fate to which each of us is condemned.

It is not just the individual self that disappears at the moment of death. It is a whole world of attachments and engagements represented in the theater of that consciousness: the world viewed and experienced from the standpoint of the dying self. That world will never come back. Its secrets will be sucked with it into the grave.

Those who think that they can preserve in their writings the discoveries of that world deceive themselves. Only a sliver of experience, edited by the halting and devious imagination, will escape to the cold page, to be read by others in the light of an alien experience. The memorialization of experience will bear a distant and contrived relation to the experience itself, which, like the body, will be lost forever.

Death is so awful that we cannot consider it for long. And so we are tempted to flee from it. In fleeing from it, however, we risk contaminating our experience with self-deception about our circumstance. We lose the most powerful inducement to our awakening to the decisive concentration and irreversibility of life, its once-and-for-all quality.

And, with that, we squander, as well, our best defense against the oppressive force of society and culture.

But is not only the recognition of death that threatens to paralyze us in return for its benefits. It is also the spectacle of life: the fact that we are alive, snatched for a brief time from the void of non-existence, against overwhelming odds—the odds against life, against humankind, and against the individual living person. Conscious life is everything: in having it we have won the prize that reality has to offer. And having come to life, we must then so conduct ourselves and arrange our societies that we can come more fully into the possession of life.

We can no more hold in our minds the significance of possessing life than we can look directly at death: for one would paralyze us by fear and the other by joy. Somehow, we must find a space between this joy and this fear in which we can make use of our time, never forgetful of the light that falls on us from these two suns in our firmament.

Our groundlessness and our mortality are the chief expressions of our finitude. What should we make of the relation between them?

To clarify our ideas, it helps to distinguish between a weak and a strong sense of what it would mean to overcome our mortality and our groundlessness.

A weak overcoming of mortality would be simply persistence in the direction humanity has already begun to take by lengthening the life span of the individual, curing many of the diseases that afflict us, and slowing, or even halting and reversing, the process of aging. The social and moral consequences of longevity have already become clear enough to suggest what much longer life spans might mean for both society and the individual. It brings, together with more intergenerational conflict over place and advantage, the threat that life may lose some of its decisive intensity. It also contains the risk that more time to live will not be accompanied by the success of the survivors in breaking the carapace of routine and resignation that begins to form around each of us and robs us of life by installments.

Longevity, even pushed much further than we have so far been able to take it, is not immortality at all. Death, postponed, would continue to await us, and many features of our experience would foreshadow its unavoidable approach. And its coexistence with groundlessness would mean that no fundamental aspect of the human condition had changed.

Strong immortality is altogether different: we would never die. Neither disease nor trauma could take life from us. That must mean as well that we could not kill ourselves, for if we can kill ourselves, something or someone else can also kill us. We would be indestructible, as the radical forms of the doctrine of the timeless one claim that we already are: but not indestructible simply as part of universal being; rather, indestructible as the embodied individuals who we are in our present earthly existence.

Such a strong immortality is not an extended version of longevity. It implies a radical change in reality: not just our reality but the reality of the world in which we find ourselves. In that world nothing is forever or indestructible, just as nothing is infinite. If one part of the world—we human beings—could become indestructible, so could anything else in that world. Nothing in our experience or our science elucidates how such a transition in the character of reality could take place, or what could bring it about.

If we were immortal in this strict and world-transforming sense but remained groundless, unable to solve the riddle of reality, as we are now, we would be like the God of the Semitic monotheisms in one way. In another way, however, we would be like non-human animals. Deprived of all urgency, lavished with endless time but denied understanding of what matters most, we would wander from one interest and one relationship to another, indulging our whims and certain that nothing mattered, because everything could be done many times again in a different sequence, without irretrievable tragedy or definitive resolution.

We would suffer the pains of boredom amid the variety that our endless time allowed us. We might try to escape boredom in diversion. Denied the final recourse of the ability to kill ourselves, we might reflect on the immeasurable evil that befell us when, in gaining eternal life, we lost everything that an ending gives to a story. We might then realize how much our transcendence depends, in each of its expressions, on our finitude.

The counterpart to longevity, as a weak surrogate for immortality, is the continued advance of our insight into nature outside and within us. For example, taking to heart the historical character of the universe, learning not to treat cosmology as scaled-up astronomy, and understanding that the stability of the cooled-down universe, with its enduring structures and regularities, is only one of the forms of nature, we might develop science in a direction different from the one that it has followed since Galileo.

Mathematics would no longer bewitch us, and we would no longer mistake it for a shortcut to the apprehension of reality. We would rid ourselves of the prejudice that the most fundamental science is the least historical one and the one that gives least space for alternative futures. More generally, we would recognize the partiality of a view that treats natural science as the royal road to reality. We would know that artistic imagination and prophetic vision, within and outside the history of religion, give us other means for the discovery of the real.

In social theory, we would achieve what the history of social thought has thus far failed to accomplish: a view that accounts for the transformation and discontinuity of the institutional and ideological structures that give shape to social life. It would do so, however, without succumbing to the illusions of false necessity. Connecting insight into the actual to imagination of the accessible possibilities of social life, it would mobilize theory against fate.

But if our understanding grew in all these ways, and many others, we would remain immeasurably distant from understanding the ground of being and the framework of existence other than as the outcome of a particular evolution. We would be more knowledgeable and less superstitious than we are now. However, granted the limited conceptual equipment with which natural evolution has endowed us, we would remain in our state of ignorance and confusion about the reality around us. Once we had abandoned every remnant of metaphysical rationalism and recognized unflinchingly that the world just is what it is rather than something else, that we cannot find outside our (collective) selves a basis on which to guide our existence, and that within ourselves we can find only bases that are interminably contestable, we would at last be ready to accept our groundlessness. The growth of our knowledge would have prepared us for such an admission rather than serve as a prelude to gaining the insight that we lack.

A strong escape from groundlessness would be something entirely different. It would accomplish the two tasks that Leibniz thought he was describing (if not accomplishing) in his philosophy. First, it would show us why the real world must be and why it must be precisely what it is. Second, it would also show us how the world, together with the larger reality in which it is enveloped in the mind of a benevolent God, gives us a basis—the only basis we can have or need—on which to guide our lives and organize our societies.

Or, to describe the same condition of escape from groundlessness free from the distinctive ambitions and methods of metaphysical rationalism, it would fulfill one (but not the other) of what the two great denials of the amazing situation—the narrative of God's creative and redemptive engagement with humanity and the doctrine of timeless one (or of the overcoming of the world and the will)—offer. It would not give us eternal life, even in the limited sense in which the idea of the timeless one offers it to us: as something that we already possess if only we could stop identifying our being with transient, embodied, and illusory selfhood and with the cravings of such a self. What it would give us, instead, would be an answer to the question that the "man in the street" addresses to the philosopher: What does it all mean?

What does it all mean? is a question at once more comprehensive and more focused than the questions that metaphysical rationalism tries to answer. It is more comprehensive because it is not about the necessity of the world but about the whole show: the existence of the world and our mortal existence within it. And it is more focused because it is moved both by astonishment at reality and by perplexity about our relation to it. The artless question, What does it all mean? is the question someone would ask—someone like me, the author of this book—if he were free from any impulse to explain the amazing situation away, to compensate for its terrors by assuring himself of the possession of eternal life, or to persuade himself that everything of ultimate significance is all right. The sign that the question remains untainted by the desire for reassurance is the absence in it of any demand that we be delivered from death.

To know the answer to this question would place us in position that is as different from the growth of knowledge as we have experienced it as strict immortality—indestructible and eternal existence—is from the indefinite extension of our longevity. Suppose we could overcome groundlessness without overcoming mortality. Remaining condemned to death, we would nevertheless see everything clearly.

Our discovery could not take any of the forms that the explanation of the world has taken in the history of philosophy and religion: it could not be like metaphysical rationalism, the narratives of creation and redemption, or the doctrine of the timeless one. We could not ask about it: But why is it that way? The *why* of its being what it is would be perfectly clear and leave nothing open to interrogation. Such insight would not be like any understanding we possess. Our acquisition of it would, like strict immortality, inaugurate a turn in the nature of the real, not simply in the human condition.

The significance of this revelation for our yet time-bound lives would depend on its content. Regardless of its content, however, it would amount to a revolution in our circumstance. It would place us, in one crucial respect, in the position of God—of the God of the Semitic monotheisms, not the gods of the Greeks and Romans. If we were strongly immortal without ceasing to be groundless, we would, I remarked, be in some ways like the gods of the Greeks and Romans: we would have become part of the furniture of the universe. In other respects, however, we would be like non-human animals, wandering the world and the possibilities of life but deprived—or relieved—of the world's fateful character.

Strong immortality and strong groundlessness would both be similarly unprecedented changes in what the world is like, not just in what we are like. The feel-good doctrines and stories that occupy much of the history of philosophy and religion have connected them. Insistence on the connection bears witness to our overpowering desire for eternal life. In fact, however, no conceptual connection—only what we intensely desire—binds them.

What we really most want is eternal life, not the answer to the question: What does it all mean? That is why the most influential answers to this question have had as their mission to explain why we will not in fact die, except as a transition from one way of being to another, or even as a transition from one experience and idea of existence to another.

Either strong immortality or strong groundlessness would amount to such consequential changes in the regime of reality that if either of them were realized, all else would be thrown open to remaking and reinterpretation. The consequences recall a standard implication of counterfactual argument, only more so. A counterfactual argument explores what might have happened subsequently had something happened differently from how it in fact happened. In the one real world everything is somehow related to everything else. In such a world we cannot tell what the effect of pulling out of the spool of fate one of the threads of causal succession, and replacing it by another thread, will be. The mistake is to suppose that we can readily confine the consequences of the modification of one piece of reality to all the other pieces.

This problem is vastly aggravated when, as in the ideas of strong immortality and strong groundlessness, the counterfactual is not simply giving an imaginary sequel, of a nevertheless familiar kind, to a series of changes. It would bring about a radical change in the regime of reality: events and power unlike any other powers and events in the world we know. All bets are off if something indestructible appears in the world, or reality can be explained by an agent in such a way that there is no longer any reason to ask: But why is it that way? Or to ask: But what caused that, or what came before?

Longing to be deathless, we may fail to appreciate that it would be no less radical a transformation in both reality and the human condition if we ceased to be clueless about the ground of being and the framework of existence, if we knew definitively what it all means. Our mortality in the context of our groundlessness and our groundlessness in the context of our mortality represent, together, the most important expressions of our finitude. They give our existence its vertiginous and dreamlike character.

Transcendence: Desire

Mortality and groundlessness mark our finitude. Our transcendence is expressed most clearly in the nature of desire, in the work of the imagination, and in the relation of the agent to society.

The core characteristic of human desire is its emptiness. Compared to desire in the non-human animals, human desire has a relatively indeterminate, unscripted, roving quality. It displays that quality even in the cravings for food and sex that we share with other animals.

Whatever we crave, we crave in double: a particular satisfaction and something else for which the satisfaction stands as a proxy and foreshadowing. We desire the satisfaction of one or another need, and experience pain or unhappiness in being deprived of it. But its fulfillment gives us only transient and incomplete relief. As soon as the desire has been satisfied, our attention turns to another unsatisfied desire. Satiety is soon followed by boredom—the burden of unused capability—and then boredom by more longing, and satisfaction of the longing by more longing, for more of the same satisfaction or for the satisfaction of another desire.

Such is the ordeal of insatiability, which haunts every aspect of our lives and from which every road to salvation offered to us promises relief. We can hope to change its forms and its outcomes in biography and history. But we cannot put an end to it without denying or disfiguring a major aspect our humanity. The ordeal of insatiable desire is one of the many faces of transcendence in the context of finitude.

What is it that we desire when we desire anything? We desire a particular satisfaction but also something else for which we make that satisfaction stand. And what is this something else? It is ultimately the affirmation of life—of our individual existence—and the fulfillment of the conditions of selfhood, discussed in detail later in this chapter: our ability to connect with others without being subjugated by them, to engage in a particular world without surrendering to it, and to form a coherent and sustained way of being in the world without being imprisoned and diminished by it.

It is also to find a way to immortality, or an alternative to immortality. Thus, a man may want to become rich because he cannot escape death. Or he may want to become powerful because he cannot escape groundlessness. Such is the endless metonymy—the trading of the ultimate for the worldly—that runs through our experience.

You may protest that this view of the ulterior reference of empty desire, seizing on objects that cannot satisfy it, shows the influence of a provincial cultural prejudice: a view of humanity emphasizing agency and therefore transcendence. This view, the objection continues, became prominent only in the last few centuries and even then only in some parts of the world.

The argument proceeds: for a much longer time than the time that has gone by since the rise of literate, state-governed civilizations, the vision of how to live, given our situation in the world, was marked by a theology of immanence and a pragmatics of sufficiency. Divine powers were manifest in nature, not beyond it. People worked, in groups, to reproduce a customary standard of living, and then stopped working when they reproduced it. Consequently, they were, or could be, at home in society and the world. They were not condemned, as we are, to an endless and fruitless quest.

Only slowly, and by steps, on this view, did we abandon the theology of immanence and the pragmatics of sufficiency, until at last we came to a conception of life that is in some respects its opposite. The idea of empty desire and of the treadmill of insatiability—and more generally the conception of the dialectic of finitude and transcendence as a unifying theme in our experience—is, according to this objection, a local, time-bound vision masquerading as an account of the human condition.

This argument has the relation between the human condition and the moral history of humanity upside down. In no society and culture were we ever at home. No ordering of life in society could ever give a human being everything he wanted, including eternal life and an answer to the question: What does it all mean? And—I will later argue—no society and culture will ever in the future be able to provide us with a home, although some forms of social life are superior to others as habitations for the context-formed but context-resisting and reshaping agents who we are. It is by action beyond sufficiency and by our refusal to see and conduct ourselves as simply wanderers in the garden of nature that we rise up, showing and developing our powers.

Were this not the character of the human condition, we could not understand how or why the successive spiritual revolutions in the history of mankind took place. Of these revolutions, the two most important and revealing of our identity are the emergence of the world religions in the thousand-year period from the rise of prophetic Judaism to the prophetic activity of Mohammad, and the revolutionary program, both political and personalist, that has aroused the whole world in the last three centuries.

The reception of these revolutions in the world demonstrates that we were never the beings who we seemed to be when the theology of immanence and the pragmatics of sufficiency appeared to rule us. We have shown our colors. Once we leave this supposed Eden, we can never return.

Our desires are empty. But as the embodied and situated beings that we are, we must give them a content. They acquire a content by means of imitation and projection.

Our desires are mimetic. To a large extent, we want what the people around us want. The mimetic character of desire amounts to a partial takeover of the self by the others. But, as Emerson wrote, "imitation is suicide." Our ambivalence toward others overshadows and penetrates the experience of desire. The mimetic character of desire becomes a source of this ambivalence.

Our desires are projected. They have a double reference: to their immediate and palpable objects and to the horizon of our ultimate concerns. Thus, whatever the immediate occasions and motives of our encounters with others, one human being demands of another: accept me and make me free.

Desire points to something beyond its immediate and tangible object. This something beyond has to do with what ultimately matters: our connection with others, our place in society, our relation to ourselves, and ultimately our confrontation with death and our attitude to the darkness surrounding us. But the something else characteristically remains hidden or barely suggested.

Thus, the experience of desire may simultaneously signal this hidden horizon of concern and represent an effort to evade it. In its former aspect, it exemplifies the presence of transcendence in each fragment of life: that everything in our existence points beyond itself. In its latter aspect, it represents an example of what Pascal called diversion: our flight from the truth of our situation, motivated by dread.

Who could blame us for taking flight from mortality and groundlessness? We take flight the better to continue living and finding in our attachments and engagements the happiness that our existence can nevertheless bring.

If we succeeded in washing from the life of desire its relation to our most intimate anxieties, we would have delivered ourselves to a self-deception threatening to corrupt and mislead every part of our experience. We would have lost the basis on which to recognize and respect other human beings as situation-shaped and situation-transcending sharers in our fate. And we would have cast aside the most powerful inducement to resist society and the script that it places in our hands.

The objects of desire may be closer to the horizon or further from it. They may be paltry surrogates for the unnamable. The distance between the unnamable horizon and its accidental proxies may become extreme and paradoxical. No expression of the central dialectic of finitude and transcendence is more pathetic and revealing.

Transcendence: Imagination

That everything in our experience points beyond itself, revealing transcendence amid finitude, shows in the character of the mind as well as in the nature of desire. We understand anything, in science, art, or any field of inquiry, by forming a view of how it does and can change.

In Chapter 2, on epistemology, I argued that not to have a view of the possible transformation of a phenomenon, given certain events or provocations, is to stare at it rather than to grasp it. We are accustomed to think that an understanding of a phenomenon informs our view of what it can become. The primary link, however, goes in the opposite direction: there is no understanding of a phenomenon that fails to prefigure an idea of what it can become.

What matters in this respect is not the idea of a set of ultimate possible states of affairs, presupposing a limit to transformation in time. Nothing in the world that we encounter, I argued in Chapter 1, justifies such an absolute limit to change and the implication of a closed list of possible states of a phenomenon without regard to the work of causation over time. What counts is the possible within reach: what can happen next under varying conditions, the *there* that we can reach from *here*. The actual must be robbed of some of its brute facticity—its just happening to be what it is—so that it can become imaginable.

The most economical explanation of why the mind works this way—grasping the actual by subsuming it under a range of accessible possibilities—is that this is what the world is like: the human mind participates in the character of reality and developed to deal with it. Temporal naturalism makes explicit and generalizes the metaphysical presuppositions of this view of reality.

To this aspect of our mental experience we can give the name imagination. Remember its two defining moves: distancing from the phenomenon and subsumption of the actual under a range of accessible transformations. The imagination becomes the instrument of transcendence by promising us the perpetual creation of the new. Its ability to keep this promise depends, however, on its association with institutions and practices that enact it in the life of society and culture and, by so doing, extend its influence on our mental experience.

Today, the strengthening of the hold of the imagination on our lives requires a form of economic life that generalizes the most advanced and mindful practice of production—what we call the knowledge economy; that opens the way for the higher forms of free work (self-employment and cooperation) to prevail over the lesser, defective form (economically coerced wage labor); and that encourages us to seek freedom in the economy, not just freedom from the economy. It calls for the organization of a high-energy democracy that overthrows the rule of the living by the dead and weakens the dependence of change on crisis. It would move to this goal by means of institutional

innovations that raise the temperature of politics (the level of organized popular engagement in political life); that hasten the pace of
politics (by multiplying sources of initiative and power in the state and
resolving impasses between them quickly); and that combine a facility
for strong central initiatives with opportunities for radical devolution:
the local or sectoral development of alternative versions of the national
future by parts of the country or of the society. It needs a civil society,
self-organized outside the market and the state, that can bring people
together in purpose-driven activities to create the new and generate
social cohesion out of social difference. And it presupposes a form
of education that equips the imagination: by affirming the primacy
of our imaginative powers, and of the analytic and synthetic skills
that serve them, over the mastery of dead information; by preferring
selective depth to encyclopedic shallowness in dealing with content;
by taking cooperation in teaching and learning, instead of the juxtaposition of individualism and collectivism in the school, as the social
setting of education; and by teaching every subject dialectically, from
opposing points of view.

This agenda, to which I return in detail in Chapter 8, on the
program of deep freedom, takes the cause of imagination from the
inner life of consciousness to the practical life of society and does so
in the circumstances of a particular historical moment. Rather than
denying our finitude, it treats the affirmation of our finitude as a
point of departure. But it seeks to widen the share of the impulse of
transcendence in society as well as in consciousness by multiplying
expressions of the imagination and opportunities for its transformative work.

Transcendence: Refusal of Belittlement

Is it natural for human life to be small, given that it is also mortal?

Refusing smallness means taking to heart the idea that everything
in our experience points beyond itself. The agent will die and be
forgotten, no matter how much he may be enamored of his own significance. His life can be greater only if it touches other lives. But it

would not be a greater life for him if it were only sacrificial, reduced to being the instrument of possibilities of collective experience in which he cannot somehow share.

Refusing smallness means as well widening the space for the expression of transcendence in our experience: the sense we have of being larger than the circumstance that we inhabit, of having an excess of experience and possibility that the arrangements of social life can neither allow and support nor fully suppress. The refusal of smallness is already implicit in consciousness, which is the sense of being alive, because surfeit, spontaneity, surprise, and fecundity, the excess of vitality over structure—are promises of extravagance in the affirmation of life.

No experience is so universal and troubling in our lives as belittlement: the difficulty of living as the beings whom we know ourselves to be. For each human being, given his or her situation, this self-knowledge takes a different form. But for no human being is belittlement ever just the enactment of a fate that has been handed out to him. If he fails to see himself as more than the performer of a scripted role in one setting (such as the workplace), he may see himself as more in another setting (such as the family).

The refusal of belittlement is a form of transcendence as fundamental and pervasive as any that we find in the experience of desire or the work of imagination. Its presence and power are obscured by the overwhelming constraints that all historical societies—some much more than others—have imposed on the spontaneous life force of the individual.

Consider first the most basic setting in which we face belittlement and either accept or refuse it: the universal turning points in every human life. The first such turning point is our decentering: the discovery soon after birth that we are not the center of the world.

This decentering is a potentially violent commotion, a mortal threat, surrounded on every side by enigma. We spend the rest of our lives trying to come to terms with it: it delivers the first and most convincing message of belittlement. Our early decentering continues to loom so large in our moral experience that it has remained the central problem for many of the most influential traditions of moral philosophy. The dominant response of these traditions is to develop a view of our obligations to one another predicated on the normalization and generalization of the decentering: they urge on us an impersonal and altruistic benevolence, premised on the idea that each of us is simply one among many, unentitled to the privileges that the agent is inclined to grant himself. Their central theme is the need to accept the decentering, to take it to its ultimate consequences, and to make our conduct conform to principles that respect its implications.

But it is not in the legalistic universalism of these approaches that the opportunity for transcendence is expressed in our moral experience. It is in the struggle to live a life in which, as survivors of the decentering, we can come terms with other people, with society, and with ourselves, without losing what the decentering puts in jeopardy: the awareness of a life that is ours alone and that, even if not the center of the world, contains worlds within itself. That the immediacy and ardor of that infantile consciousness of being the center could survive the loss of belief in its factual assumptions and, cleansed of illusion and self-obsession, elevate the quality of all our engagements and attachments, is what, as the transcendent beings we are, we can and should desire.

A second point of inflection in the arc of life occurs with the discovery of death early in childhood. This discovery may take place in steps, and its effect may be dulled from the outset by the promises of religious faith as well as by the demands and distractions of society. For someone who sees life extend infinitely before him and for whom longevity is tantamount to immortality, these demands and promises may seem to leave no room for awareness of mortality. Little by little and sooner or later, however, the discovery will not be suppressed. The tokens of death will accumulate.

The opportunity for the affirmation of transcendence comes with recognition of the fact from which death is inseparable: the urgency of our existence, its irreversible, concentrated, and fateful character. To live in the awareness of this urgency is to struggle with one's fate in time. And that struggle, waged by the individual on his way to death, is another rebellion against belittlement. The course of that rebellion is shaped by two other recurrent incidents in a normal human life.

The individual must choose a course of life. Or, if he was born into one of the oppressive orders that have marked most of world history, he will have a course of life forced on him. One way or the other, he will be mutilated. No human being is born to be one thing or another in the division of labor. Multiplicity of possible direction and development is part of what it means to share the godlike attribute of transcendence and to be the relatively unscripted animal that we are.

In rejecting many possible selves, or resigning himself to the mutilation forced upon him by an unforgiving social order, the individual suffers an amputation. Will he reduce his conception of his own identity to this diminished self? Will he continue to imagine himself in the pathways of life that he foreswore? Will such imagination become for him one of the bases of imaginative empathy with others?

The social division of labor mutilates the transcendent human being, even apart from the oppression of class and caste in which it has historically been complicit. It is a necessary mutilation insofar as it is the price of effective action in the world. But it also demands two forms of resistance, each of them an instance of rebellion against belittlement.

First, the agent must refuse to identify completely with his station: his place in the division of labor and in the professional and class structure of society. Even if the role is one that seems to suit his talents and aspirations and is free from extremes of oppression and disrespect, he must take it up with a large mental reservation. As he performs the role, he must also resist it because no place in the division of labor is entirely worthy of a human being. Only two activities come close to being worthy: philosophy and politics. They overcome it in their higher, transformative expressions, not in their customary forms. In those expressions, they are about everything, rather than about something, and they demand everything: a complete mobilization of our concerns.

Second, the refusal of the agent to identify completely with the role he performs in society must not be merely idle and ironic, a form of distancing. It must be an invitation to reshape the role, to the extent possible, in the light of an idea of the higher possibilities of social life. Such initiative is blocked in the hierarchical production systems and class societies that have, up to now, dominated history. To the extent that it remains blocked, the individual must seek refuge in his inner life and the range of personal encounters that he can influence. He must never surrender. He must guard the treasure of his transcending universality and use it as he can to perform incongruously the roles assigned to him.

Later, in the arc of a human life, the threat of belittlement revisits us in a yet more threatening way. As we grow older, a carapace of routine, compromise, surrender, and resignation begins to form around each of us. It is a mummy, composed of the rigidified form of the self—the character—and the life that it has come to accept as the only one it will ever live. In this mummy, we suffocate and die many small deaths. We die beforehand, by installments. To continue living, we must break out of the mummy. The price of breaking out of it is acceptance of a heightened vulnerability. Our reward is to die only once.

Society can make such acts of self-opening and self-subversion harder or easier to undertake. But to the extent that it fails to do so, the burden falls on the individual to make up, through the conduct of life and his relations with others and with himself, for what politics has failed to accomplish through the reformation of society.

Our rebellion against belittlement takes place in historical time as well as in biographical time, having, for its protagonist, the species and the peoples into which humanity is divided rather than the individual human being. In this guise, its most dramatic expressions have been the two greatest spiritual-political revolutions of the last two-and-a-half millenniums. Each of them affirmed the impulse of transcendence. Each of them rejected the idea that the human being is condemned to belittlement by his social and historical fate. Each of them gave voice to the dialectic of finitude and transcendence that lies at the center of our experience.

The first revolution saw the rise of the Semitic monotheisms—Judaism, Christianity, and Islam—and the emergence of Buddhism, Confucianism, and Daoism. Despite the immense differences among the theistic and a-theistic religions that appeared in this thousand-year period, the orientations to existence produced by this spiritual upheaval were united by common themes. They denied sanctity to nature; the power nature exercises over us ceased to be the main object of religious terror and fervor. They reoriented the religious consciousness around a dialectic between transcendence and immanence: the divine—the supreme source of value and reality—was projected beyond the world and beyond historical time and yet was to reengage the world that it went beyond and become manifest in it. Our relation to it, in this-worldly, historical form, became the means for our salvation. We share in the attribute of transcendence because we can connect with the divine, and we can connect with it because it has become present in the world. These religions denied the ultimate reality and value of all the divisions of class, caste, and gender within humanity and affirmed the bonds that tie us all together, even when their narratives of redemption assigned a special role to a part of mankind. Under this new dispensation, they repudiated the ethic of self-assertion and self-aggrandizement proclaimed and embraced by the ruling and fighting classes in the agrarian-bureaucratic empires that up to that moment had been the predominant entities in world history. In its place, they put an ethic of universal fellow feeling. And they moved between offering a license to escape the world, or a way to redescribe it, and a call to change it, deeply, from the heart out.

The worldwide dissemination of these religions and philosophies—in defiance of ruling interests, long-standing moral preconceptions, and even worldly wisdom and common sense—was a powerful testament to the force of the rebellion against belittlement. They spoke of a higher life, to which the whole human race could ascend. And they denied that the chains of the social order and the hierarchical pieties of high culture told the truth about our nature and calling.

All these faiths were drawn into compromises with the settled order of society and culture. But all—some more than others—retained their prophetic and subversive potential. It is impossible to understand their force without recognizing the ability of a human being anywhere and anytime to project his awareness of life beyond the part meted out to him by the accidents of his place in society and history. If the exercise of this ability was the source of a rebellion that has continued ever since, it was also the revelation of our unwillingness—indeed of our inability—definitively to surrender to the established orders of society and culture.

The second great spiritual revolution is the one, invoked repeatedly in this book, that has inflamed the world since the end of the eighteenth century. Its political side is the impulse to lift the grid of entrenched social division and hierarchy that weighs on social life in the class and caste societies that have dominated world history. Its personalist side, associated with romanticism, especially with the global popular romantic culture, is its promise that the ordinary man and woman can rise to a higher form of life, widening his or her share in the many-sided power of transcendence, with great scope, intensity, capability, and vision.

I write as one who wants to make this revolutionary movement continue living but who understands that it can live only if we reinvent both its form and its contents, its practice, and its program. We must be able to envisage its next steps, on both its personalist and its political sides, as I attempt to do in the subsequent chapters on ethics and on politics.

Both these revolutionary movements in history drew force from an affinity between the conditions of our empowerment and the impulse to affirm our transcendence over all established regimes of thought and social life. Both demonstrate our refusal ultimately to accept the real societies and cultures that have emerged in history as settings in which we can be and feel at home.

Contrary to Hegel's narrative in *The Phenomenology of Spirit*, there was never a moment in the past in which a human being lacked the subjectivity that estrangement from the way things are requires. There will never be a moment in the future when a developed subjectivity can be fully reconciled to the way things are in society and culture. And there is no single exemplary path for the development of the dialectic between our arrangements and our consciousness.

The human agent seeks the infinite, the absolute, and the unconditional, surrounded on every side only by tokens of the finite, the relative, and the conditional. We hold the power to rebel in reserve. Its ultimate source is the character of our relation to the formative institutional, ideological, and conceptual settings of our existence. We exceed them, both individually and collectively, because we have life, and they have only the life that we give them.

In this circumstance, we risk consuming our existence in a series of acts of false transcendence: mistaking the relative for the absolute, failing to place the actual within an adequately inclusive range of accessible possibilities, and giving the last word to the established order of society and culture rather than keeping the last word for ourselves.

Finitude and Transcendence as Connecting Threads in the Human Condition

Our existence is vertiginous and dreamlike. We are surrounded by darkness on every side and forever barred from solving the riddle of reality. Death-bound, we face the unimaginable contradiction between the fecundity of consciousness, evoking and exemplifying life, and the prospect of annihilation: our own and that of those we love.

Many have advised us to turn away from this terrifying and perplexing reality and to answer only the call of life, finding solace and joy in our attachments and engagements. If, however, we follow their advice we risk losing our strongest defense against the pressure of society and external reality. We consequently risk as well undermining the basis on which to recognize other people, and to cooperate with them, as sharers in a fate and in a power: the fate of death and darkness, and the power to give urgency to time and to life and to find in one another's arms what we cannot find in a world that is indifferent to our hunger for more life and more light.

Our finitude, manifest in our mortality and groundlessness, is only half the story of the human condition. The other half is our impulse to transcend: our failure to be accommodated by any ordering of society and culture, our homelessness in the world. The relation between our finitude and our transcendence would be the alpha and omega of our lives were there not something missing from it that is equally central to our experience: our relation to other people. We transcend, we become bigger, together with them or not at all.

Society and culture can be organized to make harder or easier our search for contexts that are more hospitable to the context-transcending beings that we are. We can advance, although we must always remain unaccommodated. We can change the relation of structure to spirit—if we take spirit as another name for our power to defy, resist, and reshape the organized settings of our actions. We can hope over time to create structures that are more hospitable to spirit, even if they are never a satisfactory home for humanity.

The relation between our finitude and our transcendence is a thread running through every aspect of the human condition. But everywhere it is entangled with another thread: the attempt to discover how we can be together with others without ceasing to remain and to become ourselves.

The universe must be such that it can allow for the existence of beings with these characteristics. That does not mean, as the principle of anthropic reasoning falsely supposes, that we can explain what the world is like by a reverse teleology: what it would take to make us possible. The world is what it is rather than something else; we cannot dissolve its brute facticity by taking cosmological history to be a prelude to us. It is nevertheless true that if our view of how nature works and has evolved is incompatible with our understanding of the human condition, one of the two must be mistaken.

The two leading traditions in the world history of philosophy—the philosophy of deep structure and the idea of the timeless one—prevent us from making sense of a world in which everything changes sooner or later, time is real, and nothing lies outside time. Those two dominant philosophical traditions have no space for a being who, albeit mortal and living in irreversible time, can imagine and invent the new and can trade the illusion of eternal life for the hope of dying only once. The philosophy of deep structure can be reconciled with our experience of existence only by trafficking in one of the many dualisms that have dominated the history of Western philosophy for the last six centuries and that open a unique and startling exception in our favor. To dispense with such exceptions (e.g., Spinoza's "kingdom within a kingdom") was one of the main goals of the argument in Chapter 1 on ontology as natural philosophy and social theory.

The mistakes of epistemology—and the history of epistemology can be written largely as the record of these mistakes—arise from misunderstandings of the relation between finitude and transcendence in our cognitive relation to the world. Some of these errors result from the futile attempt to jump out our bodies. We can extend the reach of our perceptual and cognitive equipment with the observational, experimental, and computational devices that we invent. We are forever tempted to mistake this empowerment for the ability to see the world as it really is, and ultimately to mistake the advance of knowledge for the overcoming of groundlessness. All these illusions exemplify a denial of finitude in our cognitive engagement with the world.

But just as we cannot jump out of our bodies and view the world definitively, as it really is, from the perspective of the stars, so we must not reduce our powers of inquiry and discovery to the established disciplines. The advance of inquiry depends on shared methods and practices that never have a claim any stronger than the value of the discoveries that, for a while, they make possible. But as change keeps changing in natural and social history, so our collective practices of inquiry are historical inventions and adaptations to the history of nature and of society.

Though we cannot hope to establish the absolute framework of understanding, our minds need never be enslaved to the present organization of knowledge. To mistake that organization for the indispensable and permanent form of inquiry and to subordinate possible vision to established method is to deny our transcendence in the realm of inquiry.

Ontology and epistemology approached in this fashion clear away false obstacles to an understanding of the human condition and to the dialectic of finitude and transcendence that is central to it. Such an understanding informs, as well, our political and moral ideas.

There is no natural form of social life. Each way of organizing society, although open to a wide range of contradictory experience, must take a particular direction. We should judge its merits by its success in creating a world in which people are able to cooperate without being subjugated, to participate in established society and culture without ceasing to resist them, and to form a way of being in the world while continuing to reinvent themselves.

Society must be able to act on the contingency of its own arrangements and to reshape them without needing calamity as the occasion for its reshaping. And the individual must be secure in a haven of safeguards and endowments that allow him to stand up and develop a unique self. Such, reduced to its simplest elements, is what the dialectic of finitude and transcendence becomes when expressed as a political idea.

The relation of ethics to that dialectic is more intimate. For here the subject is the thing itself, unaccommodated man. He is traveling to death. The great universe around him refuses to yield its secrets to him and is deaf to his entreaties. He is born in circumstances not of his own choosing: in a body that is his and yet alien, dangerous, and transient, like everything in nature; in a class and a culture that would shackle him even when, by luck, they place him in a position of privilege.

What does he ultimately have? The temporary possession of life and the company of other people. He must come into the possession of life in the time that he has, using his finitude to affirm his transcendence. But if that is his sole pursuit, transcendence will mean power worship and triumphalism. To possess life, he must find a way of relating to other people that gives him others without denying him himself.

Finitude and Transcendence Reinterpreted: The Semitic Monotheisms and Their Narrative of Redemption

As I earlier remarked, in the history of our religious and philosophical ideas about the human condition there have been two main ways to deny that it is irreparably flawed. Each of them brings good news, though one of them brings better news than the other.

The better the news, the harder we may find it to believe. We may conclude that the news is too good to be true. Trying to believe it anyway may result in a self-deception inimical to our rise to a higher form of life. Having concluded that the news is too good to be true, we may also infer that it is too dangerous to half believe in it and to use our half-belief as a source of solace.

These two famous ways of denying, or at least reinterpreting, the incurable defects in the human condition are, first, the message of the Semitic monotheisms concerning God's creative and redemptive work in history and, second, the doctrine of the timeless one, associated with the effort to overcome the world and the will. I addressed the story of salvation briefly in the prologue to this book, when I introduced the theme of our groundlessness, and the doctrine of the timeless one in Chapter 1, where it was presented as the leading alternative to the philosophy of deep structure in the global history of philosophy. Now I come back to them more comprehensively, with the aim of reckoning with the view of human life and its prospects that each of them offers. I focus on Christianity, among the Semitic monotheisms, because of its unequalled influence on the civilization of the West. I do so also and above all because the vision of this book about who we are and how we should live is, despite everything, so beholden to the Christian view.

God created the world out of superabundant love. This God needs man and intervenes in history to liberate him from sin and bring him to eternal life. The culminating form of his redemptive intervention in history is his incarnation in the person of Christ. The story of salvation speaks to both the transcendence of a God who cannot be reduced to the world he created and to the immanence of God in the world and in man, made in his image.

The mysteries of the Trinity and the Incarnation—the former regarding the inner life of God; the latter, his redemptive relation to man and to human history—lie at the center of the religion of transcendence and immanence and of the theology that develops its meaning and implications.

Nothing in this story explains why God subjects his human creatures to the ordeal of history and to the sufferings that each of us undergoes on his way to death. Nothing explains it other than God's respect for our spiritual freedom, the premise of transcendence in a world in which we would otherwise be what the behavioral sciences often represent us as being: the hapless puppets of genetic and social circumstance.

The innermost teaching of Christianity, taken out of the context of its narrative of sacred history, lies in the combination of two themes. The first is the theme of the primacy of love—of love, not altruism—in the organization of our moral experience. The second is the theme of infinity: our participation in God's transcendence and our power to increase, through love, our share in it. In multiple ways, the themes of love and of infinity connect.

We need not believe in the Christian story of creation and redemption to understand and embrace these themes. In fact, Christianity and its most influential theologians have repeatedly failed to do justice to them. If they are the touchstone of true orthodoxy, the history of Christian theology has been largely a history of heresy.

On the other hand, it is not true that—as many secular critics of Christianity and of the other religions of the Bible claim—the placement of our historical experience in a larger context of the dealings between God and mankind devalues the life, the time, and the world that we actually have. In return for the dubious solace of eternal life, we are, according to this criticism, told that our life is the prelude to another future and our world a shadowy version of an immeasurably greater reality. The result, we are warned, is to leave us estranged from all that we really ever possess: life in the present moment, which we are enticed to depreciate as it passes before us, never to return in its promised higher form. Rather than understanding our finitude as the condition of our transcendence, we diminish our highest good: life and the connections and engagements with which we fill it.

Sympathetically understood, the narrative of creation and redemption has no such life-denying meaning or consequence—if it is true. It represents human affairs as embedded within a larger framework that deepens their significance rather than annulling it. By its light, we see our relations to one another and God's relation to us as being analogous. By the sacramental indwelling of the spirit in material life, our everyday experience reveals its secret affinity to the divine and is thereby raised up. The sacrifice of the incarnate God is the model for all the sacrificial acts by which we change ourselves and the world.

That sacrifice also marks the beginning of a process that leads from our life to life eternal and from the dim light by which we see ourselves and one another to the greater light in which we stand revealed as sharers in the inner life of God.

We have no reason to accuse this doctrine, as countless unbelieving thinkers have, of devaluing the life and time we possess, estranging us both from them and consequently from ourselves. It does not devalue our worldly life; it places that life in a larger context of meaning and promise. It does not depreciate historical time; it sees the plan of creation and redemption as played out in historical time but also as moving beyond human history.

But is this faith justified? It matters whether this revelation is true on its own terms, detached from any excessive dependence on the words or forms of a bygone era. Is it only a useful and inspiring allegory for moral and spiritual truths that we can express, without loss of meaning and power, in terms that depend on no second, hidden, dimension of reality? Are we to save ourselves, together, or must the hand of God be laid upon us? Are we indeed condemned to death and forbidden from understanding the ground of being? Or are we in pilgrimage to unending life, with our way to that life lit by a light that will begin to dispel the mysteries that threaten to engulf us? If we fail to recognize that deeper order in which God's saving and creative presence is revealed, do we mistake the character of our finitude and fail to see it as a preface to our sharing, bound by love to one another, in the inner life of God? For believer and unbeliever alike, the answers to these questions are the hinge on which our fate turns and the source of the scandals of reason.[2]

The first scandal is the scandal of supernaturalism. The story of God's creative and redemptive activity requires us to believe that the causal workings of nature are suspended selectively without being overthrown. They must be suspended not only in the core mysteries of the Trinity and the Incarnation but also in their incidental features such as the virginal birth of Christ and, in the Catholic rendition of the

---

2. The argument of the following few pages closely follows my *The Religion of the Future*, pp. 225–30.

faith, the miracles performed by the saints as well as by the Redeemer himself. But any such selective suspension of natural causality raises a problem familiar in the use of counterfactual explanation. Once the skein of causality is ruptured in one place, all bets are off: we have no measure or basis on which to judge the effect of the supernatural suspension of causality on the otherwise untouched workings of nature.

The second scandal is the scandal of particularity: the universal message of the Semitic monotheisms in general, and of Christianity among them, is bound up with the details of a particular plot, marked by the actions of particular people and the occurrence of particular events in particular places and times. Why these particulars and not others? Why, for example, did Christ not become incarnate and begin his redemptive activity earlier, when his message might have reached those who died without receiving the good news, or later when, in freer societies and a more connected world, it may have been subject to less distortion. Such questions are unanswerable. By being unanswerable they highlight the disorienting dependence of the universal message on the unique plot.

The third and most fundamental scandal is the scandal of the incomprehensibility of the idea of God. According to the ancient and fallacious ontological argument for the existence of God, the existence of God is part of his perfection: the idea of a perfect being implies its existence. The inverse of the ontological argument is that a being that cannot even be coherently conceived cannot exist—or if he exists despite his incomprehensibility, we can have no knowledge of him, except by virtue of his brute irruption into historical time in accidental circumstances.

It seems that for the idea of God to perform the function that the Semitic monotheisms demand from it, God must be neither person nor being. If the counterpart to a theomorphic conception of man is an anthropomorphic conception of God, we cut the transcendent-immanent God down to our size the better to sustain the idea of the analogy between his relation to us and our relation to one another. What results is a form of idolatry.

But if God is being rather than person—"the God of the philosophers" rather than "the God of Abraham"—how can the living God who creates and redeems take on himself the sins of the world, and suffer and die? And how can his relation to us, in his triune nature, serve as the model for our relations to one another? No wonder Heidegger said that if one day he were to write a theology, the word "being" would not occur in it.

There remains a third conception of God: the conception of the mystics and of the theology of the *via negativa*, but also of philosophers such as Nicholas of Cusa, who recognized the consequences of the ideas of God as person and as being. It is the view of God as non-person and as non-being. Its strength is its weakness: its frank affirmation of our difficulty in rendering the idea of God in ways that engage the Christian faith but are also susceptible to formulation in any of the languages of discursive reason that we know how to use.

It is one thing to acknowledge that Christianity contains mysteries, beginning with those of the Trinity and the Incarnation. It is another thing to conclude that faith in the living God is faith in what a believer knows not what.

To these three scandals of reason, we can add a fourth, different in character from the other three: the overwhelming influence of family and cultural circumstance on the experience of faith. There was a moment when every Christian was a convert. For centuries, however, the vast majority of Christians have been Christians because their parents were before them. If they move from one faith to another, it is almost always from one Christian confession to another. What trust can we place in a faith in ultimate reality and in the source of our salvation that depends so ostentatiously on the accidents of our birth?

The effect of the scandals of reason is to serve as a bar to faith. Countless men and women may continue to be in the grip of religious enthusiasm; the presence of the living God in their lives may continue to seem to them an irresistible force and an undeniable fact. Their experience may nevertheless testify to the truth of William James's remark that people believe everything they can.

But in the class societies that persist under the banner of democracy, the experience of the faith tends to fall apart into two realities, both of which compromise the Christian message. Among the working class, especially in developing countries, popular religiosity may take at a discount the truth claims of the religion and reinterpret truth as resonance with immediate experience and as the power to escape the miseries of daily life and to find higher meaning in its joys. In the lives of the educated and moneyed classes and in the career of Christian theology, especially when unmoored from the magisterium of the Church, the faith may turn, little by little, into an allegory for moral and political ideas that might just as well dispense with the narrative of creation and redemption.

By these two routes—the popular and the elitist, and particularly by the latter—the experience of faith begins to give way to a condition of half-belief. In this halfway house, the half-believer neither believes in the literal truth of the faith nor renounces the religion. He believes as much as he can, or as much as his embarrassment by the scandals of reason permits.

This halfway house between belief and disbelief is dangerous. It amounts to a form of self-deception, the consequences of which for our world view and conduct we may be unable to contain. It is dangerous, as well, because it robs the religion of its subversive and transformative power. The Christianity that emerges from the dilution of faith and doctrine brought by the halfway house regularly converges with the moral and political pieties of the day. Such a religion is superfluous; it has ceased to be a storm that takes us where we did not want to go.

The promise of eternal life is the Christian response to mortality. The confession of faith in the Christian story of creation and redemption supplies the Christian answer to groundlessness. If we accept this confession, we come to believe that we are neither groundless nor condemned to death. We remain finite because we do not share in God's omnipotence and omniscience. But we do share in his attribute of transcendence, and we may even come to share in his presence and holiness: most fully by living a saintly life and by the sacramental infusion of our social and personal experience with the signs of our ascent to a higher mode of being.

Yet, increasingly, we may be unable to believe. The attempt to render the promise of eternal life credible may fail: this eternal life seems a poor substitute for everything we value most in the real, vanishing life that we have. And the depiction of the ground of being in the narrative of God's creative and redemptive activity, breaking into history and enveloping historical time in a reality that precedes and outlasts it, degenerates into the instrumental and allegorical equivocations of the halfway house between belief and disbelief.

All these concerns fall under the heading of objections to Christianity as an account of what the world and our place in it are really like. It is in this sense that I call them theoretical. I now add briefly another objection of a wholly different sort. We might describe it as practical because it bears on our reasons to perform, or to reject, the part that it gives each of us in God's plan for redemption.

Suppose that everything in the salvation narrative is true and that God, albeit unimaginable, exists, in whatever sense of existence may be compatible with his nature. Suppose further that we have overcome all the barriers to belief in his redemptive work, beginning in human history and continuing beyond it. We cannot call this belief faith, because faith implies as well that we have accepted our role in the plan of salvation, and our acceptance of that role is precisely what this argument brings into question.

God has offered us salvation: eternal life by his side. We may not accept the offer even if it includes the promise of our return, after death, to our bodies. For why should we relish a life not only without a real body but also without real historical time, and without the people whom we love?

Suppose that we have brought ourselves to take the answer to this question on faith, encouraged by the assurance that the overpowering motive of this otherwise inscrutable God is love. There remains the question of whether this motive suffices to overcome our doubts about spending the brief time of our earthly lives performing a role in a script that he wrote and that he has not fully explained to us. (His plan passes understanding. But why? With his omnipotence, he must have been able to arrange these affairs so that we could comprehend it.) Respond to my love, trust me, he says, according to his messengers and interpreters.

Should we agree to perform, ever trusting and obedient, the role assigned to us in the salvation story? Must we not renounce some of our spiritual freedom, the basis of our transcendence, to accept such a sacrifice of our little time in the world? We are told that he has given us the freedom to sin and to become estranged from him and from one another because such freedom is the condition of spirit. But are our alternatives then either to read out and enact the script that he has written for us or to rebel against his universal rule?

In *Paradise Lost*, Milton, a Christian poet if ever there was one, put in the mouth of his Satan a case for rebellion. His Lucifer would pay any price, including eternal damnation, to assert the prerogative of spiritual freedom. He would not agree to submit to a God intolerant of resistance and prodigal in his demands but economical in his explanations.

Note that this argument does not turn on the illegitimacy of inferring prescriptive conclusions from factual premises, the ought from the is. It turns, instead, on the distinctive content of a religion that represents the transactions between God and humanity by analogy to dealings among human beings. Notwithstanding the analogy, this religion allows an incommensurable disparity of insight and power to limit the analogical reasoning on a crucial point: the point at which we have to choose a course of life with the help of whatever understanding of our situation in the world we can gain.

Disregard the literal particulars of the narrative of redemption, you might say. Consider its central message of love and infinity. Recognize the larger truth and power of the faith in its ability to inform and inspire the greatest achievements of the civilization of the West, such as the plays of Shakespeare and the philosophy of Hegel— irreconcilable with Christian orthodoxy, yet unthinkable without Christianity.

The trouble is that the actual history of the faith has not been the history of the development of this sublime and ever potent teaching. If that teaching is the true touchstone of Christian orthodoxy, then it is an orthodoxy more denied than expressed by the historical development of the faith and its churches.

From the beginning of Christianity, the imitation of Christ and the practice of Christian charity, understood as inclusive and sacrificial altruism, has largely usurped the place of love. The development of a way of living and of organizing society that expresses and sustains our transcendence over context has been usurped, on one side, by 2,000 years of compromises between Christianity and particular social and cultural regimes. It has given way, on the other side, to a romanticism that sees spirit as able to live only through the shaking and suspension, rather than the transformation, of institutional structure, cultural convention, and personal habit.

Moreover, the dual doctrine of love and infinity, properly understood, implies no denial of either our mortality or our groundlessness. The flaw in the faith lies not in the devaluation of our time, life, and natural reality in favor of another life and another world. It lies in the mismatch between the revolutionary potential of the religion and its historical reality.

What is deepest and most defensible in Christianity is not what offers false escape from the irreparable flaws in the human condition. It is what points to how we can reconcile our transcendence with our finitude, and draw closer to one another, despite those flaws or because of them.

Finitude and Transcendence Reinterpreted: The Idea of the Timeless One

The idea of the timeless one has been the most powerful alternative to the narrative of creation and redemption in interpreting the human condition. We have encountered it already in Chapter 1, on ontology, as the most influential rival, in the world history of philosophy, to the philosophy of deep structure.

Unlike the story of God's intervention in history, which stands at the center of the Semitic monotheisms and has inspired three world religions, the idea of the timeless one, stated in its most uncompromising form, cannot easily be associated with another world religion or a well-defined philosophical tradition. It is best exemplified by many aspects of the world view of the Upanishads and some of the major philosophers of ancient India. Although it influenced early Buddhist philosophy, the teachings of the Buddha already contradicted it, and this contradiction became manifest in the subsequent development of Buddhist teaching and practice.

In its most radical form (to which Nagarjuna and Schopenhauer come close), it denies the reality of distinction and time. Our endless and insatiable desires leave us entangled in illusion and suffering. To overcome the deceptions of the world, we must overcome the will. The road to salvation is a reorientation that puts us in communion with one and timeless being. By understanding the phenomenal world for what it is and freeing ourselves from the tyranny of insatiable desire, we break the spell that the illusions aroused by our cravings have cast on us.

On this view, eternal life is not a good that we should hope for and struggle to achieve. It is already ours. We possess it right now—not in the transient and illusory form of distinctive selfhood as the seat of ceaseless desire but in the true and reliable form of a being that remains one and changeless under the veil of its temporal disguises. The mind emanating from the timeless one can understand this ground of being, the framework of existence, if only it can free itself from the tyranny of the embodied and desirous ego. Nagarjuna summarized the doctrine when he taught that samsara is nirvana.

As a starting point for an attempt to elucidate the riddle of reality, the idea of the timeless one suffers from defects that discredit it. By denying the reality of distinct phenomena, beings, and selves, it leaves us without a basis on which to explain the changes that we observe in the world. It has no room for causality, if only because it denies the reality of time, which any causal connection or explanation presupposes. Without causal connection, nature outside and within us becomes indecipherable.

It denies us the manifest world on account of a metaphysical conceit that we must accept or reject, but that we cannot test, revise, or improve. Moreover, it fails to explain why the world appears to us, even when detachment replaces craving, under a form that contradicts its real nature. The idea of timeless one fails to explain why the world disguises itself by generating craving animals, such as we are, whose nature prompts them to misrepresent reality.

This objection to the doctrine of the timeless one as a view of what the world is really like suggests an objection to it as a reason to overcome the life-paralyzing terror and sadness that awareness of our amazing situation may arouse in us. The idea of the timeless one promises to liberate us from our sufferings by detaching us from the objects of frustrated desire. Prominent among these objects, however, are our attachments to particular people (as distinguished from our benevolence to the strangers and life forms around us) and our engagement in the tasks in which we have a personal stake (as distinguished from all the initiatives that we might approve and admire in the actions of other people).

It is by throwing ourselves into these attachments and engagements, in the company of other people and in the struggles of our time—the time of the historical moment as well as the time of our life span, that we overcome our sadness and return to life. The idea of the timeless one, however, diminishes the reality and devalues the authority of those attachments and engagements. It places us in communion with the ultimate reality that it sees under the veil of time and distinction only by taking away from us the manifest world, with its charms as well as its dangers, and the people we love.

The doctrine of the timeless one offers both a theoretical and a practical response to nihilism: the teaching that our lives and the world itself are meaningless. The theoretical response is to expose the insubstantial and fleeting character of everything that exists and to affirm what remains when all walls are torn down. The theoretical response is in the service, as philosophical super-science has traditionally been, of self-help: *desengaño*—we detach ourselves from the habitual objects of our longing and lose or find ourselves in the reality that remains, beyond time, when the walls have come down. But the consequence is that our experience becomes progressively smaller and emptier: it is emptied out of the attachments and engagements that create meaning for us in an otherwise meaningless world and provide us with the only reliable antidote to nihilism: more connection and engagement, more life. It offers anesthesia instead of giving us life and teaches us to deal with the suffering of life by dying beforehand.

The Contradictory Requirements for Sustaining a Self

The idea of conditions of selfhood. Consider another way to view the human condition. Let us view it from the perspective of the most basic conditions for developing a self who lives, as we all must, among others, rather than from the standpoint of the irreparable defects in our circumstance: our mortality, our groundlessness, and our difficulty in reconciling our transcendence with the constraints imposed on us by our social and biological fates, our susceptibility to belittlement.

The self is consciousness—the awareness of life—embodied in an individual organism. It affirms its nature and identity by living and acting. To affirm its selfhood, it must have the experience of agency. To this experience we also give the name freedom in a sense broader and more fundamental than any that is narrowly political. This is freedom as the power to be more lifelike despite all the constraints that weigh on us, the power to exercise and to develop the attributes of life: its surfeit over structure, its spontaneity, its ability to surprise, and its fecundity in making the new. Such freedom does not imply the capacity of the self successfully to reshape its context according to its will. What it does require is the experience of being brought to life by action, both practical and imaginative, in the world.

The organization of society—the character of its politics—can support or hinder, express or suppress, this movement. In this sense, this conception of selfhood as agency and of agency as freedom has an undeniable political side. But it implies much more than anything that can be defined in distinctly political terms, although the boundary between the political and the existential remains always open and undefined. For what is at stake ultimately is the lived conviction of the individual that this life is *his* life just as the death that awaits him is *his* death. It is only by acting and becoming, despite everything, an agent that he can give effect to this conviction and make it real for him.

We should not mistake the enactment of agency and the possession of selfhood for the Western liberalism or romanticism of the nineteenth and twentieth centuries. It is neither individualist nor collectivist. Its political consequences are indeterminate. It can have moral expressions and take social forms that represent and shape the relation of the individual to society in starkly different ways.

Men and women taking hold of life, and affirming a self, discover that the conditions of selfhood are contradictory. But it is only through personal and political struggle, and by the light of experience and reflection, that they can grasp the nature of these contradictions and begin to form a view of what dealing with them requires. To become more lifelike and to strengthen our capacity to give ourselves to one another, we must deal with them.

We cannot overcome these contradictions. Nevertheless, our success or failure in reckoning with them, and in loosening the limits that they impose on our humanity, is decisive for our ability to make a self and to achieve freedom and agency, enhancing the sentiment of being.

Self and others. Everything in our self-experience depends on human connection: place and sustenance in the social division of labor, the sharing of a language and culture that provide consciousness with its medium, and the vicissitudes of the passions by which our relations to other people take on a significance and a power that is more than instrumental. We scrutinize each encounter, each attachment or each confrontation for its implied answer to the question: Is there an unconditional place for me in the world?

Without the others, each of us is nothing. The individual self exists, thrives, and makes sense of its experience—of every aspect of its life and death—only in this interpersonal context, against the background of a particular social and cultural order.

Yet every connection to another, whether in the cold distance of the workaday world or in the more than instrumental domain of passion, is also a threat. It threatens us with subjugation and loss of individual distinction. At every turn, we need the others in order to be free. At every turn, they threaten to make us unfree.

To be free and affirm the sentiment of being, we must be able to connect without losing ourselves, or rather without losing the opportunity to make a self. We must moderate the clash between our need for the others and our need to protect ourselves against the jeopardy in which they place us. We are free, we make a self, to the extent that we can connect without falling under the dominion—economic, political, ideational, or emotional—of others. How this clash is to be overcome is the subject of disputes that have helped shaped the history of moral and political thought.

In personal love we have, if we are lucky, the experience of a form of connection that offers attachment without subjugation. But love requires closeness, even intimacy. Beyond the boundaries of intimacy, we may need to appeal to a surrogate for love. The surrogate offered by the moral philosophers is an impersonal and altruistic benevolence.

Altruism is not love. The defining spirit of altruism is sacrifice for the sake of another person. But the gift is offered from a distance, and from on high. The distinctive element in love is mutual recognition, acceptance, and longing: the view of the beloved as an enhancement, even an indispensable enhancement, to the lover's possession of life. Altruism requires no insight into the consciousness of its beneficiaries, only a practical sense of their need. Love must pass an imaginative threshold: it depends on the power to imagine the other. Failure to pass this threshold opens love up to a romantic perversion: the projection onto the beloved of a fantasy shaped by the lover's self-regard. The sacrifice that expresses altruism may extend even to the laying down of one's own life. But it requires no inner jeopardy as love does. In love, this jeopardy includes the possibility of the rejection of love and the loss of the beloved.

These differences between love and altruism explain the relative inability of altruism to resolve this first contradiction in the conditions of selfhood. Its focus falls on the taming of self-interest, founded on self-centeredness, not on the effort to overcome the conflict between our need for connection and the struggle to avoid the dangers of subjugation and loss of distinction to which every connection subjects us.

In the world shaken by the revolutionary liberal and socialist challenges of the last few centuries, the true counterpart to love in life among strangers is cooperation among free and equal people. How we are to express that ideal in the institutional arrangements of the economy and politics is one way of defining the focal point of ideological conflict in this period in the history of mankind.

Both our moral and our political experience suggest that we can never overcome the clash between these two requirements of self-construction—our need to connect and our struggle to lower the price, in subjugation and loss of distinct selfhood, that we must pay for connection. But it does not follow from the impossibility of overcoming this clash that we cannot diminish it though love and cooperative activity.

Self and society. The second contradiction between the requirements for making a self has to do with the relation between the self and the social world. No one can move toward freedom as agency and self-possession without participating in a particular social world and accepting much of its arrangements and assumptions. It is only against the background of a real society and its forms of consciousness and communication that we exercise agency.

Every such social regime casts the agent in a definite place in its division of labor and imposes on him its roles, rules, and rituals. If the agent is to achieve any other way of living and of being, he must achieve it by struggling with his circumstance.

Regimes of social life differ in the extent to which they present themselves to the individual as an alien and inalterable fate. They vary in the degree to which they embed social life in an entrenched scheme of social division and hierarchy: a scheme that fails to provide for its own remaking. They diverge in how much they equate the individual with his place in the order of class or caste or endow him with the means and opportunity to change that place and to reinvent himself.

But in every regime that has existed until now, engagement in a social world—an inescapable requirement for developing a self and exercising its power of agency—has exacted a price. The price of making a self has been submission to society and culture: not submission by a self that would have any reality and shape before it submitted, but submission by a self that comes into existence through such submission, from earliest infancy; the self was never just a pre-social organism with only its genetic inheritance.

The self, however, cannot be free and enjoy the prerogatives of agency if the price of participation in a social world is surrender to that world. In some measure and by some means, with the instruments and occasions provided by the regime or without them, the individual must be able to deny the last word to the established social and cultural order and to keep that word for himself.

Here then is the clash: to strengthen its sentiment of being and enlarge its freedom, the self must be able to engage and to resist. It must be able to engage without surrendering. Or, to change the vocabulary, the agent must succeed in combining the conditions of insider and outsider. We cannot rise to a greater life and enlarge our experience of freedom unless we succeed in attenuating the clash between the need to take part in a social and cultural regime and the power to prevent it from defining the limits of our efforts.

In the first instance, we can achieve this goal politically through the making of regimes that combine several attributes. Such regimes must help us make a practical success of social life. They do so by favoring the development of the practical powers, including the powers of production, that allow us to lighten the burdens of poverty, infirmity, and drudgery. Although they cannot be neutral among divergent views of the good, they must be open to a wide range of diverse and contradictory experience. They must facilitate their own revision and narrow the distance between the ordinary moves that we make within the framework of arrangements and assumptions we take for granted and the extraordinary moves by which, from time to time, typically at the instigation of crisis, we challenge and revise the framework. And they must secure the individual in a haven of safeguards against both governmental and private oppression as well as of capability-assuring endowments, while all around him they help arouse a perpetual storm of innovation and experiment.

Just as the idea of cooperation among free and equal agents— notably in the arrangements of a market order and in those of democratic politics—has no natural and necessary institutional form, so the institutional form for the combined expression of the attributes of a regime that allows us to participate without surrendering remains always undefined and contestable.

Here, as with the clash between our need to be connected with others and our need to avoid subjugation, the political response is never sufficient. It takes place in historical time, not in the biographical time in which we live. We do not get to choose our place in history, any more than we can choose the social condition into which we are born. The difference is that the institutional arrangements of a society may allow the individual a greater or lesser opportunity to reshape his place, whereas from our place in history there is no appeal other than resistance and vision, the practical expression of which depends on historical as well as on social circumstance.

What politics fails to achieve in its historical time, the individual must nevertheless accomplish in the biographical time granted to him. To be an insider and an outsider at the same time, to deny the regime the last word and keep it for himself, he must exploit every margin of maneuver that his place in society allows him. Instead of playing out the roles assigned to him in the social division of labor, he must remain ambivalent to them, and be ready to turn ambivalence into resistance, and resistance into transformative action.

How he follows this path may count for little by the standards of the world. The practical expressions of his rebellion may seem meager and the light it casts dim. But it must result in a change in his relation to the part he plays in society: an inward distance from society's arrangements and expectations by which he affirms—if only to himself—his unwillingness to play the part of a puppet under the control of the ventriloquist.

Societies and cultures differ in their tolerance for such resistance. No society or culture can abolish it. Its foundations lie in our most defining characteristics: the dialectic of finitude and transcendence, and the ascendency of the personal and interpersonal over all its social and cultural expressions. No such compensation for the failures of politics by the struggles of the self is possible without sacrifice. Sacrifice, whether hidden or apparent, tangible or intangible, is the criterion by which we distinguish the real from the fake.

Self and self. There is yet a third set of contradictory requirements for the making of a self and the broadening of our freedom. The self must be able to form a way of being in the world. It will do so with the materials of its genetic inheritance and its social circumstance but also as the cumulative outcome of its response to that circumstance. It will settle into a course of life and begin at some point to think: this is the only life that I will ever live. It will develop a series of tropisms: of habits of perception, understanding, behavior. Thus emerges the rigidified form of the self, the character, which the Greeks called a man's fate. The combination of this rigidified self with the circumstance that it accepts or to which it is resigned becomes its way of being.

We cannot affirm the sentiment of being if we have not passed beyond the indefinition of the self in early adulthood and developed a way of being in the world—if we are forever beginning again the construction of a self. Time will bear down on us and repay lack of commitment to a path with sterility. What we mistook for the perpetual reassertion of universality will have turned out to be a fruitless wandering among particulars.

Yet if this settled way of being—the union of the character to its accepted circumstance—takes over, it threatens to become a proxy for the living self. It sucks out from our experience the attributes of life: surfeit over structure, spontaneity, surprise, and fecundity. We begin to die by installments even before the decline of our powers and the extinction of the organism. The transformation of life into a work of art, as Nietzsche proposed, amounts to the replacement of the living self by a lifeless icon.

To enlarge its freedom and self-possession, the self must be able reconcile the development of a way of being in the world with the disruption and remaking of this way of being. We need a way of being, and we need to break it open. Friedrich Schlegel remarked that it is just as fatal to the spirit to have a system as not to have one. Put the way of being and especially the rigidified self, the character, in place of system. And interpret spirit in one of its historical meanings as the self invested with the power to transcend the finite determinations of its existence. Then Schlegel's remark gives us a lapidary statement of what is at stake in attenuating the force, and changing the expression, of this third set of clashing requirements of self-assertion.

In assessing the political and moral conditions for this element in our ascent to a higher form of life, we should consider the moral conditions before the political ones: the central meaning of the task is moral and expressed in biographical time, even if the organization of society and culture, emerging in historical time, may either help or hinder its fulfillment.

To reconcile the development of a way of being with its disruption and reinvention, a person must live life as a search and exchange serenity for searching. He must throw down his shield. He must form large aims—not large by the standards of worldly power and prosperity but large in relation to the aims that the rigidified self, resigned to its circumstance, habitually pursues and large because their pursuit contradicts such resignation.

In living life as a search, one larger goal will not be as good as another. The aims and the pursuits with the greatest promise and fecundity are those that also contribute to the reconciliation of the other two conflicts in the requirements for making a self: between our needs to connect and to avoid subjugation and loss of distinction, and between the imperative of engaging in a particular social and cultural world and the requirement not to surrender to that world.

Without this qualification, our search would be both aimless and fruitless. The attempt both to develop a way of being and to break it up would risk degenerating into a romanticism or an adventurism bereft of direction.

The disruption of the rigidified self and the unsettling of the circumstance to which it has been resigned exact a price. Whoever is determined to place the living self over the lifeless icon must make himself vulnerable and accept a heightened exposure to disorientation, defeat, and derision.

In this lowering of personal defenses, for the sake of rescuing life from the rigidified self, society and culture play a powerful role by providing or denying equipment and opportunity. They are the same social and cultural conditions that support our reconciliation of the other two sets of clashing requirements of self-construction, viewed from a distinct perspective. Here, as there, their institutional forms are indeterminate and open to contest.

We can describe these conditions as regulative ideals. They mark a direction rather than proposing distinctive arrangements responsive to specific contexts. The agent should be able to rely on a haven of safeguards and endowments so that he can act free from unnecessary dependence and move unafraid in the midst of change and conflict. He should enjoy in youth access to a form of education that empowers him to understand pieces of natural and social reality by understanding how they change, and that enables him to see beyond the ideas and experiences of the society and culture into which he has been born. The state of which he is a citizen should create the practical conditions that make it possible for individuals to change career and direction. In these and many other ways, we can lower the price that those who undertake self-reconstruction must pay.

The price can fall, according to the arrangements of society, but it can never be less than daunting. The cracking open of the rigidified self will be difficult. And it will always require to be inspired by both the love of life and the love for other people. It must be both more and less than heroic; it must be the most unequivocal affirmation of our excess over the circumstances in which we find ourselves. It must signify our determination to die only once.

The conditions of selfhood reconsidered. We can never be fully reconciled to one another. We can never be fully at home in society or in the world. We can never develop a way of being of which we have reason to say: the work of self-making is completed; this is who I am, and in this way of being I can recognize myself and grasp life.

And yet the character of our existence is decisively shaped by our advances and retreats in reconciling, and not reconciling, ourselves to one another, to the social world in which we move, and to ourselves. It is not just how much, or how little, we manage to soften these clashes in the requirements of self-assertion that matters. It is how we do so: the result will be the distinctive quality of our existence.

Our inability fully to come to terms with one another, with society, and with ourselves speaks to both our finitude and to our transcendence. It speaks to our finitude because it shows that we will always be incomplete and never fully at peace. We will never be able to live in the world as the people that we know ourselves to be because we will never find a way definitively to resolve the contradictions among the conditions of selfhood. We will never quench our thirst for the infinite in a world that contains only the finite unless, by a "sacrificio dell'intelletto," we persuade ourselves that the infinite has come to us as the redemptive God or the timeless one or through the revelations of art.

But the same struggle with the consequences of our finitude and of the finitude and facticity of the world—its quality of just happening to be what it is—also becomes the vehicle of our transcendence by giving us reasons to resist and reinvent our societies and ourselves. The insistence on seeking the infinite, in a world holding only the finite, would mean nothing if it lacked a this-worldly expression. And it would mispresent our situation and our hopes if our struggle for reconciliation with ourselves were not inseparable from our efforts to come to terms with other people and with society.

The irreparable flaws in the human condition present the same reality, the same contradictions, the same interweaving of finitude and transcendence in a different register. Our mortality and our groundlessness are the two anchors of our finitude. Together, they seal our fate.

Our experience is tied to the future of a dying organism, which will never live again. We will go to our deaths without knowing why there is something rather than nothing, or why the world is what it is and not something else, or why our accidental existence, as individuals and as a species, has any significance, other than representing a momentary drawing of a lot in the cosmic lottery. Youth, engagement, and ambition may hide from us for a while the real face of our fate. If we fail to die young, that face will be uncovered before our deaths by our decline and by the deaths of those whom we love.

Yet in the insatiability of desire, in the transforming work of the imagination, and in our unending resistance to all the forms of belittlement that grind us down and humiliate us before we confront annihilation, the other side of our experience shows its face: the impulse to rise to a larger life, to become greater, which can succeed only when we become greater together.

4

Ethics (as Clarity about the Conduct of Life)

Ethics and Its Work

There is only one question that no human being can escape: how should he live, or what will he do with his life? For even if he fails to face this question squarely—as most human beings do fail—he will answer it implicitly by the way in which he lives.

The grinding realities of oppression in much of the history of civilization have imposed on people a social fate that they have been powerless to resist. In their chains, they act on beliefs that guide their attitude to their enslavement, even if those beliefs teach them to sing in their chains. The few released by their station in society from the extremes of material necessity and social constraint have found other reasons and ways to evade the question. Fear, cupidity, and sheer desperation have manacled them. Or philosophy and religion, seized upon as a series of feel-good stories designed to console them on the way to death, have assured them that all is ultimately well and taught them that the lesson of how to live is clear even if their weakness may prevent them from heeding it.

The question about the conduct of life is the central concern of ethics. Today, in the academy, especially in the English-speaking countries, a different understanding of moral philosophy rules. This understanding reduces ethics to a discussion of the ideas and of the method by which we are to specify our obligations to another. Later in this chapter I address this view of moral philosophy and give reasons for why we should reject it. Under the disguise of being a contest among the most serious candidates for thinking about ethics—consequentialism, deontology, and social contract, each wrongly associated with great philosophers of the past—this philosophy has become the expression, in equivalent vocabularies, of a legalistic and pharisaical moralism. It has turned ethics into an accounting of moral credits and debts.

Ethics addresses its central question in a space that crosses the boundaries between philosophy and religion. The ideas developed in this space share three characteristics.

First, they anchor an orientation to existence in a vision of our reality: of who we are and of our place in nature as well as in society and history. They may claim to infer such an orientation from a view of the framework of existence or from a narrative of the dealings between God and mankind. When they make such an inference, they pretend to see through our groundlessness to the hidden ground of our being.

Alternatively, they may accept our groundlessness. But they then have to anchor their ideas about the conduct of life in a conception of who we are and our situation in the world. Our groundlessness is a vital aspect of this situation. So are our mortality and our insatiability, our contradictory and ambivalent relation to one another, and our need to reckon with the hand that society and history have dealt us. We human beings must ground ourselves. But how we understand our self-grounding depends on who we understand ourselves to be—as individuals, as members of the collectivities into which mankind has divided itself, and as human beings.

Second, ideas in the space in which ethics moves break through the distinction between descriptive and prescriptive statements, between the *is* and the *ought*. The more comprehensive our ideas about ourselves and our place in the world, the less the distinction makes sense. It applies best to the relation between propositions: We cannot justifiably pass from a particular *is* proposition to a particular *ought* proposition. When we do, we commit a fallacy: no prescription can rest, all by itself, on any description.

When, however, we begin to form ideas about ourselves and the world that are comprehensive, the contrast between *is* and *ought* loses force and pertinence. It does not cease to apply at once; it becomes increasingly irrelevant. Any conception that includes a view of who we are and what we need and want, given our natural and social circumstance, will have implications for the conduct of life as well as the organization of society. From the narrowest logical standpoint, we can say that it will have implications only when combined with an additional, specifically normative proposition such as: choose your course having in mind both who you are and what the world is like. But this qualification is a pedantic extravagance obscuring a decisive point: we form such views from within, as human beings, about ourselves, not about another being or non-human nature. Such views evoke a picture of both the scene of our actions and of ourselves as agents.

Conversely, any approach to the conduct of life gains significance and persuasive force from being embedded in a comprehensive way of thinking about ourselves and our relation to nature and society around us and within us. To qualify for this role, the ideas that state it must touch widely on our condition and our place in the world. But to be comprehensive, they need not, and almost never will, take the form of a system of abstract propositions. They must represent a way of thinking, not a doctrine expressed in a manner suiting the tradition of philosophical super-science.

In the history of Western philosophy, the most familiar source of the injunction against passing from *is* to *ought* is Hume's discussion of this fallacy in his *Treatise of Human Nature*.[1] Yet in the very same work, Hume embeds a view of how we should seek to live in an account of who we are. It is a naturalistic account emphasizing how much we need one another and how little we know of the world. There is, in the discourse of the *Treatise*, an unbroken continuity from this account to a proposal for how to live; the account and the proposal are so thoroughly intertwined that it is impossible to separate them. This continuity does not mean that Hume has contradicted his thesis about the fallacy of passing from *is* to *ought*. That thesis was about the proposition-by-proposition conversion of descriptive propositions into normative ones.

---

1. David Hume, *Treatise of Human Nature*, 3.1.1.27, originally published 1739.

Third, ideas about how to live require a faith that they are never able adequately to justify. They elicit faith in the two primary senses of that word: a commitment that outreaches the reasoned justifications that we are able to supply for it, and a heightened vulnerability to other people.

The decision about how to live is the weightiest that we can make —even if it is a decision only in the sense of an attitude informing our conduct and even if we never articulate or experience it as a decision at all.

We can give reasons for such a commitment: for choosing among conflicting views of the conduct of life that we find in our immediate circumstances or in the history of moral opinion. A conception of how to live is a promise of happiness: happiness sometimes as privation of suffering but more often as fullness of activity and experience, even if bought at the cost of contradiction and suffering.

Once we translate an approach to the conduct of life into practice, the promise of happiness may be kept or broken. It may lead us toward a form of life that captivates us, or it may undermine itself. It may fit with a way of living that is available to us in our historical circumstance or it may float as a creed to which we are unable to give practical expression. It may tap into the needs and longings that we experience as most fundamental, or it may not. And it may be compatible with what we independently know to be true about who we are or can become or it may contradict such knowledge.

These are all reasons, not pretexts. When, however, we add them, and others, up, an incalculable distance remains between them and the commitment that they would justify or criticize. In the end a daunting disproportion persists between the weight of the engagement of life in one direction or another and the reasons that we can adduce for such engagement. Even when we are most ambitious and tenacious in seeking to live an examined life, and to avoid drifting into an approach to existence imposed on us by the force of circumstance or of opinion, the prejudice of our milieu, or the influence of temperament, a gap remains between the most important choice and our paltry case for it.

This cognitive gap—the gap between the commitment and its justification—is one of the many disturbing consequences of our groundlessness. In the long history of philosophical super-science, the philosophers often dealt with the cognitive gap by denying it: philosophers as different as Plato, Spinoza, and Schopenhauer claimed to have established a solid basis for the choice of an approach to the conduct of life. But in each instance, they could not make this claim without first pretending to have gained what we can never achieve: insight into the ground of being, the framework of existence, reality beyond time and history and at the end of history and of time. Here is the first sense of faith: the leap that we cannot adequately or fully justify but that we nevertheless take because we feel that we must.

From the need for faith in this first sense, there follows the need for faith in a second sense: faith as heightened vulnerability to other people. For when a man engages his existence in a way that he is unable adequately to justify, he risks being mistaken about a life, his life, that he cannot live backward or a second time. And in that very moment in which he risks misusing and squandering the only life he will live—the moment of conviction and of action in which he must unsettle, in his own life, the force of habit, custom, and convention—he puts himself in the hands of other people and makes it easy for them to hurt him.

It is in the space marked out by these traits that ethics, as reflection on the conduct of life, must do its work. The course of my argument in the first three chapters of this book has suggested two points of departure: our inability to grasp the ultimate basis of our existence and the contradictory character of the requirements for having a self.

Our groundlessness, denied by both philosophical super-science and revealed religion, leaves us with no option but to ground ourselves. The issue is on what basis, by the light of what way of thinking, and to what end. The enigmatic character of our place in the world has more than negative significance. In every aspect of our experience, it poses a threat: that it will drain away meaning and authority from all the initiatives in thought and in life by which we seek to ground ourselves. But in posing a threat it also offers a prompt to awaken us from the daze of half-conscious existence in which we risk spending and exhausting our time.

The recognition of our groundlessness arouses an anxiety that is like no other: it goes not to a piece of our existence but to all of it. When the acknowledgment of our groundlessness is combined with our awareness of our passage toward death, which marks our finitude, and with the ordeal of insatiable desire, which expresses our transcendence, it fills us with a dread that we can neither accept nor reject. A central question for ethics is what we should do with this dread. If we seek to suppress it, we risk losing our most powerful defense against all the forces that belittle us and take us away from ourselves and from one another. But if we surrender to this dread, we risk seeing the incomprehensibility of our circumstance drain meaning out of our engagements and attachments.

Another point of departure for ethics, as I have argued in Chapter 3, on the human condition, is our need to reckon with the contradictory conditions of selfhood in the relation of the self to other people, to a social world, and to itself. An orientation to existence must accommodate our need for other people and our need to escape the jeopardy in which they place us. It must deal with our need to engage in a particular social world and yet not to give it the last word. It must acknowledge the requirement both to develop a way of being and to prevent this way of being—the rigidified form of the self, the character—from becoming a mummy within which each of us dies, by installments, beforehand.

To each of these contradictions there is both a political and a moral response. The political response gives an institutional shape to society and develops in historical time. The moral response is enacted as an approach to the conduct of life and must be given in biographical time: the time of an individual human life. We do not choose our place in history any more than we chose the parents to whom or the society in which we are born. The more distant we are from an acceptable political response to these contradictions, the greater the weight that falls on the moral response. The conduct of life must make up, to the extent that it can, for the failures of politics. This is the heroic aspect of ethics.

These two realities—our groundlessness, requiring us to ground ourselves, and the contradictory conditions of selfhood, demanding some resolution in biographical as well as historical time—do not suffice to provide ethics with a place from where to begin. If they were all we had, our thinking about the conduct of life would be confined to abstractions. And philosophy would again find itself legislating to mankind from some safe and uncomprehending place in the stars.

To be fertile and usable, a conception of how to live must resonate with the requirements for making a practical success out of society. The ethical is not the political, and biographical time is not historical time. Nevertheless an ethical conception is more realistic and useful, and has a greater chance of inspiring action, if it gives expression to what I describe later in this chapter as the functional imperatives of the advanced societies: the enhancement of individual agency— the ability to see and to act beyond as well as within the context—and the development of the higher forms of cooperation, those that untie our hands to cooperate and that multiply the occasions for us to take initiative together.

Moreover, ideas about the conduct of life will mean little if they are simply the fabrication of isolated philosophers, whom Robert Musil described as despots without armies. Any theoretician, equipped with a knowledge of what pleases and with rhetorical gifts, can make up such a vision and pretend to infer it, loosely or deductively, from higher-order propositions about humanity and its place in the world. Such inventions will remain dead on the page.

Here, then, are the defining features of ethics as I understand and exemplify it in this and the following two chapters of this book.

First, it has for its central subject the conduct of life.

Second, an understanding of what life is like and an imagination of what it can become in the realm of the accessible possible inform its ideas and proposals.

Third, it does not pretend to derive these proposals and ideas from a comprehensive view of reality, but it recognizes that no view of our situation in the world can provide an acceptable background to our self-understanding if it denies central aspects of our experience. Among these one of the most important is the reality of time, which is the medium of our existence.

Fourth, it repudiates the impulse to deny the irreparable flaws in the human condition—mortality, groundlessness, and insatiability.

It has no interest in telling feel-good stories. Moreover, it attributes moral value to the acknowledgment of these flaws.

Fifth, it recognizes the power of the distinction between descriptive and normative, between *is* and *ought* propositions, with regard to particular arguments and claims. But it understands that this distinction breaks down, or loses its sense, as our ideas become more comprehensive—not about the world but about ourselves and our situation.

Sixth, in forming an approach to the conduct of life, or in dealing with the approaches that it finds in its historical circumstance, it looks to the focal points of our experience of life and liberation: the relation of the self to others, to society, and to itself.

Seventh, it recognizes the importance of the distinction between our moral and our political ideas: those that concern the conduct of life and those that regard the organization of society. But it also sees the boundary between the moral and the political as open. We live in biographical rather than historical time. Our political projects are hostage to the vicissitudes of our collective history. We must live within the time of a human life, and compensate, as best we can, in our relation to ourselves and to others, for what politics has failed to achieve.

Every established social and cultural order translates the indeterminate idea of society into a series of pictures—at once descriptive and normative—of what relations among people can and should be like in different domains of social life. These guiding images of human association form part of the terrain on which morals and politics meet.

Eighth, it faces its historical moment the better to go beyond it. The failure openly to confront the historical situation, developing our moral ideas in the form of timeless abstractions, is only likely to increase enslavement to that situation. The contest of moral visions has a history. These visions—such as the ethics of self-construction and of connection explored in Chapter 5—develop their content and acquire their force and authority by virtue of their enactment in particular societies and cultures as well as of their resonance with lasting aspirations and anxieties. To engage the approaches to the conduct of life with the greatest influence in one's own historical circumstance, to take them as points of departure rather than as points of arrival, criticizing and correcting them, and turning them into something different from what they were, is one of the most important methods of ethics conceived in this fashion.

Ninth, the approaches to the conduct of life that it studies, criticizes, revises, or proposes have a twofold reference: on one side to interests or ideals; on the other side, to practices and institutions. Our interests and ideals are always nailed to the cross of the practices and institutions that represent them in fact. The law is the site of this crucifixion.

Our ideals and interests gain much of their meaning from this largely implicit reference to their enactment in social practices and in institutional arrangements. At the same time, our institutions and practices are not like objects in nature, to be understood from without; the way in which we represent them, in relation to the interests and ideals that make sense of them, forms part of their reality and is indispensable to operating and reproducing them.

The ideas that compose an approach to the conduct of life thus always have a double reference—to ideas and ideals that communicate with a view of who we are and most want to become and to the practices and institutions that we take as the setting in which these interests are to be satisfied and these ideals realized. We can—and ultimately always must—challenge the practices and institutions as adequate realizations of the interests and the ideals. But in challenging and changing them we discover in them ambiguities and possibilities of development that were previously hidden to us. The complicated and contradictory relation resulting from this double reference and from the imagined or representational character of our practices and institutions presents endless provocations to remake both society and self and reconsider our moral and political direction.

It follows from this understanding that the history and sociology of morals—and the relation of moral visions to what I have here labeled the functional requirements of a certain type of society—form part of ethics, although the study of those requirements and of the history and sociology of morals may require no taking of moral and political positions.

Tenth, every approach to the conduct of life is a prophecy as well as a promise of happiness. It tells us: act as if the view of ourselves, of our situation, of our needs, and, above all, of our opportunities that I take to be true were true in fact. By acting as if I were true, you will make me true—or at least truer than I was before you set out to enact me.

The self-fulfilling prophecy is never fully self-fulfilling: reality in ourselves, in society, and in nature fights back. The promise of happiness may fail to be kept: the higher experience to which the moral vision beckoned may turn out to be very different from the one that was promised. It may turn out be self-destabilizing and self-discrediting. The imperfections of self-fulfilling prophecy and the failures of the promise of happiness create a basis, albeit an inconclusive one, on which to judge alternative approaches to the conduct of life.

An eleventh feature of this view of ethics is to recognize the cognitive gap, the deficit of justification, besetting our ideas about how to live. It is not that we are unable to argue, defending some views and criticizing others. This book is full of such arguments and develops an argued response to the great matter of the conduct of life. Our arguments, however, are always in the end inconclusive. Our reasons remain disproportionate to the weight of their objects.

I began this chapter by remarking that the question about how to live is the only question that none of us can avoid answering. We may answer it only implicitly by the way in which we live. We answer it nevertheless. In answering it, we are not wholly in the dark. We can find light in our experience both personal and historical—especially in the personal and historical experience of what happens when we act out some of the prophecies and promises of happiness that supply the substance of orientations to existence. At the end of the day, however, we remain far from closing the gap between our inconclusive reasons and our inescapable deeds. We must take a direction, or a series of directions, in the pursuit of the only life that each of us will have without being able to have sufficient grounds for doing so.

A conception of ethics that abandoned all pretense to grounding in the methods of the school philosophy or in the philosophical superscience of the great dead thinkers of the West would bring us, by way of moral philosophy, closer to what we need and can hope to acquire.

If moral philosophy, like all philosophy, is to preserve its critical, revisionist power without succumbing to the temptation to offer self-help on the basis of philosophical super-science, it must take its material from the real history of moral opinion and experience. And though it may find inspiration in the whole of that history, it is natural for it to find special interest in the approaches to the conduct of life that exercise the greatest influence in its own time. For they represent, almost inevitably, where we must begin if we are to hope not only to see more deeply but also to act more effectively than we have seen and acted before. Of them, we have a more intimate knowledge, a knowledge not reduced to doctrinal abstractions, because we share the ground of experience from which they arise.

In the next chapter, I engage two such orientations to existence, the most influential in our time. I call them the ethic of self-construction and non-conformity and the ethic of connection and responsibility. Each of them has been associated with great philosophers. But their strongest form is often not the one that these philosophers have given them. Each of them has a long history and enjoys immense influence. However, even after being by tested by experience and challenged by criticism, they remain unknown in their strongest forms. They are associated with the functional imperatives of the advanced societies (otherwise they would not hold the place and exercise the influence that they do): the ethic of self-construction with the enhancement of agency and the ethic of connection with the higher forms of cooperation. The tension between these imperatives helps explain the difficulty of reconciling them within a larger, deeper, and more inclusive vision.

Each of them has a privileged relation with one of the two great powers of the present day—the United States and China. But each of these nations is powerfully attracted, with good reason, to the opposite vision. And the characteristics that these two ethics have taken on by virtue of their longstanding association with these two powers prevent us from seeing each of these approaches in its most powerful form: the form that would increase its appeal to the rest of humanity. These associations with powerful societies and cultures are the dust of history. We must shake this dust off to seize and make the most of what the evolution of moral opinion in our own time has given us.

By grasping the flaws in the present form of each of these ethics, we can reconstruct them. Once reconstructed and cleansed of the limitations that the philosophers have given them—out of metaphysical conceit and of the taints they bear by virtue of their association with the societies and cultures that shaped them—these two moral visions seem to draw closer together. And indeed they do. But we would be mistaken to take their drawing closer as a promise of their reconciliation in a single unified vision. In their reconstructed forms, the shallower differences between them disappear but the deeper ones shine all the more clearly.

Practiced in this spirit, moral philosophy does not legislate to humanity how we should live. It nevertheless speaks back to history and here too remains faithful to its oppositional and transformative calling.

The argument of this chapter begins by addressing the two most influential models of how to live that we have in the modern West—the Christian and the romantic—and discusses why they do not suffice to carry out the task of ethics as I have just described it. It then turns to the school philosophy—contemporary moral theory as practiced in the academy, especially in the English-speaking countries—with its distinctive interest in the formulation and application of a method by which to determine our obligations to one another. Unlike the Christian and romantic views, which are first-order ethics, the school philosophy is a meta-ethics, both embodying and concealing a conception of morality that we should reject.

I then turn in the next two chapters, 5 and 6, to the analysis, criticism, and reconstruction of the two most influential ideas about how to live operative in the world today: the ethic of self-construction and non-conformity and the ethic of connection and responsibility. I analyze and criticize each of them in the form they take today and explore the direction in which each would have to be revised to rid itself of flaws and emerge strengthened. From this reconstruction, there results, in each instance, a tangible image of how to live.

There follows a discussion of the relation of these two views of the conduct of life to two pervasive requirements of the advanced societies: the enhancement of personal agency and the development of the higher forms of cooperation. The sociology of morals is no substitute for moral vision, but it forms part of any ethics that can meet the tests of historical experience and social reality.

This view of the relation of ethics to the functional imperatives of the advanced societies leads in turn to reflection on the relation of each of the two moral visions to the great powers—the United States and China—with which they have had the most intimate relation. This relation has philosophical interest: by freeing each of these ethics from the character that it has assumed as a result of its connection with these countries and their cultures, we can deepen each of these moral visions.

The reconstructed forms of these two ethics are closer to each other than are the forms in which we find them in the world today. This fact may arouse the expectation that we can synthesize them in a single inclusive and coherent orientation to existence. But we cannot so reconcile them other than through what would be a misleading rhetorical exercise. The understanding of this impossibility and of its consequences—for now and for the future—is the theme I take up in the final part of Chapter 6. Underlying these two moral visions is a deep and lasting duality in our moral experience.

The Christian Faith and the Conduct of Life

An ambivalent relation to Christianity marks many of the greatest achievements of Western culture. Shakespeare's plays or Hegel's philosophy, for example, cannot be said to be Christian (though Shakespeare and Hegel may have thought of themselves as faithful believers). But they are unthinkable apart from the Christian message. My interest here is philosophical (and theological) rather than historical: not to judge the chain of influence in the history of moral opinion but to ask to what extent the Christian faith, as it has been or as it should be understood, provides us with an approach to the conduct of life that we should embrace.

In Chapter 3, on the human condition, I discussed the Christian religion from the standpoint of its meaning for our approach to the irreparable flaws in our fundamental circumstances: our groundlessness, mortality, and insatiability. Now I discuss it from the perspective of its message for how to live our lives. Yet the message of Christianity about the conduct of life is inseparable from its bearing on those flaws.

At the core of the Christian religion lie both a narrative and a conception. The narrative is a prophetic story of God's creative and redemptive activity within and beyond history, culminating in his incarnation and sacrifice. The conception—I argue in this section—is centered on the primacy of love (not altruism) as the organizing principle of the moral life, on our condition as embodied spirit, and on the relation between love and infinity—our transcendence over finite circumstances and our participation in the inner life of God.

For the believer, the narrative and the conception are one: the biblical story places the Christian message of the embodiment and transcendence of spirit and of the primacy of love in the only context that secures its meaning. Our natural understanding, unaided by the light of the faith, may find its way to the moral and spiritual truths proclaimed by Christianity, although stopping short (as Aquinas and others argued) of the mysteries of the Trinity and the Incarnation.

Those who lack the gift of faith may insist that what matters philosophically is not the undoubted and incomparable influence that Christianity (and its sister religions of Judaism and Islam) has exercised on our beliefs about ourselves and about the possibilities of life. It is, instead, the truths about the human condition into which the Christian religion tapped. The spiritual power of the religion results from its relation to these truths, however inadequate its expression of them has been. Those insights are not powerful because Christianity proclaimed them. Rather, Christianity is powerful because, in some fashion, it embraced them.

The unbeliever may go on to protest that we should resist making our insight into the higher possibilities of existence depend on the conviction that we have a friend in charge of the universe and that he became incarnate as part of his plan to save us. The believer may answer that, without the light of the faith, or caught in the halfway house of the sentimental will to believe, the ideas degenerate into the platitudes of a secular humanism: the moral and political pieties of the time.

But the test of the validity of this answer is what we can make of these ideas without relying on the faith. It seems that faith has not been enough to give to the spiritual and moral inventions of Christianity their most powerful account. The polemical concept of secularization fails to capture what is at stake in the contest between the faith-dependent and the faith-independent versions of these ideas.

In considering the implications of Christianity for the conduct of life, I begin with two of the most influential conceptions of what it means to live a Christian life: the imitation of Christ and universal altruism, described as Christian charity. They are inadequate, both on their own merits as moral ideas and as interpretations of the moral consequences of the Christian religion.

I take the imitation of Christ literally, and not just in the senses in which Thomas à Kempis understood it. The best way to follow Christ's teaching is, on this view, to follow his example. For a Christian that might mean seeking the combination of visionary teaching and exemplary action that every prophetic life exhibits, recognizing the immeasurable gulf that separates the condition of a mortal man from that of the incarnate God. But the implementation of that ideal in any ordinary human existence is hostage to both the limits of inspiration and the burdens of circumstance. And even to the extent that a Christian may seek to imitate his savior in this way, the combination of visionary teaching with exemplary action remains far from indicating how we should actually live in the prose of reality.

More plausibly, the imitation of Christ might mean living a life marked by sacrifice that is informed by love. A Christian must carry the cross. Christ's sacrifice, however, was, from the standpoint of sacred history, directed to a unique purpose: the redemption of mankind. And it ended on the cross, with Christ making himself the sacrifice so that men and women might be freed from death and sin. For the secular historian, it was the outcome of a dangerous activity undertaken by a Jewish religious dissident in the period of Roman domination after the destruction of the temple. The Christian must ask himself how and for what he is to sacrifice. For him, the readiness to sacrifice is only an element in the picture of how to live. But what is that picture?

Alternatively, a Christian life may mean a life marked by the theological virtues of faith, hope, and charity—of which charity, we are told, is the greatest. And if charity is not love, it is altruism: selfless devotion to others. If service to other people is the chief moral message of Christianity, and sacrifice only its expression or instrument, the moral message of Christianity would converge broadly with that of many of the other religions and philosophies of life that emerged in the thousand-year period from the rise of the Jewish prophets to the prophetic activity of Mohammad.

This view, however, fails to illuminate what is most original to Christianity: its greatest contribution to our thinking about the conduct of life. This contribution was the primacy that it gave to love and the relation that it established between the primacy of love and the share of mankind in divinity. It is to this relation that I now turn, for here is a doctrine that bears directly on the argument of this chapter about the conduct of life. Yet the unbeliever must try to do justice to it, for Christian theology and philosophy have not.

Love is not altruism. For altruism (or charity understood as altruism) the central problem of our relation to other people is our selfishness or self-centeredness. For love, it is our trouble in recognizing other people and being reconciled with them. We must overcome the ambivalence toward others that is rooted in the contradictory character of our longing for them and our fear of them, or of the tangible and intangible jeopardy in which they place us. For altruism, the threshold difficulty is the difficulty of conquering self-interest and self-regard. For love, it is the difficulty of imagining the other. Altruism can be offered from a distance or from on high: a unilateral gift. Love seeks an answer; it demands a plane of equality, whatever the difference in outward circumstance, social station, and age of the lover and the beloved. Altruism may require sacrifice, even the sacrifice of one's own life. But it imposes no inner jeopardy. Love requires and produces heightened vulnerability. Altruism need have no physical expression; any sensual aspect is foreign to it. Love approaches the other as embodied spirit and seeks the whole other person. As in the love of the parent for the child, the physical expression may not be erotic, but it goes to all of the beloved. In its eyes, the body acquires sanctity.

Altruism can be generalized as a cool benevolence, requiring no closeness. Love wants proximity. We cannot carry it beyond the sphere of intimacy without producing intimacy even among those who were, until a moment earlier, strangers. If love, unlike altruism, cannot flourish outside the domain of intimacy, there must be equivalents to it beyond that sphere. What such equivalents are becomes a topic for both ethics and politics.

The other central theme of the Christian message is the share of the human being in God's infinity. The human being is, according to this view, embodied spirit: incarnate in a dying body as well as in social and historical circumstance, but transcendent because sharing in the inner life of God. The idea was stated, for example, by Nicholas of Cusa in the fifteenth century. By becoming God, which is to say by partaking in his nature, we become identical to ourselves. If we remained only ourselves, we would remain separated from ourselves. The same idea had been clearly expressed much earlier in the history of the Christian faith by theologians of the Orthodox Church, like Maximus the Confessor, in the doctrine that there is an exchange of natures between God and man: God becomes man by condescension, and man becomes, and is called, God by grace. Even Thomas Aquinas, above suspicion of heresy, affirmed, in his Sermon on the Feast of Corpus Christ that: "Because it was the will of God's only-begotten Son that men should share in his divinity, he assumed our nature in order that by becoming man he might make men gods."[2]

Christianity did not invent our transcendence. It was one of the many instruments by which humanity discovered and affirmed it in radical form. In so doing, Christianity embedded its discovery in its sacred narrative of creation and redemption. When we develop, outside the bounds of such a narrative or of revealed religion, an idea of our excess over the social and conceptual worlds that we build and

---

2. This passage follows closely my *The Religion of the Future*, pp. 285–6.

inhabit, as I do in this book, we are not "secularizing" Christianity. We are sharing in the collective discovery of our transcendence and in the exploration of its consequences for ethics and politics.

What I call here the idea of the infinite in our self-understanding is the thesis that we become more human by becoming more godlike. We think, live, and act in such a way as to increase our share in God's attribute of transcendence rather than (as we would in a form of Prometheanism) in his attributes of omnipotence and omniscience. It is our freedom, not our power, that is in question: a freedom that we affirm in the face of our groundlessness, mortality, and insatiability.

Just as the predominant interpretations of Christianity failed to do justice to the theme of love, by allowing altruism to be mistaken for love, so too they misrepresented and slighted the theme of the infinite. The proof of this failure lies in the approach the major Christian churches took, in the course of their history, to the relation between the faith and the organization of society. Christianity entered into ideological transactions with these regimes, supporting a series of ethical and political settlements, each of them a compromise between Christian vision and social reality, such as the feudal ethic of chivalry or the Victorian ethic of family piety and respectability. Almost always, the emphasis fell on the restraint of power and class interest rather than on the transformation of reality. When, in the years between the two world wars of the twentieth century, the Catholic Church proposed, in the papal encyclicals of that time, a social teaching with an institutional program, the program took the form of communitarian corporatism, giving precedence to the overcoming of class conflict. The liberal theology and social gospel movements of the twentieth century sought empowerment and redistribution, at the progressive fringes of the organized Churches within which they arose, but never reached the point of developing a view of structure that would carry the idea of transcendence into the organization of society and the conduct of life.

The chief countervailing tendency in the history of Christianity has been the flight from the established structures of the world rather than their spiritualization or humanization: first and always, in the countercurrents of mysticism within the faith, and later, especially in eighteenth- and nineteenth-century Protestantism, in the privatization of religion as a matter for the individual conscience. That privatization had been anticipated early in the history of the Reformation when peace with the state and the retreat of religion into the inner sanctum of private devotion and good works came to seen as the alternative to theocracy and to wars of religion.

The problem lies not solely in the working out of the implications of Christianity for ethics and politics. It lies in the message itself and in its relation to what was newest and most powerful in the Christian message. Spirit—for Christianity—must be embodied in the world; it must not float above the world. Historical time is a decisive albeit incomplete setting for the work of redemption.

To that end, the relation between spirit and worldly structure must change. In politics the Christian should work to create structures that respect and equip our power to defy and remake them. Their usefulness to the fulfillment of our material needs is only the first step. In ethics he must make up for the failures of politics by giving practical content to the command to be in the world without being of it.

When a philosopher like Hegel, who regarded himself as a Christian within the reformed church, presented, in the *Phenomenology*, his account of the path of spirit in the world, he showed, by counter example, what a view of the relation between spirit and structure that is responsive to the idea of the transcendence of spirit would have to include. For Hegel, we begin with a form of social life—the way things are—to which subjectivity, our consciousness of ourselves, offers no opposition. Then we go through a long period of estrangement up to now, or up to the time of the philosopher, in which our self-consciousness is unable to reconcile itself to structure. It must oppose the structure because the structure, riven by internal contradictions, cannot provide a setting for our infinity. And, finally, we achieve the structure in which we can accept the way things are without sacrificing the consciousness of infinity.

For the Christian, however, there never could be a moment in which we are without subjectivity, or with a subjectivity that is wholly absorbed by structure, for either of these conditions would be a denial of our transcendence. There cannot be single route of ascent, passing through an immanent logic of contradictions and disruptions, that reveals and prepares the reconciliation of spirit and structure, for such a prewritten script would amount to another denial of our transcendence. And there cannot be a final settlement in which spirit finds a definitive home in the world and no longer needs to undergo the ordeal of estrangement, for that would represent a third denial of transcendence. These three denials are Christian heresies. They recall Peter's three denials of Christ.

Having addressed the themes of love and infinity, we must now ask what the relation between them is. You might expect that the elucidation of that nexus would be the central topic of Christian philosophy and theology. In fact, it appears there almost only in indirect and veiled form.

In love, not altruism, we reveal ourselves to one another as the context-transcending, embodied spirits that we know ourselves to be. And it is because we share in God's transcendence that we can give ourselves to one another in love.

But there is a problem: we are not yet these beings who can fully love another person and transcend their circumstances. We must make ourselves into such beings in the course of both history and biography, through the reformation of society and the conduct of life. Or, in the terms of the Christian sacred narrative, we must be opened up to love and to the infinite through the interaction between human striving and divine grace—an interaction that goes on in both biographical and historical time but that continues beyond them.

We can now take stock. The most familiar images of the Christian conduct of life—the imitation of Christ and Christian charity—are inadequate in themselves and fail to express the most significant contribution of Christianity to thinking about our path in the world. But that contribution, which I have discussed under the names of love and infinity, has immense value.

It is not unique to the Christian faith. The conception of love and of infinity has worked in countless ways—many subterranean and others explicit although often stated in different words—in the history of our ideas about ourselves and about ethics and politics. It continues to live in the two contemporary approaches to the conduct of life that form the main subject of this chapter. And it bears closely on the themes of this book.

The embedding of these ideas in the sacred narrative of God's dealings with mankind changes their meaning, as the doctrine of analogy insists. But it has not worked to uphold what is truest and deepest about the message, as Christian theologians and philosophers have promised that it would, and to save it from perversion. The message has been perverted at their hands.

The Secular Romance

Another image of how to live, expressing a view of who we are and can become, results from the tradition of the secular romance. Its influence on our moral ideas, especially in the West, is rivaled only by the influence of Christianity, with which it has been closely connected, at many times and in many ways, in the course of its long history. As in the previous discussion of the Christian approach to the conduct of life, arguing for the inadequacy of the beliefs about how to live that this tradition has most commonly been taken to support is only a secondary aim. My primary goal is to seek inspiration and direction for my engagement, in the subsequent chapters of this book, with two contemporary master models for how to live.

Now the source is literature rather than revealed religion: both incomparably more significant as founts of our moral ideas than the doctrines of philosophers. Both deal with secret knowledge, gained in the midst of dense personal encounter.

The tradition of the romance, extending over more than 2,000 years, has, together with the sacred narrative of redemption and of interaction between human striving and divine grace, shaped the moral imagination in the West. I address it here at three moments of its history, which I call early romance, romanticism, and late romance.

Early romance is the narrative of life as a moral adventure that emerged in both Graeco-Roman antiquity and in the Christian middle ages, with different emphases but similar and recurrent themes. The central protagonist is the young adventurer, at once superman and everyman, who goes in search of love and distinction. To win the beloved, he must face successive trials and tribulations that remove the obstacles to his happiness and show him worthy of the beloved. The tenacity with which he seeks her shows him capable of summoning the inner force with which to liberate others as well as himself from an evil that threatens them. The central tropes of early romance are the true love and the ennobling quest.

To advance, the protagonist must throw himself into a world in which violence and illusion seem to be in command. He must undergo the intolerable and look upon the terrible. But if he succeeds, he will be raised up to a higher, exemplary way of being. In the pagan versions of early romance his struggle partners with the favoring providence that sides with those who have an excess of life. In the Christianized versions of early romance, divine grace meets human striving.

Along the way, the hero may be the victim of usurpation and mis-taken identities, denying him recognition as the master that he is in the social order as well as in the hierarchy of spiritual value. The idea that there might be no relation, or even an inverse relation, between the latter and the former has no place in this moral universe; the moral adventures that it exalts have the hierarchies and certainties of an established social order as their validating backdrop.

Here, in early romance, we have an idea of love and of a quest but no idea of infinity, except insofar as it remains implicit in the idea of vitality. Hence, the struggle of the protagonist moves toward successful resolution, for it is the radicalization of transcendence, of the impulse of transformation and self-transformation that would push the self to the limits of the reality that we know. Even in the most sublime expressions of early romance—Shakespeare's romances—we see these limits respected rather defied.

Romanticism marks a second moment in the tradition of the romance: the romantic movement culminating in the nineteenth century. We find it in dramas, in lyrical and visionary poetry, and in the novel—an art form that made it possible to represent how individuals with indefinite depth could coexist with one another in a real social world. Its most telling expressions, such as Goethe's *Faust*, present it in contradictory and self-subversive form.

Superficially, romanticism fails to break the mold of early romance. Again, we find the hero in search of true love and an ennobling task. Again, he seeks the beloved. Again, he struggles to lift the obstacles that society imposes on his winning of her and to distinguish himself among his contemporaries. Again, the condition of his courage is his vitality.

Everything is the same as it was in early romance. And yet everything is different. The longing for the infinite makes the difference. The romantic hero must win the beloved. Does he love her or is he entranced by the pursuit rather than turned to the person? He wants her. But his life with her in the routines of married life cannot be depicted because routine is the death of spirit.

To become who he is and come into the possession of life, he must struggle incessantly. But what is the goal of the struggle, other than to shine and win the beloved, a beloved with whom he cannot in fact live? Each campaign is a whim, and, as soon as brought to a conclusion, replaced by another. Was he in love with love rather than with the apparently beloved, and seduced by action rather than by its supposed goals? Is vitality its own purpose and the source of its own meaning?

Everything is different from what it was in early romance because romanticism affirms the infinity of spirit—its unlimited depth and transcendence over circumstance. But how can the agent recognize in another person, even in the beloved, the transcendence that he experiences in his own being, as if gods could converse? And how can he find in a world that presents to him only finite and inadequate beings, experiences, roles, and situations the godlike power that he finds in himself?

Animating the anguish of romanticism is the conviction that the infinite can never be at home in a world that contains only the finite. We cannot hope to change the relation between spirit and structure, routine and repetition. We are therefore called to perpetual disruption in both love and work, in the knowledge that we can never hope to be at rest without ceasing to be fully alive. We are more human the more we are godlike. And we are the more godlike the more we are more vital.

Alas, life as the romantic wants it to be may not be able to survive the routines of married life, just as revolutionary fervor may be unable to survive the experience of routine administration. For this very reason, structure is fated to regain ascendancy. Spirit is unable to provide for a future without negating itself. But then, in the interludes of rebellion that it brings about by dint of its waywardness, it enhances its possession of life. The reverse side of our elation at this prospect is our despair about the transformation of the world.

The consequences become manifest in late romance—the third moment of this tradition, at its height in the mid and late nineteenth century, ushering in the great literary movement of the early twentieth century that we call modernism. Now romance faces squarely the test of moral and social reality: its disenchantments, its resistance, its threat to leave us belittled, embittered, and overwhelmed by grief. Late romance pursues relentlessly the questions about love and action that romanticism left unanswered. And it provides an elegiacal commentary on the campaigns through which the protagonist of early romance hoped to win both glory and the beloved.

In late romance, the issue is less whether true love and a worthy quest are possible in a particular instance than whether they are possible in any instance. Our experience of the intensity of life—forever the obsessive concern of the whole tradition of romance—does not happen when and where we think it should. It is more likely to occur at the margins of existence and of society. At the end of Flaubert's *Sentimental Education*, a masterwork of late romance, the disappointed hero looks back over his life and remembers a visit with a friend to a brothel. That, he says, was the best time.

The protagonist of late romance seeks in love an escape from solipsism and self-obsession. But he never knows for sure whether what he sees is another person or a projection, a severed part of his personality, standing between himself and the beloved. When he looks for a task worthy of his efforts, he never knows whether the candidate task is more than an expression of the arbitrary prejudices of a particular culture or of his own practical and spiritual need to do something. In work and love, he seeks both sustenance from society and escape from the self. The unredeemed social world strikes back, dulling people's faculties and denying them the means with which to imagine one another.

Yet even here, beset by self-division, at odds with a recalcitrant social order, and lacking confidence in any hierarchy of value and reality against which he can judge the claims of his society and his culture, the protagonist feels the pull of ambitions that connect him to the heroes of early romance and of Romanticism: to find the other person, and to undertake actions that bring him more fully to life. The difference is that the setting of late romance, as of the modernist literature that followed it, is a real society at a real time, not a primordial, recurrent myth. The test of success must be the achievement of the heart's desire of that protagonist, in that society, in that life, at that time, or else it is nothing.

Late romance is the culmination of the tradition of romance because it poses the decisive question of practice. It poses it after giving up, as Romanticism had already begun to do, on the favor of pagan providence or divine grace; its premise is that there is no one here but us. It poses the question but it does not answer it, both because it has passed its hopes through the skeptic's flame, risking nihilism for the sake of insight, and because it is art rather than philosophy or ideology.

To achieve the aspirations of romance in practice would be to realize it as both a way of living, the subject of ethics, and as a way of organizing society, the subject of politics. The two contemporary moral visions discussed later in Chapter 5 have a fundamentally different relation to this question. The ethic of self-construction and non-conformity accepts the premises of the tradition of romance and seeks to show what it would mean to achieve them as an approach to the conduct of life. The ethic of connection and responsibility denies the assumptions of the question. It begins from a different standpoint: it refuses to take as real the situation of a self, ultimately alone in the universe and containing unimagined depths, who must find his way in the world and reconcile himself with another human being. It sees instead as its primary unit and ultimate concern the intersubjective, the interpersonal—an *us* that is prior to any *I*—and that is the closest that we come to something of unconditional value and to a standard by which we might guide our steps. It asks how we can live in such a way as to preserve this treasure and to translate it, yes, into both a way of living and a way of organizing society.

It finds transcendence in the superiority of the interpersonal to the defective and ephemeral historical forms in which we find it. It prefers an expanding benevolence—beginning in the duo of you and me and informed by the imagination of other people, of their reality and their needs—to the intransigent idea of love that Christianity and the tradition of the romance have jointly given us. Consequently, it also dismisses as superficial and relative the distinction between its moral and its political ideas. Its approach to the conduct of life can advance at any scale, but it cannot be said to be achieved until the whole of our social life has been reshaped, in how we experience it as well as in how we organize it.

The School Philosophy

The criticism of Christian and romantic ideas about how to live helps make clear the work before us. So does the contrast of the understanding of the task that animates this argument to what I call here the school philosophy: the conception of ethics prevailing in contemporary academic moral philosophy, especially in its Anglo-American form.

The school philosophy is not a first-order ethics at all. It is a meta-ethics, chiefly concerned with the definition of a method, or a way of thinking, that specifies our obligations to one another. The method is usually complemented by a contemporary version of moral casuistry —the discussion of recalcitrant moral dilemmas in particular situations, more often hypothetical than real. But the main focus falls on a set of ideas that is supposed to serve as a basis for determining what we owe to one another.

The substance of the resulting ethical conception is, as we shall see, a legalistic moralism. Its first interest is to show us what we must do to acquit ourselves of our obligations to one another. Its campaigns begin and end in handwashing: its chief concern is to leave us blameless. Our reward for following its prescriptions is to arrive at the end of our days with our moral accounts settled and our hands as clean as were the hands of Pontius Pilate after he washed them.

There are three main candidates for the obligation-specifying method: the consequentialist, associated with Bentham and his utilitarian philosophy and felicific calculus; the deontological, associated with Kant and his categorical imperative; and the social contract, associated with Rousseau and reinterpreted by contemporary moral and political philosophers such as John Rawls. Although the school philosophy invokes the names of dead great philosophers, beginning with Bentham, Kant, and Rousseau, its moral ideas bear little resemblance to theirs.

For one thing, theirs was never only or primarily a meta-ethics; like other great philosophers before and after them, they sought to mark a path for the ascent of the individual human being and of mankind as a whole to a higher life. For another thing, in developing an approach to the conduct of life, none of these philosophers—not even Kant—were chiefly concerned with the methods and standards by which to determine our obligations. Their ambition was to help show us a way to live, and their ideas about obligation were incidental to that goal. For all of them, the approach to the conduct of life formed part of a general view of the human condition and of our place in the world. Rather than continuing the work of these thinkers, the school philosophy is an original invention.

In his *On What Matters*, Derek Parfit, an exponent of the school philosophy, argued that the three main schools into which the school philosophy is divided have equivalent moral doctrines.[3] These philosophies, he wrote, state the same view in different vocabularies. They climb the same mountain. Our job is to show that it is the same mountain that they are climbing from different sides.

Parfit took this far-reaching equivalence as a sign of the validity of the moral ideas whose supposed equivalence he explored. He formed part of a generation of academics who believed that they were witness to an assault of relativist historicism on the idea of moral truth. Parfit urged them to abandon their unnecessary contest and to draw succor

---

3. Derek Parfit, *On What Matters*, vols. 1 and 2, 2011, vol. 3, 2017.

from a convergence that he saw as vindicating the objective validity of the right ideas. If they were ultimately saying the same thing, despite the difference of the vocabularies in which they were expressed and of the influences and traditions from which they arose, what they said in common must be true.

The three views were indeed equivalent though in a deeper way than Parfit supposed, as I next argue. But the inference of validity from equivalence was unfounded. To begin with, the content of the equivalence, on either Parfit's account of it or the alternative account that I propose below, was far from being universally held just because it was an object of favor among English-speaking moral theorists in the second half of the twentieth century. It stood in stark contrast, for example, to the two sets of moral ideas I have just discussed: those that were inspired by the Christian faith and those developed in the tradition of romance. And the difference was no less striking for the many subterranean ties that bound the moral program of the school philosophy to a Christian faith it had diluted and transformed by several orders of magnitude. Its relation to that faith was like that of the ideas of the Sadducees and Pharisees who lived in Christ's time to the moral ideas of the Hebrew prophets. The teachings of the Buddha, Zoroaster, or Confucius, the doctrines of the Vedas or the moral ideas of the ancient Aztecs and Incas, were even less likely participants at this congress of adherents to the obligation-focused and rule-obedient moralism of the school philosophy and of its wan, post-Christian version of the early modern Protestant and rationalistic understanding of Christian morals.

There are at least two other interpretations of the equivalence among the three major voices of the school. One of them is that they are equivalent because they are empty. The element of truth in this interpretation is that the methods of choice of the three meta-ethical variants of the school philosophy are so indeterminate that they are easy to manipulate. Depending on the premises or boundary condi-tions that we stipulate, the choice procedure can be guided to one or another conclusion; the conclusion already lurks in those conditions or premises. But it does become determinate to the extent that we identify it with a particular practice or institution: a version of the market order or of democratic politics. The trouble is that any single version of the market or democracy has a doubtful claim to represent the procedure of choice. The indeterminacy, fixed in one place, reappears in another. The thesis that the three variants of the school philosophy are equivalent only because they are empty turns out to be no more than a half-truth.

Another interpretation of the equivalence is truer and more useful. The consequentialist, deontological, and social-contract variants of the school philosophy, unlike the moral and political philosophies of Bentham, Kant, and Rousseau, are equivalent because, as they are in fact used, directed, and made determinate by this philosophy, they converge in conveying a specific message about morals. Far from expressing a universal consensus of enlightened reflection about what we should do with ourselves and with one another, they express a distinctive, even anomalous view in the world history of ethics. The better we understand this view and recognize the contest of moral visions in our own time, the stronger the reason to reject it.

Consider the six elements that together unite the three versions of the school philosophy: three statements of the same doctrine—an orthodoxy according to its advocates but a heresy when judged by the standard of the moral ideas, such as those of the romance and of the Christian, that have commanded the attention of humanity and brought about successive revolutions in our moral beliefs.

The first common element is the idea that the central problem of the moral life is self-interest or self-centeredness, and the task of both the moral agent and his society is to master and restrain them.

The second common element is the perspective of impartiality, of a universalistic altruism, giving no priority to the interests and commitments of the ego-agent. Good faith means in morals, as it does in the law, to treat the interests of the other as having equal weight with one's own. And because the individual may fail to conform to that standard, society, speaking through the state and the law, must step in and impose this standard of universal impartiality in all matters essential. We may allow some margin for the attachments and loyalties that arise from family and community life. But we dare not let them gain the upper hand lest they undermine the supreme object of morality: the containment of selfishness and self-centeredness. We may fear that such an approach to morality wars against our natural inclinations to such an extent that it dehumanizes us. The unforgiving and unimaginative personalities that it produces—unforgiving of themselves as well as of others and oblivious to the contradictions and complications of moral experience—may seem to lead us down to a lower form of life. But the school philosophy, when it is consistent, holds that severity, and the sacrifice of inclination to obligation, is the price that we must pay for being righteous.

The third common element is a conception of the basic work to be done by the morality and the moral theory that the school philosophy prescribes. It must specify the obligations that we owe to one another. It may tell us, upon recommending the chains to put on ourselves, that these restraints will make us free. But it will insist on them even if we experience as servitude what it describes as freedom. If we discharge our obligations, we will, it assures us, be guiltless and blameless. Lacking confidence, however, that we will be persuaded to accept its prescriptions, it takes care to recommend that the spiritual and temporal powers of society impose on us what we may fail to impose on ourselves.

The fourth common element is a method that embodies the perspective of impartiality and does the job of defining what we owe to one another. If the method is the felicific calculus—the calculus of the greatest happiness of the greatest number—it will be understood and practiced in the manner of rule utilitarianism rather than act utilitarianism: the calculus applied to the choice of rules rather than to the ruleless choice of acts. Otherwise, no stable moral order could subsist under the watch of the state or even in the conscience and deliberations of the individual agent. If the method is the social contract, it must be interpreted not as a primordial constitutional convention in which we together choose a way to govern ourselves not knowing the interests and identities of those who will in the future be governed by these arrangements, but as an idealized situation of choice. In that situation, which moral and political philosophy must mimic, impartiality is guaranteed because we do not know the social fate that we may have been dealt and thus our interests and identities.

We are the faceless and context-less guarantors of neutrality among real agents. And if the method is the categorical imperative—the formulation of rules of conduct that we have reason to make universal —we conceive a practice of moral reasoning that solves what seems to be an insoluble problem. It must be independent of all identities and interests, soaring above them as if handing down the moral law from a position above the circumstances of any real individual or even any real society. Yet it must have intimate knowledge of what actual lives are like as well as a view of what we are entitled to hope for from our life together. Without the support of such knowledge and of such a view, the constraint of universality remains empty and sterile; in the absence of context, it can yield no content.

The fifth common element is the search for some practical institutional arrangement that does the work of the method in practice. The appeal to such an arrangement is no minor and dispensable addition to the other elements. The method is indeterminate for the reasons and in the sense that I earlier described. It gains determinate consequence only through its association with such an institutional instrument. The two leading candidates in contemporary Western societies are the market and democracy. Through them, politics comes to the rescue of ethics. There is, however, a problem. No version of the market or democracy is incontestable. And the most important reason for this contestability is that, despite the claims of liberal political theory rooted in the distinction between the impersonal right and sectarian visions of the good, every such institutional framework tilts the scales in one direction or another, favoring one range of experience over others. There begins a struggle, of ideas and interests, for which this species of moral thinking, which wants to infer content from form and particular implications from particularity-avoiding generalities, is unequipped.

Underlying these five shared elements that distinguish this approach to ethics is an attitude. It is the attitude of those who prefer blamelessness to transformation and self-transformation. For them, the moral life is not an adventure with the power to change the character of experience. It is a book of accounts, registering what, by way of conduct, we owe to others and what they owe to us. If we balance this book properly, being careful to remain in the right, we become entitled to stand in the front rows of the temple, raise our arms to the Supreme Judge—none other than the fantastical embodiment of our moral severity—and ask: Am I not righteous and blameless? Have I not acquitted myself of all my obligations? And have I not succeeded in viewing the choices that confront me from a perspective that denies everything that is individual about me? If we found a person who had conformed to this model, we would be right to judge him a monster and to consign his book of accounts to the flames.

Yet the message that the school philosophy derived from a truncated and shrunken version of the doctrines of great philosophers of the late eighteenth and early nineteenth centuries in Europe made sense when viewed against the background of the form of life and of consciousness that prevailed in that world—a form of life and consciousness that had begun to disappear (to the extent that it was ever more than a legal and theological vision) long before the school philosophy took form.

In that early-bourgeois European world, the market order was organized around the classical law of property and contract. The unified property right was then the exemplary form of all entitlements: it drew a clear-cut distinction between the zone delimited by ownership, in which the owner could exercise the prerogative of ownership with little or no regard to the interests of other people, and his actions outside that zone in which he suddenly became vulnerable to the claims of others. The law of contract represented the agreements among people as arm's-length bargains, exhausted in a single, instantaneous exchange of performances, rather than as incomplete contracts designed to shape the ongoing relationships that in fact penetrate much of social life, and did so even in the societies in which Kant, Bentham, and Rousseau lived.

This was the world whose thinkers wanted to see it as akin to that of the porcupines described by Schopenhauer: In the cold night, they huddle together to warm themselves. But coming together they prick one another with their spines. From then on, they move restlessly back and forth until they settle into an uncomfortable middle distance. The school philosophy is the oblique moral theory of life in that middle distance.

The political background to that theory is a proto-democratic liberalism, focused on the establishment of an order of right that would be neutral among unavoidably one-sided and conflicting conceptions of the good. The historical context for the development of this idea was the settlement of the wars of religion and the creation of a state apparatus exercising power under general rules. No such neutrality was ever attainable; the claim of neutrality helped insulate from attack an institutional order that, like every such regime, favors some forms of experience, interest, and power over others.

Social and cultural difference was viewed as the problem, when in fact, for our ascent to a higher form of life, it is part of the solution. The law, laid down by the state, was represented as the source of social arrangements when in fact it has rarely represented more than a series of episodic interventions in an inherited institutional structure whose real nature remained misunderstood. When democracy came late on to the list of political aspirations of these societies and cultures, it was a low-energy democracy that left the ideal of collective self-determination largely unrealized.

A low level of civic engagement in political life, lowering the temperature of politics; a deliberate perpetuation of impasse, slowing the pace of politics; and a strong constraint on the creation of alternative arrangements in any part of the country, as a false condition for decisive initiative on the part of central government, limiting the experimental potential of politics—these were the marks of this proto-democratic liberalism. Such a democracy—the constitutional arrangements of the United States provided the clearest example—added to the difficulties of changing the established structure and assured that crisis, in the form of war or ruin, would be the prerequisite of change. Thus, low-energy democracy converged with the market order that I earlier described to naturalize the established arrangements of social life and sanctify a particular understanding of what a free society was and required. Such were the political presuppositions of the school philosophy's meta-ethics.

The most significant part of the background to that meta-ethics—the part with the most immediate bearing on its ideas—was neither economic nor political; it was religious and theological. The world religions that emerged in the 500 years before and after the life and activity of Jesus Christ had affirmed that all the divisions within mankind, inclusive of class and caste, were shallow and bereft of authority. An ambiguity remained: did the Christian faith and its sister religions offer a redescription of our situation in society or an invitation to transformative action?

These same religions (as well as, beyond the Semitic monotheisms, Buddhism and Confucianism) had replaced the ethic of proud martial self-assertion prevailing among the ruling and fighting classes of the ancient agrarian-bureaucratic empires with an ethic of universal benevolence and altruism, in one of the most astonishing reversals in the moral history of mankind. Christ taught the supremacy of love, different, as I earlier argued, from a sacrificial altruism. But it was to the supremacy of self-denying altruism rather than of love that the moral vision of the school philosophy appealed. The predominant tendencies in Christian philosophy and theology, as well as in the magisterium of the Church, supported this Christian heresy.

The altruism that became pertinent to the meta-ethics of the school philosophy was not one that required the sacrifice of the self to other people. It was one that demanded of the self that it consider its obligations to other people from an impersonal standpoint, giving no higher weight to its own interests and inclinations than to the inclinations and interests of anyone else. But the appeal to this impersonal perspective, against the background of the idea that the divisions within humanity were shallow and without authority, stood in contradiction to the economic and political presuppositions explored previously: these presuppositions made the economic and political arrangements of the class societies seem natural and even allowed those arrangements to be mistaken for the institutions required by a free society.

A particular strand within Christianity exercised a disproportionate influence on the philosophers from whom the school philosophy claimed to derive inspiration: the Christianity that emerged from the Reformation and especially from the middle period of the history of Protestantism in the eighteenth and nineteenth centuries. It was a version of the Christian faith that had made its peace with the temporal powers of the world and had privatized religion, together with all forms of the sublime, as a matter for the individual conscience of the Christian. Moreover, when it took the direction of fideism—representing religion, in Kant's phrase, as beyond the bounds of pure reason—it opened a space for a successor to that faith that would remain within those bounds. That secular and rationalistic counterpart was expressed, with philosophical depth and ambition, by Rousseau, Kant, and Bentham among others, and, in the shriveled and formulaic manner suitable to its pharisaical character and academic setting, by the school philosophy.

It is tempting to see the school philosophy as the moral theory of a vanished world: the world implied by its economic and political assumptions. It would, however, be more accurate to say that that world never existed. It has also been said often that the philosophies from which the school philosophy claims to descend are a secular proxy for the living Christian faith. However, it most closely resembles a version of that faith that was far removed from the elements in Christianity that are closest to the teachings of Christ and that hold the greatest promise of informing and inspiring us today.

The school philosophy does much worse than evade the question of the conduct of life and put in its place a rule-bound morality, concerned with our obligations to one another. It also evades and depreciates life itself: its ideas are detached from any reckoning with the contradictory nature of our relations to one another, to the social worlds that we inhabit, and to ourselves. It shows, by contrast, what we should demand of ethics.

Finding a Point of Departure in a Contemporary Contest of Moral Visions

Philosophical super-science professed to teach us how to live and how to organize society. The discredit into which philosophical super-science has fallen chills any such pretense. Reluctance to legislate morally for a humanity that has sought no such guidance is reinforced by an awareness of what at the beginning of this chapter I called the cognitive gap: the disproportion between the weight of the decision to commit our lives in one or another direction and the adequacy of the grounds that we can ever hope to marshal in favor of any such commitment. Our groundlessness, rooted in the basic conditions of our existence, confronts us in all our efforts at moral self-examination.

The school philosophy enjoys a measure of protection against these embarrassments: both because it narrows its focus to our obligations to one another and because it deals with right and wrong only through the filter of a method that lays claim, albeit falsely, to the mantle of impersonal judgment, neutral among real agents and their inclinations and interests.

By contrast to both philosophical super-science and the school philosophy, the approach to ethics developed in this and the next two chapters responds to three philosophical ambitions.

The first ambition is insistence on a much wider, more inclusive and more practical conception of ethics than the one embraced by the school philosophy: a first-order ethics, not just a meta-ethics, and an ethics that addresses the conduct of life, as many of the great dead philosophers of the past did, rather than opening the ledger of moral credits and debits in the form of a doctrine about our obligations to one another.

The second ambition is avoidance of the two most troubling features of the way in which philosophical super-science developed its justifiably broader conception of the scope of ethics. One of these features was the attempt by philosophers such as Plato and Spinoza to anchor an imperative of existence in an account of the ultimate framework of being and existence. Such an attempt pretends to a form of knowledge that our groundlessness forever denies us. The other feature was the use of this false knowledge, and of the orientation to existence that it supposedly supported, to offer us a form of self-help: denial of our groundlessness, consolation for our mortality, and an antidote to our insatiability. Just as we cannot acquire such knowledge, we should not seek such remedies. Recognition of the flaws against which they would protect us provides us with an indispensable incitement to our awakening.

The third ambition is willingness to embrace the critical and revisionist vocation of philosophy: its interest in transformation and self-transformation and its struggle to speak to what matters most, at the limit of the thinkable and the sayable. Such a conception of philosophy can and must survive the fall of the super-science. It inspires every move in the argument of this book.

To reconcile these three ambitions and find a way to develop an ethics giving voice to all of them, I propose a particular intellectual strategy. It is to engage the two richest and most influential secular approaches to the conduct of life at work in the world today: an ethic of self-fashioning and non-conformity and an ethic of connection and responsibility. I take these present-day visions of how to live as points of departure rather than as points of arrival. I explore, criticize, and revise them. And I seek to understand, in the light of the contest between them, the contradictions and possibilities of our moral experience. I deal with them not only as they have come to us but also as we can reimagine them in their strongest form.

An advantage of this procedure is to rely on the testimony of shared experience, expressed in moral ideas developed by many minds, translated into social practices and projects, embedded in national cultures, and drawing force from the functional imperatives of the advanced societies. How very different from the philosopher laying down the moral law to humanity while claiming to ground his prescriptions in insight into the ultimate nature of reality.

5

Two Ways to Die Only Once

The Ethic of Self-Fashioning and Non-Conformity

The central message. Both the moral visions with which I now deal stand on the same side of a division in the history of conceptions of happiness. On one side are the views that understand happiness as the absence of suffering and even of conflict and contradiction in existence. Schopenhauer's moral philosophy is a clear example of this view. On the other side are views that conceive happiness as a flourishing that depends on fullness and variety of experience. Such happiness cannot prescind from contradiction, conflict, and suffering.

Both the ethic of self-fashioning and the ethic of connection stand decisively on this second side. They want more life more than they want less pain. For the sake of more life, they are willing to brook more trouble.

At the core of the ethic of self-construction and non-conformity lies a view of the self, embodied in a dying organism, as the fragile and indispensable medium in which each of us has life and consciousness, which is the sense of being alive. It is in life and through life that we share both in what is most real and in what has greatest value and deserves to be called divine. By acting and imagining—by exercising and developing our powers of practical and imaginative agency—we affirm the prerogative of life. From that beginning—of vitality expressed through agency—we enter into a struggle to engage other people and the social world in which we find ourselves in ways that affirm our vitality and agency.

(But what if the would-be agent is helpless and vulnerable, or even barely holding on to life? Or what if he has repeatedly failed? Are we not bound together by an invisible circle of love? Does not love survive agency and life itself? Is the exaltation of vitality and agency not power worship, adoration of the "bitch goddess" success? The moral vision I now explore will struggle to answer—or to evade—these questions.)

The ethic of self-invention and non-conformity has as its overriding aim to bring each of us more fully into the possession of life: life in the only sense in which we can ever have it, which is existence in the present moment, right now. It seeks to make us more godlike so that we can live for real, rather than teaching us how to live so that we can become more godlike. The key concepts in these propositions are coming more fully into the possession of life, becoming more godlike, and beginning to achieve both these goals now, in the present moment.

The experience of life is the consciousness of a power that declines in infirmity and ends with death but that remains unruly and unaccommodated by the concrete determinations of our existence. It is the intimation of a fecundity, of a susceptibility to change and novelty, that comes with every opportunity to affirm life by exercising agency.

The characteristic marks of this experience of life are surfeit, spontaneity, surprise, and fecundity. Surfeit is the excess of our capacity for experience over all the particular experiences that we undergo and over all the contexts in which we undergo them. Spontaneity is the potential to defeat the script by which a society and a culture direct what we can do next. Surprise, or the power to cause it, is what the agent witnesses when he sees such disruption manifest in his existence and hopes to be saved by the overturning of his plans as much as by their achievement. Fecundity is power in making the new.

The social order—and the ideas by which we understand ourselves—can either narrow or widen the opportunities for the expression of these attributes of life. A premise of the ethic of self-fashioning is that neither that order nor this self-understanding can ever completely suppress such opportunities; they inhere in the existence of a self, in the condition of humanity.

Becoming more godlike means increasing our share in the attribute of transcendence, not in the attributes of omnipotence, omniscience, and holiness that the believers in the religions of the Bible ascribe to

God. The secular and naturalistic meaning of transcendence is our power to exceed the social and conceptual worlds that have formed us and within which we move.

The reward for the exercise of this power of transcendence is the creation of the agent who is able to act against and beyond the context as well as within it. Society may give or deny the agent the tangible and intangible equipment with which to affirm his agency—the education, the safeguards against insecurity, and the other capability-creating endowments that allow him to thrive unafraid amid change and conflict. But whether or not society is part of the solution as well as being part of the problem, the enhancement of agency is not real unless it amounts to a basis for continuous self-fashioning. The agent is not an agent if some collective ventriloquist speaks through him, allowing him only the illusion of self-affirmation.

The object of the self-fashioning is the creation of a way of being and a realm of value that speak to the innermost concerns of the individual. It does not matter that it is made of little bits and pieces drawn from here and there, from example and history. What matters is that the agent has infused into these fragments a unity of vision and intention, that he has made them his, and expunged from them the poison of imitation. What matters is that they give voice to what touches him, rather than serving as borrowed proxies for concerns that he is unable to voice.

We cannot become more godlike and come into the fuller possession of life in the future because the future, like the past, is what we never have. All we have is the present moment, life now. A sign of coming into the fuller possession of life is that every moment in the short time that we have on the way to death becomes full of incident and pregnant with possibility.

In that time, our time, living for the future must not mean allowing ourselves to become estranged from the present moment. It must mean instead living in the present as beings who are not fully determined by the present circumstances of their existence.

Coming into the fuller possession of life, becoming more godlike (in the practical exercise of transcendence) the better to do so, and awakening to the present moment describe the change in our self-experience that the ethic of self-invention and non-conformity seeks to secure. This transformation in turn changes how we experience our relation to other people.

The deepening of our self-consciousness and of our self-experience, in the decisive medium of time, is the condition for our approach to other people. With depth comes obscurity: we are obscure to ourselves. We must be all the more obscure to one another. We cannot be secure in our sense of self unless we see this sense confirmed in the eyes of others—of the others who have undergone a similar deepening, not of the others who are imitations of one another. It is only in their love and friendship, and in cooperation with them, that we can escape our isolation. But nothing guarantees that we will find them or that they will find us.

In this sense, our self-fashioning remains both incomplete and precarious. We should not compare it, in the manner of the ancient Stoics, to the building of a fortress into which we can retreat the better to steel ourselves against danger and disappointment. It is instead an invitation to a response, which may not come.

We go forward in the endeavor that I have just described by resistance to the enemy who would deprive us of the fuller possession of life. The proponents of self-invention and non-conformity variously describe the enemy as society, conventional morality, or the depreciation of life. This enemy hands out a script that tells the individual how to think, feel, and act.

The problem with the script is not just that it comes from outside and inhibits the self-fashioning required by the struggle to come into the fuller possession of life. The problem is also the content. The script that comes from outside expresses the interests and ideas of the collective—of the society, the culture, the church, the tradition. It depreciates the power of the individual agent to create value and see beyond the regime of society and culture. It represents conformity as piety, imitation as wisdom, and self-abasement as rectitude. It denounces as self-aggrandizement every attempt to defy the script in the name of the exaltation of life.

For the individual, on the way to his death and powerless to penetrate the enigma of existence, the message that comes from the outside, from the collective, amounts to a condemnation. By denying him the substance and marks of life while he yet lives, it condemns him to die many small deaths. Against this verdict, the ethic of self-invention and non-conformity affirms the prerogative of life and the power of the defiant individual—the disruptor—to escape the anticipation of death. It teaches him to live in such a way that he can die only once.

Does the ethic of self-fashioning have metaphysical presuppositions? The ethic of self-fashioning gains nothing by the pretense of relying on a metaphysical system: another iteration of philosophical super-science, exercised as it almost always is to supply solace against our groundlessness, mortality, and insatiability. The most determined attempt to sketch such metaphysical foundations for the ethic of self-construction—Nietzsche's—did more to obfuscate than to reveal the assumptions about the world and ourselves on which this view of how to live depends. In the history of the ethic of connection, the Neo-Confucianist metaphysics that reached its apogee during the Sung dynasty offers a similar example of a metaphysical foundationalism that dulled the ethical doctrine it was designed to support.

But the perils of the marriage of morals to metaphysics, exemplified by this history, do not justify us in thinking that either of these two views of the conduct of life makes no assumptions about us and the world. To us in the West today, the assumptions that the ethic of self-fashioning makes and that I list below may seem too close to views that are today widely held to require much philosophical elaboration. But that is only because of the far-reaching and many-sided influence of this moral vision on how we think about ourselves.

They are non-trivial assumptions regarding the world and us, strongly disputed in the natural, the social, and the behavioral sciences. And although, on the evidence of the history of these ideas, we need not and should not try to embed these assumptions in a metaphysical system of the kind favored by many of the great philosophers of the past, they do contradict both major traditions in the world history of philosophy: the philosophy of deep structure and the philosophy of the timeless one. We can reconcile them much more easily with the counter tradition to which I pointed in Chapter 1, on ontology, and which I labeled temporal naturalism. They are also incompatible with the structural determinism that was central to classical social theory and with the non-structural determinisms accepted by the contemporary social sciences. And, remarkably, many of them are identical or similar to the assumptions of the opposing ethic of connection and responsibility, which, for the same reason, can more easily be reconciled to temporal naturalism than to the philosophy of deep structure or the philosophy of the timeless one.

Think of these assumptions as composing a proto-philosophy rather than a metaphysical system. Seen together, in the manner in which I now present them, they exclude a great deal: most of what has been thought in philosophy and much of what has been thought in science and in moral and political reflection. But we can formulate and develop them in many different ways without compromising their significance for the ethic of self-fashioning.

1. There is one real world, and the most important thing about the world is that it is what it is rather than something else.

2. Time is inclusively real. Everything changes sooner or later, including the most basic constituents and regularities of nature and change itself.

3. The new can happen. The new is not just the enactment of antecedent possibility that was awaiting its opportunity to come onto the stage of the actual. The new reshapes our understanding of the possible, not the other way around. Insistence on interpreting the new as a selection from a closed list of possible states of affairs is a metaphysical premise intended to reconcile the occurrence of novelty with the tenets of the philosophy of deep structure.

4. Human history is open. Change always faces constraint. But history conforms to no script. And the extent to which the past shapes the future is a variable rather than a constant. We can work to establish regimes that facilitate their own revision and overthrow the rule of the living by the dead. We can also try to live in such a way that we refuse to surrender the possibilities of existence to the rigidified form

of the self—the character. In the conduct of life, as in the organization of society, we can resist fate and by resisting it become more lifelike.

5. The self has unfathomable depth. The agent contains infinities within himself—the attribute called transcendence in the argument of this book. He can experience what the social and conceptual worlds he inhabits may not yet countenance. He can discover something before he can make sense of his discovery. A consequence of this power is the obscurity of people to one another, vindicating Heraclitus, according to whom the soul of another person is a dark continent that can never be visited. But it is not just other people who are obscure to us, as we are to them. Each of us is, for the same reason, obscure to himself.

6. The previous ideas are important to all the major variants of the ethic of self-connection. This sixth idea describes only one variant of this approach to the conduct of life: the one that places its hopes in democracy as the best basis for the orientation to existence that it embraces. The ordinary holds more promise than the noble. We have reason to resist inherited hierarchies of value, as well as the restrictive social and aesthetic forms with which they are associated, not because they are elitist but because they are life-suppressing. The forms of the "noble" in art and worldly striving, based on the marriage of privilege to refinement, embody a familiar, formulaic notion of greatness. The evil that counts here, however, is not only that they carry the indelible stain of subjugation and submission. It is also that they are sterile. Comedy is deeper than tragedy because it deals in the coin of transformation, unrestrained by the need to strike heroic poses. We must seek light in the shadowy realm of the commonplace.

These six ideas describe a world in which the defining concerns of the ethic of self-fashioning and non-conformity, evoked at the beginning of this section, begin to make sense. But something is missing from them without which no idea of selfhood can speak to our experience: the relation of the self to other people. We shall later see what changes this approach to the conduct of life needs to undergo before it can begin to make up for this omission.

The three voices of the ethic of self-fashioning. In the history of moral and political ideas over the last three centuries, the ethic of self-construction has spoken in three voices. In each voice, it has provided an inadequate account of itself. The inadequacies of each help point the way to a revised understanding of this approach to how we should live.

The first voice belongs to the philosophers who gave it its most radical form, Emerson and Nietzsche first among them. Both sketched a metaphysical or theological-anthropological basis for their war on conformity and conventional morality and their conception of self-fashioning. But the speculative scaffold has counted for much less than the psychological insights and the moral guidance. Both associated the exercise of transcendence and the enhancement of agency with an idea of greatness. Both failed to develop a political doctrine to match their moral teaching.

In Nietzsche, the combination of the cult of greatness with his relative political silence suggested an implicit political conception contrasting a spiritual elite of disruptors and creators of value to a herd of conformists who had surrendered the gift of life and abandoned all claim to enhance their power of transcendence. In Emerson, faith in democracy and in common humanity kept alive the hope that we might become greater together. But the political vision remained inexplicit and in tension with the exaltation of exemplary makers of their own fates.

The second voice is that of the liberal political philosophers of the last 200 years, including Mill, Constant, Tocqueville, Humboldt, and Herzen. To them, the enhancement of individual agency had central value. Political liberty itself was valuable because it expressed and sustained a more basic and many-sided power of self-definition and self-direction, opposing any script that society, state, or even established culture prescribes to the individual.

Thus, although their primary focus was political rather than moral, their political ideas bore the imprint of a conception of what makes us human. And they offered the ethic of self-construction the political program that it would otherwise lack. It was a program, however, not accepted by either of the other two major versions of this approach to the conduct of life.

That program suffered from two related defects. The first defect regarded its ideal of agency. That ideal was framed on the model of an aristocratic idea of self-possession that came naturally in the societies in which liberal political philosophy arose, with their class structures and their anxieties about the consequences of mass enfranchisement. The association of strong central government with a passion for equality and the advance of democracy unrestrained by counter-majoritarian safeguards seemed to portend the creation of nations of conformists.

But the equivalence, by default, of self-fashioning with a form of autonomy dependent on social privilege not only made the ideal of liberty hostage to continuing inequality, it also offered a view of autonomy that was too empty and impoverished to serve the purposes of the ethic of self-construction. That view was remote from all the complications that give substance to an ideal of autonomy rather than borrowing the substance from the atavisms and tropes of a privileged class in a class society: the complications resulting from the relation of the self to other people, to society, and to itself.

The ideas of the liberal political philosophers also suffered from another defect, more directly connected with their political message: the association of their inadequate idea of agency with a dogmatic institutional blueprint, the classical system of liberal rights and the assumptions about the institutional form of the market economy, liberal democracy, and free civil society with which it was associated. These institutions promised rights without ensuring the conditions of their effective enjoyment. The property and contract regimes and the low-energy democracies that they established left in place arrangements that perpetuated mechanisms of private and public oppression. Thus, the devices for securing the individual in his haven had as their reverse side the exposure of the many to realities that denied the promise of autonomy. Represented as an impersonal order of right, neutral among clashing conceptions of the good—something that can never exist—the institutional arrangements advocated by liberal political theory were in fact a very distinctive set of institutions, pregnant with freedom-destroying as well as freedom-creating consequences.

The third voice in which the ethic of self-construction and non-conformity has spoken is the romantic voice. Little need be said about it, because I have dealt with it at length in Chapter 4, on ethics. From early to late romance, passing through nineteenth-century Romanticism, this tradition has not only been one of the main influences on the history of moral and political ideas in the West, it has also been one of the chief vehicles of this approach to the conduct of life.

The autonomy that it values above all is agency as vitality. To be fully alive is its commanding aspiration. For the romantic, such vitality may be vested in a collective entity—especially the nation—as well as in the disruptive and rebellious individual. But whether it is expressed as individualism or as nationalism, its central idea is the contradiction between spirit—manifest in the individual or collective agent—and structure. Both its heroic initiatives and its fateful illusions result from this idea. It sees self-assertion only in the disruption of structure or of routine and repetition, however transitory the disruption may be. It can have no structural projects, no plans to develop, to overcome, or even attenuate, the contradiction between spirit and structure.

The romantic vision has nevertheless helped instill in the hearts of many millions of people the hope of increasing their share in the godlike attribute of transcendence. In its popular and worldwide form, conveyed by film, soap operas, and popular music, it has persuaded many whom it has touched that the ordinary man and woman are not so ordinary after all. In opposition to the teachings of some of the philosophers and oblivious to the fears of liberal political thinkers, it has represented the ideal of greatness in a form open to the great mass of humanity. It has refused to treat such greatness as the prerogative of a tiny elite of heroes, geniuses, and saints.

The characteristic weakness of the most popular and inclusive form of the romantic vision has been its sentimentality. The mark of the sentimental is its formulaic character, which makes it easier to understand and to accept, but only at the cost of compromising its transformative reach and its power to keep criticizing and changing itself. The bias to the sentimental also reveals a contradiction in this popular romanticism: it succumbs to routine while continuing to share in the romantic equation of the routinized with the life-denying.

These three voices—the philosophy of agency, the political theory of liberalism, and the romance of becoming more human by becoming more godlike and more godlike by acting on the contradiction of spirit to structure—are far from exhausting the expressions of the ethic of self-fashioning. The most important differences among these expressions have to do with whether we become freer and bigger together, or through divisions within humanity that separate out a moral elite with an exclusive claim on the power to ascend to a higher form of life.

Developing, criticizing, and revising the ethic of self-fashioning. Both major moral visions that vie for influence in the world today suffer from evident flaws—defects that even those who accept their premises should be able to recognize. Our interest is not to discredit these two approaches to the conduct of life; it is to render them in their strongest possible form. The result will be to bring them closer together in some respects, but also to make their irreconcilable differences all the clearer in other respects. They cannot—I argue—be united in a synthesis amounting to more than a rhetorical manipulation. They are contemporary expressions of a deep and enduring duality in our moral experience. No arrangement of ideas and words can dispose of that duality.

I will call the ethic of self-fashioning that emerges in response to the criticisms that I am about to explore the corrected or reconstructed version, by contrast to the canonical forms in which the history of moral ideas brings this moral vision to us. The whole interest of the criticism is therefore constructive: to rescue the ethic of self-fashioning from an understanding of its message that diminishes its power and appeal and leaves it open to obvious objections. The point is to develop it, not to put it on trial.

The criticisms fall under four headings. The first heading concerns the relative poverty and inadequacy of the assumptions that the standard versions of this ethic make about strong and independent selfhood, including its assumptions about the relation of the self to other people: the very experience that this ethic seeks to exalt and enhance. The second heading relates to the political horizon of this

ethic—explicit in liberal political theory, largely implicit in the philosophy of agency and in romanticism—which, whether explicit or
implicit, is so deserving of objection that it compromises the moral
message with which it is associated. The third heading has to do with
what I label the Prometheanism of the canonical versions of this ethic:
its glorification of the agent and its failure adequately to confront our
groundlessness, mortality, and insatiability, with results that threaten
to undermine and pervert its proposals for the enhancement of agency.
The fourth heading is, together with the first, the most fundamental:
the emptiness of the ideal of autonomy embraced by the unreconstructed ethic of self-fashioning. To fill this emptiness requires a
far-reaching reinterpretation of this approach to the conduct of life.

To use criticism as an instrument for the correction and strengthening rather than the deconstruction of one of the most influential
moral visions alive in our historical circumstances exemplifies a
view of philosophy, not just of moral philosophy: exercising its revisionist prerogative while abandoning any pretense to philosophical
super-science.

Selfhood and its contradictions. The prevailing versions of the ethic
of self-construction rely on a thin conception of selfhood and its
conditions. That conception disregards the three sets of contradictory
requirements on which the self-construction of the individual agent
depends. The complexities these contradictions introduce are the
stuff of what it means to be a self, to affirm that selfhood over the full
range of our moral experience, and to be rewarded by self-possession.
In the absence of engagement with these complications, selfhood is
an empty fortress: its inhabitants can possess only a shadow of life.

Each of these contradictions figured in the argument of Chapter
3, on the human condition. The first has as its subject the relation
of the self to other people. The need for the other is contradicted by
our fear of the jeopardy in which he places us: fear of subjugation
and of loss of distinction. Only to the extent that we reconcile this
contradiction—politically, through the arrangements of society, and
morally, through the conduct of life—can we hope to be free, affirming selfhood and expressing our powers of agency. In love we can

hope to experience such a reconciliation. But love, unlike altruism or benevolence, will not survive outside the domain of intimacy. We look for its counterparts among strangers. The most promising of such counterparts is free and equal cooperation, which, however, has no self-evident institutional form.

The second contradiction concerns the relation of the self to a social and cultural world rather than to other individuals. No selfhood or freedom are possible without engagement in such a world. Yet engagement in it may seem to require that we surrender to it and adopt its terms as our own. The need to resist such surrender contradicts the need to engage. Unless we can engage without surrendering, we are not free. There thus begins a struggle to define and establish an order that allows us to engage without surrendering. This conflict takes places in historical rather than biographical time, and we as individuals have no control over its outcome. To the extent that the contradiction fails to be resolved in politics—and every society so far has failed to resolve it to a greater or lesser extent—we must resolve it by the way we live.

The third contradiction deals with the relation of the self to itself. To affirm a self and to be free, each of us must develop a way of living and of being. But if this mode of being becomes hardened into a rigidified expression of the self—the character—as the character is in turn wedded to a station and circumstance, our experience ceases to manifest the attributes of vitality, and we sink back into a death in life. Each can develop a self and be free only to the extent that he can find a way to be in the world without allowing the rigidified self to occupy the place of the living and contradictory agent—"the thing itself."

Without living out these contradictions and struggling to reckon with them, there is no self in motion, no enhancement of agency, no coming into possession of a life that overflows the bounds of structure. If we are to uphold an idea of self-construction, it must refer to the construction of a self that is affirmed amid these contradictions and in unceasing attempts to deal with them. We must not entrust our lives to an idea of self-construction that misrepresents the conditions of selfhood.

◈

The political horizon of the ethic of self-fashioning. The uncorrected ethic of self-fashioning either has no explicit political agenda in the form given to it by its leading philosophers or, in its romantic and classical-liberal versions, has an agenda that we have reason to reject. Its lack of an acceptable political horizon has consequences for its adequacy as a moral vision.

There is only a relative distinction between ethics and politics. An orientation to the conduct of life extends outward to a conception of what relations among people can and should be like in different areas of social life and thus into the beginnings of a political view. An approach to the nature and potential of life presupposes an understanding of who we are and can become and thus also a view of what we should demand of life. The flawed explicit or implicit politics of the ethic of self-construction casts suspicion on all its ideas.

We can distinguish three main forms of the political misadventure of this ethic. The first variant of the misadventure is clearest in Nietzsche's philosophy. It contrasts a saving remnant, the heroes of defiance and overcoming, to a conformist majority. This majority accepts the religious and moral beliefs that devalue vitality and self-assertion in the name of supposedly higher realities and ideals: God and conventional morality. Nietzsche calls this devaluation nihilism, regarding nihilism (in the manner in which Hegel had regarded estrangement) as an event rather than a doctrine. What results is an invitation to hero worship and to a moral aristocracy of self-affirmers: those who have overcome nihilism in deed as well as in thought.

The philosopher's defenders protest that he nowhere draws this conclusion from his arguments and that he was repelled by the would-be candidates to rule over the herd of submissive men and women. Nevertheless, the glorification of agency in the absence of any vision of how such agency is to be shared among many—of how we are to become bigger together—leads, in the circumstances of the class societies of real history, to the reading that Nietzsche's advocates dismiss.

The romantic misadventure is the idea of an anti-politics that shakes established structures and allows, for so long as the shaking endures, for a higher form of individual and collective experience. I have argued before that this idea is based on a failure to understand that the extent to which the institutional and ideological order of a society remains entrenched against challenge and change and presents itself to us as an alien fate is not a constant. On the contrary, it is one of the most important variables in history. The romantic illusion—a form of despair about change in the relation of spirit to structure—results in actions and omissions that are more likely to undermine than to increase the widespread enhancement of agency. By failing to acknowledge that we can change the relation of such structures to our structure-defying freedom, the romantic abandons the hope that we might become greater together.

We find a comprehensive statement of the romantic illusion more clearly in the Heidegger of *Being and Time* and the Sartre of *Being and Nothingness* than in the art and literature of romanticism. The points of contact with the ethic of self-fashioning and non-conformity are many: the emphasis on the anonymous exemplar of the median way of thinking and living as the enemy of authentic being and real life; the appeal to our confrontation with death and groundlessness as a terrorization of ourselves that awakens us from the drifting and anticipated dying to which we otherwise deliver ourselves; the way in which the strengthening of our awareness of time and its passage signals our arousal from this life-denial; and the lack of any sense of the political as an independent (though related) domain of existence, as if the fate of society were simply a screen on which we project the anguish that confirms our arousal from death-in-life.

The political misadventures of the ethic of self-construction took yet another form in liberal political philosophy, with its narrow conception of self-mastery and its dogmatic commitment to institutional arrangements and legal regimes that began as spurs, but ended as obstacles, to the enhancement of agency.

The political horizon that the ethic of self-construction has lacked is a politics of deep freedom. Such a politics rejects the contrast between shallow equality and shallow freedom that has for a long time served as the chief principle of ideological division between Right and Left. Shallowness here means the equality and the freedom possible on the basis of the established institutional forms of the market, democracy, and independent civil society. Such shallowness implies the equality that can be achieved through compensatory redistribution by means of progressive taxation and redistributive social entitlements rather than by structural changes that influence the fundamental distribution of opportunity and achievement. Similarly, it implies the freedom that can be secured within the citadel of private property and of restraints on government. It remains largely blind to the forms of subjugation and exclusion that these arrangements not only leave untouched but also help reproduce.

The politics of deep freedom must cross the threshold of structural change. But, diverging from classical social theory, it understands that such change is almost invariably piecemeal and no less revolutionary in its potential for being fragmentary. It insists on what the social-liberal and social-democratic settlement of the twentieth century excluded: the changes in private as well as in public law that can democratize access to productive resources and opportunities. To this end, it refuses to leave the market economy fastened to a single version of itself—the version defined by the inherited law of property, contract, and labor—and to leave labor at the mercy of capital on the pretext of rendering labor markets flexible. It takes the engagement of an ever larger part of the labor force and an ever broader set of firms in the most advanced practice of production—today the knowledge economy—as a mark of success in the pursuit of its goals.

In the organization of democratic politics, it wants to establish the institutions of a high-energy democracy. Such a democracy no longer needs crisis to make change possible. It heightens the level of organized popular engagement in political life (the temperature of politics), hastens the pace of politics through the rapid resolution of impasse, and combines a facility for strong initiative by central government with opportunities for radical devolution so that parts of the country can develop counter-models of the national future.

As it creates the institutional conditions for the perpetual creation of the new, it secures the individual in a haven of capability-ensuring endowments as well as safeguards against private and public oppression. It does so by settling on every individual, to the degree allowed by the wealth of society, a social inheritance: a set of resources on which he can draw at turning points in his life. It does so as well by providing varieties of early and lifelong education that form a mind capable of seeing beyond the context as well as of operating within it.

These ideas mark a direction rather than a blueprint and begin to give practical content to the idea of deep freedom—the political horizon with which liberal political theory, the romantic tradition, and the philosophers of the insubordinate self were unable to equip the ethic of self-fashioning. I return to them in Chapters 7 and 8, on politics and on the program of deep freedom. For the moment, what matters is to grasp the implications of that horizon for the notion of agency and its enhancement presupposed by this approach to the conduct of life.

It is not lordly self-sufficiency, on the model of aristocratic prerogative and self-sufficiency. Nor is it the naked notion of autonomy, whose dangerous emptiness I address later in this discussion of the failures of the uncorrected ethic of self-fashioning. It is the ability to inhabit a social world without surrendering to it: engaging and resisting it at the same time. More precisely it is the ability to act in that direction even when society is not organized to recognize and support the exercise of this power. In this way, it gives a this-worldly meaning to Christ's command to be in the world without being of it. We refuse the last word to the established regime of social life and keep it for ourselves.

But we cannot be in the world in this way unless we are liberated by a way of connecting with other people that does not present us with an insoluble conflict between our need for them and our fear of them, unless we have a way of connecting that reaffirms us in the sentiment of being. Nor can we engage without surrendering unless we have escaped the tyranny of the rigidified self and of its marriage to a social station and a historical circumstance.

Thus, the experience of agency is struggle and movement in reckoning with all the contradictory conditions of self-assertion. And for it to be a moral idea, rather than only a political one, it must be an experience of achieving such a liberation in biographical time, the time of our lives, even when the arrangements of society do not help us achieve it in historical time, the time of the collective contexts of politics.

It is the same human being, the same unaccommodated man— moving toward death and ignorant of the ground of his existence and of reality, desiring the infinite and surrounded only by the finite, riven by contradictions in his fundamental requirements of self-assertion—who must be the protagonist of both ethics and politics. The moral and political conceptions of agency in ethics and politics must converge. But our individual response to the contradictory conditions of self-assertion in an approach to the conduct of life must differ from our collective response in organizing society: what society has not accomplished in its time, the individual must find a way to foreshadow in his time and in the lives that he touches. He must do so in the only time that he has: the dramatic interval of a human life.

Agency is not an empty idea of autonomy. We can equate it with autonomy only insofar as we begin to give the idea of autonomy the content that it lacks, as I propose to do later in this reconstruction of the ethic of self-fashioning. The central theme in the discussion of the political horizon of the ethic of self-construction is the same theme that reappears in every aspect of our experience: the relation of our transcendence to our finitude.

Prometheanism and the evasion of finitude. The radical-philosophical (as in Emerson and Nietzsche) and the romantic versions of the ethic of self-invention and non-conformity bear the taint of Promethean-ism. The classical liberal version (as in Mill and Tocqueville) is rescued from an overt Prometheanism by reason of its scope: its subject matter is explicitly political and for the most part only implicitly moral. Only in the more extreme expressions of its individualism does the Promethean impulse become apparent in liberal political philosophy.

By Prometheanism I mean the belief that the individual can raise himself to a higher plane of existence. In a meaningless world, he can create meaning. He can become a creator of values and of a form of life, rather than conform to the values and preconceptions that society would impose upon him. He can even make his own existence into a work of art. He cannot, however, achieve this ascent without heroic resistance to his world and his time. He must negate all the forces—including conventional morality and revealed religion—that deny his power to ground himself and that place his agency under tutelage. As he ascends, he may have to leave behind the mass of ordinary men and women who, by continuing to accept a hapless conformity, squander the supreme good of life and resign themselves to a diminished existence. They waste it even when the grinding inequalities of class and caste leave them room for maneuver.

In its spiritual and emotional subtext, even more than in its overt teaching, Prometheanism is a triumphalism and a species of power worship. It is an assertion and a celebration of triumph not just over the social and cultural forces that would rule and belittle us but also over our mortality and groundlessness. It beats the drums in the presence of death. At the same time, it worships power: the power of the life force that flows through us and that allows the rebels and disruptors to escape belittlement and come more fully into the possession of life. "He who thinks most deeply loves what is most alive," wrote Hölderlin, invoking an irresistible force that is potent as well as seductive.

By defining Prometheanism in this way, I mean to distinguish it from the romance of the collective ascent of humanity, which represents our rise to a higher form of life as a narrative of the evolution of humanity (as in Auguste Comte or indeed Karl Marx). The narrative puts a predetermined evolutionary script in the place of the radical contingency of historical experience. It offers no answer to the predicament of the individual who cannot choose his place in history and must face the consequences of the difference between biographical and historical time.

Augustine wrote that all ages are equidistant from eternity. They are not, however, equidistant from a higher form of life that can be enjoyed only by those who are alive. Men and women who live long before the promised consummation must decide what to do with themselves. Moreover, nothing in the script of collective ascent offers a response to the sufferings of a being who even at the height of the supposed ascent will remain mortal (though long-lived), groundless, and insatiable.

Prometheanism is distinguished from the romance of the collective ascent of humanity by its individualism. If it failed to place the source of agency and life enhancement in the individual rather than in the species, it could not have the close relation to the ethic of self-fashioning and non-conformity that it does. The point of departure of this ethic is the individual represented (albeit in another vocabulary) as embodied spirit, and face to face with his society and his time, against which he must struggle if he is to come into the possession of himself and of life.

Prometheanism represents a perversion in two distinct ways. On one side, it misrepresents the relation of the self to other people and to society and thus the nature of our selfhood and freedom. On the other side, it seeks in a show of power an impossible response to our groundlessness, mortality, and insatiability.

The Promethean fails to acknowledge that no man saves himself. He remains blind to the internal relation between solidarity and self-construction. He misrepresents, in his pride, the relation between the disruptor and the society that he pretends to spurn, and the risk intrinsic to such estrangement.

The nature of this risk becomes clear when we compare the Promethean turn in the ethic of self-fashioning and non-conformity to the position of the hero in the ethic of martial valor and lordly dominion embraced by the ruling and fighting class in the agrarian-bureaucratic empires of the past. It was this ethic that the world religions rejected when they emerged in those empires. The hero claims to vindicate his worth by deeds of intrinsic and indisputable worth. Yet he receives his task from the society that he depreciates. From that society he gets a mission—often to engage in action such as violent combat that is forbidden or marginalized in ordinary social life but that is useful or necessary to the collective. In his pride, he pretends to seek validation only in himself. Yet he craves the adulation of the non-heroic majority.

The Promethean hopes to avoid this contradiction by grounding himself and becoming the creator of his own values and form of life. The lack of realism with respect to the relation of the agent to the context converges with the lack of realism about the relation of the self to other people. The result is to contradict the requirements for the making of a self. Prometheanism mistakes secular transcendence—the excess of spirit and existence over structure—for the self-sufficiency of a loveless God: a God who, unlike the God of the Bible, has no need of humanity.

If the text of Prometheanism is the claim of a fanciful independence, the subtext is the evasion of the incurable defects in the human condition. The fecundity and variety of life in the present moment meet the fate of physical decline and annihilation. We cannot grasp the ultimate setting of our existence or see into the beginning and end of time. Surrounded only by limited beings and experiences, we seek the absolute and the infinite from the relative and the finite, and demand from other people what they cannot give us: assurance of an unconditional place in the world.

Prometheanism responds to our mortality by ratcheting up the claim to life enhancement, as if a limitless vitality could defeat death. It deals with our groundlessness by celebrating the agent who grounds himself, as if agency in a void of insight and meaning, other than what it makes up ad hoc, were no cause for perplexity and anguish. It answers our insatiability by riveting the Promethean's attention on the one being whom he has most reason to treat as the missing and voiceless God—himself, as if the unconditional and the absolute could be manifest in the dying, context-dependent beings who we are.

The price of this self-deification is to make the cause of self-enhancement hostage to an illusion. The illusion is a megalomania. The fantasy of divine power (mistaken for an increase of our share in the godlike attribute of transcendence) will require a narrative to be believable. This narrative will lead back—as it did in Nietzsche's philosophy—to another version of a philosophical super-science in the service of self-help or to a religion for the Godless.

But the greatest injury that the avoidance of the unfixable defects in our condition causes is to deny us the indispensable prompt to our awakening from the death-in-life of a routinized existence. Confrontation with these flaws awakens us to time and its passage, while we remain this side of the unimaginable gulf between being and non-being. The evocation of the never healing wounds in our condition then serves to support an argument *ad terrorem* that we make against ourselves.

Triumphalism is not the solution; our best hope of regaining time and coming into the fuller possession of life is to begin by confronting the reality of our situation in the world. It is to discard the lullabies, the feel-good stories, that deny the reality of death, groundlessness, or insatiability. It is to reject Spinoza's advice to think only of life, and to turn away from death; we need to face death the better to achieve the goal of dying only once.

The emptiness of the ideal of autonomy. "I shall do such things, what they are yet I know not, but they shall be the terrors of the earth." So spoke Lear. The most basic problem shared by all versions of the ethic of self-fashioning and non-conformity is the emptiness of its ideal of autonomy.

Suppose that the individual committed to this ethic succeeds in enhancing his agency and in affirming his resistance to his time and his society. To have gotten this far, he may need to have been socially fortunate as well as morally lucky. What will he then do with this hard-won or gratuitous freedom of his?

We do not need the heroic vocabulary of resistance and non-conformity to pose the problem. All we need is the Enlightenment vocabulary of autonomy and self-determination. Brought down to the earth of a relatively more modest moral ambition, the problem remains the same. The achievement of a greater degree of self-direction leaves us with the need to supply the content. What will each of us do with our expanded autonomy?

Progressives around the world, when they do not know what to propose, propose a constitutional convention. But if you ask them what they will say in this convention, you are likely to see your question remain unanswered. Greater autonomy risks being the constitutional convention of the children of the Enlightenment. What will they do with it? Will they fill it up with the petty desires of the society in which they find themselves, benefited by a greater freedom for self-direction but defeated by the mimetic character of desire? From where will they draw inspiration and guidance once they have declared independence?

To understand the sources and significance of the emptiness of the ideal of self-determination, consider the following dilemma about agency and its enhancement.

On the one hand, suppose we accept the standard causal picture of the determinants of action. What the individual does with his freedom of self-direction will be shaped by the whole of the influences bearing on him: his society and its culture, his inherited place in them, and his genetic endowment and childhood experience. This background will speak through him: it will provide the missing direction. At least it will unless he can reshape it, use it as a source of material to serve his plans, and find direction elsewhere.

To make the idea of this first horn of the dilemma more precise and coherent, we need to distinguish between the influences in which the individual plays no part—the past of his society and culture, the social station into which he was born, his genetic endowment—on one side, and his own self-formation as he develops a way of being in the world and of interacting with other people and struggles with his social and genetic fate. The individual is reduced to the condition of a puppet and his autonomy is eviscerated if this fate reduces the struggle to little or nothing.

Suppose, by the second horn of this dilemma, that the individual makes up what he will do, with enough independence from the causal background to allow for such initiative. He uses the causal background to his ends. Physical and social causality are so arranged that they create a basis for this possibility of self-direction under physical and social influences that underdetermine the outcome of decision. The reality of self-determination presupposes that a series of social innovations and moral practices, informed by this approach to the conduct of life, can expand the frontier of autonomy, increasing the power of the agent to draw freedom out of constraint.

Here, however, there arises a secondary dilemma within the frame of the larger dilemma about agency. At this moment, when he makes his agenda up, will the individual be guided by his social and perceptual habits, the rigidified form of the self, his character? Or will he rebel against his character, lest it come to stand as another fate? He may have played a role in forming that character, but once it takes form, it becomes a fate no less tyrannical than the combination of society and genetics against which he rebelled in order to open up a space for self-construction.

The most radical versions of the ethic of self-invention and non-conformity cannot be satisfied with the substitution of the characterological fate for the social and genetic one. They must demand that disruption and revolution continue. (It is striking that, despite Nietzsche's apparent radicalism in defense of this approach to the conduct of life, he accepts the development of a coherent character or way of being, perceiving, and interacting as the exemplary outcome of self-construction. In opposition to a more radical understanding of this view of how to live, he embraces the chiseled life form—one's own life as a work of art—rather than fearing it as a substitute fate.)

Imagine, however, that in pursuit of the more radical vision, the agent insists on disruption of the character as well. He has reason to do so. The combination of the character with a social circumstance—the place that the individual occupies in the class structure of society and in the social division of labor—is fateful. It is as if the constitutional convention has already taken place and all that remains is to live under the regime it has established. To live under such a regime is to forfeit the hope of dying only once. It is to accept as unavoidable or even desirable the mummy, made of character and circumstance, that begins to form around each of us as we grow older, and in which we die many small deaths.

But what is the alternative—the more ambitious and intransigent form of the ethic of self-invention and non-conformity? It requires the individual to resist the character and its marriage to circumstance, as well as the script that society would hand him to him, telling him what to do, think, and even feel. If the agent claims, even against that duo of character and circumstance, a greater power of self-direction, by what light and to what end will he exercise this power? The radicalization of the ideal of autonomy, through the exploration of the primary and secondary dilemmas posed by this argument, puts us face to face with Lear's quandary: the apparent emptiness of this ideal—not its emptiness as real or imagined power, but its emptiness as content and direction.

If we cast to one side the scientific and metaphysical controversies about free will and determinism, we can see that the problem of the emptiness of the ideal of autonomy reveals a confusion about agency in the ethic of self-invention and non-conformity. To enhance agency and exercise the power to transcend the context, we form attachments and engagements. The attachments connect us with other people. The engagements involve us in a struggle over the shape of the arrangements and assumptions in some piece of the world that we inhabit. Transformative tasks hold the promise of self-transformation. When we try to change some piece of the world, we may, whether we succeed or fail, manage to change ourselves.

Attachments and engagements form the substance of agency. Attachments require us to make ourselves vulnerable to other people. Engagements require us to take sides in the conflicts of our social and historical circumstance. Making ourselves vulnerable to other people helps free us from ourselves and open us to the new.

Those who did not take sides, Dante Alighieri wrote, never really lived; that is why they are confined, together with the angels who remained neutral in the contest between God and Satan, to the antechamber of hell and condemned to spend their time eternal chasing empty banners. But which side will we take? Our attachments make us vulnerable to other people. Our engagements make us vulnerable to mistakes: to taking the wrong side, out of an imperfect understanding and a defective will.

The content missing from the naked ideal of autonomy must come from our attachments and our engagements, viewed in the light of epiphanies and prophecies. Epiphanies are surprising discoveries about the possibilities of experience and its transformation. Prophecies are anticipations of a greater life, informed by epiphanies.

Without attachments and engagements, seen in the light of epiphanies and prophecies, the ideal of autonomy remains hollow. Its content must come from down below. And it is the dialectic between this stuff, the real stuff of our experience, and the light—often dim, sometimes bright and even blinding but always, whether bright or dim, subject to interpretation—of the epiphanies and prophecies that gives substance and direction to the otherwise empty idea of autonomy.

It then becomes crucial to ask under what conditions—including institutional conditions in the arrangements of political and economic life—we will have a better chance of enacting in our experience this dialectic between the connections and engagements and the light of the prophecies and epiphanies. The further we remain from this goal in the organization of society, the more important it will be to develop moral practices—regarding our attachments and engagements—that make up for the omissions and failures of politics.

The reward for these political and moral experiments—the more they are moral, the less they are political—will be a fuller possession of life in the present moment. Time will appear to us, rightfully, as the defining medium of experience in which we succeed or fail in taking hold of life.

A historian of philosophy might classify this view as a species of perfectionism. It is not, however, perfectionism in the sense that this term ordinarily bears. It does not recommend that the individual turn his life into a work of art. It seeks sacrifice and vulnerability for the sake of love, and self-transformation for the sake of the attempt to increase our share in the divine gift of transcendence. Remembering time, it accepts and values imperfection for the sake of more life.

The ethic of self-fashioning corrected rather than discredited: its surviving assumptions. The effect of the criticisms of the ethic of self-fashioning explored in the preceding pages is to reconstruct rather than to discredit this approach to the conduct of life. The revised version is just the one that has absorbed each of these four sets of objections. It works with a conception of self that recognizes the contradictory condition of self-assertion in the relation of the self to other people, to the social and cultural world in which it moves, and to itself. It acquires a political horizon defined by the politics of deep freedom. It frees itself from the taint of Prometheanism and confronts our mortality, groundlessness, and insatiability as a requirement for coming more fully into the possession of life. And, above all, it trades the empty idea of autonomy for a view that sees real autonomy as the product of our attachments and engagements, inspired by the epiphanies and prophecies to which the ordinary life of an ordinary man or woman can and should be open.

Yet, in changing in all these ways, the ethic of self-fashioning and non-conformity need not deviate from its deepest and most distinctive ideas. On the contrary, once this orientation to existence undergoes the corrections I have described, these premises shine through all the more clearly. Four of them deserve emphasis: all outlast, reaffirmed and strengthened, the correction of the ethic of self-making.

The first fundamental premise of this approach to the conduct of life is its embrace of the perspective of the embodied self, requiring other people and society, and yet ultimately alone in the world: the self that will traverse the arc of a human life and that will go to its death ignorant of the ground of reality and of existence. Even when it achieves the measure of recognition and reconciliation that reaches its apex in the experience of love, and even when it finds a way to engage in a social world without surrendering to it, the chasm that separates it from everything and everyone else does not close.

This premise—the premise of the self, of the ego, of the bottom-less and all-decisive reality of individual personality—is far from self-evident. It is denied by the other major contemporary approach to the conduct of life that I examine here, the ethic of connection and responsibility. That ethic begins from a different point, insisting on the priority as well as the sanctity of the interpersonal, of joint intentionality—not I, but you and me—which it sees as the primi-tive human reality in ethics as well as in politics and epistemology. Although each of these two moral visions can go a long way toward modulating the consequences of this difference between their start-ing points, the difference never ceases to be consequential. It is not cancelled out by the four sets of revisions to the uncorrected ethic of self-construction discussed in the preceding pages.

A second premise in this orientation to life, reaffirmed by those revisions, is the view of the distinct and embodied self as transcendent over context, no matter how closed and unified the society and the culture, viewed from afar, may appear to be, and no matter how much the agent may have seemed to internalize the collective narrative and consciousness. It is the infinite view of the self: the conception of the self as always containing more possibility of insight, experience, and association than the social and conceptual regimes under which it lives can yield or countenance. It is this quality of excess, and thus of potential transgression and transcendence, that we designate as spirit when we refer to the agent as embodied spirit. By contrast, the ethic of connection and responsibility, in its canonical forms, rests on a thoroughly finitistic view of the self: one that lays no basis for an ethic of disruption and a politics of permanent revolution.

The contrast between an infinite and a finitistic view of the human agent has both epistemological and political implications. It implies the indefinite depth and hence the obscurity of the self to others as well as to itself. It demands transgression and disruption as the road to salvation, if salvation means coming into the fuller possession of life in the present moment.

The conception of the self as exceeding all the limited particulars that surround it in no way contradicts any of the four objections presented in the preceding pages. In fact, it underlies them: most clearly, the objections about self and others as well as about spirit and structure.

A third fundamental element in this view is historical and political rather than methodological and epistemological like the first element, or metaphysical and theological like the second. It is the intimate association of this ethic with the revolutionary project that has aroused all mankind over the last three centuries. This project has presented itself with two faces. One has been the political face carried by the doctrines of democracy, liberalism, and socialism. The other has been the personalist face conveyed by romanticism and especially by the worldwide popular romantic culture.

Today this project—I have argued—is both strong and weak. It is strong because it continues to command the agenda in much of the world. It is far from unopposed; it has enemies. But all other projects respond to it.

At the same time, however, it is weak because its adherents no longer know what its next steps should be. Like every endeavor in the world, it is subject to the law of the spirit, which is that we can keep only what we renounce and reinvent. We live in what I hope will prove to be a counter-revolutionary interlude in a long revolutionary period in the history of humanity. For the revolution to continue, it has to be remade in form and method as well as in programmatic content.

The ethic of self-construction is a characteristic expression of this revolutionary project. Its history and influence are inseparable from the career of that agenda. In some ways, it offered a bridge between the personalist and the political faces of the revolutionary program.

The weaknesses of the ethic addressed by the objections listed in the preceding pages have also been flaws in the revolutionary program—directly on the personalist side of the program and indirectly on the political one. For this reason, the correction of that ethic forms part of the work of reinventing the revolution and allowing it to continue.

The contrasting ethic of connection and responsibility has no such intimate and internal relation to the worldwide revolution. It is not necessarily opposed to it. But its history and concerns are separate from that program. Its adepts and ideologists can afford to be both ambivalent and selective in their relation to it.

A fourth fundamental aspect of the ethic of self-fashioning and non-conformity appears in the domain of moral psychology. It is no less fundamental for having to do with an attitude because the attitude implies a thesis and even part of a view of life and of how to live it. Nothing in the objections explored earlier discredits this attitude although much in them bears on how we should interpret and enact it.

This approach to our existence accords a moral privilege to the troublemakers: the disruptors of society and culture and above all of themselves. It treats them as the spiritual aristocracy of the human race. In this spirit, Unamuno wrote: "The winners are the ones who adapt to the world. The losers are the ones who demand that the world adapt to them. Therefore, the advance of mankind rests squarely on the shoulders of the defeated." He went on to argue that Christianity is the religion of the defeated rather than, as Nietzsche had claimed, the religion of the resentful. By the defeated he meant the disruptors; he just preferred to draw attention to the price that they so often have to pay for defiance.

The moral privilege accorded to defiance and disruption has as its counterpart another attitudinal axiom, even more anomalous and disturbing by the light of the ideas prevailing in the major world traditions of moral philosophy. The axiom is: instead of staying out of trouble (as the majority of philosophers, as well as common worldly wisdom, recommended), look for trouble. Looking for trouble means, among other things, being willing to pay the price of a heightened vulnerability for the prize of social and self-disruption. It means casting down your shield—at least sometimes—in the hope of coming into the fuller possession of life in the present moment.

Nothing in the history of moral philosophy in the West prepared us for such a seemingly dangerous and paradoxical principle of action. Even if we look to Hellenistic philosophy, with its vast range of agendas for living a life and the contrasting moral psychologies that informed them, we find nothing that resembled such advice, not even the world renunciation of the Cynics. Renunciation is not confrontation. To accept vulnerability is to foreswear serenity.

The defenders of the ethic of connection suspect that under the pretense of social and self-disruption lurks the poison of self-aggrandizement, bringing in its train a host of evils, for the individual as well as for society. Their suspicion accords with what has been overwhelmingly the predominant view in the worldwide history of moral opinion.

The objections I have outlined strike at the triumphalism and the power worship that taint both the more conventional and the more extreme versions of the morals of self-fashioning and non-conformity. They attack, as well, the unrealistic representation in those versions of the relation of the self to other people and to the social and cultural world in which it lives. But they impugn none of the fundamental aspects of the ethic itself.

From this fact comes a task: to rethink and redirect the ethic of self-fashioning, in response to these objections, without losing hold of its fundamental assumptions and commitments or of the aspirations that continue to give them force and authority today.

The Ethic of Connection and Responsibility

Its central message: all we have is one another. All we have in the end is one another. The embodied individual exists as an organism distinct from all around him. The physical reality of separation sets boundaries to the passage of life from birth to death. Nevertheless, in our experience, so long as we live, the formative reality is our connection to other people.

The cosmos in which we awaken is indifferent to our concerns. Nature, which made life possible, has also decreed our annihilation as individuals and, later, unless we become powerful enough to change the course of the history of the universe, as a species. We used to fear nature so much that we worshipped it. But we have learned to defend ourselves against its terrors and to use it more effectively to our benefit.

What we cannot expect from nature is guidance; we must provide our own light. In a meaningless world, we create meaning. The individual does not do so alone.

The source of all meaning and value is our relation to other people. Consciousness unites us as the body divides us: all understanding, even our self-understanding is intersubjective. Language, ideas, the images and conceptions by which we represent our relations to one another—all live among minds or not at all. Joint intentionality—the intentions that we form together in all our practices—penetrates and overshadows the intentions that we form as individuals. So, too, human desire, because it is indeterminate or almost empty in its expressions, is mimetic.

The *we*, which begins in the relation of me to you, and extends outward to all social relations, is not simply the overriding formative power in our experience. It is also, for all of us, the source of value. The logic of the interpersonal is the sacred in human existence if anything can be. Our supreme concern must be to preserve and develop it and to express it in both the conduct of life and the organization of society.

The difference between the moral and the political expressions of this achievement is only relative. It is nevertheless important; it gives us distinct albeit related responsibilities: in the small, face to face, to attend to the needs of other people, and, in the large, to play our part in the effort to make our life together in society a success. Making it a success implies more than the order and prosperity that enable us to satisfy our material needs. It also means turning it into a basis hospitable to the kinds of relations that we should seek in our dealings with one another.

The interpersonal is sacrosanct: it has, or should have, a valency that nothing else in our experience shares. It is, however, subject to degeneration. The exemplary form of this degeneration in our close relations with other people—the domain of morals—is use of the other person as an instrument of what we want for ourselves—manipulating him, objectifying him as if he were a force of nature rather than a co-sharer in the sanctity of the interpersonal.

As such a co-sharer, he should be the object of both our reverence and our benevolence. To revere him, we need to attend to his moral and material needs, with the means at hand and in the circumstances in which we find ourselves. To attend to his needs, we must be able to understand him and to imagine his subjective experience. Benevolence uninformed by imagination descends into manipulative objectification.

We are not born as exemplars and custodians of the interpersonal. We must be made into them, through a process of discipline and discovery that begins in childhood, administered by parents, teachers, and other elders, and that continues, self-administered, throughout our lifetimes. In that process, we must begin to master the moral grammar of social life: the reciprocal responsibilities that we have to one another by virtue of performing certain roles. Conventions, rituals, and roles, against the background of practices and institutions, form and reform the individual on the template of the interpersonal, breaking what would otherwise be his voracity and self-regard.

This external or objective element in our history as moral beings must be reinforced by an internal or subjective element: development of the power to imagine other people. Without such insight, we may be able to undertake exchange at arm's-length to mutual benefit, but we cannot hope to give practical expression to the moral logic of the interpersonal unless such an exchange is enveloped within a form of social life that conforms to an ideal of reciprocity.

Under that conception, an arm's-length, one-time deal between strangers is the minimalist threshold of a spectrum of social relations embracing the totality of social life. In each of our ongoing or recurrent relations to other people, those that we have by virtue of occupying certain roles, there must be a reciprocity that is richer, deeper, and more varied than in the arm's-length, one-time exchange to mutual benefit among strangers. If we could describe all the forms that reciprocity takes in all those circumstances, we would have a complete map of the moral culture of a society. And then we could ask to what extent each of those expressions of reciprocity conforms to the ideal of reciprocal responsibility, recognition, and reverence that the conception of the sanctity of the interpersonal implies.

The ideal of reciprocity soon turns out to be irretrievably indeterminate and incomplete as a guide to what relations among people in society can and should be like. The moral logic of the interpersonal is susceptible to perversion in the larger setting of society and its arrangements as well as in the smaller one of our direct dealings with one another. As soon as we grasp the characteristic forms of this perversion and begin to consider what would prevent it, we are dealing with problems on which the idea of reciprocity sheds only distant and faint light.

The forms of the corruption of the interpersonal brought about by the organization of society—of all societies that have advanced beyond the most primitive economic and political conditions, and certainly of all contemporary societies—fall under three main headings: subjugation, disunion, and coldness.

Advanced societies require the coordination of people and resources on a large scale. In all of them, to varying degrees, the need to coordinate has served as an occasion to organize entrenched hierarchies of class and caste. Coordination has been married to subjugation, which poisons the interpersonal.

These societies exhibit intense functional differentiation under a social division of labor. Such differentiation creates disunion: in such societies, people have little experience in common. Disunion prevents the development of wider sympathies and circumscribes the reach of the imagination of otherness on which the moral logic of the interpersonal relies.

Advanced societies rebel against the confusion of exchange, power, and allegiance—the sentimentalization of unequal exchange between superiors and underlings, or even masters and slaves, that was the most characteristic formula of social life in many of the societies of the past. They have become freer. But in becoming freer they have also become colder—consigning social relations outside the sphere of intimacy to the middle distance. The moral logic of the interpersonal would call us to be both free and warm. But that aim may seem doomed to frustration.

The program of the ethic of connection begins as an approach to the conduct of life. But it ends as a social vision. Unless we can respond—first in theory, and then in practice—to the problems of subjugation, disunion, and coldness, we cannot develop the ideal of reciprocity or give practical content to the moral logic of the interpersonal. Before proceeding further—with the aim of developing the ethic of connection and providing the ethic of self-fashioning with a worthy antagonist—I step back to consider the unfinished history of this approach to the conduct of life.

The ancient canonical form of the ethic of connection and its missing contemporary representative. The ethic of self-construction has a recent and definite history, placed almost entirely in the last two centuries. It has its philosophers and ideologists and even its canonical texts, studied as modern classics.

The same cannot be said of its chief rival, the ethic of connection. To discuss, criticize, and reconstruct it, we face a problem of a completely different order. It lacks a comprehensive contemporary formulation. We can find its deepest statement in the teachings of Confucius, who taught over 2,500 years ago in a society and a culture radically different from our own. No one in the two-and-a-half millennia since then has stated with comparable force the approach to the conduct of life whose essence I have described, in contemporary language, in the previous section.

The Confucius who taught this orientation to existence and set what has ever since remained its canonical form is the Confucius of the Analects and of the subsequent tradition of moral and political teaching that he inspired. It is not the Confucius who was reinvented by the metaphysical neo-Confucianism of the Sung dynasty. The doctrine of this canonical Confucianism is strongest, clearest, and most useful when it remains anchored in the interrogation of ordinary experience without the pretense of grounding in metaphysical assumptions.

The ethic of connection is nevertheless a presence among us. It lives in fragmentary and inarticulate form in the moral cultures of contemporary societies. But it is not Confucianism, largely confined to China, Korea, and Japan, that inspires it. It is the perceived failure of the ethic of self-fashioning to do justice to what I described as the moral logic of the interpersonal and to the truth that what we have in the end is one another. It is also, as I argue later in this chapter, its relation to a functional imperative of contemporary societies: their dependence on a moral culture conducive to the development of the ability to cooperate and to the accumulation of social capital.

If, however, we look around for *our* Confucianism—a version of this doctrine that speaks to our reality—we cannot find it, at least not as a secular ethic that does not infer its proposals for how to live, as the Semitic monotheisms do, from a narrative of God's redemptive intervention in human history. (I argued in the previous chapter the reasons for which our received understanding of Christian morals fails to provide us with an adequate image of how to live, quite apart from its dependence on faith in the revealed religion. If we developed such a vision, believers would have to struggle to reconcile it with the conventional understandings of their faith.)

Nor can we look to the secular humanism of today as the source of the vision that we lack. In the course of its history, Christianity has entered into a series of compromises with the cultures and regimes of different epochs. Practical ethics in the West has been largely the expression of those settlements. Secular humanism continues this practice, without the light of the faith that such settlements compromised, whence its platitudes, its equivocations, and its lack of any unifying conception.

We are, however, not without resources in the work of developing a version of the ethic of connection that is socially and psychologically realistic, that bears on the experience of men and women in the societies of today, and that can stand up to the ethic of self-fashioning and non-conformity. The first resource is Confucianism itself, which we must translate into words and ideas that rescue it from its setting, so remote from our reality. The preceding section, with its account of the central message of this approach to the conduct of life, offers an example of this approach. The second resource is the central strand in the sociological theory of the late nineteenth and early twentieth centuries, the strand represented by social theorists such as Tönnies and Durkheim with their views of cooperation and social union under the conditions of the division of labor in the societies of their and our times. The sociology of morals is not ethics and need not incorporate a normative direction. But ethics, as I propose to understand and develop it in this book, must include a sociology of morals. The third resource is contemporary evolutionary and cognitive psychology, which has shown the central role of cooperation in both ontogeny and phylogeny. An ethic of connection that deserves our attention and that can rival the ethic of self-fashioning must be informed by an understanding of our natural history as individuals and as a species. Otherwise, its visions of the moral logic of the interpersonal may amount to no more than a series of philosophical conceits.

Suppose that with these resources in hand we develop a view of the ethic of connection that can speak to us now. We will then discover that, once we take it beyond its basic propositions and bring it to bear on our present experience, we can develop it two different directions. I will call one of them the minimalist or relatively conservative version of the ethic of connection and the other the maximalist or relatively transformative version.

They differ according to two principles. The first principle of distinction is the extent to which each of these versions of the ethic of connection accepts the established organization of society as the template on which to realize its moral program. No version of the ethic can accept society as it is, as Confucius and his followers did not. But the maximalist ethic of connection, unlike the minimalist alternative, wants a radical reshaping of the institutions and practices, not simply their humanization.

The second principle of distinction is the degree to which our understanding of the moral logic of the interpersonal admits conflict and contradiction in its assumptions about the self and the relation of the self to other people, to society, and to itself. The maximalist version of the ethic, unlike its minimalist counterpart, views the self through the prism of all the contradictory conditions of selfhood explored in the earlier analysis of the ethic of self-fashioning. The minimalist version sees harmony and reconciliation within the self, as well as among selves, as the reward for its pursuit.

It is a matter of merely idea-historical interest which of these two variants is closer to the teachings of Confucius. It seems clear to me that it is the minimalist version, as the critics of Confucianism within China have always argued. But a student of those ancient teachings might well disagree. What matters is that we understand how much the ethic of connection, once given its maximalist voice, differs from a conservative communitarianism, and reject any attempt to humanize a world that we despair of reimagining and remaking.

The two principles of distinction are closely related. An idea of the self as riven by contradictions creates an opening for more radical change in the institutions and practices of society. And a social world peopled by such selves must seek arrangements that recognize and accept who they are.

The maximalist ethic of connection is, in the argument of this chapter, the counterpart to the reconstructed ethic of self-fashioning. Just as the latter emerges from the criticism of the uncorrected ethic of self-construction so the former results from the criticism of the minimalist ethic of connection. The maximalist ethic of connection is much closer to the corrected version of the ethic of self-fashioning than the minimalist version of the ethic of connection is to the uncorrected version of the ethic of self-fashioning.

However, the partial convergence between the maximalist ethic of connection and the corrected ethic of self-fashioning does not, I will argue, signal an ultimate reconciliation between them. As they come closer together, shedding distinctions that result from their most superficial traits, what more deeply distinguishes them appears all the more clearly. For behind the contrast between them lies an enduring contrast in our moral experience and in our attitudes and ideas about what we can expect from one another and from life.

It is not my purpose to paper over this contrast with verbal formulas or to add to the procession of feel-good stories that fill much of the history of philosophy. My aim is rather to describe the terms of a contest of visions that remains incompletely expressed. The greatest obstacle to its expression is that one of the two chairs in this debate remains vacant: the ethic of connection lacks adequate living representatives. As a result, we stand deprived of the most promising inducement that those of us who do not believe ourselves to be instructed by divine revelation can hope to have for the development and correction of our ideas about the conduct of life.

You may wonder, reader, why I proceed in this fashion. You may suspect that I am opposed to the ethic of self-fashioning and am trying to find enemies for it more formidable than those that it already has. You are mistaken. All my sympathies lie with that moral vision: with its implied image of the unaccommodated and transcendent self forever seeking the infinite amid the finite, with its bond to world revolution in both political and personal form, and with its election of the disruptors as the salt of the earth. But I recognize that in its received form it is defective. If it is to have a future, we must breathe new meaning and new life into it. And to breathe such meaning and life into it we must find for it worthy antagonists.

If these were all my motivations, I would have stopped there, with the analysis, criticism, and reshaping of the ethic of self-construction. But, while I reject the moralistic legalism and meta-ethical evasions of the school philosophy, I also refuse to share in the practice of ethics as the distribution of unsolicited moral advice to humanity claiming the false authority of philosophical super-science. And I recognize what early in this chapter I called the cognitive gap: the fact that for our most important decisions—about how to live and what to do with our lives—we always have inconclusive grounds.

Ethics must engage the most significant approaches to the conduct of life in our historical circumstance—those that have the widest appeal because they resonate most with our deepest experiences and our strongest longings. If such orientations to existence are in conflict, moral philosophy must make the most of that contest and present each of the contestants in their strongest form. It must do so in the hope that even though we may be unable to achieve a genuine reconciliation between them, the contest itself may both reveal and improve our most promising moral options and help raise us up to a higher form of life.

To develop ethics in this spirit is to remain faithful to the conception of philosophy that runs through this book. Philosophy renounces the claim to grasp the ultimate framework of reality and on that basis to direct us in morals and politics as well as in all our forms of inquiry. What it does not abdicate is our power to see and to act beyond the social and conceptual regimes that we inhabit and to challenge them even though it cannot rest its challenge on the pretense of higher knowledge. It has no special instruments for this work other than the ideas and experiences that our collective history has laid before us. It does in thought what we must all do in life: affirm our powers of transcendence without denying the reality of our finitude.

From the ideal of reciprocity to "the way things are." Having described the core message of the ethic of connection and discussed its sources and antecedents, I now develop a view of this approach to the conduct of life. My aim is to present it in its strongest form, as the leading contemporary secular alternative to the ethic of self-fashioning, without denying that we can understand and develop it in more than one way. I advance in three steps. First, I discuss the ideal of reciprocity, which roots this moral vision in the way we develop as persons and as societies. Second, I show why the commitment to reciprocity must lead, beyond itself, into a discussion of "the way things are": from the moral logic of interpersonal encounter to the moral order of society. Its meaning for the conduct of life as well as for the ordering of our social relations is revealed by its response to the problems of subjugation, disunion, and coldness. The variations of that response in turn show that this ethic can have two very different futures. Third, I explore, in the light of this analysis, the significance of the contest between the ethics of connection and of self-fashioning.

The foundation of the ethic of connection is an ideal of reciprocity. In the history of moral ideas, the golden rule is the oldest and most universal expression of that ideal. Confucius stated it in negative form: do not do to others what you would not have them do to you. Christ invoked it in positive form: do unto others what you would have them do unto you.

The formula of the golden rule is neither self-explanatory nor self-justifying. It derives its force from our dependence on one another in every aspect of existence, from our consequent need to cooperate, and from the fragility of any form of cooperation that fails to be sustained by reciprocity and must therefore be coercive. In its most completely realized form, reciprocity requires the sharing of stakes in a cooperative practice. It is realized most fully when those stakes are moral as well as material and when it gives practical expression to the idea that the *we* must precede the *I*. It demands that we engage in all our relations from the perspective of the other person as well as from our own, and that we free ourselves from submission to the isolated ego.

It is therefore a solution to what in my discussion of the ethic of self-fashioning, and earlier of the human condition, I described as the contradiction between the need to connect with the other person and the struggle to prevent the connection from undermining the self. From the standpoint of this ethic, there is never an alternative to connection. The only question is whether connection will take a form that allows us to rise together. The ideal of reciprocity expresses the hope that it will. Everything depends on the institutional details of the social arrangements informed by that ideal, once our relations to one another begin to take shape in a real society.

The golden rule and the ideal of reciprocity. Considered with respect to its practical implications for social life, reciprocity has to do with the centrality of cooperation in social life. Viewed from the standpoint of its implications for how we see and experience our relations to other people, reciprocity goes to our ability to overcome the self-centeredness of the ego and to approach these relations from the perspective of the other as well as from our own, freeing ourselves from submission to the isolated ego.

The evolutionary and cognitive psychology of our time has shown that the ideal of reciprocity has a central place in both the moral development of the individual and the moral evolution of humanity. Its phylogenetic function is mirrored in its ontogenetic role. The simple exchange of obedience for love and protection gives way, in the experience of the child, to a more subtle exchange: the willingness to work and play with others within the limits laid down by the elders in authority. The imaginative self-absorption of the child must not be allowed to become so extreme that it disrupts the group activity, sets the individual against the group, or turns the work and play of the children into a counter-model to the world for which they are beginning to be prepared.

In its ontogenetic role, reciprocity is not the free invention of society, grounded on moral and material exchange. It is not the spontaneous order imagined by the fundamentalist version of marginalist economy theory. It is, from the outset, cooperation within constraint, and the occasional deviations from its logic only highlight the severity of its limits.

The answer to the question of what it is that children exchange in the activities by which they manifest and develop reciprocity among themselves and with adults is: whatever they need to exchange to sustain a connection among themselves within the margin of maneuver they are allowed by the regime of the grown-ups. Only two forces soften the strictness of the limits that this order imposes on their play: love and imagination—the love the parents give the child, assuring it of an unconditional place in the world; and the imagination of the transformative variations of the order in the realm of the accessible possible. These forces allow the child the fantasy of play liberated from the constraints that the children must accept. Here, in this picture of constrained cooperation, giving content to an indeterminate and almost empty ideal of reciprocity, we already have all the elements with which the development of the ethic of connection must contend.

In its phylogenetic role, as a theme in the moral evolution of mankind, the ideal of reciprocity gains its force by its relation to our cooperative practices. Every aspect of our history as a species, from the development of our capacity to produce wealth and to wage war to the evolution of our thinking, has depended on our ability to cooperate. The future of that ability—its forms, requirements, and consequences—is the fate of humankind itself. By virtue of its relation to the norm of reciprocity, and of that norm to our practices and regimes of cooperation, the ethic of connection acquires immense force and appeal. It can claim to be rooted in the most basic features of our natural history as a species, not simply in moral and political abstractions.

A simple way to understand the relation between that ideal and social practices and institutions is to interpret reciprocity as good faith in the legal sense. In both the civil-law and common-law traditions, good faith has its home in contract and in our quasi-contractual dealings. To act in good faith is, on one account, to give to the interests of the other party a weight equal to one's own interests (whereas to act as a fiduciary is to act in the interest of the other party). It is to approach any transaction or relationship as a collaborative endeavor, not as an opportunity to extract the greatest advantage in the performance as well as in the formulation of the agreement. For the joint endeavor to prosper, the agreement must not be leonine, allowing one party to devour the other. Both parties must have a stake in its success, and there must be a rough equivalence between these stakes—if not by some independent, objective measure, then in the eyes of the parties themselves. Good faith excludes self-dealing, fraud, free-riding, and taking advantage of innocent mistakes and unexpected circumstances to extract maximum advantage for oneself, regardless of the effect of such advantage on the other party and on the future of the joint endeavor.

In what has been, in both the civil-law and common-law traditions, the default model of contract—the arm's-length, fully defined agreement among strangers for a one-time exchange of performances in the future—good faith can have only a peripheral place, policing both the interpretation and the performance of the agreement. But in the form of contract that in fact pervades much of social and economic life, even in societies in which the law accepts that view of contract as the default model, good faith is central. This alternative to the bilateral executory promise is the ongoing, not fully articulated, relational contract for an open-ended series of exchanges in the future. For such a relational contract, the future of the joint endeavor counts more than any momentary exchange under its aegis. And good faith, understood inclusively as I defined it earlier, is central to the development of the relationship, from beginning to end. To place the ideal of reciprocity at the center is to view all social life as a combination of such ongoing relationships, dependent for their success and survival on good faith as reciprocity, taken to heart.

How does this view of reciprocity relate to the moral logic of the interpersonal and of joint intentionality, and to the sanctity attached by that logic to the relation between me and you? The answer is that to penetrate and redeem our life in society, recuing it from degeneration, this moral logic must extend outward into all our social experience: our relation to one another as relative strangers by virtue of performing certain roles vis-à-vis one another, and our dealings with one another under the ongoing, not fully articulated contracts that form the substance of much of our social experience. Reciprocity as good faith carries the moral logic of the interpersonal into the wider life of society. The light will be fainter, and the heat lower, as it moves from the immediate personal encounter into the darkness and coldness of life among strangers, but the direction will be the same.

Nevertheless, the ideal of reciprocity is both incomplete and indeterminate. It is indeterminate because in any given situation it can be interpreted in fundamentally different ways. (I shall soon describe the interpretation that until relatively recently in the history of civilization has enjoyed the greatest influence.) It is incomplete because there is no way to go from the moral logic of interpersonal relations to the comprehensive ordering of social life in a large and complex society and then back again from that ordering to the fine texture of person-to-person relations. Institutional arrangements, and the ideological assumptions with which they are associated, intervene. The idea of society must be translated into another kind of normative logic: a series of images of what relations among people can and should look like in the parts of social life—the family, the workaday world of production and exchange under the constraints of the hierarchy of classes and castes, the state and its dealings with society. These images, enacted in institutions and practices and represented in the ideas and the language by which people understand their interests and identities, form the subtext of a real society. They provide the ultimate basis for the interpretation of the laws and for the distinction between what people can and cannot take for granted in their dealings with one another.

The regime of reciprocity and the cooperative practices that embody it must be absorbed into that larger order of social life—an institutional and ideological regime—and be reshaped and reinterpreted in the course of such absorption.

The way things are. "The way things are" is the normative order of society and culture in its double register of institutions and consciousness. The aim of the ethic of connection is to elevate the way things are, and allow it to be improved and even sanctified by its vision of the moral logic of the interpersonal.

In our biographical or ontogenetic experience, the passage from the order of reciprocity to the way things are comes when the primary aim of the child becomes to join the world of the grown-ups. All too soon the child reaches the limits of reciprocity as a guide to its dealings with others. It discovers that it cannot infer the difference between the acceptable and unacceptable interpretations of reciprocity from the golden rule or from the commitment to cooperate with others in good faith. The child will have to join a real order that it finds established and accepted worshipfully, or with resignation, by the adults. Growing up means in large part accepting their regime.

In our historical or phylogenetic experience, the passage from the regime of reciprocity to the way things are is presaged by the emergence of states in what had earlier been stateless societies. It is made possible and necessary, as well, by the rise of religions that ground our normative understanding of society in a larger narrative about ultimate reality.

The separation of state from society creates a power that can uphold and enforce a particular vision of our relations to one another. But the power that can uphold it can also transform it. Once there is a power that can change it, it ceases to seem natural and necessary. The state may sacrifice the plan of reciprocity in the stateless society that preceded it to a scheme of social division and hierarchy. That scheme may still be represented as a form of reciprocity, but it will be reciprocity under the shadow of extreme inequality. The religions and philosophies may ground this new scheme of social order in a conception of ultimate reality and value, or they may provide a basis on which to challenge it.

One way of translating the ideal of reciprocity into the way things are has exercised greater influence than all others in the history of civilization. Its authority has survived, across a wide range of societies and cultures, up to our age of democratic revolution and revolutionary economic growth. When it is finally rejected as being incompatible with the beliefs and practical requirements of the advanced societies, it becomes clear that the ideal of reciprocity can survive in those societies only if it is radically reinvented.

The formula that used to serve as a bridge from reciprocity to the way things are was the sentimentalization of unequal exchange. According to this formula, the modular social relation—between patron and client, master and underling, ruler and ruled, parent and child, husband and wife—combines exchange, power, and allegiance or sentiment. There is an exchange of benefits. The exchange is unequal because one of the parties to it holds the decisive upper hand. And the unequal exchange receives an overlay of reciprocal allegiance or sentiment that softens and legitimizes it, which is why I call it a sentimentalization of unequal exchange. Such has been the main fate of the ideal of reciprocity under the way things are.

Some of Confucius's earliest critics in effect accused him of having promoted a barely disguised version of the sentimentalization of unequal exchange—a version sanitized, but not fundamentally improved, by its association with a moral psychology that exalted the role of imaginative empathy, and by a social program that emphasized the abilities and practices that would allow one to attend to the needs of others. It is a criticism that fails to do justice to his teaching.

This criticism nevertheless contains an element of truth, which will become clear later in my argument when I explore the contrast between the minimalist and the maximalist versions of the ethic of connection. Confucius was not an apologist for the sentimentalization of unequal exchange. But neither was his teaching an antecedent to the maximalist version of the ethic of connection, committed to a view of the contradictory requirements of selfhood and to a rejection of the established social order as its basis.

What matters now is to understand that the sentimentalization of unequal exchange could not survive, and has not survived, as a bridge from the ideal of reciprocity to the way things are in the societies of this age of world history and world revolution. In these societies unequal exchange remains pervasive, even when their dominant ideologies deny its legitimacy. But exchange, power, and sentiment are no longer packed together in a single recurrent formula of social life.

Nationalism might seem to serve as a functional equivalent for the overlay of unequal exchange by sentiment. But it is not an overlay that sugarcoats the relations of social life one by one, as the sentimentalization of unequal exchange did. And because it affirms, even if only in theory, the unity of the nation above all distinctions of class and community, it retains transformative potency even when it is put to reactionary use.

What then happens to the ethic of connection? How is it to deal with the way things are?

The way things are: subjugation. In dealing with the way things are, the ethic of connection goes up a ladder of moral ambition. It wants us to expunge from social relations the element of instrumental manipulation: the reduction of the other person to a tool of our desires, or an obstacle to their fulfillment, or a screen on which to project our cravings and fantasies. Viewed from a different angle, such manipulation prevents us from connecting with other people in a way that diminishes or wholly overcomes the conflict between our need for them and the jeopardy in which they place us. In finding such connections, we begin to give content to the moral logic of the interpersonal. We can be in the company of other people without losing ourselves.

To continue moving up this ladder of moral aspiration, we must be able to imagine the other person not as a placeholder in an entrenched plan of social division and hierarchy but as the original, needy, and surprising agent that each of us is. Access to the consciousness of the other, achieved by the cultivation of imaginative empathy, beyond the limits of an arm's-length altruism, prefigures, and helps make possible, the kind of relation among people that the ethic of connection seeks.

There are two ways of defining the change that it is needed. Each of them has different implications for the conduct of life as well as for the organization of society. I name these two directions the minimalist and the maximalist versions of the ethic of connection.

The first problem that this ethic must confront in the way things are is subjugation, oppression, or domination (terms that I use interchangeably). Subjugation is the denial to the individual of the conditions of free agency by anyone or any force in the state or society. Free agency is the effective power—not just the legal right—of the agent to change his circumstance and future prospects both through his own efforts and through engagement in collective action.

In complex societies, the possibility of subjugation arises from the need to cooperate on a large scale. Such cooperation must be organized or coordinated. The state soon becomes, in all historical societies, the chief instrument of such coordination. But it is never the only instrument: coordination must continue in all spheres of social life. As soon as coordination involves a vertical element—some coordinate and others are coordinated—it provides an occasion to turn temporary advantage into vested right. The power of the state and the authority of religion and philosophy may then serve further to entrench that order in the arrangements of social life and in the beliefs by which we make sense of them.

Inequality of circumstance, if it is entrenched and extreme, undermines free agency by denying to the losers the tangible and intangible means with which to turn the tables against the context in which the agent finds himself. However, the core of the evil is not inequality itself; it is the weakening or denial of the ability to act. Aside from inequality with respect to the basic conditions of survival, the most important forms of inequality are those that disempower their victims: those who have no access to, or are excluded from, the contest over the uses of economic capital, political power, and cultural authority by which society makes its future within its present.

The hierarchical transmission of differential economic and educational advantage through the family—the essential mechanism of class society—threatens to establish inequality with respect to the life chances of individuals and the basic means and conditions of free agency. The oppression resulting from such inequality cannot be justified, as it has been in some contemporary theories of distributive justice, by its contribution to the material betterment of the circumstance of the least advantaged, subject to the integrity of the arrangements guaranteeing political freedom (as narrowly and traditionally understood).

The consequence of such a justification would be to corrupt the relations among people, which it is the central aim of the ethic of connection to elevate. Some would take care of others, in the real circumstances of class society, fattening them up as a farmer fattens his sheep, while keeping in their own hands the means for making the future within the present.

Nor can the realities of domination and dependence in class society be explained (and by being explained justified), as they were in Marx's social theory, as a functional requirement for the creation of a surplus over current consumption and for the maximum development of the forces of production. This explanation fails both retrospectively and prospectively, and results in a rationalization of history that is unacceptable to any version, minimalist as well as maximalist, of the ethic of connection.

It fails retrospectively because any given functional advantage— notably the ability to increase productivity and output at a given stage of scientific and technological development—can always be exploited through alternative institutional arrangements, some more oppressive and unequal in their effects than others. The arrangements that triumph are characteristically those among the accessible institutional options that are best at exploiting the advantage of, while mitigating the disturbance to, dominant interests and preconceptions: the path of least resistance. It falls to the enemies of the path of least resistance to exploit the potential of other arrangements to outcompete that path while appealing to a broader social base.

The thesis that our historical ordeal of domination and dependence is our fate, and a price we must pay for our future emancipation (in the spirit of what I earlier called the romance of the ascent of humanity), also fails prospectively as a guide to action now. This view seeks to persuade us to endure the realities of subjugation so that our sacrifices may allow our descendants to enjoy a freedom that we are denied. Not only does this prospective doctrine commit the same mistakes as its retrospective counterpart, it also supposes a degree of control over the future and over the consequences of our actions that our experience belies. Moreover, it allows the living to do to themselves what the ethic of connection would forbid any human being to do to another: to reduce themselves to instruments—in this instance, of the unborn.

Future freedom is unlikely to be the consequence of present oppression. It is more likely that one form of oppression will breed another. As we cut our conceptual, technological, organizational, and institutional innovations down to size to accommodate the controlling interests and dogmas of the day, and resign ourselves to the path of least resistance, we surrender to oppression and disguise this surrender as the sober acceptance of fate. The partisans of the ethic of connection, even in its minimalist form, must reject this submission and press their quarrel with the way things are.

The minimalist ethic of connection deals with the problem of subjugation in the way things are by two main devices: corrective redistribution and merit-based professionalization. Countries with a history of slavery or conquest of an existing population have also resorted to a third device, which we can generically label diversity. They have used this device to achieve a more equal representation of groups, defined by criteria other than class, in the favored places of class society. Among such criteria, the principle of diversity favors those that seem pre-political because they leave markers on the human body. However, none of these instruments—corrective redistribution, meritocratic professionalization, and diversity—nor all of them together can deal adequately with the evils of domination and reconcile the way things are with the moral logic of the interpersonal and the ideal of reciprocity.

Corrective redistribution is the after-the-fact correction, especially by progressive taxation and redistributive social spending, of the inequalities generated in the market. It leaves largely untouched the primary distribution of advantage and seeks to create, after the fact, a secondary redistribution. But the same assumptions and attitudes that encourage deference to the primary distribution in the first place— the idea that we should allow the market order as established to work its wealth-creating magic only later to mitigate its consequences for inequality and insecurity—help explain the severe limits on the efficacy of this response. These limits find expression in the familiar rhetoric of a tension between efficiency and equity.

If the inequalities to be corrected are vast and if they result from the institutional arrangement shaping the production system, the corrective redistribution will also need to be enormous. Long before it acquires the dimension required to carry out its corrective mission, it would have begun to threaten and undermine the incentives and arrangements on which the workings on the economy depend and to exact an unacceptable cost in lost economic growth. A believer in alternative institutional forms of the market order sees in these facts an opportunity to imagine and develop some of these alternatives. But the defenders of institutionally conservative social democracy or of its flexible, market-friendly successor, social liberalism, which now serves as the hegemonic position in the politics and policies of the rich North Atlantic democracies, see in them only a reason to disparage such transformative efforts.

The greatest historical achievement of institutionally conservative social democracy on its European home ground has not been the egalitarian and inclusive society on which its prophets and ideologists lavished their dreams. It has been the attainment of a high level of investment in people in their entitlements, paradoxically financed by the indirect and avowedly regressive taxation of consumption, especially as achieved by the comprehensive flat-rate value added tax or (as in France) some combination of functional equivalents to it.

The diminishment of inequality has resulted from the operation of two principles, and would be further extended by a third, which we can rank in order of significance. The first and by far the most important principle is that everything that we can do through structural change—change in the institutional arrangements and the ideological assumptions associated with them—to modify the primary distribution of economic and educational advantage—its distribution regardless of subsequent tax and transfer—far outweighs in impact and promise anything that we accomplish by corrective redistribution. The relatively greater equality attained by many European states has been the outcome of decades of conflict between reformist states and familial plutocracies over economic arrangements and political institutions: a high level of entitlements has been the epilogue to a long preceding narrative.

The second principle is that corrective redistribution may play an important accessory role in which it contributes to greater equality chiefly by sustaining the investment of society, acting through the state, in people and their capabilities. Here, however, it becomes crucial to consider the budget comprehensively, as much on its spending side as on its revenue-raising side. At least for the short-term what matters most to the impact of the budget on equality and inequality is the aggregate level of the tax take and how it is spent rather than the progressive profile of taxation.

Therein lies the explanation of what otherwise seems to be a paradox: the United States—the most unequal of the rich countries —gives pride of place in its tax system to the progressive taxation of personal income, whereas the relatively more egalitarian European countries organize their tax systems around the value-added tax or a proxy for it. By relying on a tax that is in principle neutral with respect to relative prices, but that is avowedly regressive, the Europeans are able to increase the tax take while minimizing its disruptive impact on economic arrangements and on incentives to save, invest, and employ. What they lose by way of progressivity on the revenue-raising side of the budget, they more than regain on the spending side. European electorates in the recent historical period—the period of the hollowing out of social democracy—have never been willing to relinquish the benefits of this deal. In the United States, on the other hand, politicians have preferred progressive pieties to transformative effects.

To these two principles we can add a third, emphasizing the subsidiary but nonetheless significant role that taxation may play mitigating inequality. The two chief targets of direct, redistributive taxation are the accumulation and exercise of economic power and the hierarchy of the standards of living—the resources that an individual spends on himself. Redistributive taxation can hit the second target much more effectively than the first, which requires innovations in regimes of property and of political power. The best way to deal, through taxation, with the accumulation of economic power is to interrupt it at death, by a massive estate tax under rules that the wealthy are powerless to circumvent.

The best way to deal with the hierarchy of standards of living is by an individualized tax on consumption (known as a Kaldor tax), taxing, on a steep slope, the difference between the taxpayer's total capital and labor income and his invested savings. That difference is what he spends on himself. If he earns beneath a certain low threshold, he receives an income supplement instead of paying tax. As he spends more, his tax rate may rise sharply. At the highest levels of luxury living and spending, the tax rate may be several hundred percent: for every dollar he spends on himself, he pays several dollars to the state. The only limit is political support and power. There is no technical obstacle. If the progressives were clear-sighted and sincere in their redistributive aims, this is the redistributive tax they would favor. By contrast, the personal income tax income is a hybrid instrument, hitting neither target squarely. Around the world, it serves largely as a tax on the salaries of wage workers.

The second main minimalist response to the problem of subjugation is the complex of policies and attitudes that includes professionalism and meritocracy. Merit-based professionalism would moderate the consequences if not the extent of inequality and subjugation by associating the division of labor in society with a system of roles. In that system, power and authority are wedded to professional competence.

The individual is prepared, in school or at work, to exercise his role and, by exercising it, to take care of other people. And each of these professions (the "liberal" professions more than the trades or the managers of enterprise) works under the restraints of professional standards designed to reconcile their interests with what are represented as their responsibilities. Merit-based admission to these roles, and their performance under the restraints of professional ethics, would limit the degree to which the division of labor institutes subjugation under the disguise of coordination. The ability to discharge role-based responsibilities, under such restraints, would justify both their assignment to one person rather than another and the exercise of whatever power they entail.

If any country can be said to have pioneered in this way of distributing place and power in the division of labor, it is China, the home of the early canonical version of the ethic of connection, the teachings of Confucius. However, meritocratic professionalism risks sacrificing reciprocity and solidarity to a one-sided view of how human beings use their talents to attend to others and to a short-sighted view of how they can sustain energy and inspiration in the division of labor.

The legitimate element in the demand to place people in the roles for the performance of which they have demonstrated preparation and talent is that the needs of the other—of the other who needs my work—must be paramount, especially when, as in medicine, his survival and welfare depend on it. But the rule of merit and professional specialization must be qualified by three countervailing considerations. When we add these considerations up, they point to a radical change in our approach to the division of labor.

The first such consideration is that historical experience shows how easily meritocracy can make peace with the class system, strengthening its resilience and enhancing its legitimacy. What may appear as the impersonal distribution of roles, awarded on the basis of demonstrated capabilities turns out to be tainted, from start to finish, by class privilege.

The second such consideration is the blind and arbitrary character of the lottery of genetic endowments, and our tendency to exaggerate its practical consequences by piling reward on reward for those whom we take to be the winners of that lottery. It is a species of power worship, disguised as social responsibility and corrosive of social solidary. And it results in giving to the division of labor, in class society, its poisonous winner-take-all character.

The third such consideration is our habitual failure to recognize the diversity of human excellences. They are not arranged on a single hierarchical line. A practice of education designed to kindle the enthusiasms and prophetic powers of every young person can reveal and develop them early in every human life. A reconstruction of the market order that seeks to unfasten the market economy from a single dogmatic version of itself can find ways to put the excellences that we discover to work. And an approach to technology that bets on the partnership of the algorithmic machine and the human being who imagines beyond the algorithm can help replace economic fate by transformative opportunity.

What the responses of the minimalist ethic of connection to the problem of subjugation have in common is their institutional passivity: they do little or nothing to change the institutional arrangements of the market economy, of representative democracy, and of independent civil society outside the market and the state, or to challenge the ideological assumptions that those arrangements enact. Because they are not structural, they cannot overcome an inequality so stark and entrenched that it has turned into subjugation. They are often accompanied by a moral culture that can be as punctilious about personal obligation, including obligations of respect and recognition, as it is blind to institutional structure and its consequences.

In Chapter 6, on the unresolved contest between the ethic of self-fashioning and the ethic of connection, I argue that the corrected version of the former and the maximalist version of the latter broadly overlap in their political implications. They overlap despite the obstacles to reconciling their core moral visions and the consequences of these visions for the conduct of life. The zone of overlap includes their bearing on the problems of subjugation, disunion, coldness.

I do not now explore the institutional innovations needed to address the problems of subjugation, disunion, and coldness in the advanced societies because I discuss these innovations at length in Chapter 8, on the program of deep freedom. However, the institutional goals, advancing or failing in historical time, do not exhaust the response of the maximalist to these problems. He must decide what to do about them in the meantime, in the sphere of his dealings with other people.

Such institutional and ideological innovations—some designed to render the individual safe and capable in his haven, others intended to arouse a storm of innovation and experiment outside that haven— take place in the historical time of political and ideological struggle rather than in the biographical time in which we live our lives. Under the minimalist ethic of connection, politics and morals are barely distinguished. Compensatory redistribution will, according to this minimalism, reconcile the avoidance of extreme inequality with the preservation of economic freedom. Respect for group differences and identities will ensure that life among strangers is not experienced as a perpetual assault on the dignity of the individual.

Within the conditions that compensatory redistribution and respect for group differences and identities make possible, each of us can affirm the moral logic of connection by fulfilling it through the performance of our roles and our responsibilities to other people. The development of imaginative empathy will add the indispensable support of access to the consciousness of other people and give eyes to responsibility and benevolence. Thus, there is a smooth passage from ethics to politics: politics will be moralized, and ethics will find expression in a form of social life.

In the response of the maximalist ethic of connection to subjugation, however, there is no such easy bridge between the ethical and the political. The institutional and legal antidotes to subjugation can develop only in the historical time of politics, not in the biographical time of a human life. The less those anti-subjugation initiatives have advanced, the greater becomes the need for the individual to compensate, in his own existence and his relation to other people, for their failure to progress. He must prophetically foreshadow in his experience and his circle what the species has yet to accomplish. He must affirm the moral logic of the interpersonal through this struggle with his historical fate.

A conception of the relation between two of the classic virtues of connection—forbearance and fairness—shows what this prophetic activity involves. Forbearance is the restraint that we impose on the expression of our views and on the expression of our interests so that others may have the space in which to develop theirs. To practice forbearance, we must master our ambivalence toward other people as well as our self-centeredness. (The view of personality and interpersonal encounter informing the maximalist ethic of connection acknowledges such contradictions in the self and such ambivalence about the other.) Forbearance requires the marriage of self-denial with imagination: insight into the inner world of other people. A generosity bereft of such insight turns into a form of cruelty and subjugation. In the absence of forbearance, even altruism becomes a struggle for power. Forbearance safeguards our margin to experiment while expressing reverence for the person before us.

We should not understand fairness as giving each person his due. Although each of us has obligations and commitments to others, none of us can determine (contrary to what the school philosophy supposes) the limits of what we owe one another: our obligations are proportionate to our hopes as well as to our promises and transgressions. Nor does there exist a book of accounts in which the moral credits and debits of each human being are written down. To reason as if such a reckoning existed is a perversion pretending to endow an ordinary human being with a power that the Semitic monotheisms reserve to God. Such a pretense diverts our legitimate effort to become more godlike into an attempt to put a legalistic moralism in the place of a lost faith.

We should rather understand treating others fairly as treating them in ways that diminish the price in subjugation with which every connection threatens us. In this manner, we help attenuate the conflict between our need to bind ourselves to others and our struggle to escape the jeopardy in which all such bonds place us.

We do so, however, not for ourselves but for others, as we would wish them to do for us. Practiced in this way, fairness is a form of compassion, closely related to forbearance. I will not make you denature yourself, nor will I expect you to serve my will, is what our actions say to another person when we treat him fairly. As a result, you will be a little freer, a little more assured in the sentiment of being, than you were before and a little more of society will be endowed with the sanctity of the interpersonal in a cosmos that is indifferent to our concerns.

The way things are: disunion. A change in the character of social life and especially of the division of labor in society presents the ethic of connection with a challenge distinct from oppression. At the most abstract level, it is the problem of the relation between social difference and social union. The change and the problem have been among the most familiar concerns of social theory.

The development of our powers, including our powers of production, requires increasing complexity in every area of social and economic life: specialization in the jobs that people perform, and for which they are prepared; and, more broadly, differentiation, within the same country, of forms of life and of the personal experience that such forms of life support.

Functional differentiation in the organization of social and economic life is indispensable to every feature of what we most prize in social life: the freedom that is associated with the enrichment of our experience as well as with the development of our powers. At the same time, however, it provides occasion for the hardening of class differences and for the aggravation of inequality, masking them under the disguise of functional necessity.

Moreover, change in the division of labor threatens to undermine the basis for social union: what in a particular society people have in common, drawing them together. The idea of the nation—an invention of the same revolutionary period in which this dynamic of differentiation accelerated—points to a union among the classes, communities, races, and creeds into which society is divided. Despite its demonstrated power and influence, the nation is a fabricated union, distant from the fine texture of social life—from the dealings between you and me—that represent the overriding concern of the ethic of connection.

This momentous and long-developing change in the nature of the division of labor in society presents the ethic of connection with both a threat and an opportunity. The threat is the degradation of any basis in the practical organization of society and the character of our lived experience for the ideals of reciprocity and solidarity and for our attachment to one another outside what Max Weber called "the pianissimo of personal life"—the sphere of our most intimate relations. The opportunity is to develop a higher form of attachment: one that does not depend on sameness to flourish. To be attached in the absence of sameness, and on the basis of imaginative insight into the otherness of the other person, is to be attached more deeply.

To grasp what is at stake for the development of the ethic of connection in this conundrum and in the response to it, consider first what classical European social theory—the social theory of the second half of the nineteenth century and of the first half of the twentieth—had to say about it. The best place to start is in the work of Émile Durkheim and Ferdinand Tönnies. Each of them developed in his own way what came to be the defining theme in the main line of modern sociology.

Durkheim contrasted two styles of solidarity. By solidarity he meant both the density of association among people, which sociology later came to call "social capital," and the experience of attachment, of what I have called imaginative empathy, especially outside the boundaries of the family. Under mechanical solidarity, the parts of society and of the economy, or the people within them, are alike but only weakly engaged with one another. There is a principle of juxtaposition rather than one of functional complementarity and integration. People feel connected only to the extent that they are the same. There is limited difference. The problem of social union solves itself through sameness. This is, however, a low-level union, one that can be undermined by any incipient differentiation. The counterpart to limited social differentiation is a limited deepening of individual distinction and self-consciousness.

Under organic solidarity, the parts of society and of the economy become progressively distinct. In acquiring distinct functions, they also become organized in different ways. They are now functionally related. The interaction of the different now replaces the juxtaposition of the similar as the principle of social organization. But functional differentiation is not enough to ensure the degree of union that society under organic solidarity continues to need. At the macro level, such union means loyalty and commitment to the whole to which each part belongs. In the nation-states of today and of the recent past, that whole is the nation. At the micro level, union means the disposition to reciprocity, trust, and empathy, across the lines of difference, on which much in social and economic life continues to depend. Thus begins the search—in religion, culture, nationalism, and professional ethics—for the sources of union under the new conditions. And only to the extent that this search succeeds are we justified in speaking of organic solidarity rather than merely of mutual convenience, always susceptible to being overridden by group selfishness and antagonism.

With even greater simplicity, Tönnies explored the same theme of difference and union in the form of what became the single most influential contrast in the central tradition of sociology: the contrast between community and society. Community requires shared vision based on shared experience. It brings to those who share in it a measure of security and a promise of happiness: security because under community we are more inclined to take care of one another, and happiness because to be embraced by the other is what makes us happiest. The practical and moral cost of community, however, is the heavy constraint that it imposes on the development of difference. It inhibits the development of our collective powers—beginning with our powers of production—and it restrains the individual from becoming more than an instance of some group identity and of its form of life and of consciousness.

Society is social life in the midst of difference. With difference, comes the distance of each group from the others, and even of each individual person from his fellows. Looked at in one way, this distance is just another name for freedom. Considered in another way, it is the subversion of what holds us together and makes us see our rescue in one another rather than in competition and struggle. There then begins the quest to uphold and develop the freedom made possible by society without losing what was most valuable in community: a basis for deep bonds with others, bonds that are not confined to life in the family and that can withstand the ravages of clashing egoisms and of group hatreds.

It is easy see how the idea that Durkheim, Tönnies, and many others helped develop defines, alongside the problem of oppression, a second source of danger and opportunity for the ethic of connection. Without a basis in the character of social experience and therefore as well in the organization of society, the ethic of connection will be driven out of the workaday world into the recesses of personal and domestic life. In those recesses, it will have a diminished influence and deliver a truncated message. It will speak only where it may be least needed. It will be the morality of a refuge, not the ethic of a form of life that can penetrate every aspect of our existence.

The basis for its power is what in the preceding paragraphs I called social union: the ties among us reproduced in the routines and practices of life in society. Unless the organization of society, of the economy, and of politics perennially renews the life of these ties, the ethic of connection will deliver its message to an uncomprehending social world or to one that comprehends that message as being pertinent only to the "pianissimo of the personal."

Under Durkheim's mechanical solidarity or Tönnies's community, there is such a basis. But this basis depends on the suppression of difference, distinction, and depth. And it has been undermined by changes that we are powerless to reverse even if wanted to. It exists, insofar as it exists at all, only in forms—such as nationalism, identity politics, professional ethics, membership in an organized religion— that seem inadequate to the task. They are inadequate either because (in the case of nationalism) they are remote from the small coin of interpersonal encounter in which the ethic of connection deals or (as in the other sources of partial union) because they form bonds only by sowing divisions. Union on the basis of sameness offers either too much or the wrong kind of union for the advancement of the ethic of connection. But functional interdependence within and outside the economy offers too little, even when supplemented by forces such as nationalism and identity politics, to preserve and develop union in the face of complexity and difference.

In the way things are, difference dissolves union; only the suppression of difference could bring union back in the difference-suppressing form that it had under mechanical solidarity or community. Thus, the subversion of union appears to be a fate that we are unable to escape even if we wanted to; which—when we consider the countless tangible and intangible benefits of our emancipation from sameness—on the whole we do not.

The ethic of connection seeks to change the way things are so that union and difference are no longer inversely related. Functional interdependence and complementarity in and outside the market fail to deliver this outcome. They fail to deliver it even when they are supplemented by nationalism, organized religion, group loyalties or collective identity, and the moralization of the professions and trades (professional ethics).

It is not enough to think about the relation between union and difference in a changed way. It is necessary to change the relation in fact. In the meantime, we are faced on every side with tokens of our failure to achieve or even to imagine such a change, although we are surrounded by opportunities to do so.

In the organization of the economy, the historical development of the market order took a form that disengaged market exchange from any set of reciprocities in social life. Where before our practical dealings with one another were embedded in such reciprocities, now they became free floating. This was Tönnies's society in the sphere of economic life: the destruction of social union in the arrangements of the economy. The arm's-length, fully articulated bargain, addressed to an instantaneous performance in the future, was the clearest expression of this reversal. Weber and other European social theorists taught that a moral foundation of the market (in the form that it took in the rich Western countries of the nineteenth and twentieth centuries) is the generalization of a modicum of trust—low trust—among strangers. The universalization of low trust replaced a moral culture contrasting what was owed to insiders related by blood and culture (almost everything) to what was owed to outsiders (almost nothing). The then most advanced practice of production—mass production industry—organized work in a command-and-control form that combined low trust with discretionary managerial power.

We are no longer entitled, if we ever were, to view this circumstance as an imposition of economic necessity. For we now see the emergence of an advanced practice of production—the knowledge economy—that requires, if it is to develop in its most widespread and radical form, a heightening of reciprocal trust as well as of discretionary initiative among all participants in the process of production. It also demands a fluid mixture of cooperation and competition within and among firms. These requirements point in a direction compatible neither with Durkheim's mechanical solidarity and Tönnies's community, nor with Durkheim's organic solidarity and Tönnies's society. They call for a reconstruction of both the idea and the practical basis of social union. Such a reconstruction directly concerns the ethic of connection.

The development of the division of labor creates more room for individual distinction and depth of selfhood. But it also makes the ordeal of the narrowing of the self by the division of labor harder to escape and more decisive in its consequences. The greater the hold of the division of labor over the choice of life and the range of our life experiences, the more formidable becomes the threat to our ability to imagine other people.

Our collective advance creates opportunities to parry this threat. If society is richer, we can have more free time, and in that time experiment with possibilities of experience and of creation denied to us in the workday world. Moreover, as our most advanced productive practices come to resemble more closely the work of the imagination, they may diminish, rather than aggravate, the demand for rigid specialization. Thus, as today's most advanced productive practices attenuate the contrast between task-defining and task-executing jobs, they also relativize the distinctions among all specialized work roles.

To seize these opportunities, we must have an idea: a way of thinking about difference, union, and the division of labor that allows us to see how difference and union might cease to be opposites, how we can be more different among ourselves and yet more connected in the ways that matter to the ethic of connection. A quarrel with the way things are is that it prevents us from having more difference and more union at the same time.

Consider how the minimalist and the maximalist versions of the ethic of connection understand and pursue this quarrel.

∽

Two ideas work together in the way the minimalist ethic of connection seeks to reconcile difference and union. The first idea is a certain way of understanding and performing the roles each of us occupies in the social division of labor. The second idea is a view of how, in opposition to both individualism and collectivism, the moral logic of the interpersonal can penetrate the division of labor and, having penetrated it, extend outward in ever wider circles of reciprocity, solidarity, and imaginative empathy to touch and ennoble more and more of social life.

In this account of the ethic of connection and of its alternative futures, I have returned several times to the central importance of role-based responsibilities in this orientation to existence. Reconsidering them in the light of this discussion of union and difference under the division of labor enables us to gain further insight into their significance.

For the individual, the division of labor and its evolution begin in a life-defining experience. Early in our lives, each of us must forswear the many people we might become in order to pursue a particular course of life. In many societies across historical time, we may hardly have a choice: the range of possibility before us may be dramatically narrowed by the accidents of our birth in a particular position in the caste or class order of society, in its established allocation of gender roles, or in any of the other ways in which each of us is handed a script and told to play it out.

But whether we take a course of life under duress or have some choice, we must be mutilated, casting off the selves we might turn into. Yet we cannot be fully human unless after this mutilation we are able to feel the missing limbs—our lives foregone—and to make of this feeling a source of empathetic insight into other people. Our experience of the system of roles in the division of labor bears the weight of this existential calamity.

The minimalist ethic of connection wants us to remember our other selves. It does not, like the ethic of self-fashioning or the maximalist version of its own approach to the conduct of life, cast all roles under suspicion and deny that any role can ever be worthy of a human being. But it teaches that in entering into a role and into the responsibilities that we have to other people by virtue of occupying it, we must see beyond its narrow formulas. We must perform it not just as virtuosos of the role but also as human beings bound together by the moral logic of the interpersonal. To that end we must enact it guided by our imaginative insight into other people. And we must push the limits of the constraints that the established division of labor imposes on any such attempt to soften and expand its iron limits.

This disposition to relativize the difference between relating to another person as the occupant of a station in the division of labor and relating to him as person who is always more than the performer of social roles brings us to the second way in which the minimalist ethic of connection seeks to deal with the moral consequences of the division of labor. The impulse to outreach the role for the sake of humanity—the most constant impulse of this ethic from its early Confucianist formulation to its possible contemporary forms—is the chief instrument by which we can extend the non-instrumental practice of the interpersonal into life among strangers. We do so by steps and degrees, through widening concentric circles that include at each step larger parts of social life.

As we move further and further away from the sphere of intimacy, the degree to which we may be willing to treat other people as simply means to an end increases and the opportunity to express the non-instrumental logic of passionate encounter diminishes. But there is no inflexible limit to either the scope or the intensity of that expression.

Under what conditions are we willing to treat other people, beyond the boundaries of intimacy, as something more than instruments of the fulfillment or frustration of our interests? Our willingness and ability to do so turns on our success at diminishing the dependence of sympathy on sameness. The wider concentric circles in which we show solidarity may no longer be communities in Tönnies's sense, in which reciprocal identification relies on similarity of experience and aspiration.

The chief defect of sympathies dependent on sameness is not selfishness; it is solipsism. Such solipsism undermines our ability to enact on the broadest possible terrain what is the supreme object of concern and aspiration in this approach to the conduct of life: the sacrosanct, radiant logic of the interpersonal, beginning in the you and me and reaching outward, as if it were eventually able to embrace the whole of mankind.

These remarks make clear that the political implications of this ethic are no more collectivist than they are individualist. Nor are they communitarian if by community we mean what this term has meant in the history of classical (modern) social theory. As it dispenses with the crutch of similarity of history, situation, experience, interest, and value, the minimalist version of this ethic affirms connection in the face of difference and the interpersonal beyond the intimate.

In dealing with disunion, as in all else, the maximalist ethic of connection is more ambitious. It sees difference, including the difference generated by the division of labor in society, as an advantage and an opportunity. Recognizing the threat that difference poses for social union, it does not seek to preserve union, and thus to maintain a basis for its ideals of reciprocity and solidarity, as the minimalist ethic of connection does, by multiplying restraints and counterweights to difference. Instead, it proposes to create a deeper union out of the very materials of difference. The basic method by which it proposes to do so is social recombination: the joining together of the different in common forms of action.

Consider first the significance of difference. The social democrats and social liberals of today view difference as a problem. They ask by what methods, procedures, and institutional arrangements the different can coexist in a free society. The appeal to an impersonal order of right and of the "neutral principles" on which it draws has been their principal response to difference. Their philosophers and ideologists recognize that such a putatively neutral framework is an insufficient response to the problem of difference, either because no such framework can be truly neutral, or because to the extent that it approaches neutrality it is relatively empty or indeterminate and fails to provide a basis for the content of the laws. It must therefore be supplemented by other means for the development, through the public conversation, of an "overlapping consensus" among group interests and visions. If neutrality fails, there can nevertheless be an area of convergence among the most widely shared views. That area of convergence can become the most important source of guidance. But whether neutrality fails or not, and by its failure requires some such supplement, difference continues to be viewed as a problem in search of a solution.

The liberal thinkers of the nineteenth century, on the contrary, saw difference as the solution, not as the problem. They feared that democracy would bring conformity—a society of sheep, outwardly free but inwardly submissive—and anxiously asked how to uphold, under the rule of the people, distinction of character and experience. Their assumptions were those of the ethic of self-fashioning, not of the ethic of connection. Nevertheless, the maximalist ethic of connection shares with the classical liberals the idea that difference is not to be contained; it is to be developed. The reasons of these maximalists are not those of the classical liberals.

If reciprocity and solidarity depend on sameness, they are both fragile and superficial. They are fragile because any development of new difference brought about by the changing circumstances of society will undermine them. They are superficial because the reciprocal attachments that arise in a circumstance of limited difference will be attachments less to persons than to the social and cultural categories, or the restricted stock of group identities, that they exemplify. The solidarity that the ethic of connection so prizes consists in the bonds among people, not among collective categories and group identities.

Consider a twenty-first-century example. The European social democracies of the second half of the twentieth century organized a high level of social entitlements, paradoxically financed by the regressive taxation of consumption through a comprehensive flat-rate value tax or some functional equivalent to it. The development of this high level of investment in people and their capabilities followed many decades of conflict over access to economic advantage and political power and often ended in a compromise between a redistributive and regulatory state and a plutocratic elite. The orchestration of money transfers by the state, through progressive taxation and social entitlements, thus became the residual expression of social solidarity. However, it enjoyed almost universal support as well as efficacy only against the background of strong social and cultural homogeneity. As soon as migratory flows began to erode this homogeneity the consensus around the welfare state began to weaken even as inequality increased. The result revealed that this form of social solidarity could not easily withstand the widening of social and cultural difference.

For the maximalist, solidarity amid difference counts for more than solidarity on the basis of sameness. It is then, and only then, that we connect as people who, albeit shaped by society and culture, are more than expressions of the groups into which they were born.

Moreover, the development of difference is the development of our powers. It creates the diversified stuff—of experiences, ideas, capabilities, and objects—from which the competitive practices of politics and of the economy can then select. It is on this ground, of our collective strength rather than of our collective weakness, that the proponent of the maximalist ethic of connections wants us to engage with one another. And it is also on this basis, of the development of productive powers, technical capabilities, and scientific insight, that we stand the best chance of taking care of the most needy and vulnerable.

The weight accorded to the development of new difference, rather than simply of respect for existing difference, has implications for our economic and political arrangements as well as for our educational practices. The value of competitive selection in the market depends on the richness of the material from which the competitive selection selects. One of the ways to foster this diversity is to prevent the market order from being fastened to a single, dogmatic version of itself and to insist on the coexistence of alternative regimes of property and contract—setting the terms of decentralized access to the resources and opportunities of production—within the same market order.

Similarly, our political institutions must favor the creation of new difference with the materials of existing difference. They can do so in one direction by increasing the temperature of politics (the level of organized popular engagement in political life) and hastening its pace (the rapid resolution of impasse) through procedures such as anticipated elections. They can do so in another direction by allowing parts of a country, in either federations or unitary states, to opt out of national rules under certain conditions and to exemplify a local version of an alternative national direction.

Our educational practices must be dialectical, teaching every subject from multiple and contrasting points of view. They must defy the forced marriage of method to subject matter that marks the orthodoxies of university culture and explore the study of the same subject matter by different methods. And they must give the individual access to experience and ideas remote from those that prevail in his time and place.

The cumulative effect of these economic and political arrangements and of these educational practices is to favor the creation of new difference: difference in forms both related and unrelated to the present divisions of society. The proliferation of new difference puts the ideals of reciprocity and solidarity to the test.

Solidarity and reciprocity in a context of expanding difference cannot rely solely or primarily on money transfers organized by the state, or even on a public culture, enforced by anti-discrimination law, of respect for existing difference. The sole adequate instrument of connection in such circumstances is the active combination of what was apart: doing things together with the different others, and helping to take care of them, when necessary, beyond the boundaries of family selfishness.

The doing of things together can begin in the cooperative character of education. It can continue through the implementation of a principle of social service (whether as a substitute for mandatory military service or not): everyone has, for part of his life or of his working year, responsibility to help take care of others outside his own family, as well as a job in the production system. It can be reinforced by the organization of civil society outside the state to partner with government, through cooperatives, in the experimental and competitive but not-for-profit provision of public services. It can seize on the opportunities opened up by the knowledge economy for cooperation (alongside competition) among firms as well as within them. And it can be further aroused by a way of organizing democratic politics that heightens the level of organized popular engagement in political life, enhances the transformative and experimental powers of central as well as local government, and diminishes the likelihood that political alliances and antagonisms will mirror the preexisting divisions within established society and culture.

The common element in all these changes is a principle of recombination: drawing people from different parts of the grid of established social divisions and group identities to do things together and to create new differences while bridging old ones. It is a principle of recombination and of engagement across the barriers of inherited difference—a perpetual churning of social life. Money—in the form of the social transfers orchestrated by the state under institutionally conservative social liberalism and social democracy—is too weak a social cement. The only adequate cement is joint action, or responsibility for other people, in practice.

Thus, the response of the maximalist version of the ethic of connection to the problems of sameness, union, and the division of labor is twofold: to increase difference through an organized experimentalism in every part of social life; and to overcome established difference, through the joint initiative of the different, the better to create new difference.

The multiplication of opportunities and occasions to create union in the face of difference by doing things together in the economy, politics, and education is a political project. It has moral motivations and consequences as well as political ones. But it succeeds or fails in the historical time of a country or of all humanity, not in the biographical time of an individual life. The minimalist response to disunion, like the minimalist response to subjugation, is at once political and moral: the widening concentric circles of reciprocal responsibility that it proposes elide the difference between political and moral action. But the response of the maximalist ethic of connection to disunion, like its response to subjugation, interrupts this easy passage from the political to the moral and back again.

The reason is the same in both instances, as it will be in the minimalist and maximalist responses to coldness. The maximalist version of the ethic of connection differs from the minimalist one in its refusal to take the established institutional and ideological regime of social life as the template for its moral work as well as in its assumptions about the self and the interpersonal. In committing itself to structural changes whose fate depends on the course of politics, it generates a problem that the minimalist ethic of connection, with its convergence of moral and political vision, faces not at all or much less: the need for a moral response to the problem of disunion when the political response has failed to be achieved or even imagined. And the less politics has advanced in mastering disunion in historical time, the more important it becomes for the individual to master its consequences in biographical time.

The main reason why this problem is unfamiliar to us is that the social and political theories most concerned with structural change in historical time, such as Marxism, have also been the theories most inclined to discount the potential for individual or collective action. If, as these theorists of structural change in history affirm or imply, history has a script, individual and collective action must either act out the script or resist it—in which case it is doomed to failure. On such a view, a way of action that is premature from the standpoint of our historical place in the enactment of the script is a tragic fantasy and sets the individual or collective agent up to be broken on the wheel of history.

The issue here is what virtues—meaning habitual dispositions to action—represent both the equivalent to, and the inspiration for, what I have described in the preceding pages as the maximalist response to disunion in the way things are. These virtues are more than compensations for the failures of politics; they reveal the highest aspirations of this approach to the conduct of life.

At the summit of these virtues stand openness to the other person and openness to the new. They hold, in this secular ethic, the place of the theological virtues—faith, hope, and love—in the Christian faith. They are the virtues of transcendence or divinization.

The degree to which a conceptual or social regime seizes its participants and reduces them to the condition of being its puppets depends on the character of that regime as well as on the powers of insight and resistance the participants have developed, whether with the support of that regime or in defiance of it. But no matter how far an established institutional and conceptual order has gone in entrenching itself against challenge and change and surrounding itself with the aura of a specious authority, it cannot suppress experiences that contradict its assumptions. Nor can it erase the alternative orders, the roads not taken, and the solutions rejected or subordinated, in the history of thought and of institutions.

Openness to the other is the very heart of the ethic of connection, which starts from the premise that no one saves himself and that the seat of value in human life, the part of our experience with the greatest claim to sanctity, is the moral logic of the interpersonal. But for this logic to be manifest in our lives and to lift us up, each of us (as I argued in the discussion of the role of love in the corrected ethic of self-fashioning) must pay the price of a heightened vulnerability. The need to pay that price is clear not only in our intimate relations but in every attempt to extend the moral logic of the interpersonal outward to life among strangers, including the structure-defying and structure-creating forms of collective action recommended by the maximalist ethic of connection.

Openness to the new is related to openness to the other person. Both can find inspiration in the same view of the transcendence of the interpersonal over any form it may take in history. If we were to give the last word to the structures of society and of thought, they would suck life out of us, for the first attribute of life is surfeit over such structure. They would require us to view one another and to deal with one another according to the places that we occupy in them, or the roles that they assign to each of us. We, however, are who we are because we are not simply protagonists in such role-based scripts. We cannot respect one another without disrespecting them.

Openness to the new and openness to the other come together in the disposition to connect with strangers and create forms of collective action that serve as the liquid form of new structures. Every such effort requires the association of these two virtues. But their significance in this approach to the conduct of life precedes their tie to forms of collective action. It follows directly from their relation to the central vision of this ethic: that the *we* comes before the *I* and that what makes the *we* sacred and fertile does not let itself be cabined in any one set of social arrangements.

If the marriage of openness to the new and openness to the other is of such vital importance to the ethic of connection, and if it should not depend on the fate of politics, we must ask how these two virtues and their association can find sustenance in the moral psychology of the individual agent in biographical time, regardless of what becomes of society in historical time.

The interaction between forbearance and fairness is not enough to prepare the person for the reception of these higher virtues. Between these virtues of divinization—the virtues that brings us to transcendence—and the lower but fundamental virtues of human or social connection, such as fairness and forbearance, there must be an intermediate level: virtues of purification. Their role is the *kenosis*—the emptying out recommended by the patristic theology of early Christianity.[1]

Without these preparatory virtues, the combination of openness to the other with openness to the new—resisting the established arrangements of society and the assumptions of culture—would be miraculous. The miracle would consist in the dissociation of the way in which the individual understands his interests and identity from the established social order and his place within it. There are two distinct ways in which this seeming miracle can happen: one political and the other moral.

The political way of performing the miracle consists in exploiting the duality of ways in which we can define and defend any group interest. One approach to defining and defending it is institutionally conservative and socially exclusive. It takes for granted the place that the group—for example, a segment of the labor force—occupies in the social and technical division of labor. And it therefore identifies as enemies of the group all the groups in the immediately surrounding social space that threaten its place in the division of labor.

---

1. For a more extensive discussion of the virtues of purification and of their relation to the virtues of connection and of divinization, see my *The Religion of the Future*, pp. 366–87.

The other approach to defining and defending a group interest is institutionally transformative and socially solidaristic. It sees no future in the present position of the group or in the system that underlies it—for example, a style of production that has been superseded. And it therefore fights for an alternative—for example, the conversion of that style of production into another one. To that end, it must begin to define as allies the groups in the surrounding social space that it used to regard as rivals.

The moral way of performing the miracle is to cultivate the virtues of purification. They do not soar above the earth: their cultivation depends on minimal economic, social, and political conditions, which may be denied to the individual. We are all nailed to the cross of history, with consequences that I explore in Chapter 7, on politics. Yet to the extent that such conditions are fulfilled, they create a basis for the association of openness to the other with openness to the new that depends on no breakthrough in how we define and defend group interests.

The virtues of purification, which ready us for that association, are simplicity, enthusiasm, and attentiveness.

Simplicity is the disposition to renounce the material and immaterial bric-a-brac of ordinary experience for the sake of focusing on what matters: our devotion to other people and our wrestling with the institutional, conceptual, and characterological settings of our existence. The commitment of consciousness to the trivial amounts to a lesser idolatry. It squanders our ultimate resource—time—in efforts bearing no relation to what the ethic of connection regards as sacred: the moral logic of the interpersonal and the threat of the perversion of that moral logic by the established arrangements of society and culture. By practicing the virtue of simplicity we convey our intention to recognize the value of every moment and prepare ourselves to overcome estrangement from life in the present.

Enthusiasm is the readiness to give oneself to an activity that—once found not to disregard the virtues, or to fail in the responsibilities, of connection—absorbs us for a while without residue or reservation and seems to be eternal while it lasts. In the experience of enthusiasm, we find a partial antidote to the sufferings of mortality, groundlessness, and insatiability, one that does not depend on self-deception or require indifference.

The activities to which we are able to devote ourselves wholeheartedly suspend our sense of the passage of time and offer us a temporary immortality. They draw us into an experience that provides its own justifications and sets its own terms, without pretending to solve the riddle of the world and of existence. They interrupt for a while the sad procession of longing, satiation, boredom, and more longing. Thanks to enthusiasm, the clock stops, and experience appears to be self-validating. What more could we ask? Only for something that we cannot have: that it last.

A mark of enthusiasm is the liquefaction of the arrangements, ideas, or habits within which the enthusiast moves at the moment of enthusiasm; they appear as if dissolved under the heat of a visionary impulse. It is as if, for that moment, the instruments and occasions of activity were finally adequate to its intentions.

The seemingly paradoxical outcome of this incandescent dissolution of the contrast between structure and vision is that we become relatively more open to the impressions of some aspect of reality. Before our enthusiasm, we saw through the lens, and acted at the behest, of the structure, as if another person could take our place in the same dumb service. Now the scales are removed from our eyes. Or so it seems to us, because we forget, as it is happening, that it amounts to a reprieve rather than to a salvation.

A third virtue of purification is attentiveness. Attentiveness completes the work of simplicity and enthusiasm. It is their consummation and reward. Through the virtue of attentiveness, we turn to the manifest world and come nearer to the ideal of a mind on which nothing is lost. Malebranche described attention as the prayer of the soul. The perceptual immediacy of the world in childhood, celebrated by the poet as a lost paradise, is recaptured by the grown man as intensified and discriminating vision. An aspect of the recovery of this immediacy is our capacity to regain the sense of the strangeness of what appears to be natural as well as of the excess of nature over established thought. If genius, rather than thinking better, sees more, attentiveness enables the attentive to share in the experience of genius.

Attentiveness, however, is not only a prize; it is also a fight. Its discipline is the struggle against preconception: the inescapable prejudice that every set of methods, presuppositions, and categories embodies. We cannot do without them; we need them to make sense of our experience. In surrendering, however, to any one version of them, we lose all prospect of extending our vision, and relinquish our share in the power of genius.

The virtues of purification—simplicity, enthusiasm, and attentiveness—prepare us for the divinizing and transformative virtues of openness to the other person and openness to the new.

The way things are: freedom without warmth. Subjugation and disunion have been longstanding themes in the history of social theory. The third focus of the quarrel of the ethic of connection with the way things are appears only obliquely in that history, under labels that disguise its meaning and implications. It is, however, no less important. It comes even closer than the other two criticisms to the central concerns of the ethic of connection.

Remember Schopenhauer's image of the situation of humanity as that of a pack of porcupines in the cold night. To warm themselves they come closer together but then prick one another with their spines. They move further apart but then get cold. They go anxiously back and forth, closer and further away, until they settle into an uneasy middle distance—neither close enough to be warm nor far enough away to avoid hurting one another.

That this circumstance of relative coldness is the unavoidable result of our emancipation is one of the central ideas of the social, political, and economic thought of the last few centuries. In societies and cultures before the present revolutionary age there prevailed the sentimentalization of unequal exchange: the combination, in a wide range of social relations, of exchange, power, and allegiance. Something of the reciprocal affect of our closest personal connections flowed into the characteristic dealings of society. When Talleyrand said, "Those who have not lived before the revolution do not know the sweetness of life," he was alluding to this charge of social relations by personal affect. He was not speaking solely of the privileges of an elite that concentrated in its hands political and cultural as well as economic capital. He was alluding as well to the warmth that results when the practical arrangements of society are penetrated by the affect marking our closest relations within the family.

These societies were warm if by warmth we mean the diffusion throughout social life of some of the emotional radiance of our closest interpersonal relations: those in which the other is not viewed and treated as merely a means to an end—as an impediment to or an instrument for the achievement of our desires. With warmth comes danger as well as sustenance, given the inexorable ambivalence marking our relations to one another.

Where there was warmth there was no freedom: the sweetness was the overlay of a regime of unequal exchange, the honeyed form of subjugation. When society becomes free or freer, it also becomes colder. The domains assigned to affect, exchange, and power diverge. Affect is confined within the sphere of intimate personal relations. Exchange and power, without sentiment, go to the market and to politics. Our wider life in society loses its channel to the charm, as well as to the perils, of the interpersonal and is abandoned to instrumental calculation.

In the history of social theory, this momentous transformation appears only, as in Max Weber's work, under the disguise of the categories of rationalization and disenchantment. Those categories put the emphasis in a different place: on the relation of the earthly to the supernatural, of the human to the divine. Here, the emphasis is on the relation of the personal and the interpersonal to the ordinary experience of social life beyond the sphere of intimacy.

Freud also approached this problem more closely through his concept of cathexis, the investment of affect or libido in anything from dreams to objects that evoke memories. The cathexis comes from the part of our experience with the greatest valence: in Freud's system the sexually charged complications of family life, beginning in earliest childhood, and here the domain of the interpersonal and its concentrated form in our most intimate encounters and relations.

The ethic of connection wants from the way things are something that the established social order fails to give us and that the dominant ideas deride as impossible and paradoxical. It wants a form of life that is both free and warm.

With regard to this failed aspiration, the prevailing moral and political ideas in the history of civilization fall into two camps, both of them hostile to this hope. Some of them try to ground the mixture of exchange, power, and affect in a cosmic order and to proclaim an association among order in the cosmos, order in society, and order in the soul. They offer a metaphysical or theological basis for the sentimentalization of unequal exchange and the marriage of warmth with freedom. Others—those that have prevailed in the richest and most powerful countries in the recent past—dismiss as unrealistic and dangerous the attempt to reconcile freedom and warmth.

The proponents of the ethic of connection must persist in imagining and demanding what these two sets of ideas dismiss as impossible. They must persist because in their eyes the logic of the interpersonal is the most sacred element in human experience and the relation of this sacred flame to the tenor of ordinary social life is the fateful question that it must above all address. If we can be free only by becoming cold, or remain warm only by foregoing freedom, the program of the ethic of connection for the raising up of human life is doomed.

The minimalist ethic of connection approaches the problem from the standpoint of two background conditions that it regards as indispensable to all its efforts, not simply to the hope of reconciling warmth with freedom. Neither of these two background conditions nor both together ensure the result that minimalism seeks. Yet together they do provide the indispensable foundation for the dynamic by which the minimalist ethic of connection sets the greatest store.

The first background condition is the correction of the division of labor by practices and arrangements designed to ensure the primacy of the common good and to prevent it from being converted into an instrument of narrow class or group interest and conflict. At different times, in the more than 2,000-year history of the ethic of connection, such arrangements and practices have included a commitment to promotion by merit—meritocracy; the cultivation of professional ethics and more generally of moral standards designed to guide and govern the performance of each major role in society; the development of organizations intermediate between government and the individual that would bring together employers and employees and override class conflict; and the establishment of a "responsible capitalism" that makes corporations responsible to multiple stakeholders and to the public interest. Through all these measures, the minimalist ethic of connection seeks to avoid the degeneration of social and economic life into a brutal struggle for group advantage and individual self-aggrandizement.

The second background condition is the remaking of each individual, from childhood forward, on the template of social rituals or conventions that break his self-centeredness and solipsism, liberate him from his anti-social tropisms or compulsions, and give him what is in effect a second nature: a nature suited to life in society.

The cultivation of benevolence, informed by imaginative empathy in relation to the experience of other people, can then go to work within a society that has been rendered susceptible to its humanizing effects by the establishment of these two background conditions. Against the background of those two enabling conditions something of the warmth and charm we hope to attain, and occasionally enjoy, in the circle of one's intimate relations will flow into the larger life of society. The radiance of the interpersonal as an entrancing and saving emanation will touch that larger world. Our friendliness will share in the quality of love. For the advocate of the minimalist ethic of connection, such an extension of the qualities of life among intimates to life among strangers will be our best hope of reconciling freedom with warmth in the way things are.

The maximalist protests: the likely outcome of the minimalist response to the problem of coldness is not the desired reconciliation of warmth with freedom. It is a counterfeit version of that warmth: a cheerful impersonal friendliness, bereft of any inner vulnerability of the moral agent even when accompanied by genuine acts of personal generosity and sacrifice.

Moreover, the maximalist goes on to argue, this belief about what is likely to come of the minimalist response to the evils of coldness is no idle and unsupported prediction. It is what we regularly observe, in the best of circumstances, in those cultures in which that response has been tried out: especially the societies in which Confucianism has been the leading practical philosophy. This humanizing benevolence, he will point out, has provided cover for carrying on, under another label, the sentimentalization of unequal exchange.

The maximalist approach to the task of achieving freedom without coldness must be faithful to the two decisive impulses that distinguish it from the minimalist version of the ethic of connection: its greater ambition to reconcile solidarity and reciprocity with empowerment, founded on a different idea of the self and of the moral logic of the interpersonal; and its refusal to accept the present arrangements of society as the horizon within which to pursue this ambition.

The minimalist imagines a series of concentric circles moving out from the domain of intimate relations to the wider life of society. He wants something of the character of our non-instrumental relations to one another in that domain to be carried forward to our dealings with one another in society in each of the roles that we perform. The result is inevitably a progressive dilution. The sympathy that he advocates is a weaker form of the strong bonds that can flourish among kin and friends.

The maximalist objects: Will not this attempt to sustain a counterpart to the strong affect that arises naturally in the circumstance of intimacy result at best in a cool benevolence, a faint copy of its model? And will it not then come perilously close to the uneasy middle distance into which Schopenhauer's porcupines settle? And may it not, when it fails to attain its goal, bring into life among strangers the poison rather than the love of life among intimates.

The situation of intimacy cannot, the maximalist believes, be reproduced in life among strangers. The attempt to reenact it in that life will result in a caricature of the original and an unsustainable pretense. And the pretense will serve as a spiritualizing and legitimizing halo over the real power relations of the established social order: in the old form of the sentimentalization of unequal exchange or in its many counterparts in the cultures that can no longer accept the combination of power, exchange, and allegiance as the recurrent formula of social relations.

If we are to prevent the breaking of that formula and the movement toward greater freedom from leaving us in the cold middle distance, we must find another source of warmth to complement the chain of analogies, or the multiplication of concentric circles, around the area of intimacy. This additional source must be more than an idea or an attitude; it must be the expression of a different way of living and of organizing society.

Vitality and imagination, closely linked, are the twin possible sources of such intensity of experience, radiating outward to touch wider portions of social experience. Consider the meaning of these two impulses, their relation to each other, their bearing on the interpersonal, and the general character of the changes in the organization of society and the direction of culture that can support such changes.

Recall that the two defining moves of the imagination are distancing from the phenomenon (emphasized by Kant: the image is the memory of a perception) and subsuming the phenomenon, once distanced, under a range of accessible variations. We grasp what the phenomenon is only by imagining what it can become given certain events or interventions. The most important variations are those that can happen in the realm of the adjacent possibilities: the *theres* that can we reach from *here*.

Imagination lightens the brute givenness of the world—the false impression of the finality or necessity of its present form. It lightens it by representing that form as no more than a temporary resting place in a sequence of possible changes or variations. We restore the world to time: to say that the world and the phenomena reveal themselves only through variation is to say that they reveal themselves only temporally.

The mind as imagination can combine and recombine every perception, image, and idea with every other—what in mathematics we describe as its recursive power. Moreover, it can defy its own settled presuppositions and put aside its accustomed methods the better to see or invent what it may be able to make sense of, according to changed methods and presuppositions, only retrospectively.

The attributes of vitality—invoked earlier in the discussion of the ethic of self-fashioning—are surfeit, spontaneity, surprise, and fecundity. Surfeit is the excess of experience and capability over structure: the failure of our social and conceptual worlds to exhaust what we can experience, see, and do. Spontaneity is the failure of the past fully to determine the present and future: the relativity of path dependence. We can organize our societies and conduct our lives in ways that weaken path dependence. Surprise is the potential to create the new, on the basis of surfeit and spontaneity. Fecundity is the translation of this potential into an accomplished power: the power to make the new. The really new, I have argued, is not just the realization of some antecedently defined possible state of affairs: a ghost stalking the world. It is a change in reality. As with imagination, vitality is manifest only in time: temporality is central to every aspect of it.

We can now reinterpret imagination as the way of representing and engaging the world that is characteristic of a being with the attributes of vitality. Such a being can be more or less vital, possessing these attributes in greater or lesser degree. As he comes to possess and to exercise them more fully, his vitality finds expression in a way of perceiving and explaining the world that is imaginative.

Vitality and imagination are connected through transformative action and engagement with the world and with others. Goethe remarked that the attitude of contemplation tends to irony and fatalism. The supreme expression of vitality is the creation of the new. Imagination is the shadow or the prefiguring of transformative action: the cognitive instrument and manifestation of vitality.

The maximalist version of the ethic of connection wants our relations to one another in society, beyond the range of intimacy, to be increasingly informed by the duo of vitality and imagination. Together, they will rescue us from the association of freedom with coldness. Together, they will provide a source of warmth—or of re-enchantment—that is not simply the progressive dilution of the affect accompanying our most intimate relations. The moral outcome will then not be a superior benevolence or a disinterested impersonal friendliness. It will not be the middle distance of Schopenhauer's porcupines. It will look, instead, to a version of the interpersonal bearing the marks of imagination and vitality, and awakening us to our experience and to its medium, time.

The focus will be on the relation among people—on life in society rather than on the individual self, as it is in the rival ethic of self-fashioning and non-conformity. However, the character of our interpersonal experience will itself change, taking on some of the attributes of vitality and of the imagination. We can then hope to become both freer and warmer.

The best way to understand the content of such a change in our interpersonal experience is to explore the structural changes that would make movement in this direction possible, given the circumstances of contemporary societies.

The organization of economic life must be one that allows for a wide decentralization of access to the resources and opportunities of production. In that sense, it should be a market order. But that does not mean it should take the legal and institutional form of the market economies that have evolved in the course of modern Western history. The market should not be fastened to a single version of itself: alternative forms of economic decentralization—and therefore alternative regimes of property and contract—should coexist experimentally within the same decentralized economy. The freedom to recombine factors of production within an unchallenged and unchanged institutional framework of production and exchange is not enough; it should develop into a freedom to innovate in that framework.

If the most advanced practice of production in a historical period is the most mindful one, the one that is closest to the imagination, then the largest part of the production system and of the labor force should have access to this most productive practice.

The individual worker and citizen should be secure in a haven of protected endowments and immunities so that he can flourish, capable and unafraid, when surrounded by accelerated transformation. Economically dependent wage labor should gradually give way to the higher forms of free work—self-employment and cooperation. No one should be condemned to do the formulaic work that can be done by machines.

The arrangements of democratic politics should subject the

structure of society to effective pressure without needing crisis as the condition of change. They should have the effect of narrowing the distance, for the individual as well as for the collectivity, between the ordinary moves that we make within a framework of institutions and assumptions that we take for granted and the exceptional moves by which we challenge and change pieces of this framework. To this end, they should heighten the level of organized popular engagement in political life, resolve impasse quickly, and combine a facility for decisive initiative by the central government with opportunities for radical devolution in a unitary state or experimentation within a federal one.

The form of education, both in youth and throughout life, should equip the individual to resist and overcome his context as well as to operate capably within it. It should favor capability over content and, when dealing with content, prefer selective depth to encyclopedic superficiality, approach every subject from contrasting points of view, and give access to ideas and experience remote from the present culture and its orthodoxies.

The combined and cumulative effect of these arrangements and practices is to transform the experience of life in society—of the logic of the interpersonal—and to inform it with the attributes of imagination and vitality. Thus, the maximalist version of the ethic of connection points to ideals and arrangements that converge in many ways with those suggested by a corrected version of the ethic of self-fashioning.

It will be my argument that the two moral visions cannot in the end be united in a synthesis that is anything more than a misleading rhetorical maneuver. After we expunge from the ethic of self-fashioning the excesses of a romantic individualism, and abandon the humanizing conservatism of the minimalist version of the rival ethic of connection, a gap remains between the two moral visions.

This gap can and will have moral and political consequences that are likely to become more apparent in time and that philosophy can already prefigure. Nevertheless, over a broad area, the corrected ethic of self-fashioning and the maximalist version of the ethic of connection converge in their implications for society more than in their consequences for the conduct of life. They express in two different registers the prophecy of a higher form of life. The content of this prophecy matters more, and has greater interest, than the philosophical views and vocabularies in which we voice and develop it.

These changes in the character of social life support a raising of the level of vitality and imagination that is manifest in everyday experience. They narrow the distance between the ordinary moves that we make within a framework of institutional arrangements and assumptions that we take for granted and the exceptional moves by which we challenge and change pieces of this framework.

Considered in another way, such innovations in our political and economic institutions do more than vivify our social experience; they represent the imagination at work. A high-energy democracy is fertile in generating variations on the established forms of social experience. A deepened and disseminated knowledge economy perpetually reinvents itself and its products. The education it requires seeks to form minds in which this subsumption of the actual under the accessible possibilities, with all their consequences for self and society, can live in thought before being enacted in social practice.

At each step in this account of the ways in which the minimalist and the maximalist versions of the ethic of connection deal with the problems of subjugation, disunion, and coldness in the way things are, I have been attentive to the difference between the political and the moral response to the problem: the political response developing in long historical time and the moral response in brief biographical time. And in each instance, we see that the link between the political and the moral response presents itself differently for the minimalist and for the maximalist versions of the ethic of connection.

The minimalist response to each of those problems demands chiefly a change of attitude, although one pregnant with practical consequences. It therefore need draw no sharp contrast between its political and its moral consequences. But the maximalist response requires a reorganization of society. For this reason, it renders acute the question of what the individual moral agent must do in his own lifetime in his relations to other people and to himself, while the struggle over social arrangements continues in historical time. That is why, in the argument about the moral and political consequences of a maximalist ethic of connection, I have tried, at each step along the way, to underline the immediate moral consequences of the maximalist view. I have done so in the form that is most conventional in the history of Western moral philosophy: the form of a doctrine of the virtues—of our habitual dispositions to action.

The central moral demand on what, given this understanding of the problem of coldness, we should do with and in our lives is that we must be courageous.

Courage is our willingness to overcome fear, especially fear of harms that we must risk in order to become freer and greater and to draw closer to others. We become freer and greater by standing up to the structures of society, of thought, and of character and by refusing, in our relations to others, to settle for the middle distance.

Courage is far from being the highest virtue. Its place among the virtues is uncertain. But it is the enabling virtue; without it, all other virtues are rendered sterile. It plays a role in making fertile the virtues of connection, including fairness and forbearance, of purification (simplicity, enthusiasm, and attentiveness), and of divinization (openness to the new and openness to the other). It is the first virtue of both the agent and the thinker.

We show courage in our willingness to cast down our shields and accept a heightened vulnerability. We show it when we exchange serenity for searching. We do so for the sake of our connection to others—to come closer to them and escape the middle distance, as the ethic of connection recommends, but also for the sake of vitality and empowerment, so that we may become more human by becoming more godlike, as the ethic of self-fashioning calls us to do.

The role of the will in such an unshielding is powerful but it is also oblique: to throw ourselves into situations in which we are unprotected and to do so to the end of achieving more connection and more life. The moral complications of this pursuit become explicit in our response to a foreseeable event in a normal human existence. As we grow older, a carapace of routine and silent surrenders beings to form around each of us. It is the habitual form of the self, combined with the life situation to which we are resigned. Within this mummy we slowly die, by installments, many small deaths. As life drains away from us, our relations to others are frozen into a place from which we cannot hope to wrest them.

We must escape this mummy. We cannot simply will the mummy to fall apart; we must expose ourselves to forces that break the mummy up by placing us in situations in which we are not in control and which subject us to challenges subversive of our habitual way of being. Now suppose that someone undertakes a political or social struggle out of mixed motives. He is committed to the ends of the campaign. But he also hopes that it may help him change and open himself more fully to others (in the language of the ethic of connection) or come fully to life (in the idiom of the ethic of self-fashioning).

He will have to resist two opposite but equally dehumanizing perversions. One perversion is to treat his own life as an instrument of collective aims, whose achievement he may never see. The contrasting perversion is to take the political struggle as the occasion for a romantic adventure: its professed aims serve as a pretext for experiments in the making of closer attachments or of a larger self. By contrast to both these perversions, what such a person must hope for is to act on an affinity between a society's attempt to innovate in its structure, at the cost of conflict and confusion, and an individual's effort to innovate in his habitual way of being, at the price of a heightened vulnerability. He will understand that courage is not enough unless it is joined to hope.

The object of hope can be described in many ways, including the two ways that have figured prominently in my argument here: the hope of connecting without being subjugated, of engaging without surrendering, and of forming a coherent way of being without allowing this way of being to take life away from us, and the hope of living in a complex, advanced society that is untainted either by coldness or by oppression and disunion. To be courageous and hopeful is to be ready for the dangers of the future, of my own future.

The argument and Hegel's succession. A way to restate the central themes in this argument about the minimalist and maximalist forms of the ethic of connection is to consider their relation to an aspect of Hegel's account, in *The Phenomenology of Spirit*, of the history of forms of life and of consciousness.

In Hegel's philosophical narrative, there is a history of forms of life and of their representation. Each such form of life must, to be enacted by its participants, be represented in ideas that make sense of it. Such representations, although indispensable to its workings, reveal its contradictions. The resolution of these contradictions in turn drives forward this history. Karl Marx was to recast this dialectical method as a tool for insight into the history of social and economic regimes, finding the operative contradictions in the connection between the "relations of production"—how each regime is organized and how it assigns different classes to distinct positions in the division of labor—and the "forces of production": what the development of our productive powers requires by way of social and economic organization.

Hegel's narrative distinguishes three large stages in the formation of humanity. In the first stage, we are at one with the arrangements of society. They do not appear to us as a constraint but rather as the way things naturally are. It is in and through these naturalized arrangements that we relate to other people in society as if the regime of society and culture were an elastic and transparent medium rather than the formative and distinctive context that it in fact is. In this circumstance of "immediacy" our consciousness of self remains undeveloped. The depth of our distinction from the other animals has not yet become manifest.

But because we are in fact embodied spirit, living in time and transcendent over circumstance, we cannot in the end resign ourselves to this timeless and animal-like existence. The historical experience of mankind enters a second stage in which the very ideas by which we make sense of each form of social life reveal its contradictions and unsuitability as our historical home. This is the period of spirit in estrangement. In the period of estrangement, we find ourselves at odds with the arrangements of society because we are in conflict with ourselves: the contradictions made manifest in the way in which we represent each form of life are disharmonies both in these forms of life and in ourselves. They prevent us from fully engaging in our social world without surrendering to it. They subtract from the depth of subjectivity and selfhood.

We will be free, and no longer estranged, when we can participate in social life without ceasing to affirm and develop selfhood and subjectivity. In Hegel's narrative, we are almost there; one step away from overcoming estrangement. Estrangement is not merely a subjective experience; it is an objective feature of a way of organizing society and culture. We cannot overcome estrangement simply by redescribing our situation or changing our attitude to it; we can overcome it only by developing the form of life in society that overcomes this opposition in practice.

There is much in Hegel's narrative that is useful and even indispensable to my argument here: the dual nature of forms of life, as institutional order and representation or consciousness; the idea that the succession of forms of consciousness can progress in ways that touch on our most fundamental interests and ideals; and the view that the contradictions between how we live and how we represent these ideals and interests can help drive such a progression.

Hegel understood that the norm of reciprocity is not enough to shape life in society, joining representations to practices. Only a regime of assumptions and arrangements—the way things are—has that power. Our relation to the way things are, accepting or rejecting it, reproducing or changing it, is our fate.

There are, however, also major features of Hegel's account of the history of such regimes of practice and consciousness that the method and vision developed here require us to reject. Their repudiation and replacement results in a view fundamentally different from Hegel's.

The first mistake is the characterization of "spirit in immediacy," the circumstance in which the human agent feels completely at home with the way things are—the established social order—as if it were nature itself, part of the furniture of the universe, an infinitely elastic medium, free of any tension between self and regime. There can be, and has been, a development of self and subjectivity in history. Yet not even in a stateless society, with a relatively stable customary way of life and a relatively unchallenged cosmology, do people ever become no more than hapless puppets of the institutional and ideological regime. Even then they can think, experience, and desire more than the order can countenance. Even then they can turn against the way things are and combine surrender with apostasy. The human being is never, and has never been, in the condition that Hegel describes as immediacy.

The second mistake is to imagine that there can ever be a circumstance—the final stage of Hegel's narrative—in which we are at last able to participate fully and without reservation or ambivalence in the way things are without compromising the free affirmation of our subjective life. Just as there can be no form of social life that deprives us of the powers to resist and to see, feel, and act beyond the established arrangements and assumptions, so too there can be no regime of practice and consciousness that would allow us, individually and collectively, to deliver ourselves to it without putting on chains of our own invention.

The meaning of the final stage in Hegel's narrative is to portray spirit, the human being in possession of his divine power of transcendence and transformation, as at last at home in the world, all passion spent. Such a spirit, however, is never at home in the world—which is not to deny that some forms of social life are more hospitable to the human being, embodied spirit, than others. The possibility of progression is not to be mistaken for the availability of a final reconciliation that brings the unrest of our temporal experience to an end.

The third and most important failing of Hegel's story is not to have made clear the basic content of the condition of estrangement. Hegel recounts a history of the discovery of contradictions in forms of life and in ways of making sense of them in modern Europe. It is as if the universal destiny of mankind were revealed in the vicissitudes and turning points of European culture. In representing the provincial as the universal, he also leaves inexplicit the recurrent structure of the quarrel with the way things are throughout the history of civilization.

If we are estranged from the social world, it is because in the course of that history we have been unable to connect to others without dominating them or being dominated by them; we have not managed to develop social difference without foregoing, to the same extent, social union; and we have not learned how to be both free and warm. We cannot overcome estrangement simply by redescribing our situation or developing a different attitude toward it; we can overcome it only by developing forms of life that overcome these oppositions in practice.

The minimalist and the maximalist versions of the ethic of connection represent alternative proposals for overcoming this estrangement.

The essence of the difference between the minimalist and maximalist accounts of the ethic of connection, and the meaning of this difference for the moral conversation within humanity. The minimalist and the maximalist versions of the ethic of connection differ in their relation to the established organization of society, in their quarrel with the way things are, in their proposals to overcome the estrangement to which we remain condemned by its deficiencies, and in their vision of a higher form of solidarity.

The minimalist version is the only one by which we traditionally know this ethic in the history of moral ideas. It seeks to humanize or moralize the established social order rather than radically to remake it. It places its greatest hope for the improvement of this order in the strengthening of role-based capabilities and responsibilities. But it recognizes that the efficacy of such reforms depends on their association with a force that is more fundamental and that comes earlier in the formation of the moral agent: the acquisition, thanks to social ritual and convention, of a second nature freeing us from the narcissism and solipsism to which we would otherwise be condemned. It also depends on its partnership with our empathy for other people and our cultivated ability to imagine their experience, their needs, and their longings.

The minimalist ethic of connection deals with the three major sources of estrangement—subjugation, disunion, and coldness—by proposing ideas and practices counteracting evils that it regards as unavoidable: the containment and ennoblement of power and inequality by responsibility and meritocracy; the forms of professional ethics and insight into the experience of other people that prevent social difference from resulting in social disunion; and the strengthening among strangers of a form of benevolence that represents a weakened counterpart to the stronger emotional bonds that are possible among intimates.

The vision of solidarity resulting from these impulses is one that tempers its hopes in the political transformation of society but reaffirms its bet on the good created by a disinterested beneficence. Through the combined and cumulative effect of these initiatives and practices we prevent society from degenerating into a contest of force. Above all, we preserve and expand the space for the chief source of good in the world: the non-instrumental and sacrosanct logic of interpersonal relations.

The maximalist version of the ethic of connection imposes no limit on its disposition to challenge the established regime of arrangements and assumptions as the terrain on which to enact its vision. It holds that overcoming the condition that Hegel described as estrangement, but that he failed to relate to its fundamental causes, is possible only through a radical transformation of the way things are, not simply a change in how we deal with one another given how things are. To say that the change must be radical is not to suggest that it must conform to the model of revolution that was widely accepted from the end of the eighteenth century to end of the twentieth, nor is it to accept the social-theoretical assumptions of this model—in particular the idea of an indivisible system, such as "capitalism," which must be broken and replaced if it is not to be simply managed and humanized. The transformation can proceed by steps without ceasing to be radical in its outcome. It is radical because, many such steps ahead, every feature of the way things are now is likely to have changed.

The significance of these distinctions becomes clear when translated into criticism of the societies that exist today. For the maximalist, it is not enough to restrain domination with impersonal law, compensatory redistribution, and meritocratic advancement. It is necessary to reshape the institutional and legal forms of the market order, of democratic politics, and of the formation of the individual. The economic changes will not suffice until economically dependent wage labor, bought and sold, has ceased to be the predominant form of free work, and until no one has to work to do what a machine could do instead. The political changes will have not been completed until a form of political life has been established that no longer requires crisis as the condition of change. And education will not have taken the direction that the maximalist wants until it equips the mature as well as the young with the ability to see beyond their social and historical situation as well as to move within it.

For the maximalist, the development of social difference is a goal rather than a threat. Social difference is to be reconciled with social union by the multiplication of activities that the different are called on to undertake together rather than by counterweights to the differentiating effects of the division of labor. The greatest union that is compatible with the widest amount of difference of all sorts is the aim of the maximalist.

The maximalist refuses to accept the predominance of the middle distance in our relations to one another as the inevitable consequence of our emancipation from the mixture of power, exchange, and allegiance—the sentimentalization of unequal exchange—that marked life in society before the present age of world revolution. He seeks what the minimalist dismisses as paradoxical and impossible: that we become both warm and free.

The determination of the maximalist to overcome the conditions of estrangement involves him in conflict. Everything in the development of such a project passes through struggle, not just through debate. The minimalist version of the ethic of connection has always been associated with an ideal of harmony. One of its most characteristic tropes is the avoidance of class and sectarian conflict by the joint work of self-restraint and benevolence. This ideal can have no place in the imagination of the maximalist.

Moreover, the reach of the maximalist's transformative commitments has the consequence of aggravating a problem with which the defender of the ethic of self-fashioning must also deal: the moral consequences of the failures of politics. The overcoming of estrangement in the fashion that I have just recalled is a historical and collective endeavor; there is no hope of achieving it, or even of making significant progress in its enactment, in the span of a human life. The maximalist must therefore propose a way of living that is not only informed by the same ideals that animate this political vision but that makes up, as best as possible, for what politics has failed to accomplish. This relation between the work of morals and the omissions of politics must find expression in his view of solidarity: the way of dealing with other people that he can hope to achieve now, in his own life, regardless of the persistence or overcoming of the conditions of estrangement in society.

He cannot, through individual action, make up for the burden of history. He can nevertheless aspire to live and act in such a way that his dealings with others are a testament to his vision of a higher form of solidarity and a prophecy of what he hopes for through the transformation of social life. He must despise subjugation close up, not simply in the structure of society. He must open himself to the different, forming his insight into the otherness of other people and leading in the development of joint action predicated on difference rather than on sameness. And rather than trust to superior and distant benevolence when he cannot count on either the inspiration or the dangers of intimacy, he must live by a higher standard: a disposition to be surprised and instructed by the other person at the cost of accepting a heightened vulnerability to disappointment and defeat.

Recall the reason for formulating the ethic of connection in maximalist as well as in minimalist form. If we understand it only in its minimalist form, which is the form presented to us by the history of moral, religious, and philosophical ideas, it appears as a humanizing resignation to the social order. Its claim to moral realism is then the reverse side of the limitation of its transformative hopes.

The minimalist form of the ethic of connection is the counterpart to the unrevised version of the ethic of self-fashioning and non-conformity. If all we had to go by, to understand the shape of this new moral conversation within humanity—pursued on the plane of a secular vision, without appeal to a higher-order metaphysical framework or theological narrative—were the minimalist form of the ethic of connection, then we would fail to do justice to this hidden debate. It would be as if we were presented with a choice between—to give each position the name of its most influential theoretician—Nietzsche and Confucius: a heroic individualism opposed to a morality of role-based responsibilities, other-directedness, and cultivated, disinterested benevolence. Even if we seek to present these two positions in the strongest form that is compatible with adhering to their original and canonical formulations, the result would come close to being a contest of straw men: not because the arguments and visions of the philosophers are without force, but because we have seen too much and lived too much to entrust the conduct of our lives to either of these moral conceptions.

If that is the choice, humanity will say with good reason, we had better continue to look elsewhere for guidance. We will continue to look elsewhere even if we have determined to forego metaphysical and theological props to the direction of our existence. We will continue to do so, as well, even if the meta-ethical agenda of the school philosophy—with its focus on the categorical imperative, the felicific calculus, or the social contract—seems to us an evasion of the question about the conduct of life.

The reason to develop the maximalist version of the ethic of connection is the same as the reason to formulate the revised version of the ethic of self-fashioning: so that we may have before us a choice in our approach to the conduct of life, stated in terms that we have reason to take seriously.

The version of the ethic of self-fashioning that emerges from the criticism of its most questionable and accidental features—those that it acquired in the course of the context-bound history of ideas—is in many ways closer to the maximalist ethic of connection than are the canonical versions of the ethic of self-fashioning: those, for example, that Emerson and Nietzsche, the classic liberal political theorists, or the romantics gave it. The maximalist ethic of connection is closer to the corrected ethic of self-fashioning, in similar ways, than is the minimalist variant of the ethic of connection. Yet when they are cleansed of their most obvious and superficial flaws, and wiped clean of the dross of history—the characteristics they have acquired by virtue of their circumstantial association with particular societies and cultures—these two moral visions, the corrected ethic of self-fashioning and the maximalist ethic of connection, fail to converge. Their most important distinctions stand out all the more clearly. Why are they irreconcilable, and what is the significance of their irreconcilability?

6

The Unresolved Contest between the Ethics of Self-Fashioning and of Connection

---

The Dust of History: The United States, China, and the Two Ethics

The association of each of these two ethics with one of the great powers in the twenty-first century. Each of the two moral visions that represent the chief alternative contemporary approaches to the conduct of life has a base in one of the two great powers of the present time—the United States and China. This association of an approach to existence with a nation-state is both troubling and revealing. Yet it is also loose and susceptible to radical reversal: powerful forces in each of these nations attract it to the opposing view.

If we regard ethical conceptions in the manner of the school philosophy as abstract and universal ideas and methods, any such association of moral ideas with certain nation-states would be no more than a curiosity when not an embarrassment. In explaining the national circumstances that make one such conception seem more appealing than another, we do nothing—according to this understanding of ethics—to make it any more deserving of being embraced and developed. For the practice of moral philosophy exemplified here, however, the historical career of moral conceptions has philosophical significance. Not only does it show what has happened when people have acted on their ethical beliefs, it also helps us recognize in each of these approaches to the conduct of life a central and lasting message and distinguish that message from features that the ethic has acquired as a result of its association with particular civilizations.

The two major traditions of world philosophy—the Greek philosophy of being or the philosophy of deep structure, which has been predominant in the history of Western philosophy from the pre-Socratics to today, and the philosophy of the timeless one that was ascendant in the philosophy of ancient India—represent, I have argued, inadequate philosophical settings for both the moral visions explored in this book. They demand a third position, one that dissociates reality from timelessness and makes sense of one of the most important facts about the world: that everything in it is transient and susceptible to transformation but no less real and distinct on that account.

The association of the two major philosophical traditions with parts of the world—Europe and India—is so contingent and loose that each of the two traditions has long been present, although as a minority voice, in the part of the world in which the other has been predominant. The idea that the ultimately real is one and timeless has been represented in the history of Western philosophy from Parmenides to Schopenhauer, and the philosophy of deep structure has found expression in several strands of ancient Indian philosophy.

When we turn from speculative metaphysics to moral vision, we find a more intimate and consequential relation of ideas to societies and cultures, and even to nations and states. The relation becomes all the stronger when the moral vision dispenses with metaphysical or theological props, as the two approaches to the conduct of life addressed in this book do and should.

Each of these moral visions draws its meaning from practices as well as from ideas. The ideas never fully explain, elucidate, or justify the practices. The marriage of practice to idea results in a set of experiences. And the experiences bring doubts, contradictions, and surprises. Moreover, every such approach to the conduct of life has a political message: it comes laden with assumptions and preferences about the organization of society; the boundary separating the moral from the political always remains porous. The momentous transactions between beliefs and practices, as well as between morals and politics, take place in the setting of the peoples of the world, organized by armed states. These facts account for the strange association of orientations to existence with individual countries.

This association has philosophical interest in two ways. The practices developed in their national settings harbor dangers and opportunities that the doctrines, taken out of their national contexts, may fail to reveal. At the same time, by virtue of its relationship to a country, its history, and its culture, an approach to the conduct of life takes on characteristics of this setting: a historical dust that prevents us from distinguishing the most basic and powerful tenets of a vision from those that it has taken on only because of its passage through the history of nations and states. We need to recognize this dust for what it is the better to shake it off.

No person is a set of ideas. No country is a moral creed, or even a vision defined by practices as well as by beliefs. No people accepts such a vision without reservation and ambivalence. Nevertheless, the two approaches to the conduct of life discussed here are powerful because they express aspirations that have a hold on our experience.

They draw their power as well from their relation to the two most pressing tests—at once necessities and ideals—that contemporary societies must meet: the creation of capable agents and the development of higher forms of cooperation. As the unrevised ethic of self-fashioning gives pride of place to the first imperative, the minimalist ethic of connection accords priority to the second. But both tests are indispensable to the success of a society. The problem of the relation between the ethics of self-fashioning and the ethics of connection is among other things the problem of the relation between these twin imperatives: the enhancement of agency and the development of our cooperative practices.

For these deep reasons—as well as for more circumstantial ones, discussed in the following pages, related to their historical experience —each of these countries, the United States and China, may be attracted to the moral vision that is headquartered, for the moment, in the other one. It would not be surprising to see them switch sides in the future.

The imprint of the United States on the canonical ethic of self-fashioning.
The ethic of self-invention and non-conformity, in its uncorrected and
canonical form, has set its mark on the American mind. Consider its
multiple roots and expressions in American history and civilization.

First, it had a basis in the political economy of the early Republic.
When Tocqueville visited the United States in the 1830s, only one in
every five white men worked for another man. Americans have never
entirely abandoned, in successive waves of concentration of wealth
and economic power, the ideal of a property-owning democracy of
independent economic agents who cooperate with one another, secure
in their independent citadels of property and right. Law and politics
in the United States have failed to generate alternative instances of this
ideal, compatible with the aggregation of resources at large scale and
with the multiplication of different kinds of stakes, held by different
tiers of stakeholders, in the same productive resources.

Second, the attachment to an unreconstructed version of the ethic
of self-fashioning finds support in the naturalization of the market
order as that order was defined by the classical private law of the
nineteenth century and in particular by the unified property right
as the exemplary form of rights in general. Unified property vested
all the component powers of property in a single right holder, the
owner, in contrast to the more normal condition in legal history: the
dismembering of the property right into distinct powers, vested in
different tiers of stakeholders. The unrevised version of the ethic of
self-invention gives philosophical expression to this legal and institutional reification of a market regime: the idea that a market economy
has a single natural and necessary form and that the unified property
right is its preeminent expression.

A third root of the uncorrected ethic of self-invention in American life has been the political counterpart to the naturalization of
the market order—the proto-democratic liberalism enshrined in
the constitutional arrangements of the United States. These political
arrangements maintained the people at a low level of political engagement, cooling the temperature of politics, and confused, through the
Madisonian scheme of checks and balances, the liberal principle of
the fragmentation of power with the conservative principle of the

inhibition of structural change, thus slowing down the pace of politics. The result was to deny society the political means with which to keep reinventing itself except in the enabling circumstance of crisis: war or ruin. The weakness of democracy combined with the illusions of thought to favor the view that, early on, the United States had settled on the definitive formula of a free society, which it needed only to adjust from time to time but never fundamentally to alter.

A fourth reason for the special place that the uncorrected ethic of self-fashioning holds in the American imagination is spiritual. This orientation to existence formed the core of the message of the American prophets—Emerson, Whitman, and Lincoln among them. And it bears a close relation to the most distinctive contribution of the American people to the religious life of humanity. At the center of the message of those prophets is the idea that the individual can become more human by becoming more godlike and can become more godlike by increasing his share in the godlike power of transcendence. A god in ruins, as Emerson called him, he can lift himself by becoming more like God in fact: the God who loves and suffers for his love, who loves so much that he can take on the burdens of finitude and submit to death, as well as the God who, incarnate as the Redeemer, embodies the infinite within the finite.

The message of the American prophets immediately posed the question of how society should be organized to house a being with such a godlike vocation. The naturalization of one particular version of a free society, imagined as the setting for cooperation among free and equal economic agents, became part of the orthodox interpretation of that teaching. As a result, the message came to suffer from two defects that rank high among the failings of the uncorrected version of the ethic of self-fashioning. What I earlier described as the revised version of the ethic of self-fashioning is distinguished in large part by its repudiation of these two flaws.

The first defect is a disturbance in the understanding of the relation between self-construction and solidarity. The disturbance consists in failing to recognize that solidarity is internal to self-construction, not an addition to it: the generosity of those who are strong because they are self-made. In this respect, and although formed in a Christian society, the message of the American prophets was both a denial of one of the most important truths about human beings and a Christian heresy. The truth that it denied was the contradiction inscribed in one of the enabling conditions of self-assertion: that we can build ourselves and come into the fuller possession of life only through connection with the other person, but that every such connection threatens us with loss of autonomy and of personal distinction. We cannot be free unless we succeed in attenuating this contradiction: through love among intimates and free cooperation among strangers.

This failure to recognize the truth about the relation between solidarity and self-construction is also a Christian heresy because the two central ideas in Christianity—the infinity of embodied spirit and the primacy of love (of love, not altruism)—are inseparable in the Christian faith. In that faith, our sharing in the godlike attribute of transcendence and our relation to other people are mirrors of each other.

The second defect in the message of the American prophets is institutional idolatry: the reverence of Americans for their institutions—the political even more than the economic—as the privileged form of a free society. Their impulse has been to exempt their institutions from the reach of the experimentalism that has been so prominent in all other aspects of their culture. They have refused to listen to their own thinkers—from Thomas Jefferson to John Dewey—who tried to persuade them to lift this exemption. The result has been another Christian heresy as well as a superstition dangerous to their ideals of freedom; it is a Christian heresy—known as Pelagianism—to treat any institutional order as the adequate and definitive home of the godlike spirit. While recognizing the possibility of progress, a Christian must see every regime as dust in the face of God. And his conception of such progress must lead him to act on the hope—contrary to the premises of romanticism—that we can create structures that make up for their inadequacies by their corrigibility as well by their openness to a wide range of contradictory experience.

The message of the American prophets is echoed by the religious life of the country. The ideas of the Protestant Reformation, with their focus on the direct relation between the believer and God, developed

in the middle period of the history of Protestantism into the privatization of the religious sublime and the abandonment of a theology
of social reconstruction by the major Protestant denominations. The
predominant temper of secular humanism in the United States, with
its characteristic exaggeration of the powers of the individual to save
himself and its equally characteristic understatement of our collective
power to improve society, has offered a non-theological counterpart
to the same outlook.

But the most original and revealing religious expression of the
American people has been neither in historical Protestantism nor in
the secular gospel of worldly self-improvement and positive thinking. It has been in what Harold Bloom called the American gnostic
religion exemplified by movements such as The Latter-day Saints,
Jehovah's Witnesses, and Seventh Day Adventism. In these movements we find the radicalization of the message of the American
prophets about the share of the individual in the divine life and
in the attributes of God. The deification of the person, suggesting
the communion between the human and the divine natures in the
person of the ordinary man and woman as well as in the person of
the Redeemer, is the boldest expression of a central theme in the
ethic of self-fashioning. As the ordinary human being comes into
fuller possession of life in the present moment, he widens his share
in the inner life of God.

In the most celebrated book on the American experience, *Democracy in America*, Tocqueville developed his thesis that the passion
for equality was the fundamental force in the consciousness of the
American people. He was mistaken: a narrow idea of freedom was
their ruling passion. They sought to avoid extreme inequalities of
circumstance because such inequalities threatened to undermine
freedom as they understood it. The unrevised ethic of self-fashioning
was a natural companion to their political and religious beliefs.

However, in embracing this moral vision, Americans of many
classes and walks of life have often been powerfully attracted to ideals
and practices that emphasize the importance of voluntary association,
community, and role-based responsibilities to other people. They have
then looked to movements and entities intermediate between the

state and the individual, to private philanthropy, and to associations outside the market and politics to accomplish what their economic and political arrangements are unable to achieve. We might interpret these initiatives as a spontaneous, inchoate form of the conservative, minimalist ethic of connection, gesturing in the direction of voluntary action and social responsibility without structural change. Americans have needed no Confucius to look for what the message of the American prophets left out.

It has been an inadequate response to the consequences of the failure to do justice to the relation between self-construction and solidarity and to the curse of institutional idolatry. The organization of civil society outside the state and the market is no more self-defining than the ordering of democratic politics and of the market economy. An organization of civil society that relies on the established law of contract and private associations, on the activities of churches and private clubs, and on the social campaigns and moral hobbyhorses of the rich provides a weak counterweight to inequalities rooted in the economic and political institutions and in the class structure that they help sustain.

Money transfers organized by the state cannot be an effective social cement. They will seem to be a sufficient basis for social solidarity only when practiced against a background of social and cultural homogeneity. As soon as that background is undermined, especially by the movement of people across national frontiers, the inadequacy of compensatory redistribution by tax-and-transfer as a basis for social union amid social difference will become manifest.

The real basis for social union may then become the cultivation of hardened group identities—of race, culture, religion, or even class: union based on sameness rather than on difference. One of the consequences will be the predisposition to group conformity which Tocqueville feared and denounced as the degenerate child of the democratic passion for equality when it is in fact the result of an inadequate understanding of freedom.

The shadow accompanying the unrevised form of the ethic of self-fashioning and non-conformity is thus the attraction exercised by its opposite and counterpart: the narrowest and most conventional form of the ethic of connection, the cultivation of communitarian aspirations, role-based responsibilities, and social benevolence, unaccompanied by any effort to overcome the double taint on the message of the American prophets—the idolatrous reification of American institutions and the misrepresentation of the place of solidarity in self-construction.

The imprint of China on the canonical ethic of connection. As the United States has been the national headquarters of the ethic of self-fashioning and non-conformity, China has been, and remains, the chief home of the ethic of connection. The association of Chinese society and culture with this approach to the conduct of life has a much longer history and an even broader range of expressions than the American equivalent. However, it is just as beset by ambiguity and no less subject to reversal.

China witnessed, 2,500 years ago, the public activity of Confucius—to this day still the leading exponent of this moral view. The tradition of thought and practice that he established has always had in China many rivals and enemies, open or veiled. It nevertheless entered so deeply into the institutions and consciousness of the Chinese people, and sustained its influence over so long a time and over so broad a range of circumstances, that it is only with difficulty that we can distinguish its deeper and more universal teachings from the characteristics that it acquired in its association with that people.

My earlier presentation of its content struggled to disentangle the universal message from its Chinese adaptation. To that end, it looked to classical European social theory and contemporary evolutionary psychology. And it distinguished the conventional, minimalist form of this ethic—more closely modeled on its ancient Chinese expression —from the radical, maximalist form that it would need to acquire if it is to offer a compelling alternative to the ethic of self-fashioning.

The minimalist and maximalist versions of the ethic of connection meet in the determination to affirm the primacy of the interpersonal and the intersubjective in every facet of our experience and existence. They meet as well in the effort to redeem social life from degenerating into a brute assertion of power.

Longstanding features of Chinese society and culture help explain the specific direction taken by the canonical version of this ethic: the one that we know from the form Confucius gave it. Here are four such features—examples of the dust of history, the circumstantial adaptations that an approach to existence takes during its coevolution with individual peoples and states.

One characteristic assumption is the relative denial of transcendence in this secular humanistic ethic. The larger vision of reality from which this moral vision, in its Chinese form, emerged was one that had no place for transcendence in either of the two forms made familiar in the history of religion: the transcendence of a creative God over the temporal world that he created and in which he intervenes, as described in the narratives of the Semitic monotheisms; and the transcendence of the timeless one, the ultimate source of reality and being, in the speculative monism that had a leading role in the philosophy of ancient India and that Buddhism developed and transformed. Its principal expression in ancient China was Daoism.

There is indeed transcendence in classical Confucianism (as distinguished from neo-Confucianist metaphysics). It rests, however, on the combination of two ideas: to rob nature of its sanctity and to sanctify our relation to other people. The interpersonal has a force and a value that exceed all its historical and social expressions.

What is the view of the self from which this conception of the interpersonal develops? The ethic of self-fashioning and non-conformity offers a this-worldly, secular approach to our existence and the conduct of our lives. It nonetheless affirms what we might describe as a non-finitistic view of personality: we immeasurably exceed the social and conceptual worlds that we build collectively and inhabit as individuals. There is always more in us—more possibility of experience and invention—than there is or ever can be in them. This naturalistic but non-finitistic view of the self penetrates every aspect of that moral vision and of its prescriptions for the conduct of life. In the absence of such a view of the self, the supreme value attributed to the interpersonal remains in jeopardy: the danger of confusing the moral logic of the interpersonal with its conventional, role-dependent forms. It is no mere theoretical danger: we see it enacted in the practice of the minimalist ethic of connection.

The denial of radical transcendence, founded on a non-finitistic view of the personality, occurred naturally in a culture that had not been shaken by either the revelation of a living God or by belief in the unreality of time and distinction. Buddhism came relatively late; Christianity even later; and Daoism, and other Chinese parallels to the speculative monism of ancient India, were not enough to reconcile a thoroughgoing naturalism with a radicalization of the transcendence of the personal and consequently of the interpersonal.

A second component of the historical dust that came to attach to the ethic of connection in its Chinese setting was familism: the cult of the family. In any culture that has not settled on a radical form of transcendence, distancing and devaluing the practices of society, but that has progressed beyond abasement before nature and its powers, the family becomes the true object of worship. The family became the covert object of devotion even in nominally Christian cultures. It must be all the more revered in societies that have not been shaken to the ground by the assertion of a source of value opposing both family and state. And so familism was, and remains, China's default religion.

The moral ideas and practices associated with the minimalist, canonical form of the ethic of connection come to life and gain sense and force when interpreted in the context of a society for which the family is the most convincing safeguard against the abandonment of the individual in society to a nightmare of force and guile. We can then understand much in this moral view as the extension to our wider experience in society of habits and ideas acquired in an ennobled version of family life. Those ideas and habits reach outward, in ever larger concentric circles, to touch much of social life.

In the family, power is restrained by commitment and concern. Union can and must dispense with sameness, given differences of family role, age, and gender. The larger society, reformed on the model of reciprocal devotion, can borrow some of the warmth of family life and escape the coldness of impersonal law and power.

A third feature that the minimalist ethic of connection derived from its early Chinese setting, and that it has preserved in the course of most subsequent Chinese history, has been a way of organizing the division of labor that emphasizes role-based responsibilities and admission to roles based on competitive testing. Given the early unification of China and the central part that the unified state played in its history, it was natural to take a meritocratic bureaucracy as a model for the whole division of labor in society. The division of labor was thus to be understood as a scheme of cooperation on a vast scale, legitimated by practical ability and restrained by a morality emphasizing role-based responsibility.

All the ancient agrarian-bureaucratic empires, the chief protagonists in world history before the present age of world revolution, nurtured fragments of these ideas. But none went further and more constantly in this direction than China. Viewed in this context, the minimalist ethic of connection has been the morality of such an empire as well as the moral philosophy of the family. It has seen a purified division of labor as the indispensable setting for the achievement of its ambitions for the improvement of human life.

A fourth preconception that the minimalist ethic of connection has inferred from its historical association with China is a stark contrast between order and anarchy. In that great empire, forever struggling to maintain its unity against external and internal enemies, and deficient in arrangements and beliefs suited to the management of disagreement and conflict, every gesture of resistance and divergence has been treated as an omen of the breakdown of order.

This anxiety had practical roots in circumstances common to the agrarian-bureaucratic empires. Their rulers trod a fine line between two opposing dangers. If they failed to constrain the greed and ambition of the landholding grandees, these magnates would usurp the land of smallholders and destroy the business of independent tradesmen and merchants. The money-based economy would shrink, and the state would lose a source of taxes and soldiers independent from the grandees. If, however, the rulers sided with smallholders, tradesmen, and workers against the magnates, they risked arousing a struggle that they would be unable to master and guide. They could not hope to ride the tiger of revolutionary despotism.

Management of these contrasting perils revolved around a small stock of recurrent policy options regarding vital subjects such as land tenure, the staffing of the state, and the funding of administration and of war. A more lasting success in managing them would have required the decentralization of power in economic and social life to pass a point of no return. That is what happened in Western Europe, laying a basis for the coexistence of active, capable central government with an independent civil society. In the absence of such a combination, the agrarian-bureaucratic bureaucratic empires—including China from the Chin Dynasty onward—remained susceptible to the periodic collapse of the money-based trading economy, the breakdown of unified imperial rule, and conquest by the nomadic peoples of the central Asian steppe.

Throughout much of Chinese history, these constraints and fragilities recurred. They found support in an idea: a stark opposition between order and anarchy. A deeper and more subtle set of ideas would have recognized the value of plasticity. It would have developed a vision of order that welcomed organized conflict as the condition of the ability to innovate in the face of changing circumstance and emerging opportunity. It would have understood a higher conception of order as one that splits the difference between order and anarchy.

The absence of such an idea helps account for the discomfort of the minimalist version of the ethic of connection with all forms of conflict. Aversion to conflict has gone under a long list of euphemisms, such as the value accorded to "harmony"—in the state, the society, and the soul. Contrasting attitudes to order, anarchy, and conflict rank among the most important differences between the minimalist and the maximalist versions of the ethic of connection.

To grasp the continuing practical significance of such attitudes, consider an example from contemporary China, long after the overthrow of the imperial system, in a period in which a shrunken Marxism has been juxtaposed to market fundamentalism or neoliberalism in the economy, while Confucianist teaching is regularly invoked in support of forms of behavior and consciousness promoting responsibility without rebellion.

Now, in the twenty-first century, it is widely recognized that China must reorient its economic development strategy to depend less on export-led growth and more on the deepening of its internal market. Such a reorientation, however, is no mere technical adjustment. It requires massive redistribution among classes, regions, and sectors. For that reason, it is unavoidably conflictual. An authoritarian state system, under party dictatorship, inhibits the expression and channeling of conflict in the service of experimentalism: the practice of experiments by parts of the country to generate counter-models of the national future.

A building built to sway in the wind, rather than to remain rigid until or unless it breaks and falls down—that is what statecraft and practical wisdom require and what the simplified contrast of order and anarchy excludes.

The appeal of radical reversal: shaking off the dust of history. It is unsurprising that the American and Chinese peoples should be attracted to an ethic that reverses the one with which their moral traditions have been traditionally associated. Just as the association has been chiefly with the uncorrected and most obviously defective versions of each of these moral visions, so it is the unrevised version of the opposing view that most naturally appeals to each of these peoples.

Revulsion against the evils of the moral regime of the little Napoleons out to crown themselves, at the expense of a common good, has found a voice in American religion, literature, and politics. The trouble that Americans have had, given their institutional idolatry, in imagining and developing the economic and political institutions that would allow them to become greater together has encouraged them to seek a non-institutional route to that goal: cooperation, when possible, across class and racial lines and the development of organizations and communities that would stand between the state and the isolated individual and nourish the cooperative disposition. Ideas close to what I have described as the minimalist ethic of connection and to its characteristic solutions to the problems of subjugation, disunion, and coldness have long formed the lingua franca of what passes for progressive political and moral opinion in the United States.

Just as contemporary Americans may be powerfully attracted to an ethic rivalling the one that has traditionally prevailed in the public culture of the United States, so the Chinese today have reason to feel the appeal of a moral vision that offers them what their traditions deny them. They may feel attracted to it in its least forgiving version: uncorrected, uncompromising, and unapologetically one-sided.

The reasons for this appeal are more than curiosities: they reveal some of the frustrations and longings, far beyond the dry letter of philosophical arguments, that are at stake in the contest between the two moral visions discussed in this chapter. The Chinese people live in a circumstance of extreme cultural and political repression of the self, from which only a few are exempted—by power and privilege, by marginalization, or by enjoying exceptional support from their families and communities. As state-owned enterprises and collective ownership have receded, taking with them enterprise-based social welfare and stable jobs, the state has abandoned much of the labor force to economic insecurity. The family must inherit part of the welfare-providing role, as it always has. Higher up on the scale of economic, cultural, and political advantage, the individual will be tested in a supposedly meritocratic competition in which most of the contestants must be at least relative losers.

Bereft of active belief in a Marxist and socialist dogma that elicits little enthusiasm or conviction, or of any religious substitute for the dying political faith, no living form of validation of personal sacrifice for the common good remains other than nationalism. The national impulse, however, is rendered suspect as a result of its manipulation by a self-serving power elite.

In this vacuum of faith and commitment (other than commitment to the proximate family and to the distant nation), everything in the circumstance of the individual who no longer suffers extreme poverty and deprivation inflames his narcissism. Raised (until recently) as an only child, he has been waited on and pampered only to discover later the harshness of the collective system that awaits him. All around him, he hears the drum beat of consumption and self-gratification and sees power wielded and advantage secured without excuse and with barely a pretense of any idea that could justify personal sacrifice.

In the confrontation between an aroused narcissism and an omnipresent repression, the ethic of connection and responsibility will seem to be on the side of the latter against the former. Its claim to look beyond the struggle between self-aggrandizement and conformity to a higher form of interdependence may be dismissed as empty and misleading rhetoric. The established powers in the country have helped discredit it by marshaling Confucianist doctrine to justify uncomplaining self-restraint and obedience.

In such a situation a young man or woman may be strongly attracted to the beliefs and attitudes expressed by the unregenerate ethic of self-fashioning and non-conformity. They may appear to him as the transformation of his narcissism into a mode of conduct and consciousness that is defensible and even prestigious. He may never have heard it speak in its high-flown philosophical voice. But he may have seen it all around him in the worldwide popular romantic culture, with its characteristic exaltation of private fantasies, adventures, and sublimities and its elision of any sharp distinction between material pleasures and spiritual quests. Such quests, or the idea of them, will coexist with a reluctant, outward submission to the disciplines of a repressive political, economic, and cultural order.

He may hope to "sing in his chains." The song he sings will be a version of the uncorrected ethic of self-fashioning. He will sing it within the confines of a repressive system that he cannot and will not defy.

The American people have had a favored association with the ethic of self-fashioning, as the Chinese people have with the ethic of connection. These bonds help explain some of the more striking albeit shallow and circumstantial characteristics that each of these moral visions has acquired in its long marriage to the experience and history of these great nations. The loyalties that this symbiotic relation of ethic to nation have generated are, however, qualified, riven by ambivalence, and subject to radical change or even reversal.

No individual human being and no nation will ever exemplify a doctrine, even if it is a doctrine anchored in attitudes and practices and reinforced by institutions as well as by the ideas that make sense of them and lend them authority. The partiality of these ethics, their failure to do justice to our moral experience and to our moral opportunities, is all the more pronounced in their unrevised forms—the uncorrected ethic of self-invention and the minimalist ethic of connection. The American and Chinese peoples may seem devoted to these moral visions. Their devotion should not mislead us: they may abandon them as if they were masks that can be cast off at will.

They may have good reason to cast them off, given the one-sidedness of these uncorrected moral visions and their consequent failure to accommodate the twin functional requirements of the advanced societies.

The Twin Functional Imperatives of the Advanced Societies

The idea of functional imperatives of the advanced societies. The ethics of self-fashioning and of connection would lack the force they possess if they did not have privileged ties to the twin functional requirements of the advanced societies: the enhancement of individual agency and the development of the higher forms of cooperation. If they were only philosophical doctrines, however deep and resonant, they would form part of the unsolicited advice about how to live that philosophers have offered to humanity.

Their historical association with certain national cultures—the subject matter of the previous section—would not be enough to rescue them from this condition. Far from cutting to the most significant message of these two ethics, that association covers them with the dust of history: it helps account for what in their conventional formulations is most ephemeral, circumstantial, and contestable. By contrast, their relation to these functional requirements bears directly on both doctrine and practice and on the link between their moral and their political implications.

By the functional requirements of the advanced societies I mean those most general conditions that determine whether and to what extent a form of social life can be a practical success by the worldly standards of power and prosperity as well as by the less tangible criterion of their ability to cohere without suppressing the vitality and imagination of their individual members. By naming them the twin functional requirements I emphasize their special status. They are not just useful circumstances. They can take, and have taken, inadequate and even perverse forms. But the form that they do take is fateful for both the development of our practices and the advance of the ideals proclaimed by the ethics of self-fashioning and of connection. Their importance is most clearly manifest today in the advanced societies: those in which the threefold estrangement of subjugation, disunion, and coldness has most fully run its course and in which, despite all, the transformability of social life and the transformative power of the imagination are most manifest.

The enhancement of agency. By the enhancement of agency I mean, in a first approximation, the remaking of the ordinary man or woman as an agent able to act beyond and against as well as within the framework of the established arrangements and assumptions in his society. The enhanced agent can move all the more effectively within the established context because he can see beyond it and conceive the possibility of revising it—through cooperative action—piece by piece and part by part. Because he can overstep its boundaries in thought and in deed, he can also act more effectively within those boundaries.

A simple analytic vocabulary helps express the major direction of the enhancement of agency. In any society or culture there are the ordinary moves that we make within a framework of arrangements and assumptions that we take for granted. Then there are the extraordinary moves by which from time to time we challenge or change pieces of this framework. Agency is enhanced to the extent that the distance between these two classes of moves narrows: the revision of the framework becomes part of the ordinary business of life.

In this vocabulary it becomes clear that the enhancement of agency is never just a matter of strengthening the capabilities of the individual. It involves a change in the arrangements and the assumptions that define a regime of social life. And although the enhancement of agency invoked in this conception must always find expression in the ability of an individual to turn the tables on the framework, it never involves just the power of classes and communities to act. It requires the empowerment of an individual agent. In the circumstances of contemporary society, he would be the agent both formed and presupposed by active and dialectical learning, by a practice of production (the knowledge or innovation economy) that demands initiative from every worker, and by a form of politics (high-energy democracy) that relies on the engaged citizen.

In the philosophical vocabulary of the ethic of self-construction, a crucial premise of the enhancement of agency is the transcendence of each individual, as well as of humanity as a whole, over the social and conceptual worlds that we build and inhabit. There is, according to this premise, more in us—in each of us and in the human race—than there is or even can be in them. The enhancement of agency gives operational meaning to this premise: there lies its deepest link to the ethic of self-fashioning.

The higher forms of cooperation. The higher forms of cooperation are those that support our ability to cooperate across the widest range of social and historical circumstances. This ability is a source—indeed the chief source—of worldly success. On it depends the development of our practical powers, the better to lift the burdens of poverty, infirmity, and drudgery weighing on human life.

One of the hallmarks of the higher forms of cooperation is to diminish the reliance of cooperation on sameness, allowing the different to cooperate. The less we need our partners in cooperation to resemble us in any measure—from social origin to temperament and world view—the stronger our ability to cooperate becomes.

Another mark of the higher forms of cooperation is to bring the division of labor in society closer to the imagination. The higher forms of cooperation strengthen our power to create the new because they execute by transforming. In so doing, they increase the part of our experience that is given over to the imaginative side of our mental experience by contrast to the side of the mind that is modular and formulaic.

Yet another characteristic of the higher forms of cooperation is that they attenuate the tension between the imperatives to innovate and to cooperate. All sustained practical action in the world requires us to cooperate and to innovate. Every innovation requires cooperation—for its development and implementation. But every innovation also threatens to disturb the established cooperative regime because it introduces uncertainty and arouses conflict. Who will gain and who loose from the innovation?—whether it be conceptual, technological, organizational, or institutional. The higher forms of cooperation are those that moderate the unavoidable tension between the calls to innovate and to cooperate. I later suggest what features of a cooperative regime shape its ability to achieve such moderation.

A premise of the higher forms of cooperation is what in my account of the ethic of connection I called joint intentionality or intersubjectivity: our ability to develop shared and actionable representations of the world in which we act. The higher forms of cooperation turn this premise into a task: they make it truer than it was before they set to work. In this movement lies the intimate link of the movement toward the higher forms of cooperation with the ethic of connection.

The relation of the twin functional requirements to the ethics of self-fashioning and of connection. What is the relation of the twin functional requirements of the advanced societies to the two secular moral visions discussed here? The uncorrected version of the ethic of self-fashioning seems to have a close and almost exclusive relation to the enhancement of agency, and the minimalist version of the ethic of connection to the advancement of cooperation. But this one-to-one relation between each of these ethics and one of the functional requirements is yet another sign of the inadequacy of both, when they are left in their unreconstructed form.

No approach to the conduct of life that does justice to only one of these twin imperatives can be realistic. The corrected ethic of self-fashioning and the maximalist ethic of connection each address both the twin functional requirements, although they do so from different starting points and in the light of different ideas. At the end of this section, I return to the bearing of those requirements on the contest of moral visions to which this and preceding chapter are devoted. To explain how they bear on it, I must explore how these twin functional imperatives relate to each other. And to explain that relation it helps to understand the roots of this discussion in the major tradition of modern sociology.

The relation between the enhancement of agency and the development of higher forms of cooperation was, under different labels, central to the transformation of social life that Durkheim and Tönnies took as a central theme of their social theories and of their account of the societies of their time—so close to ours. The passage from community to society (for Tönnies) and from mechanical to organic solidarity (for Durkheim) represented, for these two social theorists, both a change in the character of the division of labor, or of the social bond, and a shift in personal distinction, achieved through functional specialization. A world reliant on interdependence predicated on such difference provides individual autonomy with a basis in the actual organization of social life, not simply in professions of moral and political faith.

Both theorists recognized, however, that the refinement of cooperation and the development of autonomy were achieved at a price. The price consisted in the fundamental dangers and discontents that Hegel, in *The Phenomenology of Spirit*, had explored more comprehensively under the label "estrangement," understood as an event with objective as well as subjective expressions. This was the triple price that I earlier considered in my discussion of the ethic of connection and of its response to the flaws in the way things are.

Part of the price lay in the susceptibility of this new form of functionally differentiated social life to being overtaken by schemes of domination and dependence. Part—the part of most immediate interest to Durkheim and Tönnies—consisted in the difficulty of sustaining social union or cohesion in a society in which size, complexity, and freedom (however limited) had engendered an explosive growth of difference. And part had to do with the seeming impossibility of becoming free without becoming cold: the stripping away from social life of the emotional intensity that accompanied in an earlier form of social life—"community" or "mechanical solidarity"—the sentimentalization of unequal exchange, the overlay of exchange, power, and affect or allegiance in the same recurrent social relations.

Implicit in the evolutionary view of these two social theorists was an understanding of how the ideas of enhanced agency and of higher cooperation could be achieved and reconciled in what they took to be the advanced societies. The enormous advantages of the move from mechanical to organic solidarity or from community to society resulted in the threefold price of susceptibility to domination, disunion, and coldness. We can lower, they and their successors argued, the price to be paid through a series of ameliorative initiatives (such as the development of professional ethics, the participation of workers in the management of firms, or the cultivation of commitment to both the republic and the nation), but we cannot avoid paying the price.

This approach suffered from two major flaws from which I mean my argument here to be free. The first flaw was the implicit identification of what was in principle a world-historical shift (from community to society or from mechanical to organic solidarity), indispensable to the development of our powers and our freedom, with the arrangements and assumptions of European society and culture in the nineteenth and twentieth centuries. The second flaw was the message delivered by their social theory that any resistance to this shift (in its European form) would be, if not futile, then unacceptably regressive and costly.

The two flaws were connected: a premise of any effort to enhance agency and move toward higher forms of cooperation, without doing so at the expense of courting intensified domination, disunion, and coldness (Hegel's estrangement), must be that mankind is not condemned to repeat throughout the world the terms of the European shift and choose between the European *ancien régime* (in cultural as well as social life) and the estranged freedom of the "moderns." Denied in the way in which they approached these problems was the possibility that Tönnies's society or Durkheim's organic solidarity might take forms radically different from those that had evolved in Europe. Some of these alternative forms might address the problem of the triple estrangement more radically and successfully than anything that the North Atlantic countries had tried out or that Tönnies and Durkheim had proposed.

It is just such a possibility, excluded in their sociologies, that is crucial to this step in my argument. One key premise is the specificity and contingency of the direction taken by society and culture in this period in the North Atlantic world, and the refusal to mistake that direction for the universal path of mankind's ascent. A second such premise—to be tested in practice and explored in thought—is that we do not need to choose between the *ancien régime* and the modern estrangement, so long as we are open to the piecemeal imagination and development of alternatives. On the validity of these premises depends much in the way we approach the contest between the ethics of self-construction and of connection.

My next concern is to develop the content first of the idea of the enhancement of agency and then that of the higher forms of cooperation and, having done so, to show in what way these functional requirements of the advanced societies contradict or complement each other and what their contradiction and complementarity implies for ethics as well as for politics.

The enhancement of agency and its consequences. The enhancement of agency called for by the advanced societies demands that the agent be made secure and capable in a haven of safeguards against private and public oppression and of capability-assuring endowments. But it also requires that all around him the structure of society—its formative institutional arrangements and the ideological assumptions that make sense of them—be subject to criticism and revision. This perpetual storm of innovation and experiment is not the opposite of the haven but its complement in a comprehensive and realistic conception of the enhancement of agency.

A characteristic of much thinking about human rights and progressive political programs today is that they deal with the part about the haven but not with the part about the storm. One without the other, however, amounts to much less than half of what the enhancement of agency requires.

In a rigidified social space, the promise of the enhancement of agency cannot be fulfilled. If the structure of society and culture is shielded against attack (except by force of extreme crisis, such as war or economic collapse), the agent will not be, either in his individual capacity or as a member of groups, parties, and movements, the co-author of his own circumstance. The established social regime will serve him as a prison even if he mistakes it for the way things must be, given the implications of a higher order in the cosmos and the soul, or the inexorable consequences of a script that history has prescribed for the evolution of society. The practical and ideological immunization of the regime against challenge and change will in turn almost always be associated with the perpetuation of some entrenched plan of social division and hierarchy: the stability and legitimacy of every such plan will depend on its preservation against the corrosive effects of incessant agitation in thought as well as in politics and social life.

But if at the same time the agent has no secure place on which to stand, while everything around him becomes subject to criticism and revision, and if he is not equipped with rights and resources, both cognitive and practical, that protect him against private as well as public oppression and help make him capable of initiative, then he will live in perpetual fear. As a result, he will stand ready to give up his freedom at the first chance in return for security and protection. The content of this package of empowering guarantees must include the right kind of education—in youth and throughout life—as well as a social inheritance, a trust fund (of which the delegates of the state are trustees) on which each citizen and worker can draw at turning points in his life, for example when starting a family, buying a home, or launching or reorienting a career. The size of this fund must depend, of course, on the resources available to government and on the country's level of wealth. But the principle holds regardless of the level of wealth in society: giving everyone the means with which to stand up forms part of the effort to influence—and render more equal—the primary distribution of economic and educational advantage. And that effort is more consequential than any attempt to correct after the fact, through progressive taxation and redistributive social spending, the primary distribution of economic and educational advantage.

The tension between these two parts of the social condition for the enhancement of agency—the haven of fearlessness and capability and the plasticity of the surrounding social space—can never be wholly eradicated. And the withdrawal of the design of the haven from contention and danger is never more than relative and temporary. We can surround the rules and rights defining the haven with an aura of sanctity, albeit at the risk of hedging our admission of the contingency of all institutional and legal arrangements. We can entrench some of the elements of the haven in constitutions that can be amended only by super majorities. Nothing, however, can save the haven-defining rules from being subject to subversion and reconstruction.

Nevertheless, despite these qualifications, the two-part condition of enhanced agency rests on a deep criterion of difference among the institutional forms of social life that have emerged in history. At one pole of this spectrum stand societies—such as those with a scriptural caste system, rooting social hierarchy in a cosmic mandate—that associate the identity and thus the security and the self-worth of the individual with his fidelity to the roles and mores of his caste. Under such a regime, there can be no haven worth having without the rigidification of the surrounding social and cultural space. Any violation of the rules and demands of that order amounts to an assault on the identity and security of the individual.

Now imagine a society in which, to the greatest extent possible, the rights and resources giving the individual a safe place from which to act in the world and to his affirm his identity are disengaged from the rules and arrangements shaping economic, political, and social life. Such a disentanglement creates the basis for the two-part solution I have described: the relatively stable haven of capability-ensuring safeguards and capabilities as the counterpart to a greater plasticity and readiness for innovation in every other department of our experience.

Such a society does not yet exist. In the conditions of today, it would be the child of, among other changes, the deepening and dissemination of the knowledge economy, the creation of a high-energy democracy diminishing the dependence of change on crisis, and the generalization of an experimentalist impulse in every department of social life. The societies and cultures of today stand somewhere along this spectrum: they have disentangled only partly and half-heartedly the rights and endowments shaping the security of the individual from the arrangements defining economic and political institutions. They have, for example, developed social rights that, because they do not depend on having a job and an employer and are universally portable, help reconcile social security with economic flexibility.

But in these existing societies—with their weak, low-energy democracies and their market orders organized around the unified property right as the master device of economic decentralization, individual liberties remain identified with the preservation of political and economic institutions that limit both the empowerment of the individual and the plasticity of the social and economic order. It is not that we continue to believe—as nineteenth-century liberals did—that these institutions form part of the conception of freedom. It is rather that any attack on these institutions, or on the forms of life that they support, seem, in light of the calamities of twentieth-century history and of the failures of state socialism, to be subversive of freedom. Thus, the fate of enhanced agency becomes inseparable from the overthrow of the dictatorship of no alternatives that now holds sway in the world.

The higher forms of cooperation and their consequences. The practical success of societies depends on the strengthening of the ability to cooperate. The institutional innovations needed to address the problems of the advanced societies depend on the strengthening of the willingness and ability to cooperate.

The most advanced practices of production are the most mindful. They are also the practices that most directly and continuously associate our experiments in the transformation of nature with our experiments in the way we work together. The high-energy democracy that, without needing war and ruin as enabling circumstances, would be required to generate structural solutions to the structural problems of society, is itself an exercise in cooperation. It is cooperation concerning the future, shaped by alliances and antagonisms that do not simply mirror the preexisting social order. Otherwise, they could serve only as devices by which that order reproduces itself. The education needed to form the workers of such economies and the citizens of such democracies must exploit the affinity between imagination and cooperation as the two allied forces by which we conceive and create the new, in fact as well as in thought.

The conditions for the development of our disposition and ability to cooperate can be broadly divided into the negative and the positive.

The overriding negative condition is that the arrangements of society, of the economy, and of politics must not force upon the would-be cooperators a confining script about the terms on which they can cooperate. To the greatest extent possible, their hands must be untied. This negative condition may at first seem innocuous and self-evident. It has in fact radical implications: it is incompatible with much in the way in which contemporary societies—and indeed all societies up to now—have shaped the terms of cooperation. It is irreconcilable with a caste system that ostentatiously prescribes what the members of each caste can do and with whom they can do it. It is incompatible as well with the marriage of fixed systems of roles and class hierarchy that has characterized all historical societies to this day. It cannot be squared with the established form of the market economy that fastens the market order to a single dogmatic version of itself, organized around the unified property right of the nineteenth century, which drastically limits, in the interest of incumbent asset holders, decentralized access to what Marx called the means of production. And it cannot live easily together with the low-energy democracies of the past and present that tolerate the arousal of the people only in national emergencies, and that outside those emergencies subject the structure of society to only localized and episodic challenge. Thus, although the negative condition for the strengthening of the ability and disposition to cooperate lacks, by definition, any definite guidance about alternatives, it is far from being empty of content.

The positive condition consists in all the initiatives that anchor the strengthening of our cooperative activities in the daily routines of existence. To be realistic and effective, such initiatives must be designed to take advantage of the practical needs of these societies rather than to impose on them an inclination foreign to their experience and their problems.

What, given these ideas, is the road to the higher forms of cooperation?

First, no entrenched structure of social division and hierarchy must predetermine the ways in which we can work together. The institutional arrangements and ideological assumptions of society must incessantly undermine any such structure. The best way to undermine it is to subject it to permanent challenge. And the best way to subject it to permanent challenge is to organize a market order that allows the coexistence of alternative regimes for decentralized access to productive resources and opportunities: alternative regimes of contract, property, and enterprise. It is also to move toward a high-energy democracy that raises the temperature of politics, accelerates its pace, and combines strong central initiative with radical devolution. Such a democracy increases, even in the absence of military or economic emergency, the effective subjection of established structure to political contest.

Second, the cooperating agents should regard every exercise in cooperation as a bid to change, even if piecemeal and marginally, the established institutions. This pretense, far from being a megalomaniacal phantasy, has a basis in social reality. If the disposition and the ability to cooperate were simply a consequence of institutional facts, we could not understand why some societies have flourished under different institutional arrangements (for example, by discarding in war time, as the United States did during World War II, the way the society runs its economy in peace time) whereas other countries have failed under a wide range of different institutional models. A higher form of cooperation never takes the framework of arrangements and assumptions within which it operates entirely for granted. Its impulse is to narrow the distance between action within the framework and action upon it. The higher forms of cooperation seek arrangements that turn such a narrowing into a principle of institutional design.

Third, the individual must remain, and feel, secure in a haven of vital protected immunities and capability-ensuring economic and educational endowments. Everything in the surrounding social space should, however, be thrown open to contest and experiment. The way to throw everything open is to establish a market order that is not pinned to a single dogmatic version of itself and a democracy that does not let the people sleep.

Fourth, the economic arrangements of society must be designed to deepen and disseminate the most advanced practice of production, defined, from the perspective of the horizon of the accessible possible that we can envision today, as the practice that is closest to the imagination and to its ability to create the new, and that most closely associates our experiments in the mobilization of natural forces with our experiments in cooperation. Today that practice is the experimentalist knowledge economy, present in every part of the production system but only as a fringe, locking out most workers and firms. The knowledge economy can deepen and achieve its potential only as it spreads. But it cannot spread automatically, without the fulfillment of its cognitive-educational, social-moral, and legal-institutional requirements. The continued fulfillment of these requirements in turn depends on the radicalization of an experimentalist impulse in culture and on the development of a high-energy democracy in politics.

Fifth, no one must be condemned to do the work that can be done by a machine. Machines should do the repeatable (including inference, without rules, from large amounts of data) so that the human agents, using machines along the way, can do what no one has yet learned how to repeat. Collaboration among people, including people using machines, should not resemble the combined operations of a set of machines. It should display a feature that such a combination cannot possess: to discover or to make what our settled methods and presuppositions will not countenance, and to develop after the fact the presuppositions that make sense of its discovery and the methods that can develop it.

Sixth, cooperation should be predicated on free labor. Economically coerced wage work is not fully free. It should be replaced over time by the higher forms of free labor—self-employment (not as disguised employment) and partnership—especially when these higher forms are combined. Such a replacement is not feasible until we have the legal as well as the technical means to reconcile a radical decentralization of economic initiative with the aggregation of resources at scale. And such a reconciliation requires that the market economy not remain in the grip of any single regime of decentralized access to the productive resources and opportunities, in other words, of any one version of property and contract.

Seventh, the higher forms of cooperation connect the different as well as the similar and aim to produce the new. However, they then subject their creations to the test of radical economic or political competition. In the economy, a proliferation of incitements to creative entrepreneurial activity must be followed at every moment by the subjection of the results of this constructive fervor to relentless competitive selection.

The economic value of the division of the world into sovereign states is to create more difference. It undermines this value to turn convergence on the same set of economic institutions, practices, and rules into the basis for greater freedom in the movements of goods, services, capital, and people across national frontiers. A world economy that becomes progressively more open should instead be based on a legal and institutional minimalism: the least restraint on the power of the sovereign states to experiment in the creation of economic difference, including difference in the institutions that define the market order.

In politics, the power to take decisive initiative in the pursuit of a national direction must be met at every turn either by an opportunity to challenge that initiative at the same level of government or by an opportunity to demonstrate an alternative to it at a different level of government (for example, within a federal system). The challenge at the same level must be resolved quickly (for example, by an early election). The challenge at a different level creates an opportunity to engage the country in a contest over the national direction that is informed by tangible example and experience. Strong initiative, proliferation of alternatives, accelerated resolution of the competition among the alternative proposals and experiments, a high level of organized popular engagement in political life—this is what the combination of creative fervor with competitive selection of the products of this fervor should mean. A high-energy, experimentalist democracy is the political expression of the higher forms of cooperation.

୭

The contradictory relation between the twin functional imperatives.
The enhancement of agency and the development of the higher forms
of cooperation both conflict with and complement each other. Their
complementarity is more fundamental and consequential than their
conflict. We can best understand the general character of the tension
between them by returning to the problem of the relation between
cooperation and innovation. Innovation in which an individual plays
a distinct part is the most direct expression of the enhancement of
agency, especially if the object of the innovation is the institutional
and ideological order of social life. Even if the content of the innovation is technological or organizational rather than institutional and
conceptual, it is likely to disturb the peace of the established forms
of cooperation.

The claims that different groups—segments of the labor force or
classes—make on one another are embedded in these cooperative
regimes. The effects of the innovation may seem uncertain or especially threatening to some people and beneficial to other people. What
will be the effect of the innovation on this delicate texture of reciprocal
claims? Who will gain and who lose?

This subversive potential of any innovation is embodied not only
in the activity of disruption but in the person of the disruptor, the
troublemaker—or a whole category of troublemakers—who make
trouble for the established ways of cooperating, as the enemies of the
teamwork that is practiced at the time of the disruption. To contain
trouble and the troublemakers has been up till now the chief concern
of the guardians of the established cooperative practices and of the
institutions and ideas on which they rely.

But that is only the beginning of what leads to tension between the
imperatives to innovate and to cooperate. Every innovation requires
cooperation—in order to happen in the first place and then to be
implemented. Despite the uncertainties and conflicts that accompany
innovation, a cooperative regime hostile to innovation is doomed
to fail.

Cooperative regimes are more or less promising according to
whether they attenuate or aggravate the tension between cooperation
and innovation. And the most basic way in which they can moderate

it is by combining two principles. The first principle is to make the individuals and groups in contention secure in a set of safeguards and endowments that enable them to witness and withstand innovation without fear. The second principle is to free the potential of our cooperative practices. We free it by moving toward what I earlier listed as attributes of the higher forms of cooperation. The discussion of the fate of our cooperative practices and regimes brings us back to the essential conditions for the enhancement of agency.

As the quest for the higher forms of cooperation is embedded in the effort to enhance agency, so is the enhancement of agency internally related, by virtue of the practical conditions for its achievement, to the higher forms of cooperation. We can understand these higher cooperative arrangements as an answer to the contradictions of selfhood. How can we connect with others without losing our freedom? How can we engage in a particular social world without surrendering to it? And under what conditions do we have the best chance to avoid dying beforehand within the carapace of the rigidified self and of the social situation to which it is resigned?

Thus, despite the tension between them, the twin functional requirements of the advanced societies are linked at the top in their central conceptions and presuppositions. They are even more tellingly linked at the bottom, in their practical realization. Each feature of the higher forms of cooperation—beginning with their ability to unshackle us from any unique and exclusive institutional understanding of what cooperation among free and equal agents entails in the economy and in politics—represents a blow in favor of the enhancement of agency.

On the other hand, each way of arranging the innovation and experimentalism on which the enhancement of agency depends requires an advance in our ability to cooperate. In the economies of today, such a cooperative experimentalism requires the economy-wide diffusion of a knowledge economy thriving on a fluid mixture of cooperation and competition within, among, and outside firms. In the polities of today, it demands a higher level of organized popular engagement in political life and the combination of strong central initiative with devolution for the sake of experimentation and discovery.

In education, it favors cooperation—among students, among teachers, and among schools—in the service of active and dialectical learning.

What is the significance of this tense but intimate and reciprocal relation between the twin functional requirements of the advanced societies for the ethics of self-fashioning and of connection?

The uncorrected version of the ethic of self-fashioning has a direct relation to the enhancement of agency. But it is largely silent about the development of the higher forms of cooperation. The minimalist ethic of connection values above all our cooperative practices and relates them to what it regards as the highest source of value: the moral logic of the interpersonal. But its discourse about the self—manifest in the teaching of Confucius about the stages by which the superior person ascends in the course of his life—is only an extension of its conception of the interpersonal. The superior person ascends and comes into the possession of himself—the state in which he spontaneously desires the right and overcomes all heteronomy—by attending to other people.

The privileged and all but exclusive relation of each of these two ethics, in their uncorrected forms, to one of the two functional requirements of the advanced societies reveals their inadequacy. This inadequacy begins in a failure of moral realism: they fail to take adequate account of what human beings are really like under the wide variations of historical experience. The unreconstructed ethic of self-construction fails, especially, to recognize the vital role that our engagements and attachments play in developing our powers of agency and in giving content to an ideal of autonomy: solidarity is internal to self-construction. The minimalist ethic of connection fails, in the first instance, to do justice to the complications of selfhood: the contradictory character of the relation of the self to other people, to the social world in which it moves, and to itself—no valuable and durable forms of solidarity can be built on the denial or suppression of these complications.

If the enhancement of agency and the development of higher forms of cooperation are internally related—if they are linked, as I have argued, both at the top in their core conceptions and at the bottom in their practical implications for the organization of society—then we should expect any moral vision that can speak to us today to be responsive to both of them. The revised ethic of self-fashioning and the maximalist ethic of connection are. Each of them begins in a different place: the ethic of self-fashioning in the struggle of the individual with the world, and the ethic of connection in the priority of the interpersonal and of joint intentionality. But from that place, each of them moves in the direction of the other side: the reconstructed ethic of self-fashioning by exploring the social construction of autonomy, and the maximalist ethic of connection by confronting the contradictions of agency and selfhood.

The twinness of the functional imperatives of advanced societies may inspire the hope that we can overcome the contest of these moral visions and reconcile them in a synthesis. We may be encouraged in this hope by registering that the corrected versions of these two ethics are in many ways closer to each other than the uncorrected ones and that they can both inform and support, from their distinct standpoints, the agenda of institutional reconstruction, the program of deep freedom, presented in Chapter 8 of this book. Their final convergence would then, so it might appear, be only a matter of pushing a few steps further the narrowing of the distance between these two moral conceptions—a narrowing that the correction of their canonical versions has already begun. Such a reconciliation might seem to be justified and predicted by the reciprocal and internal relation between the enhancement of agency and the development of higher forms of cooperation.

It is easy enough to produce any number of verbal formulas that promise to dissolve the conflict between the ethics of self-fashioning and of connection and to announce that a synthesis is on the way. Such a synthesis would be in the spirit of William James's remark: "The community stagnates without the impulse of the individual. The impulse dies away without the sympathy of the community."

This conclusion, however, would be premature and misguided. The two ethical visions point in broadly similar directions. They, together, can help inform and inspire, from their contrasting perspectives, the public culture of a democracy that is committed to both the enhancement of agency and the development of our cooperative practices.

They converge broadly in their implications for the reconstruction of society, expressed in the program of deep freedom.

But it does not follow from this overlap in their consequences for society and for its public discourse that they converge in their message for the conduct of life, the subject matter of ethics. As their correction draws them, in many ways, closer together, and as they shed the shallow and questionable characteristics they have acquired by virtue of their favored association with certain societies and cultures—the United States and China—their deepest differences, in the assumptions they make and the guidance they provide, shine through even more clearly. No rhetorical formula can overcome these differences; they express a deep and lasting duality in our moral experience. I now turn to the development of this thesis.

The Impossible Synthesis between the Two Ethics

The search for synthesis: a misguided understanding of ethics. There can be no real synthesis of the ethics of self-fashioning and of connection for reasons that I discuss in the remaining pages of this chapter. What may happen is that in the future our experience and our ideas will change to such an extent that the problems of existence appear to us under an aspect to which these conceptions are no longer pertinent.

The revised versions of each of these approaches to the conduct of life are indeed closer to each other than their uncorrected versions in many ways. In other ways, however, and especially in the ways that should count most, the unbridgeable difference between them is all the more clearly manifest. Consider the reasons for which we should reject the attempt to reconcile them in ascending order of significance: the nature of moral argument; the differences between the points of departure of these two orientations to existence (differences not overcome by the corrections of each of them that I have explored); and, most importantly, their central message to us about how to live.

The impulse to find such a synthesis results, first, from an understanding and practice of moral philosophy that we have reason to reject. One view of ethics, the most influential in the history of philosophy, sees it as the provision of self-help against the irreparable flaws in the human condition on the basis of a philosophical super-science. The philosopher claims to discern the ground of being, or the framework of existence, and to infer from it a way of coping with the tribulations of a human life. He offers his prescriptions about how to live in the context of such a view of our place in the world.

If we look closely at what results, we find a feature of this operation that should arouse our suspicion. If we compare the philosophers who have written in this tradition, over the last 2,500 years in the West, we find that their top lines tend to differ from one another much more than their bottom lines. The top line is the foundational account of ultimate reality from which they claim to derive their ethical prescriptions. The bottom line is instruction in the conduct of life.

The top lines differ drastically, though each is characteristically asserted by the philosopher with great confidence. The bottom lines usually cluster around variations on the themes of altruism and benevolence. It is not the relatively arbitrary top lines that explain the convergent bottom lines. What explains them better has been the attempt by the philosophers to offer a secular counterpart to the moral teachings of Christianity, Buddhism, and other world religions.

The philosophers have characteristically interpreted those teachings in a way that expunges from them what is deepest and most distinctive about them, such as the preeminence of love over altruism in Christianity. The relation between top line and bottom line is so loose, and the attraction of the secular doctrine of benevolence and altruism so great, that on opening the moral works of the philosophers we can expect to find an unsurprising conclusion dressed up in the vocabulary of an implausible metaphysics. In this context, the idea of a synthesis comes naturally: after all, synthesis is what ethics has been providing for a long time.

It is telling that it is precisely the anti-philosophers (in Alain Badiou's phrase)—those who in the West have dispensed with the top line provided by philosophical super-science—such as Pascal, Rousseau, Kierkegaard, and (with some wavering) Nietzsche—whose bottom lines are most distinctive. The anti-philosophers have achieved this distinction even when they have been in intimate dialogue with

Christianity. Similarly, Confucius taught by dialogue, narrative, and example, free from the metaphysical pretensions dear to the neo-Confucianism of the Sung dynasty.

In turning to the school philosophy of today, we find ethics lost in another kind of misdirection that helps account for the appeal of synthesis. There the problem is not the combination of philosophical super-science with edifying self-help. It is the clothing of legalistic moral universalism, influenced by a particular strand of Christianity (the Protestantism of the eighteenth and nineteenth centuries) and expressed in the words of philosophers—Bentham, Kant, and Rousseau—who do not deserve to be blamed for the pharisaical teaching of the school philosophy.

The consequentialist, deontological, and social-contract positions have been shown to converge. But their convergence, rather than being a sign of the truth of the convergent message, is an expression of the narrowness of the legalistic moralism that they embrace, pre-occupied with the definition—by a higher-order method, which it is their chief concern to specify—of our obligations to one another. This legalistic moralism has—or had—a basis in a the political, economic, legal, and religious history of early modern Europe, a form of life that has ceased to exist. But this basis is not revealed, justified, or explained in the ideas that the school philosophers present as universally applicable.

The translation of the vocabulary of one of the schools of the school philosophy into the vocabularies of the other two schools is relatively straightforward. The shared perspective and the common foundation in a particular form of life help make it possible. And so does its legalistic character: any lawyer knows how to argue about contracts and obligations in different but equivalent ways. The bottom lines converge either because the difference in the top lines was illusory or because the relation of the line to the bottom line was accidental.

All these ways of promoting synthesis in ethics—whether in the tradition of philosophical super-science or in the practice of the school philosophy—share a defect. They treat the arguments of moral philosophy as a matter of words, detached from experience, practices, and institutions. A rhetorician can make the different look similar or the similar look different. If we adopt these methods, we can easily find formulations that appear to reconcile the ethics of self-fashioning and of connection.

What can save ethics from being the object of easy rhetorical manipulation, fertile in false syntheses and in fictitious oppositions, is engagement with historical experience—institutional alternatives in the organization of society and alternative practices in the conduct of life. The inclusion of the sociology of morals into ethics takes us out of the realm of facile rhetorical accommodation and brings us into the domain of fateful historical choices. By appreciating the political horizon as well as the moral consequences of the ethics of self-fashioning and of connection, and by recognizing their troubling association with real powers such as the United States and China, we guard against the rhetorical accommodations and make the fateful choices harder to evade.

Irreconcilable points of departure. A second reason to reject the attempt to reconcile the ethics of self-fashioning and of connection is that they have different points of departure, a difference that persists, pregnant with implication, in their reconstructed versions. The corrected version of the ethics of self-fashioning and the maximalist version of the ethic of connection make these approaches to the conduct of life stronger by ridding them of weaknesses that even their adherents would have reason to acknowledge. The association of each of these moral visions with the national cultures of the societies in which they have enjoyed the greatest authority aggravates these dispensable defects and makes them easier to identify.

But to strike down the differences that result from their points of departure would weaken them because it would undermine what makes them distinctive. It is thanks to these differences, and to the assumptions and attitudes from which they result, that each of these secular ethics exercises in the world today an influence comparable, among secular moral visions, only to the influence of its rival.

I have already described these contrasting points of departure in my account of self-fashioning and of its correction. I have now only to recall them briefly.

The first contrast in the starting points of these two ethics has to do with their premise about the ultimate protagonist and carrier of value. For the ethic of self-construction, it is the individual, incarnate in a body, formed in a social and historical setting, but separated by the abyss of consciousness and by his individual fate from everything and everyone else, and on his way to death. For the ethic of connection, it is the interpersonal: you and me, extending outward in concentric circles to include ever wider parts of social life.

The second contrast relates to the conception of the self. For the ethic of self-fashioning, we are, each of us, the infinite, by contrast to all the finite things and circumstances that surround us. If there is room in the ethic of connection for what the vocabulary of the ethic of self-fashioning calls transcendence, it is not the transcendence of the individual self, or of the state, the nation, or the culture. It is the transcendence of the moral logic of the interpersonal over all the actual ways of shaping people's relations to one another that have existed—all of them flawed by failing to avoid or to correct the perversions of reciprocity.

A third contrast in points of departure regards the relation of each of these two ethics to the revolution that has set the world on fire over the last three centuries and that has now lost its way; its defenders no longer know what its next steps should be on either its political or its personalist side. The history of the ethic of self-fashioning forms part of the history of that revolution and will share its fate. The ethic of connection looks at the revolution from the outside, free to judge it from a distance and to select what it supports or opposes.

A fourth contrast between these moral visions that survives their correction goes to their attitudes to disruptions and to disruptors and more generally to conflict, contradiction, and complication. For the ethic of self-fashioning, the disruptors are the spiritual aristocracy of the human race. The message is: look for trouble and put vulnerability in the place of serenity. In this glorification of trouble and troublemakers, the defenders of the ethic of connection see the evil of vanity and self-aggrandizement, which does not cease to be poisonous when it is democratized.

A Duality in Our Moral Consciousness

The two moral visions differ most significantly in their core messages. The difference is more patent, rather than diminished, once each of them has been revised in the manner that I proposed.

We find ourselves, the ethic of self-fashioning teaches us, embodied in an organism with a limited life span and, if it survives long enough, fated to decline into weakness and ill-health, before unavoidable death. We are placed in a historical and social circumstance that we did not choose and that the most ambitious among us spend their lives trying to overcome or transform.

If we consider ourselves from an external point of view, uninstructed by the claims of some of the revealed religions, we are dying animals, who share the fate of other animals—except that we are conscious of our mortality and of time. We are also aware, if we have a philosophical disposition, of our inability to understand the ground of being and of existence, and struck, if we are not wholly crushed by the oppression of society, by more longing than we can satisfy or explain.

From this external point of view, we are simply one more animal species among others, temporarily successful, and confined to a minute corner of the universe. The rule of animal evolution is that the individual must die for the species to live. Our species itself, like all species, seems likely to be ephemeral, at least unless we are able to escape our place in the solar system before our planet becomes uninhabitable and our star explodes.

If there is no one here but us, our disappearance is unlikely to make any impression (who else would there be to impress?), and all trace of our having ever existed may eventually vanish. If, as we now know, nature has a history, the present universe may eventually come to an end, probably to be succeeded by another. In the incalculably cold or fiery transition from one universe to another, whatever traces of our past existence may have survived the extinction of humanity will also be extinguished.

So long as we survive collectively, we observe that our societies and cultures, although having features that we do not see in other cooperative animal species, are also not entirely lacking in equivalents to them. Our civilizations are shaped by the need to contend with both nature and with one another, to organize ourselves, and to compete peacefully or struggle violently with other societies and cultures, organized at this moment in human history under the protection of armed states. The organization of these collectivities suffers the influence of our beliefs about what is desirable and possible. These beliefs are shaped by our attempts to make sense of our experience and of our powers in the context of endless struggle among the collective units into which humanity is divided.

The external point of view is not the only one available to us. It coexists with another way of thinking about ourselves, from within our experience of consciousness. From this internal viewpoint, we are not only what, according to the external view, we seem to be, even if this internal view dispenses with the supernatural light of religious revelation. Consciousness begins in the awareness of life and in the discovery of its characteristic traits of fecundity, spontaneity, and surprise. But it soon moves toward affirming that everything in our existence points beyond itself. Each of us is, to use one of the many contentious vocabularies in which the ethic of self-fashioning has been expressed, embodied spirit. Spirit is not an immaterial substance; the allusion to it implies no dualism of the physical and the mental. It is a power: the power to be unaccommodated and to reach beyond the context. This power we also call transcendence. There is always in us a residue of capability to experience, discover, invent, and connect with others. Rather than being a distinct faculty, this power is an accentuation of life and of its attributes, the awareness of which is consciousness.

Our finitude is the condition of our transcendence rather than its opposite. The enemy of transcendence is the script handed to us by society and culture, by dogma, and by conventional morality. Conformity to this script diminishes the potential of society as well as that of the individual. It is not the sacrifice of the individual to society that we have reason to fear so much as the sacrifice of the possible—of the possible forms of the enhancement of life—to the actual, to the frozen order in society, in thought, and in the rigidified form of the self. The frozen order robs us of life and transcendence and squanders our chance of making our finitude the basis for their enhancement.

Our most important resource in resisting the script that deprives us of life is confrontation with the irreparable flaws in the human condition: our groundlessness, mortality, and insatiability. In God's absence and silence, the circumstance of groundlessness, we find our lives surrounded on every side by mystery and are unable to infer a direction in life from an understanding of the ultimate framework of existence. Direction must come, if it can come, from our individual and collective self-understanding and self-invention.

Our mortality gives dramatic concentration to our lives. It awakens us to the reality of time as the medium of existence. Our insatiability enacts the drama of our search for the unconditional, the absolute, and the infinite in a world that offers only the conditional, the relative, and the finite.

As a result, we risk spending our lives in a series of acts of false transcendence, which we also call idolatry, mistaking the conditional for the unconditional, the relative for the absolute, and the finite for the infinite. Confrontation with these unsurmountable defects in the human condition does more than show us the truth of our circumstance and liberate us from wishful thinking. It arouses us from the somnambulant routines of conformity in which, half-dead, we risk dying by installments before we die for good. Our aim should be to die only once.

Our awakening through confrontation with groundlessness, mortality, and insatiability may be a necessary condition for coming into the fuller possession of life, but it is far from being a sufficient one. To make of finitude the basis of transcendence, becoming more human by becoming more godlike, the person must reckon with the contradictory conditions of self-assertion. He must find a way to connect with others without being subjugated to them, to engage in a social world without surrendering to it, and to form a way of being without allowing the rigidified character to usurp the place of the surprising self.

This freedom will come to nothing, and the promise of autonomy will prove empty, if we fail to give it content through our attachments and engagements. The attempt to increase our share in the power of transcendence will pervert us instead of empowering us if we never develop a way to become bigger together. Thus, ethics passes into politics. What politics fails to accomplish in historical time, the individual agent must foreshadow, within the sphere in which he lives and acts, in biographical time.

Remember now the central message of the ethic of connection, developed in its maximalist form. In a meaningless world, we create meaning: we develop a form of life that bears the imprint of our concerns. We do so not alone, as individuals, but together, through our cooperative activities.

We open this human clearing in a universe indifferent to our concerns as the natural beings that we are, without the help of any higher light coming to us from outside our species, our societies, and cultures. Nevertheless, this construction of the human space does not come easily. We are born as distinct organisms, not spontaneously fit for society. For the attempt to open the human space in a universe indifferent to our concerns to succeed, we must be made into social beings, able and equipped to live and work together.

We are prepared for living together by the combination of two great forces. One force consists in social rituals and conventions, associated with the roles that we perform vis-à-vis one another. The other force is the development of imaginative insight into the experience of other people. The combined effect of these two forces is to give us a second nature, suited to society.

Although the development of our second nature does not happen spontaneously, it has a basis in our first, relatively unprogrammed constitution. Our mental experience and our cooperative practices are inseparable. The ideas, the words, the language by which we understand ourselves are all social. And our tangible and intangible needs for one another are unlimited.

In our lives the interpersonal is the supreme source of value and authority. It radiates a power that no other part of our experience possesses. To remain a source of value and authority, it must not degenerate into exploitative manipulation. It must embody a norm of reciprocity.

A rule of reciprocity, however, is too incomplete and indeterminate to serve as basis for the organization of social relations in any society that has advanced beyond the most primitive conditions. For the moral logic of the interpersonal, marked by the commitment to reciprocity, to set its stamp on the way things are in civilization, it must overcome the perversions to which social life is subject in complex societies: subjugation, disunion, and coldness.

To overcome these perversions, the ethic of connection must do more than humanize or spiritualize the established order, seeking to tame our self-regard, to make us more useful to one another in the performance of our roles, and to develop our imaginative empathy. It must reinvent the norm of reciprocity and reshape its understanding of the moral logic of the interpersonal. And it must seek a series of cumulative changes in how we live and organize our societies.

The hallmark of these changes in our experience of selfhood and connection is the admission of conflict, contradiction, and confusion within the self as well as in our relations to others. It is also the intention to dispute the potential of the established social order to serve as the setting for the change in the character of social life that we should seek. Institutes and arrangements must democratize the forms of access to the resources of economic capital, political power, and cultural authority by which we together make the future within the present. And our way of living must foreshadow, in the circle of each person's actions and attachments, what politics has not yet accomplished.

We should neither deny the irreparable flaws in the human condition nor dwell on them. They represent the forward edge of a cosmos indifferent to our concerns bearing down us until it crushes us. We respond to its threat of annihilation by creating a space in which we can become ourselves. To dwell on the irreparable flaws in the human condition is a moral luxury taking us away from one another. One another is all that we ultimately have.

Must we choose between these two visions—the corrected version of the ethics of self-fashioning and the maximalist version of ethic of connection? And, if so, on what basis? We have reason to reject the unrevised versions of each—all the reasons explored in my criticism of them. But with respect to the revised versions, the problem is reversed: the arguments for both are persuasive. But they are also, as all arguments in favor of an approach to the conduct of life are, inconclusive.

Here, at the end of this discussion of ethics, we come back to the problem that we faced at the beginning: the cognitive gap in our thinking about the conduct of life. In answering the only question that no one can escape—how to live—we have reasons for preferring one answer to another. The force of the answer, however, always falls short of the weight of the question.

Recall the general grounds for preferring or rejecting an orientation to existence. It must resonate with our deepest and most persistent longings and, through them, with the widest range of our strongest desires, needs, and hopes. Both these moral visions do—from different angles, with different emphases, and with different moral and political consequences.

It must be compatible with what we independently know to be true about ourselves and our place in nature. Both these approaches to the conduct of life are compatible, provided that we correct them along lines such as those that I have described.

It must not be self-subverting when we act on it. On the contrary, it must operate as a self-fulfilling prophecy that brings our experience into closer accord with its assumptions and prescriptions. We cannot know how either of these orientations to existence would meet that test because both of them go beyond our present arrangements and practices and even beyond our widespread beliefs.

Yet both are related to powerful tendencies that have long been at work in society and culture: the tendencies discussed earlier under the headings of the enhancement of agency and the development of the higher forms of cooperation. The ethic of self-fashioning begins from the enhancement of agency and moves toward the development of the higher forms of cooperation. The ethic of connection does the reverse.

In their political implications these two approaches to the conduct of life overlap enough to coexist and challenge each other in the public culture of a democratic society. But to say that they could also coexist in the consciousness and life of a single individual would be either to imply that they can reconciled or to say that we can live—and think—in a space defined by the contradiction between them. We cannot bring them together in a coherent synthesis.

Embracing both these moral visions, while leaving each in unresolved contest with the other, amounts to a deepening of the cognitive gap. It is an admission of the limits of reasoning in the choice of a direction in the conduct of life. Such an admission may be offensive to philosophy, even to a philosophy that has renounced philosophical super-science. However, it should neither offend nor surprise the awkward moral agent, struggling to find his way without laying claim to having found it by a light that evidently fails to shine on his contemporaries. He may even admit that one of these approaches is more congenial to his temperament and to the beliefs in which he has formed his mind without pretending that the contrasting approach has anything less to be said in its favor.

Underlying the contrast between these two orientations to existence is a deep and enduring opposition in our moral experience. It is not a contrast between the external point of view, in which we look at ourselves from the outside as animals trapped in a tiny portion of universe, and the internal point of view in which we assume the position of consciousness and moral agency from within our lives and situations. It is a contrast between two ways of understanding and developing the internal point of view.

Henri Bergson distinguished a morality of aspiration from a morality of duty. If it is to be more than an attempt to read us our obligations out of a book in which the conclusions are inferred from non-human (and therefore fantastical) authority, or from arbitrary premises that already contain these conclusions under disguise (as we see in the school philosophy), the morality of duty must be accessory to the morality of aspiration. Such a morality of aspiration expresses a view of the most promising road of our ascent to a higher form of life.

The ethics of self-fashioning and of connection are two instances of a morality of aspiration. They are two prophecies and two statements of hope, informed by two different ways of understanding who we ultimately are and can hope to become.

The irreconcilability of these two moral visions is rooted in the contradictions of our nature. But precisely because the roots of this recalcitrance to synthesis run deep, there is no account of its basis that is neutral between the two visions. As there are two irreconcilable ethics, there are two irreconcilable accounts of this irreconcilability: one from the standpoint of the ethic of self-fashioning, the other from the perspective of the ethic of connection. Each of these accounts implies a distinct view of the relation between our finitude and transcendence.

Consider the reasons for the impossibility of synthesis first from the perspective of the ideas about us and our situation in the world that inform the corrected ethic of self-fashioning. All our moral endeavors are threatened and undermined from below—from our nature as dying animals—and from above—from our godlike impulse to transcend. These two threats jeopardize any way we have of coming to terms with one another. It is a gross misrepresentation of the ethic of self-fashioning, as it would misrepresent any moral program with the power to attract and to guide us, to interpret it as a radical individualism. It was never just about the isolated individual and his fate. It was always, even in its unreconstructed form, about our relations to one another and about the contradictory requirements of selfhood in a life among other people.

Each of us finds himself subject to the vicissitudes of the body and the relentless ruin of time. Each of us is on the way to death and will have to face it, in the end, alone. All our social and spiritual endeavors are hostage to the body and to its corruption. Our embodiment in a perishing organism, with highly restricted powers to receive the impressions of the world, establishes an absolute limit on our ability to relate to one another, to a particular social and cultural world, and even to ourselves. Every way of relating to ourselves presupposes a view of our relations to other people and to society.

But the body and its fate are beyond all such connection and communication even when we use it in sexual activity and erotic love, converting the instrument for reproduction of the species into a means to express our most passionate attachments. The narrator in Proust's novel lifts the veil and reveals the truth about our dealings with this strange presence. "It is in moments of illness that we are compelled to recognize that we live not alone but chained to a creature of a different kingdom, whole worlds apart, who has no knowledge of us and by whom it is impossible to make ourselves understood: our body. Say that we met a brigand by the way; we might yet convince him by an appeal to his personal interest, if not to our own plight. But to ask pity of our body is like discoursing before an octopus, for which our words can have no more meaning than the sound of the tides, and with which we should be appalled to find ourselves condemned to live."[1]

The problem is not our mortality—the corollary of our embodiment; it is the consequence of our embodiment for what must matter to any moral vision and is certainly central to the ethic of connection: our ability to affirm, in our moral experience, the primacy of the ties that bind us to others and, through them, to society and to ourselves. Imprisoned in our bodies, or conscious only so far as we are bodies, we must accept a form of isolation from which there is no escape.

The human connection is threatened from above, by our impulse to transcend, as well as from below by our embodiment—the most tangible manifestation of our finitude. We are like the God of the believers in his transcendence but not in his omnipotence or omniscience. We should seek to increase our share in that attribute by coming into the fuller possession of life and living in such a way that we can die only once.

As the idea of transcendence is borrowed from the history of religion, it may help to begin by considering the relation between its theological expression and our prospects for reckoning with one another. If there is only one creative and transcendent God, as the faith of all three Semitic monotheisms (Judaism, Christianity, and Islam) holds, and if the nature of God is love, as Christianity (according to its predominant interpretations) proclaims, then the connection among us must require us to share in the inner life of this loving God. And

---

1. In the translation by C. K. Scott Moncrieff, from *The Guermantes Way* in *Remembrance of Things Past*.

our religious imagination will begin to move in the direction if not of pantheism (we and all of nature are one in God), then of panentheism (God is a horizon of unrealized possibility beyond the manifest world). But if each human being is a God, destined to eternal life without losing the substance of individual existence (as some Christian heresies, such as the religion of the Latter-day Saints, suppose and as many earlier versions of polytheism affirmed), it is unclear how these godlike beings could ever communicate and connect. What would one God say to another? Transcendence must either suffuse or isolate. Either way it places human connection in jeopardy. It does so in one way by contradicting independent selfhood and in another way by making the bonds among independent selves unimaginable.

Threatened from below by our embodiment and from above by our transcendence, our life among other people is shadowed by an ineradicable ambivalence toward them and by the contradictions that attend our relations to others, to society, and to ourselves. The idea of a reconciliation between the ethics of self-fashioning and of connection assumes that we can place our experience of selfhood and society under the light of an inclusive harmony: a resolution of those contradictions. But we cannot.

Now consider the irreconcilability of the two contemporary moral visions I have discussed from the vantage point of the ideas about humanity and its situation informing the maximalist ethic of connection. According to all versions of this ethic, both minimalist and maximalist, our transformation into moral agents, with the practices and expectations that make us human, requires the substitution of our first nature by our second nature. This substitution takes place both in the evolutionary and historical time of mankind and in the biographical time of each individual human life.

Our first nature would be the one we would have had as the pre-social animals we never were (according to what the students of human evolution teach us). From the outset, before the development of the higher cultures and religions and maybe even before the full development of language, we were social beings. Our social practices and later our civilizations were formed in the mold of our immemorial mimetic tendencies: our second nature may, in this sense, be coeval with our first one and would not exercise its power if it did not have a basis in our natural constitution. Our desires themselves, unlike the animal tropisms that we used to call instincts, are indeterminate, roving, and subject to the same imitative influences that shape every part of our experience.

Nonetheless, the overlay of our second nature on our first is never complete. Our bodily needs, our cravings, our characteristic confusion of the physical and the social, and our slide toward death establish a recalcitrant limit to our transformation into moral agents, with our claims on one another enacted in our practices. The animal may always have been social, but the absorption of the animal into the social is always unfinished. Were the absorption of the animal into the social not always unfinished, death would lose its terrors. Despite the lullabies of religion and philosophy, it never does.

The whole aim of this replacement of our first nature by our second is to make of life in society a moral order, in which our interdependence, founded on reciprocity and manifest in cooperation, is the fundamental reality and the source of moral authority. We never fully achieve this aim. In the history of civilization, the way things are—the established social regime—is beset by the problems that I have described as subjugation, disunion, and coldness. The antidotes to these problems that minimize conflict and disruption—the characteristic tenets of the minimalist ethics of connection—are unsatisfactory. The more ambitious and transformative responses to those problems—which define the maximalist version of this ethic—require both disruption and conflict and put the fragile texture of our reciprocal commitments to one another under stress.

But that is not the end of the problems that the attempt to complete the replacement of our first nature by our second confronts. There is no natural or definitive form of social life. Every way of organizing ourselves in society, and therefore every way of dealing with subjugation, disunion, and coldness, remains contestable and contested. And the order we create is enacted in the arrangements of a particular society, under the aegis of a particular state. The irreducible and indispensable plurality of these ways of being human sets the stage for perpetual struggle. The conflict may result in a fight to the death because the sovereign states under which we develop these distinct forms of life are armed and fearful of one another.

The imperative of conflict and disruption is rooted in the defects of the way things are, in the inadequacy of the harmony-preserving ways of dealing with them, and in the indispensable plurality of societies, cultures, and states. This imperative shows the limits of any moral vision that asserts the primacy of what we can do together over what we must do alone. For even if the parties to the struggle over the way things are turn out to be classes, nations, political parties, and social movements, it is still in the end the individual who must take sides and fight or surrender. It is he who must suffer and sacrifice and resign himself to his social fate or rebel against it. And it is he who must discover in the disharmonies of our life together the sense of a loneliness that even a great love would struggle to overcome.

7

Politics (as Struggle over the Future of Society)

Finitude and Transcendence in Politics

A human being, unaccommodated man, the thing itself, torn between finitude and transcendence, is born to find his one and only life shaped for him by a double social fate as well as by the surprises that his dying body holds in store for him. He is twice crucified by society: on the cross of class or caste and on the cross of one of the distinct societies into which humanity organizes itself under the protection of states. To see this double crucifixion for what it is and to understand what we can and should do about it—both as societies in historical time and as individuals in biographical time—is the acid test of realism in political thought.

All the large and complex societies that have emerged in the history of civilization have had states. All have had a hierarchy of classes or castes assigned at birth. In all of them, the state can emerge and subsist only if it comes to terms with the class or caste structure, changing itself or altering that structure, until they are no longer acutely at odds. What has varied widely has been the extent to which membership in one of these social ranks can be traded for membership in another, as well as the extent to which the rank an individual belongs to determines what he can do with his life, how he can relate to his fellow human beings, and even how he can think, feel, and express himself.

One of the most consequential and elaborate attempts to ground this hierarchy in a general view of humanity, society, and the cosmos was the one that Dumézil and other comparativists identified as an ancient and widespread Indo-European pattern, and of which we hear echoes as far apart in their origins as the religion of the Vedas and the philosophy that Plato expounded in *The Republic*.

There is according to this pattern a reciprocally sustaining correspondence between the ordering of society and the ordering of the soul. There are three main ranks in society: the priests or philosophers; the fighters and rulers; and the peasants and workers. The corresponding ordering in the soul is the ascendency of understanding over the action-oriented impulses, and of these in turn over the sensual appetites. The hierarchies of society and of the soul sustain each other. The understanding of the cosmic order—whether in the Vedic doctrine of rebirth, Plato's theory of forms, or any other of the attempts to anchor this vision of moral and social hierarchy in a comprehensive account of reality—reassures us, if we can persuade ourselves to believe it, that the double hierarchy of society and the soul has the universe on its side. The trouble is that there are too many ways of claiming to anchor statecraft and soulcraft in reality, as the allusions to the Vedas and to Plato suggest.

The sanctification of the double order underestimates us: our capacity to surprise and to subvert, and to find empowerment and opportunity, for society as well as the individual, in the subversion and even the inversion of such an order.

The main line of sociological and economic theory has long tried to explain the persistence of this hierarchical ordering of social life by invoking its advantages: as a requirement for allowing large societies, without our technological resources, to hold together, feed their populations, and defend themselves or conquer their enemies. This is not a thesis restricted to conservative social theory. For Marx, the historical function of the class system was to serve as a basis for the coercive extraction of surplus over current consumption—the existence of which he mistakenly believed to be the chief constraint on economic growth across history, until the overcoming of scarcity.

In fact, this order never involved the inevitable sacrifice of the individual, cast into the lower rungs of the class structure, to the interests of economic progress. Any functional imperative can be realized by alternative arrangements. And one of the dimensions on which those arrangements have varied across societies, even at comparable levels of economic development, is the relative steepness and severity of class or caste hierarchy. For example, the organization of irrigated agriculture, claimed by Wittfogel to be the causal ground of "Asiatic despotism," has been achieved, in many circumstances, by arrangements more polycentric and cooperative than centralized, hierarchical, and authoritarian.

The organization of large societies and their states has nevertheless provided an opportunity to radicalize inequality and to express that inequality in the arrangements of work and production as well as in a moral logic with cosmological validation. Once a whole society and culture begin to be organized around such divisions—not only of economic advantage and political power but also of moral experience—every innovation will tend to be implemented in the form that least disturbs the dominant interests and the entrenched preconceptions.

What results for the individual is a demarcation of the space within which he can expect to live his life. In the most extreme form, society will hand him a script determining how he can live and feel by virtue of his place in the social division of labor. His sense of identity will be associated with the preservation of that place and of the whole social and cultural world that gives it life and meaning. Even then, as the transcendent being that he is, he will find occasions to deviate from the script and discover possibilities of experience that it rules out.

The societies that have resulted from the interrupted revolutions of the last three centuries have changed this reality but they have not abolished it. They remain organized around class and caste. The room for moving up in the social division of labor and for remaking the self, given exceptional luck, ambition, and talent, has widened. However, the vast majority of men and women around the world remain imprisoned within a circumstance that they are powerless to escape. That imprisonment is finitude with a vengeance, just as the revolutionary agenda was the promise of our emancipation.

To affirm our transcendence against this finitude, we would have to develop the institutional arrangements that lift, once and for all, the grid of entrenched division and hierarchy weighing, as it has in all the historical societies, on our relations to one another. Such liberation is one of the aims to which the revolutionary agenda of the last several centuries has been devoted. But the defenders of that agenda have lost their way. We must reimagine their program if we are to keep it alive.

If the shaping of life chances by class and caste is one face of finitude in the history of society, another face is our relation to the societies and cultures into which humanity is divided under the shield of states. There is no natural form of social life. Humanity develops its powers only by developing them in different directions. Each of these cultures, flourishing under the protection of states, is an experiment in a way of being human.

We are born into one of these worlds: a people, a nation, a state, a culture. What should our attitude to it be? We may identify with it and commit to it as a people—as an extension of the love that we may have for particular people. But should we identify with it as a form of life?

The form of life is what it is: the outcome of a more or less accidental history. It bears the stigmata of a class or caste system as well as of preconceptions about what the relations among people in each domain of social experience can and should look like. Should we accept it as it is, resist it and struggle to change it, or escape from it into another world, closer to our affinities?

There is one way of addressing this problem that we should reject at the outset. It is in fact the ideal to which classical liberal political thought aspires. In a free society, according to this ideal, the institutional framework should be wiped clean of any such brute particularity. It should not embody any vision of life in society other than the idea of the coexistence, in freedom under law, of people who have clashing conceptions of the good. Such conceptions will include or imply ideas about what the relations among people in different parts of social life should be like. The impersonal order of right in such a free society should remain neutral in the contest of such conceptions.

If the order of right remains neutral in that contest, people will be able to share in the life of society without having their existence shaped by the idiosyncratic features of one of the many social and cultural worlds into which humanity happens to be divided. But, as I have argued earlier, no institutional order can be neutral in this way: any such order encourages some forms of experience and discourages others. It leaves its mark on every aspect of our existence. The false claim of neutrality—an instance of false transcendence—will in fact do the opposite of what it pretends to achieve, insulating a particular form of social life against attack and revision.

We are born into these experiments in a way of being human enacted by the peoples of the world, assembled under the aegis of states. These states are armed, and ready to wage war and to demand from some of their citizens that they be ready to lay down their lives in a struggle to the death.

What are we entitled to want from these parts of humanity and from our relation to them? They used to be tribes—each of them a family of families, as if the social and cultural distinctions among them were simply an extension and sharpening of differences that had a pre-political, biological source. The unity of the people was expressed in the tangible details and the historical continuity of a form of life. To be an ancient Roman was to be born into this "community of fate" sustained through the succession of generations, and to live according to the customs of the Romans, the *mos maiorum*. Not to be part of a people was not simply to be stateless; it was not to be human at all.

But now, in the revolutionary period in which the people are supposed to rule and any customary arrangements may need to be sacrificed to the demands of national power, prosperity, and independence, the nature of the distinctions among the peoples of the world is shifting. Each nation must scour the world to identify the practices and institutions that will allow it to thrive, and remain free, in this global competition. To remain separate, they must become more alike. The will to be different, and to live independently, must count for more than the preservation of any custom.

Once we discard the classical-liberal illusion of the neutral order of right, as the institutional form of the life of a free people, we confront a surprising reality. Humanity is divided into peoples, presided over by armed states. These distinct parts of humanity are ceasing to be tribes distinguished by the continuity of generations and of customs.

They are on the way to becoming instances of a distinct way of being: a form of moral specialization within mankind. Along the way from the tribe to the moral specialization, the will to independence has taken precedence over actual difference. This will is abstract in the sense that it is not conditioned on upholding any particular set of customs. Actual differences are porous and susceptible to compromise. The will to difference is intransigent; there is nothing to serve as the object of compromise. And so it can happen that two peoples living close together will come to hate each other not because they are different but because they are becoming alike and want to be different.

The individual, born into a class or a caste, is also born into one of these peoples and delivered into the hands of the belligerent states that govern them. Each of these is a particular world, a species of humanity, that the individual did not choose, any more than he chose his parents. Each of them shapes the existence of its members and threatens to demand that they be ready to sacrifice everything for its cause.

What should we want of this division of humanity into peoples and of the relation of each of us to it, given that we are not entitled to pretend that there is a certain way of organizing society—liberal neutrality—that saves us from having to confront this problem? We should want each of these social and cultural worlds to be open to a wide range of contradictory experience. We should want the arrangements and presuppositions of each to be as susceptible as possible to contest and revision. And we should want to be able to escape, if we must, from one of these experiments in being human to another.

But these are aspirations, not realities. In the world as it is, we mostly remain in the grip of the part of society and of humanity into which we are born.

Life for a large part of humanity may already have ceased to be nasty and brutish. It will always remain short for a being who craves eternal life. But our double crucifixion—on the cross of domination and dependence and on the cross of national distinction—remains the way of the world: the nightmare from which we, in our lives as individuals, cannot awake.

The more ambitious our political ideals, the more important it becomes to recognize the reality of this double crucifixion without providing the explanations and excuses for it that the masters of a supposedly pitiless realism—Machiavelli, Hobbes, Marx, and Carl Schmitt—were prodigal in supplying.

To make clear the direction of the political argument developed in this chapter, it helps to situate it in relation to two defining controversies in the history of Western political theory. The first controversy has to do with the place of politics in human life. The second regards the relation between political ideals and political institutions.

Benjamin Constant proposed, in the early nineteenth century, the single most influential contrast in the history of Western political theory: the contrast between the liberty of the ancients and the liberty of the moderns. In this quarrel, Constant took the position of the moderns against the ancients. So do I, but with a meaning and intention different from his.

Constant encoded a programmatic conception in a fanciful historical typology: For the ancients (e.g., the Greeks and the Romans), freedom meant participation in the struggle to shape the life and future of a people. Politics was that struggle. It penetrated and influenced every domain of experience. It had inclusive significance and scope. But it also had a focus: to influence who controlled the state and to what end they exercised this control. The identity of the individual, his recognition by others and his self-respect were inseparable from engagement in this fight over the fate of a people, especially as shaped by the mastery and uses of state power. There was no properly human life to be lived apart from such engagement.

As applied to the ancient republics, this account was at best a set of half-truths combined with historical fantasies. Its operational meaning lay in the clarification of an alternative view of politics and freedom.

For the moderns, according to Constant, freedom lies in the pursuit of private concerns—in the family, work and business, and in the development of the many forms of subjectivity and individual experience that abound in modern republics. In emergencies, especially mobilization to fight in war, politics may break into private life. For the vast majority of men and women, however, politics represents a detour from their predominant concerns. When people attend to the business of the state, their chief motivation is to influence the effect of the laws on their own interests.

The protagonist is no longer the selfless citizen, for whom politics is fate. It is the flesh-and-bones individual whose main attention is directed to the sphere of private concerns. Barring calamity and the residual claims of the state on his time and even his life, his mind is turned to those concerns. It is thanks to this cabining of politics within a limited department of experience that freedom is possible.

The freedom of the moderns is the unavoidable beginning for any account of politics that joins transformative ambition to realism about history and humanity. But in the form in which Constant described it, it is the point of departure, not the point of arrival. It presupposes a distinction between the ordinary moves that we make within a framework of arrangements and assumptions that we take for granted, and the exceptional moves by which in times of crisis we challenge and change pieces of this framework. It associates structural changes with heroic action under the pressure of crisis—war or ruin—and takes private belittlement and an aspiration to modest prosperity and independence to be the normal condition of life.

The result, however, is to leave unresolved one of the contradictory conditions of self-assertion: that we be able to engage in a social and cultural world without surrendering to it. What we should desire is for the distinction between what we can change and what we must take for granted to be gradually and progressively effaced. Opportunities to participate in the collective practices by which we rethink and remake the regime of arrangements and assumptions within which we operate will then arise more continuously and naturally out of the normal business of life.

The mythical selfless citizen does not replace the flesh-and-bones individual. Instead, this individual becomes bigger: he rises to a life of greater scope and intensity. The arrangements of society and the impulses of culture encourage and empower him to tear down the wall between the ostentatious objects of ambition and their unchallenged and inexplicit presuppositions. And then it ceases to seem natural that, save for the sacrificial devotions of war and the prerogative of genius, life must be small.

The prospects for such an elevation of human life depend on the direction taken by the reshaping of society. The political arrangements have special significance because they determine, through the content of the laws, the terms for changing every other part of society.

Here we come to the other great defining controversy in the history of political thought: the debate over the alternative institutional arrangements for the ordering of political life, and especially of democratic politics. The range of live institutional options for the organization of democratic politics has been extraordinarily narrow. This narrowness is manifest in the design of constitutions. Two themes stand out over the last few centuries.

One theme is the restriction of the menu of constitutional possibilities to pure parliamentary regimes, an American-style presidential system with a rigid separation of powers, and increasingly, throughout the twentieth century, hybrid regimes that allow for a government accountable to both a parliament and a president and armed with a direct popular mandate. In every instance, society is kept at a low level of political mobilization. Even when there is undivided government (as under a pure parliamentary regime, with a government supported by a decisive parliamentary majority), politics is not organized to facilitate the reiterated practice of structural change, in societies that remain both unequal and unequally organized, except when there is a national economic or military crisis.

The second theme, ever more pronounced in the course of the twentieth century, is the constitutional proliferation of promises of social and economic rights, unsupported by an institutional machinery capable of ensuring the fulfillment of these promises. These unkept promises signal the humanization of a social world that we despair of reimagining and remaking.

In the history of politics over these same few centuries, the chief alternative to this narrow menu of options for the organization of democracy has come from the Left and taken the form of the idea of direct, participatory democracy—a democracy of popular or workers' councils. However, in every instance in which this idea was tried out it was soon cast aside, in favor of either the conventional constitutional repertoire or a despotic vanguardism. It has failed to meet the test of historical experience.

Just as in the contrast between the ancient and the modern repub-lics we must take the position of the modern republic and expand it, so too in the contrast between the impoverished inner circle of insti-tutional arrangements and the failed outer circle, we must submit to the discipline of reality without resigning ourselves to what has, up till now, been its impoverished outcome.

The aim of becoming greater together, the refusal to accept that it is natural for life to be small, the insistence on seeing in democracy a route to the elevation of ordinary experience and the empowerment of the ordinary man and woman, need to have, as their counterpart and instrument, a reformation of the institutional arrangements of democratic politics and, more generally, of a free society.

Born into a particular class or caste, in one of the societies, states, and cultures into which humanity is divided, our lives risk being crushed under the weight of an overwhelming historical fate. The struggle to become free of both these crosses—of class hierarchy and national belonging—to affirm our freedom and transcendence and to translate that affirmation into practical arrangements for the ordering of social life, may seem to be no more than the cry of an individual, misled by a false view of what individual autonomy can be, against a destiny that he is powerless to resist. But it is in fact a question about the possible futures of society. It has to do with the relation between what it takes to make a practical success of social life in historical time, in the sovereign and unequal states into which humanity remains organized, and what it requires to form and sustain an individual who can affirm his transcendence in biographical time, despite his finitude and the crosses that he must bear.

Our Moment in History and World Revolution

History is revelation. What it reveals is always ambiguous and contest-able. Nevertheless, what history shows has particular significance for politics, given that the medium of politics is historical time. I write this book during what I hope will be merely a counter-revolutionary inter-lude during a long revolutionary period in the history of mankind.

At several points in the preceding chapters, notably in my discussion of ethics, I have remarked that for the last three centuries humanity has been aroused by a revolutionary movement. This movement, I argued, has had two sides: a political side associated with democracy, liberalism, and socialism, and a personalist side identified with what we can broadly describe as romanticism, especially the worldwide popular romantic culture.

The promise of the political side has been to overthrow or lighten the burdens of entrenched social hierarchy and division that inhibit the development of our practical capabilities and corrupt our relations with one another. The promise of the personalist side has been to deepen and elevate the experience of the ordinary man or woman, and to strengthen their sense of agency: their ability to imagine themselves as sharers in a larger life and as authors of their own empowerment.

These two sides of the revolutionary movement may seem to be inseparable. In fact, they have taken largely different directions. To the extent that the personalist side becomes disconnected from the political one, it risks becoming a realm of fantasy. Instead of the enhancement of agency, the outcome then is that the would-be agent learns to sing in his chains.

This revolutionary movement remains, even today, I have claimed, the leading project in the world: it commands the agenda of humanity. But if it is strong by virtue of its commanding influence, it is also weak because its adepts no longer know what its next steps should be on either its political or its personalist side. The chief expression of this weakness on the political side is the inability of institutionally conservative social democracy or social liberalism to address, much less to solve, the major problems of contemporary societies. The principal manifestation of the weakness on the personalist side is its disassociation from the political side and its consequent confinement to fantasies of escape and empowerment.

The future of this revolution is one of the major concerns of the present work. One way to read this book is to read it as a proposal to breathe new life and new meaning into this revolutionary turn in the history of mankind. Such a proposal must conform to the law of the spirit, which is that we can possess only what we renounce and remake.

My moral and political argument explores the next steps of the movement on both its political and personalist sides. The account of the human condition in Chapter 3 anchored these ethical and political ideas in a conception of our humanity and of its contradictions. Chapter 1, on ontology, presented an understanding of what the world is like and of our place in the world that has room for the perpetual creation of the new. Chapter 2, on epistemology, developed a view of inquiry and its growth that shows by what means, and on the basis of what assumptions, we can find the ideas that the revolutionary movement needs to be reborn and to advance.

Since the late eighteenth century, the political side of this continuing but now interrupted revolution has been carried by the doctrines of democracy, liberalism, and socialism. It has proposed to rescue society from class and caste—entrenched social division and hierarchy —to lift ordinary men and women up, and to give them power. It has demanded that society be governed for the benefit and by the authority of the common people, and it has repudiated class prerogative.

Its adepts have disagreed, as liberals and socialists do, about the best way to organize an economy that serves the interests of the working-class majority and develops the productive powers of society. They have also differed over the kinds of equality that should be sought and the levels of inequality that should be tolerated, as well as over the role of the state in the direction of the economy and the moderation of inequality. But they have largely agreed on the centrality of the freedom of labor, the dignity of work, and the need to give all men and women the greatest possible opportunity to develop and exercise their talents.

Most fundamentally, they have embraced the idea that there is no elite by birth entitled to determine the direction of society, control the free work of free men and women, and hold the productive assets of society. Even those who believe that property is not a gift of the laws and has some natural form also insist that in the free order that they recommend assets will (ultimately) end up in the hands of their most efficient users, to the benefit of society as well as that of their owners.

They have disagreed about the political implications of the commitment to affirm the rule of the people. For some, the people rule only when the rights of minorities, beginning with political minorities, are protected and there can be an orderly alternation in power. For others, the political empowerment of the people must pass through a stage in which the putative representatives of the working-class majority hold power until the last remnants of class society have been eradicated and the state is secure against both foreign and domestic enemies.

Yet even these apologists of class and party dictatorship impose and exercise their dictatorship in the name of the people. And if their pretense is to be credible and effective, rather than an empty excuse, they must be able to show that it produces advantages for the many.

In no instance, amid all these variations—from the liberal-democratic to the social-authoritarian—may power be held or wielded by the representatives of an inherited class or caste order of society for the purpose of reproducing that order. And if someone says that it is exactly this that is happening under the disguise of liberal or popular democracy, then that claim becomes a challenge to the regime on its own terms: the terms on which its legitimacy depends.

We might think that this account of the political side of the revolutionary program is so inclusive and flexible that it excludes nothing and no one. In fact, however, it excludes almost all the regimes that have existed in world history prior to the present revolutionary period of the last several hundred years, with the partial exception of some city-states and stateless societies. It is only for us that the idea of lifting the grid of entrenched social hierarchy and division and of empowering the mass of ordinary men and women has come to seem the principle to which every regime must be loyal.

Once every form of legitimation appealing, as the ancient Indo-European formula did, to a natural and sacrosanct ordering of social life has been overturned, it cannot be reconstituted. The spell has been broken, and every enemy of those who hold power will have to claim that they know how to replace the sham with the real thing.

Now consider the personalist side of this revolution. Its chief vehicle has been romanticism: not just the high-cultural literary and artistic romanticism of the nineteenth and twentieth centuries in Europe but also and above all the worldwide popular romantic culture of today, conveyed by popular music, video, and film in their characteristic tropes and narratives.

The ideas and narratives of the high romantic culture of the nineteenth and twentieth centuries connect to the medieval romance and, through it, to the themes of love and infinity in Christianity. The basic elements of the romantic narrative are the true love and the ennobling quest. At every moment of its ancient and modern history, romanticism had trouble coming to terms with structure, routine, and repetition; that is to say, with what occupies most of any human life. The existence that it envisions exists only in those interludes when the romantic pilgrim or adventurer loosens the grip of routine on experience. But this true life is condemned to be exceptional and momentary. The romantic protagonist seeks the hand of the beloved, but the routines of married life defy the romantic conventions; they remain literally unimaginable.

The romantic seeks to distinguish himself by a work that raises him above the smallness of life and demonstrates that he is worthy of the beloved. The identification of the ennobling quest should come from within him and express his freedom from subservience to convention. In fact, it depends on common opinion. The result is to ensnare the protagonist in ambivalence toward the society whose recognition he both craves and pretends to despise.

The romanticism of the late nineteenth century and the modernism of the twentieth century came to doubt the possibility of both the true love and the ennobling quest. But they had nothing to put in their place, other than the worship of literature and art itself—a form of self-deification that can never satisfy anyone who has taken the Christian-romantic doctrine of love and infinity to heart.

The spirit of early romanticism has lived on in the global popular romantic culture of the present time. Its weakness is its sentimentality. The distinctive mark of the sentimental is its formulaic character: the gospel of anti-repetition is itself repetitious. It works with a small number of elements combined in familiar ways. The significance of its formulaic character is to diminish its power to generate the new and to lead from one state of affairs to another.

The shallowness, circularity, and relative sterility of much of the popular romantic culture cannot conceal the sublime message that it has carried throughout the world—into every slum, village, and shack. The ordinary man or woman is not so ordinary after all; he, she, is appointed to rise to a higher form of life: to find and give personal love against all the barriers imposed by the restraints of class and culture; to share in the subjective experience, if not the material opportunities, of the monied and educated classes; and to live life as an adventure in the making of a self, against the blindness of fortune and the injustices of society.

The message is that of our share in divine transcendence, of the supremacy of love over altruism and all else, and of the ways in which our ability to give ourselves to one another and to reach beyond the circumstance in which each of us finds himself are tied together. This is the message that romanticism, in both its high and its popular versions, took over from the Semitic monotheisms and often expressed in ways at once more powerful and more faithful to the inspiration of those religions than anything that we find in the history of religious orthodoxy.

Given this initial account of the political and moral orientation of this revolution, we can now look both back and forward and ask the only question that matters: What are the next steps of this world revolution on both its political and its personalist sides? If it has no next steps, or if we cannot define them, it must wither and stop. The counter-revolutionary interlude will not then be an interlude; it will be the future.

From this perspective, reconsider the moral argument in Chapters 4, 5, and 6. The two contemporary moral visions explored in Chapter 5 have a different relation to the revolutionary program. The ethic of self-construction and non-conformity is part of the history of that program. The ethic of connection and responsibility has no such internal relation to it.

Nevertheless, the corrected and enhanced forms of each of these contemporary moral visions provide answers to the question: What should come next on the personalist side? Unlike the school philosophy, these answers bear directly on how we can and should live our lives in historical time. Unlike the tropes of the global popular romantic culture, each of these moral visions defines a path of transformation from one way of living to another.

The impossibility of synthesizing these two approaches to the conduct of life, even after we revise them—the topic of Chapter 6—shows that there is no single answer to the question about what should come next on the personalist side. It reveals, as well, the inconclusive character of the arguments that we can make for choosing one answer over another: the cognitive gap between the weight of our commitment of life in one direction rather than another and the weight of our reasons for choosing that direction.

Once we have given each of these approaches to the conduct of life its strongest possible form, we can see more clearly how the failures of each demand political as well as moral remedies. But the less we can count on a favorable political setting for a way of living, the more we have to make up for the failures of politics by the manner in which we live and treat one another. We come to understand with greater clarity and consequence the relation between the personalist and the political sides of the revolutionary program.

What, then, of the next steps on the political side? The aims of the revolutionary project of the last few centuries for the reordering of society are far from having been accomplished. The liberals and socialists of the nineteenth century believed that there is a natural convergence between the institutional requirements for the development of our productive powers (Marx's maximal development of the forces of production) and the institutional conditions for rescuing social life from the grip of entrenched inequality.

Each faction had its institutional formula. They expected the formula that was good for one purpose—the fullest development of our productive potential—to be also good for the other—the subversion of distinctions of class and caste. We are no longer able to believe in a preestablished harmony between the institutional requirements of our material and our moral aspirations. Neither, however, do we have reason to fall into the opposite but equally dogmatic view that a tragic contradiction exists between the institutional foundations of our economic advance and the institutional bases of our emancipation from entrenched social division and hierarchy.

The question for us then becomes: Where is the zone of intersection between the first set of requirements and the second? Or, what is the subset of institutional conditions for one of these aims that also serves the other? To lift the burdens of poverty, infirmity, and drudgery that weigh on humankind, we should not need to relinquish our hope of emancipation from arrangements delivering the many to subjugation.

Here is where our poverty of direction becomes clear for all to see. The revolutionary program has lost its way on its political side as well as on its personalist one. Ambitious ideological and institutional alternatives to the arrangements of the rich North Atlantic societies were discredited by the world wars and other calamities of the twentieth century.

The last major institutional and ideological refoundation in the rich North Atlantic democracies was the social-democratic settlement foreshadowed before World War II and developed in the thirty years that followed it. Under the terms of that settlement, attempts to challenge and change the fundamental organization of market economies, democratic politics, and independent civil societies were abandoned. In return, the state gained the power to regulate the economy more intensively, to attenuate, through retrospective redistribution by progressive taxation and redistributive social spending, inequalities generated in the market order and to stabilize the economy through countercyclical fiscal and monetary policy. In its early, canonical form, this settlement relied on rules and deals that protected insiders and incumbents against outsiders and challengers: especially the organized labor force employed in capital-intensive industry and the services associated with it. The economic premise of this settlement was an economy in which mass production industry occupied the leading place.

In the course of time, this historical form of social democracy came to seem both inefficient and unfair, imposing costly rigidities on production and protecting what had become an organized and relatively privileged minority of the labor force, to the detriment of a disorganized and disadvantaged majority. Mass production industry declined and gave way to a new vanguard of production, an insular form of the knowledge economy that excluded most workers and firms.

On its European home ground, social democracy, weakened by the neoliberal criticism of it as both inefficient and unfair and undermined by the decline of its economic grounding in mass-production industry, retreated to its last line of defense: the maintenance of a high level of social entitlements, paradoxically financed by the regressive and indirect taxation of consumption. Much of the labor force found itself abandoned to precarious, unstable employment. The governing, moneyed, and supposedly informed elites embraced the attempt to reconcile European-style social protection with American-style economic flexibility, with minimal changes in the economic and political institutions. Labelled "social liberalism," this flexibilized, reduced version of social democracy had the best claim to be considered the new hegemonic project of the North Atlantic elites.

What resulted was an order incapable of solving or even addressing any of the major structural problems of the contemporary societies: the failure to create, in the age of the knowledge economy, an adequate institutional foundation for socially inclusive economic growth—a knowledge economy for the many; the failure to deepen democracy by establishing a high-energy democracy that no longer needs crisis (in the form of wars and slumps) to make structural change possible and that is fertile in generating structural solutions to structural problems; the failure to ensure a basis for social cohesion once the movement of people and the increase of social and cultural difference of all forms exposes the inadequacy of money transfers organized by the state as a social cement; and the failure to develop the kind of education, and to make possible the type of social inheritance (endowments settled on every citizen and worker), that would allow the individual to be capable and unafraid amid wider innovation and experiment.

In the rest of the world, outside the North Atlantic region, there were no alternatives on offer that deserved to be taken as universalizing heresies, as liberalism and socialism had been in the nineteenth century. Authoritarian and nationalist "state capitalism" was what remained of the ideological misadventures of the twentieth century.

The whole world, restlessly searching for alternatives, lay prostrate, bent under the yoke of a dictatorship of no alternatives. That dictatorship defines the historical moment at which I write this book.

I write it as one who believes that the revolutionary movement of the last three centuries can and should continue. But it cannot continue, and it does not deserve to continue, unless we remake, in substance as well as in form, the world revolution for which it has stood.

The larger aim of the argument is to present a view of the political life to which the finite and transcendent beings who we are can and should aspire: philosophy as an anti-fate. The narrower goal is to imagine a sequel to what I hope will turn out to be a counter-revolutionary interlude: a sequel that allows the world revolution to continue, with changed method and content. Chapters 4, 5, and 6, on ethics, considered our experience and its possible futures from the vantage point of clashing approaches to the conduct of life. This chapter, on politics, and Chapter 8, on the program of deep freedom, explore our experience and its possible futures from the perspective of alternative paths in the organization of society.

Ethics does not present the question of how to reconcile our transcendence with our finitude in the abstract. It turns it into a question about how we should live and what we should do with our vanishing time.

Politics converts it into a question about the organization of society. More than in ethics or in any other branch of philosophy, that question is necessarily historical. The successes and failures of the revolutionary agenda, and now its paralysis and disorientation, form the circumstance in which we must address it. The historical moment gives focus to the philosophical ambition.

To develop political thought in this spirit, we need two main conceptual instruments: a theory of regimes—of their nature and varieties, their making and reconstruction; and a view of the direction that such a reconstruction of society should take.

The Theory of Regimes: Imagining the Structure of a Society

The concept of a regime.[1] In every society there is a structure of institutional arrangements and ideological assumptions that shape social life. What they especially shape are conflicts over the mastery and use of political power, economic resources, and cultural authority. The course and outcome of these conflicts determine how we create the future out of the present and set limits to our accessible social futures.

The structure serves as a template for all our practical and discursive routines in every department of social life. Without it, society would be amorphous, and everything about our relations to one another would be forever in question. We might also label the structure a formative context, a framework, or, to use the word most favored in the history of Western political thought, a regime. The connotations of the word regime point toward the state: the provisions for the set up of government and for the control and uses of governmental power.

But we must give the term regime a broader scope if we want it to serve the purpose for which we need it here. The structure includes the formative institutional arrangements in every part of social life—the economy and the family, for example, as well as the state. But these arrangements can be understood, operated, upheld, and, when necessary, revised only if they are represented by conceptions. A regime is not just a collection of rules and institutions. It is also a conceptual map of what the relations among people in different parts of social life can and should be like. The structure cannot live apart from its representations: its institutional aspect is inseparable from its representational one.

Law is the most important site in which institutions meet representations. That is why Hegel and the German historicists understood the law as the institutional form of the life of a people, interpreted in relation to the understandings of interests, ideals, and identities that make sense of the institutions.

An account of regimes—of what they are, of how they are made and reconstructed, and of what they can and should become—is the

---

1. For a systematic development of a theory of regimes along the lines sketched here, see my book *False Necessity*, 1987, especially chapters 1, 2, and 4.

supreme concern of ambition in social theory. The preservation, transformation, and substitution of regimes is the highest object of ambition in politics.

The nature and origin of regimes. What is the nature of regimes? Where do they come from? We made them: they are our collective creations. But for the most part we have treated them in history as if they were more like natural phenomena that we must peer into from the outside, part of the furniture of the universe.

Because social life has no natural form, there is, in historical experience, endless fighting over the claims that we can make on one another. This fighting is the more inclusive meaning of politics. The struggle over the mastery and uses of the power of the state—the narrower meaning of politics—is only a part of politics, although often the most visible part.

The fighting stops, temporarily, or is contained, relatively. The truce lines, expressed as institutions and their representations in understandings of interests, ideals, and ideas, are what result. They are the regimes: fighting crystallized into structure. As the fighting is the liquid form of social life, the regimes, and the existence they make possible, generate its solid form.

The history of the universe, to the very limited extent that we have since the 1920s come to understand it, foreshadows this alternation: the fiery moment of concentrated energy and matter in which every discriminate order of nature breaks down and events or phenomena cannot be distinguished from the regularities governing them gives way to a cooled-down universe with its differentiated order of elementary constituents exhibiting stable laws, symmetries, and constants. The most significant difference is that the regimes of social life are our collective artifacts. We can hope to know them as our creatures and instruments in a way in which we can never grasp the phenomena of nature: the way in which the creator knows his creation.

Or think of it as a game of musical chairs. The music is the sound of the contest over the terms of our relations to one another. When the music stops, everyone sits down. The chairs are the regimes.

Once the music stops or the fighting is interrupted or contained, the order that emerges from the relative peace becomes the template of the social division of labor and of our representation of what relations among people should be like in each area of social life. Everything, from how we organize work and design machines to the ways in which we define our interests and identities, bears its stamp.

The fighting, however, never stops completely and is not interrupted forever. The peace between the breakouts of fighting is always restless and rich in surprises. The leaders and representatives of group interests—such as different segments of the labor force—may, for example, discover that some ways of defining and defending a group interest require a change in the institutional arrangements, whereas others take those arrangements for granted. They can go on to find that their view of who their allies and antagonists are depends on their assumptions about the alternative ways of organizing some part of the economy and the society. Once the thread of a specious naturalness and necessity begins to unravel, the unraveling may not stop.

The different elements of a regime may contradict as well reinforce one another. They must reinforce each other enough to stay together, informing and supporting the routines of a particular form of social life. A regime, however, is not a system with the attribute of indivisibility, as Marx imagined each of his "modes of production" to be, and as the classical liberals supposed the market economy was. Structural change—that is, change in the formative institutional and ideological order—can be more or less far-reaching, but it is always piecemeal.

To such structural but fragmentary change we can give the name radical reform. Revolution—if by that we mean the sudden, wholesale, and violent substitution of one indivisible system for another—is only the fantastical limiting case. The chief function of the idea of revolution has become that of serving as a pretext for its opposite: resignation to an order that we can hope only to humanize because we have despaired of remaking it.

It is part of the idea of a regime that it resists disruption even as it molds what can and cannot take place under its sway. In influencing what can happen under its aegis, it also shapes the futures that can emerge out of the present.

Here we reach one of the most important distinctions among

regimes. They can be organized in a way that insulates them against challenge and change: by narrowing the opportunities and multiplying the requirements for revision; by surrounding the established arrangements with an aura of naturalness, authority, and even sanctity; and by giving every major interest in the society a stake in the maintenance of the established order.

To the extent that a regime becomes entrenched in this way, it may appear to those who live under it to be a natural phenomenon rather than the human artifact that it is. Under these circumstances, the distance between the ordinary moves that we make within a framework of arrangements and assumptions that we take for granted and the extraordinary moves by which we challenge and change pieces of this framework will become extreme. And the regime will appear to those who live under it as if it were an indivisible system, even a system devised by a single mind, informed by a coherent and comprehensive conception. This appearance will be a delusion, but a delusion that the subjects of the regime will have half-wittingly perpetrated against themselves.

In the other direction, a regime can be designed and represented in such a way that it not only makes possible but also organizes, facilitates, and even provokes its own revision. The practices and ideas that give it life can emphasize its openness to reconstruction. By an apparent paradox, as I argue later in this chapter, its survival and vitality may depend on carving out from the institutions open to contest and experimentation a set of arrangements that protect the individual against governmental and private oppression while endowing him with the economic and educational equipment he needs to flourish in the midst of change around him. As a result, the distance between the moves people make within the framework and the moves they make to change it will narrow. And the regime will lose the specious semblance of naturalness and necessity. It will announce to all its nature as a revisable human artifact.

The more entrenched a regime is, the greater becomes the force of historical path dependence: the power of the past and present to shape the future. The less entrenched it is, the weaker such path dependence becomes. Our power to surprise ourselves in remaking the regime increases for better or for worse. The relative entrenchment and dis-entrenchment of regimes has no direct counterpart in non-human nature. Disentrenched structures soften the contrast between the fiery and the cooled-down forms of social life. This middle ground, if we can call it that, is the ground of experimentalism and perpetual innovation: a form of innovation that can have itself for an object.

This remarkable feature in the range of variation of regimes across history has practical significance: it bears directly on our greatest material and moral interests. Nothing is more important to the development of our practical powers than the improvement of our ability to cooperate. Nothing contributes more to that improvement than the opportunity—and the call—to experiment in how we cooperate. And nothing is more toxic to a scheme of subjugation than the incessant exposure of the arrangements on which it depends to opposition, especially when the ability to oppose is joined to the power to exemplify, in some part of society, a different way of governing and cooperating.

The making and reconstruction of regimes. Where does the content of a structure or regime come from? It does not come from a timeless typology or a periodic table of varieties of social organization. It is made with the institutional and ideological materials at hand: the relatively accidental outcomes of earlier sequences of struggle and compromise. And now, when there is worldwide rivalry, emulation, and seduction, some of those materials can come from anywhere, not just from the earlier history of a people.

But once a regime is established, it must show that it works—and indeed works better than the accessible alternatives. It is subject to a functional test: its success in supporting national power and prosperity and in allowing a broad part of the population to maintain and improve their accustomed way of life. The functional test, however, does not select types of political, economic, and social organization from a case exhibiting all the possible alternative arrangements. It applies to the regimes that actually exist, each of them put together out of our ramshackle historical and now world-historical legacy.

Consider what happens when there is an innovation in the world that promises to increase the power and prosperity of a nation relative to others and to enhance the ability of a regime to meet the functional test. One example is the advanced, experimental practice of production that we have come to call the knowledge economy. The tendency will be to assimilate the innovation in the form that is least offensive to the dominant interests and established preconceptions in the society. To this way of dealing with the innovation we can give the name the path of least resistance.

The path of least resistance in the development and dissemination of the knowledge economy is the insular form of that economy that exists today. Albeit insular, it is multisectoral. It appears, in all the major economies of the world, in every sector of production—in knowledge-intensive services and precision agriculture as well as in advanced manufacture. Yet, in each sector, it exists only as a fringe excluding the decisive majority of businesses and workers, even when this excluded majority buys its products and uses its services. Instead of spreading throughout the production system, it has remained quarantined. Its confinement is the reverse side of its failure to develop the larger economic and social potential of this new vanguard of production: to loosen or even reverse what has up to now been the most constant and universal constraint in economic life—diminishing marginal returns; to exploit the affinity between vanguard production and scientific experimentalism; and to provoke a change in the moral culture of production, raising the level of discretion and reciprocal trust allowed and required of all the participants in the productive process.

The path of least resistance is the most probable outcome. But it is never the necessary one. There is always an alternative to it. An alternative to the insular knowledge economy would be a knowledge economy for the many, spreading the most advanced practices throughout the production system. But we cannot take such a direction without far-reaching changes in the character of education as well as in the institutional and legal arrangements of the economy, diversifying the terms on which economic agents can use what Marx called the "means of production." Achievement of that goal implies the coexistence of different regimes of private and social property—including temporary and conditional claims on productive resources—within the same market order.

The path of least resistance has in its favor the weight of an existing world. It therefore offers something tangible, especially to the major beneficiaries of the established order. But it also has a frailty, which is clearly illustrated by my example of the contrast between the (existing) insular and the (proposed) inclusive knowledge economy. The solution emerging from the path of least resistance fails adequately to tap the potential of the innovations that it has cabined. And when the diminishment of that potential for society translates into restraint on its usefulness for particular classes and communities and for those who seek to lead or represent them, the conditions are met for a contest between the friends and the enemies of the path of least resistance.

The work of transformative practice and of transformative thought is to offer an alternative to the path of least resistance. To offer one, however, we need a way of thinking about regimes: their nature, their making, and their remaking. This section has presented a summary outline of such a way of thinking. However, just about every proposition in it is controversial, and gives cause for questioning.

Without such a way of thinking about regimes and their transformation—if not this one, then another—we cannot do the work of political thought. We cannot explore what it would mean and what it would take to bring the revolutionary agenda of the last several centuries back to life, with renewed meaning and force. And we cannot form of view of politics that does justice to the central themes of this book: the dialectic between our finitude and our transcendence, and our relation to one another as we live out this dialectic in our lives.

The history of social thought has been as much a history of the suppression as of the development of structural vision. An understanding of the lessons of that history shows why the theory of regimes must occupy a central place in our thinking about society. It also suggests how such a theory must differ from what it has been.

Structural vision affirmed, corrupted, denied, and recovered: lessons of the history of social theory. In the West the theory of regimes has always been at the heart of the study of society. Aristotle gave it its classic form and Montesquieu resurrected it. Both described an enduring typology of regimes—in effect, a small, closed list. They inferred the composition of this list from the nature of the group that held power in the state. They saw that control of the state had consequences for the organization of society—for example, for the status of powers intermediate between the state and the individual. The answer to the question "Who commands the state?" played, in their doctrines, a decisive role in differentiating one regime from another.

This role was incomplete because there was something else that distinguished one regime from another: the form of conscious-ness, or principle, on which its operation depended. Aristotle and Montesquieu understood that each regime had two sides. Each was a set of institutions and a way of thinking and feeling. The integrity of its institutions depended on the preservation of the habits—or virtues—required for it to work faithfully to its own vision of itself. The regime would be doomed if these virtues were lost.

Classical European social theory in the late nineteenth and early twentieth centuries produced the greatest advance in the theory of regimes that has ever occurred until now. Karl Marx's theory of society and history was the high point of this achievement. At the center of Marx's approach to regimes was a revolutionary insight: that the formative institutional arrangements and ideological assumptions of a society are not like natural phenomena. They are our creation, although we live in constant danger of treating them as if they were natural and necessary. What the English political economists had described as the universal and eternal laws of economic life were in fact the regularities of a regime—a "mode of production"—that Marx called capitalism.

Marx broke the Aristotelian mold in the theory of regimes by placing at its center the insight that regimes are artifacts of our own making, by suggesting the possibility of an irreversible transformation rather than a recurrence of the elements of a timeless typology, and by freeing the theory from a single-minded focus on power in the state. But the significance of the third of these three novelties was diminished by putting the development of production in place of the sharing of state power as the criterion for distinction among regimes. The reach of the other two novelties was compromised by a series of related necessitarian illusions: the illusions of false necessity.

The first was the closed-list illusion: that there is a predefined list of the regimes or modes of production in history. The second was the indivisible-system illusion: that each regime consists in an indivisible system, which must either be managed or replaced altogether. The third was the historical-laws illusion: that these regimes succeed one another in history according to a foreordained plan, implemented through the agency of class interests and class conflict.

The closed-list and historical-laws illusions attributed to history a pre-written script and negated the value of programmatic thought: history always has a project in store for us. The indivisible-system illusion implied that politics must be either revolutionary—the replacement of one mode of production by another—or reformist —the management of such a regime. In this way, it excluded what is in fact the chief form of structural change: revolutionary reform. Revolutionary reform—the piecemeal revision of a regime—is fragmentary and susceptible to reversal but has the potential to become cumulative and regime-changing.

Marx recognized that regimes compete on the basis of their functional consequences. But he viewed these consequences too narrowly, by their effects on the development of the forces of production. He failed to recognize the ambiguity of class interests as the chief mechanism by which the contest over alternative regimes comes to life in history. There are always ways of defining and defending a class interest that lead back to the defense of its present niche in the social division of labor or forward to the reinvention of its interests and identity under another set of arrangements. And he supposed mistakenly that the functional imperatives work against the background of a script of historical change shaped by the three illusions of false necessity.

The task of the thinkers who came after Marx was to preserve and radicalize the central insight into the made and imagined character of social life and to free it from the illusions that perverted its meaning. It was to develop an account of constraints on transformation that would no longer rely on the idea that history follows a script. Instead, many of Marx's followers in the West tried to save the theory by diluting rather than deepening it. They did so by emphasizing the "relative autonomy" of politics and consciousness from the remorseless logic of the maximal development of the forces of production through the succession of preordained regimes.

When, in the late nineteenth century and through the twentieth, social science developed out of social theory, it did not carry forward this task. It buried the vision of structure and structural change together with the illusions that had corrupted it. Each social science severed the vital link between insight into the actual and imagination of the adjacent possible. Each did it in a different way. It was as in the beginning of *Anna Karenina*: all happy families are alike but every unhappy family is unhappy in its own way. The ways in which each social science cut the bond between its views of the real and its image of transformation became its peculiar form of unhappiness.

Economics, for example, the best organized and most influential of the social sciences, did it in a way unlike any other social science. The marginalist theoreticians of the late nineteenth century set the path. Ever since, economics has been the study of their method. Anxious to produce an approach to economics that is as invulnerable as possible to the normative and causal disputes that had aroused classical social theory, these theorists developed a method that was closer to logical analysis than to a causal science. Its only close equivalent was Hans Kelsen's Pure Theory of Law. There is empiricism and analysis in their would-be science but they have little to do with each other: the causal ideas are either invented on the spot, or imported from another discipline, such as psychology. This economics suffers from a deficit of institutional imagination, especially imagination about the alternative institutional forms of the market economy itself: it is either agnostic about the institutional consequences of its propositions (pure economics) or committed to a particular legal and institutional form of the market economy (fundamentalist economics). It has no genuine account of production and its transformation, preferring to view the production system as a shadowy extension of the system of exchange under the lens of relative prices. And if offers a theory of competitive selection, bereft of any account of the creation of the diverse stuff from which competitive selection selects: the equivalent of having only half of the neo-Darwinian synthesis in the life sciences.

Once we untie insight into the actual from imagination of transformative possibility, there can be no structural vision. Thus, each
positive social science is recruited into the chorus of fate and betrays
the vocation of social theory, which is to be an anti-fate. Each is
enlisted in the effort to confer on established arrangements an unde-
served halo of naturalness, necessity, and authority as if their existence
and diffusion sufficed to prove their superiority not only over the
rivals they confronted but also over those they did not.

In the normative disciplines of political philosophy and legal
thought, the suppression of structural vision takes another form.
Instead of rationalization and right-wing Hegelianism, humanization:
pseudo-philosophical justifications of the practices demanded by the
institutionally conservative social-democratic or social-liberal settlement of the mid-twentieth century. In the theories of distributive
justice, these practices are those of compensatory redistribution to
reduce inequality without changing or reimagining institutions. In
legal thought, they are ways of thinking that misrepresent established
law as a flawed approximation to an idealized combination of impersonal principles of rights and policies responsive to the public interest,
finding or creating system where there is only a homely, contingent,
context-bound compromise of clashing interests and ideologies.

In the humanities, the suppression of structural vision takes yet
another form: escape from the realities of structure and structural
constraints into the adventurism of a subjectivity that has despaired
of remaking, reimagining, or even understanding the social world.
After the parting of ways between leftism and modernism in the early
twentieth century, the sublime—all hope of alternatives that would
afford us, without the heroic devotions of war and emergency, a
larger life—is confined, together with religion and art, to our private
experience. The public realm, rendered cold, supposedly for the sake
of both realism and liberty, is where we can seek only marginal gains
in efficiency and equity.

The aim of the theory of regimes must be to give us a way of
thinking about structure and its transformation that frees us from
this coexistence of rationalization, humanization, and escapism.
This way of thinking must do justice to both our finitude and our

transcendence. It must recognize the immense power and recalcitrance of the regimes that have emerged from our history. But it must
also acknowledge our capacity to resist and renew them. They nail
us to the cross of definite arrangements and assumptions. But we do
not have to give them the last word, or attribute to them a necessity
and authority they do not deserve. We can rethink and remake them
piece by piece and step by step. We can change their nature and modify
their power to shape our collective future.

Sources of a Direction

To find a direction, we need a way of thinking about regimes and their
revision. Without structural imagination we are lost. Social theory
represents philosophy in our thinking about society and history: it can
and should be an instrument of the philosophical aim of imagining
our transcendence over our present situation. In the pursuit of that
aim, it must also struggle to see beyond the established social sciences
as well beyond its own history, as the preceding section has argued.
The central topic of social theory is the nature and transformation
of regimes.

But although we cannot think successfully about alternatives if we
misunderstand the formative institutional and ideological structures
of social life, our thinking about them will never be enough to give us
a direction. And without a sense of direction, we will find ourselves in
the situation that Montesquieu described when he said that no wind
helps a man who does not know to what port he is sailing.

There are three sources to which we can look. The first is our
understanding of the human condition: of who we are. To consult
this source requires no essentialist idea of human nature: no view
of a core, unchanging set of behaviors and therefore no distinction
between such a supposedly immutable core and whatever in our
experience is susceptible to the historical influence of society and
culture—which is everything. What it does demand is a view of our
circumstance in the world and of our relation to that circumstance.
Our most comprehensive ideas about ourselves are a place at which

the distinction between the *is* and the *ought*, the descriptive and the prescriptive, breaks down, as I argued in Chapter 4, on ethics.

It matters whether we have a place in God's plan of creation and salvation or whether we are here on our own, without the backing of such a being. It matters whether we can understand ourselves as simply creatures of circumstance and causal determination, deluded by a false impression of creative freedom, or justifiably attribute to ourselves imaginative and reconstructive powers, and thus see ourselves from the standpoint of transformation and possibility. It matters what the conditions for developing a self are, whether these conditions are contradictory, and, if so, whether we can master these contradictions in the historical time of politics as well as in the biographical time of moral striving.

In politics, as in ethics, our ideas about our identity as human beings form part of the basis of our normative conceptions, about the ordering of society in the one case and the conduct of life in the other. In both ethics and politics, they fail to point us in a single direction. The other arguments we make in favor of one or another orientation to existence (appealing to the relative force of our desires and aspirations or comparing promises of happiness that can be kept to those that are self-subversive or impractical) represent variations on the same guiding role of our self-understanding. The result is a cognitive gap: a stubborn disproportion between the weight of a choice of direction, in the conduct of life and the organization of society, and the adequacy of our grounds for choosing.

In politics, we have sources of guidance that we lack in ethics. One of these sources is historical reality: the comparative experience of societies adapting different structural arrangements. Will they flourish or fail? Will a certain way of organizing society be taken as a model that other societies, anxious to achieve similar results, adopt? Or will it be rejected by other societies as a dead end? The lessons of historical experience serve as a second source for our ideas about a direction.

A third source of a choice of direction is the ideological debate that we find established in the world, and the division of parties and currents of opinion in that debate. A conversation about the future of society does not begin in a vacuum of philosophical speculation and inference from first principles. It begins with an existing contest. In that contest, interests are connected to ideals and to assumptions about what is feasible.

The debate that we find in the historical moment may seem the most superficial of these sources. It is the nevertheless the natural place to begin: a new public conversation must start by engaging and reshaping an established conversation. Behind the change in the terms of discourse lies the reshaping of institutions and practices. But in joining the established conversation, we can be guided by the ideas that emerge from the other two sources: about what has worked and failed historically and about who we human beings are. Let us then proceed in the reverse of the order in which I have just listed these sources of guidance: first, the criticism and revision of the existing ideological debate; second, the lessons of historical experience; and, finally, the guidance provided by an understanding of the requirements for making a self.

We have no assurance that the programmatic ideas we can infer from these three sources will point in the same direction. Yet our whole interest is that they can and will: that we can find a trajectory capable of informing the political life of the human being who is born to transcend in his finitude but who can do so only if he ascends together with his fellows. This trajectory must be one that gives every man and woman a better chance of reconciling the conflicting requirements of making a self. It must not promise to deliver what is denied to us by the coexistence of our finitude with our transcendence: a definitive home in the world, overcoming the conflicting demands of selfhood in the relation of the self to others, to the social world, and to itself. These ideas will remain powerless unless we can translate them into arrangements that allow societies to flourish and take us from the ideological debate that we have to the one we need. And nothing in them must disregard the reality of our situation as beings who suddenly find themselves alive and on their way to death in a world that exists and is what it is for reasons that we cannot grasp, and in societies and cultures that would treat us as their instruments and mouthpieces.

A Direction: From Shallow Equality to Deep Freedom

The form of the ideological contest in the flawed democracies of today pits shallow freedom against shallow equality. The Right are those who give priority to freedom under the established institutional arrangements, especially the arrangements that organize the market economy and representative democracy. The Left are those whose priority is equality of outcome or circumstance under those same arrangements.

The freedom valued by the Right is the freedom that the established market order and the existing representative democracy make possible. It assumes that a market economy will take an institutional shape similar to the one that it has now and that the inherited corpus of private law—the law of contract and property, of associations and business organizations—describes the natural and necessary form of a decentralized economy. For example, it wrongly presupposes that the two dimensions of a regime of private property—the absolute level of economic decentralization, or the number of economic agents able to bargain on their own initiative and from their own account, and the nearly absolute control that each of these agents exercises over the resources at his command—are inseparable.

It sees the strengthening of organized popular engagement in political life (raising the temperature of politics), the rapid resolution of impasse among parts of the state (the hastening of the pace of politics), and the attempt to combine opportunities for strong central initiative with radical devolution of power to parts of a country that can try out alternative arrangements as steps on the road to a dangerous collective adventure. Such an adventure threatens the power of individuals and groups to recede into their own worlds and follow their own way under what is supposed to be an impersonal order of right, neutral among conflicting conceptions of the good.

The equality valued by the Left is an equality of outcome or of circumstance, not just of opportunity. It is not, however, what it seems to be. When we combine the egalitarian profession of faith with agnosticism or skepticism about institutional alternatives, what results is the justification of retrospective and compensatory redistribution, especially by progressive taxes and redistributive social entitlements. In the absence of any attempt to alter the hierarchical segmentation of the production system, such after-the-fact redistribution can never go very far; it would soon begin to disturb established economic incentives and arrangements and to exact an unacceptable cost in foregone output. In practice, the equality prized by the Left is the humanization of an order that is to remain fundamentally unchanged, except insofar as shifting circumstances and unexpected crises require adaptations. It is the humanization of what we imagine to be inevitable.

The shallowness of shallow freedom and shallow equality lies in their lack of structural import. They do not point to an institutional reordering. Instead, they imply different hierarchies of interest and value within the existing order, only marginally adjusted. The institutional restraint is not an incidental or accessory feature of the conventional Right and Left positions; it is decisive for their significance. The goals of freedom and of equality and the nature of the relation between them depend on the institutions and practices through which each of them is achieved. The content of the ideals is inseparable from their institutional expression.

The obvious and ultimately the only way to expand the terms of this conventional debate is to relax the constraint of shallowness. There is a motivation to do so that arises from the practical needs of society, not from any merely speculative exercise. None of the major problems of the contemporary societies can be solved or addressed within the limits of the established institutional and ideological order. Far from being an exceptional feature of our present circumstance, that is what we would expect to happen, given the passage of time, in any society.

If the constraint of skepticism about institutional alternatives were removed, the Right might simply continue doing what it already seeks to do: minimize the restraints that the social-liberal or social-democratic settlement of the mid-twentieth century places on the operation and distributive consequences of the present market order. Alternatively, motivated by nationalism, it might seek an alternative set of institutions as the corporatist and fascist movements of the twentieth century did. But each of these turns would likely amount to nothing: the first because no contemporary society will tolerate the wholesale abandonment of redistributive social entitlements or be able to flourish and prosper without them; and the second because it would represent even more of a phantasy in the age of the knowledge economy and precarious employment than it did in the era of industrial mass production.

The true successor to shallow freedom is, according to this view, the generalization of the view underlying it and the explication of its premises. Real improvements arise step-by-step from experience, not from the imagination of alternative institutions. The existing forms of the market order and of representative democracy have undergone trial by experience, and any attempt to interfere with them is likely to prove counterproductive. The way to help people live larger lives is to give them more space to take initiative on their own behalf. Shallow freedom has no successor: it is its own successor.

What then happens to the Left's goal of shallow equality when we remove the constraint of shallowness? Deep equality as the commanding aim of the progressives—the would-be successors to the revolutionary agenda of the last few centuries—would mean attempting to achieve a rough equality of outcome or circumstance among the members of a society, or at least among its free citizens, and avoiding all initiatives that threaten to disrupt that equality even if they may enhance our power and wealth. No collective empowerment at the cost of significant inequality is the watchword of this interpretation of deep equality.

Deep equality, understood in this way, implies a rigid mechanism of redistribution to prevent the unequal economic success of individuals and their families from resulting in economic concentration and inequality, and ultimately in a division between the owners of productive assets and the sellers of their own labor. Such mechanisms may include restraints on alienation (especially of land), limits to accumulation, and rules of corrective redistribution to reestablish the mandated level of equality.

This is not an incoherent aim, nor is it absent from the historical experience of humanity. It characterized many primitive societies before the rise of civilization and can still be found among some of them today. And it existed, up to a point, in ancient city-states like

Sparta, usually relying on a sharp contrast between the free and enfranchised and the unfree and disenfranchised parts of the population: the combination of radical equality with a sharp contrast of class, caste, or legal status. In modern history, we find it often in pioneer societies, inspired by religious, nationalist, or socialist ideals.

But radical equality has little to do with the historical aims of the progressives, including the liberal and socialist votaries of what I have called the revolutionary agenda. They have not sought a rigid equality of outcome or circumstance. What they have most wanted is to raise up the ordinary man and woman to a life with wider scope, greater intensity, and stronger capabilities. And they have believed that the achievement of this goal requires cumulative change in the institutional organization of society.

The ideal of a stark equality of circumstance, recalling monks in their cells or comrades in arms, and of an equally shared poverty, has no appeal. It is an archaic aside from the aspirations of ordinary men and women in advanced societies. The residue of legitimate concern that it includes has to do with the effect of extreme and entrenched inequalities on the character of relations among people.

To live a larger life, not alone but with other people—to become greater together—is what I call deep freedom. Its meaning cannot be distinguished from the direction of change that it requires in the ordering of social life. At the center of that meaning is the enhancement of agency: of our ability to act, transformatively and imaginatively, especially in remaking the institutional and ideological setting of our common life.

We do not and we cannot enhance our agency alone, as isolated individuals. The idea of the enhancement of agency coexists, in the conception of deep freedom, with the conviction that we can become bigger only together. Freedom, in this context, is life, with all of its attributes of surfeit, spontaneity, surprise, and fecundity. The social form in which we affirm agency is part of its core meaning, not an afterthought.

In their revised versions, the two approaches to the conduct of life discussed in Chapter 5—the corrected ethic of self-construction and the maximalist ethic of connection—exemplify two ways of understanding the relation of agency to solidarity. Just as the corrected ethic of self-construction is not an individualism, the maximalist ethic of connection is not a collectivism. By different routes, each of them marks a route of ascent to a higher form of life that can be achieved, if it is achieved at all, only in social form.

The development of the idea of freedom must exhibit a similar richness of possible developments, indeed more so, because it must come to terms with the diversity of national circumstances and cultures. In all its many forms, however, the same two ideas must coexist: the heightening of the power of the human being to act, imagine, and transform, and the conviction that such a heightening can be sustained over time only if it finds a social form, manifest in institutions and practices that develop it. The goal of the Left must be deep freedom, not deep equality.

For the progressives of today, deep freedom cannot mean what it meant for the liberals and socialists of the nineteenth century. They worried that democracy would result in conformity and took as their model an aristocratic ideal of self-possession, dependent on the control of independent property and on the prerogatives of a superior legal status. The combination of independent, typically landed property with legal prerogative allowed the lord to retreat into a world in which he could mistake himself for being his own master and the master of many others dependent on him and pliant to his orders.

This aristocratic foreshadowing of deep freedom was triply flawed: by its direct relation to the subjugation of other people, by its insertion in the hierarchical order of a society that made the lord a servant as well as a master, and above all by the poverty and emptiness of its view of self-mastery. We cannot frame the idea of deep freedom on that aristocratic model; we need a conception of the enhancement of agency that is more open, rich, and contradictory.

Central to this more inclusive conception is the narrowing of the distance between the ordinary moves that we make within an order that we take as given and the exceptional moves by which we challenge and change pieces of that order. The latter must arise, more readily and continuously, out of the former. This is freedom as a creative experimentalism generating, through its reiterated practice, its own presuppositions.

If deep freedom is the true successor to shallow equality, what role should constraints on inequality play in its development? The overriding criterion for determining the prohibited level of inequality has to do with the exercise of agency. No inequality must be allowed to build up that corrupts the relations among people by allowing some to revel in the exercise of agency while others are reduced, by economic need, social prejudice, and educational disempowerment, to taking orders or doing the formulaic work that could be done by a machine.

Any pronounced inequality of wealth and income, and steep managerial hierarchy, exercised in the name of property, is likely to produce this effect. But even more subtle combinations of economic advantage and power can have similar consequences. Especially dangerous are those inequalities that result in giving certain groups a privileged stranglehold on the resources of economic capital, political power, and cultural authority with which we define the future. The future can be shaped, for example, by whomever can influence the evolution of technology in ways that emphasize either the substitution of labor or the enhancement of its productivity, or that either conflate flexibility with precariousness in employment or distinguish one from the other.

The struggle against inequality is not the goal. It is only an intermediate and accessory aim on the way to deep freedom.

In replacing shallow equality with deep freedom as the aim of the Left, we achieve only half of the needed change in the established terms of ideological conflict. The other, indispensable half has to do with the nature of regimes and of regime change. We advance toward deep freedom by cumulative change in the institutional and ideological structure of a society. We do so by confronting parts of the established arrangements that result in the disempowerment of ordinary men and women—such as the widening gap between advanced and backward parts of production, or the inadequacy of money transfers as a basis for social cohesion in the presence of increasing social and cultural diversity, or the importance of being able to generate alternative national paths without needing crisis to be its enabling condition. Changing any of these features of the established arrangements is likely to require institutional innovation as well as change in the ideological representations—the understandings of interests, ideals, and identities, through which we make sense of the institutions.

To this end, we need what the history of social theory and social science has largely denied us: a way of recognizing the primacy of change that is structural but nevertheless localized or episodic—radical reform. The direction and the initial steps will matter more than how far we get at any one moment.

When we think in this way, we have reason to discard and replace what has been the most constant model of ideological conflict in the rich countries of the contemporary North Atlantic region and in their outposts around the world. The formula has been the market versus the state: more market, less state; more state, less market; or compromise between the market and the state—described as social democracy or social liberalism.

Instead, the focus of ideological dispute becomes a contest over the alternative institutional forms of the market order, of democratic politics, and of independent civil society—that is, of economic, political, and social pluralism. This is the thesis of alternative pluralisms.

Consider, for example, the way in which assumptions about property enter into the definition of the market order. Does private property mean maximizing the absolute level of economic decentralization: the number and variety of the agents who can bargain on their own initiative and for their own account and gain access to the resources and opportunities of production? Or does it imply also the unqualified and perpetual character of the command that each of these agents enjoys over the resources at his disposal? The assumption that these two dimensions of private property—absolute decentralization and unqualified control—go naturally and necessarily together is patently false. For instance, we may be able to increase economic decentralization by experimenting more widely with fragmentary, temporary, and conditional claims on parts of the apparatus of production. A market order, like a democracy or a free civil society, has no single natural and necessary institutional form. We should not fasten it to a single dogmatic version of itself: a version good for some purposes will not be good for others.

Another example relates to democratic politics. A premise of conservative statecraft and political science is that there exists an inverse relation between political institutionalization and political mobilization—the level of political arousal of the people. According to this premise, politics must either be cold and institutional, or hot and extra- or anti-institutional, as in Caesarism. This premise excludes the possibility most important for the advancement of deep freedom through radical reform: a politics that is both hot and institutional. A combination of reforms regarding the electoral regime, the use of private and public money in politics, the terms of access to the means of mass communication, and more generally the incorporation by representative democracy of certain features of direct or participatory democracy, can raise the level of organized popular engagement in political life without weakening individual safeguards. Democracy is no more dependent than the market economy on a single institutional version of itself.

The contrast between conservatives and progressives, between the Right and the Left, takes on a different meaning when we have altered the terms of the ideological debate. On the revised terms, two main differences distinguish conservatives from progressives.

The first difference concerns our hopes for the reach of an ordinary human existence. The conservatives are those who believe that it is natural for human life—the lives of common men and women—to be small, except when war, emergency, and suffering require sacrificial devotion and raise us up. The most gifted, the most ambitious and the luckiest may, by their own efforts, escape this fate. But it is a perverse and dangerous political romanticism, on this view, to suppose that we can alter the tenor of our existence.

The progressives are those who hold that belittlement is unnatural. We can increase our share in the divine attribute of transcendence and become more human by becoming more godlike. But we become greater together or not at all. The struggle against extreme and entrenched inequality is accessory to the quest for deep freedom.

The second difference relates to the structure of society and its transformation. The conservatives are those who believe that we must pursue our interests and ideals within the horizon of the established institutional arrangements, especially the arrangements for the ordering of the market economy, of democratic politics, and of independent civil society. They interpret the calamities of the twentieth century as proof of the dangers of political adventurism, especially when it takes the form of the design of institutions that have not stood the test of historical experience.

The progressives are those who insist on pursuing our ideals and interests beyond the horizon of the established institutional arrangements. They know that once we begin to innovate in the organization of the market, of democracy, and of independent civil society, for the sake of realizing our interests and ideals more fully, we will confront a choice of institutional pathways. And that choice will in turn reveal ambiguities in our understanding of our ideals and interests of which were previously unaware. What begins as fragmentary but cumulative change in the institutional and ideological structure of society will soon become change in how we understand what we want and who we are.

By this standard, the vast majority of those who now count as progressives, such as the social democrats uninterested in institutional innovation, are conservative. And some of the conservatives, such as radical liberals (in either the European or the American sense), open to experiments in the institutional form of the market and of democracy, would count as progressives.

By reinterpreting the debate between the Right and the Left in this way we recast it in a fashion that represents a more significant difference than we face in the familiar contest between shallow freedom and shallow equality. We associate a difference about ideals to a difference about institutions. And we reformulate the contest in a manner that makes it much more likely to generate new possibilities rather than to reenact tried and exhausted options.

A Direction: Deep Freedom and Practical Empowerment in History

The ideological and institutional alternatives that we consider are only words until they are translated into law—that is to say, the institutional form of the life of a people, represented in a discourse about interests and ideals that makes sense of it. Under the present conditions of humanity, that expression in law must take place in a particular society under the aegis of a sovereign state.

The direction taken will not survive if it fails to be a practical success. If we are to take the direction of deep freedom, we must have reason to believe that it is not an otherworldly ideal but that it can meet this acid test in historical experience. The fundamental justification for this belief is that empowerment—the empowerment of the many—is over time more fertile than coercion in the organization of both the economy and the state, and that the collective ability perpetually to create the new is the best proof of such empowerment.

The most successful social form will be the one that can best reconcile the need to cooperate with the need to innovate and that does not need sameness to make social cohesion possible. If this proposition is true, the direction of deep freedom does not contradict what a society needs to thrive and what a state needs to become powerful and remain independent. That is not a guarantee of success in any national agenda, but it is a reason to deny that the aim of deep freedom is impractical on its face.

Beyond the most primitive stages of economic growth, the level of saving over current consumption ceases to be the chief constraint on economic growth. The hierarchical class and caste systems that have prevailed in the historical societies can therefore (pace Marx and countless others) not be explained or justified by the need for the coercive extraction of a surplus.

The chief constraint on economic growth has long been the relation between our ability to innovate and our ability to cooperate, or between our ability to innovate in technology, informed by science, and our ability to innovate in the ways in which we work together. Innovation and cooperation depend on each other. Yet every innovation—technological, organizational, institutional, or conceptual—threatens the established regime of cooperation. It arouses fear and, eventually, struggle over the effects of the innovation on each group's, or each person's, position. The best regime of cooperation is the one that does the most to mitigate this unavoidable tension between the imperatives to innovate and to cooperate. It does so, for example, by giving each person a stake and endowments that are independent of any specific set of cooperative arrangements.

In every economy there will be a most advanced practice of production. The most advanced practice of production is not necessarily from the outset the most efficient: the one that makes the most output with the least input. But it is the one with the greatest potential to reach the frontier of productivity and remain there, and in so doing to lead the transformation of the whole production system. Our understanding of what makes the most advanced practice of production advanced changes together with the succession of styles of production. From the vantage point of today's most advanced practice of production, we can look back and say: the most advanced practice of production has always been the one that is closest to the imagination, with its characteristic ability to grasp and master the actual by subsuming it under a range of accessible alternatives.

Our interest—both our narrower economic interest and our broader interest in achieving freedom in the economy (for example, by accentuating the difference between the worker and the machine), not just from the economy (through the overcoming of scarcity)—is to disseminate the most advanced practice of production throughout the whole economy. The most advanced practice of production, such as today's knowledge economy, reveals its deeper potential only as it spreads, escaping the confinement to the fringes to which today's knowledge economy remains restricted.

The readiness to innovate cooperatively and to cooperate without suppressing innovation is not enough to ensure the practical success of a society and of a state. Social cohesion must not depend on antecedent sameness of any kind. It must be compatible with difference: with heterogeneity of every kind, with complexity and contradiction.

Just as the fecundity of a method of competitive selection depends on the richness and diversity of the material from which it selects as well as on the mechanism of selection, so the power and potential of a form of social union are shown in its ability to bring the different together in endeavors animated by common purpose.

The weak and inferior way of bringing the different together is functional interdependence, as Durkheim, for example, described it in his conception of the organic solidarity distinguishing the advanced societies. The stronger and superior way of bringing the different together is to involve the different in forms of collective action to achieve shared goals. The multiplication of purpose-driven forms of collective action is the master instrument of social cohesion in a society open to conflict and contradiction and devoted to the perpetual creation of the new.

Together with the development of cooperative practices hospitable to permanent innovation, and forms of cohesion that depend on shared purpose rather than prior sameness, comes a third requirement of the success of states and societies: the formation of an individual who from early on is taught to associate capability within the framework of established arrangements and assumptions with the habit of contesting and revising pieces of this framework as he goes about the ordinary business of life.

Between the heroic transformative endeavor and the prosaic reenactment of the habits of social life lies the tinkering, the experimentalism, the endless crossing, in both directions, of the boundary between what lies within the institutional and ideological framework of society and what lies beyond it. When the practices of everyday life enact the dialectical and experimentalist lessons of a school that forms people with such impulses, the established order of society and culture is disestablished in the mind of the ordinary man and woman. In such a social world, the promise of democracy is more likely to be fulfilled: large problems will yield to the cumulative force of small, fragmentary solutions devised by the constructive genius of a crowd of common people.

The point of these remarks about what is required to make a practical success of social life is not that there is an immanent dialectic in social evolution that we need only to ride in the manner of Marx's theory of society and history. We could never just ride such an evolutionary logic for two reasons. The first reason is that it is indeterminate in its institutional forms. The second reason is that some of the forms it might take would be more hospitable to the aim of deep freedom than others. Some might use, and have used, these imperatives of practical success as an opportunity to impose new forms of authoritarian central direction on society.

There is no insuperable conflict between the ideal of deep freedom and the requirements of worldly success. But neither is there a logic of historical evolution that exempts us from having to formulate a program and to advance it amid competitive struggle within and among societies.

Over time, the most successful societies and cultures will be those that exhibit the greatest plasticity and use this plasticity to associate experiments in the mobilization of natural forces with experiments in ways of cooperating. The perpetual creation of the new is the work of the imagination, and the cooperative regime with the greatest promise will be the one that embodies that work in the division of labor in society.

In the short run, however, the path of least resistance overrides the appeal of imagination and plasticity: we develop and implement innovations in the form that least disturbs the established order and the interests and preconceptions around which it is organized. Transformative thought and practice are defined by the commitment to generate alternatives to the path of least resistance. Such alternatives have in their favor the promise of exploiting, more fully than the path of least resistance can, the potential of innovations to empower and enrich us.

That advantage will count for little or nothing unless the opponents of the path of least resistance in politics and in thought are able to demonstrate right now, in the present, the benefits of the alternatives they advocate. They must connect their proposals with the real forces and interests of existing society. They must do what the prophet always does: touch the open wounds of the present form of social life and offer tangible anticipations of a different future.

A Direction: Deep Freedom and
the Contradictions of the Self

We engage the established ideological debate and the conditions of power and prosperity from the perspective of a conception of humanity. Our understanding of ourselves and of our situation in the world is the most important source of our political ideas. In Chapter 3, on the human condition, I argued for such an understanding in two forms: at length, as an account of the human condition and of its irreparable flaws, and then briefly, at the end, as a conception of the contradictory requirements for making and sustaining a self. Each of these two expressions presents a view of how our finitude relates to our transcendence. Together, they provide an insight more important than any other in explaining the nature of politics and supplying guidance for its direction.

To make a self, we must connect with other people. But we must also deal with the jeopardy in which every such connection places us—the peril of subjugation and of loss of personal distinction. If to make the self we must also lose it, there is a contradiction in the requirements of selfhood. We may think of love as the only solution, for in love—if it exists, while it exists—we have the experience of a connection that adds to the sentiment of being rather than subtracting from it.

Love, however, is not a solution outside the domain of intimacy. Among strangers, there is not love; there is at best altruism, compassion, empathy, fellow feeling. To mistake altruism for love is to misunderstand the nature of love—a mistake that has haunted the history of Christianity.

To this problem—overcoming the clash between these requirements of selfhood—there can be both a political and a non-political solution. The political solution has priority. The counterpart to love among strangers is not just respect, recognition, and imaginative empathy. It is cooperation among free and equal agents. And it is engagement across the barriers of difference: engagement that both draws on common purpose and generates it over time.

Then there begins the struggle over the forms that such cooperation and collective action take: the institutional setting in which they can best flourish and the practices by which they can operate and develop. There lies one of the tasks of politics, a source of direction.

We can attenuate this contradiction between the requirements of selfhood but we cannot resolve it. It arises because we are transcendent. It is insoluble because we are finite.

Although we are bound to fail, we can advance. Some ways of organizing society may be better, even much better, than others by this standard. Here we have one of the criteria of political progress. It is progress toward deep freedom—the development of forms of social life that lower the price in subjugation and loss of personal distinction that we must pay for connection is one of the ways in which we become more deeply free.

Because we do not get to choose our place in history, we must find a way of living that makes up for the failures and omissions of politics. Thus, one of the concerns of the corrected ethics of self-construction and of the maximalist ethics of connection is to suggest how we can make up in our way of living and of dealing with other people for what we have failed to accomplish through the reconstruction of society.

To make a self, and come into the fuller possession of life, we must also engage with a particular society and culture as well as with other people. But insofar as the condition of our engagement in that world is our surrender to it, we cannot be free. Thus, another contradiction emerges in the conditions of self.

To make a self we must be able to join a social world while retaining the capacity to resist it and to struggle, together with others, to reshape it. We must in this sense be both insiders and outsiders. We are unfree if we remain excluded from engagement and unfree if we fail to develop the power to resist and revise. Some regimes are more hospitable than others to our nature as finite and transcendent beings. But given that nature, no regime can be our definitive home.

We must address this second contradiction in the conditions of selfhood, as we address the first one, as both a moral task in the conduct of life and a political project in the reconstruction of society.

In the conduct of life, we do so by living life in struggle and searching. We learn to refuse false transcendence: the mistaking of the relative for the absolute, of the conditional for the unconditional, of the finite for the infinite. The corrected ethic of self-construction and the maximalist ethic of connection (discussed in Chapters 5 and 6) offer two ways of participating without surrendering.

In politics the chief way in which we can seek to attenuate this second contradiction in the requirements of selfhood is to develop institutions and practices that narrow the distance between acting within a framework of arrangements and assumptions and acting to change that framework: to the difference between accepting it and transforming it. The result is to relativize the difference between struggle and normalization, between the liquid and the solid forms of social life. What lies in between is perpetual innovation and experimentalism.

A particular thesis in social theory informs this seemingly paradoxical effort and justifies its realism and its appeal. It is the thesis that there is neither a preestablished harmony nor an inescapable contradiction between the institutional conditions for the development of our practical powers, including our powers of production, and the institutional requirements for our emancipation from entrenched social hierarchy and division. There is a subset of the conditions of each that fulfills the requirements of the other. A feature of the arrangements that intersect these two sets of requirements is that they facilitate their own remaking.

It is easy to understand why that should be so. To develop our practical powers, we need to have our hands untied to the greatest possible extent. The organized anarchy of a decentralized market economy, for example, must not remain tied to a single dogmatic version of itself. To prevent the consolidation of forms of social subjugation, the arrangements and assumptions that make possible privileged strangleholds on economic capital, political power, and cultural authority must remain subject to uninterrupted challenge.

The creation of a regime that facilitates its own remaking is not, however, simply an instrument in the service of these practical and moral goals. It also stands in the service of an aim that is itself one of the aspects of deep freedom: our ability to attenuate, in the history of regimes and of our relation to them, the contradiction between the imperatives of participation and of resistance—to engage without ceasing to be unaccommodated.

Politics may seem to be less closely related to the remaining contradiction in the conditions of selfhood. Although the political implications of this third clash in the conditions of selfhood may be less obvious, they are nevertheless pervasive and profound. To make a self, we must develop a way of being in the world. But we cannot move toward deep freedom if we allow the hardened version of the self, and the place we occupy in the social division of labor, to become our fate. It will suck life away from us and leave us dead before we go to the grave. Its automatisms will take us over and leave us going around in the same circles while our time runs out.

We must break through this hardened form of the self. We can continue to live and to make a self only by loosening the hold of this compulsive form of the self on our experience. To that end, we must pay a terrible price: the price of accepting and increasing our vulnerability to loss, defeat, disappointment, and derision. In this effort we must allow ourselves to be inspired by the hope of increasing our share in the quality of transcendence and by the belief that we can become more human only by becoming more godlike.

The arrangements of society can make it harder or easier for us to move in this direction. They make it easier by establishing the relation between the haven and the storm that is the topic of the next section of this chapter and is the bridge between the ideal of deep freedom and a trajectory of institutional change, suitable to the circumstances of contemporary societies. The essence of this idea is that the individual must be capable and confident in the possession of vital safeguards against oppression and of capability-ensuring endowments. But society, in every department of its experience, must be thrown open to innovation and experiment.

As soon as it becomes rich enough to meet the basic needs of its citizens and powerful enough to defend the country, the state must assure its citizens of the educational and economic means with which to change direction and reinvent themselves during their lives. It must, among other things, offer them an education, beginning in childhood and continuing through life, that teaches them to move both within and beyond the established social world.

An agenda of deep freedom that responded only to an ideal of transcendence and found inspiration in the attempt to moderate the conflicting requirements for making a self would be impotent and otherworldly if it failed to find reinforcement in what the advanced societies need in order to flourish.

The most advanced practices of production are the most mindful: the ones that most clearly express our imaginative powers. The deepening of the knowledge economy, to reveal and achieve its productive potential, and its spread across every part of the production system are two sides of the same process. The education that these societies most require is one that builds on the basic connection between insight into the actual and imagination of accessible alternatives: we understand both natural and social phenomena by grasping how they change, and into what we can change them. The strongest basis of social cohesion is the one that results from the multiplication of forms of collective action energized by common purpose and does so across the barriers of difference rather than on the foundation of sameness. And the most useful form of democratic politics is the one that elevates the temperature of politics (the level of organized popular engagement in political life), hastens the pace of politics (the rapid resolution of impasse), and combines a facility for decisive initiative by the center with radical devolution. By these means, we increase the power of democratic politics to practice radical reform (fragmentary structural change). We render the impulse to transformation internal to democracy. We dispense with crisis as the indispensable enabler of change and allow imagination to do the work of crisis.

The Haven and the Storm

We need an idea that can bridge the conception of deep freedom and the description of a trajectory of cumulative institutional change adapted to the circumstances of the contemporary advanced societies. This is the idea of the haven and the storm. This idea must also teach us to think about politics in a way that combines the hope of becoming bigger together and the willingness to change the institutions that define the market, democracy, and free civil society—piece by piece and step by step.

Let us approach this idea through the exploration and criticism of a more familiar, kindred notion: the conception of fundamental human rights and of their relation to a free society. This notion includes both a technical or instrumental element and a substantive or purposive one. The technical element is the practice of taking at least partly out of the agenda of short-term politics safeguards and endowments that we regard as essential to freedom. Such safeguards and endowments give the decentralization of political as well as economic power a robust basis. The withdrawal of these rights and of the laws that establish them from the swings of day-to-day politics may take the form of incorporating them into a constitution that cannot be easily amended, or more generally of requiring supermajorities in the legislative bodies of a representative democracy to amend them. With or without such constitutional entrenchment, it may also take the form of surrounding them with a special sanctity. In the past, the appeal to natural rights or natural law has been one way to endow them with such authority.

Whether such withdrawal from the agenda of short-term politics has a tangible legal or an intangible ideological or theological basis, we know that it can never offer a foolproof guarantee against abrogation or revision. Views of what these safeguards and forms of empowerment are should and will change, as the arrangements and concerns of society shift. We can try to tie our hands to the mast. But we know that we can untie them—if not by the cumulative force of small changes, then by upheaval in politics or in our beliefs.

We take something out of the agenda of short-term politics with the seemingly paradoxical aim of enriching this agenda: of ensuring that it will be open to a multiplicity of powers, a variety of interests, and a diversity of initiatives. We subtract from the short-term agenda to add to the long-term one.

This observation brings us to the substantive or purposive element in the notion of fundamental rights. We must secure the individual in a haven of vital protected interests, guarantees against governmental or private oppression, and means to take initiative. Our purpose is to make him unafraid enough and capable enough to exercise his agency. The most important forms of such agency may not be individual; they may develop through cooperative action more than through individual initiative, against the background of institutions—social, economic, and political—favoring purpose-driven cooperation among the different.

There is no contradiction in arguing now for such a haven, having argued earlier in the development of the two ethics for a heightened acceptance of vulnerability, security against economic insecurity, as well as political oppression, making the risks and experiments required for the transformation of both self and society easier to undertake. The problem lies in what we must combine the haven with if it is to perform the role we should assign to it in the program of deep freedom.

Something remains missing from this account of the substantive element in the idea of fundamental rights. We can elucidate this missing element by another comparison. The parent says to the child: you are secure in my unconditional love. Now, liberated by that assurance, go out and raise a storm in the world.

But what if society has no room for the enhanced agency of the unafraid and capable self? What if it presents itself to him as a merciless system demanding that he enact the script that it hands to him? The parent may, if he is both fortunate and wise, seek to give his child some protection against the social order. But the movement of society toward deep freedom requires more than the haven.

It requires that the world in which the empowered self moves be perpetually opened up to innovation and experiment: that it be a structure with the attribute, which I earlier described, of disentrenching itself and of narrowing the distance between the moves that we make within an accepted framework of arrangements and assumptions and the moves by which we challenge and revise pieces of the framework. Such a structure is both structure-establishing and structure-subverting. In the language of an earlier moment of my argument, it must split the difference between the liquid and the solid moments of social life: the moment of active and extensive contest over the terms of our access to one another and the moment when the contest gets temporarily interrupted and relatively contained. It must dispense with crisis as the condition of change, and put imagination, translated into institutions and practices, in the place of crisis. To this change in the character of social organization—the development of a structure that subverts itself—I give the name the storm.

Such a storm—a perpetual rather than a passing storm—fails to arise spontaneously. It needs to be arranged. Each of the elements of the institutional agenda to be discussed in Chapter 8, on the program of deep freedom, adds content to this idea.

We need the storm, as the indispensable counterpart to the haven, for two reasons. We need it for the sake of movement in the direction of deep freedom, in the hope of becoming greater together and of widening our share in the faculty of transcendence. And we need it to develop our practical powers, given that their development depends on our success at freeing our practices of innovation from the restraints imposed by any inflexible institutional order.

The idea of alternative pluralisms describes the feature that the institutional innovations that we require share: they treat the established forms of market economy, of democratic politics, and of free civil society as a subset of a wider universe of institutional possibilities. We must travel in other subsets of that wider set if we are to develop our practical powers and advance toward deep freedom.

There is also a more immediate prompt to organize democratic politics around the coexistence of the haven and the storm. In the recent historical period—this counter-revolutionary interlude, marked by the ascendancy of institutionally conservative social democracy and social liberalism—the main concern of would-be progressives and leftists has been to secure the haven. They have done little or nothing to arouse the storm. They have failed to recognize that without a relation to the arousal of the storm, the haven fails to perform its most important role. As a result, they have played the part of the humanizers of the inevitable: seeking to put a more human face on the proposals and initiatives of their conservative adversaries. They have renounced the power to shape the agenda of politics, in the advancement of which those who represent the cause of creative energy, however crude and unjust it may be in its expression, always have the leading role.

What changes in the arrangements and practices of a contemporary society would take us in such a direction?

8

Politics: The Program of Deep Freedom

The Idea of an Institutional Program

The idea of the haven and the storm points back to the conception of deep freedom and forward to a program of cumulative institutional change that can implement deep freedom in the circumstances of contemporary societies.

Each part of this program plays a role in helping to arouse and organize the storm while also securing the haven. I present this program in this chapter on four axes. The first axis is the democratization of the market economy, with the reshaping of the relation of the backward parts of production to the advanced parts, of finance to the real economy, and of labor to capital. The second axis is the deepening of democracy: the organization of a high-energy democracy that equips democracy to reshape the established institutional arrangements without requiring crisis (in the form of war or ruin) as the condition of change. High-energy democracy carries out this responsibility by raising the temperature of politics (the level of organized popular engagement in politics), hastening the pace of politics (through the rapid and decisive resolution of impasse), and combining encouragement for decisive initiative by central government with radical devolution of power to parts of the country, or of the society and its economy empowered to try out, on a limited scale, counter-models of the national future. The third axis is the organization of civil society outside the market and the state, partnering with the state in the provision of the public services by which civil society builds itself by building people and their capabilities. The fourth axis is the development of forms of education, of culture, and of consciousness that equip us to live for the future and to move within the present without surrendering to it.

Such a program is not a blueprint; it is trajectory, a succession of steps. The details of the proposals for reconstruction that it may imply at any given moment are circumstantial: an expression of the form that the direction may take at a certain historical moment, in particular societies. And even the account of the direction must bear the weight of history and context—we revise our view of the direction as we move toward it. Nevertheless, what matters most in this as in any programmatic argument are the marking of the direction and the choice of the initial steps in a particular national context and historical moment.

The contrast between moderate and radical proposals amounts to a misunderstanding. We can explore any trajectory worth considering at points relatively close to present arrangements or distant from them. Here I will often prefer to describe alternatives in a form placed at an intermediate distance from the present: neither close nor remote. The reason is simple: the middle distance serves best the goal of conceptual clarification.

In transformative political practice and discourse, however, we have reason to spurn the middle distance. Proposals described at such a distance from the present—neither close nor far away—are likely to seem too remote from the present to be feasible, and yet not remote enough to arouse enthusiasm. For that reason, in politics, we should ordinarily prefer to the middle distance the combination of the proximate and the remote. The discourse of transformative practice must be at once practical and prophetic.

Failure to understand the nature of a programmatic argument and of transformative practice explains the false dilemma that, anywhere in the world today, besets attempts to defy the dictatorship of no alternatives. Proposals of structural alternatives are likely to be dismissed as either trivial or utopian. The source of this false dilemma is the failure to understand that transformations and proposals for them are about sequences of steps, not about static designs.

We can explore and describe each such succession of steps at points relatively close to what exists or relatively far away. What matters in any real change—and in the ideas that evoke it—is always: what comes next? The policies and institutional innovations that we may settle on along the way and in a certain time and place are always at best flawed fragments of a movement in a direction. Many are partial functional equivalents. What matters is the fecundity of the process in generating many of them and their persistence in that direction: a current, a flow, a waterfall. That is the sense of the remark made about Franklin Roosevelt's New Deal: all his programs failed but the New Deal as a whole was a success.

A trajectory of change is always the reverse side of a set of social and political alliances, a combination of interests and ideals. It builds its own constituency. But it does so with the materials provided by its historical circumstance. It must begin with the understanding that people in the different classes and communities of society have of their interests, ideals, and identities—an understanding that pre-supposes the established institutional order and the class and group alliances and animosities that take this order for granted. As this order changes, we discover ambiguities and possibilities of development in our understandings of our interests and ideals that had remained hidden from us before we began to reshape the institutions.

A feature of the history of our thinking about society and history reinforces the mischaracterization of programmatic proposals and of transformative practice from which the false dilemma of the utopian and the trivial results: the suppression of insight into structure and structural change in contemporary social science and its expression but perversion in classical social theory. The most important instance of such perversion is the Marxist idea of regimes as indivisible systems, succeeding one another according to laws of historical change. The failure of such a view of change leaves us with a nonsensical criterion of realism in programmatic proposals: proximity to what exists. This criterion is a declaration of intellectual bankruptcy.

A programmatic argument, like the one outlined in the following sections, must be informed by a view of regimes—of their nature, making, and remaking—free from the illusions that disoriented structural vision in classical social theory and that have suppressed it in contemporary social science. Among the aspects of the view of regimes that bear most immediately on this programmatic agenda, four deserve emphasis.

The first aspect is simply the need for such an agenda. History does not have a project for us. We cannot just ride it in the conviction that it will take us where, for better or worse, we have to go to anyway. Just as the multiplication of constraints does not amount to a project, or to the equivalent of one, so the failure of history to give us a project does not free us from constraints in advancing one. But the way in which we understand these constraints must not be to represent them as the expression of a deep, directional logic of historical change. Such a logic would in effect be a project, condemning to futility whatever direction of change we commit ourselves to.

The second aspect has to do with the way we think about the relation among the parts of a regime and therefore among the elements of a regime-changing program. A regime is not a system: an indivisible whole, standing or falling as a single piece and changing all together or not at all. It follows that we must also avoid viewing a program for regime change as a counter-system. Its elements must broadly support one another. But what matters most is their joint relation to the future: the near-term future of the possibilities that each of them opens up, and the long-term future of the direction that they signify and foreshadow. Of each of them, the first question to ask is how it changes the struggle over the future.

A third aspect goes to the species of qualitative variation among regimes that I earlier described as entrenchment and disentrenchment. Each of the proposed changes must contribute to the denaturalization of the regime: reorganizing its institutions and practices in a way that facilitates its further reorganization, diminishing the dependence of future regime change on crisis as the crutch on which revision must lean. Each must narrow the distance between the ordinary moves we make within an accepted framework and the extraordinary moves by which, pressed by crisis, we remake part of the framework. And each must therefore weaken path dependence.

The rewards are many: the enhancement of our freedom to engage in a social world without surrendering to it and to retain the characters of insiders and outsiders at the same time; the development of our practical powers, beginning with our powers of production, by untying our hands in the recombination of people, machines, and resources; and the accelerated liquifying of rigid forms of social hierarchy and division, thanks to the perpetual destabilization of the arrangements and assumptions on which they depend. The prize we seek is the institutionalized empowerment—political and cultural as well as economic—of the many.

The fourth aspect is the focus on developing the institutions and the social and political alliances required by alternatives to what I earlier described as the path of least resistance: the form that technological and organizational innovations take when they are reduced to the dimensions allowed by accommodation to dominant interests and preconceptions. No contemporary example of the significance of this feature of the agenda is more telling than the contrast between the insular knowledge economy that we have and the knowledge economy for the many that we need.

As this example shows, the obstacles to the advancement of alternatives to the path of least resistance are formidable. What nevertheless counts in their favor is that the confinement of innovations to forms compatible with the compromises imposed by the path of least resistance leaves much of their potential for production, as well as for emancipation, untapped. The task of the agents of transformation is to connect the greater use of that underutilized potential with the power interests of states and the class interests of major parts of society as well as with our larger hopes.

An example of such hopes is the hope of gaining freedom in the economy, not just from the economy. Freedom from the economy would result, as both Marx and Keynes believed, from the overcoming of scarcity—a promise likely to be postponed indefinitely. Freedom in the economy must come from the drawing together of production and imagination. It can arise from the replacement of economically dependent wage labor by the higher forms of free work—self-employment and cooperation against the background of regimes that democratize access to productive resources and opportunities. It can, as well, be a consequence of change in the relation between the worker and the machine so that no one is condemned to do the formulaic and repetitious work that machines should do for us.

Democratizing the Market Economy

The institutional indeterminacy of the market order. A premise of the economic part of the program is that a market economy has no single natural institutional form. The association of the market order with the system of private law—of property, contract, tort (delict), and corporate law—that developed in early modern Europe, on both the common-law and civil-law sides, could not have taken hold if it had failed to shape, and to be shaped by, the interests and practices of the commercial bourgeoisie and the landowning classes. But the legal expression of that market order was not just an adaptation to those interests; it was a unique and surprising invention.

Today the achievement of the most widely professed aim in political economy—socially inclusive economic growth—depends on the reconstitution of the market order, not simply on its regulation or on the attenuation of market-generated inequalities by retrospective and compensatory redistribution. Of the three things that we can do to a market economy: regulate it, soften its inequalities by retrospective redistribution through progressive taxation and redistributive social entitlements, and change it by reshaping its legal-institutional architecture, the third is by far the most important.

All hope of uniting the cause of creative energy and innovation with the requirements for giving the widest possible cast of economic agents a better chance to use the productive resources of society, and thus of achieving in fact the hope of socially inclusive economic growth, depends on such changes. The way we think about the correction of inequality reveals the extent to which we understand the implications of this truth.

The attenuation of inequality by means of after-the-fact redistribution through progressive taxation and redistributive social entitlements faces severe limits. To compensate for the extreme inequalities anchored in the vast divisions between the advanced and the backward parts of production, such retrospective redistribution would have to be massive. Long before it reached the level needed to overcome extreme inequalities, it would begin to unsettle established economic arrangements and incentives and threaten to exact an unacceptable cost in economic output. Conventional discourse about a tension between equity and efficiency is the most familiar rhetorical expression of the idea that this clash is unavoidable. However, it is not unavoidable. We can have less inequality, not as a step toward equality of outcome and circumstance as an end in itself, but as a condition for our advance toward deep freedom. Overcoming extreme inequality, as part of a broad-based empowerment that has socially inclusive economic growth as one of its consequences, can happen only through structural change: change in the institutional arrangements, including the arrangements of the market order, that shape the primary distribution of economic and educational advantage and opportunity. Compensatory and retrospective redistribution through tax-and-transfer will continue to be important. Its main role, however, is not the direct moderation of inequality, which results chiefly from structural change. It is to invest in people and their capabilities and to equalize by empowering. It is to help provide the agent with the haven that he needs to move, capably and unafraid, in the storm.

Advanced and backward parts of production: a knowledge economy for the many. The first major theme of a program to democratize the market economy and unite the causes of innovation and inclusion has to do with the relation between vanguards and rearguards, between the advanced and the backward parts of the production system.

That relation and its consequences now appear in the form of a problem: the insularity of today's vanguard of production, the knowledge economy—the experimentalist part of the production system, dense in science and technology and devoted to perpetual innovation. What makes it the most advanced part of the production system is that it is the most mindful, the one that most fully reveals our powers at the level they have now reached in the evolution of humanity. Because it is the part of production that best exemplifies the transformative powers of the imagination, including the power to change its own practices, it has the greatest potential to inspire transformation and to lead the way for the whole economy. This potential remains suppressed, with significant consequences for the cause of deep freedom.

The knowledge economy appears in every sector of production in all the major economies of the world as a fringe from which the vast majority of businesses and workers remain excluded. One consequence of this insularity is economic slowdown: by denying the most advanced practice of production to the many—workers and businesses—and by doing so in a circumstance in which the previous most advanced practice, industrial mass production, is in decline, we create reasons for stagnation when innovation seemed to herald broad-based growth. Another consequence is the aggravation of economic inequality: the deepening chasm between the advanced parts of production and the rest of the economy generates inequalities for which retrospective redistribution cannot compensate adequately without unacceptable cost and disruption.

The knowledge economy holds the promise of relaxing or even reversing what has been the most constant and universal constraint in economic life: diminishing marginal returns. It can achieve this effect by rendering innovation internal to production and perpetual rather than episodic. It brings imagination and production closer together: discovery and experimentalism are the touchstone of its method. And it requires a change in the moral culture of production: replacing the generalization of a modicum of low trust among strangers, under a system of command and control, by a heightening of the level of reciprocal trust and of discretionary initiative required and demanded of all participants in production.

In its present, quarantined form, the knowledge economy has failed to fulfill this many-sided promise. A practice of production deepens only as it spreads. In this insular form, perversion replaces promise. Production is severed into two parts: one, creative, confined to a small cadre of entrepreneurs and technologists; the other, routinized and subcontracted to relatively backward businesses around the world. A stable labor force, brought together in large productive units, gives way to a new "putting-out system" working under precarious employment contracts on a global scale.

The deepening and dissemination of the knowledge economy must satisfy educational, social-moral, and legal-institutional requirements. It demands a form of both general and technical education that turns ordinary men and women into discoverers and experimentalists. The essence of such an education, both theoretically and practically, is to associate insight with transformative capability. It must recognize that we deepen insight into the actual by broadening our imagination of the adjacent possible, and that we enhance our practical capabilities by detaching them from machine-specific and job-specific skills.

The change in the moral culture of production necessary to a deepened and disseminated knowledge economy requires the accumulation of social capital: density and diversity in the forms of association, achieved through the multiplication of forms of collective action, outside as well as within the market economy and democratic politics. As with all the requirements of a knowledge economy— educational and institutional as well as moral and social—we would never fulfill these conditions if our only motivation to do so were economic. The force driving such change must come from the all the practical and moral interests underlying the agenda of deep freedom.

The most complex and exacting requirements regard the legal-institutional architecture of the market economy. Imagine three moments in the transformation of this architecture. In the first moment, the aim must be to organize access to the resources and opportunities of production in favor of entrepreneurs, workers, and businesses from the rest of the economy: its backward periphery. That means making more advanced practice and technology available in a form that suits the ability of the rearguard and its firms to deploy them. It also means identifying what works best, by way of the practice of production, the better to disseminate it.

In the second moment, a new institutional form of the market economy can begin to emerge out of these capability-enhancing and opportunity-expanding arrangements. On the vertical axis, of relations between governments and businesses, such arrangements would organize a decentralized and pluralistic partnership between firms and government-supported organizations, with the goal of elevating the quality of a country's productive apparatus. On the horizontal axis, of relations among businesses, it would favor cooperative competition among firms: they cooperate in particular ways and areas to achieve economies of scale and scope, while competing against one another.

Such innovations demand changes in private as well as public law: an administrative law allowing the state to act experimentally; a contract law that gives a central role to ongoing relational contracts that are never the fully articulated bargains of classical contract law; and a property law that treats the unified property right of the nineteenth century as only one of several ways to organize decentralized access to the means of production. Alongside these legal developments, there should spring up derivatives of the property right —fragmentary, conditional, and temporary claims on productive resources and opportunities.

These disaggregated forms of property would make it possible for different types of right holders—workers, local governments and communities, representatives of civil society as well as investors—to hold variably shaped claims on the same productive resources. As a consequence, they would allow us to increase the absolute level of economic decentralization—the number of economic agents able to bargain on their own initiative and for their own account—at the cost (if it is a cost) of qualifying the degree and time horizon of the control that each of those right holders enjoys over the means of production to which their claims refer.

These necessary innovations in private and public law herald a third moment in the reconstruction of the market order that would bring production and imagination closer together throughout the economy and lay a major part of the basis for socially inclusive economic growth. They presage a market economy that is no longer fastened to a single dogmatic version of itself. In the distant future of the economy, the major means of production should be held in trust for society. Both as liquid capital and as technology, the means of production can be vested in independent public trusts. These trusts would run what is in effect an ongoing capital auction: they would loan out these means of production to whatever teams of entrepreneurs and technologists are able to assure the trusts of the highest return for the assets over a certain period.

Such trusts would be managed professionally and independently from the government, which would enjoy no powers of discretionary allocation with respect to them. The underlying rate of interest—the aggregate price for the use of the means of production—would replace taxation as the main source of public finance. Instead of shaping directly the allocation of productive resources, the representative democratic institutions would, from time to time, make adjustments to the legal and institutional framework within which the capital auction operates.

If we did not mind the social-theoretical objections to the use of Marx's concept of capitalism (as a supposedly indivisible system, belonging to the list of modes of production, and the product of irresistible laws of historical development, exhibiting lawlike regularities of its own), we could call the resulting economic arrangement capitalism without capitalists.

The present market economy, defined most clearly by the inherited body of private law, is supposed to be such a system, were it not for localized failures of competition or localized regulatory failures in the response to these localized competitive flaws. After all, a perfectly competitive capital market is supposed to allocate resources to their most productive uses and users, regardless of the distributive consequence of the way asset endowments are initially settled on some owners rather than others. What the theoreticians and ideologists of the market economy mistakenly imagine to be our possession (to the extent that perfect market competition holds)—that the market order assigns resources to its most productive users—is in fact our task, to be achieved only through a long struggle of ideas and of social forces.

Under what conditions are these three sets of requirements of a knowledge economy for the many—the educational, the social, and the institutional—more likely to be satisfied? There are two conditions that take precedence over all others. The first condition is the creation of a high-energy democracy, fertile in the power to generate revolutionary reforms (those that change the institutions in piecemeal but cumulative fashion) and no longer reliant on crisis as the indispensable enabler of change. The second condition is the radicalization of the experimentalist impulse and of transformative ambition in every department of social and cultural life. Both conditions form subjects of later parts of this programmatic argument: a program for the realization of deep freedom and for the arousal of the storm that, together with the haven, holds the promise of our liberation.

Finance and the real economy. A second major focus for the democratization of the economic order is the transformation of the relation of finance to the real economy—and, especially, to production.

It was a shared assumption of much of conventional economic thinking as well as of Marxism that the most powerful constraint on economic growth is the size of the surplus over current consumption. In the money-based economies that accompanied the economic history of civilization, that surplus chiefly took the form of liquid capital. In fact, once we get beyond the most primitive stages of economic accumulation, the chief constraints on economic growth become the level and pace of innovation and the terms on which we cooperate.

The relation between cooperation and innovation is crucial, and especially the extent to which the social division of labor—or the nature of our cooperative regime, the institutional framework of cooperation—is friendly to innovation in all its forms: technological, organizational, institutional, and conceptual. This relation of our innovative practices to our cooperative regime in turn determines the opportunities for both social and private gain. Private law in general, and the property regime in particular, have special importance in determining the extent to which the opportunities for private gain will be aligned with the opportunities for social gain.

What is the role that finance plays in this narrative? The surplus over current consumption, held as liquid capital, is not itself the overriding constraint on growth, when compared to the pace and nature of innovation and the nature of the cooperative regime. But it can play a role that strengthens or weakens, feeds or starves, the marriage of cooperation and innovation on which economic growth chiefly depends. Finance can be dangerous or useful. To make it less dangerous, we must make it more useful.

The best way to develop a view of finance in a reconstructed market order is to elucidate the enigmas of its role in the present order. A first enigma has to do with its relative uselessness. Under the present arrangements, production remains largely financed by the production system itself, through reliance on the retained and reinvested earnings of private firms. What then is the point of all the liquid capital held in the banks and the stock markets? Theoretically it is to finance the productive agenda of society. But external finance has, for the most part, only an oblique or episodic relation to the funding of production.

A second enigma regards the asymmetry of the relation of finance to the real economy. Finance is largely indifferent to the real economy in good times and becomes destructive in bad times. Financial volatility and crisis spill over the limits of its own domain and threaten real activity.

A third enigma takes the form of an apparent paradox. The most important responsibility of finance—funding the creation of new assets in new ways—accounts for a miniscule portion of financial activity. Even if we interpret venture capital and its associated forms of finance expansively and look at the few economies (the United States, Israel) where it is most developed, it represents but a sliver of what occupies finance.

All three enigmas have the same source: the tenuous and relatively distant relation of finance to the real economy and consequently to production. According to the still dominant ideas in economics, a perfectly competitive capital market allocates capital to its most efficient uses. To the extent that the capital market fails to achieve such an allocation, its omission must be due to a localized failure of competition in that market or to a localized flaw in the regulatory response to the market failure. That premise is simply an instance of the more general idea that a market economy has a single natural and necessary legal-institutional form.

To solve these puzzles of finance, we need to place them in the context of a broader view of breakdown and crisis in the economy. The fundamental source of economic instability is the failure of breakthroughs on the supply side of the economy automatically to ensure corresponding breakthroughs on the demand side, and vice versa. Keynes's view of this failure of spontaneous correspondence between demand and supply, although labeled a general theory, was in fact the theory of a special case: one in which "Say's law" that supply creates its own demands failed to hold, and the downward rigidity of a particular price—the price of labor—aggravated the insufficiency of aggregate demand.

Henry Ford said that he liked to pay his workers so they could buy his cars. His quip supposed there to be a contractual solution to a problem that can be solved only institutionally. The most important part of the solution is that a major part of the labor force be able to share in the work and the rewards of the most advanced practice of production. If they share in the rewards without sharing in the work, their hold on that share will always be precarious and likely to be cut down. And they will be denied the experience of creative freedom and capability that sharing in the work of the most mindful part of production can bring.

The subsidiary source of economic instability and of the breakdown of economic growth is the unstable relation between finance and the real economy. Writing in the psychologically oriented tradition of English political economy, Keynes emphasized how the liquidity of capital allows it to bear the imprint of our humors: our vacillations of greed and fear, elation and despondency. This aspect of finance is, however, only a sideshow to the principal reason for which it can cause instability and crisis in the real economy as well as in the capital markets: the variable relation between finance and the real economy.

That relation can be made deeper or narrower. Finance may consume a larger part of profits and talents without deepening. To this bloating of finance without corresponding service to the productive agenda of society we can give the name financial hypertrophy. Financial hypertrophy is the most powerful explanation of the three enigmas that I have described.

All three enigmas result from the relative detachment of finance from the real economy. And all three can be solved, in practice as well as in theory, by arrangements that tighten the link between finance and the real economy. This crucial variation in the relation of finance to the real economy represents a species of institutional variation in any aspect of the market order.

The initial step, if we are to enlist finance more effectively in the service of the productive agenda of society, is to embed it more fully in the real economy, tightening its links to production. We can achieve this goal by a combination of negative and positive initiatives.

The negative initiatives would discourage or even forbid financial activity that lacks a colorable relation to the growth of output or of productivity. For example, calls and puts, and similar financial derivatives (derivatives of the unified property right), performed a legitimate role in commodity markets by assuring liquidity. In equity markets, however, they usually lack this justification. Originally designed as safeguards against risk, they have been largely converted in the equity markets into devices of gambling.

Our aim should not be to suppress the speculative element in finance. Financial speculation develops information and organizes the allocation of risk. The problem lies in the detachment of financial speculation from the interests and opportunities of production.

The affirmative means by which to tighten the relation of finance to the real economy include all initiatives that multiply channels between saving and productive investment, especially investment in producing new assets in new ways. These may include any effort by government to mimic the undone work of venture capital, for example by creating diversified portfolios of the assets held in the public pension systems of the world and placing them in independent funds under professional management.

Such negative and affirmative initiatives represent initial steps in a long trajectory. What lies further ahead on that path is the same capital auction—the capitalism without capitalists—that I evoked in the previous description of the legal-institutional requirements for the deepening and dissemination of the most advanced practice of production. What the established ideas about the capital markets, as about the market order in general, misrepresent as what the capital markets and the market already do (subject to the limitations imposed by imperfect competition) must be in fact the outcome of a long struggle over the institutional arrangements of the market economy.

∽

Labor and capital. A third focus of the democratization of the market order is change in the relation of labor to capital. In a program designed to deepen freedom, the overriding goal, with respect to that relation, must be to assure that free labor is free in fact. In approaching this goal, we should first remember that economically coerced wage labor is only one of several forms of free work, and a form that well into the nineteenth century liberals and socialists alike regarded as inferior to the higher varieties of free work: self-employment and cooperation. Unlike the latter, they believed, wage labor was a defective and transitional form of free labor, retaining some of the features of serfdom and slavery. However, they were never able to solve the problem of how those higher types of free work might be made compatible with the aggregation of resources, including labor resources, at the scale demanded by a complex economy capable of rapid and sustained growth.

The large question of the freedom of free labor and of how it is to be achieved in a form compatible with high, sustained, broad-based economic growth in turns bears on the hope of achieving freedom in the economy, not simply from the economy. Contrary to what Marx, Keynes, and many others supposed, we are not close to overcoming scarcity, nor are we likely to be at any time in the near future. Scarcity endlessly reappears in new forms. But contrary to what they also believed, work need not be a hateful burden to cast off as soon as the overcoming of scarcity allows us to do so. It can be an instrument of our individual and collective self-construction: in seeking to change the world we change ourselves.

After the disappearance of the ancient Indo-European paradigm of three main classes or castes—the priests and thinkers, the rulers and fighters, and the workers, corresponding to a hierarchy of faculties in the soul—there have been three main ideas of work in the West. One is the idea of work as an honorable calling: the fulfillment of a social role that accords respect and self-respect as well as allowing the worker to sustain himself and his family. This view of work loses its basis when the practice of production begins to undermine the distinctions among trades and among professions (except, if at all, among the elite liberal professions) and when romanticism and democracy arouse higher ambition.

Another is the instrumental idea of work. Work loses all redemptive value and serves only to create the material means to pursue, in the family and in the private sublime, that which alone can leave us spellbound.

A third is the idea of work as a transformative vocation: we change ourselves by changing the world around us and by turning imagination into innovation and creation. Up to now, the transformative vocation has been the prerogative of a tiny elite—of talent, privilege, and luck, an elite rich in the most important resource, time. But now the convergence of imagination with the most advanced practice of production justifies the hope that the workday experiences of common humanity may share in this higher conception of the value of work.

The path toward an economy built on free labor begins in dealing with two pressing issues: the relation of the evolution of technology to joblessness as well as to the nature of work, and the situation of the growing part of the labor force throughout the world that finds itself in informal, precarious, or otherwise unstable employment.

The complex technologies that form a practice of production always have multiple possibilities of development. The form that prevails is decisively shaped by the established economic order and by the incentives and disincentives that it generates, against the background of the distribution of rights and powers in that order and of its assumptions about the social and technical division labor. Machine design and technological evolution express this hidden reality. But the evolution of technology, based on science, has no built-in direction, no autonomous logic. Its social expressions are always underdetermined. It is we who give it a direction. In most historical circumstances it takes the direction shaped by the constraints and incentives that the established arrangements and the path of least resistance support.

Today's most important technologies have evolved, and can continue to develop, in ways that emphasize either the substitution or the enhancement of labor and that combine labor substitution with labor enhancement in different ways. The precise form and effect of this combination are what matter. In each historical moment there will be types of labor that are relatively more, and others that are relatively less, formulaic and routinized.

What we should desire is that over time machines come to replace the most repetitious work and to enhance relatively less repetitious labor. It is in our interest that the substitution of labor by technology and the enhancement of labor productivity by technology operate as coeval and complementary principles. What was once non-formulaic over time becomes formulaic, and what was once impossible becomes possible as new and relatively non-formulaic production.

But this happy coexistence, by virtue of which there is continuous movement from one side of the ledger of production to the other—from the side of perpetual innovation and experimentalism to the side of what can be expressed in algorithms and rendered automatic—does not happen spontaneously. Like the larger storm that we seek to arouse for the sake of deep freedom, the coexistence of these two ways in which technology should relate to labor—replacing and enhancing it at the same time, but in different parts of the production system and the labor market—needs to be organized. We need to organize it socially, culturally, and politically as well as technically. It will not happen of its own accord. What will happen of its own accord is simply whatever suits the interests of those who exercise a preponderant influence over the allocation of capital and the content of the laws.

It must be an objective of public policy to make it happen and to shape the evolution of technology, especially technologies applicable across a broad range of sectors, in this direction. The most obvious context in which to develop such initiatives is the uplift of the immense productive rearguard of the economy, discussed earlier in this section. That uplift requires the development of the technologies and the mastery of the capabilities that we need to replace labor in some instances and to enhance it in others. A key feature of such initiatives, early in the effort at uplift, must be the coordination of access to technology, advanced practice, and capital. Any one of them, unaccompanied by the other two, means little.

The other pressing issue regarding the status of labor has to do with the expansion of all forms of precarious employment: informal or "non-registered" labor in the disorganized and illegal parts of the labor market, especially prominent in emerging economies; and precarious employment in the organized, legal labor market. The growth of this "precariat" is one of the many consequences of the substitution of mass production by the insular knowledge economy as the productive vanguard.

The recruitment of a stable force to work in large productive units such as factories, under the aegis of big businesses, had its heyday from the middle of the nineteenth century to the middle of the twentieth. It provided the most important basis for what came to be regarded as the natural forms of the defense of labor: collective bargaining and "countervailing power" in the parts of the world that adopted contractualist labor-law regimes, in contrast to the automatic unionization of the entire labor force, under a combination of sectoral and territorial principles, in the remainder of the world (e.g., Latin America), which embraced a corporatist labor-law regime.

These ways of arranging production and representing workers were preceded in the West by several centuries during which work was organized through decentralized contractual arrangements. Such was, for example, the "putting-out system," under which the capitalist provided the machines and the material and the worker worked at home with family and friends. Now we witness the appearance of a new putting-out system on a global scale.

Two discourses about this change in the situation of workers prevail in the world. A neoliberal discourse proposes to deliver the majority of the labor force to radical economic insecurity disguised by the euphemism of flexibility. There can be no sustained and inclusive dynamic of rising productivity against the background of such generalized insecurity and of the downward tilt in the returns to labor that it generates. A corporativist-syndicalist discourse representing the short-term interests of the organized minority of the labor force and the ideas of their leadership wants to ban all forms of employment that fall outside the boundaries of the employment practices characteristic of the world of mass production as attacks on worker rights. But relations of production that result from the emerging practices of production cannot be abolished by decree. The attempt to suppress them without creating ways to protect and empower the precariat can benefit only the organized minority of workers to the detriment of the disorganized majority.

The solutions of the twentieth century—countervailing power in its older form—do not suffice to deal with the problems of the twenty-first century. We need a new body of labor law to represent, organize, and protect labor rendered under conditions of unstable or temporary employment. A sliding scale applies. The more we succeed in organizing and representing such workers, the less there is need for direct protective intervention in the employment relation. But the less we are able to organize and represent these workers, using contemporary forms of communication, the greater the need for the law to protect them.

For example, the law can institute a principle of price neutrality, to be developed by a jurisprudence informed about the realities of work and wages in different parts of the labor market. Under such a principle, work performed under conditions of unstable employment would have to be remunerated on terms comparable to similar labor rendered under conditions of stable employment. In this way, we can develop arrangements that distinguish the beneficial flexibility of labor from its dangerous cheapening—dangerous because subversive of a sustained and broad-based rise in the productivity of labor and in the life chances of workers.

These two sets of initiatives—about the relation, in the near term, between technology and work, and about the relation between stable and unstable employment—represent parts of a passage to an economy in which free labor would be free in fact and we could aspire to freedom in the economy rather than just from it. I now address three connected elements of this more distant future: the relation of the worker to the machine; the relation of the lower form of free labor (economically dependent wage work) to the higher forms (self-employment and cooperation); and the ways in which transformations in both these relations depend on changes in the property regime and consequently in the legal and institutional architecture of the market economy.

Under earlier advanced productive practices, including industrial mass production, the worker worked as if he were one of his machines. His repetitious movements both complemented and mimicked the movements of the machine. So it happened, for example, in Adam Smith's pin factory and Henry Ford's assembly line. Under such an arrangement, however, the potential of technology to enhance the productivity of labor and make free work more truly free remained suppressed. Under today's most advanced practice of production and its characteristic technologies, the treatment of the worker as a quasi-machine increases the gap between what technological innovation can do for labor and what it actually does.

Everything that we have learned to repeat we can express in a formula or an algorithm. Everything that we can express formulaically or algorithmically we can embody in a physical device. From this perspective, the point of the machine is do for us whatever we have learned how to repeat so that we can preserve our most important (and in a sense our only) resource—our time—for the not yet repeatable.

Machines that we have already built may be able to advance directly from complex data to operational capabilities, such as translation from one natural language to another, without passing through the intermediate level of codified rules of inference. Similarly, we may build into them a stochastic faculty: the power to recombine complex data and reach surprising and useful results. In these ways, they may cease to be purely formulaic or algorithmic. They have achieved a level of computational power far beyond the level possessed by the unassisted human mind.

We may be able to design these high-order devices in ways that mimic our power of recursive infinity—our ability to recombine everything with everything else and, by one route or another, to skip over the explication of rules of inference. What is certain, however, is that they lack our highest power: imagination. It is by the exercise of imagination that we can grasp the actual from the vantage point of the accessible possible, make discoveries that are senseless on the basis of our present presuppositions and methods, and formulate retrospectively the presuppositions and methods that make sense of what we have discovered.

No one should be condemned by economic necessity to do work that a machine can do. To require a human being to do such repetitious and formulaic work is to deny, in the relation between the worker and the machine, the humanity-defining attribute of transcendence. A human being is an anti-machine.

Where technology can serve both the productivity and the emancipation of labor, rather than substituting for labor, this is the principle that should guide its use. It is, however, a principle unlikely to prevail so long as economically dependent wage labor remains the predominant species of free work in a society in which a small minority owns the means of production, or controls it in the interests of major owners, even when institutional ownership—for example, through pension funds—may be widespread. Such necessity-driven wage labor should give way, as nineteenth-century liberals and socialists argued, to the higher forms of free work: self-employment and cooperation, combined. In a free economy, independent economic agents join to achieve economies of scale without being driven to sell their labor.

It was only relatively late in the nineteenth century that the predominance of wage labor among the forms of free work came to seem natural and necessary. But the advocates of the higher forms of free labor were never able to show how the predominance of self-employment and cooperation can be reconciled with the requirements for the aggregation of resources, including labor resources, at scale.

The paradoxes of attempts to organize production on the basis of cooperatively organized worker-owned business reveal the essential problem. Suppose we imagine the modal unit of an alternative economy to be a cooperative of workers who are also owners of their firms. We represent ownership on the model of the traditional unified property rights, bringing all the constituent powers of property together and vesting them in the same owner—either the individual workers or the collective workforce. This is no mere conjecture: the Yugoslav system of the second half of the twentieth century showed what then happens.

That system came to grief on the same dilemmas that the nineteenth-century champions of the higher forms of free labor were unable to solve. Should the most successful individual workers or collective labor units be allowed to buy other units out, and the least successful or motivated ones to sell out? In that case, there will be a dynamic of accumulation and inequality. Eventually a distinction will arise between two classes of workers: worker-owners (individuals or collectives) and propertyless workers.

Or should there be rigid restraints on accumulation and alienation or a mechanism of corrective redistribution to cancel out the effects of such economic concentration whenever they go beyond strict, preestablished limits? Such a practice would not be palliative compensatory redistribution of the kind made familiar under institutionally conservative social democracy or social liberalism. It would rather be the outcome-oriented major redistribution that I described as the program of deep equality—envisioned there and embraced nowhere. It is embraced nowhere because it requires a degree not just of economic loss but also more generally of restraint on economic and social innovation, diversity, and experiment that no advanced society has been, or should be, willing to accept for long.

The only way in which we could solve the dilemmas that the doctrines of the nineteenth century and the experiments of the twentieth left unsolved is by innovations in the property regime and more generally in the legal and institutional form of the market economy. They are the innovations that I invoked at the end of the earlier discussions of change in the relation of the backward to the advanced parts of production and of finance to capital. We would need to develop, alongside the traditional unified property right, conditional, fragmentary, and temporary forms of rights with the aim of giving a much broader cast of economic agents wider access to productive resources and opportunities. In doing so, however, we also need to qualify the absolute and perpetual character of the power that each of those agents exercise over the resources that such rights would allow them to access and to use. In this way we would innovate in the legal constitution of the market rather than limiting ourselves to regulating it or attenuating its inequalities retrospectively through tax and transfer. The distant but direction-defining goal would be the ongoing capital auction—the "capitalism" without "capitalists"—that I earlier sketched.

Innovations in the property right stand, by synecdoche, for all the institutional transformations—in the relation of the backward parts of production to the advanced parts and of finance to the real economy, as well as of labor to capital—that would save the market from remaining fastened to a single dogmatic version of itself. Such changes—the theme of all the proposals in this section—would base a tilt to inclusive empowerment in the institutional foundations of the market order and give practical consequence to the ideal of socially inclusive economic growth.

The agenda of deep freedom—the effort to arouse the storm outside the haven, the reinterpretation of the division between Left and Right as a contest over whether it is natural for human life, the lives of ordinary men and women, to be small and whether we should take the established institutional forms of economic, political, and social pluralism as the unsurpassable horizon of our initiatives—must here become the remaking and reinvention of a free economy.

Deepening Democracy

Points of departure: the freedom of the moderns and the inevitability of representative institutions. The reconstruction of democracy enjoys a special status in this programmatic argument. In one sense, it deals with a domain of institutional change alongside others. The deepening of democracy is the political counterpart to the democratization of the market order. In another sense, however, it differs from all other parts of this proposal and has a certain priority over them: the way in which we organize politics sets the basic terms for making laws and thus for determining the basic limits and procedures of change in every part of social life. That would be true, in a society with a state, even if the struggle over the mastery and uses of governmental power made no pretense to be democratic. It is here that we determine, in the most comprehensive and decisive way, how the future is to be made and become law.

The starting points of my discussion are the two ideas by which, in the previous chapter, I situated my political argument in relation to two formative contrasts in the history of political thought. First, I took the position of the "modern republic" against the ancient one in Benjamin Constant's antithesis. The protagonist is the real agent, immersed in the cares of private life and in the concerns of the groups to which he belongs, not the imaginary selfless citizen for whom civic life and the affairs and defense of the state stand at the center of existence. If the scope of that real agent's concerns is to broaden, and the distance between the moves we make within the framework of the regime and the moves by which we change the regime is to narrow, this broadening and this narrowing must begin with that real agent, such as he is, in the real and resistant social world that he inhabits.

Second, I accepted as a point of departure for thinking about the institutional arrangements of democracy the very limited repertoire of live options for the organization of democratic politics that we find in the contemporary societies. And I rejected, as misunderstandings and failures, the occasional attempts, in revolutionary moments and movements, to jump out of the confines of representative democracy into a direct, participatory politics, of popular councils, even in large countries with complex economies and societies.

But to say that I take the highly restricted range of available institutional alternatives as a point of departure is not to say that I take it as a point of arrival. We can serve the purposes of deep freedom, arouse the storm that complements the haven, and reconcile our stake in the development of our practical powers of production with our interest in emancipation from entrenched social hierarchy and divisions only by innovating in the institutional arrangements of democratic politics. Once we have traveled in this direction for a certain distance, the hope of enhancing, rather than of replacing, representative democracy with elements of direct, participatory democracy returns with greater clarity and purchase on reality.

Weak and strong democracy. All the democracies that have existed up to now are weak, low-energy democracies. They are deficient by the standard of representing the political instrument of a movement toward deep freedom. These weak democracies are weak in several connected senses. We can define the strong, high-energy democracies that the project of deep freedom requires by contrast to them.

First, they are weak because they fail to realize in practice the idea, which even a conventional, minimalist conception of democracy accepts, that under democracy the terms of social life—the way things are—must result from collective choice. They must not be imposed, involuntarily and even unknowingly, by a part of society that holds the decisive power in the state or by the blind force of custom.

A criterion of whether a democracy meets this minimalist test is the nature of the laws. The laws of a democracy that meets this minimalist standard must not resemble, in this respect, the relation between the *jurisdictio* and the *gubernaculum* in medieval European society. Law was then and there announced and elaborated in two different ways, characteristic of pre-democratic states.

As *jurisdictio*, it was the elaboration of a common law that described, especially through private law, the way things are, or were. Nobody was supposed to have made such law, though the jurists were its custodians. It carried well into relatively recent centuries the idea of a natural form of social life, slowly refined—or worked pure in Lord Mansfield's phrase—by a long dialectic of collective custom and legal reflection. Its expression as method was, and remains, the idea of legal doctrine or of legal dogmatics.

As *gubernaculum*, the law was made by the edicts of the prince, whose responsibility was to deal with the urgent and circumstantial matters that the common law left unaddressed, or at most to adapt the common law (the *ius commune* of the civilian tradition) to changing circumstances. As such it consisted in a series of episodic and localized interventions in the otherwise unchanged way things are, made explicit, as customary order, purified by doctrine, in the common law.

In the conventional, minimalist conception of law under democracy as the outcome of collective decision according to constitutional procedures that enshrine majority rule, subject to minority rights, the law should be neither of these two: neither *jurisdictio* nor *gubernaculum*. Yet it seems that to a large extent it is the *gubernaculum*: a series of episodic and localized interventions in the way things are. And if that equation of the law with the *gubernaculum* fails to account for all of what the law is, that may be because the idea of an unchosen common law, describing the way things are, survives residually, as a ghost, in the basic institutions of private law, especially as it continues to be decanted by jurists and judges by the methods of legal doctrine or dogmatics.

The large question that stands behind these observations about the metamorphoses of law is the relation of the law—the instrument by which democracy should do its transformative work—to the way things are: the dumb, unjustified, unchosen, and even unseen structure of society. If the actual law of the existing democracies takes this structure for granted and intervenes in it only occasionally and in fragmentary form, democracy will be weak. It will be weak in its most important attribute, of mastering and remaking the structure: rejecting it as fate and recreating it as artifact.

It is possible to object by a lawyer's argument. If the democracy fails to change the structure, the ways things are, beyond such localized and episodic interventions, that failure must occur, the objection would go, because the majority has chosen to make its own what custom and tradition have bequeathed to it. *Qui tacet consentire videtur*—he who remains silent is thought to consent, St. Thomas More reminded his tormentors when he was trying to escape the gallows without renouncing his faith. It is a vain objection, which adorns unthinking submission to history and fate with a pretense of choice and commitment.

By contrast, a strong, high-energy democracy would be one fertile in its ability to conceive and bring about structural change. Rather than bowing down to fate and custom, it would be forever reckoning with the constraints that the established regime places on the development of our powers and the range of our experience. Its commitment would be not to perpetual change but to change chosen in the light of experience, deliberation, and regulated conflict.

A second, related criterion by which to distinguish weak and strong democracy has to do with the relation of structural change to crisis. In a weak democracy, structural change does not come naturally. It needs crisis to make it possible. The two characteristic forms of such structure-enabling crisis are ruin and war. If the impulse to structural change, especially change in the institutional arrangements and in the ideological assumptions associated with them, is not endogenous to the regime, a shock external to the routines of social life must provoke it and make it appear to be unavoidable. Transformation must come, when it comes, as the dangerous gift of trauma.

This second criterion by which to distinguish weak from strong democracy in turn leads into a third. Under weak democracy the dead rule the living. The dead rulers may be certain dead people: especially the architects of a regime and its written constitution. Their rule over the living may rely on the idea that the regime was a once-and-for all invention, inspired and matchless, by an individual or a collective Lycurgus. But then what was once an invention must later be turned into a tradition, at least until some terrible ordeal of the republic requires the achievement of the architect or architects of the republic to be reenacted, usually at a lesser scale.

More often, however, the dead who rule will not be, and never were, named dead people. For when they were alive, they too were ruled by the dead: the nameless dead who could contribute to a collective practice because they submitted to it and who did their work more effectively because they could not grasp its meaning. That meaning would become manifest to their successors: the temporarily living whom they, the unknowing dead, rule.

By contrast, under strong, high-energy democracy the living rule themselves and obey Christ's command to let the dead bury the dead. They do not deny the power of history both to constrain and to equip. They recognize that they must build with the materials at hand, in their own history as well as in the histories of all the peoples of the world. But they also know that prophecy counts for more than memory.

The living see democracy as more than the rule of the majority qualified by the rights of minorities, beginning with political minorities. They see it as the perpetual creation of the new in the service of the development of our practical powers and of our advance toward deep freedom. We can never hope to take any regime as our definitive political home, any more than we can find any situation in our existence that would allow us to say: here we can rest; we need look no further. Forever denied such a definitive political home, we must search for the next best arrangement: a regime that equips us to revise it in the light of our experience and of our epiphanies and prophecies. In such a way we seek to develop a political life that can do justice to both our finitude and our transcendence.

In this spirit, I now describe four sets of institutional changes that would mark a movement toward strong, high-energy democracy. As with my discussion of institutional changes needed to democratize the market order, they are not in any order of temporal or causal priority, except that the fourth—the enrichment of representative democracy by traits of direct, participatory democracy—presupposes that we have already gone some distance in the achievement of the other three. I explore each of them with an emphasis on the middle distance from the present: neither very close to established institutions nor very distant from them, in my previously stated conviction that the middle distance lends itself best to conceptual clarification, my primary concern here. What my argument consequently lacks is the combination of the immediate and the remote, of the practical and the prophetic, that we most require in transformative practice and discourse.

Each one of the four sets of proposals draws on examples or anticipations in contemporary experience and debate. It is only when taken together, as markers of a turn in our goals as well as in our institutions, that they may seem to describe a steep climb to an unfamiliar mountaintop.

By the same token, the four sets of institutional arrangements marking this direction support one another without, however, constituting a system. The idea of structure, not system, important to the theory of regimes and of regime change outlined in Chapter 7, teaches us to appreciate the logic of combined and uneven development: we can move forward with some of the changes before advancing others. At some point, we will find that what we have failed to change inhibits further movement in what we have changed.

Even more important than the direct relation, of constraint or opportunity, of each part of this agenda to the others is success or failure in creating over time the constituencies that will support it because they have come to see their interests and identities as well as their ideals in its light. The deepening of democracy, like the democratization of the market, is about the enhancement of individual and collective agency and thus ultimately about the vitality of both the individual and the group—from close communities to whole nations.

In the circumstances of a wide range of contemporary societies and cultures, commitment to the enhancement of agency implies that the citizens of a high-energy democracy begin to view themselves as doers and makers, with increasing powers, more than as either victims or beneficiaries. They cannot be empowered as isolated individuals. They can become bigger, and live larger lives, only by becoming greater together. The institutional form of this shared ascent is the recurrent theme of this path of regime change—in politics, as well as in the economy, civil society, and education.

Raising the temperature of democratic politics. A first set of institutional changes has to do with the temperature of politics: the level of political mobilization or of organized popular engagement in political life. One of the senses in which the democracies that have existed up to now are weak is that they are cold: they are organized to favor a relatively low level of popular engagement in political life. They heat up—with more popular engagement, on and off the streets—when the established form of politics has failed to deal with emerging structural problems.

An example of such problems is the inadequacy of money transfers arranged by the state to ensure social cohesion in societies that can no longer rely on a high degree of ethnic and cultural homogeneity to ensure that cohesion. It is not enough for the wound to be open. Some force and leadership must place their hands on the wound, as authoritarian, ethno-nationalist right-wing populism has recently done in many countries. It is one thing, however, to arouse agitation that the established political institutions fail to channel. It is another thing to change these institutions in a way that results in a lasting elevation of the temperature of democratic politics, not simply in ephemeral waves of discontent and disillusionment. A leader or a party may rise to power on such a wave, but no society will be changed by it unless and until what began as a negation of the way things are leaves a lasting institutional legacy.

A premise of conservative political science and statecraft is that political institutionalization and political mobilization are inversely related. Politics must in the end be either cold and institutional or hot and anti- or extra-institutional. Hot anti- or extra-institutional politics is what we call Caesarism because its real career has depended on leaders who arouse the discontented mass, which would otherwise lack direction, or profit from its arousal. In the end, according to this conceit, we must choose between Madison and Mussolini.

What this thesis denies is what even the limited variations of comparative and historical experience show: one of the most important ways in which political institutions vary is in their receptiveness and encouragement to political mobilization. It is by an extension of this historical variability that we can conceive the project of developing the institutions of a form of democratic politics that is both institutional and hot. Such a politics would sustain a higher degree of political mobilization, or organized popular engagement in political life, and give it institutional shape.

Our ability to achieve this aim is no mere theoretical curiosity; it bears on every aspect of the changes envisioned and the goals embraced in this agenda of deep freedom and of high-energy democracy as part of that freedom. A politics fertile in the potential for continuing structural change is necessarily a high-energy politics. Such a politics weakens the dependence of change on crisis. Its arrangements rest on the principle that the imagination does the work of crisis without crisis.

A high-energy democracy accomplishes this work provided we can devise political institutions that do in practice what the imagination does in thought: subsume the actual under a range of accessible variation. In this way, we rob the actual of some of its brute and immovable facticity, its just thereness, and allow the accessible possible—the *theres* to which can get from *here*—to share in the reality of the actual. On this basis, of connection between insight into the actual and imagination of the adjacent possible, we begin to form an understanding of what we would otherwise just stare at. The institutions of a strong, high-energy democracy help carry out this work in practice, by generating alternatives, such as those that I earlier described as revolutionary reforms, without needing to lean on ruin or war as the condition for undertaking them.

In the false idea that politics must be either cold and institutional or hot and anti-institutional, we can recognize a close cousin of the romantic mistake about spirit and structure. Only the political spin differs. For the romantic, spirit can flourish solely in those brief interludes when it disrupts structure. For the defender of the idea that hot politics can only be extra-institutional (Caesarism being the most salient example), the same contradiction between spirit and structure holds.

For a romantic who has lost hope in politics and especially in changing the relation of spirit to structure, the place for spirit is the private sublime—the recesses of our intimate experience of religion, art, and interpersonal life. Spirit has no place in politics, where its introduction must be destructive to both liberty and sound judgment. The same romantic lack of hope in our power to change over time the relation between spirit and structure, creating a structure that no longer spells death to spirit, reappears in another form: it then wears the disguise of sober disillusionment about alternatives rather than of romantic enthusiasm about what our interludes of defiance to structure can bring about.

The raising of the temperature of politics—that is, of the level of political mobilization—must not be so rapid or extreme that it disregards the first point of departure of this programmatic argument, its refusal to accept the premise of Constant's mythical ancient republic: the displacement of private life and its concerns by all-consuming civic commitments and passions. The modern republic begins with the contrast between the ordinary moves that we make within a framework of arrangements and assumptions that we take for granted the better to engage our private concerns and the exceptional moves by which from time to time, under the pressure of emergency, we challenge and change pieces of that framework.

By raising the temperature of politics (and taking the other initiatives outlined in this chapter) we diminish the distance between these two sets of moves rather than put the second set in place of the first. Our revisionist and transformative activity emerges more constantly and naturally out of the normal business of life. We are better able to participate in our social world without surrendering to it.

It follows from this conception of the goal that we should seek to raise the temperature of politics in small cumulative steps rather than by a sudden change in the place that politics holds in the lives of ordinary men and women. It also follows that we should want the direction of change in political life to be reinforced by the changes we seek in the economy, civil society, and education. Consider, for example, the deepening of the knowledge economy and its dissemination throughout the production system, the organization of civil society around purpose-driven shared concerns and the multiplication of forms of collective action, and the development of a way of teaching and learning that focuses on capabilities to move both within and beyond our present form of life and treats the inherited body of knowledge with skeptical distance. All these initiatives, taken together, will sustain the enhancement of individual and collective agency in politics. The idea that revisions to the framework of established arrangements and assumptions are a perpetual outgrowth of the normal activities that we conduct within the framework will not appear as an extravagant ambition, belied by the normal tenor of social life.

The specifically political initiatives by which we can hope to raise the level of organized popular participation in political life in contemporary democracies fall into three groups.

The first group has to do with the relation between money and politics: the public financing of political activity and the imposition of strict curbs on the private use of money in politics. The defense of such use on the ground that "money talks" misrepresents the problem as if it were a principle. All contemporary societies continue to be class societies in which the life chances of individuals remain powerfully shaped by the differential transmission of economic and educational advantages through the family, and the lion's share of assets is owned or controlled by a monied elite. A high-temperature democracy accentuates the contradiction between class society and democracy.

We muffle the transformative potential of this contradiction to the extent that we allow money to buy political voice.

The second series of initiatives regards the relation between the means of mass communication and politics. Time on the most important means of mass communication—television and social media advertising today, something else tomorrow—should not be available for purchase. For example, the television companies must make broadcast time available for free to both political parties and organized social movements under standards that take into account the present standing of each such party or movement in representative institutions.

The third set of initiatives, and the most complicated, has to do with electoral regimes. Almost everything that can be done by way of voting rules to raise the temperature of politics is likely to depend on the path-dependent effects of particular circumstances. For example, the substitution of first-past-the-vote majoritarian, district-based voting by proportional representation may in many contexts allow for the energizing of politics through the partisan expression of implicit contradictions and suppressed alternatives in a country. In the presence, however, of a highly fragmented party system, locked into a series of paralyzing political deals among themselves and with the organized interests in society, the same intended effect may be achieved by the opposite means: an at least temporary substitution of proportional representation by first-past-the-post voting.

In many countries, a rule of mandatory voting, under which a voter has the privilege to abstain but must pay a small fine if he fails to vote, can dramatically raise the level of political engagement. No country that has adopted such a rule of mandatory voting—and several rich and developing countries have—has ever yet abolished it. Once acquired, the habit may become hard to shake; it may enter into the consciousness and culture of the people.

The argument against it, citing the oppressive character of such an obligation, makes little sense. For in those countries, like the United States, in which this argument is most likely to be made, the individual is or has been faced with much more burdensome obligations than the obligation of turning his mind every few years to the affairs of the republic with the privilege of abstaining: for example, in the recent past, military conscription, and today jury duty and the preparation of personal income tax returns.

In the nineteenth century, the classic liberal justification for property and educational qualifications to the suffrage was that they helped prevent the enfranchisement of voters who lived or worked under some form of subjugation or economic dependence. But these liberal objections underestimated the extent to which even the flawed present form of mass politics could allow the moneyless to oppose the stranglehold of the moneyed classes on political power. Similarly, they failed to recognize the force of class interest in the political preferences of the enfranchised minority.

These fragmentary examples of the temperature-raising effects of certain voting rules, especially when adopted against the background of the arrangements about money and media access that I have described, merge into initiatives that I will discuss in the fourth set of institutional innovations marking the path to a high-energy democracy: those that confer on representative democracy some of the features of direct, participatory democracy without, however, abolishing representative institutions.

Among these initiatives are those that involve the mass electorate, through plebiscites and referendums, in resolving impasse among the branches of a divided government, the regions of a divided, multinational country, or the parts of a fragmented class society. Most promising among such forms of popular engagement in law are those referendums and plebiscites that address whole national directions, or alternative packages of innovation in policies and institutions, rather than single issues.

Another instance of the consequences of popular participation in law making for raising the temperature of politics is the direct involvement of organized local communities in local government. Such involvement may, for example, take the form of a system of neighborhood associations that partner with local government but have their own independent structure, powers, and funding. This duplication of power from the ground up may strengthen rather than weaken local government and combat the bane of representative democracy: the expectation that the citizenry will fall asleep politically, unless awakened by emergency, in the periods between elections.

All these initiatives designed to create political institutions that heighten the level of organized popular engagement in political life, and overcome the false choice between cold institutional politics and hot anti-institutional politics, converge in the same direction. Their combined effect is to energize democracy and enhance both individual and collective agency in politics without abandoning the realistic ground of the "modern republic," in which politics, in its narrow sense of struggle over the mastery and uses of governmental power, does not and should not dominate life.

In many countries, people often attribute political disengagement to national culture. Thus, that which is created through the achievements, failures, and omissions of national politics is cast as the expression of a form of experience and consciousness that institutional change would be powerless to reshape. But give me any significant subset of the changes I have just described, and I will show you how the unpolitical become quickly disillusioned with disillusionment and spring to a political engagement that their longstanding attitudes and ideas seem to have foresworn.

Democracy and class society. A second series of institutional changes concerns the pace of politics and the relation of the pace of politics to the participation of civil society in the inner life of the state. To deepen democracy, we must hasten the pace, as well as raise the temperature, of democratic politics. Our aim should be, as Karl Popper said that it is in science, to make mistakes as quickly as possible.

To say that politics is slowed down is to say that it remains mired in impasse and indecision. It is to say that we experience politics as a succession of each party's second-best solutions. Each can claim, at the end of its time in office, that its proposals did not fail. Instead, they were never really tried out.

Hastening the pace of politics deals, however, with only half of the problem that this second set of institutional innovations in the organization of democracy addresses. There is also the matter of the extent to which, and the way in which, society sets the pace and the direction of politics, and prevents political life from being controlled by a cadre of professional politicians and the organized interests to which they are beholden.

A hastening of the pace of politics may seem to be favored by a concentration of undivided power. Such power may be concentrated in a party dictatorship. A regime of this kind is unlikely to be long-lived unless it is a collective dictatorship with a strong conception of its historical project. Alternatively, power may be concentrated in one of the weak democracies of today under a constitution that dispenses with divided government, concentrating power de jure in parliament or de facto in a strong-willed executive supported by a parliamentary majority.

The societies in which democratic states exist are divided along class and other lines and very unequally organized. Thus, a dilemma arises for the democrat and for democratic theory. To fragment the state and open it up to society is to open it up to this unequal and divided society, not to a multitude of equal and independent citizens.

Then at least two things can happen, and probably both will happen in some combination. The richest and best organized sections of the society will take over parts of this fragmented state or exercise decisive influence over it. But they will be opposed by other interests that will take over other parts of the state, or resist, from outside the boundaries of the state, in the economy and culture. The result will be a slowing down of politics, unless there is a constitutional mechanism by which impasse can be broken.

But suppose that, for the sake of decisive action, power in the state remains unified in either of the two main ways in which it can be unified: by collective dictatorship or, under weak democracy, by a government supported by a parliamentary majority and unencumbered by any constitutional division of powers. The state will still exist in an unequal and divided society.

Under the collective dictatorship, power will turn into economic advantage. And the organized interests of society will clash in the shadows within and outside the state. The collective dictators may repeatedly crush the emergent interests outside the state to prevent any rival to their power from consolidating its influence. But then they will face a fragile, amorphous civil society. Such a society will leave the dictatorship strong in appearance but weak in reality: the state will have no reliable apparatus other than its own with which to work its will and steer civil society.

An undivided government under weak democracy in a divided class society will face choices that are not so stark. But it will find that the more ambitious its transformative programs, the more they require, to advance, organized partners beyond itself: in local government, in the production system, and in civil society. These prospective partners will not be there as mere puppets of those who sit in the high offices of state; they will have interests and minds of their own. Their presence will bring with it complication, contradiction, and the risk of impasse.

In the light of these variations, we can define the problem. To deepen democracy, we must hasten the pace of politics without leaving the state lonely. The division of powers may provide multiple ways through which the rest of society, outside the state, can engage the state. But this division of powers may come at the price of impasse among the branches of divided government.

The consequences of the relation between a divided class society and a democratic government, however, overshadow the dilemmas of the division or unification of powers within the state. The quickening of the pace of politics will be illusory if we achieve it at the cost of the isolation of the state. We will have quickened the pace of a politics that is bereft of transformative potential because the state lacks adequate partners outside itself. And we will have done so all for nothing: the impasses that we suppose ourselves to have avoided by unifying power in the state will return in doubled force in the relations between the state and society. The divided, unequal, and unequally organized society will exert its restraining influence to slow politics down. It will do so in discordant voices: hence the tendency to impasse.

In one matter, however, these voices are more likely to be unified: in opposing all initiatives that seek to resolve in favor of democracy the contradiction between democracy and divided, class society. The impasse then will be between the would-be transformative state, bent on remaking society in the image of democratic society, and the privileged and organized parts of society that look on the state as the instrument by which to satisfy and, when necessary, to reconcile, their interests.

The question then is: What does it mean to quicken the pace of politics when the democracy exists, as all democracies up to now have existed, in the context of such societies? The hastening that matters most is not just any acceleration of the pace of politics, not even just an accelerated ability to generate revolutionary reforms. It is the ability to do so in a particular direction: the direction of overcoming the contradiction between democratic politics and divided, class society.

I am not referring to democratic politics as we may idealize it but as it exists. As every political scientist knows, there is rarely a stable, one-to-one relation between place in the class structure, or in the social division of labor, and political position. People are united and divided by opinion, beginning with opinions about their interests. And every feature of their experience and identity influences their political preferences.

A democratic society would have a similar fluidity: in the opening of wider access to the resources and opportunities of production; in its multiplication of the varieties of purposive-driven collective action; in its commitment to a form of education that helps its citizens see beyond the established order of society and culture; and, in all these ways, in its weakening of the hold of established places in the social division of labor on the exercise of our powers. Democracy, rather than being turned into an instrument of the divided, class order, should disrupt that order and make it more like itself.

Corporatism and Weimarism. Contrast this response to the contradiction between democratic politics and the unequal social and economic order with two responses that played a major role in the constitutional evolution of the twentieth century: corporatism and what I will call Weimarism. Of these two, corporatism turned out to be shorter lived and less consequential. Weimarism has defined the main line of constitutional development. It has failed both to quicken the pace of politics and to moderate the conflict between democratic politics and an anti-democratic social and economic order.

Corporatism is the attempt to solve the problem of the relation of civil society to the state by representing the classes and chief corporate entities in the state. It sought to suppress class conflict without abolishing the class structure: cooption, cooperation, and compromise would replace conflict. They would replace it under the watchful eyes of a state intent on putting controlled popular mobilization in the place of uncontrollable mass politics.

Corporatist doctrine appeals to several related illusions: that the problems of the market order result from class selfishness: that the important choice in the development of market society is the choice between its conflictual and anarchic form and its cooperative and corporativist form; that conflict, including class conflict, can be replaced with a lasting deal or a series of collective deals; that the state can fix its relation to society by organizing the whole of society and then bringing the organizations that represent each class and part of the labor force into the structure of government; and that the state can draw power and legitimacy from incorporating an otherwise disorganized and directionless mass of workers and producers into itself. The constitutional arrangements of such a regime would distinguish themselves by the automatic enrollment of the whole citizenry in unions and associations that would become at the same time instruments of political representation, always under the guidance of officials of the central government. No wonder corporatism was a project dear to dictators—not collective and nationalist dictators but individual dictators anxious to found their dictatorship on institutions without having to give up any power in return.

Weimarism has been the dominant line of constitutional evolution in the West from the end of World War I to today. It survived when corporatism failed and vanished, but its success consists partly in the idea that it represents an inevitable failure. Weimarism has two parts: constitutional dualism—a proposal for how to set up governments so that that they can act decisively (hastening the pace of politics) without ceasing to be accountable; and social rights—a way to deal with the anti-democratic character of the social and economic order, without having to reconstruct it.

Weimarism has been the constitutional counterpart to institutionally conservative social democracy and social liberalism. But as Weimarism emerged before the social-democratic settlement, so too it seems to be surviving it. I call it Weimarism less because of the Weimar constitution, soon amended, than because of the ideas that surrounded the drafting of this constitution and that have ever since influenced constitutionalism around the world.

The first half of Weimarism—constitutional dualism—has to do with the set up of the central government. It appears on the surface to be little more than a combination of features of the parliamentary and presidential regimes. This hybrid character, however, fails to reveal its driving motivations and distinguishing features.

Its first concern is to ensure that government can act quickly and decisively while being held to account. It wants to make such action possible without allowing it to serve as a pretext for runaway executive authority. For this reason, it designs a sitting government that can lean on both a parliamentary majority and a directly elected president. Its second concern is to duplicate and strengthen the expression of popular sovereignty in the composition of government; thus, it provides for both parliamentary institutions and a strong president with a direct popular mandate.

We can interpret constitutional dualism—the two vehicles of popular sovereignty, the two popular powers to which the government must answer—as an undeveloped and inadequate attempt to hasten the pace of politics while tightening the links between government and the citizenry. But it does nothing to quicken politics where the quickening counts most: in the production of initiatives designed to moderate the clash between a democratic politics and an undemocratic social and economic order. And it is timid even on the narrow ground of preventing impasse among the parts of government that it creates, as the lingering paralysis brought on by "cohabitation" (a president and a parliamentary majority at odds) under the constitution of the French Fifth Republic shows. It amounts to a minimal enlargement of the constitutional repertoire.

The second half of Weimarism has had a career at once fabulous and disheartening. Ever since the aftermath of World War I, constitutions have been packed with promises of social and economic rights.

They have promised every source of comfort to their citizens, from abstractions like human dignity to detailed offers of employment, housing, health care, and education. They have assured the citizenry that property must serve a "social function" and that economic freedom will prevail in concert with social solidarity. However, they have made all these promises without establishing any of the political, economic, and social institutions that would ensure they could be kept.

The social rights talk in the constitutions has been a way of acknowledging the contradiction between a democratic politics and an anti-democratic social and economic regime—and then providing a fake solution. And in this too, Weimarism has paralleled the stratagems and omissions of institutionally conservative social democracy and social liberalism. It is not copious—and largely unkept—promises of rights that humanity needs. What it needs are the transformations that can make us free.

The social-rights aspect of Weimarism is, in the eyes of the world, its most successful endeavor. The practice of making such rights promises and of pretending that they can and will be kept—and, being kept, will overcome the contradiction between democratic politics and an anti-democratic economic and social order—has been received and repeated all over the world, even by collective dictatorships that might have been thought less prone to such pieties. Yet an ineradicable sadness surrounds this practice and its practitioners. They suffer from what Nietzsche, comparing Brahms to Beethoven, called the melancholy of impotence.

Hastening the pace of democratic politics. In considering what should replace corporatism and Weimarism, we can begin by returning to the narrow, seemingly technical problem of the hastening of politics under the constraints of divided government (e.g., the United States–style constitutional arrangement, with its characteristic distinction of three separate and coequal branches of government), and the apparent lack of constraint on the hastening of politics under undivided government (e.g., a British-style parliamentary system, with a government wielding the power and authority of a sovereign parliament). The point of departure offered by each of these arrangements differs, but the central task remains the same: how to quicken the pace of politics in a way that helps first moderate and then overcome the clash between democracy and an anti-democratic social and economic regime.

The premise of divided government is the existence of a natural and necessary relation between the liberal principle of the fragmentation of power and the conservative principle of the slowing down of politics. Power is fragmented by being distributed among the three branches of government, none of them under the control of the others. Politics is slowed down by endowing each branch of government with a limited power to stop the others. The result is to establish a correspondence between the transformative reach of every political project and the severity of the constitutional obstacles that it must overcome on its way to being carried out.

There is no such natural and necessary connection between the liberal and the conservative principles. They are connected by intention and design rather than by necessity or logic. Their connection amounts to a triumph of conservative statecraft.

From the standpoint of the program of strong democracy and deep freedom, we should reaffirm the liberal principle and repudiate the conservative one. The multiplication of distinct branches of government creates more than an opportunity for the state to speak with several, discordant, voices: it gives society multiple opportunities to speak to the state and through the state. To that extent, it holds open the prospect of diminishing the isolation of the state from society.

However, in so doing, it also increases the chances that an impasse will arise between at least two of the three branches of government. Rather than resolving this impasse, it perpetuates it. In this way, it throws sand—and more than sand—in the gears of any attempt to use governmental power to change the social and economic regime. Whatever justification this procedure has must derive from reasons to slow politics down, not from the liberal principle of the fragmentation of power, provided that we accept two ideas.

The first idea is that a free society has no natural institutional form in its arrangements for the economy, for politics, and for independent civil society, that every specific form is defective and ephemeral, and that we must be able to renovate such forms if we are to advance in the construction of a free society. The second idea is that we can uphold the fragmentation of power, but avoid the slowing down of politics, if only we develop constitutional procedures to resolve the impasses that may result from divergence among the branches of a divided government.

To accelerate democratic politics, we must resolve such impasses quickly. And to associate the quickening of the pace of politics with avoidance of the isolation of the state from society, we must preempt stand-offs among parts of the state in ways that involve the mass of citizens in their resolution.

Consider the impasses that may arise in the relations between the executive and the legislative branches of a divided government under a US-style constitutional arrangement. Under the Madisonian scheme of checks and balances, such deadlocks are prolonged. In the thinking that inspired this constitutional tradition, the perpetuation of impasse is less a problem than part of a solution: it represents a way of inhibiting the transformation of society by politics. If a free society has a natural order that needs only be reinterpreted and readjusted from time to time, in the light of experience and circumstance, then the defense of freedom requires the adventurism of structural change to be contained or even avoided altogether.

To maintain the liberal principle of the fragmentation of power, under divided government, without accepting the conservative principle of the slowing down of politics, we need only to develop the constitutional machinery for the rapid resolution of impasse, especially between the executive and legislative branches. One way to achieve this result is to grant both the political branches the prerogative of responding to a deadlock between them over the direction of the country by calling early elections. Such elections would always be bilateral: for both the Presidency and the Congress. Thus, the branch that exercised this constitutional prerogative would have to pay for its exercise the price of running the electoral risk. As a result, it is more likely that early elections would be called too rarely than they would be called too often.

By this simple device, extending by analogy a procedure familiar under parliamentary and semi-presidential regimes, the Madisonian logic of the presidential system would be turned on its head. Such a system would become a machine to accelerate politics rather than to slow it down. Two powers in the state, with strong and direct popular mandates, confront each other directly in an election that has the programmatic divergence between them for its subject matter. The whole citizenry (especially under a role of mandatory voting) can either break the impasse or deliberately maintain it. But now the bias of the constitutional logic shifts from the perpetuation of deadlock to its prompt resolution, not by deals between the political branches (which may nevertheless be provoked by the effort to avoid an early bilateral election) but by the judgment of the universal electorate. Here, as often, a limited institutional innovation can have far-reaching consequences.

Now consider undivided government under weak democracy, as in the case of a pure parliamentary regime in which the parliament speaks, in principle, for the virtually unlimited sovereignty of the people. In practice this means that the sitting government, supported by a solid parliamentary majority, finds no restraint in other branches of government, save for the power of the judiciary to act in the name of a written or unwritten constitution.

That government, however, exists in an unequal and divided society. The real restraints on the government are those that result from the resistance of the organized interests of the society to it and to one another. This circumstance puts squarely the problem of how to overcome impasse, not between branches of government, but among powers of society. The aim is to overcome impasse in ways that supersede or diminish the contradiction between democratic politics and an undemocratic social and economic regime.

Every proposal applicable to this circumstance applies as well to the situation of divided government. The difference is that here we have to worry only about impasse beyond the frontiers of the state, in the relation among powers in society. There we need to concern ourselves as well with the important but lesser matter of impasse within the state among the branches of government.

The same procedures and practices that can hasten the pace of democratic politics in an unequal and divided society can also lessen the contradiction between this society and that politics. They thus show the direction in which to look for an alternative to Weimarism.

One version of such arrangements would create a set of parastate entities or public trusts to administer an increasing part of the productive capital and capital-intensive technology of society through an ongoing capital auction: the capital auctioning regime—capitalism without capitalists—that I earlier described. Whichever entrepreneurial teams can provide the highest rates of return for the use of those assets, over time horizons that would differ among the funds, get to use the productive resources of society.

The funds that look to assess returns in the relatively shorter term would be the ones most resembling an auction. For the funds that assess returns over the long term, the distinction between such an auction and quasi-public venture capital funding is effaced. And the difference between gains to the funds and gains through the funds to society also wanes.

Both the shorter-term and the longer-term funds would be managed by independent directors or trustees nominated and approved by the representative institutions of society. And their performance would be independently and competitively judged by a higher-order directorate of the same character, and ultimately by those same representative institutions. In these arrangements, the interest of society lies in experimental diversification, not just in the time horizon but also in the approach of all the funds to capital auctioning, in the range of economic agents with which they would deal, and even in the nature of their staffs and leadership.

The capital market that currently exists is already supposed to be this capital auctioning regime if only we could purge that market of localized failures of competition and of similarly localized failures in the regulatory response to such competitive flaws. This is a point of view that denies what should be fundamental in a discussion of the market economy: to acknowledge that the market, including the capital market as one of its aspects, has no single natural and necessary form. Varieties of the capital market differ in the extent to which they either tighten or loosen the relation of finance to the real economy. The capital auctioning regime is simultaneously a project to democratize access to what Marx called the means of production and a project to deepen finance, enlisting it more fully in the service of production and productivity.

A second set of arrangements by which to diminish the conflict between democratic politics and an unequal social and economic order is the inverse of the first set. Here the goal is not directly to widen access to productive resources and opportunities in favor of a larger cast of present or potential economic agents and plans of production. It is to rescue groups caught in situations of disadvantage and exclusion from which they are unable to escape by the forms of cooperative economic and political action available to them.

Just as the existing capital market is supposed to be the capital auction regime I have described, minus localized failures of competition and regulation, so the existing democracies are supposed not to witness such inescapable varieties of collective disadvantage and exclusion. Yet they do, as their relatively peaceful coexistence with an undemocratic social and economic order implies.

The defect lies in the political as well as in the economic and social institutions. If a group cannot escape from entrenched disadvantage or exclusion by the means of collective action available to it, then the democracy must come to its rescue and free that group from its prison. If nothing in its established arrangements and practices allows it to offer such rescue, then its practices and arrangements must be reformed accordingly. Not content to develop institutions that broaden access to resources and opportunities of production, the democracy will also create other institutions that ensure the forgotten orphans of those institutions will have champions in these additional institutional creations.

A state prepared and equipped to offer such rescue must include a practice distinct from the legislative, judicial, and executive or administrative functions. Consider the nature of such a practice by contrast to adjudication. Its aim is not to pass judgment on alleged violations of specific rights by an identifiable agent and restore the situation that existed before such violations. Instead, it is concerned with the extent to which particular social organizations or areas of social practice may be complicit in the exclusion, subjugation, and exclusion of certain groups. Its subject is not the violation of specific rights of individuals; it is the subversion of collective agency. If the individual is disempowered, he is disempowered as a member of the group. And if the group is disempowered, it is disempowered as the result of a combination of disadvantages and obstacles, which may be both institutional and cultural, but which, whatever their specific nature, leave their imprint on many organizations and areas of social practice.

The protagonists in such dramas are not individual right holders, or even discrete corporate entities. They are groups (whether organized or not), their leadership, and the state. The evil to be redressed is a circumstance of subjugation or exclusion that contradicts the presuppositions of the democratic order even under weak democracy.

This evil is structural but is also concentrated in particular parts of the organization of society. Nevertheless, it has a causal background that may extend in many directions. The redress consists in intervening in the parts of social life in which the evil is most manifest, and then invading—and reshaping—at least part of its proximate causal background: for example, practices of recruitment or admission to jobs and schools, or the administration of businesses and non-profit organizations.

No part of the contemporary state, under either divided or undivided government, is designed, equipped, qualified, staffed, and financed to do this work that is at once structural and localized. In the United States, in the three-branched state, the branch that wanted to do this work—the judiciary—has done it, up to a point, until it has run out of power and legitimacy. So long as it could, it justified its engagement as an extension of the idealizing and systematizing interpretation of law in the language of impersonal principles of right and of policies responsive to the public interest. However, deficient as it is in the resources and capabilities that this selective invasion and reshaping of the causal background of social life requires, it has confined itself, in this reconstructive practice, to relatively marginal social organizations such as schools, prisons, and mental hospitals, leaving untouched the central organizations of production, finance, and power.

Under undivided government, parliamentary sovereignty, and governments that speak in the name of a parliamentary majority, any attempt to undertake this work has more often taken the form of legislation, extended by administrative action. But it is unsuited for legislation because it is localized, and for administrative action because it is structural.

We would need to create the agent together with the practice and endow that agent with the resources and powers that it would require. Under divided government, it would be a fourth branch; under undivided government, a part of the state enjoying something like the distinction and authority of the judiciary, from which it would be entirely separate, and, like the judiciary, speaking in the name of the (written or unwritten) constitution. Its leadership might be chosen, for fixed long terms, by the two political branches under divided government, and by parliament under undivided government.

Its most important work would be to select for reshaping the organizations and practices most immediately responsible for the evils that it seeks to redress. Everything is causally connected with everything else. Once the thread of the causal background to the evils that this rescue seeks to redress begins to unravel, it can eventually touch every quadrant of social life. The thread must stop in the immediate background to the evils that it seeks to correct, on pain of losing both the distinctiveness and the efficacy of its practice.

When it stops, however, it will already have given the democracy examples of how we can begin to overcome the contradiction between democratic politics and an unequal, divided social and economic order. It will have shown how we can replace promises of rights with instances of empowerment, and Weimarism with high-energy democracy.

Combining decisive central initiative with radical devolution. A third set of institutional innovations that define the path of a high-energy democracy consists in arrangements that make it possible to combine decisive initiative by the central government with the devolution of power to parts of the country or of the society and economy. The power that matters most is power to initiate and exemplify alternative directions for the country. The core idea is that as a country travels a certain road it can hedge its bets and enable parts of itself to try out and exemplify different models of the national future.

The conceptual basis for this third series of institutional innovations, as for the other two, lies in the theory of regimes. Here two tenets of that theory have a crucial role to play. The first tenet is the primacy of structural change: the ultimate topic of both theoretical interest and practical concern in politics. The second tenet is that alternatives consist in a succession of steps—the conception of which we do and must revise as we move ahead—not in blueprints and systems. We should, I have argued, follow the liberals and socialists of the nineteenth century in giving primacy to structural—meaning, above all, institutional—alternatives. But we should differ from them in our refusal to succumb to a structural dogmatism.

The association of strong initiative by national government with radical devolution—radical because distinct and developed enough to signal a different national trajectory—violates two assumptions of conservative statecraft and political science. The first such assumption is that when power is divided between the center and the periphery in a state, its distribution must follow a hydraulic model: the more power that goes to the center, the less power can go to the periphery. We can, on the contrary, give more power to both the center and the periphery by combining arrangements that raise the temperature and quicken the pace of politics at the center with arrangements that expand the constitutional instruments of devolution. Such a combination depends on the detailed arrangements shaping the assignment of divided and concurrent powers between center and periphery.

The second such assumption is that the potential to combine devolution with strong central initiative is, if it exists at all, limited to federations, and not available to unitary states. The truth is that unitary states and federations or confederations have different advantages and disadvantages as settings for such a combination. No reason exists to prefer, in general, one to the other for this purpose.

We can imagine two stages through which the combination of stronger initiative by national government and devolution progresses. In the first stage, the primary instrument of the combination is cooperative federalism and its counterpart in unitary states. The cooperation should be both vertical among the three levels of a federation or the equivalents of these levels in unitary states, and horizontal among states or among municipalities in federations and among local authorities in unitary states.

The enabling technical distinction is the distinction between divided and concurrent powers in the way of organizing the relation between central and local power. The powers of the central and state or municipal governments would be—and, in some degree, always already are—divided in some areas and concurrent in others. The initiatives of an inclusive productivism—designed today to deepen and spread the knowledge economy—are a prime candidate for such concurrent powers. And so are the initiatives that are needed to reconcile in large, unequal, and federal states the local management of schools with national standards of investment and quality. A national movement engaging thousands of schools and teachers in an endeavor to change teaching and learning practices depends on cooperative federalism to advance.

On the horizontal axis, of relations among states and among municipalities, cooperative federalism takes the form of regional organizations or consortia bringing such local governments together to pool experience, insight, and resources in the development of economic, educational, and other alternatives. Horizontal cooperation is the favored setting for the formulation of strategies of regional development, especially in large countries. It is only when national development programs touch the ground of regional reality that they come to life. They cannot touch that ground effectively unless the regional development strategies are conceived as well as implemented at least as much from the bottom up, by the regions themselves, as from the top down, by national governments. And to be made bottom up they require the cooperative engagement of state and municipal governments.

Nothing prevents unitary states from developing—as several have —such practices of vertical and horizontal cooperation. They represent a preeminent means for the step-by-step development of structural alternatives unblinkered by structural dogmatism. Cooperation between center and periphery serves the experimental development of alternative institutions and policies. It makes it possible to develop a series of variations on similar themes, and to compare the results across a range of circumstances that are bound to be similar in some respects and different in others. It arms structural innovation with experimental diversity.

A second stage in the coexistence of strong central initiative with devolution begins when we inaugurate a practice of what I propose to call wide divergence. Under certain conditions, part of a country—or later parts of the production system or the school system, or any other major area of social practice—could apply for rights of exceptionally wide divergence from national policy and law, the better to develop a consequential alternative to some aspect of the main road traveled by the society.

It would be vital to subject such applications for wide divergence to a twofold vetting—by the representative institutions (especially the national legislature, under both divided and undivided government) as well as by the judiciary. Devolution brings the advantage of experimentation and the danger of serving to entrench group privilege or oppression. Wide divergence is radical devolution, which accentuates both the experimental advantage and the accompanying danger. It can be allowed only when there is assurance that it will not be used to escape national legal restraints on any form of subjugation, exclusion, or disempowerment, or to give any class, race, or party privileges that it would not otherwise possess.

In the first stage of the innovations by which we combine strong central initiative with devolution, federations have an advantage: they offer a readymade template for such a combination. Unitary states must make up for the lack of that template by creating new entities such as regional or combined local authorities. In the second stage, of wide divergence, however, unitary states enjoy an advantage. In a federation there is a presumption that every part of it will simultaneously have the same measure of right to develop its own laws and policies. So long as this presumption remains in place, there cannot be wide divergence. In a unitary state, no such presumption exists: the principle of wide divergence confronts no initial obstacles. Thus a unitary state, the United Kingdom, has found it possible, if not easy, to strike different deals of devolution with the nations that it unites.

Endowing representative democracy with features of direct democracy. There remains a fourth set of institutional innovations that define this alternative form of democratic politics: those that add to representative democracy some of the features of direct, participatory innovations. These additional traits of direct democracy do not supersede the need for representative institutions. Nor do they reverse the preference for Constant's freedom of the moderns over his freedom of the ancients as the only realistic point of departure for the transformation of political life. Their outcome is not to rob politics, in its narrower sense of struggle over the mastery and uses of governmental power, of its relative marginality to the concerns of everyday life. Nor does anything in such innovations signal an end to the domination of politics by a cadre of professional politicians, who devote much of their lives to developing a career in party politics.

The transformations heralded by this fourth set of innovations are nevertheless profound. When seen in relation to the changes in the economy, civil society, and education that define the agenda of deep freedom, they point to an enhancement of agency: of our power to act and, in acting, to rethink and reshape the habitual presuppositions of our action. The promise of such an enhancement becomes intelligible and forceful because it is not unique to any domain of social life; it is common to all domains. The message of a high-energy democracy will not then be contradicted and undermined by the practices of other parts of social life.

The least important ways in which we can add features of direct democracy to the institutions of direct democracy are those that take explicit constitutional form. The most important ways are those that have to do with the organization of all the other parts of social life. Direct democracy is about the participation of the individual in the collective or cooperative activities by which we remake society. The opportunities for such participation outside the domain of constitutional reorganization vastly exceed, in variety and significance, the opportunities for it within that domain.

There is a role for direct democracy, as I earlier suggested, in the breaking of impasse between the political branches of government —the executive and the legislative branches—under divided government. An example is the constitutional prerogative, which both political branches should possess under divided governments, to break the impasse by calling early elections, provided that such elections are always for both branches.

Another example is the appeal to comprehensive programmatic plebiscites or referendums. Such referrals to the general electorate would be about alternative directions of national development, embodied in combinations of initiatives, by contrast to single-issue consultations of the people. They would in effect be extemporaneous elections about the national future.

A different enhancement of representative democracy with features of direct democracy would focus on local government rather than on central power. For it is in the relation of local communities to local government that we can expect to find the most numerous and significant examples of popular engagement in self-government. We can imagine, for example, creating alongside the formal structure of local government a second, parallel structure of neighborhood associations and community groups addressing paramount local issues such as the public schools and the police. A new body of social law—neither public nor private—might make available a legal framework for the self-organization of civil society outside the state. And civil society, thus organized, would both monitor and propose. Thus, the whole citizenry can have a chance to participate in active self-government, without becoming professional politicians or career civil servants.

All such constitutional expressions of the marriage of representative and direct democracy are much less important than the ways in which the transformation of society outside the state can convey the larger message of direct democracy: self-government as an expression of individual and collective agency.

The deepening and dissemination of today's most advanced productive practice, the knowledge economy, as part of the democratization of the market order, would bring production and imagination closer together. It would weaken the distinction between conception and execution, between jobs of direction or supervision and tasks of implementation. And it would require a rise in the level of discretionary initiative and reciprocal trust required of all participants in production. The result would be to efface the sharpness of the contrast between self-government in and through the state and the organization of production.

The multiplication of forms of purpose-driven collective action, joining people across the barriers of social and cultural difference, would make the creation of the social future out of the social present a focus of deliberate action rather than an unintended and automatic outcome of a society's mechanisms of self-reproduction. As a result, it would give larger expression to what is most appealing in the ideal of participatory democracy but what should not be, and is not, confined to political life narrowly considered: the collective solution of collective problems through forms of collective action that create union supported by shared purpose rather than by the antecedent similarity, or shared heritage, of the collaborators.

An important example, of great practical significance, is the participation of civil society, alongside the state, in the experimental provision of public services. The state continues to provide all citizens a universal minimum of public services—a minimum that becomes higher as society becomes richer and more demanding. But beyond that universal minimum, the state partners with independent civil society, acting through not-for-profit cooperatives of specialized professionals and interested publics in the experimental and competitive supply of such services. Such a partnership is the most promising way to improve the quality of public services over time. The significance of this example and its affinity with direct democracy become clear when we remember that civil society builds people and defines its own future by how it provides public services and develops human capabilities.

A way of teaching and learning that seeks to develop our ability to move both within and beyond the established order—and refuses to honor, in the education of the young, the forced marriage of method and subject matter characteristic of the university culture—represents the educational counterpart to the empowerment of the citizen under strong democracy. Such a democracy recognizes, and seeks to support, the diffusion of prophetic powers among the broad mass of ordinary men and women. The exercise of such powers in our everyday experience is a more telling response to the concerns motivating the ideal of direct, participatory democracy than any constitutional arrangement could ever be.

Cohesion and Freedom: The Self-Organization of Civil Society

Civil society as a site of institutional innovation. We move toward deep freedom by establishing the haven and arousing the storm. We combine the haven and the storm by innovating in the institutional forms of economic, political, and social pluralism: the institutions of the market economy, of democratic politics, and of independent civil society. The counterpart to a democratized market economy and a deepened democracy is a civil society organized outside the state and outside the market: organized ultimately by itself, not by either the market or the state. To this end, however, it needs help, provided that the help does not compromise its independence from the state.

Only an organized civil society, self-possessed and confident of its powers, can generate alternative futures for society and act on them. A democratized market order and a deepened democracy existing alongside a disorganized civil society or one that is very unequally organized will be fatally weakened. Neither politics nor economic life suffice to generate out of themselves an inclusive structure of association among people. A market economy that doubles as a market society, reducing social connections to self-interested material exchange, lives on the verge of disassociation. A form of democratic politics that claims, in the manner of Constant's ancient freedom, to impose its concerns on the whole of our experience, destroys the recesses of intimacy and phantasy, of love and concealment, on which our humanity depends.

Social organization, outside the market and politics, is power and freedom. What can and should its sources be? Let us identify by exclusion its possible and necessary sources.

In most societies and cultures of the past, association has been ascriptive: people have been born into a caste, class, or community as they are born into a family. Often their group belonging—a collective identity—has a physical expression. The human body bears the stigmata of a social fate.

Such ascriptive bonds help inform prophecy with memory. But if they are the sole, or even the predominant, source of association, the self-organization of society outside the market and the state cannot come into its own as a basis for movement toward deep freedom. We cannot use the forms of association to reinvent and free ourselves if they work in our existence as if they were natural and immutable. Nor can we count on them as devices of emancipation if we believe that they make up a readymade toolbox rather than a set of tools that we manufacture as we need and use them.

Purpose-driven association bringing together people who have no antecedent social bond is the most significant and promising prompt to the self-organization of civil society outside the state and the market. Such purpose-driven association will be more fertile if it is not restricted to a single task and exhausted by achieving it. There can be, there should be, a continuous dialectic between the purposes that draw people together beyond the frontiers of the market and of politics and their practices of association.

Ascriptive bonds—inherited forms of belonging and affinity—may play a role in the background to help sustain connections before the force of a common endeavor has begun to work its magic on our attitudes to one another. The more the varieties of purpose-driven association dispense with any antecedent sameness of nature or identity, and cross the barriers of social and cultural difference to produce union out of difference, the more powerful they show themselves to be and the greater their potential to use the union of the different to develop new difference.

The second major source of association outside the state and the market is law. We may think of law as the institutional form of association rather than as its source. The institutional form, however, must often precede the associational outcome and be part of its genesis. The self-organization of civil society requires the development of a third branch of law distinct from both private and public law as they have developed and exist today.

It may at first seem that the inherited private law—especially the law of contract and of private association—suffices as a legal vehicle for this part of the agenda of deep freedom. It has been common to regard private law as the equivalent of a natural language in which we can think any thought about the endeavors that would bring us together within or outside the domain of market transactions. This view of the perfect elasticity of private law was reaffirmed, mistakenly, when the architects of the social-democratic or social-liberal settlement of the mid-twentieth century superimposed a new body of public law—the law of the regulatory redistributive state as well as the constitutional law that I labeled Weimarism—on a largely unrevised body of private law.

There are two reasons why the established private law represents an inadequate instrument for the self-organization of civil society. One of these reasons has to do with the relation of the voluntary or optional character of much of private law to the unequal and unequally organized society in which it exists and for which it was made. The other reason relates to the specific, historically unique character of this existing body of private law.

In the context of the combination of class society and weak democracy that we find in even the freest and most egalitarian contemporary societies, the voluntary and optional character of the devices of private law—especially the law of private contracts and associations—means that they are more likely to be useful to the organized minorities than to the disorganized majority of society. For this deficiency to be remedied as part of the movement beyond weak democracy and class society, it would be necessary for the associational structure of this new body of social law to be a default that prevails in the absence of its explicit rejection by the interested parties.

We can form some sense of what this change in the character of the law of associations—the core of a future body of social law—means by considering an example from the legal history of the twentieth century. The predominant labor-law regime was contractualist: collective bargaining as a countervailing power to reestablish the reality of contract, given the inequality of bargaining power in the employment relationship. Unionization was voluntary, and the unions were independent of the state. But part of the world—much of Latin America—followed a different path and established, under the influence of European corporatism and fascism, a corporatist labor–labor regime. All workers, in the formal, legalized parts of the economy, were automatically unionized. The unions stood in the shadow of a Ministry of Labor as instruments of controlled mass mobilization.

Imagine a hybrid regime, taking from the corporatist regime the principle of automatic and comprehensive unionization but from the contractualist regime the principle of the complete independence of the unions from the state. The focus of such a labor-law regime shifts from the achievement of association, a gift of the law, to the decision on how to use this gift. The inclusive character of unionization gives a solidaristic tilt to trade-union activism and counteracts the temptation of workers in the capital-intensive parts of the economy to make deals with their employers to the detriment of the rest of the labor force. Different labor movements, connected or not with political parties, compete for position in this unitary structure, just as political parties compete for position in the (weakly democratic) state.

Established private law fails as the natural language of a self-organizing civil society for another reason, which has to do with its distinctive historical development over the last several centuries. Its central ideas have been the unified property right, vesting all the constituent powers of property in a single right holder, the owner, and the bilateral executory promise: a fully articulated, arms-length bargain for a one-time exchange of performances at a future time, exhausted at the moment of performance.

The independent organization of civil society is more likely to demand the disaggregation of unified property: the superimposition of different types of claims, held by distinct tiers of right holders, on the same resources. It will also emphasize ongoing, incomplete relational contracts—and the varieties of association they prefigure—rather than instantaneous fully articulated bargains. Every association amounts to the development of such a relational contract.

If existing private law is inadequate as a setting for the self-organization of civil society, so is the extant body of public law. It has developed as the law of the state, democratic or not. Insofar as we might understand social law as an extension of public as well as of private law, its subject matter is the public sphere that does not pertain to the state. But when we seek to define the distinctive character of what refers to the public but not to the state, we come back to the social: to social capital and to the law, the practice and the varieties of association.

If private and public law were transformed and developed in the ways suggested by these remarks, they might meet each other in the middle. The historical cores of public and of private law would then appear to be an extension of the main, social concern of law: private law as an extension dealing with the market order, and public law as an extension regarding the state. Rather than waiting for such a transmutation, we must fill the hole in the middle of law and create the default legal order of civil society.

Association in politics and in the economy. The power that results from association is above all a power to open a path to the future, to alternative futures. Association, and the empowerment it makes possible, exist as well in the market economy and in democratic politics. A democratized market and a deepened democracy make distinctive contributions to the accumulation of social capital.

In a democratized market order, oriented to the development of a knowledge economy for the many, the moral culture of production changes. Earlier productive vanguards, such as industrial mass production, relied on a command-and-control style of management. And command-and-control production, like its setting in a market economy depending on arm's-length transactions, required the generalization of a modicum of trust—of low trust—among strangers. The strangers were the workers confined to their highly specialized niches and working in ways that reflected the repetitious movements of their machines. The strangers were also the market agents—traders and firms—transacting with one another at arm's length.

By contrast, a knowledge economy requires an increase in the level of discretionary initiative and reciprocal trust expected from all who participate in production. As in special forces or guerrilla operations, discretionary initiative and reciprocal trust represent two sides of the same phenomenon.

The wider market order in which such a practice of production flourishes is one in which cooperative competition often replaces the assignment of cooperation and competition to starkly separated domains of economic life. In all these and other ways, the production system and the market order become settings for the accumulation of social capital.

A deepened democracy requires a higher level of popular engagement in political life. It involves the popular sovereign in the overcoming of impasse among parts of the state as well as between the state and the organized interests of society. And it creates a basis on which parts of society can seize the opportunity created by the devolution of central power to develop alternative versions of the national future.

None of these changes turns the democratized market or the deepened democracy into self-sufficient sources of social capital or substitutes for the self-organization of civil society outside the market and the state. All of them, however, make it possible for that self-organization to find resonance and confirmation, rather than contradiction, in the character of economic and political life. The example of empowerment resulting from the self-organization of civil society would soon be discredited and abandoned if it were no more than a solitary impulse. We must now turn to this impulse to gain deeper insight into its motivation, basis, and consequences.

The motives and significance of the self-organization of civil society outside the market and the state. The motivating force driving cooperation in civil society, outside the economy and politics, must be the struggle to achieve practical goals through collaboration. In this way of speaking, association is the means and the practical ends for which we work together are the goal. But, as in any ongoing and necessarily incomplete relational contract, the association is also, and even chiefly, the goal, and any particular result that it may make possible represents a fragmentary instance of its potential and an opportunity to keep it alive.

For purpose-driven collaboration to flourish and justify the development of distinctive practices and even of a new body of law, it must amount to more than a social equivalent to self-interested market exchange. It must perform a function in the life of the advanced societies, just as the two ethics discussed in Chapters 5 and 6 gain their force from their relation to the twin functional imperatives of those societies: the strengthening of personal agency and the development of the higher forms of cooperation.

The deeper role that purpose-driven association, developed across the barriers of social and cultural division, performs in these societies is to supply a basis of social cohesion. That basis must survive the erosion, or the deliberate overcoming, of sameness: preexisting similarity of group belonging, class, and culture. It must also achieve a degree of social union that mere functional differentiation and interdependence can never hope to attain.

Here we face, once again, a problem that classical European sociologists saw no way, or only false ways, to solve. Sameness is, morally as well as materially, an onerous basis for social cohesion. By excluding difference, it inhibits complexity and contradiction. By inhibiting complexity and contradiction, it restricts innovation of all kinds. It exacts an unacceptable cost in constraints on economic growth and growth in productivity. It arrests the development of political freedom and robs it of substance. It prevents the deepening of subjectivity.

But functional interdependence is no substitute for sameness as a basis—albeit an oppressive and impoverishing one—for social cohesion. Durkheim himself was aware of its inadequacy as a social cement. He had once thought that he had found the necessary and sufficient supplement to functional independence in the sharing of an ideal of autonomy. No ideal, however, can suffice as a source of union; union must derive force and authority from the experience of acting together for a purpose. What Durkheim described as the ideal of autonomy—a relatively unreconstructed version of what I earlier explored as the ethic of self-fashioning and non-conformity—is an especially unpromising candidate. For how can gods have an experience of union among themselves unless it is imposed from above, as it was on Olympus, or arises more powerfully from below on the wings of love and of the imagination?

In one contemporary society after another, sameness has given way to contrasts of experience and of vision. Two forces have played a leading role in this transition. One force has been the aggravation of an inequality that is reinforced by the hierarchical segmentation of the economy into worlds that allow for very different experiences as well as very different rewards. Another force has been a form of migration in which the migrants seek to uphold in their new land the culture of their old one. What once may have been something close to a tribe—the nation—begins to become something else.

Money transfers organized by the state cannot contain or counteract either the inequalities or the divisions of experience in the emerging form of social life. The only adequate basis of social cohesion becomes the multiplication of forms of collective action: ways for people to do things together outside the economy and politics as well as within them.

This link of social cohesion to collective action, and the communities of purpose and ultimately of fate that such action builds, were always there; they are not the result of aggravated inequality or greater cultural and ethnic heterogeneity. Now, however, collective action cannot be based solely or even chiefly on inherited sameness. And it must be able to cross the barriers of many-sided difference and to gain strength and inspiration from crossing them.

The most distinctive and dangerous feature of the change that we witness in the character of the national difference is the evisceration of the concrete collective identities expressed in national custom. This evisceration results in the replacement of a commitment to actual and therefore porous national difference by a will to national difference. This will is intransigent precisely because the identity it seeks to reaffirm is increasingly emptied out of tangible, customary content. It wills a difference that has lost much of its substance.

In a world in which actual difference wanes, rescue does not lie in the sacrifice of difference on the altar of cosmopolitanism and enforced institutional convergence. It lies in the empowerment of difference. Difference of all kinds—including among nations—is not the problem. It is part of the solution. But new difference counts for more than inherited or remembered difference.

A people creates new difference by doing things together, and by providing a setting in which many groups, motivated by the desire to achieve particular goals and solve particular problems, can do things together. Even as they continue to wane, inherited affinities and traditions may facilitate such purpose-driven collaboration.

In such circumstances, however, cohesion will be more a consequence than a cause of the joint endeavors. Endeavors will often survive and transcend the purpose or purposes that originally motivated them, suggesting new uses of a collaboration that has already proved its usefulness.

The more such associations join people whom the inherited order of culture and class have not previously brought together, and the more widely they range over the recognized and not yet recognized problems of social life, the stronger a source of social cohesion they are likely to become. They give the answer to the question posed by those classical sociologists: how a society unable to rely on the similarity of the people, experiences, interests, and values that form it can nevertheless hold together. The multiplication of new ways by which people do things together, especially when they cannot rely on either the market or democracy as vehicles for doing them, is the most promising source of social cohesion. It gives us our best chance of reconciling our movement toward deep freedom with the strengthening of our ties to one another.

Each such purpose-driven instance of collective action must have a practical focus, helping to solve a problem that the market and the state have left unsolved. Each must create union out of difference and accomplish what functional interdependence alone cannot unless some significant collective purpose motivates it. Those who participate in it must be able to experience a living connection between this public purpose and their own interests and values.

To vindicate the idea that the self-construction of civil society is a terrain for institutional innovation distinct from democratizing the market and deepening democracy, we need to identify initiatives that can advance it. The cumulative effect of such initiatives must be to leave civil society outside the market and the state more organized, and therefore more empowered, than it was before.

In this spirit, I now give examples of two such species of collective action. Each addresses an unsolved problem and unseized opportunity in the life of the advanced societies. In addressing the problem and opportunity, each adds significantly to the store of social capital. It does so without relying on the containment of difference as the condition of union. Each is both a source of social union and a way to create new difference.

Public services and association. A major opportunity to give purpose and density to association is the engagement of civil society, together with the state, in providing public services and enhancing their quality. Such an engagement requires civil society to organize itself and to come to terms with both the market and the state without allowing itself to be absorbed in them. Far from representing an invention *ex nihilo*, it builds on a role that civil society, sometimes under the label of "the third sector," already performs today in many countries.

Public services, beginning with health, education, and support for those who are unable to take care of themselves, are more than responses to particular social needs. Such services build civil society and build its individual members. When civil society shares in the development and provision of such services it makes itself and it equips the people who compose it to make themselves, cooperatively as well as individually. Here is a form of association that has the sustenance of association as its object.

Civil society, however, cannot do this work without help from the state. Nor can it accomplish it without being able to rely on law that establishes the associational forms suited to the practical role. The question is then whether it can get the help that it needs from the state and the basis that it requires in the law without compromising its self-direction. Notwithstanding its need for that state help and that legal basis, civil society must in the end organize itself more than be organized by any force external to itself.

Consider what these aims imply in the circumstances of the advanced societies now. Throughout the world, the dominant, if not the exclusive, way of providing public services is what we might label administrative Fordism, by analogy to the name sometimes given to the most advanced practice of production before the emergence of today's productive vanguard, the knowledge economy. Fordist mass production was characterized by the large-scale production of standardized goods, made by semi-skilled labor, working with relatively rigid machines and production processes and assembled in large productive units, organized on the basis of specialized and hierarchical work relations.

Administrative Fordism is the provision of standardized, low-quality public services by the bureaucratic apparatus of the state. To say that they are low quality means in this context simply that they are of lower quality than the comparable services that might be acquired on the market by someone with money. The only alternative to administrative Fordism has often seemed to be privatization: the hand-over of public services to profit-driven firms.

There is, however, another alternative: one that shows how the provision of public services can serve as a vehicle for the independent organization of civil society. The state must, under this alternative, continue to guarantee a universal minimum of public services—a floor. It may also work to develop the most advanced, complex, and expensive services—the ceiling—as it does in the development of the most advanced defense technologies. However, in the broad middle zone between the floor and the ceiling, the state would help engage independent civil society. Civil society would partner with the state in the varied, experimental, and competitive provision of public services.

The immediate reason for this arrangement is practical: engaging the varied talents of specialists in civil society in the design and distribution of public services is the best way to enhance the quality of those services. It is an anomaly that the administrative equivalent of a knowledge economy, bent on experimentalist and perpetual innovation, remains in its early stages.

The more far-reaching consequence, however, of this way of providing public services is to endow civil society with the strongest axis around which it can organize: to reshape its own future profile and capabilities through its participation in the design and distribution of those services. To this end, the state would actively recruit specialists who do not belong to the professional civil service—the bureaucratic apparatus of the state—and who would not become public servants as a consequence of their participation. It would help equip and finance civil society. It would, as I next describe, set up the legal framework under which the associations and cooperatives of civil society would work. It would monitor them through judicial or prosecutorial authorities independent from the sitting government or the executive. And it would establish a similarly independent system to monitor and evaluate the results, the better to identify and to disseminate what works best.

In the countries, such as the United States, and the fields, such as medicine, in which there is now the clearest foreshadowing of such a system, these anticipations rely on the marriage of private philanthropy to the elite professions and the universities. But if such a system is to be independent from the monied classes and their charities, and applied across the whole range of public services, it must not depend on the gifts of the rich.

Part of the money reserved by the state for the financing of public services, including the money committed to public health insurance, would be vested in multiple, independently managed public trusts, with a mandate to develop their own agendas and experiments. And these resources would in turn be used to finance associations or cooperatives of specialists in the different areas in which public services are provided.

The universities, professions, and professional associations would play a role, as they do today in many countries, in shaping the engagement of their constituencies in the distribution of their services. That engagement, however, would also have to be shaped from below, by teachers, physicians, social workers, and other professionals and experts, and by the movements and agendas that they formed.

The whole arrangement would be subject to two distinct types of checks, implemented by different entities and authorities. On one side, there would be the managerial monitoring of efficiency and effectiveness, conducted by an independent part of the state. On the other side, there would be the judicial and quasi-judicial monitoring of integrity and fidelity to public purpose.

Health, education, and social welfare accounts for a major part of total spending in all the advanced societies. The relation of such a system to the workings of the market economy therefore becomes a matter of utmost consequence. And the reinvention of the competitive mechanisms of the market in what would, from the beginning, be one of the largest parts of the economy, would be vital to its success.

The ultimate responsibility for the evolution of this system would fall on democratic politics rather than on this extension and adaptation of the market economy. For it is the democracy that must ultimately decide the direction and make the laws defining the institutional framework. A self-organized civil society, engaged in the work of shaping its own future, is the natural counterpart to a democratized market and a deepened democracy.

Social solidarity and association. My second example explores the potential of cooperative action as a source of social cohesion in a particular setting: the organization of activities by which we share responsibility to take care of other people beyond the frontiers of the family and of family selfishness. The premise of my first example was a rough equality among the participants in collective action: all are able to be agents. The assumption of this second example is that some people are not able—at least, not fully—to exercise agency. They stand in need of care. The delegation of care to helpers paid by the state or by the family is not enough: not enough to provide the care with the devotion and humanity that it demands and not enough to turn the way in which the care is given into a source of social cohesion.

Consider two aspects of the social and historical background to this problem and this opportunity. I take as my context a society in which, in many ways and for many reasons, the family has been weakened; we can no longer count on it to exercise, or even to acknowledge, the responsibility of care. Even when it can and does, it may subcontract its responsibility to professional helpers and external organizations.

I also assume a circumstance in which a nation has ceased to be a tribe marked by ethnic and cultural homogeneity, if it ever was one. The development of difference of all kinds has exposed the inadequacy of money transfers, orchestrated by the state, to serve as a social cement. In a country with a higher degree of homogeneity, in which people look, feel, and act more like one another, they are likely to be more willing to make sacrifices for other people's children and parents than they would be in a country in which they have drawn apart—even the sacrifice needed to finance, through taxation, a well-funded public system of social care.

Moreover, the care thus financed and provided may also be more likely to share the spirit of the family. If society is broken up into communities, and caring, albeit financed by the state, is internal to those communities, something of the spirit of the family writ large may survive. It will survive, however, at the cost of a failure to produce social union across the barriers of difference and even on the basis of difference. It will, as a result, be an inferior form of union, one that must be an incubus on the cause of deep freedom rather than serving as an instrument of that cause.

Given these circumstances and the intimate, internal relation of self-construction to solidarity, we should seek to establish the principle that every able-bodied adult ought to hold two positions in the social division of labor: one in the system of production and skilling; the other in the caring system—the responsibility to minister to other people's needs. Here is a form of collective action that expresses most directly the ideal of solidarity.

Imagine two major variations on the institutional realization of this principle: one mandatory, the other voluntary but encouraged and supported in multiple ways. The mandatory variant is social service in youth. The voluntary, but favored one, is engagement in helping other people in need—with time rather than money—outside one's family.

In many countries around the world, including the rich North Atlantic democracies, military conscription has been replaced by professional armed forces: a mercenary defense force. The armed forces, especially of any major state, must be able to count on a significant element of professionalism if they are to combine advanced technologies with radical versatility in the field. Their enlisted ranks, as well as their officer cadres, must include men and women with relatively long-term commitments and the extended training that such commitments make possible.

But a deepened democracy cannot dispense with an ancient republican principle: the armed forces (meaning all land, air, and sea forces) must in a republic always remain the nation in arms. They must never become a part of the nation, paid by the other parts, to defend them. They must not degenerate into a force of poor people hired by the propertied classes to defend the country.

Most states, however, will not need active military service from more than a fraction of their youth. Those who are exempt from military service should then be subject to social service. They should serve, preferably, in a part of the country and a social milieu different from their own. The focus can be on building the country and helping its people in some area of expertise related to the one in which they are being—or hope to be—educated. They would begin or continue their education in the course of their service.

The sovereign nation-states that compose the present world order double as class societies. To assert the republican idea of the army as the nation in arms, and to extend that idea into the development of an equivalent form of social service, is to create a space in which the hold of the class order is loosened. It is to understand nation-building as the building of one's own nation at a moment in every young citizen's life span when experimentation with one's life can be most readily associated with the discovery and reimagination of one's country. Solidarity ceases to be sugar-coating. It becomes instead an expression of collective energy in the making of national union.

Later, during adult life, everyone should be encouraged to spend part of his working year in service to others, according to his trade, profession, or walk of life, and respecting the limitations of his circumstance—service to the vulnerable and the needy. Money, even if given by the individual rather than by the state, is no substitute, as a source of social cohesion and solidarity, for the gift of time. Everyone is troubled and busy. But we know that in many countries those who give most of their time are those who have least time to give, because they have more children. Time and the heart expand together.

It may be futile and counterproductive to make such adult service mandatory: the variation of personal circumstances is too wide, and the peril of imposing generosity too great. The state can nevertheless act and spend to make such social engagement financially neutral for the majority of the working population, through subsidies of one form or another.

For such voluntary service to become a recurrent part of the working year, it has to be organized as well as subsidized. The key agent in that organization of voluntary service should not, indeed cannot, be the state. It must be civil society itself. The organization of voluntary social service, sometimes supplementing and sometimes replacing the provision of welfare services by a governmental bureaucracy, requires a dramatic advance in the density of association. It calls for a multitude of associations extending outward beyond the existing associational structure of civil society—its churches, clubs, and benevolent organizations—to connect those who give their time to those who need it.

One human being knocking at the door of another is more than a piece of a transformative program. It is a promise of secular salvation if anything can be.

Education: Capability and Prophecy

Education and deep freedom. To democratize the market, deepen democracy, and encourage the self-organization of civil society is to reshape institutions. The cause of deep freedom requires more than institutional change. It requires as well change in consciousness and in the formation of the mind. The part of this vast and intangible domain that most lies within our grasp to influence is education: in the first instance the education of the young but also of the fully formed human being throughout his life.

To those who doubt that our mental experience and capabilities should be the object of a transformative project, the answer is that they always are. Civilization depends on it. No human society, not even societies before literacy or before states, has failed to develop more or less explicit programs for the education of its members.

In the cause of deep freedom, informed by a recognition of both our finitude and transcendence, and conscious of the social character of the practices by which we affirm and develop our power to transcend all the concrete determinations of our existence, the character and content of education must rank as one of the foremost concerns.

In this view, education must equip us to deal with nature, society, and ourselves given the order that is established in society and in culture and our limitations as the natural beings that we are. The school acknowledges and confronts our finitude.

But we are also the beings in whose experience everything points beyond itself. To increase our share in the quality of transcendence, to develop our powers of insight and of action, and to enlarge our freedom by reckoning with the contradictory requirements of self-construction, we must form a view of how best to educate ourselves. We must think of education as not only an effort to equip ourselves for the world that is at hand but also as an attempt to acquire the instruments with which to reimagine and remake that world.

The ability to orient ourselves to the future and to the possible changes our cognitive and practical relation to the present and the actual. It increases the reach of our insight precisely because it robs the actual of some of its false semblance of finality and necessity and allows us to subsume it under a range of proximate possibilities. It equips us to engage the social and cultural order in which we move without giving it the last word. The last word we keep to ourselves. Keeping the last word to ourselves amounts to another definition of transcendence.

Under democracy (seen in the light of the idea of deep freedom) the school must recognize and engage the student in three ways. First, the school must acknowledge each student as an agent, and work to enhance his or her ability to act imaginatively and practically, and, most importantly, beyond the present order as well as within it. Second, the school must see each young person as a prophet in waiting, on the assumption of democracy that prophetic powers are widely diffused within the whole of humanity and that the gates of prophecy are never closed. A prophet is the agent who sees our present experience, or some part of it, as susceptible to a transformation that brings us more fully into the possession of life or to a higher form of life. Thus, he is able to seize on elements of our present experience that convey the promise of more life, more being, more freedom. Prophecy is not prediction; it is the identification of potential, to be realized through transformative, including self-transformative, action. Third, the school views each youth as possessed of imagination and sees imagination as a bridge between agency and prophecy. By robbing the actual of some of its brute facticity—its just-there-ness, which may suggest to our bewitched minds its naturalness or necessity—we make it imaginable.

Imagination informs both agency and prophecy. Agency and prophecy give existential weight and social consequence to imagination. All three together enter into an idea of education under democracy.

The first-line objection to these ideas and hopes is that they disregard what the vast majority of young people—the presumed beneficiaries of such an educational program—are really like. They are, like most of their parents, worldly and sullen, except when they are aroused by diversions and pleasures, or by anger and fears. They have been taught to seek preferment through competition, or to resign themselves to the fate signaled by their social inheritance. The struggles of thought neither energize nor repel them but simply leave them bored. The educational program addressed to the supposed agents, prophets, and masters of the imagination will in practice be tortured to death by mediocrity and risks becoming, after an all too foreseeable struggle with its reluctant beneficiaries, a travesty of itself.

These and similar objections are both true and not true. They describe part, but only part, of what we are like. They are deficient in hope. But they do lay down the challenge to which any educational program as ambitious as the one I outline here, as part of the project of deep freedom, must respond: to show how such an ascent can begin from where we are, and reckon with the shared element in all the failings that the skeptic would invoke—our common acceptance of belittlement and our habitual denial of transcendence.

ॐ

Jumping over the established reality. Hic Rhodus, hic salta. The central paradox of education considered from this point of view is a variation on the theme of finitude and transcendence and of the collective character of our power to transcend. To equip the student to deal with the established context of society and culture by reaching beyond it, the school must itself achieve this goal. But it must somehow do so with the instruments that the present society and culture provide and in a struggle with three forces in that present that vie for the power to set its direction: the state, the family, and the university.

For the educational program that I outline here to advance, the supporters of this program must both placate and resist all three. That requirement deepens the paradox: we may well ask—as we may of every aspect of the agenda of deep freedom—from where will these supporters come?

The state has usually wanted the school to supply servants of the established order, willing and able to produce and, if necessary, to fight. Proficiency in the knowledge and skills required to operate the existing productive apparatus, perform one's role in the established social and technical division of labor, and master the core practices of the current society and culture has been its overriding concern. It has wanted to provide for an education that reconciles the demands of the specialized trades and professions with the possession of an elementary core of widely shared common knowledge. In the pursuit of this goal, the state has often allowed education to lag behind what the emerging forms of production require from the worker.

Under weak democracy, its representatives have also stressed the need for citizens to have the abilities and information needed to participate in deliberation over common affairs. However, in the real circumstances of the coexistence of weak democracy with class society, this profession of faith in popular enlightenment has generally come down to a harsh compromise: those born into the monied and governing elites, or candidates for incorporation into them, are educated in the discourse needed to master the management of the state and of production. Everyone else is taught a formulaic minimum and then prepared, if at all, for doing a narrowly defined job.

The emergence of the knowledge economy, albeit in its present shallow and insular form, modifies this situation. It demands a higher set of capabilities from even the users of its products and services. But what would reshape the state's demands on the school would be movement toward a knowledge economy for the many, a high-energy democracy, and a civil society able to organize itself outside the market and the state and to generate social cohesion through the multiplication of forms of collective action across the barriers of social and cultural difference.

Every part of such a program limits the other parts, not as an indivisible system but as a divisible structure, subject to the logic of combined and uneven development. Reciprocal constraint, open to breakthroughs, is especially evident in the relation of the reform of education to institutional innovation. What the state will regard as necessary and possible in the reform of education will be shaped by changes, or failures to change, in these other domains. And every advance or setback in their reformation will have consequences for the school. In the meantime, we should regard the state's demand that the school provide it with capable workers and managers as a movable obstacle.

The second force that seeks to determine the direction of the school is the family. In *The Republic*, Plato proposed a radical solution: to remove the child, soon after its birth, from the family. We may ask, however: to what problem was this a solution? For Plato, it seems to have been an imaginary device by which to escape, in one move, the constraints of established society on our transformation. If it were to be applied in its literal terms, it would have a starkly dehumanizing effect by taking the child away from the primary source of love and acceptance vital to his ability to flourish as a person. No human institution is harder to replace than the family. Moreover, the ability to enforce this solution on a mass scale presumes a power so great that it implies all other powers, and risks making the reconstruction of the rest of society either unnecessary or impossible and, in any event, unintelligible.

There is nevertheless a real problem, demanding not one fantastical cutting of a Gordian knot but real solutions. The problem has two main aspects: one of them has to do with the consequences of the class structure of the existing societies; the other, with the invasion of the family by worldliness and the dangers that worldliness presents to enlightenment and emancipation.

We know from abundant empirical evidence that the family milieu is the greatest determinant of the cultural resources that the child brings to the school. Both the class structure and the culture of the nation or the community set their mark on that milieu. The republican ideal, professed in even the weak democracies that we have had up to now, implies that the school should do whatever it can to neutralize the influence of class inequality. The greater the inequality in the surrounding society, the stronger becomes the need for the school to counterbalance it by offering to its young wards alternative sources of intellectual encouragement and ambition. Contrary to Plato's plan, it must find a way to do so without undermining or disrespecting the family and its culture.

In the real societies of history, the family has most often stood for worldliness as well as for inequality. Parents usually want the child to succeed by the standards of the world. If the family is privileged, it uses its advantages to arm the child with the best possible opportunities and instruments in the struggle for advancement. If it is bereft of privilege, it will want the child to escape to a higher station, to shine and prosper. Even if it professes belief in one of the world religions, or in their secular romantic counterpart, teaching that life is nothing if not sacrificial, it rarely instructs the child to taste the bitter pill of sacrifice for the sake of change and transcendence.

Under the light of the conception and agenda of deep freedom, the school must do more than struggle to neutralize the influence of the class structure on the education of the young; it must also strive to neutralize the influence of this worldliness. The most promising way to do so is to contribute to the diversification of forms of excellence and achievement rather than to embrace the thankless cause of a forbidding saintliness. It must struggle against the influence of worldliness not by proposing world renunciation but by contributing to the diversification of ways of flourishing in the world. An idea about who we are and about how we can become free underwrites this complex commitment: the view that to be free we must participate without surrendering.

The search for engagement without worldliness, for participation without surrender, leads to an idea that should occupy a major place in the educational program of a free society: the importance of helping each young person find a subject and an activity eliciting passionate intensity from him, and then allowing him to adapt his educational program to its pursuit—to the study of the ideas, and the mastery of the skills, that help him pursue that passion. Absorption and enthusiasm overcome the contrast between worldly surrender and flight from the world and in this way connects education with empowerment.

The third force with which the supporters of this educational program must contend is the university culture, the custodian of canonical knowledge and methods. As discussed in Chapter 2, on epistemology as inquiry into inquiry, one of the organizing principles of the university culture is the forced marriage of methods and subject matters, naturalizing the study of a subject by a particular procedure: cosmology, for example, by an anti-historical method and evolutionary biology by a historical one, and the pseudo-science of economics by the quasi-logical, hypothetical method that the marginalist economists introduced at the end of the nineteenth century and associated with empirical data without the benefit of causal theories that can be overthrown.

Another organizing principle of the university culture is the confusion regularly established in each branch of inquiry between what it has actually discovered about the world and the sense it makes of these discoveries, and then, in how it makes sense of them, between its account of why part of the world is the way it is, as well as of how it might change, and the characteristically unexpressed metaphysical presuppositions of such accounts—presuppositions typically justified, if they are justified at all, only by the approaches to the explanation of reality that they inspire.

The alternative possibilities of thought are regularly suppressed by the university culture. Revolution in thought most often takes the form of recovering some of these suppressed possibilities and acting on them to develop a different approach to part of the world.

The national curriculums disseminated around the world translate the university culture and its organizing principles into a form suitable to the understanding of the young and of their teachers. They are the infantile version of the canonical knowledge guarded and conveyed at the heights of the academic system. With greater transparency than their equivalents and sources in the university, they induce the young to mistake the dominant ideas for reality.

Education under democracy cannot settle for such a role. It cannot avoid engaging canonical knowledge. Much of the most developed understanding that we have of reality is to be found in the university system. There are not two sets of disciplines—one orthodox and the other heretical, as the Marxists were in the habit of contrasting "bourgeois science" to their own theories.

But the contingent and contestable association of method and subject and of empirical discovery, causal explanation, and metaphysical presupposition on which the university culture is based must not serve as the foundation for the education of the young in a society that seeks to root education in fearless inquiry. What ordinarily remains shrouded in mystification at the heights of academic life must be—and can be—demystified at every stage of education. I later argue that a central principle by which to achieve this goal is to approach every field of knowledge dialectically, from contrasting points of view, and that it is possible to do so, effectively, even at the initial rungs on the ladder of our cognitive ascent. The reward, if we are successful, is to deliver the young to the higher stages of education with at least partial immunity against intellectual emasculation and servility.

Against the background of these remarks about the three forces that struggle to set the direction of the school, we can ask once again: How is a society to jump over itself in the education of the young? Who can resist, contain, or redirect the combined claims of the state, the family, and the university culture on the direction of the school, and how can they do it? There are two basic answers to these questions.

The first answer is that in its early stages an educational program must do the work of a movement engaging, in any large country, thousands of teachers and hundreds of schools. It must have its thinkers or ideologists. Such programs can acquire authority as projects of national liberation, as they repeatedly have during this revolutionary period in the history of mankind. Domingo Sarmiento in nineteenth-century Argentina, José Vasconcelos in twentieth-century Mexico, and John Dewey in the twentieth-century United States proposed to rebuild their countries through education—whether holding power as Sarmiento and Vasconcelos did, or exercising influence only through their ideas, as Dewey did.

To succeed in advancing an educational agenda like the one I outline here, the reformers must be able to nurture such a movement in their country before they wield any direct governmental authority. They must be able to produce tangible examples of the educational practice they propose. They must open a space in which their examples can flourish and be interpreted as expressions of their doctrine. They must hold the state, the family, and the university culture at bay. To that end, they must be able to use each of these three as a restraint on the other two.

The second answer is that movement in the direction of this educational program depends on its resonance with convergent movements in the organization of the market, of democracy, and of civil society. According to the logic of combined and uneven development, the movement in education can advance for a while before the convergent advances in other domains take place. But the message of the movement will remain insecure and even unclear if the arrangements of the rest of social life contradict it.

If there is such a convergence, the educational reform will acquire extraordinary significance in the program of deep freedom. It benefits from its proximity to the idea of transcendence that informs the whole of that program. It translates that idea into practices and conceptions that presuppose, exalt, and build the person as agent, prophet, and master of imaginative powers.

The economic and institutional conditions of educational reconstruction. Before turning to the approach to teaching and learning that should mark this educational program, consider the institutional and economic conditions for its implementation in an important subset of contemporary societies: countries that are very large, very unequal, and federal in structure, like the United States and Brazil.

The requirements applicable to them apply as well, with adaptations, to a much wider range of states.

The most fundamental practical imperative will be to reconcile national standards of investment and quality with local management of the schools. To achieve this goal, it will be necessary to deploy three instruments.

The first device is a way of assessing educational outcomes, school by school and student by student. This system of assessment must do justice to basic verbal and numerical skills, as the present comparative international tests do, but it must also be responsive to the higher ambitions of this educational program, as the current tests obviously are not. And it must enlarge its testing methods to accommodate the pedagogic goals that I next describe. Moreover, it must find a way to register success and failure in the pursuit of individual passions and in the educational practices that allow them to develop. So long as the present testing regime prevails, a country—especially a small and rich one—can raise its standing in the international tests with relative ease by investing heavily in the conventional verbal and numerical skills of the bottom part of each class. This beneficent achievement does little to bring the country to the threshold of the educational ascent that I later explore.

The second tool is a mechanism to redistribute resources and staff from richer places to poorer places. The dependence of schools on local finance is a crippling infirmity incompatible with any democracy, much less a strong democracy, or even with an undemocratic society determined to exploit the potential of advanced productive practices and technologies. But even a far-reaching redistribution of resources within a federal system will have limited efficacy if the monied classes can opt for an independent system of expensive and well-endowed private schools.

The third method is the one with which we have as yet least experience: cooperation within the federal system in assisting, and, if necessary, taking over, a local school system that, despite the available mechanisms of redistribution from richer places to poorer ones, persistently falls below the minimum acceptable level of investment and quality. The principle is straightforward: the quality of the education that a young person receives should not be determined by the happenstance of where he is born. Would that we could add: or by the class into which he is born—but that depends on the changes in economic, political, and social institutions that I earlier discussed.

The three levels of the federation should be associated in organizations that can, when necessary, take over the temporary administration of a failing local school system, entrust its management and reform to independent administrators, fix it, and return it fixed. If the problem cannot be solved through such a time-limited turnaround, the procedures of redistribution within the federation will have to be strengthened. If, as is likely, these procedures turn out to be insufficient to negate the effects of the class system on the hierarchy of communities and their school systems, further progress will depend on institutional change in the organization of the economy, politics, and independent civil society. Here, as always, structural change trumps the redistributive correction of the consequences of the established economic, political, and social institutions.

The path of liberation. Any program for education must distinguish itself by its approach to learning and teaching. I now offer an account of an approach that is responsive to the aims of the project of deep freedom and to the view of humanity developed in this book. It would be foolish to pretend that this pedagogic model is the only one compatible with these requirements—it is but one example of how to interpret their educational implications.

This way of education applies to both general and technical education. It makes it possible for us to turn them into two variations of the same approach rather to treat them, as they generally have been treated, as radically distinct.

The prevailing style of technical education has given priority to job-specific and machine-specific skills. The most influential national example has been German: skilling in the use of the core machine tools of the conventional industry of the recent past and in the skills and knowledge demanded in traditional trades, followed by apprenticeship and on-the-job training. The predominant practice of general education has emphasized basic verbal and numerical skills as well as mastery of an abbreviated encyclopedia—the skills and mastery supposedly vital to the performance of non-manual and especially managerial or executive responsibilities.

Initially, technical education was conceived as suitable for the working class. Now it is offered to what is in fact a relatively special-ized and privileged part of the labor force being prepared to perform non-managerial roles. By the same token, general education, in its European version, was an adornment of the elites. Now, in a simplified form, it is the education given to most of the population, including in the richest and relatively most educated countries: a form of school-ing, continued in university education for the masses, that is neither theoretical nor practical.

The education of elites has had to be redrawn as a contrast between two styles of general education, as the experience of the United States in the recent historical period shows. General education for the man-agers and rulers has been reinvented as a dialogic practice in the mastery of a set of problem-solving and argumentative skills, worked out in a group setting and emphasizing the acquisition of a certain style of sociability. The aim of the sought-after style of sociability is to cast over one's peers an ingratiating and self-effacing charisma that removes any sting of superiority. Such a way to educate amounts to a degraded version of elements that ought to figure in an education respecting our powers of transcendence and serving the cause of deep freedom.

The first attribute of a way of teaching and learning should be to equip the student to engage with reality in society and nature, both imaginatively and practically. In every domain we understand how a phenomenon works by grasping how it changes and what it can proximately become as a result of such change. Insight into trans-formative possibility—in the domain of the adjacent possible—is insight into the actual.

In the service of this focus, we must develop each young person's powers of analysis and synthesis: their ability to take ideas and infor-mation apart and put them back to together. We do so the better to enlarge the stock of conceptions that we deploy in moving back and forth between phenomena and their transformative variations. In each area these analytic and synthetic operations take a different form. We must not allow such differences to obscure the fundamental unity toward which all cumulative understanding reaches.

It is futile to pursue this ambition until the student has mastered basic verbal and numerical skills in reading, writing, and quantitative calculations. But it is possible to begin pursuing it much earlier in the education of the young than is commonly supposed. How early we can do so, and in what manner, is an empirical question of pedagogic practice. But it is also likely to be a question about our assumptions regarding the area of study.

Whether, for example, in the teaching of mathematics, set theory and number theory can and should precede the extensive teaching of arithmetic only for a small elite of mathematically gifted students is not a matter about which it makes sense to entertain dogmas. It depends on our ingenuity in the development of teaching methods and materials that present abstract ideas in ways that make them palpable and accessible.

It also requires that the architects of the educational program not be themselves bewitched by illusions that may divert them from the pursuit of these aims. If, for example, the first aim of Hilbert's program in mathematics and the one for which he was most known— to represent and vindicate all of mathematics under a system of finite axioms and rigidly defined methods of inference—turned out to be justified, it might result in an insuperable obstacle to the imaginative exploration of mathematics. But, despite the misleading example of Euclid's geometry, this aim turned out to be misguided. Once we cast it aside, we can turn to the two other ambitions of Hilbert's program: to affirm the unity of mathematics against the subfields into which it threatened to fall apart, and to move the focus of attention from mathematical objects (whether spatial or numerical) to mathematical methods. Contrary to what Hilbert supposed, the failure of the ambition to reduce mathematics to a closed axiomatic system strengthened rather than weakened the basis for the pursuit of these other aims. They can justify and orient the teaching of mathematics in a spirit consonant with this first element in the pedagogical program outlined here.

In each area of thought, we face similar problems and find similar opportunities. In each area, the obstacles to thinking about reality in the spirit of transformation result from illusions. Overcoming those obstacles in the discipline is always difficult. But to the extent that they are overcome, the door is open to presenting every subject, from its rudiments up, in a way that approaches everything from the standpoint of its possible, proximate changes.

We cannot develop our powers of analysis and synthesis, enlisted in the service of transformative insight into the real, in a vacuum of content. With regard to content, selective depth counts for more than encyclopedic coverage—the second trait of this approach to education. From this fact result the advantages of teaching and learning organized around themes and projects. The preference for selective depth over encyclopedic scope is the second feature of this approach to education.

Is there then information—for example, about global and national history and about the history of nature and of life in the universe and on our planet—that everyone must master to be able to orient himself usefully around such projects and themes? Yes, we cannot abolish the encyclopedic orientation completely. We must retain some element of the abbreviated encyclopedia, combining it with the preference for selective deepening over shallow coverage. We interrupt the generalities from time to time to focus on a theme in depth.

A third feature of this pedagogic model extends and qualifies this relation between skills and contents. It does so by generalizing and diversifying the principle underlying an education in the classics in civilizations as different as the European and the Chinese. To be free, the mind must gain a distance from the present society and culture that surround it. But, in communication with alien experience, it must be able to reengage, equipped by the perspective it has acquired, in its immediate social and cultural setting. Then it sees with double vision.

For European civilization, the second eye looked to Graeco-Roman antiquity. For China, it looked to the Confucianist canon of the pre-imperial period as well as to the poetry and philosophy of earlier stages in the country's long history. The subject matter of such an education was removed from present experience. Yet it could speak to the present, and its ability to do so found support in its genealogical relation to the living culture of the society in which the school existed. The relation was also just a thread, albeit an important one, never the whole story: Christianity had a stronger claim to be a source of European beliefs than did the world view of the Greeks and Romans; and in China, the Confucianist canon had rivals from the outset.

Double vision, yes; a closed canon privileged over other expressions of humanity, no. The way to rescue for our project what is most valuable in the practice of classical education is to insist on the search for double vision but to cleanse it of the taint of commitment to a narrow and closed canon. Every student must, through the practice of selective deepening, engage with the experiences and beliefs of a part of humanity distant from him in time or space. Such an exposure will help him loosen the hold of the idea world that surrounds his imagination and help him become freer and more alive.

A fourth characteristic of this approach to teaching and learning has to do with its social setting. Cooperation among students, among teachers, among schools, as well as between students and schools, should prevail in place of the juxtaposition of individualism and authoritarianism marking the traditional classroom. The cooperative practices of advanced science can live in the school.

Cooperation in teaching and learning is the indispensable social basis of any critical and experimental approach to inherited knowledge that can be widely shared. It is there, in the early formation of the individual, that we begin to build the makers and agents of a knowledge economy for the many and of a democratized market order, the citizens of a high-energy democracy, and the agents of a civil society that organizes itself outside the state and the market.

Students and teachers can work together in groups, exploring variations on the themes or projects that the group selects as its focus. In this way the cooperative educational practices are more than just useful to the exercise of the imagination; they serve as instances of it. And by serving as instances of it they also exemplify an impulse that runs through the entire agenda of deep freedom: the effort to become bigger together.

A fifth and last characteristic of this educational program is the most ambitious and the hardest to reconcile with the conventions and traditions of schooling. It is also the one that most clearly clashes with the assumptions underlying the university culture.

Every subject should be taught at least twice, from contrasting points of view. It is the best way to liberate the mind by preventing it from mistaking the dominant ideas in each discipline for the way things are. The practical condition for this procedure is the sacrifice of encyclopedic coverage to selective depth.

It is not a principle that can be applied at the most elementary stages of education, where the focus falls on the acquisition of basic verbal and numerical skills. Neither, however, need it or should it await the higher levels of education. It is, after all, from the university culture, with its enforced marriages of method and subject matter and its confusion of empirical discovery, theoretical explanation, and metaphysical presupposition, that the problem comes.

The aim of this fifth feature of the educational program is to prepare the mind to engage with the received body of knowledge without surrendering to the superstitions of the academy. The young can then advance to higher education insulated against those superstitions.

The goal of this dialectical method is not simply to guard students against the path-dependent illusions of the established disciplines. It is to help them discover as early as practicable in their education the enigmatic character of reality and the impossibility of advancing in our grasp of the real without subjecting ourselves to the discipline of a contest between ways of thinking.

The pertinence of this insight is not limited to the upper reaches of theoretical knowledge in science and philosophy. It applies as well to all our practical or technical knowledge. The reason why it applies to all our knowledge and experience is that it expresses the coexistence of transcendence and finitude that is the rule of our being. Here as always each of us may face our finitude alone, as we do in facing death. But we affirm our transcendence only together.

The style of general education defined by these five traits can inform, as well, a distinctive approach to technical education. That approach will no longer focus on the job-specific and machine-specific skills that were central to traditional technical training. It will emphasize, instead, the higher-order, flexible capabilities required for the operation and continuous adjustment of the numerically controlled machine tools of a knowledge economy. Rather than being contrasted to general education, such a style of technical education will be on a continuum with it.

The commanding aim of education in a free society is to introduce us to the practices described by this program of teaching and learning. We come to understand that they are not the prerogative of an intellectual or spiritual elite. They must become the common possession of humanity.

Deep Freedom and World Order

The price of difference. The cause of deep freedom must flourish or fail in a world divided into sovereign states. Under the guard of these states, the peoples of the world develop distinct forms of life, each of them an experiment in a way of being human.

The division of the world into sovereign states comes at a terrible price. To be able to defend themselves and to say no to those who would subjugate them, these states are armed. Facing one another they are also fearful and grasping. They live on the verge of waging war against one another. When war comes, it can destroy everything that men and women hold sacred and take away life itself.

Each of these states, justified as the home of a people, can become, and often has been, a prison. The hierarchies and divisions that its laws impose, in the name of national distinction and practical need, commonly cast the vast majority of the people under a servile yoke.

The price of the division of humanity into sovereign states is high. But it is not as high as the price of bringing the entire human race under the control of a world state. We can rise only by diverging. No form of national life, and no collection of such forms, exhaust the powers that we have reason to develop and the experiences that we have reason to undergo. Without a dialectic of contrast, defiance, and rebellion—without the unlimited capacity to surprise, nourished in different lands, by different peoples, living under different institutions and assumptions—our impulse to transcend would be placed under a constraint from which it might never recover.

We have no reason to believe that the nation-state, as it exists today, will forever remain the predominant form of the division of humanity. What matters is that different peoples retain the power to develop distinct forms of life and express them in institutions and practices as well as in beliefs. Unless these forms of life can take institutional form, their differences risk being nothing but folklore. To take institutional form, they must be expressed as law, and be underwritten by whatever power can ultimately determine the shape of society or set the limits of its variation. That this power exists in the world only in multiplicity, not in unity, is what matters most. We can diminish the price that we pay, in the risks of war and oppression, for this multiplicity. But if we refuse to pay it, we risk losing a greater good.

I have argued that the nature of the differences among nations has changed in a way that we do not yet fully grasp. We used to be united by similarity of experience and belief as well as by common descent. Our collective identities were manifest in our customs.

We are becoming something else as each people sacrifices some of its customs to worldly ambition and revolutionary aspiration against the background of the worldwide struggle of states. In this transformation, which we could not forego without failing to rise to a higher form of life, we encounter an unexpected peril. The reproduction of actual national difference gives way to something much more dangerous: the affirmation of a will to national difference that is uncompromising because it lacks the tangible content of distinct customs, sacrificed long ago on the altar of worldwide competition, political rivalry, and ideological emulation.

Liberal cosmopolitism proposes to suppress national difference. Reactionary nationalism wants to preserve or reaffirm inherited and remembered national difference. But the best response is to equip the peoples of the world with the institutions and the capabilities that would allow them to create new difference.

Difference—real difference—is not the problem. It is the solution. But the differences that we create matter more than the ones we inherit or remember: prophecy above memory.

Governing the world without world government. In the interests of our ascent, we must find ways in which the world can govern itself without world government. In such a world, sovereign states remain in command. They nevertheless cooperate to achieve global public goods and avoid global public harms, such as war and destructive climate change. Of these harms, the one most to be prevented is armed conflict between the great powers.

The price of the division of humanity into sovereign states, however, is not simply the danger of war. It is also the risk that much of humanity will remain imprisoned within oppressive states.

A diversity of forms of experience must be sustained by a plurality of power in the world. But a qualified pluralism of power is better than an unqualified one. Different forms of life, supported by a wide range of institutional arrangements, should be able to flourish under the protection of states. But in each of these forms of life the individual should be able to stand up, expressing his power of agency, and, through that power, his transcendence.

In each of these distinct societies and cultures, the individual citizen should have at his disposal a haven of vital safeguards against governmental and private oppression and of capability-assuring endowments. In each, the empowerment of the people should have as its counterpart the empowerment—and protection—of the individual person. In each, the structure of society should be open to challenge coming from all quarters of the people, and the contradiction between democracy and the class structure of society should be resolved in favor of democracy. In each, no economic, political, or cultural elite should be able to capture for long the power of the state and to work its will on a cowed population.

The world of sovereign states should be a world of free societies. A qualified pluralism of states would be one that tended to prevent, isolate, and defeat instances of national life organized in defiance of these hopes.

This qualified pluralism remains so distant from our reality that the attempt to impose it, or even to profess it, might serve only to discredit it in the eyes of those who have no patience for dreams that are dangerous as well as idle. They are dangerous because they are overwhelmingly likely to be misinterpreted in ways that make the future they envision harder to achieve. In the course of being discredited and misinterpreted, they may also make it harder to organize the inclusive and varied forms of cooperation among sovereign states that we need in order to secure the greatest global public goods and avoid the greatest global public harms, including the danger of war between the great powers.

How are we to lower the price that we pay for the necessary division of humanity into political units that are able to organize society in different ways, under different assumptions? How can we avert the evils that may follow from this division, especially war among the great powers, and secure, without establishing a world state, the benefits of cooperation among states? And how can we then later create the conditions to establish a qualified, rather than an unqualified, pluralism of power in the world—a coexistence of free societies—without eviscerating the force of state sovereignty?

Consider the basic elements of a direction that supplies the practical answer to these questions. I invoke them in an order that facilitates understanding rather than in any temporal sequence.

Historical experience shows that there is only one way, not a plethora of ways, by which the world can govern itself without world government: cooperation among states. Everything else is a fantasy, and almost all such fantasies point toward a world state.

In the recent experience of humanity, such cooperative activity has taken three main forms. Under one form, states cooperate to solve specific problems: single-purpose coalitions. Under a second species of cooperation among states, states in a region of the world cooperate to achieve goals that they cannot fully accomplish by themselves: regional coalitions. An example is the European Union, founded to secure perpetual peace in Europe and to lay the basis for a form of social and economic organization different from the one established, across the ocean, in the United States. By a third variety of cooperation, states that are similar in their magnitude and level of development, or the role that they play in world affairs, cooperate to work out shared responses to shared problems: similar-state coalitions. Examples of such coalitions at the present time include the G20, the

G7, and the BRICS (bringing together China, India, Russia, Brazil, and South Africa).

From the initiatives of such coalitions of the willing there emerges over time an accumulation of shared practice. This legacy of practice enriches and reshapes international common law: the law of nations. You may well ask who will settle the conflicts that may arise between the rules and policies established by these multiple coalitions. The answer is: no one. The conflicts will have to be settled without appeal to a higher power, as we might expect to settle them within a single state or empire. We may settle them by using, for example, a counterpart to the reconciliation panels that deal with divergence between the two chambers of a bicameral legislature. We will develop international common law without the cadres of emperors, imperial jurists, and bureaucrats on which a world state would rely.

Of all the forms of cooperation among states, the most important would be cooperation to avert war, especially war among the great powers—today the United States and China. Here arises the need for a fourth type of coalition of the willing: an initiative of middle-level powers to engage those greatest powers in an entente of shared commitments and of reciprocal understandings, assurances, and ultimately guarantees of their vital security interests, as well of the vital security interests of these lesser powers. Vital security interests are those that relate directly to political independence and territorial integrity.

Such an entente would have two broad aims. One goal would be to engage the great powers in a range of initiatives shared between them and with other powers, in the hope of prompting them to turn from reciprocal belligerence to peaceful competition. The other purpose would be to identify the vital security interests of the great and lesser powers and explore the extent to which, and the ways by which, these interests can be both assured and reconciled; their reconciliation is a large part of their assurance.

The assurance would initially stop short of a guarantee with armed force. The entente, however, would work toward making such a guarantee possible, with the commitment of the armed forces and technologies of the participant states.

Such an arrangement would have to develop outside the rigid

limits of the Security Council of the United Nations, paralyzed by the veto powers granted to five actual or presumptive victors of a war that ended in the middle of the past century. Whether it could later inform and inspire a transformation of the UN system that allowed the entente and the UN to converge is a question that depends on the ability of the UN to free itself from the arrangements established at the end of the Second World War.

This cooperative action of states to pacify the world has two principal precedents in the last two centuries. One precedent was the nineteenth-century Concert of Europe and the practices by which, in an age of empire, it tried to create a system of counterweights and guarantees that would prevent any country from having to choose between war and surrender. Its advantage was its flexibility and susceptibility to evolution. Its disadvantage was its subordination to the interests of the elites and autocrats who governed the participating states.

The other precedent was the League of Nations, which, more clearly than the United Nations system that replaced it, sought single-mindedly to pacify the world. Its advantage was its clarity of focus on the avoidance of war and military aggression. It sought to achieve this purpose by putting a wide array of nations on the side of any state whose independence and territorial integrity might be threatened by another state. Its disadvantage was the rigidity of a structure disconnected from the realities of power in world politics and rendered sterile by the lack of armed force. The entente would need to combine the flexibility of the Concert of Europe with the clear and narrow but exacting aims of the League.

Another globalization. For the world to govern itself without world government and move toward a qualified pluralism—one that encourages a wide range of national experiments in ways of being human and recognizes the agency of every people and of every individual person—cooperation among states is a necessary but not sufficient condition. The world must also become open, which is what we call globalization. But the globalization that it builds should differ from the one that it has built. We can best understand the character of the globalization we need, in contrast to the globalization we have, by seeing it developed in the setting of one of its aspects: the world-trade regime.

The commanding purpose must not be to maximize free trade, which is not an end in itself but a secondary, relative, and conditional good. It should be to develop an open world economy in the manner, and at the pace, best calculated to encourage the coexistence of different experiences of civilization and strategies of national development.

The rules under which world trade is conducted, whether set in a worldwide regime of commerce or in multilateral trade pacts, should open up the greatest possible space for institutional experiments and alternatives, including alternative ways of organizing a market economy. By contrast, the World Trade Organization treaties of the late twentieth century, and the multilateral trade pacts that followed and replaced them, exemplified an institutional maximalism. They required the participant trading countries to adopt not just the market economy but also a particular version of the market order.

Under the label of subsidies, for example, they outlawed the forms of strategic coordination between governments and firms that the now rich countries used in the course of becoming rich, but that they now want to forbid the latecomers from deploying. Similarly, they required the trading countries to incorporate, as a condition of their participation in world trade, a legal regime of intellectual property, developed at the end of the nineteenth century, that leaves many of the intellectual innovations of greatest importance to humanity under the control of a small number of multinational firms.

We know that it is possible to organize trade on the basis of institutional minimalism: the greatest degree of openness that is compatible with the minimum of restraints on institutional divergence and experimentation, including experimentations with the institutional arrangements defining the market order. The General Agreement on Tariffs and Trade, which preceded the WTO, preferred minimalism to maximalism. But so more generally did the law merchant, in the early modern period, over the centuries of its evolution. The law merchant developed a legal regime for international trade that could coexist with a wide diversity of legal rules and arrangements in the participant countries.

The attempt to present legal and institutional convergence as nec-essary to avoid the crippling transaction costs that result from a disharmony of national rules misreads the history of international commerce and of the law that has governed it. The whole point of trade is to turn difference to mutual advantage. Difference in productive specialization is likely to be related to all the other economic, social, and cultural differences that are expressed in rules. The argument for legal and institutional convergence—or mandatory "harmonization"—recalls the logic of the dove evoked by Kant in *The Critique of Pure Reason*: as it flies, the dove thinks that if there were no air it would fly even faster. How far we can go in reconciling a diversity of national legal rules and institutions with exchange across jurisdictions is not something that we can establish *a priori*: it is a matter for experience and experiment.

The established form of globalization is distinguished as well by the stark contrast of its treatment of mobility for goods and services and for capital, on one side, and mobility for labor, on the other. It seeks the maximum freedom for things and money to cross national fron-tiers. But it also wants to imprison people in nation-states or in blocs of relatively homogeneous nation-states like the European Union.

The movement of things and of capital across national frontiers is sometimes useful and sometimes harmful. But the movement of people is sacrosanct: it forms part of the process by which humanity develops its powers and becomes both unified and diverse. Greater labor mobility across national frontiers trumps all other measures in its potential to diminish inequality among nations.

We cannot institute freedom for people to move across national frontiers instantly and universally without causing revolutionary dis-ruption of the nation-state and of its provisions for social welfare and the protection of labor. But we need not accept a regime that seeks to give immediate and total freedom of movement to things and money but arrests people within the nation-state. Goods and services, capital, and people should gain freedom to cross national frontiers together, in small cumulative steps. We can protect the receiving countries by safe-guards and gradualism: the long road from temporary work permits to permanent residency and citizenship. And we can compensate the sending countries—those that lose workers—for their investment in the education of the skilled labor that goes elsewhere.

An open global economy in a world of free societies must be based on free labor. Countries must remain free to compete on the basis of unequal returns to labor, so that labor-rich economies not be deprived of an indispensable advantage in their competition with capital-rich and natural resource-rich economies. Unequal returns to labor, however, must have a limit in the principle of free work. And for that limit to point toward a future of deep freedom, states must be free to experiment with institutional innovations and legal provisions that point beyond economically coerced wage labor to the higher forms of free work: self-employment and cooperation. Such a direction implies, as I have argued, changes in the law of property, contract, and association that make it possible to reconcile those higher forms of free labor with the imperative of economies of scale.

This direction, illustrated here with respect to trade, stands in contrast to the globalization that has developed in recent history. That globalization mispresents the maximization of free trade as an end in itself, embraces a doctrine of convergence to an ever smaller and more unified set of institutions and practices, denies to people the freedom of movement that it wants to grant to things and to money, and fails to bring us closer to a world in which free labor is really free.

What I have described in the trade context is neither more nor less globalization. It is a different globalization.

Against the background of this other globalization, and so long as peace is maintained, especially in the dealings among the great powers, we can hope that the strengths of a society that loosens the stranglehold of established structure and encourages the perpetual creation of the new will be manifest. The peoples of the world, unquiet today under a dictatorship of no alternatives, will look around to find signs of the alternatives that empower ordinary men and women.

Until then, we must play for time. If the world is forced to choose between autarchic nationalism and a globalization that suppresses difference, it will prefer autarchic nationalism. And if it is forced to choose between embracing the cause of economic and political freedom in the institutional form that it takes in the rich North

Atlantic countries of today and rejecting that cause, it will reject that cause.

Grotius and now. As we look back on the main lines of this agenda for governing the world without world government, it may be useful to compare it to another project of world order, formulated in the early days of the modern state system as it developed in Europe: the thought of Hugo Grotius. There are four elements in Grotius's visionary yet practical scheme for the making of global public goods: the idea of international society as a society of sovereign states; the law of treaties as the contractual element in world order; public international common law as the pre- and post-contractual component in this order; and natural law as the guide to what would otherwise be a state system without inspiration or direction.

My argument here reinterprets, sometimes radically, each of the first three parts of Grotius's system and replaces the fourth. The division of humanity into sovereign states is more than a brute fact. It is the expression of a deep truth: that humanity develops its powers only by developing them along different lines and can be unified only by being allowed to diverge. Treaties among states represent a fragment of what states can do by acting together in the distinct forms addressed in my discussion of coalitions of the willing. Public international common law is less a legacy than it is a prophecy; it can draw its material from the work of all the coalitions of the willing and make explicit the wider implications of that work for the future of mankind.

Here, however, Grotius's conception of natural right gives way to a moral and political ideal enjoying unrivalled appeal today: the idea of the enhancement of agency—of the potential of every man and woman to stand up and lead a larger life, to become more human by becoming more godlike, and to live in such a way that he or she dies only once. We know from experience that we cannot hope to develop this power as individuals unless we also exercise it as peoples, organized, now, under the shield of states. To that end, we seek a world that needs no world government to govern itself.

Epilogue

Everything in our existence points beyond itself. Our transcendence and the reckoning of our transcendence with our finitude define the human condition. They have been the subject matter of this book, explored in many parts of our experience and in each branch of philosophy. To address them in this way, I have had to rethink what philosophy is and can become.

The struggle of our transcendence with our finitude takes place, for everyone, along the arc of an individual human life. Throughout our existence, each of us, a product of countless improbable accidents, verges on nothingness. Each of us faces alone in death the definitive expression of his finitude. But none of us transcends alone, even when we flatter ourselves that we do.

The exercise of our transcendence involves, at every turn, other people. The best way of involving others is to love them, and the next best way is to cooperate with them. Transcendence is manifest in empowerment, but it develops through cooperation and culminates in love. The most real and promising forms of empowerment are those that allow us to become greater together.

Society may be, and for much of history has been, so oppressive that it hands each of us a script, adjusted to our place in the social division of labor, and tells us, or forces us, to enact it. We need to do whatever we can to resist the script imposed on us—if not to replace it with one that we wrote, then at least to prevent it from robbing us of the sense of being alive and in possession of our own selves.

Our troubles are not over when our power to chart a direction strengthens. As we pass through childhood, each of us, a storehouse of alternative ways of becoming a person, may imagine many different courses of life. However, we cannot be everything in the world. We must choose a path and reject other paths. This rejection, indispensable to our self-development, is also a mutilation. In choosing, as we must and to the extent that we can, we cast aside many aspects of our humanity.

If we cast them aside completely, we become less than fully human. We must continue somehow to feel the movements of the limbs we cut off. To learn how to feel them is the first major work of the imagination and a source of our ability to imagine the experience of other people.

Later, as adults, we fight in the world and against it. We settle into a habitual way of living and doing. A mummy starts to form around each of us. It diminishes our reach and our vision by accommodating them to our circumstances. In this mummy we suffocate: we begin to die many small deaths.

We can continue to live only by breaking out of the mummy. We can break out of it only by denying ourselves some of the safeguards with which we shield ourselves against the frustration of our longings and the defeat of our ambitions. Our reward is to die only once.

Life comes before goodness: vitality is the condition of sustained and magnanimous empathy. We are plunged into an encompassing and mysterious darkness, which our minds can penetrate only at the edges. Luck and misfortune, beginning with the accidents of our birth in a particular class, nation, and community, shape much of what happens to us.

We would be almost nothing if we failed to fight against the consequences of this fate and to recognize in ourselves the unaccommodated and uncontainable spirits that we all are. As we rebel against our belittlement by the alliance between chance and society, we cease to be small. We become greater: unshaken and unsubdued.

Our struggle, which is the condition of our ascent, would also be the cause of our perversion, were it not transformed by love. To love another person and to be driven by a vision defining a task are the two decisive events that a person can experience. They make us godlike, not just like the God who creates, but also like the God who suffers and dies.

Through them, we become hostages to other people, who may rebuff our love and destroy our work. This dependence on others is not our doom. It is our salvation.

Index of Proper Names and Works

Index of Subjects